PELICA
A.

THE DEMOCRATIC ROOSEVELT

Rexford Guy Tugwell was born in 1891 in Sinclairsville, New York, and educated at the University of Pennsylvania, where he received his Ph.D. in economics in 1922. He was a professor of economics at Columbia University when he became an adviser to Roosevelt in 1932, and he served under the President as Under-Secretary of Agriculture from 1934 to 1937. He was appointed Governor of Puerto Rico in 1941, and he was a member of the Caribbean Commission from 1942 to 1957.

Mr. Tugwell has taught and lectured at the University of Chicago (where he was Director of the Institute of Planning from 1946 to 1952), the London School of Economics, Howard University, and other colleges and universities. He is a member of the American Political Science Association and the International Institute of Planners, and in 1958 he was the recipient of the Woodrow Wilson award.

Mr. Tugwell is the author of nearly twenty books; his most recent include *The Art of Politics* (1958), *The Enlargement of the Presidency* (1960), *The Light of Other Days* (1962), and *How they became President: Thirty Five Ways to the White House* (1965). He is presently at the Center for the Study of Democratic Institutions at Santa Barbara, California.

REXFORD G. TUGWELL

THE
DEMOCRATIC
ROOSEVELT

A Biography of
Franklin D. Roosevelt

PENGUIN BOOKS INC
BALTIMORE · MARYLAND

Penguin Books Inc, 7110 Ambassador Road
Baltimore, Maryland 21207

First published by Doubleday & Co., Inc. 1957
Published by Pelican Books 1969, with the
permission of Rexford G. Tugwell

Published in The United States of America

INTRODUCTION TO THE PELICAN EDITION

Reviewing this account of Roosevelt's life twenty-five years after his death and fifteen years after writing it, I neither have much to change nor much to add. Professional historians have been at work during this time. To the latest of them Roosevelt has been just another prominent past American. To those of us who lived when he did he was more than that; and to those of us who knew him, much more.

Frank Friedel and Arthur M. Schlesinger, Jr., come in between. They were young men in the Roosevelt age, and did not know the man himself; but they could understand what differences he made in the lives of all his contemporaries. Something more than historical interest influenced their extensive accounts of his life and times. Detachment was even more difficult for me because I had known and worked with him. There was, however, one advantage in this. I had been able to study him from close by as he performed his political miracles. I realized very early in this association that a facile manner hid a formidable determination. I was challenged to understand his intention. When I came to write about him I was most concerned to explain what by then I conceived to be a master plan.

Especially during the terrible depression I had seen the resolution form that Americans should never again have to suffer such an ordeal. Besides imposing hardships, it stole people's old faith in their country's future. This for Roosevelt was inadmissible. He was able to do something to make them more secure against the risks of joblessness, old age and the other ills they had always feared; and their faith in their government and in themselves was measurably restored.

This is really the theme of this book: how one man, so generally thought by those who had known him before he became President to have a very ordinary intelligence, and to have only a scattered interest in anything but his own advancement, should have proved to be the nation's hero in the gravest circumstances of its history.

Would he have been able to do still more? We shall never know whether, if he had lived, he would have succeeded in his plans for peace in the world after Hitler was defeated. He died, as Lincoln had, in the tumult of victory, leaving his conception to be worked out by others. They bungled his scheme, or thought they had a better one, and long years of acrimony were entered on. I have always thought he would have managed the transition more successfully; but that is conjecture and was beyond the scope of this book. What was not beyond it, and what I tried to show, was the relentlessness of his drive toward those ends he meant to see attained. The foundations were laid for the domestic ones; but peace, the most consequential of all, was just beyond his reach. The few years more he needed were denied him and so the immense effort of the war yielded far less than might have been won.

I think it fair to say that recent discoveries, with the exceptions I shall note, have added nothing really substantial to the account here; and my interpretations seem to have been generally accepted. There are, however, two differences I have had with those who knew him and who may have been nearer the truth than I.

The first of these was with Aubrey Williams who felt that I was mistaken in saying that Roosevelt thought he might contain Hitler by political means, and, for this reason, felt that going to war would be a defeat for himself as a politician. Williams believed, from talking with him in the later 'thirties, that Roosevelt was convinced even so early of the need for force and quite ready to see it used. As Aubrey recalled it, he said plainly that Hitler would recognize nothing else and would have to be destroyed.

During the years of negotiation, when Americans were so reluctant to arm, did he always know that war was inevitable, or did he think that the threat of it was a sufficient counter to Hitler's plans for conquest? My conversations with him left me with a different impression from Aubrey's. Still I was made uneasy by a clear recollection of what, as President-elect, he had told me in 1933 about the Japanese. He had said then that war with them was coming and that it may as well come earlier as later. When I had protested he had answered out of what he said was "considerable experience" in trying to encourage the liberals in Japan, that they had lost control; the military had taken over; and it would take a war to dislodge them.

He had repeated this conviction when we were conferring over the first allocation of public works funds in the early days of the New Deal. He had insisted on putting aside a substantial sum for enlargement of the Navy, saying that it would presently be needed in the Pacific.

So Williams may have been right. Roosevelt may have made up his mind must earlier than I had thought, that war must come on both sides of our continent. What I had interpreted as political maneuvering was perhaps no more than temporizing while he prepared opinion and strengthened the Armed Forces for conflict.

The other concession I must make—although the evidence hardly seems substantial enough to carry the weight it is being asked to carry—is the relationship with Lucy Mercer who later became Mrs. Winthrop Rutherford. This seems to have begun in 1917, as a passionate summer affair and to have gone on throughout their lives as a continuing friendship. It did not disrupt his marriage; but there is reason to believe that it altered his relations with Eleanor. How much it altered them is not clear; but it does seem probable that things were never again quite as they had been between them.

What seems to me likely is that Eleanor, then pregnant, took the small children to Campobello, their place in New Brunswick, early in summer. Franklin was left alone. Lucy Mercer's duties as Eleanor's part-time social secretary brought her to the Roosevelt house several times a week. She is described as a lovely young lady, cheerful and richly affectionate. He fell in love with her and she with him.

Their affair was interrupted when Eleanor heard what was going on and rushed home to confront the lovers with the familiar choice. The decision was that they must give each other up; but how stormy the interviews were, and what threats were made, is not known and never will be unless some still undisclosed account turns up. Relatives and friends knew about the affair and news of the confrontation got around. It was suspected that the circumstances had just been too difficult for divorce. There were his children to be thought of; and there was his career, certain to be gravely risked; then, too, Lucy was a devout Catholic.

Evidence of further relations is equally elusive and circumstantial; but that there were some it is impossible to deny. Jonathan Daniels has gathered up and interpreted what relatives and friends had to say; and it adds up to something substantial.[1] Lucy married, somewhat later, Winthrop Rutherford, a formidable representative of American wealth and prestige. He was twice her age and a widower; but she graced his household and bore him a son.

Her loyalty as a wife seems to have been tempered with a lingering regret for a lost love fully matched by Franklin's affection. They certainly met many times in later years, far too many, and in circumstances much too varied, not to have been planned with persistent care.

[1] In *Washington Quadrille*, N.Y., Doubleday, 1968.

They were not just two people belonging to families and social circles that made occasional meeting inevitable. They sought each other out.

During the worst strains of his war-time Presidency, when he was closely guarded and his social life was extremely restricted, they continued to meet. Her husband had died after a long illness. She was, then, a wealthy widow; and it was she who commissioned the portrait being painted by Madame Shoumatoff at the time of Franklin's final collapse at Warm Springs. She was, in fact, one of the four women in the room when his head twisted downward and the massive hemorrhage infused his brain. The others present, besides Shoumatoff, were his cousins, Laura Delano, and Margaret Suckley, two maiden ladies who often gave him the undemanding company he never had from Eleanor and who may have given Lucy's presence a needed respectability on other occasions than this.

Jonathan Daniels reports a general conspiracy of silence about their meetings, although Roosevelt himself made no strained secret of his visits or hers. There must have been many people around him—the secret service men, for instance, who arranged the rendezvous, as well as members of their families—who knew of them. But those who would have known consistently omitted any mention of Lucy's presence on many occasions when notes were made of what went on. Eleanor had long since developed her own concerns; and the household was one with numerous visitors. A President, of course, travels a good deal and visits many places. They met, and others covered up for them; but if their relations went beyond a consolatory friendship there is no record of it.

When, a few hours after his collapse on an April day in 1945, Roosevelt was known to be dying, the Secret Service rushed Lucy away to her Southern home in Aiken. In the accounts of his last hours no mention is made of her presence. This does have the air of conspiracy.

What sort of journey from Warm Springs to Aiken that must have been for Lucy can only be imagined. The summer romance and the lasting friendship must have been a poor substitute for the life together they may have hoped for but sacrificed to ambition and public decorum. Now even that was over. But it had at least been something.

This is all much too circumstantial; but with Jonathan Daniels I feel now that it must have been a glowing pleasantness in Roosevelt's life. Also, it must have made a difference in his relations with Eleanor. In my own book I noted that they gradually grew apart and that she developed a most unlikely, but most successful, career of her own as a public figure. I thought there had been no thought, ever, of separation. I now agree that there must have been thought of it, however quickly it was discarded. At any rate she continued to be the wife of the President; both acknowledged the full relationship but what intimacies they continued to share we do not know.

Aside from these amendments, neither of them satisfactorily supported by evidence, I have found no changes necessary. The world since 1945 has been a place at once of dread and marvels, some of them not anticipated by the war-time President. If I have since believed that he would have withheld the nuclear bomb from use, would have encouraged the emergence of a friendlier China, and would have prevented relations with Russia from assuming the poisonous nature of the succeeding decades—these speculations were not germane to this book. When it was written he had for some years lain in the rose garden at Hyde Park beneath the simple monument he had planned; and what had happened to the world was beyond his power to change.

It was Eleanor who was to lie beside him there. The inscription on the marble slab said so from the time of its installation at his direction; only the date of her death remained to be carved. There was no recognition anywhere that Lucy had had a part in his life. Whether this is a reflection of his and Eleanor's marital relationship or is only a concession, even in death, to the image both felt they owed their country, it is impossible to say.

Santa Barbara, California   Rexford G. Tugwell
January 1969

INTRODUCTION

Counting only Presidents, of course, Theodore was the first, and Franklin Delano the second, Roosevelt.

This book is about the second, a man who sometimes described himself as a bridge between an old and a new America. He called the old one a horse-and-buggy world; the new was a world of machines and power and great enterprises. And it is true that he did facilitate our transit from the old individualism to the new collectivism. This involved, in economists' terms, a change from unlimited to regulated competition with some direction and some weighting in favor of those with the least power to bargain; and from individual responsibility for all the risks of life to security for all in sickness, unemployment, and old age. In a larger context, it involved change from a world organized for war to one organized for peace. The bridge did not reach quite from the old to the new. How could it when the old was not quite abandoned and the new not quite in being? Firm ground at either end was not yet available.

The world seemed to go to pieces after the war. And Franklin Roosevelt was no longer around to help lay better foundations. Yet in spite of the renewed dissension, several footings remained firm. Collective bargaining, social minima—these and some other achievements, including a certain willingness to regard the economy as one whole—were well begun. But forthright national planning, the subordination of private interests to public ones, the liberal freedoms, an organization for peace —these objectives he had in mind were either not accepted or not fully so. Collectivism at home and collective security abroad were only reluctantly consented to, but their oncoming could be seen to be inevitable in the post-Roosevelt years.

9

As I have worked at this book I have always been aware of writing about a man who attempted much more than he was able to carry through. I became quite certain also that he was finally conscious of his role and had a clear focus on his aims. When he fell short, moreover, he knew better than anyone else the extent and significance of the failure. He was a political man, a democrat; he believed in getting things done with full, if not always complete, consent. Getting this approval very often required compromise. He took what he could get for what he had to give. He thus subordinated the important to the necessary, trusting his judgment to yield a public profit. If there was a residue of hatred from those who were beyond the margins of compromise, he accepted it. He did not like it, but it was inevitable and it did not unduly worry him.

When he died our society was measurably farther forward in every respect than when he became President. He grasped leadership when we were economically paralyzed and socially divided. The nation was a giant in chains of its own forging. He loosened the chains by relieving the paralysis of fear; he reduced the divisions by attacking poverty; and he began a reconstruction. His reconstructive plans had to be postponed because of first the prospect and then the fact of war. But there were clear indications—as we shall see—that he would have come back to them if he had lived. He did not think himself a failure; he was simply not finished.

When he is criticized—and he still is, and bitterly—the criticism comes either from those who dissented from his conception of the future or those who would have had him get there by different means. But no one who believes in the democratic method can honestly say that he did not earn the right to define the future or to choose the means for approaching it. He was an elected leader, not one who had his power from force or from unauthorized chicanery. Some critics may not agree that what he wanted was sufficient, others may not agree that what he wanted was desirable, and neither may admire the methods he used; but none of them can claim that he did not take expert advantage of our complex and peculiar way of doing things. As we look back, it is more and more apparent that a political genius of a rare and effective sort was at work. He accepted both problems and conditions for their solution and found his own answers. Usually a majority approved, and approved emphatically.

To accomplish his aims he adopted—or perhaps he always had—the same view of the presidency as his most effective predecessors. He used the office as an instrument to enhance the well-being of all the people and to maintain the securities of the nation itself. It was his view that as President he had powers co-ordinate with and equal to those of the Congress. They were derived from the same source. The President, he believed, was much better equipped to understand national needs and to define the means for satisfying them than the legislative branch; and so he must be a leader. On the whole, it can be said that no President before him grasped more completely or met more fully the responsibilities of his office. He made the presidency an institution more commensurate with its obligations than he found it because he saw so clearly what those obligations were and because it was his natural bent to accept and carry out public duties.

We are a lucky people. We have had leaders when the national life was at stake. If it had not been for Washington we might not have become a nation; if it had not been for Lincoln we might have been split in two; if it had not been for this later democrat we might have succumbed to a dictatorship. For that was the alternative, much in the air, when he took charge. It is important that younger Americans who did not know him should understand what he found, what he left, and, above all, how he went about his work. His attitudes and the devices he used are the ones called for among us. They will have to be improved and used again. Our troubles are not over; they will never be over. We must hope for other such leaders in other days of crisis. They can learn from studying the Roosevelt technique.

Many of those who have written about this second presidential Roosevelt have said that his was an unusually complex nature. I have never thought this an illuminating characterization; but I could understand why Frances Perkins, for instance, said so. There was always much that was hard to explain, many actions that seemed inconsistent, many things begun and apparently abandoned. It was impossible to develop a recognizably simple personality from the known facts, one exactly typed and reduced to rule. It did seem complex. But that, I think, was because so much of it was hidden.

No historic figure ever lent himself less well to preconceived patterns of behavior than Franklin Roosevelt. His most ardent partisan has to explain embarrassing lapses from the strict code he himself accepted, and his most malevolent critics find themselves losing their prolonged struggle to prove him a spendthrift—if not a traitorous—leader with an overmastering mania for power. He was consistently neither a puritan nor an unscrupulous schemer. Approaching the development of his character and the history of his behavior in this polarized fashion will not explain what posterity needs to know about so consequential a career. But that he was not really more complex than most of us are I am fully convinced: he may well have been less so. He believed in an external guidance not all of us accept as a reality, and he was certain of a commanding destiny most of us have no reason to anticipate. He considered himself appointed to be a leader, but that was because there was work to be done which he judged he could do. If these controlling forces operated on his nature more powerfully than is usual, there is ample explanation in his environment and in the encouragement flowing in upon him from every side.

There is something beyond all this, something internal, to be understood. It was known by the shrewdest of his contemporaries—people like Charles F. Murphy, who was the Grand Sachem of Tammany when young Franklin was in the State Senate and who later helped nominate him for the vice-presidency; or like Josephus Daniels, who, with every reason to distrust and punish a contumacious subordinate, understood that he was dealing with a young man marked for preferment even when he seemed to be distressingly brash and immature; or again like Ed Flynn, who, being much smarter in this than his colleague Jim Farley, always knew that a Roosevelt was an irresistible force, not one to be taken lightly. Yet it should be noted how many of his contemporaries there were who did not feel the heat of this political energy. Walter Lippmann made himself famous in 1932 by denying that it existed; and so did Heywood Broun, who soon regretted his mistake. Many business and labor tycoons who challenged his leadership never felt it until too late, and many of those who write about him still do not recognize its irresistibility.

The ferocious drive behind this progression toward destiny is hardly describable except as it issues in behavior. It cannot be located specifically in intelligence, in attractiveness, or in any other quality of temperament or character. It consists in an impulsive urge so deeply seated and so primitively energized that it activates and controls every other impulse. Looking back on the Roosevelt career, I find its most persistent as well as its most astounding feature is this fierce flame burning at its core. The head of steam it generated allowed its containing vessel no rest even in invalidism, much less in seeming defeat; it drove his turbines with a merciless impatience. Its source was certainly an original force which is shared very unequally among men.

We can divide his contemporaries, as I have suggested, into those who recognized that he was a man thus possessed and those who did not. It marks the degree of their sensitiveness and understanding. They did not need to become followers to show this perception. Such diverse political enemies as old Elihu Root and the younger Wendell Willkie recognized what they were up against. But Herbert Hoover, Alfred M. Landon, Thomas E. Dewey, and many others, not all of them enemies, would always be puzzled.

There were a few fellow leaders who were similarly driven. How diverse their other qualities were shows as nothing else can how utterly irrelevant such possession is to any moral criterion. For Hitler, Mussolini, and Stalin, as well as Churchill, had the same kind of fire in their vitals. All these were Franklin's rivals for world leadership; he knew them as such, and they knew him for what he was. Churchill accepted subordination; the others were crushed. There were some pretenders in the United States. Among these were Huey Long and Upton Sinclair. There were also Wendell Willkie, Douglas MacArthur, Henry Wallace, Harry Hopkins, Harold Ickes, Burton Wheeler, and Philip La Follette. These were ambitious men. All were frustrated by the fiercer concentration, the wilier talents, the greater power of the Roosevelt personality. None could compete successfully. He was, as Willkie said, "the champ."

I have tried to show in this book how the deep volcanic pressure had its way with the individual, how his mind coped with the responsibilities it brought him, how he rose to the occasions of national crisis, how he sometimes dodged and temporized in the interest of eventual victory, and how the obligations he felt, as well as the lessons he learned, controlled his actions. The force within him always demanded and got some kind of response, although it was often masked by falsification of intentions or concealment of objectives. But, as we must also see, he could, when necessary, hold the pressure in check and wait his time with extraordinary patience. This often misled opponents and associates alike who thought he had quit when he was only waiting the right moment.

But this Roosevelt was, in any case, a man of enormous consequence; and I have tried to explore him fully and to report my discoveries. It will not do, I have felt, to leave the impression with posterity that all those who knew him believed him to be the product of a goody-goody education who was made President by a people who recognized spontaneously the desirability of his candidacy and who followed him through the years because they thought him infallible as a leader. His career was both less and more noble than that. It began as a fight for preference, sometimes an ignoble one, down among the local politicians; it ended in a conquest of self, an abandonment of pretense, and a return to the highest and purest ideals, far removed from considerations of ambition, of party, or even of narrow nationalism. There was much that was worthy of praise; there were some things to be deplored; there were some disastrous decisions; but there was nothing of inconsequence and nothing we ought not to tell about because it does not fit the stereotype of statesmanship.

Apologists have complicated the Roosevelt case and set up an added hazard for the interpreter of his work. He can in fact be misinterpreted so easily that it is sometimes done even by those who should know better. Nothing could be farther from actuality than to picture him as a scion of aristocracy who found his way into public life because of his family position and who rose because influence was used in his behalf. The reverse was true. Yet this is not an unusual version of his story. I regard it as due him to say with some emphasis that his position, his wealth, and his easy education were handicaps that had to be overcome in his first campaign for election and in every succeeding one; that they did not help but hindered; that he overcame them, and did it so thoroughly that they afterward seemed to have been advantages when actually they were not. I would go further and say that this is the kind of genius he showed all the way through. All the hard things were made to seem easy. He left nothing to help us see how magnificent his achievement was. On the contrary, he put every possible obstacle in the way, so much so that a biographer often finds himself baffled. There are carloads of papers, records galore, correspondence in reams; and remarkably little of it is of much essential use unless it is subtly interpreted in its context.

Yet the historian knows that because of its fascinations he will not be able to let go a task that may be inherently impossible. So I have pursued to the end the account of a life I have found myself admitting that I cannot wholly explain. By this I mean that I often cannot account for important decisions and cannot trace the origin of crucial policies. I have sometimes been forced to admit that I do not actually know and cannot document even what I have come to believe.

There is hardly a dependable record of a conversation in Franklin Roosevelt's whole life. There is no actual recording of any one of several hundred cabinet meetings, and there are very few full transcripts of high-level conferences. This seems so incredible that stories have been invented to explain the lack of materials. There was a persistent one, met with often at the Hyde Park library, that there was a secret recording booth in the White House basement below the presidential office and that conversations were taken down and put away for future reference. Alas, it is not so. There never were any recordings.

We do have transcripts of the press conferences, of which the number is roughly the same as that of cabinet gatherings. And as one who attended, as a substitute, a certain number of cabinet meetings during the first administration, I register doubt whether, if stenographic reports were available, they would reveal any more than the press-conference transcripts. The cabinet was not a consultative body, at least not regularly; it was an appendage of the presidency not valued very highly as a source of collective wisdom. There do exist many accounts of conversations and of conferences—including meetings of the cabinet by others who took part—and these are valuable to the historian if he takes them strictly for what they are and constantly recalls that none of the note-takers was admitted to the inner chambers where the decision-making took place. Even if his memory was infallible, he seldom knew what was in the President's mind.

Taking such accounts too literally can have appalling results. Consider the often-repeated story concerning the gold-buying operation of 1934 in which the day's price was reported to have been set by a flippant presidential drawing of numbers from the air. The solemn repetition of this incident as evidence of an incorrigible irresponsibility—in which his detractors were anxious to believe—is an illustration of historical irresponsibility, but not of Franklin Roosevelt's. He often covered a prayerful calculation with a pleasantry. He is perhaps to be criticized for having about him those stupid enough to retail such a remark as serious, but not for having actually behaved as the remark would have us believe.

There are many less striking illustrations of somewhat the same thing. The serious student is forced to conclude that this man deliberately concealed the processes of his mind. He would rather have posterity believe that for him everything was always plain and easy, that he undertook all his projects with certainty and pursued them serenely, than ever to admit to any agony of indecision, any serious study of alternatives, any misgiving about mistakes. But it was not so. Not less for him than for others, his burdens were burdens, carried with pain and endured with fatigue. But it was part of his conception of his role that he should never show exhaustion, boredom, or irritation. Even those who served him longest and in the most intimate capacities can recall very few times when the real Franklin was for the moment nakedly exposed. That this was so is the most serious of all the problems any biographer must face.

I myself had a special difficulty, aside from that of attempting to penetrate the walled-up mind from which such world-shaking conclusions issued. I would not allow myself to run beyond what I judged to be the tolerance of the readers I wanted to reach. Those readers were well represented by my two sons, one born in 1939 and one in 1942. I felt it important somehow to convey to them the significance of the Roosevelt experience. Several times I took them to Hyde Park, and often I tried to interest them in pieces of the history I—but not they—had lived through. But they needed something more, a coherent but contained account; and it is this that I have undertaken to write. Innumerable times the temptation to overdevelop incidents, to dwell on fascinating determinations, to recount at length achievements and failures had to be resisted. I was moderately successful; the shortness of my account of a long public life amidst vast affairs is attributable to the hope of interesting a new generation in the one man to whom no one in my generation was indifferent.

I had sympathy and most generous help from everyone I consulted. I cannot begin to enumerate all of these. They include many old colleagues from New Deal days and many others I had not personally known but who had some relationship to the President. Many acknowledgments have been made in footnotes to the text. I have made use of everyone else's research as well as my own. All of us have cause to be grateful to the civil servants at the Hyde Park library who never show impatience with importunate requests and who respond unfailingly to appeals for help. I have worked also at Warm Springs, at the Archives in Washington, and at the Congressional Library, and I am indebted to people in those places for assistance. The library of the University of Chicago has been a place of constant resort. But this account would not have been undertaken or carried through if I had not been listened to through three courses of lectures by students and friends at the University of Puerto Rico. Many of the chapters here were shaped first as talks in those series. To the chancellor, Mr. Jaime Benítez, to the dean of the College of Social Sciences, Mr. Pedro Muñoz Amato, and to many others, including my old friend, the librarian, Mr. Thomas S. Hayes, I commend my written words as I once did my spoken ones in the hope that they will be found acceptable.

To the late Marshall Field and to the Social Science Research Council I am indebted for certain financial assistance which made my research easier.

One further matter: I have throughout my history referred to the President as Franklin and to Mrs. Roosevelt as Eleanor. I did this partly because it was appropriate to speak of them this way in infancy and youth and because there was no logical place where a change of form seemed indicated. I went on even into the presidential years writing of "Franklin" and "Eleanor," even though in my association with them I never addressed either of them in so familiar a way. It seemed natural, because from long consideration of their lives I had come to think of them much as a clergyman might who asked a divine blessing on "thy servant Franklin" or "Eleanor." No disrespect was intended; quite the contrary; I hoped my use of the given name would indicate a certain affectionate detachment. Of the affection there is not likely to be doubt; of the detachment, I hope I have achieved it to the degree necessary for capturing truth.

When I had finished, I asked Mrs. Roosevelt to read what I had written. With her usual kindness she agreed, saying that she would not comment on my interpretations, because everyone is entitled to his own; she would only point out errors of fact. This she did, and I am naturally grateful. This consideration seems to me a logical extension of the openness, the toleration, and the helpfulness which have been the characteristics of her life.

A brief chronology of the Roosevelt career follows immediately. Preliminary study and frequent reference to it may make the sequences in the text easier to follow. It has not been possible in so brief a book to explain fully the background against which our historic character moved or to discuss satisfactorily the many issues he helped to resolve. To remedy this, many references have been made to other biographical and historical works, and the appended timetable is meant to be a further convenience.

THE ROOSEVELT CHRONOLOGY

1828	Birth of James, Franklin's father.
1854	Birth of Sara Delano, Franklin's mother.
1882	Birth of Franklin at Springwood in Hyde Park Township of Dutchess County, New York.
1884	Birth of Anna Eleanor Roosevelt on a nearby estate.
1885–90	Franklin is tutored at home and goes on journeys abroad with parents.
1891	First experience of school at Bad Nauheim for six weeks.
1896	After more tutoring and travel, is entered at Groton School.
1897	Establishes himself at Groton with some difficulty.
1898	Still at Groton, watches Theodore Roosevelt's campaign for governor, his father James·having bolted the Democratic party to support the Republican candidate Roosevelt.
1899	Is taken to Theodore Roosevelt's inauguration in Albany.
1900	Enters Harvard; tries for athletic teams but has no success; father dies.
1901	Tours Europe with mother; begins to report for *The Crimson;* fails of election to Porcellian; is chosen for Fly Club.
1902	Protests British treatment of Boers; works hard at reporting; very busy with Cambridge society.
1903	Elected president of *The Crimson;* becomes engaged to Eleanor, a distant cousin; substantially finishes college course with average grades.
1904	An extra year at Harvard; studies economics, political science, and history. Takes a winter trip to the Caribbean and Panama. Graduates in spring. Enters Columbia University School of Law in fall.
1905	Goes to Theodore Roosevelt's inauguration as President. Is married to Eleanor and they have a long honeymoon in Europe.
1906	Daughter, Anna Eleanor, is born.

17

1907	Admitted to the Bar; becomes clerk in the firm of Carter, Ledyard and Milburn. Son, James, is born. Begins to buy acreage of his own at Hyde Park for farming and forestry experiments.
1908	Predicts casually to fellow clerks that he will be President and tells how he will manage it.
1909	Son, first Franklin Delano Jr., is born in March and dies in November.
1910	Nominated for state senator by Dutchess County Democrats and elected. Son, Elliott, is born.
1911	Involves himself in protest against election of Sheehan for senator, thus incurring Tammany enmity but making a name for himself. Is spotted by Louis McHenry Howe, Albany newsman, as likely to go far politically. Gradually becomes a ticketed Progressive. Decides to support Woodrow Wilson as a way of entering national politics and escaping Tammany wrath.
1912	Organizes Wilson's support in New York; goes to Baltimore convention; is re-elected in spite of sickness during campaign, Howe taking charge.
1913	Is appointed Assistant Secretary of the Navy; resigns as state senator and escapes from Tammany.
1914	Is unsuccessful candidate for governorship nomination against Gerard and learns more about Tammany's power. Second Franklin Delano Jr. is born.
1914–17	Supervises labor in Navy yards; handles Navy contracts; comes under admirals' influence and is known as a big-Navy man. Is separated in policy from Daniels concerning preparedness. Interested in Caribbean, especially Haiti and Marines; also visits Cuba and Santo Domingo. Irritated with Wilson and Daniels, who are not sufficiently martial to suit him. Develops social life in Washington; makes many friends among the diplomatic set. Gradually makes peace with Tammany and is urged to run for governor in 1916 but declines.
1916	Last child, John Aspinwall, is born.
1918	Wilson suggests that he run for governor, but he decides on war service. Goes abroad to see war after many attempts and tries to become officer on his return but is too late.
1919	Goes abroad to visit Peace Conference and settle Navy affairs. Returns on the *George Washington* with Wilson and becomes a convert to peace organization.
1920	Is nominated for the vice-presidency (with James M. Cox, the Democrats intending his selection to soften the slight to Wilson of Cox's nomination; actually Wilson did not approve); campaigns widely and, although the contest is lost, builds up party acquaintance all over the country. Becomes vice-president of the Fidelity and Deposit Company of Maryland with office in Wall Street. Also practices law with Emmet and Marvin.
1921	Attacked by poliomyelitis.
1922–24	Works at convalescence; tries various doctors, places, and cures.

Goes to Florida Keys for winter exercise in warm water. Eleanor works with Howe to encourage Franklin and discovers her own personality. Warm Springs is found and seems to be a place where exercise in the pool will assist in recovering the use of his lower body. Participates in Smith attempt to gain nomination for presidency. Makes "Happy Warrior" speech. Has Smith and Davis at Hyde Park for reconciliation. Eleanor becomes politically active.

1924 Forms law partnership with D. B. O'Connor.

1924–28 Gradually gains prominence in the Democratic party as a disinterested elder. Eleanor continues political work too; becomes a teacher and a practiced public speaker.

1928 Puts Smith in nomination at Houston convention, making second "Happy Warrior" speech. After reluctant evasions, feels forced to take nomination for governorship and is elected by narrow majority even though Smith is defeated for the presidency.

1928–30 Develops independence in the governorship which involves coolness in relations with Smith.

1930 Is re-elected by largest majority registered until that time. Becomes presidential candidate.

1932 Nominated for the presidency against Hoover and wins election in midst of depression.

1933 Gives the nation action to combat deepening economic crisis. Eleanor becomes effective collaborator.

1934–36 Very gradual economic recovery and continued experimentation; but gradual erosion of control over the Congress.

1936 Is re-elected in overwhelming victory over Alfred M. Landon.

1936–40 Accelerated loss of power. Disastrous Court fight contributes to fading out of New Deal by strengthening reactionaries. Preparedness becomes chief preoccupation as war breaks out in Europe and line-up against dictators takes place. Tries for conciliation but fails.

1940 Is re-elected by narrowed majority over Wendell Willkie. Makes first decision to proceed with work leading to fission of uranium.

1941 Leads the nation into war against Japan and Germany after the provocation of Pearl Harbor. Luckily, Hitler has attacked Russia and a general nutcracker strategy is possible.

1942 Assumes substantial leadership of Allies. Churchill conforms. War reached crisis as Germany and Japan spread their empires with amazing speed.

1943 War turns toward eventual victory; tremendous war effort in the United States begins to have effect. Franklin becomes strategist-in-chief, communicating with Churchill and Stalin, but always having the last say because of immense U.S. power. January, Casablanca Conference; August, Quebec; November–December, Cairo-Teheran, where Stalin is met face to face for the first time.

1944 Victory approaches, and outlines of organization for peace take

19

shape; Franklin is their sponsor and negotiator. D-Day: invasion of Europe occurs on June 6; after stubborn fighting in Normandy, armies sweep across France. Opens negotiations with Wendell Willkie for new party alignment to unite the nation's progressive forces. Willkie agrees but postpones action until after election. Is re-elected to the presidency over Thomas E. Dewey. Feels Dewey most unscrupulous of all his opponents, but wins by still narrower majority.

1945   Final conference at Yalta in February gives shape to coming peace. Begins to believe the post-war world may be made secure not only from war but also from want. In his last months he turns again to the progressive agenda for prosperity and fair sharing. Yalta arrangements begin to come apart in the unskillful hands of seconds as San Francisco meeting to establish permanent United Nations approaches. Dies as Germany crumbles and before Japan has finally collapsed, but in the clear prospect of military victory; also before he could carry further his scheme for party realignment; aged 63 years, two months.

THE DEMOCRATIC ROOSEVELT

1

January is deep winter in the Hudson Valley of New York State and the most unpleasant month of the year is just ahead. The James Roosevelts were, however, staying home in 1882. On the thirtieth a big healthy son was born to them at Springwood, just south of Hyde Park Village, and they were very happy. James was already fifty-four, and this fine son must have seemed to him another kind of bonus in a singularly fortunate life. Sara, the baby's mother, who had been a Delano from Algonac, an estate across the river, was twenty-eight. For her this was the culminating blessing in a deeply happy marriage. Almost ecstatically she nursed him, and as he grew into a smiling and vigorous youngster, she hovered over his ventures into the world with endless and often expressed wonder at the miracle he represented.

There are various trite ways of describing the circumstances of Franklin Delano Roosevelt's childhood. He could be said to have been born "with a silver spoon in his mouth," or to have spent his early years "in the lap of luxury." Neither would be factually inaccurate. But the implication that he became a spoiled child would be quite wrong. The stigmata of spoiledness are nowhere evident in his life story. He was protected from some of the harsher physical experiences of childhood and was kept from knowledge of the uglier realities; but this did not result in the petulant egotism of the spoiled. As a baby he grew quickly into health and intelligence; as a child he was required to assume the responsibilities appropriate to his years. The consideration his parents had for each other, for those who served them, and for their neighbors and friends was an example he absorbed as he grew. He was a normal child—what a later generation would learn to call well adjusted.

His eyes first opened to an old and well-used home set in wide fields and surrounded by magnificent trees—elms, maples, chestnuts, beeches —whose tossing branches in winter and whose shelter from the sun in summer would always be a lively and lasting remembrance. All his life

Franklin was to feel a special bond with trees, as though they were a friendly and permanent element in a changing world. His first venturings outside the spacious house took him out under those trees, and presently beyond the lawns to where field and gardens, tended carefully in the English tradition under his father's superintendence, stretched away parklike and open. From the first he was shown the duties and pleasures of country life. He understood how plants and animals were made to grow productively in an ordered scheme. There was no beauty, he was taught, so appealing as that of a landscape in guided use and under strict control. The field crops and the pastures for cattle and horses surrounded the house beyond the lawns. Further in the distance on one side there lay the valley with its great river, and on the other, the distant rising hills, partly open, partly wooded. Most of what could be seen this side of the river belonged in a real sense to the Roosevelts.

He learned from his father that man's first duties were to those who lived about him and to the land on which all of them lived. He was, it cannot be too much emphasized, a child of the country. Cities, he knew, were clustered out there on the periphery of existence, curious agglomerations to be visited on occasion; but they were not by any means the center of things to him as they were to so many of his contemporaries. He would never really regard them as other than a perhaps necessary nuisance. Moreover, he could not quite believe that people raised in them could have the whole worth of others with country backgrounds. His idea of an ideal enterprise would be a farm, one suspiciously like Springwood. The cold and impersonal way he would be apt to treat the businessmen of a more sophisticated pattern, when he became a statesman, would be a grief to many important people who could not believe that wealth and its appurtenances, so impressive to others, were something Franklin Roosevelt did not recognize with any of his sensitized emotions. They were interlopers in a civilization that had once been pleasantly rural. They had no legitimate complaint if their activities were brought within the bounds of decency and they were required to behave as countrymen thought they ought to behave. Family standing was different. He recognized class, but it was not wealth that made the difference.

The James who was Franklin's father, who taught him the elements of management, who showed him how to swim and skate and ride, and who required him to care for his own pony, explained to him gently, in a hundred situations, the meaning of "noblesse." But the father was also a businessman. He was, in fact, what Franklin on a particular occasion and in a never-to-be-forgotten phrase would describe as an "economic royalist." But if the son had understood this from the first about his father, it could hardly have made any difference. The businessman who went off to the city a couple of days a week and sometimes to distant places for longer stays was not the father Franklin knew; the business connections were too remote to seem very real. James Roosevelt was a capitalist, not very active any more in the management of the various enterprises represented by his investment, glad to get large dividends, incurious about labor policies or conditions of work, or even about the exploitation of consumers or resources. But to his son he was a country gentleman and in every way the model of what a man should be. James was not, so far as that went, wealthy or powerful, as were the Astors, the Vanderbilts, and others of a similar sort. But he belonged in their class. When he went to the city he went to Wall Street, and when he came home he came to a neighborhood where they too had estates. He was very anxious as his son grew up that he should follow his own pattern, so much so that when Franklin spoke rather prematurely of wanting to go to Annapolis and have a Navy career, James took him in hand with a seriousness that had its effect. Franklin complied, even if with some lingering regret. It was characteristic, however, that no one knew how disappointed he was. He made the sacrifice cheerfully.

Not far from the Roosevelts there were the Frederick Vanderbilts and the Astors; next door there were Rogerses, and up the Hudson a few miles there was a classic mansion on a hill where Ogden Mills was being raised. Ogden was to be Herbert Hoover's Secretary of the Treasury, following Andrew Mellon. And he and Franklin were to meet on a historic occasion in the White House just before Hoover left it forever. Somehow Ogden, and most of Franklin's contemporaries, raised in similar circumstances and having what was apparently the same education, would develop political attitudes quite different from his own progressivism. They were more usually and normally occupied as capitalists and as conservative statesmen than as reformers or even liberals. Franklin's father and mother may have been economic royalists and Springwood may have been an estate rather than a farm, but somehow Franklin learned from parents and environment a sympathy, a determination to right wrongs, and, moreover, an indifference to the claims of wealth, which in apparently similar circumstances produced Robert McCormick, Richard Whitney, and Vincent Astor, among others. And practically all the others emerged into adulthood lacking Franklin's conviction that the nation's ills—and the world's—waited the reforming leadership of the more fortunate.

Such a dedication, however gained, does not necessarily carry with it either the talents or the knowledge to make it effective. When in rare instances it does, the resulting public figure is apt to be one of those about whom disturbance always seems to center. He is likely to be much loved and much hated while he lives and, after he is gone, to be remembered with prideful nostalgia as the controversies which had centered in him fade. Greatness, it will be recognized, went with him to his grave but was never granted by his detractors while he lived.

The small boy on the Hyde Park acres being so carefully introduced to life by his father and so lovingly watched by his mother had no observable marks of such a greatness. He was quite ordinary in intelligence. He did have an unmistakable charm, which is universally testified to, a kind of sweet reasonableness and an anxiety to please which reduced all those about him to an uncritical affection. He had his way about most things, but his parents' concern for his future required discipline; from his first days he moved within it almost unknowing. He was unconscious of restriction because pains were taken to make the rules seem reasonable. He became a gentleman as easily as any youth ever did.

But he acquired more than manners and attitudes in the first fourteen years of life before he went to school. The Hyde Park routine was leisurely and rural. But there were many visits to New York City; and, more important, there were visits abroad almost every year. His father habitually took the cure at Bad Nauheim; and on the way or returning, there were stays in France or England. Often, too, while he was in Germany and England he was allowed to travel with carefully selected tutors. And once, for a while, he went to a German school. Thus he became aware of contrasting customs, other languages, and foreign scenes. He became, in fact, cosmopolitan. As he entered his teens he was almost as much at home in Germany as in the United States, and he was familiar, from long visits, with that country-house life in England, then entering on its closing decades, which was so much like that of his own Hudson Valley.

He had gone to have his early lessons with neighboring Rogers children; he had then had a German and a Swiss governess, and as his teens approached there had been capable tutors; so that in the languages, at least, and in mathematics he was not behind more formally educated boys when it came time for him to go away to school. That, his father recognized, was at the age of twelve. But his mother could not bear to part with him. And for two years more he was privately tutored and went on developing a life of his own on the family estate. He graduated into more strenuous sports. He rode hunters, played tennis, and in winter skiied. Among the mementos of his youth, so carefully assembled at the library and museum which now adjoins the old house at Hyde Park, are several successive models of the iceboats that were used when the Hudson was frozen over. So he sailed both in winter and in summer. And iceboating, as those who have tried it know, is one of the most thrilling of all outdoor sports. There can hardly ever have been a better place for it than the wide curving river just below the Hyde Park slopes.

The Roosevelts not only possessed the home estate and often went for extended stays abroad, but they also had a summer home at Campobello. This retreat was on an island in the Bay of Fundy, part of the Canadian province of New Brunswick, not far from the Maine harbor town of Eastport, where old established families had "cottages." Its four acres had been acquired after an exploratory visit in Franklin's second summer. It was nothing luxurious; it was primitive by Newport standards—but then those were standards the assured and established Roosevelts never tried to maintain. Theirs was a more modest and composed existence, rich with association and furnished with every convenience, but never in the least pretentious. Pretentiousness was something the Roosevelts had outlived generations before.

In the cold, deep waters of the Bay of Fundy, where dangerous tides of twenty-five feet and more rip and roar through constricted channels toward the shore and out again to sea, Franklin learned about ships and oceans. His father tutored him as carefully in the arts of sailing and navigation as he had in the management of Springwood. And when he was about sixteen and old enough, he was presented with what may have been, outside his first pony, the most precious possession of his life: the *New Moon*, a twenty-one-foot knockabout. Until then he had had to use the *Half Moon* under one or the other parent's superintendence. The *Half Moon* was fifty-one feet long and so rated as a yacht. He thought himself a genuine sailor when he shifted from the larger to the smaller boat. The graduation gave him a satisfaction he remembered all his life as one of the really adequate compensations for growing up. Summers from then on were marine seasons. He came to know every cove and headland of the rocky coast, every tide and current of the dark, dangerous waters. But he did not need to learn about the sea so much as just to be near it. He took to boats as some boys do to motorcars, as though he had been born in one. He spent his days idly cruising in the sun or adventurously testing his skill against wind, fog, and tide. Many a future admiral of Franklin's age would never have the sea in his blood as Franklin did. And none would more instinctively understand the uses of ships.

But life changed for Franklin at fourteen. What should have happened at twelve was finally allowed to happen then. His mother gave way and he was escorted to Groton. Groton may not have been the school of his dreams, if he had any dreams about school; but he had been enrolled there since the age of two, and it had always been part of his expected future. It was not an ancient institution. Its relative newness was perhaps made up for by its undoubted exclusiveness; but the fact was that it had been founded soon after Franklin's birth. It was sheer chance that James and Sara Roosevelt had visited the James Lawrences of Groton in 1883 just as the school was rising on land given by the Lawrences to Endicott Peabody for a school. The apparent impulsiveness of Franklin's sedate and cautious parents in entering him at a school not yet established is accounted for by knowing something about Headmaster Peabody and the list of the school's trustees. This list included such names as Phillips Brooks, the famous clergyman, and J. Pierpont Morgan, the financier. And these were not unrepresentative. The other boys similarly enrolled came almost altogether from what would be described as Social Register families.

But the main attraction was undoubtedly Peabody. From September 1896 until June 1899 the person of reference in Franklin's life was this large, athletic, and professionally Anglican headmaster to whom his parents had entrusted him. He, and to a less degree other teachers, took the place of the father Franklin had now left behind and the tutors on whom he had depended.

Groton was a small school on the English model, devoted to the development of character in boys who might otherwise have been softened by pampering and might never have come to realize their responsibilities as members of the nation's ruling group. This was precisely the way Peabody put it; and what he said, he meant. He had an ideal of dedication which was to be fulfilled by the gift to the nation of worthy men. The Christian life included, along with good works, the cultivation of games and sports as part of a rigorous and frugal regimen. Peabody also believed in the humanities, and Groton's curriculum was biased in their favor with some compromises to develop economic and political understanding. The playing of games and the study of Greek, Latin, and the modern languages—those were the Groton disciplines, as they were those of the English church schools. The boys slept in bare cubicles, took many cold baths, and lived on fare so plain that most of them, otherwise happy enough, complained of it. But they had chapel every day; and Franklin, at least, did not object. He liked to hear the plain but elevated words of Peabody and to repeat the familiar litanies. He would like them all his life.

Groton was not a place where intellectual interests got first attention. There were teachers, and good ones; but athletics were furiously pursued, and a close group life with norms natural to teen-age boys monopolized most of the waking hours. Franklin is not supposed to have been unhappy there. But it has to be noted that he did not do very well at anything. He never came under Peabodian rebuke, but he was never much praised, either. He was not a leader among his fellows, but neither was he solitary. He accepted the going standards, struggled to perform as he was supposed to perform, and was not conspicuously disturbed by his comparative failure.

Peabody spoke of Franklin in after years in a kindly way when most graduates were treating Franklin to chilly disapproval "as a traitor to his class.[1] He was a good Grotonian, something not to be deleted from his record. And the headmaster himself, as Franklin might have said, very often came close to stating the principles Franklin would have said had guided him into traitorousness.

The comparative submergence of Franklin throughout his school life is sometimes said to have been caused by his late entrance. And this may very well have been important. At puberty or thereabouts boys make friendships of a sort they will never make again. These bonds are so close and so unconsciously strong as to become almost a projection into a common personality of what had been before, and would be again, separate individualities. And in a closed society of boys, such as a boarding school becomes, a whole group may be welded together into an undifferentiated mass. Living together as they do, playing, working, sleeping, suffering a common discipline, sharing common victories and defeats, they become a hard-and-fast, one-for-all-and-all-for-one group which outsiders may hope to penetrate only by paying a heavy price in resentment. His form had had two years of this welding when Franklin entered it. Until his last day at Groton he never quite broke down the last resistance of those who had made up the original group.

But there was something else about Franklin at that age which must not be overlooked. He was not only late in arriving at Groton; he was delayed in his whole development. In spite of his quicksilver charm and his easy perception of others' reactions to himself, his understanding developed rather slowly. This mental and psychological accompaniment of physical growth was not an arrest; it was a delay in development. It happens to many boys. At fourteen, when he went to Groton, Franklin was no more than five feet three inches in height and he weighed not much more than a hundred pounds. During his first year he sang soprano in the choir; his voice had not yet changed. By the following autumn he had reached a weight of 112 and dropped out of the choir because his soprano was no longer dependable. But that was when he was full fifteen.

Franklin's letters home during his Groton years were charmingly boyish compositions. If they are read with some understanding of puberty they are a little pathetic for avoiding the painful moods, the maladjustments, the questionings, which torment every boy. The hearty and outward-turning Peabody was not one to listen sympathetically to a

---

[1] It is true that a short list of public figures of progressive leaning could be compiled from the graduates of Groton. It would include Bronson Cutting, Dean Acheson, Averell Harriman, Sumner Welles, and Francis Biddle. But the percentage of these compared with that of those who became notable reactionaries would be infinitesimal. If Groton graduated Franklin Roosevelt, it also turned out Robert R. McCormick at the same time, whose Chicago *Tribune* would certainly be the most effective objector to every liberal impulse in America for several generations.

boy's disturbances, nor were any of the other teachers. These elders would have been embarrassed by the revelation of what would have seemed to them abnormality. They would no doubt have advised more cold baths and more exercise. Boys thus driven in upon themselves may develop a deceptive exterior which conforms in every apparent respect to the standards of behavior set and enforced by authority and by group influence; but what goes on within may be something that in the long run will explode into non-conformity at inconvenient, perhaps disastrous, times.

Such a boy may undergo racking ordeals when the long-delayed results of suppression emerge into action—the more so because their origins may by then have become hopelessly obscured. Transition from boyhood to manhood is never easy. For those in whom the change goes slowly the agonies are prolonged; for them the psychic injuries resulting from such a bland pretense that nothing of the sort can or should happen, such as hearty, athletic, and practical elders are apt to assume, may be profound. The guilt of dreamings and of the disparity between ideals of conduct and the welter of primal urges toward sinful deeds—these are crises in which a youth needs love and understanding as he never needed them before and never will again. The rough handling of his fellows, their careless invasion of his reticences—these may be a good enough corrective, used occasionally and with insight, for over-developed self-regard and inner turning; but in a boys' school there is no escape from such brutalities. In these years the haven of a father's understanding and his yearning guidance is a priceless guarantee of normal emergence into adult life.

There is no record of the struggles and trials through which young Franklin must have passed while he was at Groton. The student who reads his letters to his mother or to other relatives and friends forms the picture of a youth so gay and careless, so full of local interests, so intent on gaining approval, that he is apt to overlook entirely what is never mentioned. The very fact that the surface is so cheerful and uncomplicated is plain warning of an area all too carefully hidden. This was the time and these were the circumstances in which Franklin was learning how to present to the whole inquiring world the image of himself that he had reason to believe they would approve. He was also learning to carry completely hidden his trials and experiments, his thoughts about serious matters, and even the way he saw the world and men's relations with each other as they came and went in it.

Just here I turn to something for which the evidence is not at all satisfactory. There are, however, hints, and these are so compelling as to command acceptance as a supposition. My guess is that in these years Franklin came to depend with a great abiding trust on divine support. One of the curious traits of his later life was that he would never discuss certain of his deepest emotions, including his religion, even with his wife Eleanor. One reason for this, so far as religion goes, is, I think, that he came to his conception of its role in life—at least in his life—in a difficult adolescence. He found the comfort he needed in this as in nothing else. He found, in the society of a boys' school, perhaps, that anything more than acceptance of form and ceremonial is discouraged in somewhat the same way as is being too earnest a student. He learned, therefore, to find and keep the support of religion without argument and without ostentatious practice.

This belief in and reliance on a fatherly God to take the place of the earthly father who was retreating into the shadows of age became so settled and fixed in his life as never again to be questioned. He found the Anglicanism of Peabody and of the St. James parish in Hyde Park satisfactory. It required of him no testimony, no embarrassing externalizations of his inner torments and resolutions. It was simply there, the atmosphere and ceremonial of an institution in which divinity was present but not demanding.

If it seems peculiar that Franklin had no adult doubts, no doctrinal difficulties, and only a serene faith which nothing could disturb, that is because the philosophy of religion was not his métier. He had other reticences. As to these, but most of all as to his religion, it can be guessed that they were too precious a reliance, too much needed by a man in the continuous buffeting of public life, to be risked by examination after complete acceptance. This is, of course, speculation, and psychological speculation at that, and so I enter on it with due tentativeness and modesty. But I do know that Franklin found religion as a boy. If he never let it be questioned, that may well have been because he had found it in circumstances so utterly convincing that re-examination was unnecessary.

This is important even if only its practical consequences are considered. Franklin would always be a man in robust spiritual health. This gave him a sense of balance and perspective capable of supporting him firmly when grave decisions had to be made and when counsels were confused. It enabled him, moreover, to sleep long and restfully at night, when he felt that the day had been given to the service of men —who, along with him, were God's children. If the men he served were God's children, they were also his—Franklin's—brothers and worthy of equal sharing in all the opportunities of life. He was not the sort to make this kind of thing explicit, but that he thought of himself as a practicing Christian there is every reason to believe. The concept may have been broadly interpreted to include indirect activities, but it must be recognized to have existed. How easily this builds up into a social program something like the New Deal is not too difficult to see. This was still a long way in the future and across numerous crises. But the thoughts in boys' minds are often the forerunners of adult policies.

I am quite willing to argue for the structure I erect on Franklin's boyhood inclination toward religion. I feel certain of the personal as well as the public consequences. I went to church with Franklin a time or two in later years. I sat with him in confidence on occasion as consequential matters were brought to decision. He felt, I judged, that he had a duty to do and that he was under a certain general direction to work it out through politics. His touch with divinity was renewed when he sat in places of worship making responses, joining in song, just as he had done at Groton. And always, when new undertakings were before him, he asked all his colleagues in it to accompany him if they would in asking for divine blessing on what they were about to do.

It must be understood that one who asks and feels that he receives support in this manner, and with sincerity, cannot, even in his own estimation, go disastrously wrong. If an error is made it is an understandable one and nearly always unavoidable in the sense that the best has been done and that no one could have done more.

There appeared later in his life the inevitable difficulties into which a non-self-examining mind may fall—he had trouble separating ends and means and sometimes used means he ought not to have used; and he found that loyalties are not always single and simple. These are the inevitable accompaniments of a political career, of public life and statesmanship. They should not be neglected in the examination of his career.

But that he felt justified or excused by a consciousness of having done his best, and having done it with divine approval, seems to me obvious. The secret of his unassailable serenity and his easy gaiety lay in this sense of oneness with the ongoing processes of the universe and his feeling of being, as Emerson said, in tune with the infinite. A person relying on such comfort and assurance can work happily and cooperatively with and for others. He can, moreover, work for objectives far beyond his own expectation of survival, taking a wholly sufficient satisfaction in being part of a swelling tide of human effort rolling toward climactic betterment.

Franklin worked thus for conservation, for instance, and found in it the kind of lasting interest I describe. It was his first assignment as a young legislator. He was happy in it. But it was gradually transformed into more than concern for the land and natural objects; it became a concern for people as well. And this gradually opened out, as we know, to caring for all the resources and all the people of the nation. Conservation, well-being, and security were controlling words in the motivation of his whole career. And in the end this preoccupation was consummated in the plan for such a society of nations as would, he hoped, secure the peace and well-being of all the people on earth.

32

It was all, as I understand it, quite logical, all in pursuit of quietly arrived at objectives. He was doing, he believed, the work of the God with whom he had so confident a relationship. He was doing it each day, using the political means for which he had a talent, and being rewarded day by day as he went along by the progress he saw, by the affection which came to him, and by his own confidence that what he did was done under the fatherhood of God.

There is another pervasive characteristic I have come to regard as of almost as much importance in his life. It is something so evident to the understanding student as to forbid its neglect. Franklin felt a necessity for emotional concealment which was extremely persistent. I am quite certain, also, that this was very much complicated by the continual delay in his development. A boy in the throes of adolescence sees the world through troubled eyes. When he approaches it slowly—more slowly than his intimates—he shares, yet does not share, their experiences. And since they are ahead of him, leading him, as they move into manhood, what he really thinks and feels needs to be concealed because his emotions would seem infantile to the intimates for whose approval he yearns. Those emotions seem unworthy even to him by the standards he has accepted. Outwardly he professes feelings and reactions he actually does not have. And those he does have he distrusts and would not under any compulsion expose.

It is my belief that Franklin was the victim of such circumstances and that his handling of his difficult problems at Groton became the model for behavior in later similar situations. If it is accepted, as I believe it must be, that he came late to each stage of his development, the successive latenesses begin to reveal themselves as having appeared in a similar order of time, or not far from it. For instance, at Harvard —where he was a student from the age of eighteen to twenty-two—his activities were more than usually simple for an undergraduate. Although he became an editor of *The Crimson* and president in his senior year, an inspection of his editorial writing shows an almost incredible outpouring of incitements to "school spirit," a heated interest in circumscribed local issues, and almost no awareness whatever of realities beyond the undergraduate horizon. At the Columbia University School of Law, although he was then married and had settled on a profession, he still had discovered no deeper interests and not even any considerable feeling for the law—so much so that he did not bother to take his degree after passing his bar examinations in the spring of 1907. The years of law practice that followed were desultory and unmotivated; he was still marking time.

Not until 1910—when he was twenty-eight—is there any evidence whatever that he had found himself or discovered any purpose to whose devotion he felt any responsibility beyond that of being a good citizen

33

in Hyde Park and a practicing Christian. There may have been intimations of something larger. But they can be uncovered only by looking back from the presidency and straining somewhat to fit them into a meaningful development. The same sort of delayed coming to one mature level after another keeps up even further, though the difficulties of penetrating to so cleverly hidden a psyche become more difficult. The Assistant Secretary of the Navy in his thirties developed no very creative view of the great events in which he was an actor. He was as conventional as he was busy, except of course that by now he was a professional politician and developing big-Navy ideas. It was not until his campaign for the vice-presidency, with Cox as his superior, that he displayed any cohesive view of national and international affairs. And even then he seemed to have drifted into Democracy and mild progressivism because of the circumstances of his first elections and his inheritance from Uncle Ted; also, perhaps, because it was, he judged, to be the American leaning rather than because he had yet discovered that this was the way to satisfy his deep but as yet unfocused aspirations.

When Franklin should become President there would be much speculation concerning the origin of his social and economic leanings. This would have been better informed if it had been realized that from his first year at Groton he had had some contact with politics and economics as academic subjects. What he learned in his courses certainly had no direct and specific effect on his later policies, but in a general way the influence was lasting.

The doctrines he was exposed to were those familiar in that generation. The classical system of free enterprise in which competition was the force at work was taught in all academic departments. By now it was beginning to be modified by governmental interference. A good deal was said about maintaining fair competition—especially by preventing monopolistic practices, and sometimes even by regulating hours of work, minimum wages, and factory conditions. This was a loosening of the earlier rigid rule that completely free competition must govern all business relationships and that governments had only police functions.

It may be noted here that Franklin remained within this ideological pattern all his life. He would strain it on occasion, but not severely. Its hold on his mind would never be loosened.

The study at Groton, as we know from a surviving notebook, was not a mere indoctrination. There were discussions. And the first of them took advantage of the contemporary heat aroused by Bryan's free-silver campaign in 1896. Political argument was an excellent educational device and modifies considerably the view that Groton was an establishment given wholly to rote learning of orthodox subjects. Even fourteen-year-olds could not have escaped absorbing some attitudes about the monetary issue. Bryan had polarized the whole country with his Cross of Gold speech at the Democratic convention; and the business community was seriously alarmed by the threat of inflation implied in his candidacy. It can be imagined that the boys of wealthy families at Groton were alerted; and Franklin's notebook reflects the arguments being used. Money must be stable if it was to be a measure of value; gold offered stability; free coinage of silver meant a depreciated dollar. This would injure even workers, whose wages would buy less because their real wages would fall. This concern for labor was a notable feature of the discussion.

This particular issue, and the contention about it, may well have made a lasting impression on Franklin's mind. We can imagine that he went on considering it from time to time in a casual way over the years, until suddenly it became important to him as an issue he must deal with. The solution he found would not correspond with that entered in his Groton notebook, but the arguments on either side would not have changed in the course of the several decades. Gold, in his mind, would no longer seem so stable, nor would stability in itself be so desirable a quality; but the relation of gold to prices and of prices to prosperity would still seem to him the same.

There were other issues considered in this course which would later be ones he would have to make up his mind about. How prices are fixed and what can be done to manage them; how "the trusts" operated; how levels of wages were arrived at and the inevitable effect of artificially raising them—the wages-fund doctrine; tariffs and their incidence. All these were discussed. The statement was orthodox and classical; it did not tend to undermine the going system, but it did give a boy's mind a certain familiarity with such matters. This is important. It would often be noted in after years, even by those inclined to disparage Franklin's policies, that he approached the discussion of them with ease and without hesitation. There was none of the embarrassment a really ignorant politician shows in such matters. The body of doctrine, the terms used in exposition, the viewpoints of those who had thought most about such matters—these were all known to him.

There is no doubt that he accumulated technique as he went along. But this is not necessarily a sign of maturity. In his case I am convinced that it was not. Technique in politics can rise to the level of strategy when used for statesmanlike ends. It can also stay at the level of tactics, concerning itself with the devices for getting oneself elected or for pushing other candidates. Even Franklin's work for Al Smith during the years of his convalescence from disease after 1921 was not a considered support. It was just going along because of political expediency; when he came to take a good look at Smith and summoned his reserves for laying out a course ahead, he saw at once that a break with him was in

35

charm   *Flexibility*   *pragmatic*

fact necessary. There was more than expediency in this; there was also a failure to realize the essentially reactionary policy for which Smith stood and from which he himself would have to dissent.

All the members of the Brains Trust and their associates will testify, I think, to the flexibility of the Roosevelt mind even when the presidency approached. He was a progressive vessel yet to be filled with content. He was in fact slow and late in maturing all the way along. And always he had to conceal his lateness from those about him who did not understand that it was so. He became, in consequence, a consummate actor.

He was the kind of man to whom those who wanted him convinced of something—usually something in their own interest—could talk and argue and insist, and come away believing that they had succeeded, when all that had happened was that he had been pleasantly present. He may or may not have understood the issue. But no one would ever know whether he had or not. What he did understand, because of his long defensive training, was what the motives were with which he was confronted. About that, no one was ever more shrewd. And no one got much from him that he was not inclined to yield for another reason than that it was urgently sought.

There was something else about Franklin—a gift evident from his earliest days—that assisted and protected him in what I conceive, in spite of outward appearances, to have been a difficult course through education and illness into an established career. It was even then a notable characteristic. That was his persistent and unconscious charm. I speak of something now that is easily recognized when encountered but not at all easily described. It had a double effect on the development of his personality. As he came somewhat late to each stage of maturity, no one noted or made allowances for lateness. His associates merely underrated him as a pleasant fellow. They thought of him as permanently several levels lower than he would presently reach. They were therefore constantly unable to believe in his achievements. They assumed that the individual they had known a short time ago must have been arrested at the level they had observed.

Because he was treated with condescension, he made secret resolves, I am quite sure, as any spirited person would, to show the condescender how mistaken he had been. These resolves do not need to be openly stated or even secretly recognized. They are, nevertheless, an ever present goad. Meanwhile approval can be had for other characteristics than maturity. Franklin had so much success with his charm and relied on it so much that practically everyone assumed it to be about the only quality he had—this and a kind of superficial brightness which seemed part of the same characteristic. That he was likable, even lovable, everyone who knew him as a boy, as a youth, and as a man testifies. But no two people seem to agree on anything else.

He moved as a boy through an environment essentially ununderstanding but not hostile, thinking it to be, as boys do, something simply there to be made the best of. What he would have been like if he had had to fight his way through the public schools, as, for instance, Al Smith, Bob Wagner, or Fiorello La Guardia—all political contemporaries —had to, and then begin as a young lawyer hanging around a political clubhouse looking for an opportunity, it is hard to say. He might have been killed off, or he might have grown tough and capable. The student of his career has to take circumstances as he did. What it amounts to is that he led a relatively protected early life but one which nevertheless had serious problems to be met in his own individual way.

What Franklin had to contend with was a very different kind of temptation. From every delayed level he reached he had to climb to the next through the smothering layers of assumption that he was incapable of getting there. Things were obviously so pleasant where he was; he was so agreeable and so well adjusted; he was so handsome, rich, and wellborn! His present good fortune was obviously enough for anyone. It had been enough for thousands of others apparently just like him. Why should it not be enough for him? Especially, why should it not be enough when he was neither brilliant, worldly-wise, nor very much at odds with his circumstances?

From Groton he was to go on to Harvard. And no one paid any particular attention to the one intellectual adventure of his later schooldays. He was introduced to Mahan. A sixteen-year-old boy whose passion was the sea and sailing discovered the greatest of all exponents of sea power. From that time on Franklin's one exploratory activity, all on his own, was the reading of naval history. That this was important, it is not necessary to insist. To study the role of the Navy in American development was to understand the relationship of the nation to other nations. How independence was gained and kept was not a secret to be discovered by studying land campaigns or even the opening of the West; that secret lay off the coasts, from Labrador to the West Indies. It lay in the approaches from the East and in the use of ships to take advantage of jealousy among potential enemies and favor among potential friends. The nice weighing of strength deployed over space and maneuver carried out in time was something Franklin came to as a scientist does to his laboratory or a littérateur to his books. It lay unused in his mind for a long time; but the assistant secretaryship of the Navy when he came to it was a kind of fulfillment.

No one noticed that he was acquiring this competence. His interest led him to collect pamphlets, documents, and prints which had to do with maritime history. It was a harmless and quite understandable

Struggle for acceptance

hobby for a wealthy young man. So were his stamps. He played with stamps, and in his play learned more than anyone supposed possible. This was the kind of geography that not only places identifiable areas in relation to each other but assesses their relative importance through historic changes. It was a nice supplement to naval history. If those who were inclined to take his potentialities overlightly had been watching the meaningful signs, they would not have been confused by his apparently superficial preoccupation with conventional pleasures and his apparent disinterest in affairs of importance. But everyone—not excluding wife and mother—regarded his hobbies as nothing more than the appropriate hobbies of a gentleman. Plenty of stamp collectors, connoisseurs of naval or sporting prints, and enthusiasts for old books have never become consummate politicians or, in fact, public men of any sort. For Franklin these turned out to be merely interesting adjuncts to a career.

As he passed on to Harvard from Groton some difference developed in Franklin's relation to those about him. He had never been important at Groton, but he had come to be accepted as a conforming and even a useful member of his group. His most important victory in the struggle for acceptance had been the managership of the baseball team. He schemed to get that responsibility; and, having got it, he strove to carry out his duties acceptably. This, in schoolboy rating, is a relatively low honor, given to those who would be athletes if they could but who for some reason have not been able to succeed. Franklin did not think athletics unimportant. He agreed completely, so far as anyone knows, with the order of prestige which ranked a football captain first in the regard of his fellows and which ranged lesser athletes in descending scale. It was not until, far down the scale, most of the athletes having been left behind, the baseball managership appeared in the ranking— just above the literary honors.

This kind of non-recognition followed him into and through Harvard. The chief characteristic of all this experience, from the psychological point of view, was failure to achieve what he knew to be first-rank places, together with a consciousness of competence which ought to have brought them within his reach.

True, he was a Grotonian, and Groton was an exclusive school; but what Groton was in the world had no impact on members of the small school community. What counted was what he was within Groton. So at Harvard. Harvard was a first-choice university. At Harvard, because he was Grotonian, he became a member of an inner circle of good-school graduates from which midwest high school boys were as effectively excluded as if they were lepers. He had gold-coast quarters, furnished with luxury, and had an entree to the society of Boston and its suburbs. But he was not invited to join Porcellian (as Uncle Ted had); the Fly

38

Club (Alpha Delta Phi) was not quite so select; and altogether he was rated among the inner circle—and he must have been conscious of it every hour of every day—just about as he had been at Groton.

Part of this failure to achieve what in his heart he must have felt would have been suitable ranking was because of his slight retardation —in this case mostly physical. A boy of sixteen who is slight and lathy and who shoots up without gaining much weight will not be a very noted athlete. Those who knew him only in after years always had trouble visualizing him in his youth. He fought the limitation his physique enforced, but he never overcame it. His co-ordination was good; his muscles were long and supple; he once won a high-kick contest at Groton—but he was not a bruiser. He was not able to take punishment as were boys who were built closer to the ground. He gradually came to have a tall slenderness which, when the gangling awkwardness of youth had been overcome, was wonderfully graceful. His mother had been what in those days was described as a Gibson girl; her son was a Gibson man. Later on he was a good tennis player and golfer, but he was never a great collegiate athlete.

Neither his adeptness at pleasing those whose opinions he valued nor his physical beauty counted on the playing fields of Groton or of Harvard. He tried. His letters continued to be full of the earnestness of his long effort to succeed. He was always, it seemed, in a more or less battered condition. But he was always on a fourth or fifth team or crew. Never in his school or collegiate life was there ever a cheer for Roosevelt; and that in itself was failure enough to be recalled far down into later years.

At Groton he attained that doubtful prize, the baseball managership; at Harvard his best mark was represented by the editorship of *The Crimson*. This was second-rate, if that; but it was something. And those who note what remarkable spirit Franklin expended on his *Crimson* work, and how wholly devoid of originality or imagination it was, miss the point. He was still making the very best of what he could get under the going rules. He was proving that he could function acceptably without breaking out of the conventions, even if his maturity was slower than that of his companions. It would have been in character if, just at the last, he had startled everyone by suddenly seeming to have grown up and evinced interests beyond the Harvard yard. It is true that he was stirred by Uncle Ted's 1904 campaign and there was even some interest in the Boers, who were just then being badly treated by the imperial British; but these are explainable in other ways. Uncle Ted was a family hero; the Boer business was not original with Franklin. At Harvard he never seemed to have reached maturity.

There was one occurrence at Harvard, however, which a biographer afterward noted—whenever there was an election and he was eligible, he was elected.[2] The exception to this, which taught him a valuable lesson, was the Class Day elections in his senior year. These were, as in other Ivy League colleges and universities, controlled by the inner circle of the elite clubs. He was one of six nominees for class marshal, of whom the top three would win. He was fourth and so was eliminated. One thing about this was that only about half the eligibles had voted; another thing was that the three who were elected obviously constituted a club slate from which Franklin had been omitted. He had neither organized the electorate nor got himself selected by the machine. He had been remiss in the most elementary political precautions. It is not unlikely that in the succeeding days he did some talking and even some threatening. At any rate, he was subsequently elected permanent chairman of the class committee. The number voting was not much larger than before, but his majority of those who did vote was large.

He had found out something about politics. It might be taken as a portent of the future.

[2] Frank Freidel, *Franklin D. Roosevelt: The Apprenticeship* (Boston: Little, Brown, 1952), Chapter IV.

2

Franklin, all through his Harvard years, was a very busy young man. There was not only his freshman and sophomore athletics—he tried with little more luck than he had had at Groton to play freshman football and as a sophomore earnestly worked at his rowing with only slightly better success—but he tackled his *Crimson* career with almost desperate energy. For three years he probably averaged half of each day during the term time on the paper, using all his resources of energy and persuasiveness to succeed. In this he also displayed a determination that might have been a warning to some of his later competitors if they had not been too careless to assess such a collegiate activity at its true worth.

As has been remarked, it cannot be shown that his rise to power on *The Crimson* was motivated by any desire to use it for a public purpose. He had no novel ideas concerning its possibilities when he did come to control. It was exactly like the struggle to become stroke of the crew. He responded to an inner compulsion in pursuit of an objective difficult but not impossible to achieve. The achievement would be a sufficient end in itself because of its established prestige. If it ever occurred to him that such a dedication of time and effort ought to be for some more general or communal objective, there is no evidence of it. And his conduct as editor does not support such a supposition.

It may be straining an interpretation to project this intensive *Crimson* drive into the future, but there is certainly some reason for saying that his efforts for election as state senator, as Vice-President, and as governor, at least, were somewhat similar in motivation. He was still trying to become stroke of the crew or end on the football team; still trying to rise from second to first. This is another way of saying that his was to be a careerist's life, not one dedicated to a cause—being thus like Lincoln's or Theodore Roosevelt's, not like La Follette's, for instance; or like that of Hoover, for another example, who coldly set himself to abolish poverty, no less, by the application in public life of engineering

41

principles. If this seems a contradiction of his humaneness and Christianity, as it might also of Lincoln's, the seeming is, I think, superficial. The *use* of the offices he attained in later life was for great public objectives; there can hardly be any doubt about that, considering the policies he consistently pursued. But he still may not have worked to attain them in order to use them for these public purposes. This is a distinction of some importance. Keeping it in mind may help to follow his development from stage to stage with heightened understanding.

As in later dedications to absorbing activity, *The Crimson* editorship was handicapped by his lateness and immaturity. He was not really very good at the job. His was not, like Theodore's, a literary gift, and his editorials were only passable. But such advantages as he did have he developed to the limit; and he exhibited a cautious discretion that foreshadows his later political efforts. He never rashly committed himself or went beyond the positions supported by convention or, if convention was changing, by a clear majority approval. The result was that he got to the very top of this particular heap and stayed there without challenge until he was ready to leave. And, as in other instances, when he had acquired the power of position, some use for it finally did occur to him. It was nothing very substantial, but it was beyond the usual undergraduate concern. Just at the end of his *Crimson* term he began to speak of reform. He was not yet mature enough to think of reforming society; he thought only of reforming Harvard—physically. He campaigned politely for better fire protection, new walks, and other improvements.

Not only did he hardly ever speak of the world outside, he never even questioned the kind of education Harvard was furnishing. It was a little early yet to notice the ferment which by then must have begun and which was to revolutionize collegiate education from 1920 on; and anyway, Harvard's authorities were to be late in recognizing the need for change. But it might have been supposed that the undergraduate paper would have some reaction to what was gestating in so many collegiate minds. No Roosevelt editorial ever mentioned education or, for that matter, anything with what might be called an intellectual interest. This was partly because of his immaturity and partly because of his cautious keeping away from controversy, but it was also a faithful reflection of average undergraduate aversion to classroom disciplines. Athletics and other "campus activities," the pleasures of society—these came first. Studies were to be got through; but, pretty much as at Groton, they did not have prestige rating sufficient to motivate serious pursuit.

Franklin's academic average was about a C. This meant that he "got by." He was distinguished in nothing; but no subject was so difficult that he could not absorb enough of its elements to pass an examination.

42

Comparison with Theodore in this, as in other matters, is naturally inevitable. Theodore's attention to his studies and his competence in them won him a Phi Beta Kappa key. Franklin became Phi Beta Kappa too, but not for scholarship. He was given an honorary key when he became a prominent public figure. But that was far from being the same thing.

To follow Franklin through a week or a month, sharing his activities, would, I suspect, have exhausted the most energetic observer. He was, by his sophomore year, well past the worst of adolescence and well into a regime of youthful social activities far more demanding than those of the usual undergraduate. He was, after all, a Roosevelt; and the neighborhood of Boston had a well-developed high society into which his entree was automatic. Moreover, by then his mother had come to live in Boston for the winters. His father had died (in December 1900 at seventy-two) and she could no longer stand separation from her son.

This decision of his mother undoubtedly gave Franklin some uneasiness. As a good son he would have been solicitous about her loneliness now that the father to whom she had devoted so much care in his last years was gone. The uneasiness would have been for his own independence, not of action but of thought. For Sara had grown more domineering with the years. That may be too harsh a word, but she was an imposing lady, conscious of her every virtue and jealous of every prerogative pertaining to her position. If she really came to Boston to assume a more intimate direction of her son's life, as seems probable, she was disappointed. The time was rapidly approaching—may already have arrived—when Franklin had an inner life of the spirit, if not quite yet of the mind, which was closed to everyone, not excepting his mother. I have always felt that it was this move of his mother's which taught him finally to keep the doors locked that closed away the slowly evolving life within. The processes were at work, like fermenting wine, which would emerge in the end refined and matured; but meanwhile there would be no explorations and no tamperings. So what Sara intended worked rather in reverse.

But mother and son were already separated by more than the interval between her generation and his. After all, Franklin was touched by the history he studied, and there must never be forgotten the influence in his life of the then active career of Uncle Ted. It seems likely that even the fugitive, and not very frequent, conversations between these two may have penetrated deeper than any other of the exchanges of Franklin's university years. The older man was sensitive to youth. He may have divined the ferment working in Franklin's mind and encouraged its excitement. He was, we know, a very special kind of hero as well as a relation: and his career was the kind Franklin's feelers were exploring even before he woke to what they were doing.

What Sara wanted of her son was no secret. She wanted a conforming country gentleman in the image of James, capable of managing the estate and the business interests to which he would fall heir. She feared departure from the pattern and put up barriers to adventure wherever she could. Franklin simply ignored them. His response when such matters were discussed was to change the subject blandly and present an agreeable but perfectly blank front, quite impenetrable to probing. After a few attempts Sara must have held her peace more or less, but she never gave up. The militant old lady went down into age fighting for the soul of a son she thought she ought to control.

Franklin was able to dispense liberal hospitality under his mother's superintendence, something that gave her happiness and satisfied part of her need for participation in his activity. And he spent many weekends at country and suburban houses; he played tennis and golf; he skiied and skated; he dined and danced and went to teas. What with athletics, *The Crimson,* and society, he cannot really have had much time for strictly academic work.

Vacations were not very different, except that they were spent elsewhere than Cambridge and that there was no classroom routine. At Hyde Park or at Campobello he had a continuous stream of guests; he visited in others' homes; he played games; he sailed and fished; he traveled. Once in a while in an odd hour he got out his stamp books and worked over them or looked into an account of naval adventures. Perhaps on going to bed he read a little history or a detective story— a habit that would stay with him all his life. He developed a flair for clothes and dressed carefully in the rather elaborate fashion of the young gentlemen of that day. Often the additions to his wardrobe were English. English tailors were, after all, the most approved.

His health was basically good enough to support the strain. He was subject to colds which lingered bothersomely, and not infrequently he was laid up with other ailments. He was not as robust as those who knew him supposed him to be. But he looked and, when he was in action, behaved like an Adonis. He was altogether a tall, handsome, well-co-ordinated, highly favored, and agreeable young man.

He was also, it must be remembered, wealthy. He was not yet the owner of the Hyde Park estate or of the Roosevelt fortune, but he was the heir; and his mother never allowed him to lack for cash. She did not let him have his way in management. She could be very stubborn and, on occasion, haughty. She felt that she had instructions from the departed James and insisted on things being done as they always had been. It was this insistence that first led Franklin to buy additional land. He wanted to try out some new ideas, especially the setting out of many trees, and his mother would not let him do it on the old acreage. He was also, in his thirties, to make important additions to the house, yielding to the first manifestations of the builder's urge which would

44

be one of his notable characteristics as a public man. His definite conceptions concerning the planning of public works would amaze and disconcert many a subordinate in future years.

This was the first emergence, too, of his lifelong preoccupation with conservation. The earth and its inhabitants—plant and animal—he always treated as something especially precious. There was no outrage he would so indignantly prevent, or punish when he could, as the maltreatment of farms or forests, either as the result of carelessness or of rapacity. Trees and grass, well-tended crops, contented animals—these belonged to the round and rhythm of nature. His father had started him on this lesson. He developed it for himself, and its application was persistent. It was part and parcel of his religion. He would learn presently—indeed he seems always to have known—that compromise was necessary. Compromise and dissimulation were to be characteristic in his career. But about conservation there was something so special that when it was involved he seldom gave way to expediency.

Perhaps to the student, however, the most curious—and most important—thing about all the records and observations of these preparatory years is that Franklin seems always to have been turned outward toward the interesting and multifarious world. He seems never to have looked inward at all. It was certainly extraordinary the way he concealed his inner life.

No young man comes easily through the trials of youth any more than he does through the stresses of adolescence. The necessary readjustments in all his relationships as he accepts the direction of his own career are profound in any case; and if he is not helped and if he has other problems, his difficulties are greater. It is a mistake to assume that because Franklin was handsome, rich, and charming, and was, moreover, a Roosevelt, his way was smooth and his progress easy. That this cannot have been so is to be deduced from consideration of his situation and especially from small but revealing evidences.

Think, for instance, of the standards set for a Roosevelt and of the hedge of taboos that surrounded him. He had always to remember that a long line of ancestors on both sides—the Delanos almost as much as the Roosevelts—had in each generation advanced the family toward the position in life to which he had succeeded. He was the inheritor of a landed estate which he must leave in better condition than he found it; it must also, if possible, be enlarged. The home on that estate must be protected as a family retreat, a secure and fixed center. The house must be filled with another generation after him which he must be prepared, as his father had been, to rear in the Roosevelt-Delano tradition. The wealth supporting the family and making it secure must be so managed that it increased rather than diminished.

These were the demands of family. There were also the demands of

45

the wider world. His father had participated in modest but active and generous fashion in the public life of the community, sitting on boards and committees, being helpful in all good causes, and especially mitigating distress whenever it appeared. The Roosevelts had nearly always done this in their time and way. And then there was the shining example of Uncle Ted. There was never much love lost between the Oyster Bay and the Hyde Park branches of the family.[1] But the familial jealousy was more in evidence in the generation following Theodore the President than in any earlier one. After all, Theodore had no reason to be jealous of James. And for James' son, Franklin, he always had a warm regard. Franklin returned this affection, almost to the point, I should say, of a fixation. He would have others as time passed, but this one was permanent because, I suppose, of the circumstance that Uncle Ted was in the White House. This sentiment, however, only deepened the responsibility that devolved upon him as a Roosevelt and may have given him more anxiety than happiness. He lived in a reflected glory which for him was a strong directive to emulation. Franklin was a familiar visitor at the White House. This had been true since his father had taken him to see Grover Cleveland. But during his Harvard years, when Uncle Ted was President, he was often a visitor. Such a connection, besides being a source of pride, can be a kind of scourge. Where, in himself, were the qualities displayed by Uncle Ted? This may well have been a kind of special torment from a relatively early age.

Franklin, as he grew more mature and accumulated experience, gained in intelligence. But it was an intelligence that was more and more at the service of a compulsion to achievement which had taken hold of him, which he no longer resisted, and which he did not quite always successfully conceal, although he grew more clever and more cautious as he developed.[2]

Taken all together, the influences bearing on the young Franklin were very complicated. But somehow or other they all come together to make a mind, to create a character. And if his development surprised his contemporaries, that was because they did not look below an unusually deceiving surface.

[1] It came out at its bitterest in the persistent unpleasantness of Alice, Theodore's daughter, to all the Hyde Park clan, especially when Franklin committed the unpardonable sin of succeeding, instead of Theodore Jr., to the White House. It can even be seen in Cousin Nicholas Roosevelt, who became a newspaperman and diplomat. Cf. his *Front Row Seat* (Norman, Okla.: University of Oklahoma Press, 1953). Cf. also Alice Roosevelt Longworth's *Crowded Hours* (New York: Scribner, 1934).

[2] It is not too soon to point out that, to Franklin, Uncle Ted was never really a Republican; he was a progressive using Republicanism for a purpose. Is there not a hint in this of the later relationship of Franklin and the Democratic party? Parties, to Roosevelts, were instruments of their mission. The mission was to all Americans and finally to all mankind.

There is one thing about this that can be said with some certainty. Such of it as he owed to his Harvard educational activities—or to those that followed, for that matter, at Columbia—was very minor. It is well enough known what courses he selected with the help of his adviser, who was the eminent historian, Archibald Cary Coolidge. But there is something unexplained about the approach he made to the whole matter of his studies. It is generally agreed that he achieved no more than a passing competence in any of them, and it has already been noted how busy he kept with non-academic activities. He was in no hurry, and he became something of a dilettante collector of books as well as stamps. Why, then, did he take the maximum number of courses allowable and those not the "snap" courses so much favored by gold-coast lads? The fact is that he pursued this policy over three years and was ready to graduate a year ahead of his class. Then, during his fourth year, he signed up for an array of studies in history, politics, economics, and philosophy which ought to have kept him up nights. He never got the master's degree for which he was registered in that fourth year, but he passed all those courses in spite of the important diversion of becoming engaged and being away for more than six weeks on a winter's cruise. Why the hurry and crowding in that last year? Was it an instinct for acquiring what he would later need?

As a freshman he was introduced for the first time to the formal study of government under A. Lawrence Lowell. He also began what must have been a quite extensive exploration of English literature with Kittredge, Baker, and Wendell. He studied French literature, too, with C. H. C. Wright and Irving Babbitt and European history with A. C. Coolidge. These are famous academic names. These were teachers whose influence was strong on Franklin's generation and doubtless on Franklin too, but not in a professional way. What they had to give him went into the general cultural reserve he was building up. He might never have any use for the specific items of that reserve, but he could always use the income it produced. Perhaps he undertook so much because he did not really respect it greatly; it was an amateur activity, not to be taken too seriously.

There are two particularly revealing letters to his mother, written just as he entered his fourth year.[3] The first of these explains that he had had some difficulty in choosing between the law school and the graduate school. He had, he said, finally succumbed to unanimous advice against the law school. But the advice was evidently only against entering "this year." It seems to have been already decided that he was to study law and that it was being postponed only because it would

[3] They are both to be found, with some explanatory notes, in *F.D.R., His Personal Letters: Early Years,* ed. by Elliott Roosevelt (New York: Duell, Sloan & Pearce, 1947), pp. 504 ff.

interfere with activities of greater priority. How the decision in favor of law was reached, what alternatives he considered, and whose advice was asked are not at all as clear as they ought to be. Being a lawyer may not have been preliminary to later political adventures. He was thought of by the politicians of Dutchess County for the state legislature more because he was not taking his lawyering seriously than because he was a success. He was by that time cultivating his Hyde Park connections rather actively—joining the volunteer firemen, renewing interest in the estate, and the like. And it is certain that being well known about the neighborhood commended him to the local Democrats more importantly than his being a lawyer. But still it was a kind of springboard. He was not just a country gentleman turned politician. He was to be a member of three metropolitan law firms in the future, even if in none of them were his services to be prolonged or intensive. In later years he spoke of his legal status about as often as he did of his claim to being a farmer; it was a respectable affiliation; it gave him a place in a world which seemed to him, I can't help feeling, transient and insubstantial.

It is supposition on my part to speak of his loneliness and fear of impermanence; and it is a bit premature, in his life's story, to speak of it when he was an undergraduate. But it seems to me to have accompanied quite naturally his feeling of being present but of not quite belonging and the worry of never being quite up to the tests he had to meet. Later it will be more clearly seen what barriers and defenses he threw up and what resources he tried to marshal; shoring up courage and damming off the incursions of eternity may have been what he was doing when he cultivated so earnestly the esteem and affection of his fellows, which he never, to any absolute degree, captured as some youths do. The whole *Crimson* démarche needs some such rationale also; and we shall see how preoccupied he was, as he became an important figure, with the physical apparatus of life. He would always want to improve the earth and men's works. No man in the whole history of the nation caused so many acres to be improved, so many buildings to be built—as he thought they ought to be built. He went as far as anyone could go in the transfiguration of the nation. It is allowable to speculate whether it may not have been partly because what lay under his hand was so precious and so fleeting; he would do with it what he could. Law at the moment seemed a way to go on with what he must do. It would not seem so for long. And even now he was hesitant, as though he had a premonition of its insufficiency.

The point of reference about that fourth year at Harvard was, clearly enough, that if he undertook the law school courses he would have to give up his other activities and concentrate on academic

48

work. But these "other activities" were ones in which he had made a heavy investment and which were just promising to yield the satisfaction he had anticipated. That formidable array of social science courses for which he signed up was not intended as a commitment to the demanding tasks it would seem to involve. It was an overdemonstration that in not going on to law he was not wasting time. He was going to listen to some famous lecturers and fill in some enormous deficiencies. He would find that he could not read their books, and he would not be drawn into their research. That too was not, he discovered, his métier. He did not admit this even to himself, I suspect—later he tried some very academic enterprises such as historical writing, but the fact is that he quietly succumbed to the law when this year was over. It is of some interest that at this juncture he definitely abandoned the humanities for the social sciences. Except for one English course, what he elected was all history and economics—and the economics was quite specialized. As yet he may not have understood himself in a positive way, but some negative limitations were apparent.

The second of the letters to which I have referred was written a week after the first, when he was just beginning that fourth year:

Alpha Delta Phi Club
October 7, 1903
Wednesday

Dearest Mama,

I am now fully in the Graduate School—too deep to get out or change my mind. I am taking five courses in the Department of History and Political Economy—which interests me much more than English but which is also much harder. I have few hopes of getting an A.M.—indeed I am quite indifferent about it, but the courses will do me lots of good, whether I get B or D in them and to do the former would make me work so hard that I could not do justice to my Senior year.

My courses are History 11, on Middle English History, very hard but excellent; History 16, the Hist. of Continental Europe from 1715 to today; Economics 8—the history & theory of banking; Economics 9, the history of Transportation (railroading etc.) in the U.S.; and English 11, a course on Bacon which is good & which I was allowed to take.

After the football game Saturday at which I ushered, I went to the Beals at Beverly, & attended a small dance at the golf club. Sunday we spent at the Sohiers' camp & had a swim. Alice Sohier is still on her back after having her appendix removed last week. I came back after dinner on Sunday & wrote my editorial— What do you think of them so far? The address to the Freshmen scared me to death but I survived—I drooled on journalism here & also on strenuousness etc.

Please wire who is coming on the 16th, Friday. Are H. (Helen) Cutting, Eleanor & Moo all coming to us? I bring home H. Peabody, Livingstone

Davis probably & I may have one other. Jimmy Jackson can't come. The paper takes every moment of time.

Ever

F.D.R.

Franklin wrote frequently to his mother, but she often did not think so. A week or two without a letter when they were apart seemed to her outrageously long. But considering Franklin's busyness in those years, the number of his surviving letters is really amazing. It shows him to have been an unusually dutiful son. He recognized this as he recognized other obligations. He knew how concentrated were his mother's affections, how unlimited her ambitions for him, and how essentially lonely she was after the death of his father. Nevertheless, nearly all of his letters were like the one just quoted. They provided information and expressed affection, but they conceal more than they reveal. They can be studied over and over without discovering any hint of the decisions he must have been making which would affect his whole career.

It is impossible not to conclude about Franklin in his Harvard years what was still true of Roosevelt the President—that he allowed no one to know his inner life. This applied as obviously to his mother and Eleanor as it did to others—Lathrop Brown, for instance, his Grotonian schoolmate who roomed with him at Harvard and who went on being a friend in Washington. This is often said to be a characteristic of the reticent Englishman; and Franklin's early training, participated in by father, tutors, Peabody, and his fellows, was of the same sort. So far as the betraying emotions were concerned, they must not be allowed to show. He suffered pain, embarrassment, and defeat with becoming stoicism; he learned early not to be enthusiastic, and equally early not to whimper. But concealment went far beyond anything he could have got from his training. He was obviously, I believe, hiding the weaknesses in his nature, covering the areas which were most vulnerable to hurt, concealing the vast but vague designs shaping in his dreams. One of the weaknesses most noticeable and most significant was that lateness to arrive at the various stages of maturity. This had the effect of making much that went on about him slightly incomprehensible. He knew that certain things happened and would happen, but he was not quite certain why. And he did not want this insufficiency to be known. He went to great lengths to keep it hidden. That repository of concealment by now begins to seem bottomless.

Franklin was vulnerable in another way, as his mother never learned, but as Eleanor, in the warm rush of her love for the handsome cousin who so unexpectedly chose her out of so many, very early divined. He had a weakness for struggling humanity which rose to a feeling of responsibility. Those who were oppressed and suffering touched a spring of indignation in him which welled up persistently. It is one clue to

50

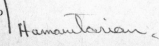

his whole life's orientation. It explains what he always did with po[wer] after he achieved it. He was forever turning to the righting of wro[ng,] the correcting of injustices, the recovering of the disadvantaged, the placing of the poor in a better position. The hard judgment of nearly all his contemporaries that poverty was the fault of the poor, that unemployment existed because men would not work—a familiar sort of upper-class social philosophy ever since there had been an upper class —was not a judgment in which he joined. He felt that the system was rigged and that disadvantages had been institutionalized. There grew in him a persistent impulse toward reform.

That he was growing into such a determination could not have been guessed from his correspondence with his mother nor, evidently, from his exchanges with his fellows, and it may be that I put its recognition a little early. He was not a campus radical. He seems never to have discussed or espoused socialism, for instance, as he might very well have. Nor did he belong to any study group or circle. But the only alternative to suspecting that even at Harvard, in the midst of his superficial busyness, he was generating these conclusions is to hold that he was at some time or other converted. This seems to me fantastic. I think the fascination for him of Uncle Ted's career was centered in an interest in that ebullient statesman's progressivism. I think his preoccupation, so obvious when looked for, with political techniques almost from the very first, and certainly at Harvard, was an interest essentially in the leverages for change. Whether or not he recognized it yet, it would be difficult to say. But any student is likely to be baffled by the problem of locating in time the Roosevelt recognitions. He had no intention of letting anyone discover them, then or thereafter.

This apprehension was undoubtedly approached slowly and almost unconsciously. It came together with his acceptance of the going standards of conduct, his strenuousness, his athletics, and his *Crimson* competition. It also merged with the intense, almost feverish careerism so characteristic of his whole development up to the presidency. He went for the editorship because it was an accepted thing to do; but I think that, dimly and unrecognized, his drive for power and prestige was motivated not only by wanting to show that he could do it but because he sensed that he could put it to better use than his competitors; and because it possessed the potential power, in his hands, to correct injustice and to relieve distress.

That he was deficient in comprehension of what the specific uses of power might be was always a fact; and it was this fact which he knew to be a serious weakness in himself. He concealed it with that care and persistence which seem to me almost his most amazing characteristic. It came to be granted later that he was a great master of political techniques, not only at the tactical but also at the strategic level. The

51

Harvard — not a preparatory

same persons who recognized this talent were often moved to speculate on its motivation. Some unkindly insisted that he always wanted something they usually called "personal power." Those who were technicians too—like Jim Farley or Ed Flynn—and who knew that such marvelous techniques could be motives in themselves, were inclined to impute no other motive than this. And some observers—like John T. Flynn and Franklin's cousins, Theodore Jr. and Alice—were quite certain that Lord Acton's aphorism about power corrupting its possessor was true of Franklin.

It took the common, ordinary person, without inside information or any talents of his own, to understand finally what had been going on in the Roosevelt mind. He hadn't known all along, of course; he had voted the first time more against the other fellow—against Ottinger in 1928 in New York State, against Hoover in the presidential campaign of 1932—but he had not been too slow to catch on. He recognized in Roosevelt a convinced, an able, a dedicated champion. People were his people. He might not say so all the time; he might even deny it; but there was never a time from 1928 until his death when Franklin Roosevelt was not politically unassailable; and it was because he was the people's man, adopted and, in a sense, consecrated.

It seems to me simply not sensible to believe that preparation for this dedication did not begin at Harvard in spite of all the superficial evidence to the contrary. And when the signs are looked for I think them easy enough to discover. One of the most revealing, apart from the obvious seriousness of his experimentation with political procedures when he was ambitious for Class Day honors, is, however paradoxical it may seem, his concealment of it, as though it were—as undoubtedly he thought—a weakness.

How did he explain to his mother his concentration on political and economic studies? They were the alternative to law school, which would keep him from pleasurable pursuits. How cleverly he dwelt on the social activities he knew she would approve! But she must have been aware of an undercurrent toward a professional interest in public affairs. The teachers with whom he occasionally consorted were mostly those whose subjects were economics or politics. The name of A. Piatt Andrew, for instance, often appears in his correspondence. He went on Sunday or weekend excursions and sometimes rode with him. Andrew was a youngish assistant professor of economics with whom Franklin took courses in his sophomore and senior years.[4] His mother need not

[4] Andrew was an unusually sparkling lecturer, according to most accounts. He left Harvard presently to go into politics and became Assistant Secretary of the Treasury in Taft's administration and later congressman from Massachusetts. Franklin's first course with him was the general course in economics in which Andrew lectured and a number of even younger men conducted discussion groups. It is noted in the volume of *Personal Letters: Early Years* that one of

have been disturbed by Andrew's influence. He was not an economic philosopher likely to be leading a younger friend into dangerous explorations of alternatives to capitalism. He was interested, in fact, in the operations of the business system. He accepted classical economics; he was a student of money and banking and would become a competent, conservative public official in Taft's administration.

W. Z. Ripley, another of his teachers, was one of those extraordinary American academicians who, like a number of others, did not confine his interests to any one field.[5] He was as well known for his ethnological investigations as for his economic essays. His *Races of Europe* was an accepted text long before he interested himself in the business system. When he turned to economics he brought to his work an original and penetrating intelligence. He lent powerful support to the movement for corporate reform. It is not too much to say that the New Deal regulatory acts—the Truth in Securities Act, the "death sentence" bill condemning public utility holding companies, as well as the acts separating the commercial from the investment banking function—would be in direct descent from his teaching. His book *Main Street and Wall Street* was a sensation in the days when financiers were riding high. There were others as well: but Ripley was certainly influential. Franklin may not have studied his economics with serious professional intent, but that he remembered Ripley's strictures on corporate finance is obvious.

The others would include Brandeis, who was not formally a teacher but who somewhat later reached Franklin through Felix Frankfurter of the Harvard law school. When the time came for action it would be Frankfurter (and his helpers, Landis, Corcoran, and Cohen, as we shall see) who would be available for the actual drafting of regulatory acts. But the beginning of it all in Franklin's mind has to be attributed to Harvard and his teachers. There was left a residue of bias, never to be quite dissipated, against big business, and especially the corporations of that day, and in favor of governmental interference.

Ripley published a book of readings, *Trusts, Pools and Corporations*, the year after Franklin took his course. It must have been much in his mind when his influence on Franklin was being exerted. Daniel Fusfeld,

---

these instructors was Gilbert Holland Montague, who became chairman of the New York Bar Association's committee on the NRA. It is also noted that, speaking at a 1935 meeting of the Academy of Political and Social Sciences, Montague said some harsh things about NRA, including the following: "[It] snatched at a form of executive law making that was unconsciously but nevertheless essentially fascistic. . . ." The significance of this will appear a little later.

[5] Such others as Amasa Walker, Franklin H. Giddings, Simon N. Patten, John Bates Clark, Thorstein Veblen, John Dewey, and Charles Horton Cooley, to name only a few of a generation. All these were names Franklin must have become familiar with from his assigned readings. Their influence was not more than a general one. He was not a close student. But their thinking was part of the body of social study in his day.

who has explored more carefully than anyone else this Harvard educational experience, is inclined to stress Ripley's dominance, and I think he is right.[6] Ripley certainly made vivid the evils of corporate finance, and he had no reticence in affirming that regulation by the federal government was called for.

How much persisting influence is traceable to Andrew's courses in money and banking, it is somewhat harder to say. But Franklin must have had his interest engaged. There were still some remaining agitators for free silver in spite of Bryan's defeat, and there was widespread dissatisfaction with the banking system. It was believed that booms and depressions were considerably affected by monetary policy. It is probable that Andrew discussed all the issues leading to the appointment of the National Monetary Commission in 1908 and to the passage of the Federal Reserve Act during Wilson's administration.

As we shall see, Franklin was fascinated all his life by the mysteries of money. Andrew believed in what was then called the "quantity theory," whose central tenet was that the price level was definitely affected by the amount of circulating medium and that the circulating medium had a relationship to gold. This was the sound position of his day. He believed in stable prices and the gold standard.

This position was reinforced by O. M. W. Sprague, whose course dealt with banking systems. At the heart of his teaching there was a strong belief in central banking and credit controls as devices for stability. In this sense Sprague was a reformer. He wanted order brought out of a contemporary chaos. He had much to do with preparing the way for the Federal Reserve Act of 1913.

It may have been that Franklin's attendance at lectures and discussions was desultory and his reading not carried out systematically, but the resemblances between the Harvard thinking on these economic matters and the policies he afterward adopted are striking. One who is trying to discover the origins of New Deal economic policies cannot ignore the Harvard classrooms.

It is not unlikely, however, that, conservative as the influences were which must be supposed to have been brought to bear on Franklin at Harvard, they did serve to start a ferment, or to further one, which was to issue in the later Roosevelt methodology. The courses of his last three years in economics or politics must have centered on questions of public policy. Certainly those of Ripley, Sprague, and Andrew did. And even if Franklin's last year was not notably devoted to studies, he must have sat through a good many hours when his professors were analyzing leg-

---

[6] *The Economic Thought of Franklin D. Roosevelt and the Origins of the New Deal* (New York: Columbia University Press, 1956).

islation, discussing proposals, and referring to the consequences of government action.[7]

What happened as a result of Franklin's associations of this sort at Harvard seems to me not difficult to assess. He found this whole area of technique interesting in a way none of his other studies had hitherto proved to be. His inquiries were elementary and preliminary and he came to no conclusions, though it is not reasonable to suppose that he sat in all those classes and associated informally with all those teachers without discussing, and very likely at length, many of the issues comprehended in these fields of money and banking, transportation, and so on. But what ought not to be overlooked is the heavy weighting of history in his study program. Even in that fourth added year there were five history courses. Most of them, as before, were European history. These, taken together with his repeated trips to Europe and his study of French and German literature, must have given him an orientation in civilization much more adequate than most Harvard students could have had.

The history courses were given by a very select group of historians, ones who would have dwelt not only on the battles and royal successions of the periods they covered but would also have, at the very least, analyzed the public issues under discussion and the notable decisions taken. Franklin must indeed have got from his introduction a coherent conception of history as a series of events involving debate and decision, with democracy gaining hard-won positions and public welfare rather than the fortunes of the royal houses coming to be the center of consideration.

It is true that he did not work very hard at his reading. Nevertheless, he was getting an outline knowledge of the past which would serve him very well in his life as a statesman. He would always have a sense of perspective, of time running on, and of events assuming sequence, which is one of the marks of the man who has placed himself in the unfolding of historical processes. It was probably not a bad thing that he should have had so much more knowledge (from his courses) of European than of American history. His American background was something he acquired in other ways. It should not be forgotten that Uncle Ted had written a good deal about the West, for instance, and no doubt had engaged Franklin's imagination. No one could have been a

---

[7] O. M. W. Sprague is another name which was to turn up again. Early in 1933, when the World Monetary and Economic Conference impended in which a new administration would be involved without any adequate preparation, Sprague would be turned to and made a special assistant to the Secretary of the Treasury. He would for some time be regarded as the central figure in American policy making. But he, along with others, would be repudiated in the famous "bombshell" message to the conference and would resign with some bitter comments.

Roosevelt, and especially so self-conscious a one as Franklin,[8] without knowing a good deal about the American past.[9] And the Delano past was in his mind too. In later years, on historic occasions, he would refer to it as part of his own personal tradition.[10] He thought of himself, I am convinced, as a kind of American symbol; and his responsibilities were enormous because that was so.

There are two specific events with intense emotional implications which occurred in Franklin's Harvard years. His father died in his freshman year, and in his senior year he became engaged to his distant cousin Eleanor. The influence of his father had gradually diminished during his Groton years. The elder Roosevelt was slowly succumbing to a heart ailment. His place, as a matter of fact, had been taken more or less by tutors for several years before that—from the time Franklin was about eleven. There is some importance to be attached to this tutorial influence. Being under masculine direction from the age of eleven is something not experienced by many American boys, most of whom have had women teachers all the way to college. It must have gone some way to counteract the smothering effect of his rather imperious and doting mother. On the other hand, the discipline was quite different from that of either a father or a public school society. His intellectual interests would have been encouraged—his bent toward reading history, mostly; his life would have been a bit solitary too—although he was so gregarious and had such an interest in people that the solitariness seems to have had, if anything, the effect of making him more appreciative of company when it could be had. It was as though he longed for close touch with others and sought to ingratiate himself so that they would yield.

His father's long illness tended to reduce his mother's concentration on him. He had a good deal of freedom during those years when his parents were abroad or his mother was nursing his father at home. And

[8] There is an essay in the library at Hyde Park, written by Franklin in a Harvard history course in December 1901, called "The Roosevelt Family in New Amsterdam before the Revolution." Many of Franklin's letters refer to genealogical matters, especially those to his mother. That lady often seemed to her friends much too insistent on the aristocratic lines of descent which converged in her son from both sides.

[9] Not very much importance is to be attached to his sitting under Frederick Jackson Turner for a course in his senior year. To begin with, he was away for six weeks of the term on a Caribbean cruise. It is likely also that from reading Uncle Ted's books he was familiar with the range of history Turner taught.

[10] For instance, in 1933 when he accepted the so-called Stimson Doctrine concerning the Japanese in Manchuria, Franklin told Moley and me, who protested, that he had a special reason for taking such an attitude. That reason was the Delano connection in former generations with the China trade. This is also mentioned with bitter humor in General Stilwell's memoirs concerning his relations with Chiang Kai-shek. The general was also told by Franklin that he had a special feeling for China and the Chinese.

56

FDR's mother upset about his marriage

when during his first year at Harvard his father died and his mother transferred her complete concern to him, he was very largely immune to her demands. When, in his last years, she persuaded him to go on the Caribbean cruise it was an act of desperation on her part and serves to illustrate how definitely she was even then—and ever afterward—excluded from Franklin's decision-making about important matters. In taking Franklin away she thought she might be recouping her position after a severe defeat. That defeat was her son's determined announcement that he intended to marry Eleanor Roosevelt. The truth was that the *grand dame* had been pretending to herself that her admirable son was under her thumb; and the revelation that, without consulting her, he had chosen a mate was a rude shock, one that she found hard to accept. She did everything she could think of to break up the match; and never to her dying day did she really accept Eleanor's pre-emption of Franklin's heart. She was to make life miserable for the young wife, with a curiously laissez-faire acquiescence on Franklin's part, which I can account for only by supposing that Franklin assumed that Eleanor approached the matter just as he did.[11] He bent to his mother's direction but did not let it affect in the least his deeper concerns. She never had the slightest notion what was going on in his mind, and when slight suggestions did convey themselves to her she reacted mostly by pretending that nothing had happened. She obviously hoped that ignoring his embarrassing tendencies would banish them. When she could not quite achieve this she sometimes complained to him or to others; but the gentle rebuffs she encountered taught her indirection. And in Franklin's more mature years she was resigned to that method.[12]

Part of Franklin's defense against the persistent attempts of his mother to direct not only his activities but his thoughts was a certain jocularity, at once gentle and decisive, which served to keep her on

[11] It is referred to in Eleanor's *This Is My Story* (New York: Harper, 1937), and, somewhat more frankly, in *This I Remember* (New York: Harper, 1949).

[12] On an occasion (in 1933) that both embarrassed and amused me, she backed me into a Hyde Park corner and demanded that I stop Franklin from going on with the rumored recognition of Russia. I could not make out whether she thought I had something active to do with the Russian matter or whether she was appealing to me as one who would naturally share her repugnance. I rather think she mistakenly regarded me as sharing to some degree her aristocratic reactions, although I came from far upstate and she would not have known of any family connections. I found it hard to put her off. When I suggested that she appeal to Franklin directly she made a very revealing remark: "Oh," she said, "he's so stubborn about such things." Such things, I concluded, involved all public affairs. The old lady still presided at Hyde Park in semi-feudal style, but Franklin's political career brought into her house some very queer specimens. She looked at them askance but bravely assumed their adherence to all her prejudices and standards. This made for some amusing conversations with people like Jim Farley, Louis Howe, the newspapermen, and the Secret Service. They came to call her "the Duchess" and to accept her as part of the rather strange entourage of their chief.

notice that his inner life was his own. The flavor of this can best be got by reading the *Personal Letters* collected after Franklin's death. Most of these illustrate a delicately humorous affection at once respectful and concealing. He began this at Groton, continued it at Harvard, and went on with it—although the communications were of course far fewer—into his public life. Of all the long series of letters, none was more filled with tenderness and gentle persiflage than those written on his honeymoon voyage with Eleanor, every minute of which the elder lady obviously resented with quiet fury.

His mother never did quite know how Franklin managed to carry out his wooing without her getting wind of it. She must have seen too late that she had even been party to what she could only have thought was an eminently safe cousinly association. There were half a dozen other young females in Franklin's circle about whom she was much more concerned. She simply found Franklin's choice incredible. She found also, though, that he was going to be stubborn about it. He would go for a curative cruise and enjoy it greatly, but her heart sank to see how little effect all her diversions were having on his central determination. The truth was that she had been defeated in her most important campaign. She would have to share her Franklin with another. She was not for an instant conciliated by Franklin's repeated promise that she would now have two children instead of one. Eleanor was an intruder. She should be made to feel it every day of her existence. She was not only an intruder, she represented the forced recognition of Franklin's escape. There could be no reconciliation. One of the most pathetic passages in Roosevelt annals is Eleanor's long attempt to placate the old lady, which failed so miserably and caused Eleanor so much agony.

That Franklin either did not see this going on or that he felt nothing could be done about it is one of the not very numerous instances of cruelty in his personal life. Eleanor, in her reminiscences, glosses it over; but the hurt is only too apparent, and the implied criticism of her husband, even in the years of their closest and warmest association, can very easily be read between the lines. But for the historian the important thing is to recognize Franklin's seizure and protection of an essential independence. It might have to be got by dissimulation and kept by a continual tactical management, which meant sacrifice and exclusion even for those who were dear enough to him; but he was determined to have it and to keep it. He was his own ego, not someone else's, even when he was hardly yet an ego at all.

3

Franklin's mother was right to suppose that his wife would be very important in his life. Eleanor was. She never did Franklin's thinking for him, any more than his mother did, but she was vitally important to him in the other ways that any good wife knows about. No one, indeed, will ever be able to understand Franklin very well without understanding Eleanor as well. It is far from enough to say that their association, beginning when both were very young, continued into fruitful marriage, was confirmed and matured in her determination that he should become a whole man again during a long convalescence, and went on into a unique partnership in public life. No wife of any American President, certainly, and none of any prominent politician ever played a more important part. With consideration always for Franklin's problems as she knew them, she still had her own views, expressed them frankly, and became, as time went on, an elder stateslady who was greatly respected and widely influential.

Eleanor's ultimate development into a personage of consequence is the more remarkable because of her suppressed and subdued girlhood, her modest and retiring young matronhood, and her apparent indifference, until she was middle-aged, to public affairs. Where her progressiveness came from is at least as much a puzzle as where Franklin's originated and of almost as much importance. But then, of course, she was a Roosevelt. That alone could account for the energy, and it helps to account for the progressivism.

It may be that the most significant cause is to be found in her original and exceptional outgoing warmheartedness. The suffering of others was, to her, an unbearable responsibility. She was powerfully moved to do something practical about it; and there came a time when she could interfere effectively on behalf of those who were distressed. She was everlastingly doing it—as all those around her knew. It was evidence of a power of growth in her that she came to understand finally how little good it was possible to do individually and directly, and how necessary

59

Eleanor Ridiculed

it was to sublimate the philanthropic impulses into social programs and permanent systems.

It was at least as unlikely that Eleanor would turn out to be a practicing progressive as it was that Franklin should. She was born to and lived in circumstances of luxury; she was guarded and protected from the harsher realities of life; she was educated by governesses and at exclusive schools; until she was middle-aged her knowledge of events was incredibly limited and naïve. Yet, in spite of all this, she became a shrewd political associate of her husband and she gained an exceptional knowledge of government and its possibilities. As in Franklin's case also, her close friends seemed to share none or little of her social sensitiveness. They became in their time the matronly counterpart of Franklin's classmates, presiding over large family establishments, administering estates, and retreating with the expected reluctance into the twilight of the leisure class in Britain and America.

There is no reason why anyone able to read should not know all about Eleanor from birth. It was not until she was over forty that she emerged into the glare of publicity which would follow her all the rest of her life. But that glare was so intense that it lit her past as well as her present. It was remarkable how little she had to hide. There can, I should think, hardly ever have been so good, so simple, and so energetic a woman. She was a precious gift to her husband and to her nation at a time when such a gift was especially needed. But it cannot be denied that her very goodness and innocence were often exasperating to those about her; and to her husband's political enemies she was the target for ridicule on an unprecedented scale. Like the ridicule to which he also was subjected, it served more than anything else to betray her effectiveness. But it sometimes did penetrate the protective covering of goodness that surrounded her. And there were bad times from these causes for even so saintly a woman.

Her detractors, failing to find flaws in her character, looked for them in her naïveté with somewhat greater success. But the attempts to paint her as a self-righteous prude were no more successful than any other attacks. She was, in fact, extremely realistic. If she had faults they were of a sort her enemies could not use. She lacked something of a sense of humor, or perhaps perspective; she did tend to be somewhat literal-minded, and she gave up rather ungracefully to the necessities of politics. Franklin had some difficulty with her because she pressed too hard for the causes she felt strongly about, especially at that juncture of his career when he was managing things so that his selection as President should be inevitable; many compromises in that interest were ones he preferred not to discuss. And sometimes, after he had become President, she seemed somewhat too much in evidence as a public figure. But the truth is that if the reverse of this had been true she might well

60

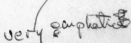
very emphatic

have been more savagely attacked for *that* kind of conduct. There was no appeasing the reactionaries whose privileges were curtailed by the New Deal. And quite as much as Franklin—even more, as some felt—Eleanor was the personification of New Dealism.

There were other women who were her contemporaries in public life, some of them admirable in character and activity. They all paled beside her shining selflessness. Her school friend, Isabella Greenway, was one of them; so was Lady Astor, and so were Frances Perkins and Mary Rumsey—to name only a few rather like her. Then there were among her contemporaries another sort—her cousin, Alice Roosevelt Longworth, for one instance, and Mrs. Robert Bacon and Clare Booth Luce. This sort ridiculed Eleanor and got a kind of feline satisfaction from it, evidently; but the amusement, to their exasperation, was confined within a small and impotent circle. Eleanor's appeal was very wide. Even after her final retirement from public life—as United States representative to the United Nations—she was still in demand as a writer and lecturer, and her daily newspaper column was still reaching millions of readers. She commanded a very large income from these sources, and most of it went to the support of such good works as were carried on by the Friends Service Committee.[1]

Eleanor had come to this fulfillment through stages which an observer would have thought made such a result most unlikely. She had been the very prototype of the poor little rich girl. Her mother had died when she was only a child, her father when she was a young girl. And until she was fifteen she had been brought up by her maternal grandmother at Tivoli, farther up the Hudson than Hyde Park, and in New York City. She had had a protective affection for her father which had been constantly and rudely frustrated by his alcoholism. His death had left her forlorn and bereft, wholly at the mercy of singularly unloving female relatives who did their duty by her—and little more. She never even had a governess she could really love. And she grew from girlhood into young womanhood with a rich accumulation of affection waiting to be asked for but never wanted. At fifteen she was sent to school in England and stayed there for three years, being "finished." She was

---

[1] I saw something of her during summers in the fifties at Hyde Park. On one occasion in 1952, in the home she had made for herself a few miles from the old estate house which had now become part of the Franklin D. Roosevelt Library and Museum, she was surrounded by nearly a score of visiting grandchildren, grandnieces, and grandnephews, who splashed all day in the swimming pool and expected her to read them bedtime stories as well as to keep the peace. She was besieged by the telephone—reporters asking her views on public affairs, chairmen of causes wanting her to appear, and just plain people wanting her advice. She presided serenely over the turmoil, nearing sixty-eight, a little hard of hearing, but showing no sign of diminished energy or any frailty attributable to age. She had obviously no regrets: her eyes were on the future and she still thought things could and would be improved.

put to a regime of manners, art, music, and languages. She already knew the manners, she learned the languages, she agonized over the piano without result, and she studied art without feeling any response.

She came back at eighteen to a senseless regime with elderly relatives—more than one of whom shared her father's weakness—and rather marked time until Franklin, a storybook Prince Charming, came into her life. Such a miracle was beyond her most extravagant hopes. She had been a big and awkward girl, always growing out of her clothes and always dressed below her years. She agonized at parties over skirts above her bony knees when all the other girls already had theirs lowered in adult fashion. She danced badly, she had buckteeth, and her feet were big. Her relatives were brutally frank with her. She was an awkward and ugly girl and they had not the least idea how anything could be done about it.

Nature, however, as she grew up, clothed the large bones with attractive flesh. Her face, if not pretty, became a glowing representation of the warmth and energy within. She was no longer an ugly girl. Far from it; she offered the promise of grateful response to the man who would unlock the stores of love she had to give. Franklin was by then one of the greatest prizes, matrimonially speaking, in the large circle of Eleanor's acquaintances. It all began by his being kind to her again, as he had been before when they had met as children. It can be imagined that all of a sudden sometime, dancing perhaps, he realized what he had in his arms. At any rate, he was not a young man to lose time. Nor was she any girl to resist the rare fortune of his attention. There was nothing in the way. She had an income of her own which took care of the objections that he had very little except what his mother gave him. There was only the opposition his mother had to any other woman coming into his life. This, he thought, Eleanor's sweetness and submission would dissipate.

They were married in 1905 on March 17, St. Patrick's Day. Eleanor, in her literal style, told about it in *This Is My Story*:[2]

After graduating from Harvard, Franklin went to law school at Columbia University. His mother took a house at 200 Madison Avenue, and we had many gay times during the winter of 1905 with his cousin Muriel Robbins, who often came to visit her Aunt Sallie, and the other young members of the family. Parties were given for us, wedding presents began to come, and my Cousin Susie helped me to buy my trousseau and my linens. It was all very exciting, and the wedding plans were complicated by the fact that Uncle Ted, at that time President of the United States, was coming to New York to give me away, and our date had to fit in with his plans. . . .

Uncle Ted was coming to review the St. Patrick's Day parade on

[2] P. 122.

Fifth Avenue. But he was no doubt glad for once to do something for the ugly overgrown niece who had suddenly become a lovely bride-to-be. Uncle Ted was that kind of man. His affection for all the family was real. He made none of those nasty comparisons of his own with that other branch of the family up the Hudson which were to be so characteristic of his children. He had always liked Franklin. And the marriage was one he thoroughly approved, even if Sara, the scion of the Delanos, did not.

A preliminary to the wedding was an invitation to both young people to stay in Washington with an aunt who lived there, for the inauguration of Uncle Ted. This was the "Auntie Bye,"[3] about whom so much is heard in all the Roosevelt annals. This was by no means the first White House visit of either Franklin or Eleanor. Eleanor, it must be remembered, was a closer relative of the President than Franklin; and Uncle Ted had succeeded McKinley in 1901. She had then been seventeen and still in England, but she had come back at eighteen, and on a number of occasions she had visited at the White House. I speak of this familiarity because I believe it to have some importance. When Franklin and Eleanor moved into the White House in 1933 it was in critical times. It was very fortunate that neither had to go through the sometimes prolonged conditioning process most of the other Presidents and their wives have had to go through; if they had, something terrible might have happened to the nation. As it was, they came to their occupancy as though they were coming home. They had seen Presidents at work; they had shared the play of presidential children; they had slept in hallowed beds and danced in the great East Room. Franklin did not have to learn that Presidents have to be leaders, that they have to coerce the Congress and maintain a steady and independent rapport with the people. He was there as if by some long-anticipated appointment with destiny and he knew how to behave from long imagining. And Eleanor did not have to begin by excessive caution; she could enter on an active helpfulness at once.

The honeymoon in 1905 was a little delayed. Franklin had to finish his year at the law school. About the only flaw in a real storybook bridal trip was the news, received in the midst of it, that he had failed in two of his courses.[4]

<hr>

[3] Anna Roosevelt Cowles.

[4] Franklin was the same sort of student in the law school that he had been at Groton and at Harvard. He was not a natural scholar. The courses he failed to pass were made up by re-examination in the fall. He passed his others but, having passed his bar examinations in the spring of his third year, he did not bother to finish all of them. He never got his LL.B. degree, although in course of time he would accumulate several LL.D.s just as he would an honorary Phi Beta Kappa. This makes an interesting contrast with Uncle Ted, whose career

That honeymoon summer can be read about in Eleanor's *This Is My Story*, and all the letters written to "Dearest Mama" have been published in *Personal Letters*. It is hard to imagine, in later more restrained and restricted times, the spacious freedom the handsome and healthy young couple enjoyed as they explored each other's personalities and savored the first joys of married love. Those were the days before the automobile was common, and they made long journeys in the mountains of Europe by carriage, slowly enough to soak up the scents and sounds and views. Their senses were open to the beauties about them as they made slow progress through the stages of their grand tour. Italy, Venice, the Dolomites, the Tyrol, south Germany, Paris, London, the English and Scottish countryside—that was the itinerary. As they went they tried all the foods and wines and bought whatever they saw that pleased them: books, linens, furs, clothes, furniture, silver. There was money enough, although Franklin kept some accounts and pretended always to be short. He wrote home to his mother at every stage, retailing imagined extravagances—something he always felt was very funny, and perhaps the two did enjoy the byplay together. Eleanor was incredibly blissful: she adored her husband, absorbed the world's beauty, for once did not notice the comparative disadvantages suffered by the less fortunate, promptly became pregnant, as was wholly becoming, and wrote conciliatory newsletters to her mother-in-law.

It was a fruitful marriage: Eleanor bore six children—the first Franklin Jr. died—in the next ten years. It has also to be rated as a happy one: there is not the slightest evidence, so far as I know, that either ever thought for an instant of separation or even that either's affections ever wandered. There were some flaws in the perfect composition. Eleanor had mother-in-law trouble in spite of all preventive and conciliatory efforts. Sara, given an inch, took the proverbial mile. And there were times when Eleanor wept bitterly in exasperation. The older lady chose the young couple's residences and furnished them, and found the servants and instructed them. When the babies came she assumed they were more hers than their mother's. When Eleanor rebelled Franklin blandly refused to recognize the cause, and gradually she gave up.

Eleanor had poor defenses against these aggressions. Her first source of weakness was the gratitude she felt for rescue from the long insecurity of a parentless childhood. She sank into the comfort of protection with a relief so deeply felt that she would on no account jeopardize it. Then, too, she had had that awful education furnished by finishing schools for the daughters of the wealthy. It was incredible how ignorant she was and how embarrassed it often made her. On her honeymoon

he so consistently paralleled. Theodore always had high marks, was remembered as a brilliant student, and would have been a noted author if he had never had a public career.

she was asked by an Englishman to explain the difference between federal and state governments in the United States. She was confused; and the excuses she made were an emotional scar forty years later when she told about it.

On quite another side, she discovered well along in her first housekeeping venture that she had not the faintest idea what went on in a kitchen. She could have starved in one; and evidently she nearly did when a cook left and another was not readily to be had. A girl of a later age, in any family, however wealthy, would not have had such embarrassments. She might prefer many servants and relief from every practical worldly concern, but she would not be completely helpless if deprived of them momentarily. To Eleanor a house without some five servants was practically a desert. This was the worse because she was as unassuming, thoughtful, and modest a person as ever lived. Later visitors were struck by the insistence with which she approached the preparing of scrambled eggs in a chafing dish, with her own hands, both in the governor's mansion at Albany and in the White House. They were very ordinary scrambled eggs, but they were symbolic for Eleanor of a certain important freedom.

Circumstances never required Eleanor to become a housewife. She never had to cook a meal, she had nurses to look after her children, and she was never without a personal maid. But I think she always rather regretted these advantages. She would have loved to cook for and wait on Franklin as other girls had to on their husbands. It would have brought her closer to him. It may be thought that she could scarcely have been distant from a man who fathered six children for her in ten years. But the truth was that Franklin was never intimate in the ultimate sense with anyone, including Eleanor; and this may well have been a grief to her and may account for many things about her which have never been very well understood. The place she made for herself in American life may have been a kind of substitute for the place in Franklin's life she never had.

It is true enough that all of us make our short journeys through this life essentially alone. There are the mitigations that come to us from friendship and co-operation in tasks to be done, but these do not touch that inner loneliness of the soul at the center of every personality. Only marriage sometimes penetrates that well-defended fortress. Two do sometimes nearly become one. Eleanor shared everything with Franklin that she was allowed to share and opened her faithful heart completely to his desires and needs. But Franklin himself did not possess the key to his own unconscious reticences, and there was very imperfect reciprocation. His defenses had developed strongly at Groton, had been reinforced at Harvard, and were, by the time of his marriage, completely impenetrable. He also knew by now that he could protect them.

The world he lived in was a multifarious one. There were pleasures and activities of many sorts to choose from in every day and suited to every mood. He seemed to be turned outward toward each of them in turn, giving to each his whole attention. This is how it appeared to those people who were around him. He had a trick of seeming to listen, and to agree or to differ partly and pleasantly, which was flattering. This was more highly developed as he progressed in his career and was responsible for some misunderstanding. But it was part of a whole apparatus of defense, becoming more formidable every year. Finally no one could tell what he was *thinking*, to say nothing of what he was *feeling*.

Even Eleanor, most of the time, had little idea of his real feelings. And by the time he was President she knew very little more what he was thinking than did any of the rest of those around him. A complete confession might have been very good for Franklin about the time of his marriage. Among other benefits, some self-surrender might have opened his heart to his wife and given him a comfort he never possessed. Eleanor gives hints of all this in her autobiographical accounts of their association. Sometimes the revelations are poignant. I am quite sure that Eleanor never understood Franklin's religious reactions. She knew that he believed; he insisted on outward observance. But he would never discuss it with Eleanor. On one occasion she tells how he abruptly refused to discuss the spiritual guidance of the children, saying simply that what was usual was not to be questioned. This was the stranger because Eleanor herself was a loyal communicant of the same church.

Such sharp repulses were unusual. Franklin much more often evaded all such cornerings. I regard myself as having been very deeply trusted indeed to have been allowed to penetrate some distance behind the curtain of his reticence on occasion. But it happened to very few people, and to them very seldom. And Eleanor was not as exceptional in this as a wife might have expected to be. Of course she began wrong. She never aspired to equality in the early years, in anything. The outpouring of her love was disarming, but it aroused mostly the protective instincts of her husband—except when the mother also became involved.

So the two of them, linked by indissoluble bonds but not lost in each other as husband and wife might sometimes be, went on into a world which was to be very different because they had lived and worked in it.

The honeymoon over and the household temporarily established in one of several houses they were to live in—all on upper East Side streets in New York—a rhythm of family life was established in New York, at Hyde Park, and at Campobello, which went on pretty much unchanged until Franklin went to Washington in 1913. And even then the wrench was not too severe. Instead of living on East Sixty-fifth Street, in one

of the adjoining twin houses that Sara had built to keep the family together, they then lived at 1733 N Street in Washington during the winters, in the house they had already visited when Uncle Ted was
inaugurated and which indeed was known as "the little White House"
because Uncle Ted had lived there before moving to the White House
itself.[5]

By that time Franklin would be on his way upward, stars in his eyes,
the future bright before him, and his beloved Navy under his official
care. But meanwhile he still had to earn his entry to the political derby;
and even though he was a Roosevelt, he was no more than an obscure
Wall Street lawyer doing lowly jobs for his respected firm—Carter,
Ledyard and Milburn. That firm, moreover, was a firm of corporation
lawyers. They represented several of the "trusts" about which Uncle
Ted was fulminating.[6] And Franklin's identification with them could
not, even by the most imaginative, be thought of as a prelude to a
career in public life carried out as a Democratic progressive. Such a
suggestion would have seemed fantastic at any time before 1910—when
he was twenty-eight.

It has been hinted that by 1910 Franklin was pretty bored with the
law; and it may be that he was, and that his enlarged activities in the
Hyde Park neighborhood were the obverse of a certain neglect of his
duties in Wall Street. However this may be, he had built up enough
good will at home so that to the local politicians he seemed an appropriate choice for nomination in 1910 to run on the Democratic ticket
for the state legislature—the Senate, as it was finally determined. Judge
John Mack of Poughkeepsie actually made the suggestion; and he,
Mayor Sague, Tom Lynch, and a few others carried it out. Franklin
appears to have accepted without the slightest hesitation. Rather as an
afterthought he then asked for and got the blessing of Uncle Ted, who
thought he ought to go ahead, although it was to be regretted that it
had to be as a Democrat.

It may be that the elder Roosevelt thought the matter of slight importance. It was unlikely that any Democrat would be elected from
Dutchess and Columbia counties, which were as Republican and conservative in politics as the backwoods of Vermont—and conservatism
can go no further. As it turned out, it was Uncle Ted's machinations
that made 1910 so successful a year for Democrats, including Franklin.
From the succession of events immediately following, it is not difficult
to reconstruct Franklin's frame of mind. It is my firm conclusion, which
I may as well state dogmatically, that he conceived the presidency to
be possible almost at once, and that although he must have had months,
even years, of discouragement he never subsequently doubted for long

[5] Auntie Bye's.
[6] Standard Oil and the Sugar Trust, among others.

that he would succeed. The worst discouragement would be his illness. He might well have been permanently put out of the running by the polio which hit him so hard in 1921; and there were certainly months when such a possibility must have lain with him in the successive beds in which, as he later told friends, he willed with an intensity he had never used in any other cause to move his left big toe. A man fighting with a paralysis so complete must necessarily have been diverted from any other physical ambition. But the truth is that in less than a year he was back at his preparations and never again dropped them.[7]

But the polio crisis was years ahead as he began his career with an energetic acceptance speech in Poughkeepsie—energetic but not an example of effective political oratory. This was indeed one of his deficiencies which, he realized, he would have to study to overcome. He mentioned this difficulty more than once—which seems a little ironic, considering how artful an orator he was thought to be twenty years later. Perhaps practice improved his style. He started out at once to get plenty of that.

What Franklin, who was then twenty-eight—and a young-looking twenty-eight at that—said on the occasion of his first acceptance to the experienced politicos gathered in county convention was almost a parody of all acceptance speeches: ". . . I accept this nomination with absolute independence, I am pledged to no man; I am influenced by no special interests, and so I shall remain." This is exactly what he would have felt compelled to say, as many other candidates have, if

[7] A letter to Louis B. Wehle, written in November 1922 and printed in *Hidden Threads of History* (New York: Macmillan, 1953), pp. 89–90, shows how deep he had already got into state politics within a year of being stricken. In that fall the New York State Democratic Convention had nominated Al Smith for governor and he had been elected. Franklin had taken an active part, as this letter shows:

Dear Louis:
  It is fine to get your letter and we can all congratulate ourselves upon the fine results of election day. I had quite a tussle to keep our friend Hearst off the ticket and to get Al Smith to run, but the thing went through in fine shape and I am glad to say that the Democratic organization in New York is in better condition than at any time since 1912.
  I have been down to New York several times this autumn and move down for good on December 4th. Do come to see me at 49 East 65th sometime soon after that.
This letter was written on the letterhead of Emmet, Marvin and Roosevelt, one of the firms he and friends were to set up as he pursued his career. Louis Wehle was a Harvard friend and a prominent New York lawyer. He was also a friend of Brandeis and had been useful in the Wilson administration as he was to be in Roosevelt's later on in several responsible jobs.
  Much earlier even than this Franklin had begun to interest himself in political affairs after being stricken.

he *had* been pledged to a boss and his machine. And of course the truth was that he had been picked at a small meeting of bosses—extraordinarily fine men, all of them, but still bosses—and that he owed his nomination to them—notably John E. Mack, then district attorney of Dutchess County.[8] The chairman, Edward E. Perkins, dissented. He took a lasting dislike to the young dude from Harvard but is said to have been persuaded by argument that Franklin could be separated from a generous amount of money for the campaign.[9]

Perkins was justified in his misgivings. Franklin was not in the accepted political tradition of the United States. And probably the county chairman blamed himself to his dying day for having consented. This would not have been because Franklin was not a winner but because he was. For when the newly budded candidate said he was pledged to no man it was notice to Tammany, if any Tammanyites had had sense enough to foresee what Franklin would become and how he would behave, that he was going his own way and not theirs. Another Roosevelt had appeared who would rise by thrusting the party organization down, imposing his terms on it, and proclaiming loudly and at length his virtues as an independent. But neither Murphy, Cohalan, and Sullivan of the New York Wigwam nor Perkins in Dutchess County had any premonition of what was to come.[10]

There never was such a thing as an independent in politics who got anywhere. But there have been some famous politicians who made or enhanced their reputations by claiming to be independents. In fact it is almost a rule that the most famous of them thus repudiate the forces to which they owe their rise. La Guardia did it, Wilson did it, and Theodore Roosevelt had done it. But none was more successful than Franklin Roosevelt at both using the bosses and the machines and gaining a reputation for repudiating and opposing them.

There is a preliminary to this Poughkeepsie proceeding which anyone studying the Roosevelt career must not overlook, especially if he gets to wondering, as he very well may, why Franklin accepted the unlikely chance of being elected as a Democrat to the State Senate from the notoriously Republican Twenty-sixth District. Grenville Clark, a reputable witness, remembered afterward something of significance that might well have been expected to turn up, very likely more than

[8] It would seem to Judge Mack, before he was through, that nominating Franklin Roosevelt was almost a profession in itself with him.

[9] Franklin knew this; but, being an opportunist, he was not disturbed. The fact was that he did not have much money. His mother and friends, however, did contribute some twenty-five hundred dollars, not enough to appease Perkins, but enough to justify Franklin's choice to the others.

[10] But somewhat later Elihu Root had. He told Josephus Daniels, who had courteously consulted him, that Roosevelts were "apt to want to ride in front." This was in 1913, when the assistant secretaryship of the Navy was in question.

once. Franklin said in the hearing of several colleagues as they sat around talking one day in the big office of Carter, Ledyard and Milburn, where a number of them had their desks, that, as for him, he "wasn't going to practice law forever, that he intended to run for office at the first opportunity, and that he wanted to be and thought he had a very real chance to be, President."[11]

When John E. Mack suggested to Franklin that he might be nominated for some office that year he was lucky not to have had Franklin jump down his throat. He was waiting for a chance, and that he saw this as a much better one than the other politicians did seems quite certain; if he did not, the astuteness he showed from then on must have appeared quite unaccountably after his first election. It seems altogether likely that he perceived the revulsion from Taft reactionism as likely to become a Democratic opportunity. Uncle Ted was deep in the Republican struggle, especially in New York, which would result in the Progressive split in 1912 and mightily assist the election of Wilson. In 1910 T.R. forced the nomination of Henry L. Stimson for governor against Boss Barnes's opposition. Barnes and the regular Republicans sabotaged the campaign and a Democrat, John A. Dix, won.

Franklin Roosevelt, the evidence is, saw this coming before Tammany did. If Boss Murphy in New York and Perkins in Poughkeepsie had anticipated a state-wide Democratic victory, some regular Democrat would have got the opportunity so carelessly offered to bumptious Franklin.

It was thus that Franklin boarded the escalator to the first floor of the political house. When he got to that floor, whether because of or in spite of a spectacular campaign, which by rights ought to have turned Dutchess and Columbia County hayseeds against him—he toured all over the countryside in spectacular style, automobiles not being so common then as they would soon become, scaring horses, wearing collegiate clothes, and making speeches in an unmodified Groton accent—he knew exactly what to do to prove his eligibility for a ride to the next floor. He had hardly got to Albany when he opened a fight on Tammany which kept him for weeks on the front pages of the New York newspapers and got some little attention all over the country.

When it was over he was a made man. He was, for one thing, fortuitously labeled at once as a progressive, a label he had the wit to accept with enthusiasm, thus aligning himself with Woodrow Wilson, who, in the same political disturbance, was elected governor of New Jersey. Also, his Albany fight against Sheehan was quite like the one in New Jersey against Smith and a very similar one in Illinois. He was noticed not only by Wilson but by all those progressives who were in those days

11 *Harvard Alumni Bulletin*, April 28, 1945, 47:452.

so hot on the heels of bosses and reactionaries everywhere and whose power was so rapidly rising that even Uncle Ted, shrewd politician that he was, saw that if he was to make an ex-President's comeback it must be as a progressive. He was setting out to take the Republican party away from Taft and the reactionary bosses. He would become so committed, and yet make such limited progress, that the bosses would defeat him for the nomination; whereat there would be nothing for him to do but lead a third-party movement.

Uncle Ted was moving into a cul-de-sac, but that was not evident to anyone in 1910—unless it was Franklin. More likely he had no more than the hunch on which he so often proceeded—after a careful survey of the possibilities. At any rate, it was his first stroke of that political luck which later came to seem so fabulous. Perhaps the first and most important observation to make is how far he would have progressed from those beginnings by 1920, when his more serious campaigning began.

When it was over and he had won, even he could see how naïve, ignorant, and ill prepared he had been. His winning was attributable first to the Democratic landslide of that year and only secondarily to any contribution he himself made. But he knew with a great certainty that he had found his career. He improved as he went along, gaining confidence, studying the technique of political communication, and seeing that his sheltered life, his schooling, and his Wall Street lawyering were handicaps, not assets, in his ambitious enterprise. His beginning awkwardness in getting into communication with ordinary folk made him shy, and his incompetence to discuss any issue of importance left him very little to talk about. He fought his shyness and discussed small and close-by subjects, refusing, usually, to be led into wider topics. He did object on occasion to criticism of Uncle Ted, and he said right out that he thought Charles Evans Hughes had been a good governor. The response to this chance-taking taught him something he would not have forgotten in 1932—one of the prominent incidents of that later campaign would be the wooing of Hiram Johnson, Republican progressive. All his political life he would look to the Democratic party for his nominations, but he would always take pains to woo such Republican voters as could be detached.

As in several future campaigns, his election was materially contributed to by Republican votes. He paid no attention to the city of Poughkeepsie, which was a Democratic enclave in Republican territory; he went after Republican farmers (just as he was always to do later on), and he learned how to meet them. With them he could capitalize on his connection with Uncle Ted, and he often talked about him familiarly (he had made sure, it will be recalled, that Uncle Ted was not going to repudiate him). Beyond that he talked mostly just about

71

"good government"—whatever that was. But in those days, it seemed, that phrase meant something. It was not necessary to be a radical in any real sense to be a reformer. As a matter of fact, the Cleveland Democrats in New York were the most active anti-Tammanyites in the city, prominent among them Edward Shepard, who would be Franklin's first alternative to "Blue-eyed Billy" Sheehan for United States senator. And Cleveland Democrats were far from being radicals. Indeed they had some close Wall Street connections. John A. Dix, who was to be governor, was one of them; and there were others in Albany still left over from Cleveland's governorship back in the eighties who would welcome Franklin to Albany as potentially one of themselves because his father had been a lifelong Cleveland supporter.

But "good government" in the West and Midwest was a large part of the progressive focus. The American democracy was just in process of getting direct instead of legislative election of United States senators, home rule for cities, direct primary instead of convention nomination for candidates, judicial and administrative reform for cities and states, the acceptance of the merit system instead of patronage appointments in the civil service, and some kind of protection for those who were injured in industrial accidents and for women and children in industry. Full social security was still a dream; but factory laws, the regulation of hours of work, the prohibition of child labor, and a hundred other reforms which would seem so commonplace once they were attained, all had to be fought for in bitter battles, and by heroes later generations would think it unnecessary to honor greatly because it would be impossible to conceive how evil and angry the opposition to them could have been.

The progressives of 1910 were the American middle class, and especially farmers; and it was a Republican dissidence, not a Democratic one, which carried it on until Wilson's time—in spite of Bryan, who challenged again and again but without success. And great gains were to be made by Wilson—among them the income tax, the popular election of senators, and the Federal Reserve System; but these were all in the future as Franklin campaigned in Dutchess County in 1910. And being not too well informed, he would much rather expatiate on the principle, rather than the specific items, of that good government which all but the most reactionary—and even some of them—wanted but which was much more wanted undefined than specified.

Franklin never exhibited more clearly than in that first campaign the lateness and immaturity I have spoken of before which would always be a characteristic weakness as he entered on new stages of his career. He was a boy doing a man's job, just as he would seem to Walter Lippmann to be in 1932 when he was challenging for the presidential nomination. Lippmann, who had known him a long time, had worked with him in Washington, and had watched him as governor. He knew he was unprepared. He had reason to think him unfit for the presidency in a great crisis. But what Lippmann had not noticed, and as others usually failed to understand, there was in Franklin, because of his dedication to the career he had chosen, because of his sense of destiny, or perhaps because he had an extraordinary way of reacting to challenge, a phenomenal capacity for growth. He never seemed capable when he was given a job to do; he never failed to rise to its demands; and it was always turned to the interest of common folk.

He went to Albany fortuitously, then, as a state senator, was welcomed by the remaining Cleveland Democrats, was looked at askance as a kind of gilded amateur by those rising professionals, Robert Wagner and Al Smith—who were to be leaders, respectively, of Senate and Assembly for that session—and immediately undertook another adventure which seemed far beyond his capabilities but which proved to be his entry fee to the escalator that would lift him to the second floor of the political house. He refused to accept the Tammany candidate for United States senator. "Blue-eyed Billy" Sheehan is still a symbol in American political history. It was the young senator from Dutchess County who created that symbol and kept it alive for a generation.

4

In 1932, telling us about it, Franklin always spoke of his famous first essay in Albany as "the Sheehan business." After hearing it the first time, when I had caught him in reminiscent mood and with an evening ahead, I went next day to look at the house on State Street in which so much of it had happened. It was still there and looked as though it might be for a long time. And I could dwell in imagination on the scenes of that long-ago spring. The inside of the Senate building had been burned out that very year, so the picture of twenty-nine-year-old Franklin, fresh from his gilded surroundings, among the heavy desks, spittoons, and the leather furniture of 1911, could not be recaptured. I fancied I could see him staring down his long nose at the presiding officer, getting a reputation for arrogance, when he was more shy than proud. It was a faint materialization. But I was intrigued by the scene and the actors, and my imagination was quite adequate to supply the missing décor. The year I was trying to call up had been, in fact, I suddenly realized, the year in which I had begun what might have been a career of reporting on the Buffalo *Courier* at the other end of the state. As a cub I had heard about the Sheehan fight from my elders, since Sheehan had come from Buffalo and had opposed Cleveland, who was a Buffalo hero. But what I recalled by 1932 was very little.

The old three-story house I went to see on State Street was a brash appurtenance for a new legislator, to begin with, and Al Smith and his fellows must have eyed it with appropriate East Side disdain. Most legislators, on their fifteen-hundred-dollar salaries, lived in boarding-houses and left their families at home. Franklin seems also to have appeared on some early occasions in the cutaway or Prince Albert, tall hat, and spats of formal occasions among the Edwardian wealthy. And this was something that, caught in a photograph, he did not live down for years. Also, instead of more plebeian eyeglasses, he wore what the voluble Al Smith called "pinchers"—pince-nez. Altogether, he had an

74

air of patrician superiority and youthful disdain which annoyed a good many people—including Frances Perkins, who had occasion to solicit assistance from him for labor legislation for which she was lobbying.[1] Frances, being a woman, should have known that the chilly airs Franklin assumed were the cover for a sense of inadequacy. There were others whose annoyance was more consequential, including the alcoholic Tom Grady, who was irritated on the slightest occasion that year because on account of his habits he was being replaced as presiding officer of the Senate by Robert Wagner. But so tolerant and kindly a fellow as Bob Wagner occasionally thought the young senator from the Twenty-sixth District intolerably self-seeking. It is reported that on one occasion he shouted from his dais: "Senator Roosevelt has gained his point. What he wants is a headline in the newspapers. Let us proceed to our business."[2]

This last incident showed that the other professionals, even those no older than himself, knew perfectly well what he was up to. He was "making a name for himself." And it is improbable that they were fooled in the least by the clothes, the manners, or the swank of a rented house. Perhaps they even understood the awkwardness with which he was struggling. They, in their own way, were doing the same thing. And all three—Roosevelt, Smith, and Wagner—were to have a certain success. Since they were all Democrats, their ways would run together for many years. Sometimes the concurrence would be pleasant and mutually helpful, but sometimes it would prove to be the reverse.

"The Sheehan business" seems not to have happened in quite the way Franklin afterward described it—for instance, to me in 1932. But this only goes to show that Franklin, even if he was first a governor and then a President, was in many ways quite like the rest of us. For him as for others the past was apt to improve in the telling. The point of the tale as he told it was the struggle to prevent Tammany from putting over "Blue-eyed Billy" Sheehan as United States senator in succession to Chauncey M. Depew, whose term was expiring. As the tale went on being repeated Sheehan became more and more a villain and his rejection more and more a victory for the righteous. Somehow the attitudinizing of young Franklin dropped out of the account. The truth was not greatly different; but Franklin's version did, I am afraid, suffuse the episode with a justifying light.

The events of 1910–12 all seem, as we look back at them, to have had an intricacy that defeats simple recounting. Those were the years of Taft's decline, and with him reactionary Republicanism; of Uncle Ted's growing impatience with what had been a premature retirement and his seizure with an impulse to occupy again the center of a stage

[1] *The Roosevelt I Knew*, by Frances Perkins (New York: Viking, 1946).
[2] Freidel, op. cit., p. 119, from a newspaper clipping in the Roosevelt Library.

75

he had dominated so long; of the entrance of Wilson on the stage that Uncle Ted thought was his to recapture; and of Franklin's first splurge of publicity and his emergence as a budding statesman.

The effect in New York State of Theodore's maneuvers was, as has been said, to split the Republicans and allow the Democrats to win—the process which carried Franklin into the State Senate. But Franklin was not the only shrewd assessor of these events. Sheehan also saw what was coming, and he too had ambitions. In fact he wanted, as had been the fashion with rich men, to finish his career in the United States Senate. He thought he saw a way to do it, because senators were still elected by legislators, and legislators were not too difficult to manage. Especially was New York's legislature amenable to management if the Democrats controlled it, because then it was only necessary to have the good will of Charles F. Murphy, the boss of Tammany. And Sheehan had bought that with magnificent contributions.

The senatorial elections went this way: Senators were elected in joint session by a majority of both houses. There were 200. But each party's decision on how to vote was made in caucus and was binding on all those present. It required 101 votes to elect, but it required only 58 to control the Democratic caucus of 114. In betting language this would be called a "parlay," and that is probably just how Al Smith described it to Franklin when that neophyte asked him how it worked. But Franklin was smart too; he saw that if enough votes could be kept out of the caucus to prevent the mustering of 101 for Sheehan, the hold-outers could prevent any choice being made. They could at least bargain. Truth to tell, it was not Franklin who saw this first; it was another legislator, Edmund R. Terry of Brooklyn, who had reason to be peeved at Tammany[3] and who explained the possibilities to Franklin. But that young man grasped the indicated tactics rapidly and made some overnight decisions, which, if he had made them differently, might have affected his whole career.

If he joined Terry and defied Murphy, he was defying the Tammany tiger in its moment of victory. The reputation of Tammany was seldom to forgive and never to forget, and very well Franklin knew it. He would be likely to be fighting the New York organization from then on as long as he was in politics. And there would be no pains spared to retire him permanently at the first opportunity. On the other hand, such a defiance, if made good at all, would earn him a reputation for independence of the same sort that had made Uncle Ted famous. It might get him also the kind of publicity not available to young Albany legislators, than whom, as Louis Howe later pointed out, no one is lower in newspapermen's regard. Louis was then the New York *Herald's*

[3] He seems to have felt aggrieved about patronage.

Albany correspondent and as such was having his first rather startled look at the young man about whom all the rest of his life was to center and in whom all his hopes were to find embodiment.

Louis could have told Franklin too—and perhaps he did—that to defy Tammany was a good bet for a senator from the Twenty-sixth District. It was Republican anyway, except for the city of Poughkeepsie, and a fight of this sort might well be the only thing in his record that would be of much use to Franklin two years hence, in a year not marked by a national Democratic sweep. At any rate, Franklin overnight did decide to join Terry, and within a week he was an active member of a full-fledged revolt of twenty-one Democrats who held up the senatorial election for two and a half months. As the most noticed of this courageous crew he multiplied by many times the notice he rated as another Roosevelt in Albany. He was suddenly the archfoe of Tammany. By implication, which was just as important, he was a Progressive, even if he was a Democrat, and never afterward would he lose the label.

It is not at all clear that Franklin foresaw this last development when he joined Terry. He had not emerged from his campaign with any such label except as he had claimed to favor that good government which was synonymous with virtue. There is often, among those who are merely curious but not students of the Roosevelt career, a certain wonder about this. On the face of it, a patrician member of the Roosevelt and Delano clans, with a Groton-Harvard-Wall Street background, would hardly be marked for a progressive political career.

To understand fully the emergence of the most successful of twentieth-century progressives, all the events of 1910–12 have to be studied. But two of them were perhaps more significant than the others. The first was this defiance of Tammany; the second was the escape from Tammany's retribution by way of Wilson. Both were purely political moves, but both were also progressive commitments. As such they carried with them presumptions of support for a whole program, some of which Franklin liked and some of which he did not, but none of which he could henceforth altogether escape. Conservation he embraced with enthusiasm; woman suffrage he had doubts about and gave in to with some reluctance. In between he supported labor legislation with some reservation and the various items of good government with various degrees of readiness. But all of it was part of the role for which he was cast; he could not, if he had wanted to, escape.

But on the whole, although he had some qualms about the way his neighbors were likely to view the more forward-looking items in the progressive program, he found his new-found philosophy congenial. He also, being then, as ever, shrewd in sizing up the long-run future, saw that progressivism—Democratic progressivism—was good politics. How right he was. No conservative, from then on for ten years, could have any real political success; and, after an interval, progressivism would carry him to the White House. What would any Roosevelt follower not give to know what went on in the young senator's mind on the night and day of January 19, together with a few subsequent nights and days. If in Wall Street he had seen his way ahead to successive steps ending at the presidency, in Albany he saw the political conception necessary to his climb and embraced it then and there.

The Sheehan business was only an incident; it did not originate or end as Franklin was later inclined to interpret it, but it had far consequences, and they were of precisely the sort he wanted. If he preferred to make a good story of it, so did everyone else. What he did was mostly to accept the general interpretation. This was that he won, almost singlehanded, a notable victory. Louis Howe knew how far this was from the fact, and so did all the other newspapermen; but, like the apocryphal Washington story of the cherry tree, it came to be far more true than the facts about it. If it did not happen the way it was supposed to, it still made more sense in story than in fact.

In the affair, as it turned out, the man Sheehan is of no particular importance except as the occasion for Franklin's commitment; he was never heard of again, and his efforts to punish Franklin failed (though they succeeded with some of his co-operators). Edmund Terry sank into like obscurity. These and the other gentlemen involved were reduced to footnotes in the Roosevelt history. Whether or not he intended that they should merely be useful instruments in his climb to power, that is the purpose they served. Because Terry had no *pied-à-terre* in Albany, the revolters made their headquarters in Franklin and Eleanor's house on State Street while they held out against Tammany pressure. This gave Franklin the appearance of being in command and the opportunity to be interviewed by the reporters.

Sheehan himself had come up out of the shadows of the underworld, as had that other famous Buffalo character, Fingy Conners. But Sheehan was a lawyer who had gradually come to control several utilities, to be counsel for others, to become wealthy, and move on to New York City. He had always interested himself in politics. Utility magnates had to. And believing that 1910 was to be a Democratic year, he had organized a pool of utility contributions to Tammany's war chest in return for Murphy's promise of the senatorship.[4]

---

[4] There is an excellent account of "the Sheehan business" in E. K. Lindley's *Franklin D. Roosevelt* (New York: Blue Ribbon Books, 1931), a book which remains the best account of Franklin in his Albany years. These events occurred before Lindley's time, but he heard about them repeatedly not only from Franklin himself but from numerous newspapermen who recollected what went on. As for Sheehan himself, a few sentences from Lindley's book summarize his career: "To the Progressives of that time 'Blue-Eyed Billy' Sheehan was the epitome of standpattism. As a young man he had made himself Democratic leader of

Political bosses do not go back on pledges, and Murphy of Tammany was bound to see that Sheehan was elected if he could. Terry and Roosevelt's little band were not so bound; and all, for one or another reason, felt able to defy Tammany. Some of them had, they thought, been badly treated in the campaign by Murphy, who in those days was a capricious and autocratic boss, even though by comparison with John Curry, who would be his successor when Franklin was governor, he would almost rank as a statesman. Some of the conspirators were old Cleveland Democrats, conservative but honest, who hated Tammany as a matter of taste as much as anything else. True conservatives react violently against the smells of corruption inherent in the policies to which they give consent, and occasionally they revolt.

That the holdout should be so cohesive and should go on and on into a third month must have surprised everyone. That, as the weeks passed, young Senator Roosevelt should become the spokesman of the group—though, as all agree, in no sense its leader—may have been largely because the daily meetings went on for hours and hours at his house. He naturally became the front man and presently, by a process not difficult to reconstruct, began to be more confident of his position. After a while he began to find, almost daily, small items and large to feed the press. The larger of these connected themselves with national affairs. The State Street insurgents were presently made to seem part of the movement for the direct election of senators and of the same fight on the bosses as was going on currently in so many other legislative centers, including New Jersey, where Wilson was operating.

Murphy's authority being at stake, he could not afford to give up easily; but he was getting a bad press, and the other items of his legislative program were being held up. His promise to Sheehan was only one of a good many, and he was defaulting on all of them. He and Franklin had a conversation after a few weeks; as Franklin afterward reported it, nothing was settled. Indeed Murphy politely said that he did not doubt Franklin's sincerity. Franklin had a rather more embarrassing session with Sheehan himself at the State Street house—Eleanor entertaining Mrs. Sheehan while the men had their talk—in which threats were used. Franklin and all his co-operators, Sheehan said plainly, would be ruthlessly hunted out of public life unless the affair

Buffalo, then leader of the party in the Legislature, and finally Lieutenant-Governor during the three-year term of Governor Roswell P. Flower, beginning in 1892. He had been National Committeeman for five years and Chairman of the Executive Committee of the State Committee for two. He had fought Cleveland, in Buffalo and in Albany. At the end of his term as Lieutenant-Governor he had come to New York to make his fortune as a lawyer. In 1911 he was the partner of Alton B. Parker, Democratic nominee for President in 1904, and counsel for, as well as director of, a dozen public utility and railroad companies, including the principal lighting and traction corporations of the city."

This was the entrenched political power Franklin was challenging.

was ended at once. Franklin did not doubt that this was so; in fact the punishment had already begun. The scion of the Roosevelts and Delanos was not very vulnerable, but not all the others were so fortunate. Mortgages were foreclosed; loans were called; privileges were canceled; political exiles were arranged. Incidentally, this would go on for years, as Sheehan had promised it would. Being politicians, the legislators were not optimists about winning; and anyway, they had only a negative pressure to exert. They talked about electing Edward M. Shepard, who would have been suited to their requirements. But they knew well enough that in the end it would not be he who would be chosen.

The compromise, when it came, could well have been interpreted as a defeat for the insurgents, because the candidate to whom they agreed was Judge James A. O'Gorman, who had been a Tammany man all his life—had in fact been a Grand Sachem; and the truth was that after the long winter weeks of struggle the coalition was breaking up and something had to be done quickly. The newspapermen knew what had happened; their reports pictured the end as a Tammany victory. But Franklin's genius for communications stood him in good stead. It was not long before the impression was general that Franklin had come out on top, that in fact he had forced Tammany into a corner and gained a compromise. O'Gorman was a Tammanyite, but he was also a reputable judge; and Franklin pictured him as a kind of Alger hero and himself as his discoverer.

The importance of the whole affair in the end appeared to be, so far as Franklin was concerned, that he had earned the enmity of Tammany, along with a reputation as a progressive insurgent. Louis Howe taught him how to use both to good advantage. It was indeed not unlikely, although their formal connection had not yet begun, that Louis showed him how he might avoid the political demise Tammany was preparing for him. Wherever the inspiration came from—the origin is not in the record—he went that fall to visit Woodrow Wilson in Trenton. There he was received in the manner befitting a somewhat younger participant in the same struggle Wilson was in. Smith in New Jersey was an even more typical specimen of the political boss than Murphy in New York. And he had made Wilson governor. He failed to understand his man. Wilson, having got so far, now was turning on the author of his political career. He saw that he could go no further in pawn to a boss. It was not going to be very gracefully done, and Wilson would be open to charges of ingratitude, at the very least; but his eye was firmly fixed now on the presidency. Such a fixation is a wonderful justification for the use of otherwise doubtful agencies and methods. And Wilson was having luck outside New Jersey. If he was thought of at home as having been rescued from an impossible situation at Princeton and been made governor, only to turn on his sponsors because they were useless in his further ambitions, that was not what was understood elsewhere. He was conservative enough, it was believed; but, like the Cleveland Democrats, he was supposed to have a revulsion from the odors of machine politics. He was a "good government" man. He had already journeyed widely and talked much, and he was rapidly gaining in reputation.

Franklin, with a shrewdness that could be suspected by now to be characteristic, judged that Wilson would succeed. His specific opposition for the presidential nomination seemed to be Champ Clark, who was such a confused fuddy-duddy, as against Wilson's sharp intelligence, that Wilson's victory seemed a very good risk indeed. The two amateur politicians evidently got along very well, although neither said anything about what went on. They were neither of them pressed for a report because no importance was attached to the interview.

It was clear, however, that Franklin had made another commitment which would, if it succeeded, take him out of Tammany's vengeful power. It remained for him to behave becomingly during the rest of his stay in Albany and to show his political permanence by re-election. Both these conditions were met by 1912; and in 1913 he was to occupy Uncle Ted's old post in the Navy Department. The escalator would have taken him up another flight.

Before that rise began he went through a long session of the New York legislature, stumped the state in an effort to prevent the punishment of his co-conspirators at the polls (in the fall of 1911, when he himself did not have to run), busied himself in support of Wilson, went through another Albany session, and won re-election to his Senate seat from a sickbed—he had typhoid fever, and Louis ran his campaign. Even this sickness was lucky, in a way, since it immured him safely at Hyde Park while Uncle Ted was making his strenuous bid for a comeback.

The legislative experience always loomed large in his recollection afterward. It was then that he found himself at last engaged, at the age of twenty-eight to thirty, in activities suitable to his powers and his ambitions, and he threw himself into them without reserve. From his own point of view there was really only one thing wrong with it: New York State had no navy. There was, however, an entirely adequate substitute in the state forests, game refuges, and parks. These became his special preserve; he worked for their improvement and enlargement in the same spirit that he added to the Hyde Park estate, improved the fields and the stock, and every year planted thousands of trees. The historians will note that here again he was cultivating an interest of Uncle Ted's. It was to remain an interest throughout his career—at least until all such physical matters lost themselves in his last years in the imponderables of war and peace.

Franklin had older colleagues whose love for the New York forests and parks was enduring; Osborne is a name at least as much honored by conservationists as Roosevelt. But Franklin has to be given credit, if along with these others, for some reorganization of the state's conservation work, for an approach to new protective laws, and especially for the solidifying of a state tradition of care for the face of the earth. He enlisted Gifford Pinchot, who had recently had a historic difference with President Taft, and altogether made friends in this kind of work who were to remain close to him throughout his career. I think he felt toward the end that this, perhaps, was as satisfying a phase of his life as any he could look back to.[5]

As a legislator with a widening progressive reputation, however, he was besieged with importunities of other sorts. This was, it must be remembered, just at the beginning of the movement toward reform, both in government and industry, which would, within Franklin's lifetime, revolutionize the conditions of life and work for nearly every American. Government would be forced to assume regulatory duties that would have seemed altogether beyond reason to a former generation. Many of them would have their effective beginnings in New York during the successive governorships of Al Smith, with Franklin supporting him. At the moment they were the items of a general progressive program to which Franklin was very quickly introduced by proponents as soon as he became prominent. He was at first rather reluctant about some of it. The truth was that it was all new to him, and besides, he was not certain how his mostly rural Hudson Valley constituents would regard such innovations. Regulations governing the conditions of urban life might be a distant interest indeed for upstate farmers. But as Uncle Ted became officially progressive, replacing La Follette as the titular leader of the movement, and as Wilson transformed himself with an almost unbecoming rudeness from what had seemed to be a rigidly conservative professor into a bidder for progressive leadership, Franklin gained courage to follow what was undoubtedly his bent.

By the time Franklin left the legislature, the Congress had been petitioned to resolve in favor of the direct election of senators, a direct

---

[5] I must say, for myself, that I feel especially proud to have been his agent in some of this work at a critical time. I organized the preliminaries to the Civilian Conservation Corps; as Undersecretary of Agriculture I had for a while jurisdiction over the Forest Service at a time of expansion, and I was repeatedly urged by him to take charge of an enlarged land-use division in the government. Once I was even entrusted by him with the carrying of a message to a conservation celebration in Albany when it was impossible for him to be there. I can testify at least to the continuing happiness he had in contributing to one of the finest traditions of the American people.

primary law had been passed—after he had fought long and hard to make it better—and a good deal of social legislation was under way. This, in addition to his contributions to conservation, always gave him great satisfaction. He looked back on Albany as the school where he had learned his trade and found his footing.

In the fall of 1911, although there was no compelling reason why he should, he spent weeks in traveling and speaking all over the state. He was learning more of his trade. This campaign of 1911, in which he was not even a candidate, was a kind of dry run for those more consequential ones to come when his own fortunes would be very much engaged; it was the first campaigning he had done beyond the boundaries of his own district. The excuse was that his friends of the insurrection were being martyred. It is not clear that he saved any of them. The high Democratic tide of 1910 was definitely receding anyway; and the new Assembly in 1912 had thirty-seven fewer Democrats than its predecessor had had. But when the fall activities were over, Franklin had had physical touch with most of the state's communities, he knew the leaders, and thousands of New Yorkers had heard his voice.

The legislature in 1912, instead of a Democratic majority, had a safe Republican one. It was therefore somewhat dull for Franklin. He continued his work for conservation with the backing of the rather lethargic Governor Dix. Here, curiously enough, he ran into Tammany again. He could not at first understand why Murphy should oppose protective measures for the forests and watercourses, a matter which was cleared up when certain contributors to Tammany funds openly demanded their pay; these were the dealers in game and millinery supplies who wanted no restrictions. He was unable to put through the comprehensive bill Pinchot had helped him frame for the "Protection of Lands, Forests, and Public Parks"; here again the lumber and power interests were too much for the conservationists. So, after all, his conservation efforts had immediately disappointing results. He was seized with an indignation at the rapacity of the resource plunderers which never left him and which colored much of his policy when he moved into positions of far greater power.

In 1912, during the spring, matters seemed not to develop so favorably, either, for Wilson. As the professionals approached the national convention an amateur candidate seemed less attractive. After all, he was an unknown, and lately he had seemed to be emerging as an independent, something the professionals detest with a hard instinct. This was especially true in the East and the Midwest, where the big-city machines were so powerful; the West and the South seemed more favorable—an indication that became fact in the election.

As every politician knows only too well, election and nomination have sharply different conditions and probabilities. There are years when almost any Democrat can win, and 1912 was one of them, although this did not appear clearly until after the Republican convention and the defection of T.R. and his Bull Moosers. There are also years when almost any Republican can win, and Franklin was to run into one of them as vice-presidential candidate in 1920. But 1912 was pretty obviously a Democratic year, and that made the Baltimore convention one of the most bitterly contested in history. The professionals wanted one of their own, since there was no great need to make a show of devotion to the public interest.

A nomination that is a fairly certain prelude to election is one that intensifies all the sectional and factional rivalry so endemic in both big political parties, but especially the Democratic party with its solid South which can never have a candidate but which furnishes so many electoral votes. This causes a feeling of inferiority and resentment which is expressed in some way in nearly every convention. But such a year is one in which the professionals do not hesitate to express their criticism by choosing what seems to them a safe and steady man. Harmon was their first choice in 1912, but Clark was acceptable.

The Democratic advantage was not so obvious in the spring as it later became. Wilson had broken with the New Jersey professionals, and, as Franklin had to confess to him, he could not count on any delegates from New York: Tammany would have a big majority among them, and the New York vote would be governed by the unit rule. Wilson's inquiry was notice enough, however; and Franklin went furiously to work. He told Wilson that even if he could not count on the New York delegation at the convention, he would have New York's votes in the election. This might not be much comfort to a candidate who was beginning to feel that his main problem was the nomination, but Franklin set out to make of it what he could.

With the help of some other non-Tammany Democrats he formed a New York State Wilson Conference. On the call for the first meeting of this group there were the names of two prominent Democrats from each congressional district, eighty-six in all. Among those who were members of a committee of twelve appointed by this conference there were some respected but not very influential names: Edward M. Bassett, Lawrence P. Dunham, George Haven Putnam, E. J. McGuire, and Thomas Mott Osborne.[6] They were somewhat at a loss to know what they could

[6] The State Democratic Convention met in New York April 12, 1912. Franklin invited twenty delegates to a Wilson dinner on the eleventh. Seventeen declined, which shows Murphy's power and the reason for Franklin's discouragement. About the middle of May, when Franklin came back to New York from a trip to the Caribbean, William F. McCombs, W. G. McAdoo, and Senator O'Gorman had begun a Wilson movement. Thomas Mott Osborne had organized a similar one upstate. Franklin was made chairman of the New York State Wilson Conference at once, and with funds furnished largely by Osborne, organization was

do that would have any considerable effect. What they decided was that they would somehow manage to appear in Baltimore with a hundred and fifty Wilson supporters. They would make as many contacts and as much noise as they could. Their object would be to convince the delegates from other states that only the Tammany organization in New York City opposed Wilson. The upstate Democrats were for him, they would urge, and if he was nominated the state would surely go Democratic. They hoped this would have a real effect on the delegates from elsewhere. Besides, there were about thirty New York delegates who were Wilson men, even if their votes were made impotent by the unit rule. On the whole they hoped to have a real effect; and, if Wilson came through successfully, they aspired to form the nucleus of a reformed party in the state. Tammany on the losing side could be punished, as Franklin's personal resentment indicated would be no more than just.[7]

It is impossible here to tell the story of that fierce battle in Baltimore. Wilson emerged the victor: but that old war horse of the Democracy, William Jennings Bryan, was the hero. He who had been three times a Democratic candidate and who had been influential if not dominant in conventions since 1896, when he had captivated one with a single speech, was still a power. If he was through running he had neither forgotten his cunning nor lost his friends. He hated the city machines, and especially Tammany. And he resented the appearance in a Democratic convention of such men as August Belmont and Thomas Fortune Ryan, and made another famous speech saying so. Tammany had begun by voting for Harmon, then switched to Clark, whereupon Bryan switched to Wilson, "for as long as Tammany supported Clark." Clark's vote rose at one time above a majority; but the old two-thirds rule of the Democrats was still in effect, and he was checked there. Then he began to lose. The trading and shifting went on ballot by ballot, until on the forty-sixth Wilson got the necessary two-thirds, and it was, according to custom, made unanimous.

Franklin was wonderfully stimulated by the excitement. He cannot be said to have been an important figure, but he was more conspicuous than the run of the delegates. There were many of those present who were to recall afterward the pleasant and mercurial young fellow who

---

pushed. It was at this time that Franklin hired Louis McHenry Howe to direct the publicity for this group. They were never after, as long as Howe lived, to separate.

[7] The New York State group occupied a building across the street from the Wilson and Clark headquarters and issued a manifesto to be put in the hands of the incoming delegates. It began like this: "New York has a large 'Progressive' vote. Unless you give us a candidate that will get this vote, we shall lose the state." And it ended with a typical Howe touch—the attempt to popularize: "Nominate Wilson—that's all!" This obvious reference to the advertising slogan for a popular whiskey may or may not have had fortunate connotations. But it did have some currency during the subsequent campaign.

had taken pains to become acquainted, had shown considerable knowledge of their part of the country, and had argued so earnestly for Wilson. They remembered him also because he was a Roosevelt, a Democratic Roosevelt. After Theodore, most politicians had forgotten entirely that there had been a Cleveland supporter in upstate New York named James Roosevelt. It came back to them as his tall and active son reminded them that not all the family centered in Oyster Bay. Not a few delegates, moreover, had, however casually, noticed the emergence of this other Roosevelt as the most conspicuous member of the Albany insurgents. They recalled it as they watched him circulate among the professionals gathered here from all over the nation.

Among those who turned a benign eye in Franklin's direction was Josephus Daniels, another old war horse with almost the rank and seniority of Bryan himself. The Daniels recollections of that convention were sharp, and they were set down at length in his memoirs.[8]

This was the first—but it was far from the last—time the older man was to work with the younger one. They would have, to begin with, seven and a half years together in the Navy Department; and that was not to be the end—far from it. At the moment Daniels was a very busy man. He was an important professional. Not only had he been chief clerk of the Interior Department in Cleveland's administration but he was also an important southern leader. He was national committeeman from North Carolina, and he was also a newspaper proprietor. It was natural that he should be near the center of things. Daniels, moreover, was an old Bryan man in more than just the political sense; he was an ardent churchman and a teetotaler—a typical representative of the Bible belt, except for his tolerance, his geniality, and his genuine progressiveness. He wanted Wilson and made no secret of his preference.

Daniels was to have an important part in the campaign, so important that there could be no question but that he had earned a post in the Wilson cabinet. Franklin, after his first elation at Wilson's choice, went back to New York to see what could be done for the candidate in his upstate country. He also had his own political problems. There was actually some talk of nominating him for governor to succeed Dix. Uncle Ted killed that idea by splitting the Republicans so effectively that Boss Murphy knew he could elect anyone who was not positively repugnant to the upstate Democrats. He would certainly not take Franklin. He chose "Plain Bill" Sulzer, a curious character who turned out so badly for Tammany purposes that he had to be impeached. But by then Franklin would have gone on to new opportunities.

The Democrats were likely to win the state: but there was a question

[8] *The Wilson Era* (Chapel Hill: University of North Carolina Press, 1946–49), 2 vols.

whether Franklin would even be renominated. There was the Sheehan business just behind him: and there was Perkins, the Tammany-controlled county boss, who disliked Franklin anyway, to be circumvented. What seems to have won against these handicaps was a genuine popularity among the voters, together with a nucleus of firm friends among his original supporters. At any rate, he was renominated in August without any fuss. Meanwhile he had carried the Wilson support somewhat further by setting up an organization called the Empire State Democracy. This, again, was dependent largely on Osborne funds, which ran out along in August: as a matter of fact, the organization was just about dead by mid-August when the state convention was held. At most, its organizers earned a credit for trying. Franklin, however, with his usual luck, could avoid responsibility for this failure. He came down with the timely typhoid fever which allowed Louis Howe to run his whole campaign and demonstrate his indispensability. It was done in masterly fashion, with the use of several innovations in the way of appeals to voters; and Franklin won. Of course a good many Democrats won that fall, among them Wilson. And that, as it turned out, was a good deal more consequential for Franklin than his own victory.

Many harsh things have been said about Franklin Roosevelt. Among them have been allegations, stated with absolute certainty, that all he ever had in view was rising to the presidency and staying there as long as possible. This, I think, is to confuse political methodology with public policy. Franklin could have had no influence on his times if he had been, as his father was, a desultory businessman and a country gentleman. He could have had a good life with his farms, his collections, his sports, his travel, his friends, and his family. He need not even have gone on with Milburn, Carter and Ledyard. He had money enough, counting his mother's share of the Delano fortune and the considerable income Eleanor had inherited. He could simply have settled down in Hyde Park among the surroundings he loved as few people do love their home places—or can, for that matter, because so very few are as lovely as the Roosevelt estate above the bend of the stately river.

Even those whose nerves were set most on edge by Franklin's personality and his behavior have been utterly unable to think of him as behaving other than as he did. He meant from the first to be President, they say of him, as though that will be taken to be an unquestionably derogatory characterization. I too do not doubt that the young Franklin meant to be President, or that it was an ambition held to all along; there are many evidences of it. It is true, too, that there are few reasons to believe that he had any obvious qualifications for that high post. But who has qualifications for it at thirty? And is there any limitation on the time for ambition to seize a man?

If they are looked for in the Roosevelt career, alongside the evidences of restless ambition, there appear to the searcher multifarious evidences of preparation for responsibilities beyond those he had at any stage of his progress. I have made the point before that he always seemed late. It continued to be so. When he went to the legislature he was immature almost beyond belief in the affairs of the state. Al Smith could have passed an examination in such matters with a much higher mark than Franklin. So could Robert Wagner or perhaps many another young man. But Franklin caught up. He progressed amazingly in the two years of his senatorship. Then a very characteristic thing happened. He moved on. From 1913 he was no longer a New York Stater: he became a national man. And in spite of the fact that later he was to have two terms as governor, he never really went back to being a New York Stater.

In an interval of the year before he moved on to Washington—1912— Franklin had an experience just as stirring—maybe more so—as that of the convention at Baltimore whose various excitements he experienced with the exaltation of the born politician. This was his visit to the Panama Canal, then in full spate of construction. What he saw filled him with an almost unbearable pride. He was also charged to the exploding point with the ambition he now fully understood: to have such power that he too could cause, as Uncle Ted had, things of this magnitude to happen.

One of Franklin's most notable characteristics had not, up till now in public life, had the opportunity to develop. He was a natural builder and arranger. He felt in himself a talent for design, and it is true that he had a flair for laying out and for managing and for helping things to run more efficiently. It had never yet had any expression, and never would have had if he had stayed in the legislature. But he was about to find himself in still another sense. His bent for managing and building was to have full scope in the Navy, was to be one of his contributions to the governorship of New York, and would come out in the magnificent works of his presidency. So far it had been exercised only in miniature at Hyde Park, at Campobello, and in his conservancy efforts as a legislator. There was some cramping even in these: his mother continued to be obdurate about the Hyde Park estate. And his conservancy work was frustrated. In 1915 his mother would give way and allow him to build an addition to the old house which about doubled its size. He claimed to be his own architect—as he was to be later for various other buildings at Warm Springs and at Hyde Park;[9] and, as everyone who had occasion to work with him knew, he had stubborn ideas about the look of government edifices—post offices and the like.[10]

[9] Although there were sometimes professionals, and they probably contributed more than he admitted. Henry Toombs was one of these.

[10] The changes at Hyde Park involved taking down the wooden tower which was the main feature of the old house and putting on a stucco front, but the

At Campobello, to be sure, he had been able to do something. For there the younger Roosevelts had been presented by Sara with the next-door place. This was very precious to Eleanor as the first home which was truly hers to do with as she liked. The New York houses she had lived in had been chosen and furnished by her mother-in-law, and she had been an uneasy addition to the family at Hyde Park. She had tried very hard to be a daughter; and doubtless Sara had tried, too, to make accommodation. But, as Eleanor later admitted in her autobiographical books, it was never very successful and doubtless accounted for more family derangement than was at once apparent. Now, as before, when they were newly married, Franklin simply refused to see the problem. As a matter of fact, it never was mentioned between them after he discovered Eleanor one time dissolved in tears in the first New York house and professed complete bewilderment. Eleanor simply went on living without complaint. In those years she was a wife and mother—nothing much more. Her metamorphosis was to come in the aftermath of tragedy.

There was a kind of escape from this at Campobello. Not only did Eleanor have her own house and servants, but there were the freedoms of summer and the open air, children busy with country and seaside pursuits, and Franklin arriving as a welcome visitor when he could. But the children kept coming, and Franklin sometimes escaped altogether from the household. Usually he went for a few days or weeks on his favorite vacation—sailing up or down the coast. A time or two he went to Nova Scotia for hunting or fishing. But in 1912 with Hall Roosevelt, Eleanor's brother, then an undergraduate at Harvard, and J. Mayhew

---

most important change was the addition of the large library on the south with suites of rooms on the second floor, which from then on were his favorite living quarters, and some other additions on the north. Those of us who worked with him and were asked to stay at Hyde Park became most familiar with the library and with the small dark "office" in the old building. The library of that house at teatime was as sheerly pleasant a room as I have ever seen. There was a veined Italian marble fireplace at each end in which wood fires burned and over which family portraits presided. In a corner there were the desk and chair from the *George Washington*, used by President Wilson as he labored over successive drafts of the League of Nations. By that time also there were his "governors' chairs"; and the rest of the furnishings of that spacious room were quite as Rooseveltian—cases for stamps, books, naval prints, rare volumes he had picked up on his travels, every one of which meant something to him. And then, besides, there were the French windows opening out to the lawns and slopes shaded by the ancient trees. No one who sat in that room with him, surrounded by the memorabilia of a long and secure culture, could doubt the perfect fitness of its creator to be President of the United States. It seemed no more than natural. Incidentally, the remodeling work at Hyde Park was done by Elliott C. Brown, a New York contractor, and so pleased Franklin that Brown was called in by him several years later to do some emergency camp building during the war. He and Brown together broke a good many regulations—and did a job about which Franklin especially liked to brag in after years.

Wainwright, a Republican Senate colleague, later to be a long-time congressman, he went down again, as he had done in his last year of Harvard, to the Caribbean, a part of the world he was drawn to as to no other except the Hudson Valley. This time he went only to Jamaica and Panama. Jamaica reminded him of his other visit with his mother, and he wrote her one of his many considerate "Dearest Mama" letters.[11]

But the few days he had at Panama aroused in him the really heroic mood I have spoken about.[12] There was something spontaneous and boyish about the engaging enthusiasm aroused in him by the sights he saw. After several pages of detailed description of his journeyings about the project, he spoke of coming to the Pedro Miguel and Miraflores locks:

> I can't begin to describe it and have become so enthusiastic that if I didn't stop I would write all night. The two things that impress the most are the Culebra cut, because of the colossal hole made in the ground, and the locks because of the engineering problems and size. Imagine an intricate concrete structure nearly a mile long and three or four hundred feet wide, with double gates of steel weighing 700 tons apiece!
>
> Goethals said in his quiet way last night: "We like to have Americans come down, because they all say it makes them better Americans" . . .
>
> I only wish you could see this wonder of the world, greater than the Tower of Babel or the Pyramids.[13]

These words start up in our memories Franklin's own great projects yet to be conceived—so far as anyone knows—the TVA, Grand Coulee, Bonneville, Shasta, Fort Peck, the Florida Ship Canal, the St. Lawrence Seaway, and Passamaquoddy. Some of them were carried through; others fell victim to the private interests they threatened. He regarded all of them as special contributions to the nation. He hovered over the estimates, studied the blueprints, visited them with an author's pride. Surely there was some element in the Roosevelt blood that made them builders on the grand scale, Franklin no less than Theodore. But I sometimes wonder if even Theodore would have seized on the atomic bomb as Franklin did and risked two billions of dollars secretly on its success.

It was this strain in the Roosevelt character that most infuriated those of a more conservative bent. What they said—meaning to be scornful —was that the Roosevelt projects were grandiose. Even Louis Howe often spoke of them that way when he was in a no-saying mood, as he so often was with Franklin. He said no so often, however, that his opposition served as no more than a moderate brake on Franklin's run-

[11] *Personal Letters: 1905–1928*, p. 184 ff.

[12] The excavation work on the canal was nearing completion in 1912. The vast construction enterprise was already a success in contrast with the French failure, a result largely due to Gorgas and Goethals, one a public health expert, the other an engineer.

[13] *Personal Letters: 1905–1928*, pp. 186–87.

away imagination. And sometimes in a puckish mood he was known invent what he called "crazy schemes" just to enjoy Louis' reaction. There were times when not even the closest observer could tell whether he was serious in proposing something new. Passamaquoddy—to harness the tides for power at a cost of hundreds of millions—would, I suppose, be an example of this. Not until the Army engineers actually went to work could the senators believe so fantastic a proposal was actually to be implemented. They stopped it then, to Franklin's deep disappointment.

Franklin was at his best when he was making plans for national improvement. He was not always so good in the more abstruse realms of policy. He came to these as a rule later than to building and improvement projects. In the period of his life being considered here, he occasionally tried his powers tentatively in a wider field than state affairs and in less specific ones than conservation, to which he was making so important a contribution. The results were not too happy. A speech in March 1912 before the People's Forum of Troy seems particularly significant because of its groping and unsuccessful attempt at exposition. If it is read carefully in the light of later events, it is not difficult to understand what he was getting at—which was the statement of a modernized progressive faith—but it must have left his hearers at the time in a state of complete confusion.

"Competition," he said, "has been shown to be useful up to a certain point, but co-operation, which is the thing that we must strive for today, begins where competition leaves off." He did not want to call this "community interest," because that was a socialist term, nor even "brotherhood of man," which implied a hopeless idealism. He preferred to call it a "struggle for liberty of the community rather than liberty of the individual." This, he said, was "what the founders of the Republic had been groping for."

This attempt by Franklin to rewrite Jefferson, Madison, and Hamilton, three of the most effective political expositors in all history, who were always able to say exactly what they wanted to convey, must have seemed somewhat pretentious. What he meant to do was to go beyond current interpretations of the Constitution's meaning and to argue that his was a truer interpretation of original intentions than those which had been imposed in the meantime. What he meant is best understood if it is taken as a kind of vague preview of NRA and various other New Deal measures. He was saying that industrial regulation had been a failure and that it had failed because it was negative. He was searching for a way to state a more positive policy. That, I think, was the meaning of "liberty of the community." Taken that way, its shadowy outline of something that a long time later would become national policy has a significance no historian ought to neglect.

As an example of a field where co-operation was essential he spoke of conservation—something that by now he knew a good deal about. "If," he said, "we can prophesy today that the state [or, in other words, the people as a whole] will shortly tell a man how many trees he must cut, then why can we not, without being radical, predict that the state will compel every farmer to till his land or raise beef, or horses? For after all if I own a farm of a hundred acres and let it lie waste or overgrown, I am just as much a destroyer of the liberty of the community, and by liberty, we mean happiness and prosperity, as is the strong man who stands idle on a corner refusing to work."

He went on to show how the same reasoning applied to the trusts, so much talked about in those years. There, too, there must be co-operation. "If we call the method regulation, people hold up their hands in horror and say 'unamerican' or 'dangerous,' but if we call the same identical process co-operation these same old fogies will cry out 'well done.'" Trusts, he said, run upon the theory of monopoly. But co-operation "puts monopoly out of date . . . We now understand that the mere size of a trust is not of necessity its evil. The trust is evil because it monopolizes for a few and as long as this keeps up it will be necessary for a community to change its features. . . . What we want today is not laws aimed at this, that, or the other business or class or system of government off hand in the hope that some target will be hit somewhere. . . . Every new star that people have hitched their wagon to for half a century, whether it be anti-rebating, or anti-trusts, or new fashioned education, or conservation of our natural resources, or state regulation of common carriers, or commission government . . . [each is part] in the evolution of the new theory of the liberty of the community."[14]

The alert political theorist can see what Franklin was driving at well enough. It had something in it of Uncle Ted's New Nationalism, somewhat less of what Wilson was to call the New Freedom, and a good deal of what by 1932 was to be called "national planning" or "partnership with government." That happy epitomizer, Wilson, was to put much of it in a pithy phrase: "No monopoly should be private." The conception was to lie dormant in Franklin's mind for almost twenty years and then to issue in measures to meet a crisis.

Just to point a contrast, to show how much happier Franklin was in dealing with matters his mind really comprehended, consider the sharp impact of a paragraph from a speech made at the Saturn Club in Buffalo (which must have been heard by whatever old Grotonians or Harvard men there were in that vicinity, the Saturn being that kind of club) when he was stumping the state for his threatened insurgent colleagues and incidentally arguing for a state-wide direct primary:

[14] Poughkeepsie *News-Press*, March 5, 1912.

The good work has begun and it gathers momentum with each succeeding week. Cassidy in Queens went out on the toe of a boot last week. McCooey is hanging on by the skin of his teeth in Brooklyn. The Bronx has thrown off Murphy's domination, and Lou Payne and Odell, on the Hudson River, are losing their grip on the Republican machines. McCabe, in Albany, will be succeeded in the spring by a young Democrat who can defeat the Republican machine of Boss Barnes. Cornelius Collins has lost his grip. Murphy and his kind must, like the noxious weed, be plucked out, root and branch. From the ruins of the political machines we will reconstruct something more nearly conforming to a democratic conception of government.[15]

It seems almost inconceivable that so vehement and forthright an opponent of Murphy and his Tammany should, within a few years, come to some sort of accommodation with them. But Murphy was some sort of prophet too. He must have been, to foster the generation of Smith, Wagner, Foley, and others who would be the later collaborators of Franklin. He must especially have been able to accommodate himself to realities to have offered Franklin the governorship in 1918. But he would; and he could have delivered it. But by then Franklin would be seeing himself in Navy uniform and, for the moment, not interested in immediate preferment. He could nearly always see around political corners, and around this one he could see a dead end. Dead ends, he considered, were not suitable for Roosevelts.

[15] Lindley, op. cit., p. 101.

5

Between 1912, when Franklin was damning New York's great and lesser bosses up and down the state, and 1918, when Charles F. Murphy's peace offer was made on behalf of Tammany, there was to stretch that part of his career which would be spent, as Freidel remarks, "in Professor Wilson's School of Public Administration." His services at Baltimore, his shrewd early contacts with Wilson, and his efforts in the campaign, even though he was ill during its latter part, would have commended him to the Wilsonians. This would include both McAdoo, Secretary of the Treasury, and Daniels, so strangely given the Navy post.

As Daniels afterward told it, he asked Franklin without preliminaries in the Willard Hotel lobby at inauguration time whether he would like to be his Assistant Secretary, and Franklin accepted on the spot. This was another throat he nearly jumped down, as he had nearly jumped down Judge Mack's in 1910. But we know that before this McAdoo in the Treasury had given him the choice of being his Assistant Secretary or Collector of the Port of New York—the latter one of the choicest of the political plums of that time, and especially so for him in view of his feud with Tammany. There is no record of what was said. He turned this offer down in an unrecorded interview. But it seems certain that there must have been preliminaries to Daniels' invitation, and Franklin probably told McAdoo what he most wanted. Franklin would not have been averse to working and scheming for the Navy post. It was his next step along Uncle Ted's path; it united, as he said exuberantly to a friend, "vocation with avocation"; and it furnished not only an escape from threatened Tammany harassment but a means, instead, of harassing Tammany, not to mention all the other bosses in the state. There would be a lot of patronage in the Navy, and it could be kept away from Murphy in New York City and from Barnes and others upstate where the Republicans were in control. The brash young man could make

94

good his hitherto rather empty threats. He was about to become a politician with a certain power.

In the whole story of Franklin the Navy appointment has the significance of a move out of a local situation and into a national one. The young state senator from New York's Twenty-sixth District was now to stretch his wings in a wider environment. It would be quite possible to write the history of the Wilson administration and never mention Franklin Roosevelt. Most of the histories written soon after Wilson's passing hardly mentioned him. Yet one of the most significant occurrences of that regime would seem to be, for those who looked back several decades later, the nurturing of this future President.

Those who have examined Franklin's service of seven and a half years as Assistant Secretary agree on some judgments concerning it, but they disagree on others. In fact it is quite easy to gather from the accounts two completely contradictory interpretations. One of these would have him a simple, naïve errand boy for the active admirals; the other pictures him as a hard-working and effective administrator, attending strictly to business, and responsible for reforms in Navy administration of the utmost importance for its coming test in World War I.

The truth appears to lie somewhere between the extremes. Those who have studied Franklin's whole ongoing life are aware of several deep-running impulses and several limiting characteristics. Among the impulses were the strong ones to succeed in politics and to be forever building and changing; and these were complementary in the sense that one gave scope to the other. His state senatorship made possible the conservation work that was one of the most satisfactory preliminary expressions of his building instinct. Being second in charge of the Navy opened out new possibilities of the same sort. Working for bigger and better ships and more of them was as much an expression of Franklin's personality as the enlargement and improvement of the Hyde Park estate which he undertook so happily in this period. Years later the whole nation would benefit from this builder's impulse when he was President and could allow it scope he had hardly dared to imagine theretofore. It was an insatiable desire. It went on from one thing to another. It got so that he could hardly see anything anywhere without considering how it could be improved or whether it ought not to be replaced.

This double drive is characteristic of many successful Americans, businessmen as well as politicians; and America has been a land where the possibilities for this sort of personal achievement have been unexampled since the days of Rome. Americans, indeed, have been described as latter-day Romans, and it is a comparison that helps a good deal in understanding the national history. I should not be surprised if a good many of those who had so much to say about Franklin as a Roman dictator had in mind, although they may not have been conscious of it, not so much the contemporary Mussolini as the ancient Augustus. It was hard to think of Franklin, ever, in Mussolini's fancy uniforms, popping his eyes and screaming exhortations to crowds of frenzied black shirts; it would have been shocking bad taste if nothing else, and no Grotonian would have risked the ridicule he would have merited. But it was not at all difficult to think of him in a toga, scheming with the senators for the extension of the empire, for the improvement of its administration, and for enhancing welfare. The Romans were practical governors.

The two necessary talents—for political success and for strategic engineering—do not necessarily go together. A good many successful politicians have had no building instincts at all, and a good many great engineers have had no political talents. In some of the greatest statesmen they have been combined—not in all. In Franklin they were, as they were also in Jefferson and in Theodore Roosevelt. Lincoln lacked the engineering impulse almost altogether, and so did Wilson. Not only were they combined in Franklin, but they were almost ideally combined. Also, it has to be said that his rise to presidential power was to be concurrent with unexampled opportunities for vast constructive projects. The immense productive capacity of the nation was half paralyzed. Franklin was given the opportunity of setting this great machine in motion, under his direction, to achieve the kind of rebuilding that exactly suited his talents and that satisfied his deepest aspirations. An America made whole and beautiful, fields and factories shining as they fulfilled their purposes, because the people who worked there were happy and secure in the kinds of homes and communities which were worthy of God's children. That was Franklin's dream.

His presidency was still two decades away when he began on the Navy. But those who are puzzled by the varying accounts of his role in this first tour of national duty will do well to keep in mind what kind of man he was. They will continue to be confused if they merely study the documents. There never was a public figure, I believe, about whom the paper records were so voluminous and the reminiscences so voluble. He began to save everything himself when he was at Harvard, and he kept it up all his life. He set up a whole institution years before his death to hold the collection and make it available to those who would come after him. All of this and all the recollections do not necessarily reveal the man or explain his behavior. The elaborate and successful actor while alive prepared a gigantic trap for historians. What made him believe they might be deceived into accepting the picture was the same sort of defense as the bland unwillingness to recognize what he did not want to recognize in his family surroundings, the same also as his assumption that everyone acknowledged the standards of Peabody and, moreover, accepted them without probing. Those who did not, like many businessmen and bankers, must be made to conform. They would, because they too knew the standards and accepted them, even if they violated the code. Good historians did not go behind documents; there would be plenty of them to explore. They would be too busy exploring to ask embarrassing questions.

No, Franklin did not like probing. He was a simpler fellow than even some of his close associates thought, and not so complex a one as they have been inclined to picture. So, at least, it appears to me. He intended to behave as he had been taught to behave, and others might be held to the same standard of conduct. This included worshiping God, holding singly to wife and to family, standing well in the community, helping others when he could, and working to get ahead. There was nothing wrong about gaiety and no need to be dour. But there ought to be real punishment for those who betrayed others, wasted nature's resources, or engaged in what he sometimes called the "flim-flam" of business. These impulses and these limitations were, I think, the chief motivating forces and the channeling barriers of his whole career. There were times when he strained the limitations, a few occasions when he breached the barriers, but this did not affect the standards and principles which on the whole he respected.

A relatively simple man of this sort is bound to run into trouble which he may or may not allow to bother him. His loyalties will become mixed, as Franklin's were mixed about wife and mother; and he will confuse ends and means, as Franklin was forced to do repeatedly in the exigencies of public life. As to this last, the danger is that means will become rather too easily justified by the ends. Because many decisions will not be easy on these accounts, such a man is apt to pretend that he has not made any decision and to drift into a course of action by avoiding the making up of his mind. A good deal of Franklin's apparently contradictory conduct *actually was contradictory,* some of it so conflicting as to result in mutual cancellation. But it must not be assumed that, because as an observer you yourself can see it now, he could see it then. He was apt to see the importance of immediate ends more readily than the consequences of doubtful means. And besides, he had very effective suppressive mechanisms. They protected him from some convictions of sin that others thought must be worrying his soul.

A philosophical and questioning person is not one who is apt to get much done. His conscience will not let him. He is not likely, in the first place, to get into such a position that he *can* do much. He will not be able to choose ruthlessly, put the decision behind him, and make more choices tomorrow. His face will not be turned toward the multitude of those who can help or hinder and present the appearance of interest, appreciation, and outgoing charm. He will be "sicklied o'er with the pale cast of thought." If there is one true observation made about Franklin by all who saw or knew him, it was that he was never "sicklied o'er." This did not mean that he was liking or accepting what he was seeing or being told; it meant that he was interested in it. Eleanor said of him in *This I Remember* that he had an extraordinary ability to see and listen without having his decisions in the least affected. And this was certainly true.

Franklin made his decisions not so much because of what he saw or heard or read as because of what he was. There was a reaction between his basic observation—which was, of course, due to his acute senses, but not to any single or any few impacts upon them—and his fundamental impulses. It was already evident that he would be likely to go far in politics; he was also, it seems to me equally clear, going to do a job of building. He would use power as it came to him for the building purposes he had in mind. And his personal conscience would always be the servant of his public conscience. There are those who say of him, partly because they recognize this, that he had no personal conscience. About this, I myself have doubts. But I would put it another way, and perhaps it is a justifying way. I should say that he would not reject any resort which would give him the leverage he needed to do the things he thought he must do—that is, within reason, within a margin of tolerance defined by "getting into trouble."

The mainspring of his life was, it must be understood, what he must do. If ethical quibbling had been allowed to interfere constantly or private conscience to assume the control it has in many lives, he would never have become President in the circumstances he had to meet. This is not to say that an examination reveals any considerable personal departures from the governing codes or even any straining of the bonds of custom. His departures were all in a longer interest, calculated for the large purpose which dominated his life. That justified them for him: and it must satisfy us.

Considering his old love of the sea and his preoccupation with naval history and ships, the Navy was almost an ideal place for Franklin to begin his experience on the national scene. The only other locale as congenial would have been the Department of the Interior or Agriculture. The one had parks, the other forests. He was not offered either of them; and the Navy post was so natural that he probably never thought of anything else. But something might be made of the fact that his closest older friend, among all the host of casual friends he moved so gaily among in these Washington years, was Franklin K. Lane, who was Secretary of the Interior. They must often have discussed the great subject of their mutual interest—conservation. But Franklin's Washington years were remarkably single-centered. He was happy in being a Navy man, except, of course, that he was always a politician as well.

One of Franklin's most determined detractors, J. T. Flynn,[1] made a good deal of the supposed indiscipline, even outright disloyalty, to his chiefs, Wilson and Daniels, implied in the big-Navy drive Franklin lent himself to during his first year in Washington. But anyone can see that this, even if not exactly allowable to a young Assistant Secretary, was neither so jingoistic as Flynn said it was nor so disloyal as he claimed. Franklin did think it incredible that neither Wilson nor Daniels was fascinated by ships or even by a fleet or impressed by the admirals who planned and sailed them. Even his admirers would not deny that he went too far, but it can be seen that the impulse to which he was responding was the demand for recognizing the Navy's role in statesmanship, for the improvement of this rusted tool, and for recognition of a fine brand of men who represented the nation out at sea. If he had to convince Wilson and Daniels, he would; if he could not do that, he would argue in public. He said much too much. He ought to have been spanked, and probably was, which may account for a few cryptic passages in letters. But events rescued him from severe disciplining. What took place in Europe from 1914 on was argument enough for Navy-building. The Assistant Secretary being Franklin Roosevelt, he was having Roosevelt luck. His building instincts and his contriving talents were exercised to the full, and no real penalties were incurred. He even got some credit for prescience which he did not deserve. He did not know better than his elders about what was likely to happen internationally, but there is no doubt that it looked afterward as though he had.

It is a little difficult to explain why Franklin was allowed to run on so loose a rein at the beginning. It is, all things considered, one of the least admirable phases of his career. And Mr. Flynn capitalized on a real weakness. Franklin definitely tried to commit the administration, in which he was very subordinate indeed, to policies at variance with those the President and the various department heads were trying to develop, and he was on occasion bold and provocative in the effort. In several instances he went so far as to offer an interpretation of American policy unknown to the national tradition, although quite possibly held to by the more independent admirals. It outdid Mahan in Mahan's own field. It can only be described as imperialism, even if of a rather benevolent sort.

It must be remembered that, although war in Europe began in the year following Wilson's first inauguration, the official policy of the United States until after his second election was strict neutrality. All this time, from the very beginning, Franklin was pushing publicly and privately for the kind of Navy needed for war; and with this he was without doubt the least neutral official in all Washington. With his op-

[1] Who wrote *Country Squire in the White House* (New York: Doubleday, 1940) and *The Roosevelt Myth* (New York: Devin-Adair, 1948).

99

portunities and connections, the impact of his campaign (for it can hardly be called anything less) for intervention must have been a real embarrassment to Daniels, especially, who was an avowed pacifist, and Wilson, as well, who had a delicate and difficult neutrality policy to shape and to maintain. In these circumstances Franklin greatly exceeded the tolerable limits of free expression for a member of a group.

It was during his first month as Assistant Secretary, before he can have thought extensively about the problems of the Navy—except as he had always thought about them—and before he can have straightened out his ideas about foreign relations, that he began. He said to a group in New York:

This is not a question of war or peace. I take it there are as many advocates of arbitration and international peace in the Navy as in any other profession. But we are confronted with a condition—the fact that our country has decided in the past to have a fleet and that war is still a possibility.[2]

This relatively moderate statement had progressed less than a year later (January 1914) to this Mahan-like pronunciamento:

Invasion is not what this country has to fear. In time of war would we be content like the turtle to withdraw into our own shell and see an enemy supersede us in every outlying part, usurp our commerce and destroy our influence as a nation throughout the world? Yet this will happen just as surely as we can be sure of anything human if an enemy of the United States obtains control of the seas. And that control is dependent absolutely on one thing—the preponderant efficiency of the battle fleet.

Our national defense must extend all over the western hemisphere, must go out a thousand miles into the sea, must embrace the Philippines and over the seas wherever our commerce may be. To hold the Panama Canal, Alaska, American Samoa, Guam, Porto Rico, the naval base at Guantanamo and the Philippines, we must have battleships. We must create a navy not only to protect our shores and our possessions but our merchant ships in time of war, no matter where they may go.[3]

It is difficult to know whether this obstreperous Franklin who was seizing every opportunity to write and speak and was rapidly formulating a full imperialist doctrine to be supported by the attainment of "a navy second to none" was simply being heard by a small audience to whom these ideas were congenial, in which case the embarrassment to his superiors would not be very great, or whether he was left alone because Wilson himself did not mind this point of view being expressed along with the more pacifist views of Daniels. Presidents do that kind of thing. This Assistant Secretary would do it when he became President —no predecessor would have been more adept, as a matter of fact, in

---

[2] Lindley, op. cit., p. 119.
[3] Ibid., 120.

the use of the trial balloon or of this even more extreme settlement by controversy. Such differences can be allowed to develop, with the President remaining apparently ignorant and above the battle, until it becomes clear which side has the better of it—either because conditions have developed as one or the other side said they would or because public opinion has been clearly won over. He can then plump for one or the other, having escaped the responsibility for adopting, or even favoring, the losing side. He may even appear to have been all the time on the side that won.

Wilson, it must be remembered, had plenty of pacifist and neutralist opinion available in his official family. Besides Daniels, there was Bryan, who until June 1915 was Secretary of State, and whose resignation was a kind of resolution of the first Wilsonian dilemma. Thereafter the policy was to be, if still neutral, a stronger and more positive neutrality. At that time there would be a good deal of talk about Daniels following Bryan into retirement since their views were almost identical.[4] And to the later students of the Roosevelt career there seem to be rather numerous suggestions that the Assistant Secretary would have been a more appropriate Secretary than the old gentleman in the string tie and broad-toed shoes. This is perhaps only seeming. Franklin's career was accompanied by numerous of these cleverly suggested promotions, and they can seem more important because of his later prominence than they actually were. They were often "inspired," and easily recognizable as such. It must not be forgotten how persistently and single-mindedly Louis Howe worked for the advancement of his divinity. These sallies were often part of his technique. This one, I think, was not.

Louis had come to the Navy with Franklin and would stay there with him straight through the Wilson administration. He appears to have carried a heavy load of naval work besides his perennial promotion and guardianship of Franklin. And much of his watchfulness would have been cautionary. I should think that in those years he would have been forever warning Franklin about going too far and risking the displeasure of his superiors. He must have been especially nervous during the period of known coolness between Daniels and his subordinate in the pre-war period. Neither principal would acknowledge afterward that this was a serious matter. Daniels spoke of Franklin in later years as having been somewhat young and impulsive; Franklin was even less committal—by that time he was a good deal mellower and was inclined to value Daniels' political acumen much higher than he had in earlier days. Besides, he may have come to think that Daniels was right about

[4] Daniels afterward explained his failure to resign by saying that he had not agreed with Bryan that the stern note to Germany—the famous second or "strict accountability" note on the *Lusitania* sinking—would lead to war.

the admirals, about the businesses they had favored, and about the welfare of the Navy "boys." At any rate, both were so much inclined to gloss over the differences of their service together as to give historians some difficulty in deciding how serious they may have been. But Daniels in a reminiscent mood did confide to his diary once that he was on the whole glad that he had not punished the young man. So evidently he did on occasion wonder how Franklin ought best to be handled.

In the first few years they differed about policy; once policy had been settled by the beginning of the war, they continued to differ, but less sharply, about methods. Franklin was impatient, aggressive, intolerant, and completely certain. Daniels was cautious; he was also suspicious of many of those Franklin accepted without question—officers and suppliers. He was also reluctant to agree that war was coming, and was doggedly anti-imperialist. Then too, they moved in entirely different social circles. The Roosevelts were hardly ever in the Daniels home. The Danielses, in fact, were not happy in the glittering diplomatic and official set; the Roosevelts moved in it as a matter of course. The officers, the officials, and the diplomats of Washington were often friends, sometimes relatives, and very frequently old acquaintances of the younger people. Especially among such foreigners as the French and British representatives there were many families with whom they had the genuine intimacy natural to so cosmopolitan a couple.

Daniels was typical of an American tradition Franklin could not understand or appreciate. He had none of that upper-class background which distinguished his younger colleague. He had made his way to a place of distinction out of poverty rather than out of riches. He had also a set of indignations which contrasted sharply with those of Franklin. There can be no doubt that he was good for the Navy's popularity among people who tended to be irritated by Franklin and his presumption. For one thing, his Methodist morals involving teetotalism and suspicion of cardplaying and dancing were better understood than the less restrictive Anglican practices. He was plain; he wore baggy clothes and a parson's broad hat; and he was a little fat. He looked a good deal like Bryan or like a hundred congressmen who were his contemporaries. It was no wonder that he was accepted without reserve as one of the Washington professionals who knew their way around and could be trusted to return a favor. He understood the importance of giving jobs to congressmen's relatives and hangers-on. Political debts were as important as any other kind. Others around Washington understood, too, that the dust on his shoes was North Carolina dirt, not mixed with an accumulation from foreign sources. He made no secret of his preference for plain American things and, for that matter, for plain Americans. He distrusted big business and all those who dealt in money. He made no pretense of learning, although he had an appropriate store of knowledge.

When Daniels sat in a circle of congressional friends in the somewhat incongruous surroundings furnished by the afterdeck of the *Dolphin,* he was indistinguishable from them. An opinion from him concerning the naval budget was taken as coming from one who thought as they did, and he was likely to get what he wanted. What he wanted was a better business organization for the service, more closely figured contracts with suppliers, and an end to collusion in bidding from ship-builders, armor fabricators, and gunmakers. He wanted the Navy to take care of the boys entrusted to it—their health, their morals, and their education. He did not worry about the officers because he knew that they would worry about themselves. That he was a pacifist seemed to many people—naval officers included—to make him ineligible for the secretaryship. He thought it just the place for a pacifist to be. He would keep the service from being provocative while it got ready for any real emergency there might be.

It is impossible not to feel at this distance—and even the most ardent Roosevelt admirers betray the feeling too—that, compared with the older and more effective Daniels, Franklin was immature, impulsive, and unwise. What makes the contrast worse is that he did not conceal his opinion that the older man was incongruous in the secretaryship and slightly ridiculous as a man—acceptable neither socially nor professionally. The admirals despised the Secretary, the diplomats deplored his manners, and the younger officials regarded him as obstructive. He was against war in general and against the particular war Franklin could see appearing over the horizon. The old man would do nothing to further its coming; even specific preparations often came under that interdiction, and this infuriated Franklin most of all.

In the period of their widest difference concerning policy they could and did work together for the improvement of the Navy. But there is evidence that Franklin came close to being insubordinate in advocating participation in the war and in breaching neutrality. He deliberately cultivated Spring-Rice, who was the British Ambassador and, as is now known, the head of a vast propaganda organization devoted to bringing the United States into the conflict. If there was another particular diplomatic friend it was La Boulaye, an attaché of the French Embassy. With the La Boulayes the Roosevelts became so friendly, indeed, that the French would take advantage of the fact, when Franklin became President, and make him Ambassador.[5] These friendships were made good when events did lead the United States into war. But their cultivation was doubtfully proper in the preceding years.

[5] Eleanor mentions Madame La Boulaye as one of the finest women she ever knew.

Taken together with Franklin's public advocacy of an expanded overseas responsibility, his friendships with those who represented one side of the European conflict, and his tendency to allow naval officers far more latitude than Daniels would, the relationships between the two responsible officials must have been reduced for long periods to mere formality. Franklin made disparaging remarks in his letters to Eleanor which show how he felt. He referred to both Bryan and Daniels, when they did not react as he felt they should to the beginning of war on the continent in 1914, as "dear good people" who "understood no more than Elliott" what was happening in the world. And in a hurried note on a significant date (August 1914) he said to Eleanor:

Dearest E.

Alive and very well and keen about everything. *I* am *running* the real work, although Josephus is here! He is bewildered by it all, very sweet but very sad!

Not very hot so far.

Your devoted

F[6]

[6] *Personal Letters: 1905–1928*, p. 243. A note appended to this letter—written presumably by Elliott, who at least nominally edited the letters, is revealing. It shows that even he felt this not to have been a period in which Franklin is displayed at his best:

The somewhat derogatory remarks about Josephus Daniels in the letters of this chapter are far more illustrative of the growth of F.D.R.'s personality than of Daniels' competence as a Secretary of the Navy. Because of the entirely different backgrounds and personalities which J.D. and F.D.R. brought to the Navy Department in 1913, it was almost inevitable that at first the younger man should find fault with his superior. Daniels' lack of concern for longstanding traditions of naval etiquette, his preference for prolonged deliberation at the expense of quick decisions, his shrewd, country-editor type of mind, and his mature understanding of Washington politics were characteristics that clashed with F.D.R.'s youthful and impetuous enthusiasm.

Daniels was never disturbed by his own very limited knowledge of navigation and of naval techniques, but always felt that his task was an administrative one in which a command of naval science was not a prerequisite. However, he considered naval etiquette to be an administrative question, a question of morale, and thus antagonized almost all the high-ranking officers by attempting to replace outworn naval traditions with a more democratic system. He housed officers and enlisted men in the same barracks, reformed the promotion system, allowed enlisted men to enter the Academy at Annapolis, changed the uniforms to provide greater comfort, and altered many other traditional restrictions which were no longer applicable to a modern navy. At first F.D.R.'s fondness for the traditions of the Navy caused him to agree with the protesting officers, who also resented Daniels for his limited understanding of technical naval matters and for his insistence upon keeping final authority in civilian hands. As a result the admirals played up to F.D.R. and brought him all their complaints, thereby further encouraging his early criticism of Daniels; indeed, in order to obtain official approval of their requisitions and other papers, some of the officers even went so far as to hold the documents until J.D. left Washington, and then presented them to F.D.R. for his signature as Acting Secretary. On the other hand, the enthusiasm which made F.D.R. the favorite of the ranking officers did not produce the same results

Get this

It ought to be said about this that Franklin changed. He ultimately had sense enough to see how he must have appeared to the older and wiser man. In the years of the war they worked together rather better, Franklin having developed some administrative competence and having gained, as well, some needed lessons in the utility of patience and political care—and some, perhaps, in deportment as well. If in later years Franklin was inclined to gloss over this period, there is ample reason for supposing that he recalled it well enough. If there were no other evidences, the really tender attention he paid to all the honorific details of a younger man's admiration for an elder would betray his concern. I first sensed this when he introduced me to the Danielses on the train carrying all of us to the inaugural in Washington in 1932. Taking the older man's hand fondly in his, he said, "Rex, this is a man who taught me a lot that I needed to know." Daniels seemed like a patriarch then—one of the Democrats surviving from the Bryan era—but he was still to be a most useful Ambassador to Mexico for nearly nine years. And he would, in fact, outlive the man who had once been his Assistant Secretary.

I have to call attention here to something rather remarkable: the suggestion of future policies to be discovered even in the brash and irresponsible expressions of Franklin as a junior member of the Wilson administration. There are two of these with particularly important after-developments. His imperialist leanings were eventually transmuted into assistance for weaker peoples, which is a more Christian version of his ideas in 1914; but his undisguised chauvinism and eagerness to punish the Germans did not die out. It seems to me to have issued again unchanged in the unconditional-surrender formula to which he committed the Allies at Casablanca. In even more virulent form it showed itself in the Morganthau Plan for German punishment to which he consented.

Neither Daniels nor Wilson seems to have sympathized at first with Franklin's persistent cultivation of the New York political garden. In fact there were times when a rather discouraging hand was laid on certain of his activities. The worst of these, from the administration point of view, was when in 1914 Franklin entered the senatorial primary against James W. Gerard. For Gerard was Wilson's Ambassador to Germany. This ambassadorship had been Tammany patronage and it signalized, as Franklin ought to have recognized, Wilson's unwillingness to have any part in New York feuding. As President he needed support from wherever it could be got. He had forgiven Tammany for what had happened at Baltimore, thus showing how practical he had become. Franklin, in this incident, suffered one of his few outright defeats, and

---

with Congressional committees. . . . Although they agreed on the necessity for expanding the Navy, their differing opinions of the world situation often made F.D.R. quite contemptuous of "Mr. D." in the early years of their association.

much the most humiliating, for Tammany won by a wide margin, although Gerard did not come home to campaign. This display of political naïveté is only understandable as following a disappointment about the governorship—which is undoubtedly what Franklin wanted in 1914 but which Wilson discouraged him from seeking.

The fact is that Wilson told Franklin in a cold note that he thought it would be best "if members of the Administration should use as much influence as possible but say as little as possible in the politics of their several states." Moreover, he refused a request for a conference. This could have been interpreted as an invitation to resign and at best shows Wilson's general feeling about Franklin. But it was let go without further comment. Franklin did not really want the senatorship and would not have been elected had he been nominated in that year—as he should have known. His way forward led through the governorship, as had been the case with Uncle Ted. But the ebullience that was distinguishing his Navy service seemed to be pushing him irresistibly. He was riding very high. The campaign for the senatorship was one more activity he could not resist. Even his love for the Navy was not an effective deterrent. He would have left it without regret, apparently, for what he regarded as a political promotion—a step up.

This whole affair was very unhappy as well as hard to explain. Daniels advised him against the attempt but believed afterward that McAdoo had urged him to run. Daniels loyally enough tried to straighten matters out by asking Wilson if he should—as he could—pull Gerard out. Wilson refused to interfere and Franklin was in the unhappy position of having to praise—or at least not to dispraise—his opponent. And this made it difficult also to attack Tammany. He retreated to Washington with scars on his knuckles but with another political lesson learned in a way never to be forgotten.

In spite of this reverse he went on building an upstate following as best he could, giving a good deal of time and energy to correspondence, visiting frequently with leaders, and being very free with advice whether asked or not. By 1915 some curious changes were happening in his relations with Tammany. They seem to have come by way of John J. Fitzgerald, a representative from Brooklyn. The initiative, however, was Franklin's; and the manner of its happening suggests that he was either learning from Daniels or was setting out in pique to show that he could practice politics as well as any old-timer—something he had so far failed to demonstrate conclusively. It is not unlikely that Louis Howe was involved in this small enterprise which had such large consequences. It has that look.

Fitzgerald had an annoyance in 1915. He thought the administration had outrageously ignored his claims to patronage. Franklin, knowing about this, unofficially arranged for the two Fitzgerald sons to have

106

places of vantage at the laying of the *California's* keel at the Brooklyn Navy Yard. This began a series of curious interchanges, Franklin at first doing most of the giving. Fitzgerald was allowed as much of the Brooklyn patronage as could be managed. And in the fall, making a speech in Greenwich Village, Franklin, guided by Fitzgerald, praised Tammany's candidate for sheriff. That candidate was Al Smith. From these small gestures of Franklin's there were to be results of great importance running on until 1928.

It was the same sort of foresight that was responsible for offering the New York postmastership to Robert Wagner, who was also a Tammany product. The offer was not accepted because Wagner wanted a judgeship. But the gesture was appreciated. These younger men were the best evidence of Tammany's current venture into relative political probity under Murphy's guidance. It was to last long enough for Franklin's purpose, since Murphy would be influential at San Francisco in 1920 when a nomination for Vice-President would be in question. And Franklin could say that the Tammany of Smith and Wagner could not, after all, be so bad as it was sometimes pictured.

This phase of Franklin's New York efforts was continued in 1916 when he came to the State Democratic Convention at Saratoga Springs with credentials from Wilson and McAdoo. He brought a demand that Samuel Seabury should be the candidate for governor. Tammany yielded on this, but it was a Republican year again and Seabury lost, perhaps because Tammany was not very enthusiastic. But for Franklin the recognition by Tammany that he was as necessary to them as they to him was an inevitable preliminary to any future.

This rather uneasy peace could be said to have been sealed when on July 4, 1917, Franklin was the honor guest and speaker at the 128th Tammany celebration of Independence Day. Commemorating this event is a surviving photograph of three consequential people in one group, as ironic a pictorial record as exists in American archives. The three individuals are Charles F. Murphy, John A. Voorhis, and Franklin himself. The two Tammany chieftains are in full Wigwam regalia, Franklin eagerly propitiatory in a double-breasted suit, bow tie, soft straw hat—and pince-nez. It may be reading something into the ensemble to say that the tall, patrician-faced, and utterly serious Franklin, alongside the slightly rakish Murphy and the iron-jawed Voorhis, looks in this picture remarkably like the kind of "front" Tammany needed. But the suggestion is actually too plain to miss.

In Freidel's *Roosevelt* this photograph is given a place just before one of Franklin and Daniels, both in a smiling mood, looking across, as Franklin admitted next day, toward the White House from a balcony of the old State, War and Navy Building. The end and the means are all too easily connected by anyone who studies, with the earnestness deserves, the maneuvers of this rising President-to-be. After this point in his career no one can doubt his intentions. That was a preliminary possessive look he was taking, and Daniels, old professional that he was, does not seem averse to furthering the younger man's schemes.

There was, however, a dilemma which by 1918 was quite clear to the sharp sight of the politically alert Assistant Secretary. Uncle Ted, when he had run for the governorship, had had his Rough Rider reputation behind him. Franklin knew that his civilian Navy service had been far more valuable than any he might have performed in uniform, but a civilian would be at a disadvantage in post-war politics no matter how strong his other claims might be. This, added to what was already a strong urge to wear a uniform, led him to discourage the numerous suggestions for an active candidacy in 1918. If he had realized that the end of the war would be in clear prospect by election day and that his desire for commissioned rank would be frustrated anyway, he might have accepted Tammany's offer of support for the governorship when it came. But he could not know that. Even Wilson, usually so reserved, came around this time. Daniels' report is flat that Wilson said, "Tell Roosevelt he ought not to refuse to run for governor if it is tendered to him." Daniels, too, seems by now to have been heartily on Franklin's side.

Franklin's subsequent behavior about this opportunity is equivocal. He was obviously pleased by the message Daniels brought. Nevertheless, he made apparently sincere efforts—through Judge Mack—to prevent the nomination. He was just leaving on a mission he had been scheming to set up for a long time. He wanted to see the war. And now he was going, officially to inspect, personally to participate at least a little.

He moved in the highest naval, Army, and diplomatic circles during this 1918 trip.[7] It was some satisfaction—one often denied to those whose work had to be done mostly in Washington—to see the action resulting from those mountains of papers which had gone across his desk, those endless conferences, and all the maneuvering. The Navy had done well. The whole war was moving rapidly into its final phase. It was not realized by anyone, except Wilson and a few others, how close Germany was to collapse; and when Franklin was shown by Ad-

---

[7] It was on this trip that Franklin ran into Robert Dunn, who was at the moment an assistant to Admiral Sims in London. Dunn had been born to Newport society, was an explorer of some note, and a reporter. He had joined the Navy at the outbreak of the war and soon found himself in intelligence work. Franklin spoke to him as one member of the upper class to another. Dunn reported it in his autobiography, *World Alive* (New York: Crown, 1956), p. 276:

Squat old Sam Gompers came over to see his East End birthplace. Franklin D. Roosevelt turned up next. "How's the job? And Josephus?" I asked him over Scotch. His eyes fell to the glass. "Gosh. You don't know, Bobby," he said gravely, after a pause, "what I have to bear under that man."

miral Plunkett a set of naval guns mounted on cars ready to move up to the front, he asked the admiral whether he might not command them. And it was with this in view that he hurried home. But he got there with a severe pneumonia, and by the time he had recovered and asked to be allowed to resign to put on uniform Wilson told him the armistice impended. So Franklin never wore the navy blue he loved so much. Also, he never had in his record the spectacular military interlude that had done so much to boost Uncle Ted.

As things turned out in New York, Al Smith was nominated for the governorship and so entered on his bid for the presidency. Franklin, if he had been elected then to that office, would probably never have been President. There were to be no Democratic Presidents until Harding, Coolidge, and Hoover were through. If Franklin had run in 1920 for President instead of Vice-President, as he would have been entitled to do if he had been governor, and perhaps again in 1924 and in 1928, he would almost certainly, as a three-time loser, have had to give way to another in 1932.

It was Roosevelt luck that a series of circumstances kept him out of the governorship in 1918 and, indeed, until 1928. Anyway, the student of his career must conclude that he was not yet ready in these years for the major responsibility. Uncle Ted had become President at forty-three; Franklin was now thirty-six and would have been thirty-eight in 1920. It was too soon. There is also something more than age to be considered; he was not yet of statesmanlike stature. It was true that he had come on wonderfully in his Washington service. He was wiser, humbler, and far more experienced. But all of this was not yet enough. It would go into the making of the man he would be in 1932, along with much else that was yet to happen; but in itself it was far from sufficient. He was fortunate, and the nation was fortunate, that his bid for power was delayed for more than a decade.

Franklin would be so far removed from public notice for several years of that interval, and public memory would be so short, that his re-emergence in 1928 would fail to call up in most people's minds the services of past years. It would simply be said then, when he was spoken of, that he had been a satisfactory wartime Assistant Secretary. Assistant Secretaries in Washington are much like vice-presidents in industry: they are not regarded as of much importance and they never get much attention. But this was an injustice in Franklin's case and something of a handicap besides. If he needed the succeeding interval for maturing, it was unfortunate that it allowed him—after 1920—in spite of strenuous preventive efforts, to fall into relative obscurity. If he had gone on quickly, as Uncle Ted had done, he might not have been really ready, but he could have capitalized politically on what was really quite a good administrative record.

He had not actually demonstrated any maturity or wisdom, but this would not have mattered. Assistant Secretaries are not policy-makers. In Franklin's case he had had occasion to learn something of that sort of thing too, some of it the hard way, by experience, not always happy, and some of it merely by observation. These lessons were sometimes negative ones. He had watched Wilson bring the nation carefully into the world struggle. He must have learned from that how naïve his impatient pushing and carping had, after all, been. But there were positive lessons too.

Out of the unhappy interferences of the administration in the affairs of Latin-American neighbors in those years, he formulated, during later years of reflection, a far better policy, which, when it was fully developed, was a really magnificent conception, ranking with the old Monroe Doctrine—this, of course, was the Good-Neighbor Policy. With naval diplomacy he had, as a responsible official, a good deal to do. At that time he was moved, without any deep realization of its significance, by the challenge of disorder in other lands. He thought it not too difficult to "straighten out" Santo Domingo and Haiti, and it was "his" marines who did the active work. In the more serious case of Mexico, when Wilson's schoolmasterish impulses got the better of his judgment, and naval and military power was used to discourage certain dictators and support other political leaders thought to be more democratic, Franklin had a chance to see that helpfulness was one thing but that interference was quite another. It required some time for this to occur to him; during his vice-presidential campaign he would seem not to have changed greatly. But the transformation was already in the making.

The student of Mahan and the disciple of Uncle Ted thus gained at least some wisdom through experience. If it seems to have come rather slowly and to have arrived somewhat late, that is what we have already seen to be a norm of his career. As his appropriate collegiate maturity arrived only when he was about to leave Harvard, so he began to have statesmanlike qualities only as he prepared to leave the Navy. Sometimes before that he had exhibited qualities which his admirers could well wish were not in the record. Consider, for instance, what kind of person is revealed in this passage of a letter written to Eleanor (Dearest Babs) in 1915, a couple of months after Lansing had succeeded Bryan as Secretary of State:

> Last night I attended the official dinner by the Lansings to [certain diplomats] and it was a delight to see a Secretary of State who is a gentleman and knows how to treat Ambassadors and Ministers from other civilized nations.[8]

[8] *Personal Letters: 1905–1928*, p. 285.

ending of superficiali (handwritten annotation at top)

Unfortunately there is quite a lot of this kind of thing to regret. As everyone of his generation knew, there was very little of this elite superiority left in the gubernatorial or presidential Roosevelt. There was self-respecting consciousness of an aristocratic heritage, but it had mellowed and been transformed into an appreciation of people's selves, not their manners. The mature Roosevelt would recognize genuine human qualities when he saw them; and it would be difficult to find anyone less regardful of differences in appearance or more tolerant of contrasting customs.

The beginning of this change from supercilious superficiality to a deeper and richer appreciation of humanity can even, I think, be roughly dated. There is a letter that seems to betray Sara's hurt as she came to realize, perhaps after some sharp exchange—in itself most unusual, since Franklin was so reluctant to expose his real mind—how far her son had departed from the rigid code she had prescribed for him and had hoped he still observed. Passages from that letter of October 14, 1917, follow:

Dearest Franklin and Dearest Eleanor,

I feel *too* badly that I let you go without your pearl collar, *too* stupid of me! . . . I think of you almost in New York and I am sorry to feel that Franklin *is* tired and that my views are not his, but perhaps dear Franklin you may on second thoughts or *third* thoughts see that I am not so far wrong. The foolish old saying "noblesse oblige" is good and "honneur oblige" possibly expresses it better for most of us. One can be democratic as one likes, but if we love our own, and if we love our neighbor, we owe a great example, and my constant feeling is that through neglect or laziness I am not doing my part toward those around me. After I got home, I sat in the library for nearly an hour reading, and as I put down my book and left the delightful room and the two fine portraits, I thought: after all, would it not be better just to spend all one has at once in this time of suffering and need, and not think of the future; for with the *trend* to "shirt sleeves," and the ideas of what men should do in always being all things to all men and striving to give up the old fashioned traditions of family life, simple home pleasures and refinements, and the traditions some of us love best, of what use is it to *keep up* things, to hold on to dignity and all I stood up for this evening. Do not say that *I misunderstood,* I understand perfectly, but I cannot believe that my precious Franklin really feels as he expressed himself . . .[9]

What this rigorous old lady meant to say was not that she could not believe that her precious Franklin had changed, but that she would not. But he had; or, perhaps more accurately, he was changing. He was discovering that men are not to be judged by class standards but rather by the test of worth. If Professors Wilson and Daniels taught Franklin Roosevelt that, it is added luster for already lustrous reputations.

[9] Ibid., p. 274.

6

Franklin was to enter presently a sticky interlude in his career. His progress, in fact, had already been interrupted, and specific possibilities in the future cannot have been very clear. If his decisions during this time seem somewhat confused or uncertain and his actions seem to have no pattern, it is because he was feeling the way to a new start. The same old objectives held, but the immediate furtherance of progress toward them was a problem. The truth was that for an aspiring politician he had been overlong at his Navy assignment. A pause of seven and a half years in one place is quite likely to be fatal to a political aspirant, and especially if that place is a minor appointive job in Washington. Even members of cabinets almost never learn that they are ineligible for the presidency; they are notoriously hopeful of succession. There are always exceptions; Hoover was one and Taft was another; but it is necessary to go far back in the national records to find other cabinet members—or any officials other than Vice-Presidents—who succeeded to the presidency. And it is not difficult to see why this should be true.

The rule is that inferiors are identified with superiors. They seldom seem to be reconciled to this subordination, and their ambitions often interfere with their usefulness as members of the cabinet; but the fact is that their efforts and risks are wasted. They almost never succeed. The superior has usually during *his* time worn out the party welcome, and a second candidate from the same party has little chance. Much the best way to the presidency is through a state governorship. Governors have a political organization of their own and so a nucleus of convention delegates. They have not been involved in Washington affairs and so can claim to have policies of their own, which is important in the rhythm of American political change. One who has been a governor while his national party was out has not shared in discredit or defeat and is ready to offer himself when the upswing comes—as come it will.

Incidentally, it can be argued that governorships, other things being equal, produce the best Presidents as well as the largest number. This is partly because a governor has had administrative experience, but even more because he has had practice in the management of legislatures. Above all, he has learned that he must be a leader—a leader of his party and more especially of the Congress. One writer on the presidency has called the occupant of that office Chief Legislator,[1] and there is much truth in that characterization. A President who comes to his office as Harding or Truman did, from the Senate, comes with a "legislative point of view." Everyone who has come from that source has wasted a year or more in discovering that the President must lead and not follow, and this is fatal, because that period includes the months of the "honeymoon" which will never come again. Such a President is not likely to accomplish much.

Franklin, if we speculate about his state of mind in the years just ahead as the war came to a close, must have known all about the most usual and desirable way to the presidency. He had both positive and negative examples before him; but especially he had Uncle Ted and Woodrow Wilson within the sensitive area of his experience. He knew something at least of presidential origins.

He had behind him a foolish grab for a senatorship which he must now regret; but also he had to think over the recent missed chance for the governorship. He may have foreseen the long Democratic exile, but it is unlikely that he did. Up to the second journey of Wilson abroad, in 1919, the terrible struggle over the Treaty of Versailles, his compromise in Paris, his trouble at home with the recalcitrant isolationist senators, and his breakdown in the midst of the battle for ratification—until somewhere in the latter part of 1919—Wilson seemed almost a godlike figure, far above political battles, the recognized savior of the world. Yet for a sign of what was to come there had been the humiliating loss of the congressional elections of 1918, and that after a special appeal for support; and even in 1916, although he himself had been elected, there had been losses in the House of Representatives. The signs were there to be read by one detached enough to read them. How quickly so magnificent a figure could lose his prestige and how completely the power flowing from his hold on the people could fade away, Franklin was in process of learning. And it would leave him momentarily confused. The way ahead would be far from plainly marked. It would indeed be very obscure. It may have seemed thus obscure from the fall of 1918 on.

These would be years of fumbling, of pause, of uncertainty, of defeat, and of slow and anxious recovery. Part way along he would fall into the deeper abyss of illness so serious as almost to end everything. The

[1] Louis Brownlow in *The Presidency* (Chicago: Public Administration Service, 1948).

climb out would be slow, and for some time it would be a faltering one. Eventually, however, he would renew his grip on his own career, signalized by a few flashing reappearances as he lifted himself on his crutches to catch the eye and ear of the political world; and then opportunity would come. It would come disguised: he would by then be too sophisticated to believe in the unlikely and he would nearly miss it altogether. The campaign for the governorship in 1928 must have seemed to him a wholly chimerical undertaking, and probably he never satisfactorily explained to himself why he undertook it. He would win by an incredibly narrow margin. This victory would be the lever he needed. When he had it firmly in his hands, he would use it, from the first, powerfully, delicately, with the sure touch of the expert, to force open the door to the presidency. He was ten years delayed. But they were maturing years. And maturing was something he could use.

Taken as a whole, Franklin's behavior in his first Washington experience shows that he understood what way he must go. He never for a moment lost touch with New York politics. There was no electoral year from 1913 to 1918 when he was not talked of, prominently suggested, or actually offered some nomination. Sometimes the talk seems to have been stimulated by Louis Howe, but much of it was spontaneous. He was, in fact, upper New York's representative in the Wilson entourage and, as we have seen, by 1918 he had reached a reconciliation even with Tammany. All this is evidence that he knew the political worth of his Washington job. It gave him prestige at home, a prestige to be used as Uncle Ted had used his Navy years.

The rejection of the governorship nomination in 1918 must almost at once have seemed to him a serious mistake, and especially when Al Smith was elected. It was the last of the generally Democratic years for a long time to come. From then on Al would be on his own, without national support, as Franklin might have been. But regardless of the doubts Franklin may have entertained about his judgment after Smith's winning, fate was being kind. Al's apparent success would stop short of the pinnacle, and Franklin would be able to build on his predecessor's failure.

Anyway, there were nearly two years more in the Navy. His trip abroad in 1918 was barely recovered from when he began to agitate for another. The effects of influenza plagued him all fall, but in the postarmistice confusion it was clear enough to him where the focus of events would be in the immediate future. That was in Paris, where the terms of peace were to be settled. He resolved to be there.

Wilson was in process of making the most disastrous mistake of his presidency. Instead of staying securely at home, negotiating firmly from the midst of an America united under his leadership, he went himself to negotiate with those hard realists, Lloyd George, Clemenceau, and

114

Orlando, on their home grounds. In doing this he sacrificed the reserve position so important to a chief of state; but what was even more important, he lost the opportunity to recapture the national unity needed for ratification. It can be understood why he was moved to go. He saw the war as having been in vain if the League of Nations, which was to prevent future wars, was not made part of the treaty of peace. And the other allies, eyes on territorial gains and the punishment of Germany, had less than no interest in the League. He went to insist on its acceptance, intimating that all the power of the United States was behind him. To get his way in intimate negotiation he was forced to make compromises—ones he knew to be unwise—so that the treaty he brought home was unworkable. But it was not this that defeated its ratification. It was the disillusion of a whole people with international co-operation. There was widespread feeling that the United States had been used by the old European powers for purposes in which the American people had no interest—to which they were hostile. And Wilson's idealism stirred them no longer.

He proposed to abandon the traditional isolationism and to use American power in an organization for peace to prevent future wars. What he did not reckon on was the American post-war temper. Impatience, disgust, disillusion, withdrawal—all these were in the air as the boys began coming home from "over there." The crusade was ended; its afflatus had evaporated. Let ungrateful Europe go hang!

There were, as always, senatorial enemies of the presidency, waiting like political buzzards for signs of weakness in the White House—led this time by an effective strategist, Henry Cabot Lodge. The national reaction from the tensions of war rapidly became a reaction from the President who had led the way into it, who had imposed the disciplines necessary to its winning, and who now proposed a further commitment to sacrifice and involvement. Wilson had never been a national hero, except at the moment of going to war in 1917 and the other moment of acclaim in the first months of 1919 as he came home from Paris. In 1920 his following was sadly diminished and his enemies were encouraged to make really vicious attacks.

Franklin saw all this happen. He was close enough to follow it in detail, yet not so much part of it that his analysis was wholly confused by loyalty. The lessons he learned would guide him more successfully through a later and similar crisis than Wilson had been guided through his struggle. Franklin's United Nations would at least be official policy by ratification at home, and even in the inevitable post-war reaction it would not be repudiated.

His plea to go abroad was a somewhat sophistical one. Daniels had better let him go, he told the old man, so that the business of winding up the Navy's extensive affairs abroad could be carried out under proper civilian authority. There was going to be an investigation: that had been ensured by the Republican congressional victories of 1918. Daniels ought not to risk any carelessness in the forthcoming liquidations. The Navy's affairs were, as a matter of fact, in good shape. It had been a well-conducted war: and if Franklin had had any idea that there were risks of scandal he might far better have stayed home and let Admiral Sims, who was then in charge in London, take the blame. But he pressed, and Daniels let him go.

He started this trip just at the beginning of 1919. The staff he took was exceptionally able; and a good job was done, although there was an acid exchange or two with the irascible Sims—who, turning out to be a Republican, was to try to make trouble later. Because others did the work, Franklin could spend a good deal of time in doing what he had really come for. This, of course, was to watch from close by the goings on in Paris. Eleanor was with him, and their joint letters back to "Dearest Mama" yield a kind of slanting but revealing light on the Peace Conference. Even if they show little understanding of what was under negotiation or of Wilson's trials, they convey well enough the confused and febrile atmosphere of Paris in the conference months.

As Roosevelts always were, these young members of the clan were besieged with hospitality. There is mention of the La Boulayes, as well as dozens of other diplomats, of friends among the well-to-do in France and England, and of distant relatives on both sides of the family. There were dinners, teas, visits to country houses, shopping expeditions—an almost giddy activity. Eleanor showed no more sign yet of interest in public affairs than any of the other graduates of her English finishing school—several of whom she went to visit. She was a little breathless, but she was also anxious about the children and her thoughts were always turning toward home. Her letters are somewhat wistful with notations about the children of other families they visited, but there is almost nothing about the events which were of so much consequence to all the world.

Uncle Ted had died while they were at sea, and in Paris there was a memorial service. For a moment the rising Roosevelt and his Roosevelt wife paused to recall and regret. Uncle Ted had lived magnificently; glory had shone all about him, not a little of it on Franklin and Eleanor. But whether Franklin thought instantly that now *he* was *the* Roosevelt, with the family's prestige in his care, no one knows. If he did, no one was allowed to share his feeling, and the only surviving comment is Eleanor's. "We were shocked," she said somewhat conventionally, "by the news of Uncle Ted's death and I think much of Aunt Edith . . . Another big figure gone from our nation and I fear the last years were for him full of disappointment . . ." How Franklin felt was to become evident later on when, making a campaign as a Democrat, he would nevertheless express public admiration for the dead Theodore and perhaps inflate his qualities a little, as was suitable for a successor.

Reading Eleanor's comment in the volume of letters, it is easy for a reader's eyes to drop to the concluding sentence of the same paragraph. It says: "I have nearly finished 'Henry Adams,' very interesting but sad to have had so much and yet find it so little." The Adams blood had run thin in this generation; but the Roosevelt blood was running rich still and vigorous. Franklin, it can be presumed, had brought that book aboard and was reading it after he went to bed. That was his habit. But what he thought of the wizened and disillusioned little old scholar with the famous name, watching and writing in the Adams house across the square from the presidential mansion, no one seems ever to have heard him say. It would have been revealing, coming from one so secure in his faiths—faith in divine support, in progress, and in his own eventual destiny. He might have momentary doubts about direction, but he had none at all about human ends, Adams' chief preoccupation.

The return trip was on the *George Washington*. The ship was carrying Wilson home to his final ordeal. The President, tired almost to death and trying to brace himself for what was coming, was not very gregarious. The picture is of a gray-faced man in a golfing cap staring out at the inscrutable sea as the old ship made her slowish way homeward. But Franklin did talk with him once, and Wilson seems to have made of him—what he had not been until then—an enthusiast for the League. Whether he merely caught fire from the President's flame and renewed his loyalty to a fighting chief, or whether he was suddenly made to share the older man's vision, it was, anyway, from then on, along with his progressivism, a major item of his political luggage. He would sometimes carry it lightly, sometimes seem not to recall that he had it: but how far he would carry it, and with what fidelity he would guard it, would be evident to everyone when the work began at Dumbarton Oaks which would issue in the charter of a new league.

I myself have sometimes thought, having in mind Franklin's qualities of ebullience and sympathy, so little encouraged by Wilson during the past years, that Franklin responded uncritically to this sudden attention of the President and may have been carried beyond his own judgment. Shipboard conversion may very well have been deepened also by the spectacular scene in Boston as the President came home to his accounting. The active front of the opposition to the League may have been the vindictive little senator from Massachusetts, but the people of that state were in a mood, if only temporarily, for acclaim. They all but mobbed the President. Through a sea of cheers he rode to the scene of the first of those great persuasive speeches he was to make in the next few months; they encouraged him to think that the recalcitrant Lodge and his senatorial conspirators could be defeated by presidential appeal.

It was a false impression. The Bostonians were echoing the European approbation. Tomorrow they would turn coldly away from today's implications.

But the whole scene must have affected Franklin deeply and aroused in him a loyalty which hitherto had had such slight foundation. It must be recalled that, to accept the League, what was required of him was a giving up of that super-nationalism which had characterized all his public attitudes since he had gone to Washington. He was a big-Navy man, perilously close, in fact, to being an imperialist. He was now to talk about international co-operation, the reduction of armaments, substitutes for war, and the coming of an era of peace. I do not doubt that it was sincere. He was to demonstrate that it was. But the imperialist instincts did not all die out at once. He was still the Franklin of those prideful inspections he had made in Haiti and Santo Domingo of the marines' custodianship, and in Panama of Uncle Ted's vast public work. Pride in the Navy and belief in its benign behavior would never vanish from his calculations. But from now on he was a League supporter and ready to sacrifice what must be sacrificed for its establishment.

On that winter day in Boston even the cautious Calvin Coolidge, then governor of Massachusetts, soon to be Franklin's opponent in a national campaign, seemed to negate Lodge. He said some warm words of welcome. He went further. He praised the League. Franklin was not the only one to be moved by the Wilsonian fervor and the people's apparent response.

As the elections of 1920 approached, the Democratic party was disorganized by the defeat of the treaty and the anomalous position of its leader. Wilson had undertaken to rally the American people when he belatedly discovered the strength of the Senate conspiracy against the League. On the return leg of a speechmaking swing to the Pacific Coast he had broken down. From then on, until he appeared on March 4, 1921, the wasted ghost of his vigorous years, to ride with his successor down Pennsylvania Avenue in the traditional handing-over ceremony, he was immured in a White House bedroom, and all business was transacted through his wife and his physician, Admiral Grayson. It was, because of this, a time of even more rapid dissolution, both in national and party affairs. Nothing new was begun, and the disestablishment of wartime institutions was about all the administration was equal to.

Franklin was busy with his Navy routine, and he and Eleanor did rather more entertaining than they had done before, mostly of European notables, of whom there was so large a supply in Washington just then. This widened their diplomatic acquaintance, but it did not contribute to the furtherance of Franklin's career. Just where that tended no one could say; the immediate future grew murkier rather than clearer. It was only necessary to look around to see that the Republican trend, so

118

evident by 1918, had not been arrested. Only a miracle could save the Democrats in the presidential elections of 1920. As always in these circumstances, there was a good deal more scrambling for Republican nomination than for the Democratic. It was worth more.

Both Governor Lowden of Illinois and General Leonard D. Wood, an old associate of T.R., were prominent contenders. So was the progressive Hiram Johnson of California. The energy with which the nomination was pursued resulted in a deadlock: and this, as in so many cases, gave the professionals their chance. That was the year they enriched the American language with the "smoke-filled room" phrase. The room was in the Blackstone Hotel in Chicago. And the result of the deliberation was the incredibly cynical choice of Warren Gamaliel Harding, United States senator from Ohio, as the candidate. Harding was the product of one of the most corrupt machines in the country and himself a slick, good-natured "sport" without a trace of capability.

Looking back, the observer might generalize, if he cared to, that for once the professionals overreached themselves. The scandals of the Harding regime would haunt the Republican party for a long time; but the honest observer would have to admit that, although some worry must have been caused among the participants by the results of that June night's trading, there were no actual party penalties. There might possibly have been if Harding had not died in office, a blowzy, worn-out old roué, and made way for the dry and cautious Coolidge, the Vice-President, who had not been touched by the scandals because he was seldom touched by anything. But the fact was that the professionals got away with it; and Republicanism, in spite of Harding and the Ohio gang, was to have a run of twelve full years, and then it was to be a depression, not the politicians' betrayal of the voters, that would be responsible for their displacement.

The Democrats met in San Francisco later in the same month that Harding and Coolidge were nominated and the Republican "retreat to normalcy" platform was adopted. Every one of them knew how the prestige of Wilson had declined and into what disrepute the whole party had fallen. The war had not settled anything. True, the Germans had been beaten and there was gloating over the victory, but the overwhelming disposition was to let it go at that. This seemed so incredible that it was almost impossible to accept it as final. The war had been a party war, and it had been won in glorious style. There had been no turning up of the usual post-war scandals, either, which was just next to a miracle in such a time of pressure. The party ought to have been able to rely on a people's gratitude; instead its leader was discredited, its policies were unpopular, and it was forced to face, amazed and impotent, an imminent repudiation at the polls.

The administration crowd did, however, come to San Francisco in force, and there they had the strategic position that went with eight years of office. They could write the platform; and if they had a really outstanding candidate they would just possibly have a fighting chance against the weak contender the Republicans had nominated. There were two possibilities—A. Mitchell Palmer and William Gibbs McAdoo. Palmer, the Attorney General, had lately won a place in American history by the first of those strange security crusades that were to torment the body politic recurrently for a generation. He thought his crusade entitled him to the nomination, and so it did if public notice was a qualification. McAdoo was Wilson's son-in-law as well as Secretary of the Treasury. By this double bond he was committed to the Wilson policies. But also he had been Director General of the Railroad Administration during the war. He had done a magnificent job; he had brought the first order into American railroading that it had ever had, suffering as it was from the effects of repeated lootings and careless management. But in the post-war malaise this was "socialism," and his excellent record was rather to McAdoo's discredit than to his credit.

Even the administration men at San Francisco recognized that what was indicated was a candidate who was as far removed as possible from Wilson and from the war. So strong an impulse toward survival as this might have been checked, however, if Wilson had spoken. The party might have undertaken an honorable suicide. But the sick man in the White House was staying silent. There is reason to believe, incredible as it seems, that he hoped the convention would nominate him for a third term—something that must be put down to the combined effects of the adulation he had received in Europe so short a time before and the disease that had now withered and enfeebled the once strong body and dominant mind. Watching from his invalid's chair, he gave no lead to the aimless delegates. Lacking it, they nominated James M. Cox, Ohio governor, and very quickly, as they prepared to leave, Franklin D. Roosevelt of New York as his running mate.

There were several reasons for choosing Franklin. Since Cox was not an administration man, his running mate had better be one. But Franklin, to tell the truth, was a rather anomalous Wilsonian. There could hardly have been anyone in the official family so little really identified with it. Before the war he had been almost insubordinate in pressing for action; while the war was going on he had had no part whatever in shaping policy and he had in fact been outside the decision-making circle. Also, he had a good many friends who were not only not Democrats but were very active Republicans—he was closer to General Wood than to President Wilson and shared that proconsul's views, especially about the treatment of lesser peoples. Those views were also, it must be remembered, Uncle Ted's. There was reason to believe, besides all this, that Wilson still regarded Franklin with a rather chilly and questioning eye.

Concerning domestic policy, Franklin persisted in rating himself as a progressive. But what that meant in 1920, beyond what had already been achieved by Wilson's measures, it would be hard to say. The progressives were at a low point just then. Most of the ambitious program set out in the Bull Moose platform of 1912 had been taken over by Wilson, and there was no encouragement in the temper of the electorate for further advance. Public ownership of the great utilities and of heavy industry, further limitation of hours and the establishment of a minimum wage, and general social security—such things were not to be thought of. There was a revulsion against labor's stiff fight to hold gains made during the war, just as there was against the government seizure of the railroads. And the "wobbly" (I.W.W.) scare, along with Palmer's agitation against the "Reds," was at its height. Franklin was not out on the progressive frontier. He had been advocating none of the items on the further progressive agenda, nor had he been defending the civil liberties so freely being violated. He had had no occasion lately to define his political beliefs in any detail. On the other hand, he was not at outs with Tammany any more; if Charles F. Murphy did not push him forward at San Francisco, he did not oppose him. What that astute strategist had in mind no one knows; but New York bosses had pushed Roosevelts onto the national stage before as a way of getting them out of the state. And Franklin in Washington had for seven years been tolerable to Murphy. He might have thought it better to have him running for Vice-President than for governor or senator. And anyway, Murphy could not have missed the plain political signs. No Democrat would win in 1920; that was evident even after the Republicans had nominated Harding.

Franklin, of course, thought—or seemed to think—that he and Cox had a fighting chance. He had had time to size up the situation, and when he was chosen he was able to reply without hesitation. He put on some show of surprise, but actually numerous suggestions had warned him, and he had gone West with an entourage explicable only on the theory that they were to assist him in some major enterprise. Since he was by now a fairly seasoned politician himself, the conclusions to be drawn from his acceptance are not too difficult. If his ticket did not win, he would have a claim on future Democratic consideration when the situation had improved. He would be a well-known national figure at a time when new names and faces would be looked for—when the Wilsonians had departed and the younger men remained.

His own most noted activity at San Francisco was the seconding of the nomination of Al Smith. But before that he had brought attention to himself by seizing the New York standard from Jerry Mahoney when a parade for Wilson started during Homer S. Cummings' keynote speech. Tammany men were sitting sour and silent while the delegations from all the other states were cheering and marching. There was something of a scuffle; then the New York standard, in Franklin's hands, joined the parade. This, he must have thought, was the least respect the convention could show the stricken leader. Before this, also, he had had something of a victory when he persuaded the Rules Committee that New York's delegates, having been chosen by primaries in separate congressional districts, need not be bound by the unit rule. Tammany could not thereafter vote the whole delegation; Franklin's upstaters were freed, for what it was worth.

After these incidents Murphy could not have held any very kindly feelings for Franklin, but he was not one to allow a grudge precedence over judgment. Nor, at that time, was Al Smith. Al made one of the seconding speeches for Franklin. The mutual political alliance of these two was becoming noticeable. With Tammany willing and Cox approving, Franklin was quickly nominated.

In all this affair Wilson had remained inscrutable. So when Franklin suggested to Cox that their first duty was to visit the President, there must have been some uneasiness about what kind of reception they would receive. It was, in fact, far from cordial. Nevertheless, they were deeply affected by the President's helplessness. And they resolved that they would make the League a genuine issue and not try to bury it. For Franklin at least this was clearly more than just a quixotic gesture. He was by now much more internationalist than ever before, even if the imperialist tinge was noticeable. Besides, since he had been fired by his talk with Wilson on the *George Washington* and the outpouring of emotion he had witnessed in Europe and again in Boston as Wilson landed, he had persuaded himself that the League was not the cause of the falling away of Democratic popularity. That, he considered, was the natural aftermath of war. It was not beyond possibility that so great a cause could yet be a winning one.

At any rate, both candidates made the League and progressivism the issues. The Republicans offered a disestablishment of all the hated wartime restrictions, freedom for business, a lowering of the tormenting high cost of living, and a withdrawal from international complications of all kinds.

There was a clear issue about foreign policy, and presently the general difference between the parties about home affairs began to take shape. If the Republicans offered "normalcy," the Democrats had to offer—at least they did offer—what Franklin called "organized progress." Because of the outcome, what Cox said as the presidential candidate is of scant historical importance. Obscurity overcame him promptly.

The whole campaign was distinguished by apathy. This could be because, even with Harding running for the Republicans, the conclusion was hardly in question. Harding was shocking to Nicholas Murray Butler and to William Allen White, very different kinds of Republicans but alike in feeling that the integrity of democratic institutions had been outraged by the buying of a President by business. White afterward spoke of Harding as a "he-harlot" and wrote of the convention that he had never seen one "so completely dominated by sinister predatory economic forces." But the extent to which the public simply did not care is almost beyond belief. This was the first national election in which women voted too; but even that, which might have been thought to favor Cox and Roosevelt, since they stood for the organized peace, seemed to make no difference.

Senator Lodge, making the keynote speech, stated the Republican creed:

We must be now and ever for Americanism and Nationalism, and against Internationalism. There is no safety for us, no hope that we can be of service to the world, if we do otherwise.

Harding bungled and bumbled his way through the campaign; he was dignifiedly silent at first, but his employers now and again sent him out to speechify. What he said, when not meaningless or inconsistent, was each time another way of saying what he had said better in the famous Boston speech in May. What the nation needed, he had said then, was

not heroism but healing, not nostrums but normalcy, not revolution but restoration, not agitation but adjustment, not surgery but serenity, not the dramatic but the dispassionate, not experiment but equipoise, not submergence in internationality but sustainment in triumphant nationality.

Cox, in a moment of inspiration, summarized the opposite of this reactionary blather:

The house of civilization is to be put in order. The supreme issue of the century is before us, and the nation that halts and delays is playing with fire.

That fire would blaze up in 1939. But in 1920 there were few to believe it. Cox did his best, but it was like wading through feathers; there was no response.

Franklin was not far behind Cox. The impression now can easily be got that he was, indeed, out in front. But of course it did not seem so then. Later attention naturally centers on the vice-presidential campaign of the man who would be so consequential in the national annals. Even at that time, when no one could have foreseen that it had any special significance, Franklin made more stir than secondary figures usually do. No one, for instance, in 1916 had taken very seriously what

123

homas R. Marshall had to say when he was running with Wilson. His
existence was that of a modest flower in the shadow of a great oak. And
Calvin Coolidge, Harding's second, is best described as having maintained a "dignified silence." But Franklin behaved quite otherwise. He
was looking to the future.

Franklin's political position, even if it had got for him second place
on a national ticket at the age of thirty-eight, still did not please him.
He might be fairly well known in New York, agreeably regarded by
those who had some reason to know about his Navy service, and rather
vaguely present in the consciousness of certain others. But actually he
had no hold on the regard of any significant number of supporters. How
could an Assistant Secretary of the Navy have made any notable impression on American voters? He had not been encouraged to put
himself forward in any of the national campaigns while he was in Washington; and when he had, he had mostly been confined to talking about
the Navy. True, he had enlarged that into propaganda for sea power,
going often against Wilson's apparent wishes, but that was of less than
no use to him now. The voters were no longer interested in an instrument of national aggrandizement.

The vice-presidential candidate had very little in his record to build
on except vague memories of his past opposition to Tammany and the
progressive label attached to him by the double circumstance of being
a Roosevelt and having been a member of Wilson's official family. Beyond that, he had been an acceptable administrator left untouched even
by the partisan post-war investigations.

If Franklin's behavior in the 1920 campaign seems to differ from the
usual pattern, the reason is not really obscure. This was his chance to
make himself prominent. If he was ever to go farther, his identification
with the policies of the future must become firmly fixed in the minds of
voting Americans. He thought he knew what his commitments ought
to be. They were, in fact, the same ones Wilson had sorted out of the
various alternatives before him. He had to be an internationalist and
he had to be a progressive. His task was to fill each of these concepts
with Rooseveltian content so that he and no other would be their known
champion.

He could not do this by following along as Cox campaigned; nor could
he do it by modestly confining himself to an innocuous speech or two
in the fashion of predecessor candidates; in the fashion also, it might
be remarked, of his Republican opposite number, Calvin Coolidge. Cox,
he must have seen, was unlikely to win and so would never really be a
leader to whom he would owe subordination. He never admitted doubts
and cheerfully deferred to his principal; but actually he ran an otherwise unaccountably active campaign all on his own, and when it was
over he had made himself, rather than Cox, the actual party leader in

124

succession to Wilson. This was a political feat of really astonishing cleverness.

To define the international issue was not an involved matter. It had already been done by Wilson. Franklin approached it bravely in his acceptance speech, which, by the way, set the pattern for later ones when he would have first place on the ticket. To assembled party men and neighbors, and speaking from the portico of the Hyde Park house which in later years would be so familiar in picture and story, he said:

In our world problems, we must either shut our eyes, sell our newly built merchant marine to more far-seeing foreign powers, crush utterly by embargo and harassing legislation our foreign trade, close our ports and build an impregnable wall of costly armaments and live, as the Orient used to live, a hermit nation, dreaming of the past, or we must open our eyes and see that modern civilization has become so complex and the lives of civilized men so interwoven with the lives of other men in other countries as to make it impossible to avoid, except by monastic seclusion, those honorable and intimate foreign relations which the fearful-hearted shudderingly miscall by that devil's catchword, "international complications."[2]

This was duly followed by other pronouncements of the same sort, some of them ingenious; but the argument had reached the point of tiresomeness long before. Some of the shrewder participants realized this—for instance, Tom Lynch and Steve Early—and Steve warned Franklin that the voters' interests were much nearer home. It was a time of readjustment. There was unemployment because war work was finished and peace work had not yet been resumed. The cost of living refused to come down from its inflated levels. The agricultural surpluses resulting from an acreage vastly expanded during the war were piling up. Farmers were frightened and their complaints were to be an insistent problem throughout the next decade. All these troubles had to be accepted as Democratic responsibilities. In the end they would defeat Republican ingenuity too; but that would not be for some time. Meanwhile there was no adequate alibi and no policy.

Franklin did his best, but it seems now to have been a poor attempt. Its fault was generality at a time when specific new suggestions were needed. The best he could do was to fall back on the promise to inquire and to adjust. But his use of the word "definite" before "study" was not convincing. It served to underscore the emptiness of the whole phrase. What he said was this:

A greater America is our objective. Definite and continuing study shall be made of our industrial, fiscal, and social problems. Definite and continuing action shall result in reform, and neither the study nor the action shall be left to emotional caprice or the opportunism of any groups of men.

[2] This acceptance, quoted here and below, is to be found in *Personal Letters: 1905–1928*, pp. 500–8.

These were intended to be brave words. To many Americans they seemed to have false overtones. It was a plea in avoidance. And it was sheer whistling in the dark to say, as he did:

It is the faith which is in me that makes me very certain that America will choose the path of progress and set aside the doctrines of despair, the whisperings of cowardice, the narrow road to yesterday.

This speech was carefully calculated and constructed. Franklin thought it very good. So did the listeners before him. But he and they were partisans. It was unmistakably reminiscent of the Wilsonian speeches—eloquent and high-minded, but vague. And Americans had had too much of eloquence. They were sick to death of Wilson. And they preferred the Harding brand of vagueness.

Steve Early, who was out ahead as Franklin's campaign circus took the road, sensed the American tiredness. He caused the candidate's tune to be changed so far as that could be done, within the limitations of his secondary position. The campaign became an exhibition, so far as Franklin was concerned. Twice he made cross-nation circuits, speaking seven to ten times a day and making side journeys as well. When it was over he knew practically every Democratic leader in the country. Also, he had added to an encyclopedic geographic knowledge which always left those who were exposed to it openmouthed with admiration.

In view of what happened afterward, several features of the 1920 campaign ought to be noted. One of these was a concentration on the West which was unprecedented but which broke the ground for later forays of the same sort. It is quite apparent that Franklin already had glimpsed the grand strategy of uniting West and South which would be so effective in 1932 in spite of opposition from the city machines. Such a strategy seemed obvious later; it was by no means obvious in 1920, although Wilson's narrow successes owed something to such a coalition.

Another characteristic was the conscious development of the Roosevelt identity. This, too, would still be potent in 1932. That others than Franklin feared his monopolizing of the family name was shown by the haste with which the Republicans sent a representative of the Oyster Bay branch out to denounce the usurper. The Republicans themselves were not at the moment proud of their Roosevelts, but they had a lively fear that the Democrats were developing one who might be troublesome. At Sheridan, Wyoming, Theodore Jr. told the world that Franklin was a "maverick" who "does not have the brand of our family." He was too late. Franklin had already walked off not only with the name but with the Roosevelt tradition. Late in October, certain of this, he boldly brought it into the open. "I wish Theodore Roosevelt were alive today," he said. "He at least had definite convictions." He went on to praise him as a fair fighter and an example to American youth. The implication was obvious. The Roosevelt of 1920 was named Franklin. He too was a fair fighter and full of forthright convictions.

But political historians do not grant Franklin this kind of claim. There were things said by this Roosevelt that were far from forthright, and positions taken about which the kindest word to be said is "ambiguous." The truth is that Franklin, feeling his way into the heart of the American conviction, determined to identify himself with it; and, convinced that it was generally progressive, still was uncertain concerning the content of future progressivism. In view of his old feeling for conservation, it is a little sad to know that one of his biographers felt that even about this he "trimmed" in deference to pressure from go-getting Westerners who were not at all interested in nature but had very practical interests in water power, grazing rights, and timber concessions. He called his new policy "development," but it had every appearance of exploitation.

Perhaps the worst affair of this sort, however, was the curious performance at Centralia in the state of Washington. I am unable to account for it except by assuming that in this, as in the instance of conservation, he accepted the direction of local leaders, which was always more or less his habit, about what to say so far from home. At Centralia he seemed to endorse the indefensible invasions of civil liberty being carried out under A. Mitchell Palmer's direction and to take his place with the cheap super-patriots who were defining everyone's loyalties for them. Centralia, a year before, had been the scene of a bloody attack by the American Legion on a gathering of I.W.W.'s, utterly unprovoked and in the purest vigilante tradition. Franklin chose to praise the Legionnaires in ridiculous, blown-up phrases. Perhaps he was oversensitive still to the political danger from never having got into uniform. But talk about a "high form of red-blooded patriotism" in connection with what was plainly embryonic fascism does no credit, in retrospect, either to his sincerity or his prescience.

Neither these nor other lapses from principle did any immediate political harm. In the expedient sense they had this much justification. But their very lack of penalty may have made the young candidate more likely to follow such a design in later campaigns. To my mind they are sinister notes in an otherwise judicious effort, unsuccessful in itself, but thoroughly justified as part of the long-run enterprise in Franklin's mind.

How strenuous it seems! It induces fatigue simply to contemplate Franklin's activities during August, September, and October. And always he must have been tormented by not knowing what to say. He had with him in his special car Marvin McIntyre, Tom Lynch, and several other loyal supporters; but none of them was, in political terms, more than simply shrewd. They knew the campaign was a losing one; but it was not losing for any reason they were capable of comprehending. The truth was that the reasons were beyond Franklin's power to influence. He could not repudiate Wilson, nor could he turn his back on the League. He could and did push them somewhat into the background. But his worst difficulty was that the Democrats had only a vague domestic policy left over from Wilson essays in filling out the progressive agenda. Even this was wrong for the time. They could talk all they liked about "going forward," but this only annoyed a people who were stubbornly determined on reaction. What they wanted was not to go forward any more at all.

It would be a long time before the Democrats would achieve a coherent and persuasive domestic program—not until three Republican presidencies had intervened; and then they would be returned to office less because they professed to know what to do than because the Republicans obviously did not. At that time Franklin's renewal of the "going forward" theme would have a good deal more appeal. The American people would by then have had plenty of normalcy.

But in 1920 "normalcy" had a dulcet sound. And even if Franklin had then and there, by some legerdemain, conjured up the itemized New Deal of 1932, it would not have changed matters much. But in view of what was to happen, Franklin's own summary of Wilsonian progressivism early in the campaign is interesting. It was from this as a base that he was to resume in 1932. This was his own summary claim:

In the six years prior to the present Republican Congress there was more legislation of a constructive nature put on the statute book than has been placed there by any administration since the formation of the Union . . . the income tax, the federal reserve system, publicity of campaign expenses, the eight hour day, safety appliances on railroads and mines, Workmen's Compensation, farm loan banks, federal aid for good roads, soldier's compensation laws, war risk insurance, pensions for soldiers of all our wars, establishment of the Department of Labor, establishment of the Department of Commerce, the Federal Trade Commission, our Merchant Marine, our Naval Forces . . .

This statement was in pursuit of a tactic he would use repeatedly: to affirm that the Democratic party was the progressive party. Partly the idea was to commit even its reluctant southern wing to progressivism; partly it was to attract to it those progressives who were enrolled as Republicans. This splitting of the enemy was ineffective in 1920; in other times it would be very useful. In spite of discouragement, Franklin would never really change his belief that progressivism was the wave of the future.

If his definition of progressivism seems inflated and empty, that is because so definite an end had come to an era. A Navy and a Merchant

Marine were padding; by no stretch could they be called progressive. The legitimate claims to the Federal Reserve Act and farm legislation were the furthest extension, in the fields of finance and agriculture, of progressive thinking. They had been achieved, and there was nothing more. There was no Democratic promise in 1920. And in that sense Cox and Roosevelt hardly deserved to win.

But in spite of the humiliation of 1920—Harding's and Coolidge's vote was sixteen million to Cox's and Roosevelt's nine million; in electoral votes, 404 to 127—Franklin still thought the progressive wave would carry him into the White House. He said so to Tom Lynch, who was somewhat downcast. He put it specifically, saying, "Tom, 1932 will be our year." This bit of forecasting I might doubt if Tom Lynch himself, with Mrs. Lynch corroborating, had not related it to me with utterly convincing circumstantial description. I am compelled to accept it.

It can be seen now how admirably the campaign of 1920 served Franklin's purpose. It had given him license to roam the nation, exhibit his charm, and become acquainted with hosts of professionals. If he was not yet Mr. Democrat, he was the heir apparent of not only the Bryan-Wilson tradition but that of Uncle Ted. His judgment that by 1932 he would come into his inheritance seems a bit startling, and I doubt if Franklin was as certain as he seemed; I doubt whether the way and the method were clear. This still has to be set down as a sticky interlude in his career. But it cannot be denied that he was faithful to progressivism even if he seemed hardly to know what it meant; and it cannot be denied that he did say to Tom Lynch that 1932 would be "the year."

7

The period of Franklin's life which began in November of 1920, after the Republican victory, has to be considered against the background of normalcy. His sallies into business adventure, his cheerful but industrious keeping up of contacts with his fellow exiles among the Democrats, and his occasional invasions of the political arena can be understood only as counterpoint to the dominating theme of booming business and supine government. The Harding complaisance was quickly taken advantage of and corruption invaded the body politic. When Coolidge succeeded in 1923, endemic scandals were in process of exposure. They went on with that moralist's reluctant consent; so far as he could he ignored them; and, strangely enough, most Americans felt that he was right. Nothing is so bizarre about the 1920s, even the bust which succeeded the boom, as the stubborn public indifference to corruption.

On occasion this turned positive. Those three majestic ornaments of journalism in New York City, the *Times*, the *Post*, and the *Tribune*, united in villifying Senators Walsh and Wheeler as "Montana scandalmongers" and "assassins of character." The exposures were "contemptible and disgusting"; they arose out of "twittering hysteria." And naturally the journalists got around finally to averring that radicals and internationalists were responsible for this undermining of the American way of life. If this seems a curious reaction to the kind of conduct in public life which forced the resignation of three cabinet members and put one of them in jail for receiving bribes, which was marked by the suicide or conviction of several other presidential intimates, which disclosed that the White House had been turned into a kind of saloon for the Ohio gang, it is nevertheless characteristic of those years of reaction. It is also characteristic that although Albert B. Fall, Secretary of the Interior, was convicted of receiving bribes and sent to jail, Edward L. Doheny and Harry F. Sinclair could not be convicted of giving those same bribes. *They* were big businessmen.

It was the mark of normalcy that business and businessmen were free from any effective restraint. Government was in check, held there by the occupants of its offices. Coolidge said it: "The business of America is business." Government ought to keep out of the way except for imposing tariffs on imports and performing a few police functions. Coolidge's program, reiterated again and again, was "economy and lower taxes," and the country got both. He was sour, suspicious, fearful, and solitary; but he knew who was responsible for his rise and his support. Whenever he was called on to trumpet the virtues of business he responded in his nasal New England voice over the radio, for radio had now arrived to revolutionize the arts of politics. He seemed to give the nation comfort. He was very nearly idolized by grateful speculators who surged toward fantastic riches while he turned a blind eye on the doubtful methods they employed in the chase.

Coolidge was succeeded in turn by Hoover, who had been Secretary of Commerce throughout the Republican years. It was appropriate that a Secretary of Commerce should become President in so exclusively commercial a regime. It might have been even more appropriate if Andrew W. Mellon, Secretary of the Treasury, had succeeded. He was credited with four successive reductions of taxes heavily weighted in favor of the wealthy; and since the wealthy were in a dictatorial position they might well have gone the limit. True, Mellon himself benefited from the reductions—one of them was worth eight hundred million to him—and much ought to have been made of that fact in a campaign; but he would not have lost, not in 1928; no Republican could have lost.

Hoover, even if he had been Secretary of Commerce, and properly assiduous in that office, was nevertheless a slightly incongruous choice for triumphant capitalists to have made. He was not a politician as Harding and Coolidge had been; he had had a career as an international business consultant, starting from a base in engineering, but he had left that behind to become the most noted doer of good works on the grand scale of any person in history. After being Food Administrator for Wilson during the war, he undertook to rescue devastated Europe from starvation and pestilence and succeeded with an efficiency hitherto unknown among public administrators. Until just before the election of 1920 no one knew his politics or his philosophy; and since he had been a Wilsonian, it was rather generally thought that he was a Democrat and there was some suspicion that he might have progressive leanings. There is little doubt that he could have had the Democratic nomination in 1920 if he had been willing. Suitable candidates were very scarce and he stood out above any other. Even Franklin thought it suitable—he said so in a letter to a friend—and there were many others. There is something almost inexpressibly ironic in contemplating the developments which might have followed his acceptance; and not the least of these is the possibility that his running mate might have been Franklin himself. Hoover and Roosevelt—that would have been a mixture, odd even for American politics.

But Hoover knew something about himself that others, including Franklin, were to discover only later. He was a conservative of hard conscience, of strict adherence to principle, even if hitherto a silent one. This hardness and strictness made him inflexible. And inflexibility is a quality no person in political life can well afford. The technique of compromise, of trading the important for the essential, of accepting even doubtful means for desirable ends—these are the distinguishing possessions of most successful politicians. All this would be revealed during the next few years. For Hoover was to sit in the cabinet with Fall and Daugherty, and in Coolidge's administration he would on many occasions have to overlook some doings of which he could hardly have approved. But then he would not be responsible. And it may be that he would do more protesting than came to public notice; Coolidge is supposed to have resented the thought of his possible succession to the presidency. He always regarded Hoover as a kind of nuisance. "That man," he said, "has offered me unsolicited advice for six years, all of it bad."

Hoover, however, was what the people wanted in 1928, even if he seemed to the professionals something of a risk. He was believed to be the epitome of engineering efficiency. He would cut down government, reduce taxes even more, and so encourage business—not that business was in need of encouragement; by now the signs of runaway boom were apparent to everyone. The atmosphere of speculation and quick, even if doubtful, profits had transferred itself to New York. The fever of fast riches had its center there, but the infection had spread to every corner of the nation. Wall Street was bonanza country. Everyone was trying to outdo everyone else in that trading center which William O. Douglas a few years later would call a "Casino."

Hoover has since said that he was aware of the danger that this gigantic bubble of inflated values would burst; but, like everyone else, he found it hard to follow his conviction or to accept the likelihood that the time for bursting had arrived. It is indeed almost impossible for the historian to convey in any convincing way the fever of those years. The sickness had invaded the nation in the aftermath of the war and, beginning in 1921, had built and built in an ever-mounting tempo toward the events that were to occur when the edifice collapsed. That collapse would ruin Hoover, but it would furnish Franklin that opening for which he had so long waited and worked. He would exploit it to the full.

As Harding sagged toward his end, as Coolidge presided over the New York orgy reassuringly, seeming to deny its illicit nature by his hard-shell respectability, and as Hoover stepped into the presidency, ready, as he said, to end the poverty men had suffered throughout their history on this earth, Franklin played his part in the evolving drama with obvious impatience. He did not enjoy obscurity; but, so far as politics went, there was nothing to be done after 1920 but to accept the prospect of a prolonged exile. But even out of office the careerist of politics has necessary activities to keep up. He must maintain his position. He may not have the leverage of government, but he must find ways to keep his prestige. He must be the available man when the turn comes for the party to organize a succeeding government.

It is bewildering to follow Franklin's many ingenious recourses, especially between 1922 and 1928. During these years his seemed to be the prominent name associated with every respectable cause and especially those sure to attract publicity—such as campaigns for funds, for instance. He was chairman of drives put on by the Boy Scouts, the American Legion, and the Cathedral of St. John the Divine. He sought opportunities to make statements, to present his opinion, and to support every worthy institution. To recount all these efforts would require pages of listings. But all of it can be seen to have had one end—the keeping of the Roosevelt name in the popular mind.

This effort was, however, no more than a supplement to his direct political efforts. These involved an extensive correspondence with all the leaders whose acquaintance he had made during his vice-presidential trips; with most of them he assumed himself to be on a first-name basis, and with all of them he was confidential on party prospects. This was the broad endeavor—to keep his name known and to keep local leaders aware of his continuing occupancy of the titular Democratic position. The narrower and more critical tactical decision was one similar to those shrewd ones he had made when in 1911 he had attacked Tammany, when in 1912 he had attached himself to Wilson, when in 1918 he had made up with Tammany, and when in 1920 he had run for the vice-presidency as a progressive internationalist Democrat. He now espoused the cause of Smith.

Al Smith had lost the governorship in the debacle of 1920, but in 1922 he had been re-elected. This was to happen repeatedly until the new situation of 1928 would supervene. He was then to move on to higher things, leaving the governorship to Franklin. But meanwhile there would be 1924, the year of Smith's defeat for the presidential nomination. But that year in political history is less known to later times for the phenomenon of Smith than for the re-emergence of Franklin. He would in that year be the manager of Smith's campaign for the nomination and at the convention would make his "Happy Warrior" speech, only slightly less famous in the annals of political oratory than Bryan's "Cross of Gold" speech in Chicago in 1896. Something has been

made of his not having written this himself—Judge Proskauer, Smith's
mentor, seems to have been its author—but politicians seldom write the
speeches they deliver. They are not usually capable compositors, and if
they are they recognize themselves as being based on movements for
which they are no more than the spokesmen. Only when they reach
the top can they even determine what their pronouncements will convey, and then within limits and subject to modification or even veto
by the group will.

The "Happy Warrior" address was, for Franklin, however, one of
those miracles every politician hopes for. It immediately placed him
where he wanted to be, where he had been back in 1920—the second
man in the party, ready to step into first place when first place would
have supreme value. In 1928 at Houston he would repeat his 1924 performance. The results would not be so striking. But that was to be a
decisive year, nevertheless. For against his judgment he would be persuaded in the fall to take the nomination for the governorship and he
would win. At the same time Smith, as presidential candidate, would
lose and, moreover, he would lose in New York where Franklin had
won. So there Franklin would be, number one now, with events tum-
bling the nation toward acceptance of the renewed Democratic bid for
control.

If, having lived through this eight years of exile and having at the
end of it emerged within striking distance of the presidency, Franklin
felt that he was traveling under a star, there was some justification. It
may seem to the casual observer that what happened was nothing extraordinary. But Franklin did not act as though he felt that way. He
thought it extraordinary; but that did not, I think, surprise him. He
was appointed for events to center in. Crises happened so that he could
dominate them. History itself waited to throw him up when what was
called for was the man needed to complete the logic of her unfolding
events.

When the Harding bravoes were taking Washington for their own,
Franklin was being initiated into business in Wall Street—not a speculative business but one, nevertheless, that existed for the purpose of
making profits. As became one who had been a vice-presidential candidate, even if a defeated one, who had (on January 7, 1921), moreover, been introduced to his new surroundings by a most impressive
testimonial dinner attended by Frank A. Munsey, Adolph S. Ochs,
Owen D. Young, and others of a similar sort, he took up the role of
the "younger capitalist." He had been put in charge of the New York
office of the Fidelity and Deposit Company of Maryland. This was a
surety-bonding house whose head was Van Lear Black. Black was himself a person of wealth and some notoriety for his sporting proclivities.
He was much better known as a yachtsman and a flying enthusiast than

134

as a businessman. It has been suggested that Franklin appealed to him as another of his own sort, although of course what was stressed in the publicity for the occasion was Franklin's executive ability, his legal training, and his "unusual freedom from specialization." When it is questioned whether Franklin was worth the twenty-five-thousand-dollar salary he was paid it has to be remembered that, after all, he had had that relatively long experience as an executive in the Navy Department.

Opinions differ as to whether Franklin was as valuable to the firm as Black had hoped. There is no very good way of judging, because before his first year was up he was invalided by infantile paralysis. Thereafter his position was somewhat nominal, although he held it until he became governor seven years later. What he certainly did do, however, was to attract business through his various ramified connections. He seems to have had no reluctance to do this. His political prominence was capitalized on with skill and perseverance. Among those whose business came to Fidelity and Deposit through him was W. G. McAdoo, who still had ambitions for the presidency. McAdoo was attorney for E. L. Doheny, the oilman who was soon to be caught in the Teapot Dome scandals. At the moment Franklin, in writing to McAdoo, claimed Doheny as a friend.

Closer at home, he increased the company's business with the State of New York more proportionately than the rival concern, American Surety, was able to do; he "spoke to" James J. Walker when he became mayor, and he gave company jobs to sons of Tammany chieftains. Also, he got the business of the American Federation of Labor. This kind of thing did not require morning-to-night daily attendance at the office during his long struggle to recover from paralysis. And Black refused to consider his resigning. When he became able he went to his office a day or two a week and did the rest of his business at home; but he was away from New York a good deal, first under the care of a physician in Massachusetts, then in Florida during the hard winter months, and finally at Warm Springs in Georgia, a place that was to mean much to him all the rest of his life.

There is endless argument as to whether Franklin used improper means to get business for his company, but there is even more about his various other business ventures. These ranged all the way from almost continuous speculation on the Stock Exchange to investment in what the oil promoters call wildcatting. There were schemes for dealing in foreign currencies, taking advantage of the wildly fluctuating exchange rates of those days; there were several ventures having to do with ships and shipping, and at least one for organizing a dirigible transport line between the United States and Europe. In 1922 he tried to form a syndicate which would buy and operate privately a tract of forest land as was done in other countries; a somewhat similar idea was to grow southern pine as a crop. All these were in one way or another the outgrowth of old interests. So, it could be said, were others, such as the scheme to set up a chain of resorts from Warm Springs in the South to Lake Placid in the North.

Some of these ventures made a little money; others lost a little; but a few of them returned to embarrass him in later days. The lobster business was a favorite example, frequently cited by Louis Howe when he wanted to remind his principal of his propensity for extravagant and risky investments. In this one he lost the fair sum of twenty-six thousand dollars, but it was a straight business of catching lobsters and holding them for market. Cameo and Photomaton were more doubtful. Cameo was intended to exploit the modern vending machine by having whole stores made automatic. He afterward protested that he and Henry Morgenthau, Sr., had got into the affair merely through an exchange of stock and that his connection was a nominal one. But the fact is that he was a director until he became governor of New York, something the Chicago *Tribune* delightedly recalled in 1934 when in a fireside chat he spoke of the twenties as an unfortunate decade "characterized by a mad chase for riches." At that time Cameo was petitioning for reorganization; its shares had fallen from a high of eighteen dollars to two for a quarter. Photomaton also succumbed to the depression. But while it was prospering Franklin made a profit from it almost without knowing that anything had happened. Morgenthau bought and sold its stock for him. He was not, as he had been of Cameo, a director; but that did not prevent criticism.

There was a sort of pattern to which these ventures conformed. They were schemes for getting a profit from novel ideas or new gadgets. There were many such schemes afloat then, stimulated by the booming rise of the stock market and the quick fortune-getting which was so common. What Franklin did has to be set against that backdrop of business ebullience and easy commercial morals. It is true that on one occasion he was rebuked by the general secretary of the Society for Promoting Financial Knowledge for lending his name to doubtful enterprises. He replied that it was hard for a man more or less in public life to prevent his name from being used without authorization. He tried to be vigilant in the matter, he said, but the record will hardly sustain this explanation. The truth is that he was naturally venturesome and that he did get into a variety of things just because both his imagination and his cupidity were appealed to.

Something more needs to be said about his finances and his miscellaneous attempts to get hold of his share of the easy gains of those days. It has usually been assumed that Franklin had a large income at his disposal; but largeness is relative, and the fact is that his income was never enough to meet his obligations. For this reason he always felt himself to be pinched. Some of his speculations in the twenties arose out of sheer venturesomeness, the attraction he felt toward bizarre and imaginative ideas which with some capital and a good deal of ingenuity could be brought into being. But some of them were undoubtedly intended to make him rich.

The same wide-ranging imagination used in his speculations would infuriate his critics when he came back into public life. Before then he had been cautioned often enough—caustically, on occasion, by Louis Howe—so that the propensity was under fair control. There was, for instance, not much visible sign of it while he was governor, a period when he was being extremely cautious. The circumstances of the presidency, however, called for "bold, persistent experimentation," and this was the time when he really let himself go on a grand scale—but not, of course, in private ventures for profit. This delighted his followers and occasionally worked his enemies into frenzies which he blandly ignored.

But there was the other reason for his many attempts to tap the springs of easy money during the boom. He had a family of five children and a wife whose homemaking virtues were not her most conspicuous ones. She had a considerable income of her own which she used for the common expenditures, but until he began to be carried on the Fidelity and Deposit payroll Franklin never had much of his own. The salaries of state senators and Assistant Secretaries of the Navy would hardly pay the travel expenses of the Roosevelts. Travel expenses cannot have been insignificant, what with moving about from Washington or New York to Campobello with a family entourage. But the expense also of domestic establishments on the Roosevelt scale, together with the kind of entertaining which was a regular and routine obligation, must have been high. Then, too, Franklin had his "contacts" to maintain. This required a staff. Louis Howe managed this, but his ideas were expansive too. Franklin seems to have been extraordinarily preoccupied with expenses; he was always trying to get Louis Howe on others' payrolls and sometimes having trouble about it. His first quarrel with Robert Moses —one that would go on to more and more vindictive lengths—was about his effort to enter Louis on the rolls of the Taconic State Park Commission (of which he was a member) while really keeping him as a personal assistant.

After 1921 there were the terrible burdens of sickness and convalescence to be carried. The bills seemed mountainous to the man, helpless in bed or laboring, with a horrible feeling of frustration, at the exacting and exhausting regimes prescribed by doctors who, he always realized sooner or later, were just guessing. It is not to be wondered at if he took a few chances in the hope of a windfall. The twenty-five-thousand-dollar salary can hardly have met his invalid expenses alone.

It is sometimes said, and oftener intimated, that these rather fanciful risks of the twenties illustrate a basic lack of ethical responsibility. Close examination does not bear this out, especially when considered in the setting of those times. Some ventures were doubtful, none of them came out very well, and if he had kept out completely he would have been just as well off financially. But to impute to him any significant departure from customary ethics is to go beyond the facts. His behavior may not always have been becoming in a national hero, but the student who follows his adventures with sympathy can find a good deal of amusement in the ingeniousness of the schemes, in his irrepressible hopefulness about their outcome, and in a kind of unkillable faith that something rare and fortunate was bound to happen to him sooner or later. It never did, but he never gave up.

Politics, his real métier, it must be recalled, was more or less closed to him in those years, except for spectacular emergences on widely separated occasions. He cultivated the political field with persistence but under the most discouraging conditions. His investment of effort grew larger and larger, but toward the latter part of his exile the prospects improved so considerably that he could begin again to visualize in detail the way ahead. The pay-off did at last come within view.

But in 1921 this consummation was across a deep and dark gulf of physical torture. How he fell into this gulf and climbed out of it, how he even made it serve his permanent purposes, is a kind of tale to be eloquent about. It is impossible not to feel unqualified admiration for the sheer quality of the performance, the naked courage it required, and the resources of determination which supported the effort. Several of his biographers have described this incident so well and with such understanding that I should only be repeating their stories if I dwelt at any length on the occurrence. I shall be as brief as I can; but the reader must remember that anyone who speaks of it at all must be moved by those same sympathetic emotions. Besides, I should like to say what I have come to believe about those incredible reserves of fortitude which had to be used down to the last small measure to overcome so overwhelming a disaster.

The seizure was a most unlikely one. To begin with, Franklin was thirty-nine years old; then the sickness occurred at Campobello. Neither his age nor the location seemed appropriate to such a disease, and the first doctors can perhaps be excused for not recognizing it. But a famous Philadelphia diagnostician can hardly be forgiven for so categorically diagnosing it as a blood clot in the lower spine. That mistake led to torture by massage for some time before it was stopped by a more careful successor. By then the typical paralysis had made recognition easier; but by then, also, a good deal of damage had been done.

The family had been summering on the island; his mother was in

Europe, and Franklin himself had been going through an unpleasantness in Washington which had disturbed him deeply. He had been the subject of an investigation by a Republican-dominated subcommittee of the Naval Affairs Committee of the Senate. There had been during Franklin's time an inquiry into homosexuality. It was alleged that the investigators had joined in the unnatural practices in order to trap the offenders and that this was known to the Assistant Secretary. It was a ridiculous business but, for an aspiring politician, an extremely dangerous one. The Republicans succeeded in overreaching public tolerance, and the affair collapsed. But Franklin had been really frightened at its possibilities and had exhausted himself in the Washington heat trying to get a fairer hearing. It was later recalled also that he had a short time before visited a Boy Scout camp at Palisades Park with a group of notables. But immediately before the attack he had been aboard Black's yacht, *Sabalo*, voyaging back to Campobello to resume the vacation interrupted by the Washington emergency. Black stayed over a day to fish, and that day Franklin, crossing the deck while baiting hooks, fell overboard. The water was icy as always in the Bay of Fundy, and the shock seemed unusually paralyzing after the heat of an August sun.

Next day the family was sailing, although Franklin felt a little ill, when they spotted a ground fire on one of the islands. They landed and fought it with green branches for several hours, emerging grimy, sweating, and exhausted. The story is that, back on Campobello, they dogtrotted some two miles to a fresh-water lagoon, swam for refreshment, took a dip in the cold bay waters, then ran home again. In his wet bathing suit, Franklin sat reading an accumulation of papers for a while; then at the supper table he remarked that he guessed he might have a little lumbago and went upstairs to bed.

That began it. Next morning his temperature was high, but the local doctor in Lubec thought it was only a cold. Eleanor was frightened. She sent the children and some guests off on a three-day camping trip. Next morning Franklin was paralyzed from the chest down, and Louis Howe began a search for more reliable medical advice in the nearby resorts. It resulted in the diagnosis of a spinal blood clot. Not until two weeks later, after Uncle Fred Delano had consulted several specialists, did Dr. Lovett of Boston arrive and confirm the suspicion of poliomyelitis. He stopped the massaging and made Franklin more comfortable; he also raised his hopes by saying that it was a mild case and that complete recovery was likely.

Dr. Lovett was too optimistic; so were several successors. Franklin had been crippled terribly, and for life. And there now began the trial of endurance between his will and the stubborn paralysis of his legs which would not end for years—until he reluctantly accepted the permanency of his helplessness and in a way made virtue of it. What lay between Dr. Lovett's encouragement and this reconciliation with implacable fate was such a test of strength as few men ever endure.

It is not necessary to follow in detail Franklin's eager seizing of one hope after another, the gradual growth of knowledge about the after-treatment of the disease, and the prescriptions of exercise and strenuous regimens which, one after another, disappointed his expectations. But I must remark that he met each new suggestion with optimism and expended limitless energy on cures. All of them failed.

Dr. McDonald, with whom he worked for several summers, required of him hours of swimming and other hours of various exacting exercises. Mrs. Charles Hamlin, interested in Dr. McDonald's work, later wrote an article, which in turn is quoted in the second volume of the *Letters*.[1] Her account is calculated to wring the most hostile heart:

> For two or three hours a day he went round-and-round an oblong of wood with a railing around it. He leaned on the railing, and hand-over-hand he talked, laughed, and dragged his legs after him . . .
>
> . . . One night Franklin and Eleanor came to visit with me in Mattapoisett. Two men carried him in to a seat at the dining-room table. He told the men not to return until 9:30.
>
> When dinner was over, Franklin pushed back his chair and said, "See me get into the next room." He got down on the floor and went in on his hands and knees and got up into another chair himself.
>
> It seems that Dr. McDonald taught his patients this way of helping themselves so they would have a feeling of freedom to move if necessary. . . .

This was four years after the attack. He was still not defeated, still trying. And his most considerable effort was still to come. That, of course, was at Warm Springs in Georgia. This was at least a pleasanter experience, as were also his several houseboat winters cruising among the Florida Keys. There he could fish and while away hours lazily in the sun as well as exercise in the warm water.

There his mind was enough at rest so that characteristic projects began to drift into and out of his thoughts. This time they took a new form suitable to a man who was chained to a chair. He would write. This he could do sitting down. After all, Uncle Ted had done it, and had not he himself been editorial writer for *The Crimson?*

He started a history of the United States. Telling me about it years afterward—I had heard of it and asked him how far he had got—he laughed and said that it had been "something to do." "But I had a real idea," he went on. "I thought all our histories lacked movement and a sense of direction. The nation was clearly going somewhere right from the first. I thought I could do better with that idea than had been done before."

[1] P. 589.

His history began too far back—with the explorers. It seemed to him, having written some fourteen pages, that the job would be longer than he could endure. He gave it up; sitting in the sun with his stamps or idly fishing, he never picked up the tale again, though the numerous emendations in the surviving draft show how often he thought of it. This abandoned effort is the evidence that Franklin was not a writing man as Uncle Ted had been. When he was President and in the midst of war he would betray to Harry Hopkins some chagrin that his colleague Winston Churchill was so skilled at an art he himself did not possess. I myself think that if that history had gone on to a successful end Franklin might well never have become President. The satisfactions of authorship are an end in themselves. He might have discovered that; and if he had, he might possibly not have been willing to trade even the pleasures of politics for the painful joys of the writing craft. But he lacked the talent; and, bitter or not, the recognition was accepted.

It was warm water that drew Franklin to Warm Springs. He could stay at his everlasting exercises longer in the warmth, and the withered muscles might come to life again when they were buoyed up and had less load to assume. The Springs in Georgia were not only warm, the water was heavy with minerals; and this, too, helped to carry the burden. After years of effort elsewhere Franklin first believed that he felt life in his feet there and first had real reason to think that he might fight free of his crutches, then his canes, and at last be able to walk alone.

The possibilities of the place were first suggested to him by George Foster Peabody, who had an interest in a dilapidated inn there. He had heard accounts of the remarkable improvement of a polio victim from exercising in the warm water, and had passed the information on to Franklin. In October 1924 he went there for a three-week stay and a first trial of the cure.

Eleanor went with him on this trip. The children were gradually growing up and the succession of boys going to Groton had begun. Currently James and Elliott were there, with Franklin Jr. and John yet to enter. Until now Eleanor had been separated from him a good deal while he sought relief. Especially she could not often join him on the *Larooco* in Florida waters. But while he was acutely ill and bedridden, and in his first year of struggle, she had resisted despair and defeat along with him. She had hardly been out of call. When she had not been there, Louis Howe had; and this care of a helpless man created an alliance which was to last for life. Until then Eleanor had been something less than enthusiastic about the wispy, wheezy little man who had clung to Franklin like a burr. She came to appreciate him now, and gradually appreciation became the fondness which joined endeavor so often leaves behind even when the efforts are over.

It was these two who fought a dangerous secondary engagement with Sara. The elder woman saw her chance. She would now persuade Franklin to leave all the unbecoming activities in which he had become entangled and retire to Springwood. The house had been remodeled to his order; the library was a gracious setting for a leisured invalid; and in summer there were the lawns and the trees, grown older and less well tended now, but the same ones he had loved as a boy. The dowager eyes shot fire. Her boy should not be tortured back into public life; he must be resigned to her care.

Of course the critical engagements of this campaign went on in Franklin's mind, but that the betraying restfulness of Springwood was appealing was too obvious even to be mentioned. Eleanor and Louis accepted battle where it had to be fought. They bullied, shamed, hauled, and lifted Franklin out of his bed and into his braces and exercises. He soon responded. Presently he had to be restrained rather than encouraged. But their early urging was crucial. With their help and, as he was certain, with divine help too, he entered life again on its own terms. He asked no favors and rejected any that were tendered.

Warm Springs was the last of his experiments. It seemed so likely to give him back his legs that he accepted it as a permanent part of his environment. To Eleanor's slight dismay, he adopted it also as a project. Before he died so quietly in a small house he had built there in 1932, it would be what Roosevelts made of everything they took an interest in, the most outstanding thing of its kind. It became the most famous of all treatment centers for polio victims. Compared with the scraggly, dilapidated old resort it had been before the Roosevelt magic was applied, the transformation was astounding. That story must be left to one side. It too caused a good deal of controversy at one time or another. But no one can say that it was not a magnificent achievement or that the crippled Franklin did not create it. There are those who still say that it was done, as all Roosevelt projects were, to glorify its creator. Perhaps there was that about it. I myself have not been able to separate that motive from the sheer builder's instinct which in this, as in so many other instances, was at work. It remains true that thousands of sufferers have benefited from its care, and millions more from its amazing offspring, the National Foundation for Infantile Paralysis. That seems to me an overwhelming argument.

Before going on to the main business from which Franklin was diverted temporarily by treacheries of disease and the struggle to recover, I must tell about one more of his significant contacts with the economic system—the Construction Council. I must do this because it so clearly follows from the cloudy speech we saw him making at Troy in 1912

and so clearly foreshadows the policy embodied in the National
covery Administration in 1933. The experience between 1922 and
with the Council served one very good purpose: it taught him that
purely voluntary self-regulation did not work. When it came to organizing NRA, the next obvious device in the scale, moving out from complete laissez faire, was "partnership with industry," a phrase obviously
intended to soften the fact of government intervention. Many of the
quarrels of that time would center in the extent of intervention: would
government be the senior or the junior partner? As we have seen, Franklin was disillusioned about competition as an organizing principle, even
as modified by the earnest attempts at regulation of the past fifty years.
It was time to abandon it and go on to the co-operation that would
ensure the "liberty of the community."

NRA would in its time be abandoned, and before his first presidential
term was over Franklin would revert to the old policy of regulation.
But that would be an expedient action, not one he believed could be
permanent for modern industry. This whole train of events clearly began back in 1922, when he undertook to help the construction industry
organize itself. Even then, after a little experience, he saw that some
government aid was necessary.

Franklin seems to have approached the then Secretary of Commerce
in a gingerly way; but just at that time Herbert Hoover was having his
troubles with the Supreme Court about trade associations—of which
this was one of many—and he refused any encouragement, even what
Franklin had requested, which was only the collection and dissemina-
tion of statistics. Of course Hoover did not mention the Court; he based
his refusal on quite other grounds—that businesses could organize more
successfully with government left out. Government inspiration, he said,
would scare off co-operators.

When Franklin's proposal was turned down by Hoover, he announced
that the Council itself would issue a weekly forecast of building conditions so that members could be guided in planning. It was never done;
he could not get the funds. In fact he got very little co-operation from
the constructors, so little that at the end he felt that his efforts had
been completely frustrated and that voluntary self-regulation was not
the answer to "industrial chaos," as he had hoped. The attempt to
smooth out the curve of boom and bust in building operations failed.

I do not suggest that Franklin undertook and carried on this work
with the Construction Council in order to learn about business behavior,
or that he did it because he foresaw that when he became President
an industrial organization policy would be needed. He undertook it for
a much simpler reason; it was another way of occupying himself in a
semi-public role of considerable importance and attended with appropriate publicity. The effect he wanted was much the same as that

143

Good

resulting from his Boy Scout, American Legion, and Cathedral of St. John enterprises. It was incidental that a future statesman learned something of importance. Of all his interim experiences in the years of exile which were not directly political, this had the most significance for the future.

Some time before he formally ended his presidency of the Council it had ceased to have much present interest for him; he was busy again with politics—not because he anticipated re-entry into public life as soon as it happened, but because his influence in the party was obviously growing and sooner or later, he could see, he was to come into the central role for which he had waited so long. As a matter of historical interest, it is amazing how persistently and how energetically he participated in political counsels between 1920 and 1928. For one who held no office and sought none, those eight years were surprisingly crowded with political correspondence, with counseling, with planning and maneuvering, and, on occasion, with spectacular participations.

Of these last, the most important were his appearances at the national conventions in 1924 and 1928. In both of them he was a prominent figure, the more so because he was regarded as a gallant, almost heroic, survivor of personal disaster, and because he sought nothing for himself. This last is an attitude politicians cannot understand and they are therefore intrigued by it. When Roosevelt made his "Happy Warrior" speech in 1924 supported by his crutches, and when he appeared at Houston in 1928 with only canes, there was no one in the whole assembly who did not note the change and feel for him the kind sympathy an exhibition of sheer courage can always command. But, besides, both addresses were carefully devised. They had upon them his own mark. It was recognized. The New York *Times* correspondent said of the Houston speech that it was "high-bred":

There was nothing strained or fantastic or extravagant in what he said. It was the address of a fair minded and cultivated man, avoiding the usual perils of national convention oratory and discussing in an intelligent way the qualifications which should be sought for in the President of the United States. . . .

This was the way the original "Happy Warrior" speech in 1924 had been received also. Since these addresses were nominating speeches for Al Smith, they point up the long support Franklin gave to the Smith cause. It is interesting to follow this during the twenties as Smith consolidated his hold on the New York State electorate. Smith's reign began with the victory in 1922, when he was elected by the biggest plurality in the history of the state; and it went on—with one defeat—until he ran for President in 1928. In September of 1922 Franklin held a reception for Smith at Hyde Park, and the county sent a wholly Smith delegation to the state convention. This was the year when Hearst would have got the nomination for United States senator if Smith had not refused to run with him. A compromise resulted in the nomination of Dr. Royal S. Copeland, a Hearst medical columnist, with whom Smith would run, and Franklin became honorary chairman of Copeland's campaign committee.[2]

That was the most he could do in 1922, but by 1924 he had recovered sufficiently so that he could become the active manager of Smith's pre-convention campaign. It failed, but it brought Franklin great credit as a practical manager. Smith was still governor when in 1928 he was given the nomination for the presidency, after Franklin's speech, on the first ballot. It is not strange that Smith, who was worried even about New York, felt certain that Franklin would strengthen the ticket if he would make the run for governor. The only thing strange about it—or which seemed strange at the time—was that Franklin consented. He was very generally considered to be beyond the governorship stage. He was a national statesman, recognized and deferred to—not far from the number-one man among the Democrats. In every election year there were suggestions of his nomination for something, usually the United States senatorship. And it was at no time unlikely that the Democrats might turn to him in convention and nominate him out of hand for the presidency. This was so even in 1924. A writer for the New York *Herald Tribune* who signed himself "Looker On" wrote a piece on July 1, 1924, the day after the balloting began. He said:

. . . While the results of the futile ballots were droned from the platform in the Garden yesterday, there sat in the exact center of the great hall the one man whose name would stampede the convention were he put in nomination. He is the only man to whom the contending factions could turn . . . And that man does not want the nomination and actually would be alarmed if he knew what people were saying about him in the delegations . . . From the time Roosevelt made his speech in nomination of Smith . . . he has been easily the foremost figure on floor or platform . . . without the slightest intention or desire to do so, he has done for himself what he could not do for his candidate. . . .

I may be risking the suspicion that I have imposed on the successive events of those years an interpretation to be got only from seeing their outcome. Also, I do not minimize the intensity of Franklin's concentration on regaining the use of his legs. He thought the Warm Springs regime, if persisted in, would eventually rehabilitate the lost muscles. Nevertheless, it is fact that Smith—and with Franklin's active concurrence—made his successive bids for power in 1924 and 1928, when no Democrat could have won. He and McAdoo killed each other off in

[2] Both would recall this in 1933 and later when Franklin was pressing for food-and-drug legislation that Hearst and his advertisers opposed.

1924 and left the field to John W. Davis, who made a miserable showing even with La Follette splitting the Republicans again as Uncle Ted had in 1912. It did seem, with that defection taking place, as though a Democrat had a chance. But "keeping cool with Coolidge" was exactly what the nation wanted to do and did. In 1928, with Hoover as the unusually attractive Republican nominee, and party differences healed, the professionals—including Franklin—could hardly have felt that the Democrats had a chance.

Smith was hopelessly defeated. Even the solid South was split by the religious issue. He was politically dead from that moment. But the Democratic day would come; and with Smith out, who was there to succeed? No one could miss the obvious answer. And especially since by then Franklin had been governor of New York for four years and Smith had been retired to private business.

It is an indication of the change in Eleanor's life that she was a delegate to the State Democratic Convention in 1928 at which Franklin was nominated for the governorship. It was a change that had begun during Franklin's convalescence and was partly due to Louis Howe, who acted as her mentor in political education. When Franklin's activities were mostly confined to correspondence, she could be a kind of substitute. She went in by way of organizing the Democratic women, but presently she had earned a place of her own in party councils.

When Smith had been nominated in 1928 there was a decided increase in the volume of suggestions that Franklin take his place as governor. It at once appeared that the state convention might nominate him. Franklin replied, when he could not ignore the pleas, that he had a private campaign to complete. He was at last, he said, getting some response from his withered legs. If he really thought that, it was an illusion, born of hope so long deferred. He still could not take a step without braces, and he never would. He was keeping up his everlasting struggle. He was forty-six now, and he had been fighting his stubborn legs for seven years. He seems to have been convinced that two more years of his rigorous devotion to exercises would see him on his way. It is not thought now that he would ever, under any circumstances, have come any farther. But he was not yet resigned to being a cripple. Or so he told those who urged him to become a candidate.

But there was—as always in his case—another consideration. All three, Franklin, Eleanor, and Louis Howe, were realistic enough to recognize that 1928 would be an overwhelmingly Republican year. Franklin often said that Republicanism was bound to end in a debacle and that when it did the Democratic opportunity would open up. But that had not yet happened.

He became more and more convinced during the weeks before the state convention that Smith would lose the presidency, and he was more and more determined not to be drawn into the campaign for the governorship. Louis told a newspaperman during the summer that Franklin would run for the governorship in 1932 and for the presidency in 1936, but there is no direct evidence that Franklin saw it this way. It may be that he thought the moment for the governorship had passed. His candidacy for the presidency would be just as valid in 1932, with Smith out of the running, whether he had been governor or not. And defeat in 1928 might be fatal.

But Smith was desperately determined, and Franklin was finally, after frantic efforts during which he resisted stubbornly, half persuaded by the unanimity of the pressure; and when the convention nominated him and then adjourned, he was in for it. He had deliberately absented himself and was in Warm Springs to emphasize his intentness on recovery rather than politics. Louis, moreover, was in New York. If Louis had been with him in Warm Springs, it is likely that the refusal would have been stiffer. As it was, that little man could only exhort and plead by telephone. When he saw that he had lost, he was far from sure that this would not be the end of all his long efforts. Franklin would lose; and a loser in politics has a heavy handicap for any future preference.

Once nominated, Franklin took the bit in his teeth and behaved in New York as he had behaved during the campaign of 1920 throughout the nation. He had a smaller territory to cover, and his energetic attack could take him into hundreds of localities and put him in direct touch with millions of voters. When it was over and he had won, even though Smith had lost, the rest of what was to happen to him was marked out for all to see.

The Roosevelt who became governor of New York was not even yet a finished product even if he was forty-six—the age at which Uncle Ted had been running for his second term. But he was far nearer it than he had been when he had run for the vice-presidency with Cox. There were warring impulses in him still, general policy decisions yet to be made, and a clear view of the future yet to be formulated. But he was confirmed in his general belief that his party must be a progressive one and that he was destined to be its leader. That was enough to go on as he entered his new stage. It was the kind of entry he always made to new stages, uncertain concerning what was ahead, perhaps even a little thoughtless, but eager to succeed and certain that he could master the circumstances he was about to meet.

He was to do double duty now for four years—he was to be the governor of New York, true, but he was also to be a candidate for the presidency every moment of that service. Nothing he did would be done without this end in view. This being so, it would hardly be expected that he would be a notable governor, and he was not. But he was a

147

notable candidate. That was to be proved by success in being nominated and elected in 1932.

Looking back down the years from 1928 to 1910, the student, as he surveys them, realizes with something of a shock that there are, after all, only eighteen. So much seems to be crowded into them that a lifetime might well be needed for so many and such varied experiences. Think of all the political battles, if nothing else; all the conventions attended, and all the preliminary maneuverings. But the interludes actually were long—the Navy service was seven and a half years, the employment in New York about the same length. So the appearance of crowding comes from all the efforts and activities that were directed toward keeping the political leaders aware that there was a Roosevelt in the wings waiting to come on stage and the public in a mood to receive him. It had been a consistent and single-minded progress, full of adventures, yet cautiously pursued. In retrospect, the risks seem fewer than they must have seemed when they were undertaken—the attack on Tammany, the attachment to Wilson, the reconciliation with Tammany, and, when Murphy died, the rapprochement with Al Smith. But every one had worked out exactly as it had been planned. The timing may have been uncertain, but that was because extraneous forces had made variation necessary. The Republicans, however, were sure to stumble into trouble, even if the occasion was delayed. And even before the expected trouble came, Franklin was back in public life, more strategically placed than he had been before, still waiting for the debacle to happen. It would be delayed only one year longer. Then there would begin the three-year immolation of Hoover, the Republican, and the corresponding rise of Franklin, who was the Democratic alternative.

8

Judge Rosenman has written a firsthand account of Franklin's approach to the governorship.[1] Rosenman was one of Al Smith's young assistants who was loaned to Franklin and worked at his side throughout the campaign of 1928. Later, when he came to assess the relevant content of Franklin's campaign speeches, his inaugural, and his messages to the legislature, he was struck by the similarities in the declarations about public policy with those that were later given the generic name, "the New Deal."

The impression of similarity was intensified by a review of the commitments to policy during Franklin's second term as governor. The significance of this, of course, is that the great depression arrived in 1929 and that Franklin made his second (1930) gubernatorial campaign in its aftermath. A catastrophe of this magnitude refused to be ignored. Franklin's acknowledgment of its existence and his suggestions for remedies do indeed remarkably foreshadow the New Deal. The anticipations are not of detail; they are topical and general. The content of each item changed or remained to be filled in, but it is true that not very many new categories were added in Washington to those worked out in Albany.

Rosenman catalogues this program in a few concise paragraphs:

After Roosevelt became President, writers and commentators expressed surprise at the rapid succession of legislative proposals urged by him during the "first hundred days" of his Presidency in 1933. . . . Many have wondered where they all came from in such a short time. The fact is that the basic

---

[1] In *Working with Roosevelt* (New York: Harper, 1952), Chapter II, "The First Campaign for Governor." The chapter following has the significant title, "The Genesis of the New Deal: The First Term as Governor." The relevant documents can be found in *The Public Papers and Addresses of Franklin D. Roosevelt*. One set of these (2 vols.) contains the governorship papers. The other (13 vols.) contains a selection of these and the presidential papers. The references here are all to the presidential papers. These were published at different times and by different publishers. The first four are numbered volumes; the rest are designated by the year they cover.

philosophy and social objectives of the New Deal proposals can all be found in Governor Roosevelt's speeches and messages during the four years *before* he became President. . . .

In [them] you will find proposals for appropriate state action in the same fields in which he later urged action by the Congress: minimum wages and maximum hours, old age insurance, unemployment relief through public works and other means, unemployment insurance, regulation of public utilities, stricter regulations of banks and of the use of other people's money, improved housing through the use of public subsidies, farm relief, public development of water power, cheaper electricity especially in rural areas, greater use of state funds for education, crippled persons and the mentally and physically handicapped, repeal of prohibition laws, reforms in the administration of justice, reforestation and proper land use.

You will also find extended discussion of many of the themes that he was later to use so frequently that they came to be well known as a part of the Roosevelt philosophy: the interdependence of all groups of the population; regional planning; bringing industry into rural areas; conservation of natural resources; separation of legislative from executive functions.[2]

Thus Judge Rosenman, who was more intimately concerned in formulating these ideas than any other individual. But even if his testimony were not available, the same conclusion would necessarily be arrived at from the documents. Franklin's fallow years did indeed have their uses. It is impossible to imagine the vice-presidential candidate of 1920 putting together a program of this sort. In those years he and the Democratic party shared a poverty of ideas which only the depression seemed to relieve. It should perhaps be repeated that as a governor's agenda it was tentative and gradually reached, that its content was sometimes inconsistent and that Franklin was as yet not clear in his mind about the division of responsibilities between state and federal government; but, as Judge Rosenman says, it indicates that "his basic philosophies and principles had been pretty well formed."

If after their service the members of the Brains Trust of 1932 had been inclined to overmagnify their contributions to the New Deal (as I think I may say they were not), ample evidence that they were merely helpers existed in Franklin's already formulated program. The governor's mind may have been a *tabula rasa,* but the *tabula* had clearly labeled pages to be written on. He did not very much care *what kind* of farm relief, or *how* the principle of cheap and universally available power was arrived at. Banking regulations might be of any practicable sort, and the methods used for relieving the unemployed were open to argument. But he was committed to *some* action in all these matters. That he was committed does indicate, as Judge Rosenman insists, that Franklin had identified his problems, or at least many of them, and had considered some of the solutions. When he had been out of office, with

[2] Op. cit., pp. 31–32.

very cautious

no actual prospects of one, and when he appeared to be pretty much an opportunist looking for an opening, he still had imagined himself in charge. He knew in what direction moves ought to be made.

There is further significance in his not having been committed to a program before he was nominated in 1928, and it is interesting to see how much and what part of the whole he ventured to formulate in the first campaign. For Franklin, it must never be forgotten, was a politician and so knew what his first concern must be. I was amused to discover in Judge Rosenman's book the report of a remark about this, which was similar to one made once to me. It explains a good deal. Franklin, now President, was speaking to Rosenman:

You know the first thing a President has to do in order to put through good legislation? He has to get elected! If I were now back on the porch at Hyde Park as a private citizen, there is very little I could do about any of the things that I have worked on. So don't throw votes away by rushing the gun—unless there is some good sound reason. You have to get the votes first—then you can do the good work.[3]

The point about this is that the Roosevelt I have been writing about up to now, and the one who was to be governor of New York for four years, was on his way to the presidency. He was carefully not saying or doing anything that would jeopardize progress toward this ultimate place. If he had, it would have lost him the opportunity to become the leader and teacher of the American people. It would have been unjustified in a practical sense; and it would, besides, have been immoral because it would have risked defeat for the reconstructive measures he believed were needed if the American dream was not to end in a chaos of individualism. A strong government, directed by a courageous executive, had to furnish the leadership and bring about unity. Who that strong executive was to be was ever in his mind.

Franklin became a thorough political professional—how thorough only those who worked with him really knew. But even casual study reveals the persistence of the political criteria in all he did. Being consciously guided as he was by these considerations—that is, the arrival at and the maintenance of a position of power—the fact that in the fallow years he gradually sorted out of the available possibilities the items enumerated by Judge Rosenman and that he gradually revealed them during his governorship shows that he considered this a platform he could run on. This, he had made up his mind, was what the American people could be persuaded to approve. What was omitted from the program was, on the contrary, what would have resulted in more opposition than support. I find it remarkable that all this should have been

[3] Ibid., p. 30.

worked out in pre-depression days, not in detail, but substantially. It has to be accepted as the platform of a presidential candidate.

Only incidentally, the historian is tempted to say, was it regarded by Franklin himself as a program for the times, a remedial agenda. Disparaging comments are sometimes made. But this is to overlook his theory of leadership. The leader was not to take chances with his gaining of power; but he was to discover—and this was the most subtle of the political arts—what people wanted, people in great numbers, a majority, even if they did not themselves yet know it. What was latent in the public mind was the most important thing of all for a politician to be able to divine. If he had the talent for this, a good deal of the rest would be added unto him. And what he lacked would very likely be forgiven.

Yes, most easily forgiven would be omissions; and, remembering this, the political leader ought never to allow himself to be "smoked out." This, too, Franklin never did allow, even at the urging of old hands, who, although they should have known better, were more inclined than he to panic in emergency, to feel the pressure of hostile questioners and repeated criticisms in the press. He picked his own issues and his own time. He had the talent. It amounted to genius.

Thus equipped in principle and method, Franklin was able on this first campaign trip to amaze skeptical young Sam Rosenman, who had been appointed by Al Smith to be his mentor. Sam had been counsel to Smith as governor. It has been remarked before that Tammany could on occasion nurture talent and public spirit. It was done unknowingly. Tammany was a practical school of old-fashioned, hard-boiled politics. It was inherently corrupt because it sold governmental favors for money. But there were always those who refused personally to accept pay other than as public servants. The price of their preferment was that they would go along. They would not oppose; they would, up to a point, join in doing what the chieftains directed them to do. They helped change municipal regulations and state legislation without examining reasons, closing their eyes to exploitation. They voted as they were told. As they became trusted they rose in the organization. They then gained a certain independence and, using their Tammany connections, could become reformers of a sort. The outstanding example of this process at this time was Al Smith, and Robert Wagner was another almost as conspicuous. Younger men, among whom was Sam Rosenman, felt themselves justified in following in the same way.

Sam was indeed just such another. He had been a protégé of a notorious ward leader and had risen because of his Tammany services. Jimmy Hines, his sponsor, afterward went to jail for proven and flagrant corruption, but it was a taint that never touched Sam except as it generally did everyone who was part of the organization. He was young to be counsel to the governor, but he was able and eager; and Franklin accepted his help without question. As a gubernatorial candidate, coerced into running by the organization, he was willing to emphasize the organization's responsibility to him.

It was different when it came to emphasizing his responsibility to the organization. This was confined to his enthusiastic support of Smith. When he began to develop his own state campaign it turned out to be very much his own, a foretaste of what his governorship was to be like. He did make his support of Smith conspicuous. He began, even before his own nomination for governor, by making addresses in a number of strategic cities. And his first few speeches as candidate were so much oriented to Smith support that Maurice Bloch, the state chairman, protested.[4]

But that this enthusiasm for Smith was like a number of Franklin's attachments has already been hinted. Like others of them, too, it began tentatively and reached full force only when it became altogether plain that it was right and useful. It does not need to be insisted that he did approve of Smith, whose long record as governor was as notable for practical reform as any in New York's history. A long list of extremely detailed and effective regulatory laws had been passed and their enforcing organizations set up, usually as a result of public pressure built up by Smith to coerce reluctant Republican legislatures. Employers generally, and capitalists of all sorts, resented him; but so long overdue were his remedial measures and so effective were his appeals for them that public approval was overwhelming.

Franklin had first begun to realize how necessary this program was by people Eleanor brought to him. This was one of her most useful functions, then and later. In this case it opened Franklin's eyes to a range of affairs completely unknown to him before the effort to educate him began. Frances Perkins speaks of it in *The Roosevelt I Knew:*

In the years of his illness Mrs. Roosevelt developed a remarkable reportorial quality. She had always been an observant woman. She learned to be more observant and to be able to repeat in detail what she saw and heard. This was of priceless help to him, handicapped as he was, longing to be in touch with the people, and having to learn to take vicarious instead of direct personal experience. . . . With great perspicacity she brought him people with whom he could share the things going on in his mind. She realized she could introduce new and stimulating ideas through people who were thoughtful, had had a variety of experience, and wanted to know what he thought. She began to take out to see him two friends in the Women's Trade Union League —Rose Schneiderman, and Maude Schwartz. These intelligent trade unionists made a great many things clear that he would hardly have known in any other way. . . . He saw [trade unionism] in a new light. . . . He had never

---

[4] "Tell the candidate," a telegram to Rosenman in Buffalo said, "that he is not running for President but for Governor; and tell him to stick to state issues." Rosenman, op. cit., p. 17.

understood . . . the purpose of the movement. He had neither seen the background of exploitation in industry from which the movement had grown in England and in this country, nor had he been a technical academic student of the movement itself. I doubt that he had ever read any of the standard works on trade unionism.[5]

Smith had also been an earnest if not consecrated worker for conservation.[6] On all such counts his predecessor had Franklin's approval. But more than anything else he felt bound to declare himself because of the kind of opposition which had defeated Smith's bid for the nomination in 1924 and was now threatening his defeat for election in 1928. This was, as Franklin bluntly called it, "bigotry." Smith was a Roman Catholic, a devoted, even a militant, one. And it was freely being said in the "Bible belt"—and in plenty of other Protestant strongholds in the rural areas—that to elect him would "bring the Pope into the White House." It was an undeniably liberal and spiritual impulse that caused Franklin to react again and again to this opposition with an otherwise unprecedented directness, an almost bitter denunciation.

This genuinely felt support for Smith must not, however, prevent the recognition that it had a hard core of political utility. Smith had to have his run before another Democrat could have the right of way. It had been Franklin's judgment—and that of Louis Howe—that Smith ought to have had the nomination in 1924. He would not, they had thought, be elected then unless things went badly for the Republicans or unless Coolidge did not run again. But Smith's traditional two terms would be over by 1936 if he should win this time; if he did not, he would have had all the chances to which he could be thought to be entitled.

He had to be got out of the way. That was the inescapable fact. To support him was to help him on a course that must be followed. To support him, also, was to earn his favor. And if he was to be nominated, even if he was not elected he would have much to say about his successor. It could not be anticipated, even by so shrewd a forecaster as

[5] Pp. 30–31. Frances, who was at this time Industrial Commissioner of the state of New York, a body which was one of the products of Smith's regime, and who was to become a member of Franklin's state cabinet, naturally speaks of what she knew. What she does not mention is that there were others who were responsible for Franklin's developing social awareness. Henry Morgenthau, Jr., brought him into touch with rural problems, first those of conservation, then of rural sociology; and Louis Howe, as well as others, including Doc O'Connor, brought innumerable businessmen, bankers, and industrialists as well as politicians to see and talk with him; and now as later, much of his view of the world was shaped by the lawyers who, after all, he most admired and with whom he was always in somewhat diffident touch. This had already begun to include those who had helped him on power problems; it had also included Frankfurter and Moley.
[6] He was an East Side boy; the regulation of sweatshops was something to engage the emotions; conservation was admirable, but it was not something to excite a passionate drive.

Franklin, just what would happen—that Smith would exhaust his credit with the Democrats in one woefully unsuccessful campaign, so that the way would be cleared for a successor by 1932. Franklin's strategy was obviously based all along on Smith's winning either in 1924 or 1928. That he might not would upset Franklin's timetable.

It can thus be reasoned that there was more than met the eye in Franklin's working for Smith. The calculating second man might feel himself in line to succeed, but he must do something also in his own behalf. In this instance it came to nothing. It was luck more than good management that would bring about the joining of favorable events in 1932; and in 1928, Franklin was still quite unaware of that coming climax. He hoped for Smith's success, not only because he approved his work as governor and because he resented the rising of religious prejudice against the candidate, but because Smith had to have his day, get through and get out of the way.

It was Maurice Bloch, the state chairman, who had sent Sam Rosenman on campaign with Franklin, even though Smith had suggested it. At any rate, Bloch felt entitled to give directions through Sam. Franklin perhaps heard with some approval what Bloch had telegraphed about his sticking to his own campaign. He had certainly done his whole duty by Smith; no one would question that. He could turn his campaigning now to the issues and the methods he judged to be those that would win his own contest. He undoubtedly continued to think that the national and the state campaigns would result in the success of the same party. It would be most unusual for the one to succeed and the other not to; at any rate, he went to work with that startling individual energy, that exploitation of the Roosevelt personality, which came so natural to him. And he found upstate New York a peculiarly agreeable campaign ground.

He started off, as Sam recalls, by touring the southern tier of counties by way of the Erie Railroad. Sam began his job of assisting in a skeptical mood; he had heard that his candidate was aristocratic, cold, aloof— all that sort of thing—which shows that he had been indoctrinated by the Tammanyites; it was from them that the stories had come. But Sam was in for a surprise. The man he had to deal with was unexpectedly sensitive, voluble, and helpful. Sam had only to listen as the first speeches were made in Binghamton, Wellsville, and Jamestown. Franklin spoke without notes or any apparent preparation. But then what he said was what he had been saying all along; aside from local references, it was in support of Smith. This was familiar country to the man who had been raised in Dutchess County. And Franklin needed no tutoring in his approach to its people.

These upstate counties—the region where the Finger Lakes lie, long, gray, and quiet, between hills so high as almost to rate as mountains—

had a kind of loveliness that never failed to move Franklin. It was a country that had been abused—overfarmed. As migration from New England had taken place a hundred years before, moving along the water-level route of the Erie Canal, driblets of it had turned southward down the numerous valleys. Pioneers had settled in them and on the enclosing hillsides. For several decades at the beginning of the nineteenth century, local historians say, there was always smoke by day and fire by night among those hills as the forests were burned off to make farmland. Gradually an economy of self-sufficient farm and village life was established. It had some six or seven decades of prosperity before decline set in. For the decline, western competition, as the plains were settled, was mostly blamed. But equally responsible were the abuses for which the pioneers were themselves responsible. By 1928 the pastures were overgrown, the hayfields were choked with the weeds which grew better than grass in eroded soil, and the homesteads—the white houses built out of the famous carpenter's book—and the great red barns calculated to hold a long winter's supply of feed for livestock had fallen into miserable condition. On top of the secular decline in New York farming there had been imposed the general agricultural depression of the post-war years.

The towns along the Erie Railroad showed the poverty of their hinterlands. The red brick and white clapboard buildings were shamefully shabby; there was a pervading pessimism that had turned to a kind of sour reactionary determination that what was left must be held onto. It was hard-shell Republican country. But Franklin knew it, and knew its people, as he knew little else in the world. From these hills several of those who had been with him in the Sheehan fight back in 1911 in Albany had come, and over this territory he had campaigned to support them as the bosses had brought punishment to bear.

The way Franklin responded to the immediate challenge of this, his first campaign since 1920, was revealing. It showed how natural it was for him to do this kind of thing—that he moved into its trying rhythm with a smoothness and ease which are born in some men. It showed that he had been too long away from the sights and sounds of political battle; there was a special kind of joy in getting back to it. It showed, also, that it was a happy chance which had forced him into a state campaign quite against his judgment and his wishes.

Franklin was, moreover, on the verge of a belated love affair with the Empire State, and he moved into its mysteries as a lover might woo a mistress—sensitively, warily, but with a commanding grace. This was the deeper motivation for his campaign. It goes far to explain its ardor. Throughout the next four years, from a very powerful position indeed, he would do all he could to repair the damage done by the pioneers in the upstate country. His restless mind would look and listen for suggestions. He would organize, he would urge legislation, and he would get some results.

Because of Franklin's governorship the hill country of New York would be brought measurably nearer to sound land uses and useful reconstruction. Not very much, actually, could be done in four years, but much could be started. The visitor going about the state can see how many changes dating back to his time were begun. There would for all the future be an incomparable chain of parks, among them the great Allegany, Catskill, and Adirondack reserves; and scattered everywhere there would be recreation spots: along the Great Lakes, beside the Finger Lakes, among the hills and gorges, and bordering the state's swift, clear brooks and rivers.

The villages and small cities of the hill country would not grow much any more—one of Franklin's less practical conceptions, and, at the same time, most characteristic, would be his notion that industry could be returned in small units to rural sites with benefit both to industry and the country—but decades later, after not only his governorship but also his presidency, new paint would be on the houses and the barns, the streets and roads would be improved, and the stores would be prosperous. The decline would at least have been arrested. For this, many remedies would have been responsible, not by any means all of them Franklin's. But he would have presided over many of the changes, and they would always be associated with his name.

When the candidate got to Buffalo on his first campaigning journey, he put Sam to work. He was to talk now about something with which he was not familiar. There was to be some use for those suitcases full of documents and data that had been lugged along in anticipation of speech writing. Franklin casually indicated that tomorrow he could use a speech on labor. Young as he was, Sam was not an unpracticed ghost writer; but Smith's had been a different method. For Smith the facts and their related ideas had to be gathered and arranged so that he could absorb them. He was unable to use written memoranda; he had to be told. Franklin, however, could read. He could have a written speech before him—written by someone else but reworked by himself—and make it sound extemporaneous and sincere. Even in this first state campaign he had no trouble doing this; in later and busier times it became a well-mastered technique.

It was not easy for Franklin to break in ghost writers who could be helpful in this. He took a lot of pains with Sam on this trip. By the end of several strenuous weeks Sam had acquired a valuable facility, and Franklin commanded his services from then to the end of his life except for his first four years in Washington. There would be other successive ghosts, some of them much more competent than Sam in a literary way, and some of them better economists or political scientists.

Sam would break in most of them, teach them Franklin's way, and with most of them make a team that would serve Franklin well.[7]

It seems necessary to explore at some length the methodology of campaigning and the content of the addresses used in this appeal for the New York governorship. There are in it so many anticipations of later methods and policies that their examination at this stage is necessary to an understanding of their origin and their evolution. For instance, I find it interesting that Franklin was enough at home in the subject matter of agriculture to make a wholly extemporaneous address in Jamestown, with some apt references to the local situation, but with unhesitating comments also on national policy; but that when he talked about labor in Buffalo, education and welfare in Rochester, or even parks in New York City, he took the precaution of having before him a prepared manuscript. His pores had been open to agricultural discussion; on other matters he might have picked up something, but not in an organized way. And much had already been done by Smith for which it was appropriate to claim Democratic credit.

Even on agricultural relief, however, he had not fought through the brambles to any sharp policy. What he had to say—and what he repeated throughout the campaign—was a mixture of what might be called back-to-the-land-ism together with what we later learned to call Peekism. The first of these will be understood without further description as an echo of utopian notions out of the past—the idea that men are better off close to nature and working with their hands on their own acres. This was an old weakness with both Eleanor and Franklin and was shared by Louis Howe. They were amateurs. It would require some disappointing experience with homesteads to dispel the illusion. The second—the national policy—requires fuller explanation.

Both in 1928 and in 1932, as it turned out, agricultural policy would be an important issue. In 1928 the nation was at what proved to be the high mark of a very perilous prosperity. But even in the midst of good times the farmers were already depressed. They had not recovered from their post-war troubles. Responsible for these were (1) the sudden uselessness of the new land called into production by the demands of war, when much of the Western world had had to be fed and clothed from America; (2) the changes in diet from starches to proteins; and (3) the development of synthetic fibers. There were other contributing causes, such as the overcapitalization of farm lands in prosperous years and the complete inability of farm owners to discharge

---

[7] Curiosity concerning the ghost-writing technique is better satisfied by reading the Rosenman book than any other account. There is in it not only a full explanation of the Roosevelt method but a comparison of it with the contrasting methods of Smith and of Truman, both of whom Rosenman served in the same capacity. But of course there is much to be got, too, from Sherwood, Moley, and High, all of whom were used and wrote accounts of their service.

Rest of the
World wanted
to be self-suff.

their debts with the income from cheapened crops. A bale of cotton, a bushel of wheat, or a hundredweight of pork would now exchange for so little factory-made goods that farmers were being pressed year by year into deeper poverty. The vital productive agricultural plant was running down and many farms were being abandoned.

To argue in such a situation for a return to the land made no sense; it would not make much more sense in the depression years to argue that the unemployed could be cared for in this way. But to Franklin it seemed axiomatic that in the country they would have shelter at least and, if they would work, something to eat. It was not that simple, as he was to learn at some cost. But he resisted the lesson for a long time.

What has been referred to as Peekism did not make much more sense in the circumstances, but at least it had its origin in traditional American policy. Even its most stubborn refusal to recognize reality was understandable. The reality was that foreign markets were closed to American products. This was not only because the war was now over but because another non-military war had begun. All the importing nations had been frightened by the quick exhaustion of their food supplies and by the risks involved in dependence on America far across submarine-infested seas. They were initiating determined programs of self-sufficiency which meant paying bounties to their own farmers for raising the very products which were in surplus in America, and the creation of a synthetic-fiber industry at far greater cost than cotton from our South.

The impact of agricultural distress had been severe enough to create and hold together a farm bloc for some years past. This group had come to uneasy agreement on a program. It was well known in those years to every newspaper reader as the McNary-Haugen scheme—after the names of its sponsors in Senate and House. The McNary-Haugen bills had been in and about the Congress for years; many individuals had had a hand in shaping them; many organizations had made suggestions and taken positions on them. In them there centered the hopes, finally, of the distressed farmers of the whole nation.

But if there was one individual more than another who could claim authorship—or perhaps original sponsorship—it was a farm-implement manufacturer from the Midwest named George N. Peek. His was far from an original mind, and the ideas were more those of various agricultural economists than his own. Also, as would appear, an associate of Peek's, a former brigadier general named Hugh Johnson, had exercised a very fertile mind on the problem. At any rate, discussion, propagandizing, and appraisal of what farmers wanted or would accept had had as much to do with working out the McNary-Haugen scheme as had an honest attempt to discover a realistic cure—realistic even if hard to swallow.

Farmers censored of S E D

The nub of the trouble, the reason why a really remedial solution could not be found, was stubborn opposition to acceptance of the necessity for reducing production to accord with demand. This also was the reason for the popularity of increased exports. Peekism relied always, in one way or another, on exporting surpluses; it avoided completely the alternative of cutting down. This was partly because farmers resisted the idea but also because processors and middlemen resisted it even more.

Here we come to an important and troubling phase of the agricultural problem, one nettle no public man wanted to grasp if he could avoid it. It was one that would bedevil Franklin and his agricultural administrators throughout his regime in Washington. The processors were more influential in shaping policy than the farmers, even though powerful organizations now represented agriculture. Lobbyists for millers, packers, middlemen, and financial houses were clever and powerful. They "owned" many legislators. They could not be ignored. They were determined that there should be no reduction in the volume of products passing through their hands.

I explain all this now to make plainer much that must be spoken of later. I should also say that George Peek had gone to Houston—the Democratic meeting place in 1928—and had sold his program to Smith. It was embodied in the Democratic platform and was what Smith was committed to. Smith, however, had had a certain caution. If there was one subject about which he was conscious of complete ignorance, it was this one. And he had hedged his acceptance of the unrealistic export idea with a commitment to set up, and to accept the findings of, an agricultural commission—after he became President.

It was evident that Franklin had watched and listened to all this with interest. What he said extemporaneously at Jamestown in October is therefore of interest in itself and because of its foreshadowing of important things to come:

If you will read the Republican platform and in connection with it the speeches on farm relief made by President Coolidge, you will find that the Republican attitude . . . is covered by a general pledge of help in the first place, and secondly by the suggestion that they will work it out in some way through the expansion of the cooperative movement among the farmers. . . .

The whole plan is very vague; and when you come down to what the agricultural interests in the wheat and cotton and corn belt States are chiefly interested in, namely, the question of dealing with surplus crops, both the Republican platform and the Republican candidate have been singularly reticent. Nobody knows today what the exact attitude of Mr. Hoover is. . . .

On the other side, the Democrats, both in their platform and through their candidate, have recognized that the crux of the matter, the meat of the cocoa-

160

nut, is dealing with this problem of the surplus crops. Governor Smith in his campaign speeches has pledged definitely that if he is elected next November sixth, he will immediately call together the best farm experts that he can find to devise a definite way and means for taking care of this exportable surplus.[8]

This seems to me almost the best of all possible illustrations to show the stage of competence Franklin had by 1928 reached in an important public issue. The extemporaneity of his speech has been emphasized because it was important that it was his own observation and thinking which had brought him to the identification of the crux of this matter—the surplus. He had not gone beyond this to any suggestion, actually, for a cure. He perhaps gave away his own acceptance of Peekism when in the last quoted sentence he called it an "exportable surplus." Nevertheless, it shows serious consideration.

He was even more assured when he turned to the state platform and his own ideas as to the state's obligation. The surplus was a national problem; but there were responsibilities at home. These, he said, centered in tax relief and a reduction in the costs of distribution. This is recognizable as Cornell doctrine. The experts there thought—and would continue to think—that this was the sort of attack to make. They were convinced laissez-faire economists, and they rejected any notion of interfering with the "laws of supply and demand." They would cause a good deal of trouble about this later on. But it was true that there were inequities to be corrected. And Franklin made the most of them. His campaign, in fact, would draw the Cornellians into his advisory family. When Henry Morgenthau, Jr., would become chairman of the Agricultural Advisory Commission which Franklin would set up as governor, the Cornellians would be most heavily leaned on. Henry, who was not an original thinker, would have his mind so monopolized by their ideas as to exclude others. But for a governor's program their advice was unexceptionable. By following it Franklin was to make a record in agriculture which would be something to point to with pride when he made his bid for the presidency.

But I must add one thing more in praise of this Jamestown speech. In it Franklin came very close indeed to stating what proved to be the single most important principle of national agricultural policy during the New Deal. This was the principle of parity. He put it this way:

I want our agricultural population . . . to be put on the same level of earning capacity as their fellow Americans who live in the cities. . . .

This was really getting close to the cause of depression as well as to

[8] The quotations from this and other 1928 campaign speeches in this chapter are from *Public Papers,* Vol. I.

the farmer's disadvantage. He got this close by his own thinking. He was indeed maturing.

It is, however, possible to cite an example—one of many—which shows far less able analysis, which is, in fact, superficial in the extreme. It is best to cite it here for comparative purposes and for the sake of completeness. It has to do with a story he told as a kind of parable. He was, he admitted, repeating something he had said back in 1920, but it still seemed to him relevant. He called it "the story of the four bears":

There are four different kinds of bears in the United States, and, of course, all these bears come under the jurisdiction of one government department or another. I think it is the brown bear that comes under the jurisdiction of the Department of the Interior, and I think the black bear comes under the Department of Agriculture; and the Alaska bear comes under the Department of Commerce; and the jurisdiction over the grizzly bear comes under the Department of War. That has been going on from time immemorial in Washington.

He went on to say that he had told this story not only to illustrate government inefficiency and the need for reorganization but because the Republicans had stolen it from him. Harding had used it, Coolidge had used it and, much to his amusement, Hoover had again trotted it out to use in his acceptance speech of last June. The Republicans had promised each time to reform the conditions illustrated by the supposed mix-up about the bears. They were no more likely to do it now than they had been in former years.

The point about the use of this story is a double one. First, it sounded like a homely illustration, simple enough for anyone to understand, of governmental inefficiency under the Republicans. Second, however, it was thoroughly meretricious and demagogic. If Franklin by 1928 did not understand the weakness of functional administrative organization, he was unfit to be governor. Did he really mean to imply that there ought to be, in the federal government, a Department of Bears where they could all be got together? That was the inference if anyone cared to make it. What a shambles the government would be if every function had its administrative corollary had been pointed out by numerous experts. Franklin's seven and a half years in the Navy had certainly brought him beyond this kind of administrative thinking.[9]

Administrative organization is an important matter; no governor or President would consider more seriously or make greater progress, in

[9] I am reminded of an acid comment made by the then chief forester, Ferdinand Silcox, when he heard of Harold Ickes' proposal to change the name of the Department of the Interior to the Department of Conservation. He awaited now, he said, someone's proposal that there should be a Department of Life in which there would be assembled all the activities relating to wildlife, child life, and night life.

the long run, than Franklin himself. When he was on the hustings, however, he catered to the know-nothing, the anti-expert weakness in his hearers. He did it more than was allowable in a responsible leader. Perhaps I exaggerate, but I find in this illustration from 1928 the beginnings of a tendency that was far more important when he was President. For instance, when he protested at Chautauqua his hatred of war and said that he would repeat "again and again and again" that so far as he could prevent it there would be none, he would be playing on fears he had no right to play on, and at a time when he knew there might be war and was actively preparing for the possibility of American participation.

In this 1928 campaign there are to be found many, even most, of the characteristics of his later days. There is the appealing charm, there is the skillful simplification of issues, there is the tremendous drive—and there is also the willingness to stretch very far the limits of truth. This is not uncommon in politicians; it is in fact almost universal among them, and perhaps it means no more than that Franklin had become a thorough technician.

In a speech in Rochester and again in Troy, he referred directly to his crippling, something he would not feel compelled to do in presidential years, being content merely to show himself in strenuous action without argument. He was not yet so sure of himself in 1928, and so he said, speaking of the need for expanding the state's welfare services, and particularly those for assisting the crippled:

I suppose that people readily will recognize that I myself furnish a perfectly good example of what can be done by the right kind of care. I dislike to use this personal example, but it happens to fit. Seven years ago in the epidemic in New York, I came down with infantile paralysis, a perfectly normal attack, and I was completely, for the moment, put out of any useful activities. By personal good fortune I was able to get the very best kind of care, and the result of having the right kind of care is that today I am on my feet.

And while I shall not vouch for the mental side of it, I am quite certain that from the physical point of view I am quite capable of going to Albany and staying there for two years.[10]

[10] Al Smith had already said all that was necessary about Franklin's physical condition. In a statement following the convention he had referred to it in this way:

Frank Roosevelt today is mentally as good as he ever was in his life. Physically he is as good as he ever was in his life. His whole trouble is his lack of muscular control of his lower limbs. But the answer to that is that a Governor does not have to be an acrobat. We do not elect him for his ability to do a double back-flip or a handspring. The work of the Governorship is brainwork. Ninety-five per cent of it is accomplished sitting at a desk. There is no doubt about his ability to do it.

This statement to the press is printed in Lindley, op. cit., p. 21. Lindley was present when the statement was made.

Referring in another way to the same subject in Troy, Franklin recounted for his audience two weeks of campaign activity. He was answering, he said, "a good deal of sob stuff" written by Republican editors about "that unfortunate man" who had been drafted for the governorship.

We started off nearly two weeks ago from the City of New York, consisting of a caravan—a whole flock of people, candidates, the press, the stenographic force, etc. We started in in Orange County and we went on through Sullivan, Delaware, Broome, Steuben, and so forth, out through the Southern Tier, all the way to Jamestown. One day we covered 190 miles by automobile and made seven speeches. Then we worked our way up to Buffalo and back to Rochester and Syracuse; because we were getting into our stride, we took a little side trip up to Oswego and Watertown, and then we dropped back to Utica. We left Utica this morning, intending to have an easy day of it. We got to Herkimer, where we all made speeches; then we expected to come through to Schenectady, but when we got to Fonda, there were forty or fifty automobiles in line blocking the road, and we were literally kidnapped. It threw the whole schedule out. We were told that up in that neck of the woods, Gloversville, where in the past there had been occasionally two Democrats, and sometimes three, that had gone to the polls, there were two thousand people waiting for us on the street, and that all the talk of the owners of the glove factories there could not keep them off the streets. So we changed our plans a little and went up to Gloversville. There they were, all of them going to vote the Democratic ticket. When we came on down, we were kidnapped again. We got to Amsterdam. We expected to go through Amsterdam just as fast as the traffic cops would let us, but there were sixteen hundred people in the theatre in Amsterdam, waiting. They had been waiting there two hours.

And then, for good measure, we just dropped into Schenectady and spoke there earlier in the evening, and now here we are in Troy. Too bad about this unfortunate sick man, isn't it?[11]

This is the picture, impossible to misinterpret, of a man vigorous, zestful, enjoying his job. And it is literally true that he did enjoy it.

[11] But Frances Perkins, op. cit., pp. 44–45, recalls something of the impression got from watching one of Franklin's appearances. He was to speak in New York at a hall to which the only possible entrance for him was by way of a fire escape:

I stood in the wings backstage, being among the fifty-odd people who were to sit on the platform that night. I realized with sudden horror that the only way he could get over that fire escape was in the arms of strong men. That was how he arrived.

Those of us who saw this incident, with our hands on our throats to hold down our emotion, realized that this man had accepted the ultimate humility which comes from being helped physically. He had accepted it smiling. He came up over that perilous, uncomfortable and humiliating "entrance," and his manner was pleasant, courteous, enthusiastic. He got up on his braces, adjusted them, straightened himself, smoothed his hair, linked his arm in his son Jim's and walked out on the platform. . . . Then he launched into his speech. . . .

Something in the movement, the excitement, the swirling crowds and the crowding supporters, the opportunity to talk down toward a sea of faces, feeling the cheers and applause rise up to him—something in all this, or all of it together, spoke to his emotions. It was for this he had been made. This he knew how to do best, and better than anyone else.

So acute were his senses in this kind of excitement that he learned in the midst of it at a rate of intake far greater than he could have achieved in repose. He absorbed information unconsciously, he smelled the truth as the crowds saw it; everything he saw and heard taught him lessons. All this he stored away. It made an amazing collection, astonishing to everyone who came in contact with it. Before the campaign was over he even made an extemporaneous speech about labor, something he had not dared to do at the beginning. It was a competent performance on all counts—appeal, content, timeliness; it was the kind of thing that defeated his opponents then and thereafter. He drew it out of his own experience and thus made it doubly effective, even if it was a bit careless with facts:

. . . I remember particularly one of the first things I got into awful hot water about up in my country district—and mind you, I come from an unfortunate district up there on the Hudson River where organized labor had mighty hard sledding, and still has, in the city of Poughkeepsie. . . .

And one of the first measures that we started in 1911 was the fifty-four-hour law for women and children in industry. In those days a fifty-four-hour law was considered the most radical thing that had ever been talked about. . . .

Those three years were very interesting years and I learned a lot. I think that it was those three years spent up there in Albany that made it possible for me to go down to Washington in 1913 with some understanding at least of the problems of the Federal end of things.

I remember when I got down there. I had not been there more than about a week when a delegation from the Brooklyn Navy Yard came down and said, "Mr. Roosevelt"—they had not started to call me Frank; they did in about another week—"there is one thing we want you to do. You know, you, as Assistant Secretary of the Navy, have charge of all labor matters." I said, "That is fine; I did not know it." "Will you do something to change the present method of working out the wage scale paid in the Navy Yard?" I said, "Fine. How is it done?" "Well," they said, "do it yourself." I said, "Why, hasn't it been done by the Assistant Secretary in the past?" "No, it has been done by the officers." And then they went on to tell me how unjustly the wage scales in all of the Navy Yards on both coasts and on the Gulf of Mexico had been arranged each year by a special board of naval officers.

After I had been there I think three days longer, I got Joe Daniels to sign an order making it the duty of the Assistant Secretary to fix the wage scale each year. I am very proud of one simple fact, and that is that during the seven and one-half years in Washington, we did not have one single major dispute, no strike, walk-out, or serious trouble in all of the Navy Yards, all over the United States.

This was a potent campaign appeal. Franklin was obviously offering himself as labor's man. He may have been spoken of in his Navy years as an officers' stooge; he may have been called a Hudson Valley aristocrat; he may have gone to Groton and to Harvard; he may have spent years in Wall Street. Nevertheless, or so he intimated, he was now labor's man. The point is that he was able to get himself accepted as such, then and for all the future. This was transformation by political magic.

As the governorship canvass progressed, Franklin rapidly assumed the ways of behaving, the attitudes, and the postures which New Yorkers first, then other Americans, and finally all the rest of the world would come to identify with him. The picture of a patient, harassed, and melancholy Lincoln bowed down under burdens he could hardly support but could not abandon; or that of the other Roosevelt, Theodore, boundingly vivacious, jumping from one issue to another, showing all his teeth, shouting "Dee-lighted," and making savage gestures that frightened no one—neither of these is more characteristically and indelibly identified in the American mind than that of their successor, Franklin—St. George on a prancing steed riding to meet his dragons, furnished with a golden voice and caparisoned with money, position, and a paradoxical progressivism. The cigarette holder in his teeth, the charming smile, and the toss of his head were indelibly impressed on American memories. He was indeed, as a sourish radical would later say, "a gay reformer."

This picture is not accidental; anyone who cares to can see it in process of being composed. Or, to change the metaphor, he can see the actor studying his part, experimenting with his lines, and gesturing before the practice mirrors; he can see the stages of development from a shy and supercilious young apprentice, first to secondary roles and supporting parts, and then, after a hiatus of trial and disappointment, to the center of the stage. The hero's role was natural to the man Franklin had now become.

But there cannot be a St. George without a dragon, and an actor must have a drama. There has to be a villain if there is to be a hero. The foil who was to serve Franklin well emerged in the 1928 campaign. It was all very well to support the presidential candidate, to ingratiate himself with farmers and with workers, and to speak for everyone's welfare and security. But in the course of these excursions no really satisfactory villains turned up, or else they were numerous and, since they could vote too, had best not be too definitely antagonized. The farmers had traditional enemies—the middlemen; and Franklin waved a sword

166

in their direction. The people at Cornell—and Louis Howe, curio
enough—would have had him engage them hotly. But he never dia;
even during his presidency, tenderness toward middlemen would seem
to some of his assistants a curious weakness; but to Peek and to a powerful figure who had not yet appeared in Franklin's company, Bernard
Baruch, they would be objects of special tenderness. They had exceptionally able and well-financed lobbies penetrating all branches of government; they would have served very well as a villainous foil for a
reformer. Franklin chose not to select them for the role.

Equally available were the bad men among the employers of labor.
In the late twenties—years difficult to recall with the vividness they deserve—the principle of collective bargaining was far from being accepted by American employers, and the capitalists lurking in the dens
and underbrush of Wall Street were troglodytic in such matters. The
cliché by which they were guided was that labor had to be kept in its
place; its place was to work for what employers thought they could
afford to pay and under conditions they found it preferable to maintain—both of these governed by the competition among them to achieve
low costs and high net profits. If workers struck they should be fired.
If they picketed they should be jailed.

The appeal was, it will be seen, to force. Conciliation was regarded
as a weak policy which would be regretted when, because of it, labor
"got out of hand."

It was beginning to be good strategy to take sides in the running war
between employer and employee. It was open to anyone just slightly
gifted with foresight to see that full collective bargaining would evolve
during the proximate years. To advocate what is going to happen is apt
to pay in politics. Franklin, as we have seen, did plump for collective
bargaining as a principle, and he did declare plainly for generous reforms of other sorts in working standards—thus identifying himself with
the Smith tradition so well established in the state. But Smith had never
denounced employers as such, and Franklin did not either. To do so
would have been to declare war on businessmen, and war on businessmen could easily become war on business. This was dangerous in New
York and, indeed, in most parts of the United States. Even the progressives at their most enthusiastic had invariably called themselves the
champions of business—small business.

Politicians had often made ogres out of big businesses; but these were
always identified as "Railroads," as "Wall Street," as "The Trusts" or
"The Money Power," either narrow and voteless corporations, or entities so vague that they escaped identification. Franklin recalled that
Uncle Ted had taken out after "malefactors of great wealth," but he
could recall also that nothing very punitive had come of it; the malefactors were allowed to reform and be accepted if they abandoned their

reprehensible practices. Meanwhile no one really knew who they were. Because they had not been identified they could remain—as they did— the most reliable support of Uncle Ted's party.

Franklin knew a better dragon, one that lived in a noisome cave. This monster breathed conspicuous fire, everyone knew about him, and the electorate was widely convinced of his abandoned wickedness. Al Smith had identified him and had brought him to battle again and again, going to the people for support and having the good fortune to have a Republican legislature make its usual mistake and defend him. No more satisfactory ogre ever existed. He could be engaged and destroyed again and again; he would reincarnate with amazing facility; he would always be there to serve as a foil. He would never reform because it was not in his nature to reform. He would be a perennial issue. Every investment made in war against him would be a permanent one from which the dividends would go on accruing through one campaign after another into the far future.

Until totalitarianism, incarnated by Hitler, turned up, power was the most satisfactory of all Franklin's political *bêtes noires*. There was one period when "the money-changers" were hauled onto the stage and castigated. But in this instance, as in others, the denunciations were softened because the object of them had to be rehabilitated rather than eliminated; and, as we know, the honest financiers were eventually allowed to retire unharmed, even if a bit discomfited. The two really satisfactory foils of Franklin's sixteen years on stage were the electric utilities and the totalitarians—the one early, the other late. His zest in these pursuits was uninhibited, perennial, and effective. A majority of Americans followed him into battle without hesitation.

See how forthright, convinced, and unreserved was this first challenge in 1928. He began thus:

This is a history and a sermon on the subject of water power, and I preach from the Old Testament. The text is "Thou shalt not steal."

It was, from there on, a recounting of sordid machinations on the part of the utility companies and the financiers. He went back twenty-one years and, introducing his villain, revealed the evils he had done. The worst of these was the suborning of the legislature—a Republican legislature, of course—and the stealing of privileges and rights belonging to the people. He showed Al Smith exposing and assailing all the wicked cohorts and organizing regiments of voters in his support. Two individuals were named among the enemy—one Machold and one Ottinger. Machold was Speaker of the Assembly; Ottinger was Franklin's present opponent, the Republican candidate.

He ended this way:

. . . it is a simple fact, which Mr. Ottinger cannot deny, that the gubernatorial campaign of 1926 was waged in large part on this issue. As all know, Governor Smith was re-elected by an enormous majority, and it seemed clear that the people of the State had set the seal of approval on his policy. As a result of the 1926 election, however, there came that episode in our State history which will be recorded in large letters for all time.

Immediately after the votes had been counted in November, the power interests of this State realized that unless prompt action were taken, their chances would be gone, for the plan of reorganization of the State Government, which had been adopted by the people the previous year, was to go into effect the following first of January. Under that plan the old Water Power Commission was to die. The power interests had less than two months to get something done, seven weeks to go. Through the subservient Republican leaders they controlled four out of five members of the Water Power Commission: the Speaker of the Assembly, the Majority Leader of the Senate, the State Engineer, and Albert Ottinger, the Attorney General of the State of New York.

In this situation the water-power interests became desperate. They induced the Water Power Commission to consent to grant them a lease on the St. Lawrence River which would have deprived the people of most of their water-power resources forever. The Governor, hearing of the plan of the Commission, promptly protested . . . But in spite of that this Commission had the consummate nerve to reply to the Governor that they intended to go through with the granting of the lease. . . .

Public opinion was thoroughly aroused in every section of the State. Litigation was threatened. The situation was critical. There, on the one side, was the overwhelming and definitely proven opposition of the great majority of the citizens, demanding that this steal should not be consummated at the eleventh hour.

There, on the other side, stood the Water Power Commission, listening to the pleadings of the power magnates. . . .

I see a picture of a table: four men, among them the Attorney General of the State, the lawyer elected by the people to defend the interests of the people . . .

There stood these four men, their pens poised. . . . Telegrams poured in, protests from public meetings and editorials in the newspapers of all parties flooded Albany. And in that crisis came the decisive move, the open dare of the Governor of the State of New York, challenging the Water Power Commission to affix their names. . . . But in the nick of time the face of the Water Power Commission was saved. The power companies themselves lost their nerve . . . they decided that rather than arouse public opinion they would wait . . .

. . . It was a drama that has had a happy ending in the first act; the curtain is about to ring up on the second act. . . .

One election, just one day, two weeks from today . . . stands between the rights of the people . . . and the loss of their priceless heritage . . . Those who would steal our heritage are within one day of success. I have been placed by my party on duty as policemen to guard that heritage. I ask your support in that difficult and great task. . . .

9

It was suggested earlier that for Franklin the New York governorship was a kind of anticlimax, a turning back or deflection from the straight line of his career: the point being that he was already, and had been at least since 1920, a national rather than a state figure. He had served an apprenticeship in Washington under notable party auspices; he had been the party's candidate for the vice-presidency of the United States; and, by assiduous and persistent cultivation of Democratic leaders all over the country, he had established a reputation as a concerned and industrious formulator of party policy. He could almost be called the custodian of the Democracy. It had been a long time since he had taken more than a nominal interest in state politics. He was not even a delegate to the state convention that nominated him in 1928.

To an extent difficult to realize in a later generation, New York State belonged politically to Al Smith. He had labored long and faithfully for the interests of its people, and he had demonstrated again and again his hold on their gratitude. Only once—in the general debacle of 1920 —had he been defeated. He had been elected four times, always with a Republican legislature—thus demonstrating how personal his popularity was.

It required some readjustment for Franklin to come to grips again with state affairs. It was made harder, not easier, by his predecessor's monopoly of the state leadership. To succeed Al Smith was far more difficult than it would have been to succeed any other governor within memory. Also, it must be remembered, Al was not moving up to the presidency as he had hoped; he was not moving anywhere except back to New York City and his private affairs, whatever they might be—he did not even have a job until his good friend Raskob made him manager of the Empire State Building. He found it hard to contemplate separation from work which had come to seem to him something he alone could do. As he thought about it he was more and more concerned, and no small part of this concern came from a lack of confidence in his successor.

There was prevalent, and especially among the hard-boiled Tammanyites, a conception of Franklin's qualities and abilities that had refused to be dispelled, as stereotypes often do, by any of their actual experiences with him. It was a conception, moreover, that was shared by newspapermen and, to an extent, by the public as a whole in the East. He was regarded as a high-minded fellow with an inclination to fancy notions, not radical, but impractical, undependable, and an individualist. This picture of Franklin, as it turned out, was one that was not held at all by southern and western leaders, or even midwestern ones. Beyond the Mississippi, Franklin was a progressive politician, strangely arisen in New York in spite of Tammany and Wall Street. His election marked him as a man to be watched, and eastern disapproval was rather a commendation than otherwise. But to Al Smith departing, and to his official family, as well as to others with a stake in Al's particular kind of practical reform, the reservations they had about Franklin aroused grave misgivings. They tended to forget his years of administrative experience—it was a measure of their provincialism that they should regard as very little account a good record in Washington —and to recall only that he was a Hudson River aristocrat who had behaved unorthodoxly in the New York legislature.

Worrying about the continuation of his policies, Smith felt that the least Franklin could do would be to keep in office the team so carefully assembled by himself. It had performed faithfully for years and was now experienced and tested. In particular he would have liked Franklin to keep Mrs. Belle Moskowitz and Robert Moses.[1] They too thought they ought to stay, and undoubtedly there was a good deal of talk among them about how it could be managed. All the interests involved were mobilized, and Franklin was fairly besieged with demands that the administration should have little more than a titular change. It was quite evident afterward that this plan was fully expected to succeed— which shows a really amazing carelessness and superficiality among those presumed professionals. They really thought that Al's retirement could be made only nominal. Franklin could be persuaded to leave the management of affairs in the capable custody of Mrs. Moskowitz, Bob Moses, and the others, who would take their directions, as they had got used to doing, from Smith. Nothing much would be changed, except that they would have the nuisance of manipulating a figurehead.

It would seem incredible to later historians that capable and respon-

---

[1] Mrs. Moskowitz had been credited with persuading Smith to adopt the reform program for which his administration had been so noted, and she had by now become almost his alter ego; Moses was Smith's Secretary of State and already a hard-driving and ruthless administrator.

sible persons should have so misjudged the man they had to deal with.
But they were not only capable, they were egotistical to the point of
having excluded from consideration the kind of measurements really
competent people use. To say of Belle Moskowitz, after her extraordinary services to the state, that she made a stupid blunder in this instance is, in spite of the incongruity, not to overstate the case. But it
must be said of her in all candor that elevation to the role of President-
maker seems to have inflated her ego to the point of practical im-
potence. She had, as a matter of fact, completely mismanaged Smith's
presidential appeal. Not only had his campaign been a losing one, but
nothing had been done to overcome his most obvious handicaps. They
had rather been persistently enlarged. The picture of the East Side
sport in the brown derby was the one too many voters saw rather than
the responsible and experienced public executive. What made the
Smith managers think this would appeal to the nation was an incorrigible provincial self-approval. The same arrogant belief that their own
good qualities must be the only ones available made them think that
Franklin would make the obvious concession. When he showed some
reluctance, they thought he could be forced to agree.

This last was an even more inexcusable mistake. It shows conclusively
that they had made no appraisal at all of the man they had to deal
with. Franklin had not wanted to run; he had consented as a party duty.
But he had made his own campaign, a strenuous one, and against all
the odds he had been elected at the same time that Smith had lost.
It was apparent from the election returns that the moment for which
he had waited since 1920 had arrived. Smith's defeat had been more
than the loss of an election; it had been a repudiation from which no
recovery was conceivable. This left the stage empty. It awaited a new
star. What the newly elected governor of New York ought to do in these
circumstances might not be clear in all respects, but about this one
thing there could be no doubt. To have become the stooge of Smith
and his crowd would have been to share repudiation rather than to
accept the designation so plainly indicated by his electoral success.

It was afterward intimated that Franklin had been ungrateful. He
had run on Smith's record, it was said, and had promised no more than
that he would continue the policies of the past years. He now turned
his back on his political sponsor; he ignored the urgent recommendations of a wise and experienced tutor. This charge was one that Franklin nevertheless felt compelled to risk, and he formed an official family
of his own. It was well known that, from the day of his inauguration on,
communications between him and Smith were all but discontinued.
Their relationship would never afterward be more than formal.[2] The

---

[2] It would not be true to say that all communication stopped; but it is true
that Smith waited in vain, after Franklin's inauguration, to be sent for. There are

sad political end of Al Smith as an ally of the Liberty Leaguers, denouncing Franklin as President and "taking a walk" from his party, was inevitable, not because Franklin had declared his independence on January 1, 1929, but because the American people had refused Al their votes in 1928. But it was only natural that he and his should find another reason; they preferred to blame Franklin. It is one of the many ironies of his progress that Smith's unfriendliness was a political asset rather than a liability. This was true even in the succeeding campaign of 1930, although then, as we shall see, Smith smothered his personal dislike and accepted party chores.

Frances Perkins, whose position until then as chairman of the Industrial Board had been a semi-judicial one, was, however, asked to go on with Franklin as industrial commissioner—administrative head of the department. This, for Frances, was an unexpected promotion. She was, in fact, his concession to the feminists and to the welfare workers who had joined in urging that he retain Belle Moskowitz.[3] Frances was to please him so much that, as everyone knows, he would take her with him to Washington. She would be the first woman cabinet officer; she would also establish a record for length of service among all cabinet officers.

Franklin at this time also paid a debt to the Morgenthau family by taking Henry Jr. into his official circle. The elder Morgenthau had helped with funds and advice; Henry Jr. had an estate not far from

---

several notes to Smith in the *Personal Letters*, and they show Franklin in an affable light, but they are not about important matters. In December, before inauguration, writing from Warm Springs, he asked Al to speak to Robert Fitzmaurice about a job in the Executive Department. The duties would have to do with living arrangements, mostly on journeys. There is a pathetic note in Franklin's nickname for Bob Fitzmaurice—"Commissioner of Ramps," he called him. It is a reminder of Franklin's physical helplessness and the cheerful manner of his acceptance of it.

That November, Al was in Biloxi, Mississippi. With him were Bill Kenny, a wealthy New York contractor; Jim Riordan, a banker, president of the County Trust Company, who was to commit suicide after the crash of 1929; and Senator Pat Harrison, whose home it was. This was the company Al kept. Franklin wrote to him there about appointments to the Transit Commission and invited him to Warm Springs. Smith did not accept. This is the closest they came to consultation in the post-election period.

[3] Frances saw something of the campaign; she knew Eleanor and Sara and had often been at Hyde Park. She was among those—perhaps the principal one—who had been responsible for Eleanor's education in welfare matters. She also saw, and finally understood, the break Franklin made with the preceding regime. But she owed much to Belle Moskowitz and to Smith, and the transition was not carried out in the way she would have approved. She was amazed at Franklin's offer to make her industrial commissioner and a little inclined to make conditions. She was not much more certain of Franklin's liberalism than others were of his competence. Her account of these matters in *The Roosevelt I Knew* is a firsthand one. Her recollections are clear and dependable. But she, hardly more than others, penetrated the surface Franklin displayed to the world.

Hyde Park and had cultivated Franklin assiduously. It has been noted that his interest in agricultural matters had extended to contacts with the professors at the State College of Agriculture and that he was made chairman of Franklin's Agricultural Advisory Commission. He now enlarged these relationships. The Advisory Commission was appointed even before inauguration, which does show, I think, both a concern on Franklin's part for long-depressed farmers and a sense of where the votes had come from which had turned the election his way.

Henry Morgenthau was no more a farmer than Franklin was. He had an estate which he ran very well, but his knowledge of the working farmers' problems was not a firsthand one. This was not important at this time or later, perhaps, except in a political sense: he could not be accepted as an authentic farmers' representative, even as publisher of *The American Agriculturist*.[4] On the other hand, Henry may have been responsible for Franklin's early acceptance of the Cornell definition of agricultural relief. This limited the program to tax reduction, financing for co-operatives, better roads, marketing regulation, production research, extension advice, and the like. It excluded any governmental economic interferences with supply, demand, or the market. The McNary-Haugen measures, which were the center of the farm bloc's agitation, seemed to Professor George Warren and his colleagues, who were depended on by Morgenthau for advice, thoroughly bad. It was government interference, and this, to convinced free-enterprise adherents, was anathema.

It was a curious thing, however, that Warren, who was the most influential of the Cornellians, believed in monetary manipulation by the government. To him, as to other of his contemporaries—for example, Professor Irving Fisher of Yale[5]—management of the dollar was a superior substitute for management of the economic system. A "compensated"—and therefore stable—dollar was the alternative to "socialism" in all its varieties. There were various ways of reaching this stability; that which Warren had in mind was the manipulation of the dollar's gold content. This was a process, he believed, that could prevent monetary fluctuations. If prices were stable, farmers' disadvantages would largely disappear. They would never have to repay debts,

[4] *The American Agriculturist* was a farm paper with a large circulation in New York State and so was obviously useful politically. It was his knowledge of farmers rather than of farming that made Henry Jr. useful. It was he who suggested after Franklin's inauguration that an office be set up in Albany to feed news to the rural press. This was done and it was one of the influences that enabled Franklin to keep and enlarge his hold on the country voters. It was Republicans who split their votes who were responsible for his election both in 1928 and 1930. This was not a surprise. He had, in fact, counted on it.

[5] And more important still, that curious group known as The Committee for the Nation, of which more will be heard later.

174

for instance, in dollars worth more, and therefore harder to get, than those they had borrowed.

This is a subject that cannot be adequately discussed here. It is mentioned because it was the Cornellians' excuse for objecting to farm relief of the McNary-Haugen sort and, to anticipate, the sort that would be developed during the New Deal.

But these were early days, as Franklin took up the governorship. Morgenthau's Agricultural Advisory Commission made a number of prompt recommendations and Franklin as promptly passed them on to the legislature. This process was successful enough so that when Franklin approached the re-election campaign of 1930 he really could claim substantial accomplishment.[6]

Before leaving for the moment—it will have to be returned to—this subject of agriculture, it ought to be noted that in that same year, 1930, Franklin, in addresses to farmers, spoke of further measures. One of these had to do with the "spread" of prices between the farmer and the consumer. For this, regulation of the markets would be necessary. Another had to do with a curious regional theory. A New York "milk shed" had been set up; Franklin at least toyed with the idea of its extension to other products. This would cut off from outside competition a whole market to be reserved for local farmers. The original justification had been a sanitary one—that inspection could be carried out only in a limited area and that no milk should be consumed that had not been inspected. A picture arose of regionalized production and markets. Nothing came of this proposal for further extension, and of course it accorded very poorly with the general theory of laissez faire in which he otherwise believed, or, at the moment, appeared to believe.

His laissez-faire commitment was to be considerably modified when he got down to campaigning for the presidency in 1932 and looked around at the debris of the business system, but as he entered the governorship he was simply not considering the possibility of any departure from orthodoxy. He would, as the economic crisis developed, become intrigued with planning, and it may be that his agricultural observations predisposed him to its acceptance. But if they did, that was something his Cornell friends would not have countenanced.

There were other matters of importance to which Franklin gave thought with some result in his early governorship. Frances Perkins' testimony is that the first months—in fact, the first year—"were mostly 'carry-on' months, continuing with the program started in the Smith and Dix administrations." There were, she says, some advances in administration, but nothing new. This shows, I think, that Frances was overly concentrated on her own specialty. Nothing new did happen in her

[6] It was with obvious pride that the statement concerning this was issued on April 24, 1930. It is to be found in *Public Papers*, Vol. I, pp. 145 ff.

department, but there were developments in several other fields, such as public utility controls, the administration of justice, and the organization of government. On the whole, because of these successes, I doubt whether any responsible student will be able to write condescendingly of Franklin's first gubernatorial term. Numerous theorists had been trying to persuade public officials to adopt several of the principles to which Franklin at that time gave unhesitating adherence. In the matter of the public utilities and their regulation, he argued on a number of occasions that the Public Service Commission in New York, as a part of a general perversion, was mistakenly conceiving itself as a judicial body. This allowed it to "arbitrate" between the public utilities and the public. Public Service Commissions, Franklin maintained stoutly, were public bodies. They were created to protect and further the public interest. They should stick to it.

In this same field he also committed himself to the important but very technical principle of "prudent investment" for the valuation of utilities. The companies had invented the alternative theory of "reproduction cost." This is a matter I cannot explore at any length. But it is fundamental to the adequate control of quasi-public businesses. There are libraries of argument pro and con about this question alone among others in the utility field. But the basic fact is that rates are established for utility services by discovering the valuation of the properties and allowing a "fair" return on that valuation. There can be argument about "fairness." It can be construed to be 8 per cent—as it often has been—or more or less. But it is far more important what the 8 per cent is 8 per cent of. And much of the fight for decades had centered on just this question. It is certainly greatly to Franklin's credit that he allowed himself to be briefed by academic people he trusted and committed himself without reservation to "prudent investment."[7]

In these rather complex matters, which might otherwise have been difficult to present as public issues, Franklin was accommodated by the Republican legislature. The stupidity of that body in offering itself as a continuous foil is amazing. But it went on doing so for Franklin just as it had done for Smith. Time after time Franklin was able to load and fire, with enormous effect, at proposals, drafts of bills, and political maneuvers of the majority as it sought to serve the utility interests and otherwise to favor the few rather than the many.

In this, as in other matters, Franklin adopted an old and time-honored device. This was the appointment of a commission to report, following which legislation could be drafted. A person elected as Franklin was, rather unexpectedly, had to find his feet in each situation. Be-

[7] His adviser in this matter was probably James C. Bonbright, a professor at Columbia, to whom he turned in several instances and who was consistently kept busy with successive posts of importance in power and utility matters.

Rep. leg. wanted to supervise expenditures

sides, the appointing of a commission, then its report, and then the fighting through of legislation served the purpose of public education, helped to arouse support, and called attention to a leader's faithfulness. In several instances, beginning with the Agricultural Advisory Commission, Franklin followed this method. On the whole it worked very well, although when Hoover began to use it, Franklin allowed himself to be critical and to see in it an excuse for inaction.[8]

The whole electric power fight was drawn out and dramatized by this method. It turned conveniently before long into a struggle over the vast potentialities of the St. Lawrence, and this presently became a source of contention between the state and the federal government—between Franklin and "his old friend" Herbert Hoover. This whole matter is stated and argued in Part IV of the first volume of the *Public Papers*. There can be no doubt, in these after years, that Franklin was justified in all his contentions. But that he should have been able to make effective political capital of such unlikely material is still a matter for wonder.[9]

There is another matter of great importance in public business, but awkward in the extreme as political material, for which Franklin must be given good marks in his early days as governor. This can generally be labeled: "the case for the executive budget." The matter came up because of attempts by the heavily Republican legislature to extend its appropriating power to include the supervision of expenditures. This is the basis of a permanent quarrel between the legislative and executive branches in the American system of separated powers. It was not a novel issue. But in New York State it was at that moment important because as Franklin came into office a new budget system became effective. This was the culmination of long efforts for reform in state administration, part of a nationwide agitation. Concern that democratic institutions should be improved had been expressed by scholars and more thoughtful public officials for a long time. But a kind of cumulative crisis arose as the burdens and duties of government increased with the growth of population, the industrialization of the country, and the proliferation of services and controls necessary to protect the public.

One focus of this reform movement was the making of the executive more responsible and more efficient. Under the old haphazard system many subordinate officials had been elected and so were independent,

[8] The famous Wickersham Report on the Volstead prohibition law was the most notorious of Hoover's avoidances.

[9] The St. Lawrence Seaway and Power Development would remain an issue throughout Franklin's presidency. He would never be able to conclude the matter. It was not until 1954, when another Republican would be President, that eastern seaboard representatives and power lobbyists would find it convenient to allow the arrangements to be made which should have been made in the twenties or thirties.

more or less, of the governor. And many autonomous agencies had been created—so many that real administrative control was no longer possible. Widespread agitation had led to the adoption of a federal budget in 1921 after many years of evasion by the Congress. And the same process, with the same reluctance in evidence, had gone on in New York State. Franklin himself summarized the situation in an address to the City Club in New York after he had had a substantial victory over the legislature in his first clash with it. He had, in fact, won a suit and was understandably disposed to make the most of his triumph:

Starting with the Constitutional Convention of 1915 a large body of public opinion . . . sought a reorganization of the State Government in order greatly to reduce the number of executive departments—118 of them—and in order to create a responsible Budget System. As you know, the departments were duly organized and are now eighteen in number. This was followed by the adoption of the amendment to the Constitution providing for the Executive Budget. The purpose of this budget was to center financial responsibility for making estimates in the Governor, to center administrative duties in the executive departments, and to limit the functions of the legislature to making appropriations and other strictly legislative duties.

The amendment to the Constitution, spoken of by Franklin, came into effect on January 1, 1929. But there had been an interim period, while Smith was governor, during which the segregation of appropriations had been, by arrangement, shared by him with two legislative committee chairmen. They liked this and, when the new budget went into effect, refused to relinquish the privilege. Franklin disagreed and carried the matter to the Court of Appeals, where he was upheld. Said Franklin to the City Club:

I was very certain . . . that this was not only contrary to the intention of the people of this state but also contrary to the scheme of American Federal and State Governments.

The decision of the Court of Appeals sustains my contention in every particular. Let that be understood once and for all. That statement is not open to challenge . . . members of the legislature can appropriate moneys but cannot carry on administrative or executive duties. This is a constitutional question, and the decision is so far-reaching that this particular case will be regarded for generations to come as one of the pivots on which the Government of this State and of other States rests.

Nothing could be more seemly than that such an instance should appear and come to issue in the first months of Franklin's return to public life. He spoke of it as a constitutional question. It was far more than that to him. It confirmed his intention to center responsibility and power in himself. He and no other was to be the author of good things and the bringer of them to the people. What he meant to bring had already taken shadowy shape in his mind. It could begin with a tinuation of Smith's small reforms—improvements in working condi. tions, shorter hours, protection for women and children, and the like. But it would widen into a grand design for an ordered land with secure and happy people living in it. Parts of that design could be approached through the governorship. More would have to be deferred until the presidency was achieved. But much is discernible, even if only as thoughts for the future, in the public papers of this reluctant candidate who turned so quickly into a contented governor.

Where these ideas came from, specifically—and this is true of every part of what became a complex whole—is sometimes very puzzling. About many of them there can never be, for a very good reason, more than guesses. The reason is that Franklin was determined to conceal their origins. He never gave credit; he never had to. He always had at his disposal fertile minds with an incorruptible public orientation. He robbed them cheerfully; and the authors, being concerned only that some social consequence should come of their inventions or discoveries, were glad to have made a contribution.

There was a certain unique atmosphere in the Albany of Franklin's governorship. Smith who preceded and Lehman who succeeded him were governors who deserve to be listed among New York's most capable; but there was an élan, a sense of largeness and capability, in Franklin's administration which came with him and went with him when he left. This, I think, is not imaginary. It radiates so strongly from the effulgent personality at the center as to throw a kind of glow on all the doings of those years. Even the quarrels with the legislature were good-tempered, in a sense, because, like good drama, before the bitterness of frustration and anticlimax set in they were invariably resolved in favor of the hero in the statehouse. The *Public Papers* reveal an expanding personality having its way with affairs, making a swimming progress toward those indefinite but consequential goals we bind up in the bundle labeled "the public good," interpreted, of course, in the special way suited to contemporary politics. And the letters of those years are even more revealing. They confirm the reports of the onlookers and helpers who have written about their experiences. Franklin was growing and succeeding. He was proceeding happily and uninterruptedly toward a larger destiny. Meanwhile he was performing well in a role of secondary significance.

It would have been said even by experts that the government of New York State was in good operating shape when Franklin became its chief executive. Smith had never been tolerant of inefficiency or slack in his work. He had whittled and tinkered the machinery into a smooth-running whole, and there had been one complete overhaul which had brought New York up among the best organized of all the forty-eight states. But Franklin set out, nevertheless, to make improvements. And of all the possible ways, he chose what seems now to have been the best—and not only from the point of view of effecting change, but also from the point of view of politics. The assignment was given to a capable man.

Herbert H. Lehman was a New York banker. His firm, Lehman Brothers, was almost as representative of everything connoted by "Wall Street" as J. P. Morgan and Company—at least two of whose members, by the way, Franklin knew on first-name terms: Thomas S. Lamont and Russell Leffingwell. But Herbert Lehman, in spite of the Wall Street connection, was a man in whom the worm of conscience gnawed incessantly. He could be reasonably at peace with himself only when he was working in the public interest. He was a small and unpersonable man, not an orator and not a politician. Yet his qualities of honesty and serious purpose were so evident that he was always being used by more brilliant contemporaries. He was fairly content in a secondary role. He had a talent for administration and a shrewd judgment of people which had been sharpened in his business career. He was Franklin's lieutenant governor. He might very well have been something of a problem. Louis Howe from time to time suspected him of intrigue. But finally even he concluded that there was no danger from that direction. Franklin knew it all the time.[10]

On April 11, 1929, Franklin wrote the following letter to his lieutenant governor:

Dear Herbert:

There are two reasons for the following suggestions:

1. It seems evident that the Republican leaders are going to try to analyze and criticise every possible expenditure made in the departments, commissions, etc., and secondly, I think the time has come in the nature of things for us to make a very careful check-up of our own on the actual business administration of the departments.

It is, therefore, my thought that we should start immediately an examination from the inside, covering three main points.

1. The method of purchases.

(a) I have already started this in the Division of Purchases and Standards through Mr. Auld and the representative of the New York Central. This will cover all purchases made through the Bureau.

(b) Something should be done to cover the purchases made by the departments direct, and which should go through the Purchase Bureau.

2. To check up very carefully on the progress of all construction work. I

[10] Jim Farley is authority for the belief that Lehman had been among those—Justice Scudder of the New York Supreme Court being another—who were preferred by Smith as his successor over Franklin. And Louis might well have felt that Smith and Lehman were too close for Franklin's good. Cf. *Behind the Ballots* (New York: Harcourt, Brace, 1938), p. 79.

am confident that things are going much better under Haugaard than they did under Sullivan-Jones, but there should be a very definite progress chart covering all construction.

3. I think a general survey of departmental administration is advisable and can be conducted without stepping on anybody's toes. This would go into two general questions of better cooperation and prevention of duplication between departments, and into the question of employees' efficiency, necessary employees, etc.

Please consider yourself in charge of starting this.

It may be worthwhile to consider the appointment a little later, say in June, of a special Advisory Commission of three leading businessmen to make a full report on insuring administration efficiency. If you would conduct a preliminary survey, and we decide to appoint such an Advisory Commission, we could turn over to them the preliminary facts as something to work on.

A second look at this letter will show how shrewd Franklin could be in the handling of a delicate situation. The letter led to some improvements in public business. But it is cited rather to show a political leader at the top of his form. Notice what it accomplished.

1. It transferred Lehman's loyalty from Smith to himself.

2. It avoided some prospective dangers—for instance, that of Republican criticism about administration, and that of possible investigations which might be especially embarrassing to a presidential candidate.

3. It actually brought into use the genuine talents of the lieutenant governor.

It is not too early to remark that this was really typical. It represents a method that would be used all through the presidency as well as the governorship. Again and again these seemingly forthright and innocent essays would turn out to be of cumulative significance. As to the specific subject matter here, in the end the assayers of Franklin's contributions to public life would have to rate very high his impact on governmental efficiency, and this in spite of the fact that there would be a persistent and nagging criticism of all his efforts. His contemporary reputation would be that of an indifferent administrator but perhaps, having been overcredited in some respects, it was to be expected that he would be undercredited in others—a kind of compensatory adjustment.

It is equally revealing to survey the range of his suggestions, while still governor, concerning the role of government in contemporary society. He was relatively free of those trammels that bound so many other leaders; and many limitations, such as they were, can be understood as imposed on himself for purely political reasons. It would not yet be discreet to go farther. And it would not, if there were a reaction, further the causes he had in mind. His special sense about this was nearly infallible and he allowed it to guide him in almost every instance. There had been unusual attention, all through Smith's administration, to welfare legislation. Much had been done. But there were two hazards of life for workers for which there were no provisions. One of these was old age, and the other was unemployment. They would in time be brought together with other protections into the Social Security System of the New Deal; but even while he was governor, Franklin made attempts to reduce both these risks.

Typically, in both instances, he began with an investigative commission. With neither could he advance very far, and for obvious reasons. No state by itself could accept and shoulder these enormous burdens. Unless all the states were in it together, any one would find itself meeting its neighbors' obligations and swamped by the demands. But he made a beginning; from the response, he learned that he had touched the most sensitive of all political nerves. People wanted security more than anything else, and they wanted the responsibility for it to be accepted by government.

It is a little difficult to understand, from the picture that has survived, the real nature of the booming twenties. There was afterward a tendency to think of the period as one of universal prosperity. But this was a long way from being the fact. There was much unemployment before October of 1929, and the high cost of living had been for years a difficult political issue, thus indicating a consumer squeeze of some significance. And wages had not gone up in proportion to living costs. This, taken together with the continuing farm depression, shows how superficial was the whole theory that a "new era" had opened. The boom was a financial one, resting on an uncontrolled expansion of debt; its underlying foundations were shaky, but the perils were obscured by a mist of optimism.

Economists, of course, knew the facts; and a bust to follow the boom had been anticipated in professional circles long before it occurred. Many of the experts had predicted a collapse so often that when the break came they were about as startled as anyone else that it had really come. But their predictions, except for timing, had not been inaccurate. That Franklin knew all about these expectations is evident; they were, after all, filled with political potentialities. But the nature of the depression, its catastrophic proportions, and its duration were no more anticipated by him than by others. In view of the prevalent atmosphere, it is a little surprising now to realize how sensitive he was to the markers along the road to disaster. He was very quick, also, to react when depression did begin. It reinforced the pleas he had already made for unemployment and old-age insurance, especially; he had only to add one more category—relief.

But during his first term the spotlight was kept on the public utilities and especially on the power interests. The depression would make it possible to switch to Hoover's responsibility for business collapse. While

182

the boom lasted, no more than preliminary intimations of such an attack were in order. While he worked at the utility campaign he showed an extraordinary ability to analyze the problem, extract what was of use, and carry to the people a set of sound conclusions. Having done this, he was ready to begin on the accommodating Republican legislature. Judge Rosenman, in *Working with Roosevelt*, attempted to give his readers an idea of Franklin's method of preparation; he used the instance of power. The following seems to me an unusually enlightening vignette:

Leland Olds, invited to meet Roosevelt for the first time, was quite nervous and excited as he was shown to his room in the stately old Executive Mansion . . .

The Roosevelt greeting made Olds think that the Governor had been waiting for this opportunity all his life, and that his whole legislative program depended on what Olds was going to tell him. As experienced as I was with it, I used to get the same impression . . .

When dinner was over, I got his chair and wheeled him from the dining room to . . . the small study where we all had coffee.[11]

Franklin, says Judge Rosenman, had been doing all the talking during dinner. Now he thanked Olds for coming and proceeded to outline the matter at hand as he saw it. He spoke of the rural need for electricity, using Dutchess County and the back-country folk to make his point. He was being concrete. But presently he talked himself around to a theory he had in mind. Olds tried to interrupt, but he had no luck. Franklin was going to finish first:

"Now I've been thinking that the whole reproduction cost theory of valuation is the bunk and that overvaluation is as bad now as overcapitalization was in the old days. Tell me what you think about the prudent investment principle . . ."

I pulled out my pad and pencil . . . as Olds began to answer. I knew I would have to prepare the first draft of a speech or message on the subject . . .

Roosevelt interrupted Olds frequently . . . If he did not quite understand, he frankly said so . . .

"Yes, but what do you think the courts would do about it—what has been the latest trend of the decisions?" he asked.

And a long series of other questions:

"Isn't the accounting of these companies questionable; shouldn't there be a uniform system of accounts?

"Shouldn't the function of the Public Service Commission be less judicial . . . and more administrative . . . ?

"What do you think of a People's Counsel to protect the consumer in rate cases . . . ?

[11] Op. cit., pp. 33–34.

"Don't we need a real club in the closet that we can use to make the companies behave decently . . . ?"

Some of these questions I had heard him put to other people. Some were new and had been suggested by his talks with others . . .

By eleven o'clock, the Governor rang for refreshments. He usually took what he called a "horse's neck"—a long glass of ginger ale with lemon peel . . . Later, after the repeal of prohibition . . . he would, at this late hour, take beer. . . .

When the time came for bed, the Governor expressed his thanks, and, as usual with his overnight guests, he asked Olds to come into his bedroom in the morning . . . to say good-by. By this time Olds—as nearly every other visitor who came up on a similar errand—was a little the worse for wear but completely "sold" on Roosevelt, on his sincerity of purpose and on his determination to fight for his objectives.[12]

It will be recognized, I think, how true a picture this is of the political leader at work. It would not be true to say that Franklin was not interested in public power, or in the other issues he developed so superbly; but just how intrinsically interested he was I certainly am not prepared to say and it seems to me likely to remain a puzzle. If he was vitally concerned he would not have needed to educate himself in this way *after* he had announced it as an issue. He would already have been deep in the subject. On the other hand, we all take fire over issues which have hitherto gone unnoticed and have to dig belatedly for information. It was part of Franklin's immaturity that he did not know very much about any organized body of knowledge—even the law, which, as we have seen, was involved here. He had a general—what his detractors called a superficial—acquaintance with most questions under current discussion; and about most of them he was disposed toward what he understood to be a progressive opinion, but about only a limited number of them was he prepared to take a position or to defend it in public discussion.

During his first gubernatorial term his reluctance to extend his commitments was a matter for some criticism. But the most caustic comments concerned his avoidance of issues which others would have liked him to be committed on—prohibition, for instance. This was not because of ignorance; it was a determination to govern his own timing. Another and even more serious issue about which there was a good deal of forcing was his equivocal relationship with Tammany.

The prohibition issue loomed larger in those days than afterward would seem conceivable. It was the kind of relatively trivial thing that can excite people when no really significant issues are pressing. In earlier days, or later ones, Americans had to think of their liberties, their welfare, even their very existence. These were days of interlude. Soon

[12] Ibid., pp. 35–36.

the depression would tighten its grip, the economic system would be paralyzed, and concern for their livings would move into first place with Americans everywhere. But in Smith's time prohibition had been a favorite object of attack. Even though he had not been elected he had sensitized the whole electorate to the issue.

It was thus, so to speak, left to Franklin to be disposed of. It is not strange if he did not know what to do with it. He did not know what to do with the League of Nations, either. This did not mean that he had no preference; it meant that he judged the majority preference to be different from his own. It therefore had to be played down. Prohibition he assessed at its true value—as unimportant in the nation's future and therefore an improper cause of division. It meant little whether it was settled one way or another. And he did not intend to lose any votes by crusading for something of that sort. He therefore temporized, and his critics were inclined to take this as evidence of weakness. It was used by the Smith forces (Raskob was still chairman of the Democratic National Committee), who wanted to embarrass him, to illustrate what they called "pussyfooting."

They seemed to think him, in the terms of those days, a "dry"; if he could be embarrassed by refusing to say one way or the other, a point might be won. They had the Committee make a "wet" statement. But Franklin contended that the Committee had no right to make policy determinations, and precedent was on his side. The incident did not pass without some worried moments, but he refused to accept the challenge.

Meanwhile he pushed the other issues which seemed to him more important—those the progressives were agreed on—and especially the control of utilities in general and power concerns in particular. He lost something, perhaps, in the prohibition matter. It was partly responsible for the "wishy-washy" reputation he had with many people who saw or heard of public affairs only casually and through the medium of the press. But there was the other issue of Tammany corruption. And this was his thorniest problem. It involved his most delicate organizational relationships, and it required the most careful handling. Looking back, it can be seen how superbly it was done. At the time, as he was working his way through this passage, it seemed to some observers another instance of temporizing, of weakness, of failure to act decisively in a matter that was notoriously his concern. Walter Lippmann spoke of it in those terms. Actually it deserves to rank with Franklin's most successful tours de force.

Soon after he settled down in the Victorian governor's mansion in Albany, perhaps after the first excitements were over, perhaps even after certain old accounts were settled, he realized that what faced him was not so much a race for the presidency—that was a general and distant end—as the absolute necessity of re-election to the governorship. His term was two years. If he should be defeated in 1930, his now reburgeoning career would wither and die. Not only was this success imperative, he had taken certain steps which had made it unnecessarily difficult. These must be reversed or neutralized.

He had suddenly to accept the fact that he had not approached his situation correctly; he was not, for the moment, the national figure he had got used to being. He was governor of New York. His eye might be on Washington, but his base of operations was in Albany, and Albany could easily be the end of his diverted career. To be governor until the next presidential election was the central problem, which, if it was not solved, could make further problems moot. The first essential for going on into a second term as governor was renomination. He could not be renominated unless Tammany agreed. And he had broken, even if tacitly, with Tammany's pride, Al Smith. Al was known to be in a vindictive mood.

By his first summer in Albany, Franklin realized what he was up against. This is plainly enough shown by his firm denial late in July that the presidency was in his thoughts,[13] and in his affirmation that the governorship had his whole attention. He was bound to make an effort to conciliate Smith although that now would probably not succeed. That failing, as it probably would, he must go around Smith to Tammany's head, thus flattering him with official recognition. So he wrote John Curry, who was now Grand Sachem, in October of 1929, suggesting D. Basil O'Connor as a kind of permanent go-between.[14] As early as May of that year Franklin had set up personal communication by asking Curry to visit him at his New York house,[15] but a liaison man in these affairs is a convenience. Judge Rosenman says that at the same time he was also carrying messages back and forth. This establishment of communication was not done for nothing on either side. Tammany, in exchange for favors, was co-operating. This co-operation, to serve Franklin's purpose, must be continued through 1930. But the going was not smooth. Curry was no Smith or Wagner; he was not even a Murphy. There was widespread and flagrant corruption in New York, so much so that Franklin's political roots were in danger of being uncovered in an

---

[13] There were a number of drafts of this statement. One by Louis Howe, together with the revision that was finally issued, may be found in *Personal Letters: 1928–1945*, Vol. I, pp. 67–69. In this he said he was "definitely disturbed" by persistent newspaper stories about his presidential ambitions; and he affirmed that he had "made it perfectly clear in Albany immediately after inauguration" that he was to be concerned only with New York State for the next two years. It was, he said, "a man-sized job" and he would not "be devoting any time or thought to purely speculative matters" not concerning the state.

[14] *Ibid.*, p. 86.

[15] *Ibid.*, p. 59.

extremely noisome dung pile. There was an election in New York City in 1929, and the issue was corruption. The notorious Rothstein case was current. Jimmy Walker's insouciant defiance of the conventions, as well as the canons of honesty, was under daily attack by the New York *World*. Walter Lippmann was riding Franklin hard. But worst of all, the opponent of Jimmy Walker was another rising hero, Fiorello H. La Guardia.

In the course of the campaign La Guardia disclosed that a Tammany magistrate, one Vitale, had borrowed twenty thousand dollars from Rothstein, and the changes played on the corruption theme were loud and various. Walker, however, was re-elected by a half million plurality, which was one kind of answer to the *World*. And Franklin breathed easier for the moment. But the outcries were not stilled, and they were directed more and more pointedly toward Albany.

Franklin managed to stave off the necessity for acknowledging Tammany's corruption until after he had got what he needed in 1930.[16]

This is a shrewd guess. The liaison with Curry was working.

It was not a costless postponement. He suffered in many people's regard, but they were not people who had any power to affect the nomination in 1930. He could only hope that some means could be found to slough off the resulting opprobrium. Perhaps he hoped that the elec-

---

[16] A shrewd guess about this, although evidence is lacking, is offered in H. F. Gosnell's *Champion Campaigner, Franklin D. Roosevelt* (New York: Macmillan, 1952). After the stock market crash had exposed official corruption in New York City because of bankruptcy proceedings which probed the affairs of many defunct concerns, and because of investigations of stock swindling which involved the magistrates' courts, the failure of the Tammany district attorney to take any notice forced Franklin to ask his state attorney general to intervene. The rising unemployment, also, by creating frantic competition, increased the pressure on the patronage system. Weak central control under Curry of Tammany allowed the buying and selling of jobs to become a notorious traffic. After noting this Mr. Gosnell explains how, as he thinks, Franklin handled his dilemma:

In the investigations of corruption, the New York Democratic organization dragged its feet. . . . The leader of Tammany was called before the Grand Jury in one of the magistrate's cases and he refused to waive immunity preliminary to being asked to testify. After this example all the Manhattan district leaders, the majority of whom held city offices, followed suit. The metropolitan press soon pointed out that this stand was an enormous blunder.

These events gave Governor Roosevelt the opening that he was looking for. In a letter to Mayor Walker he demanded "that the pleading of immunity by public officers in regard to public acts shall cease." Apparently this letter had been discussed with the Democratic leaders, for Mr. Curry put the pressure on them to support the entire state ticket, including Roosevelt, for renomination. *Public officeholders had to sign the waivers of immunity indicated. It is to be noted that the Governor did not demand that these public officials sign waivers with reference to all acts that they may have committed . . . [they] were restricted to public acts. Thus the Governor found a formula which permitted him to come out on top of a difficult situation. He appeared as the advocate of investigations of corruption and at the same time held the support of the Tammany organization.*

torate would pay little attention, or that he could create effective diversions. What went on in the inner chamber we can only guess. But that much did go on we must infer.

He almost did not succeed. The Republicans in 1930 demanded a special session to deal with the situation in New York County. This threat was staved off. But almost at once new judicial corruptions came to light. I quote from a note appended by his son Elliott to Franklin's reply to a letter of remonstrance from W. Russell Bowie, pastor of Grace Church in New York.[17]

After the collapse of Republican demands for a special session to deal with the situation in New York County, new evidence came to light of traffic in judicial offices. When the grand jury convened by the Tammany district attorney found no indictments, F.D.R. placed the case in the hands of the Republican attorney general and designated a Republican Supreme Court justice to convene an extraordinary grand jury on September 15th. At the same time F.D.R. requested the Appellate Division of the Supreme Court to make a general investigation of the magistrates' courts. The division undertook to do this, and, at F.D.R.'s suggestion, named as its referee to conduct the inquiry Samuel Seabury, long-time enemy of Tammany, former judge of the Court of Appeals, and Democratic candidate for Governor in 1916. Although these were regarded as hostile acts by Tammany they did not appease the Republicans. . . .

Bowie cautioned Franklin that the nation was watching and was asking who was the master, Roosevelt or Curry. Franklin's answer was a careful one referring to the demands upon him that he proceed in ways that were really illegal, forgetting that a long tradition of Anglo-Saxon rights was involved. "In thinking it over," he said, "for the love of Mike remember that I am just as anxious as you to root out this rottenness, but that on January 1st, 1929, I took a certain oath of office."

It was a narrow squeak. But Franklin made it. The timing was delicate. Tammany was not too much alienated before the nomination. Afterward it did not matter so much; he could make his own campaign. He could say, without perhaps convincing his friend Bowie or Walter Lippmann or the careful historian, but with that dead-pan look he sometimes used, that he was not involved, that he had done all he could, and that if there was corruption in New York there was corruption elsewhere also. He was only the governor. His power to intervene was limited.

Every campaign has its own interest. Each of Franklin's produced some item of peculiar political significance. From the campaign of 1930 I treasure most as a curiosity what Al Smith said about his successor

[17] *Personal Letters: 1928–1945*, Vol. I, p. 148. Bowie was a Harvard classmate.

in his nominating speech (for it was he who demanded and got the privilege):

In all my experience, no man has accomplished more in the office he occupied than Franklin D. Roosevelt. He has a clear brain and a big heart. For humanity, the love and devotion he has shown the poor, the sick, and the afflicted, Almighty God has showered down on his head the choicest graces and his choicest blessings.

It was well known that Al had long since exhausted his patience with Franklin. To friends he was using explosive language to express his annoyance. But he was a party man, and the party's candidate was also his. There would come a time when this loyalty would break down, but it had not yet arrived.

10

The life of the Roosevelts in the governor's mansion might seem not to have changed very much. The domestic hubbub went on as before; their children came and went—somewhat older and even more boisterous and insistent children now, although much of the time they were away at school. A procession of guests moved sporadically into and out of the mansion, but then that was true in every house they inhabited—in Hyde Park, in New York, in Warm Springs, and now in Albany. Father Franklin sparred with the legislature, entertained the great, dealt with piles of papers, held long conversations with people of knowledge, closeted himself with politicians of all sorts, and presided over a table and a fireside gay with conversation, furnished with amplitude, and bright with optimism. Franklin himself was developing a paunch in spite of continued exercise, and his jowls were noticeable; but the lines of character in his face were gradually giving it a new cast. Youth was no longer there, but then it had not been there since 1921. All seemed to be much the same as before except for the normal encroachments of age on its individuals and the molding of time on its things.

Actually, a revolutionary change had taken place. As soon as he began to operate from the governor's mansion and the statehouse, Franklin was transformed from an ingratiating party counselor, even if an important one, into the generally recognized head of his party, the center and source not only of gubernatorial power but of the whole newly challenging Democracy spread out over the nation. That Democratic power was coming to life after years of discouraging defeat even before the crash of 1929. After that debacle it seemed to be infused with an irrepressible energy.

Naturally, as Democratic hope enlarged, the hopes of individual Democratic aspirants also enlarged. Al Smith had said he was through with politics; Democratic optimism, however, worked on his mind, and gradually he and his friend Raskob began to act very much as though they were maneuvering for position. Smith protested that this was not true—to Ed Flynn, for instance—but Franklin knew better. Nor was Smith the only hopeful who began to stir himself; there was McAdoo, now something of a leader in the West; there was Garner, who became Speaker of the House in 1931; there were Byrd and Ritchie, hoping they were not too southern to be considered; and there were Young and Baker, old-time Wilsonians, without McAdoo's continuing claims to power, but strong in the hearts of many elderly Democrats.

It was Franklin, however, who possessed the enormous advantage of the New York governorship. This was a center from which to operate not equaled by that of any other possible contender. Instantly, when Franklin occupied it, the radiating influence was felt in the farthest corner of the land. Howe and Farley now had something to work with; they used the position for all it was worth. Their first objective was renomination and re-election to the governorship in 1930; their second was the ensuring of nomination—this time for the presidency—in 1932; their third was a successful presidential campaign. Presently it became obvious that these objectives were of successively diminishing difficulty one after the other; the second would become more attainable when its predecessor had been passed; the third began to appear easy for any eligible candidate who made no mistakes. Howe and Farley were energized by the prospect.

These political twins worked out of New York City. Only occasionally were they seen about Albany. That was Franklin's seat, theoretically dedicated to the state's affairs, but actually now the staging base for the march on Washington. There was much activity, but he conducted himself with grace, his dignity only occasionally disturbed by such critics as Walter Lippmann and other New York liberals who read weakness instead of shrewdness into his reluctance to discipline Tammany. They accused him of buying Tammany's favor by turning a blind eye on corruption in the city. But most public men have this sort of difficulty. Their ability to maneuver, to barter what they have for what they hope to get, is conditioned by their ability to maintain a screen behind which to do it. Franklin's flair for maintaining a deceptive front was never more effectually used. It often seemed incredible even to those who were more or less aware of what was going on that the machinations they knew of were taking place. Such duplicity seemed utterly foreign to the frank and agreeable public figure who could be seen going about his affairs from day to day. Only when they themselves were part of a scheme, in the sense of carrying out a fraction of it or seeing to it that someone else carried out a fraction, did they have a look behind the stage set for the star of the performance. It spoiled the ensemble to have critics always trying to penetrate backstage, and Franklin did not like it. He could not always prevent it, but he could and did pretend that nothing went on behind the scenes.

Close collaborators, however, were never allowed for an instant to forget that the principal was an actor-manager and not merely an actor; it was his production, and nothing concerning it was beyond his notice. No one knew enough, either, to replace him as manager, to say nothing of replacing him as actor. This applied even to Louis Howe, who, for all his ubiquity and familiarity, was by now treated to a certain much-resented exclusion, not to the degree of others but still so noticeable that he began to exhibit the jealousy often remarked by later helpers. Sam Rosenman was oftener at Franklin's side in Albany than anyone else, even though he had as yet little to do with the preparations going forward for the venture of 1932. He was helping to make the state job a success. But he had continual trouble with Louis.

Louis was thick-skinned himself, and even a little that way where Franklin was concerned, something that Franklin never understood in any of his associates and that is indeed seldom understood by any public man. Franklin was inclined already, even if he put a good face on the matter publicly, to regard criticism as unfriendly at best and malicious at worst. He decidedly did not relish any probing of his intentions or any inquiry about his motives. There was an evident compulsion in this. He tried to control it, and Louis constantly counseled restraint; but not infrequently it broke out in one or another way—in press conferences, interviews, or conversations. It was a discordant note; it was also a betraying one. The implication was that he felt himself entitled to privilege, the privilege of one who was exempt from criticism. Those who did not recognize this and grant the immunity he needed were ticketed in his memory. He had an elephant's recall for injury. Someday the offender might be surprised not to have a favor granted. In the long run there were a good many such individuals. No pleading would ever change their status or admit them to the circle of trusted collaborators. So far as Franklin was concerned they were permanently cast out.

Critical comment became a serious problem toward the latter part of the first term as governor when the Tammany trouble was in process. Much of it was traceable to the power interests, and some came from Smith's friends. But more originated among the progressives themselves, especially the group centering in the New York *World*. But in the early days it had not yet appeared to disturb the prevalent cheerfulness. The sense of going on to bigger things was strong in the Roosevelt household.

It was in those days that the pattern of life for the family was formed which persisted throughout the governorship. It was not exactly in contrast to the pattern of the fallow years; it was an enlargement and extension of the family with Franklin at the center. Somehow or other even casual visitors to one of his houses seemed for the moment a member of the clan. This was partly Franklin's ease and informality—he called everyone by his first name on the slightest acquaintance, and he always assumed that visitors' habits and standards were the same as those of the Roosevelts. He also assumed that everyone would be pleased to join in what he was doing. It was partly, also, the atmosphere created by the young people. They made everyone feel at home. Then, too, the quiet but lovely Missy LeHand, Franklin's secretary, was a member of the household; so, presently, was her assistant, Grace Tully, a buxom and cheery Irish girl. Their charm was pervasive. Sam Rosenman also more or less lived in the mansion, sparing what time he could for his family in New York. His wife, Dorothy, grew to be a favorite with Franklin, and she was often about. Louis Howe had a room, too, and was present often enough to keep his family franchise, even if most of his work was in New York.

Guests were easily absorbed into this menage. And it was done as easily—or more so—in Hyde Park as in Albany. Even Sara, now that the dignity of the governorship clothed her son, was more reconciled to the vulgarities of politics. She graced the lower end of the long Hyde Park table, looking past not only family faces but some that seemed to her incongruous. Her son sat at the head, but this did not always compensate for the manners of some of his guests. She even offered advice on occasion, irrelevant advice usually, proceeding from an obsolescent aristocratic mind, generous but not very tolerant. What she had to say was listened to kindly enough by those present, but it was never heeded. She thought herself entitled to a word, evidently, since her home had been turned into a rallying center for Franklin's final essay in high politics. As Eleanor remarked, however, Sara had come upon times during the depression when her household would have had to contract, and she might have had to give up Springwood altogether if it had not been for Franklin's opportune success. She was not a really rich woman, and she had lost heavily in the 1929 crash. Franklin from now on could draw on public resources. But no acknowledgment of this new support was ever made by the old lady. She presided as she always had, with the assurance of unassailable position.

The official establishment at Albany was an ample one. The Smiths had run it on a generous scale, and the new incumbents needed to make only minor changes. Franklin and Eleanor had no intention of altering very much the physical situation. Theirs, they knew, was not to be a long stay. Eleanor speaks of changing some minor arrangements and some of the household customs. One that she recalled was the habit the Smiths had had of requiring huge desserts. The new emphasis was on an ample service of plain, substantial food. But in Albany as elsewhere the household got very little of Eleanor's attention. It was managed by a capable steward. Many witnesses have testified to the generous, almost lavish scale on which it was run; they have also testified uniformly to the inefficiency everywhere evident—the poor food, the slipshod service—so incongruous when matched with the formal, rather English routine of tea in the afternoon and eight o'clock dinner, which seemed to call for a meticulous regime.

Eleanor was a busy woman. She had a furniture-manufacturing business at Val-Kill, she was a part-time schoolteacher, she was more and more active in politics, and she was beginning what was to be a whole career of public speaking, one that eventually would earn her an independent living. She spent at least two days a week in New York, often more, and she traveled a good deal. In these circumstances she was not the mistress of the house as far less energetic women often are. Missy LeHand was much more regularly present and of necessity she arranged matters to suit Franklin's convenience. But Franklin was no more desk-bound in Albany than he had been anywhere else. From January to March, when the legislature was in session, he was tied to the mansion, except for weekends at Hyde Park and occasional visits elsewhere to speak or confer.

Such occasions were carefully scrutinized; he went only if something was to be gained. It was necessary that he should be the principal figure at any such gathering, and the paterfamilias impression was more easily conveyed from his own ground. As the procession of various visitors went on, it slowly swelled in volume. There gradually spread, in ramifying fashion, the knowledge of his availability.

It became customary for him to be in Warm Springs at Thanksgiving. A few autumn weeks there always served as a restorative. And the ceremony of turkey-carving on the holiday was invested with ritualistic importance to all concerned. The New York house was not used much except as a temporary convenience, but Franklin was often at Hyde Park, a less-than-two-hour drive from Albany. This was partly because he enjoyed the ride along the Hudson in the big limousine, accompanied by friends and escorted by outriders from the smart state police. The countryside to him was as familiar as a much-read book, a well-loved classic, full of an always new interest. The river, seen through the trees and across the meadows, the farms and forests along the road, the distant Catskills—he was a proprietor in all this now in a more real sense than ever before. It was his and it was being improved.

In spite of the special problems furnished by the unexpectedness of the governorship, Franklin really did take everything in course without visible strain; and there were some satisfactions no one but he knew of —except, perhaps, Eleanor, who loyally would not speak of them. One of the most interesting, to the later historian, is the belated conquest of Harvard. That citadel, which had never been quite conquered by the undergraduate Franklin, surrendered totally to the newly invested governor. In the first spring of his incumbency he was grand marshal of his reconvening class, was given the degree of Doctor of Laws, *honoris causa*, delivered the annual Phi Beta Kappa oration, and was made an honorary member of that purely intellectual fraternity. If I read correctly between the lines of the letters during that spring, the balm to his old, never-quite-healed wounds represented by these capitulations had a healing efficacy not matched by many other of his achievements. His victory was the sweeter, naturally, because it was incidental. It was not intrigued for; it came as recognition of an outstanding position in public life. Universities present these distinctions not to honor the recipient but to advance their own interests. No better evidence of Franklin's secure position could be imagined than that Harvard wanted him on its roster of familiars.

This was, however, no more than a treasured symbol. Dartmouth and Fordham also gave him honorary degrees that June, and these were only items in a long list of such honors. Other organizations and other people now sought association with him in some degree and in various manners. The organizations to which he now belonged require several pages to list; and the number of his correspondents—just those he addressed by their first names—runs into hundreds. If it appears incredible to the student that any personality could stretch itself so far, reach its tentacles into so many lives, and draw support from such diverse approval, he must realize that he is observing a rare political phenomenon. The real cause for amazement is not how far and how wide Franklin's net was flung but with what ease and naturalness it was done. A few experienced and cynical commentators among the New York liberals had those acid remarks to make which annoyed Franklin so much, but they were actually lost, however he felt about them, in an overwhelming wash of approval; almost no one attended them with any care except Franklin. But it has to be reiterated that he caught every discordant note. In the symphony of his public performance these discordances sometimes seemed to him intolerable, and control of his resentment was difficult.

But his progress went on. It enlarged and spread, even if under a surface of critical newspaper comment; how well the thing had been done could be seen when the returns came in on election night in 1930. In spite of the strains and stresses of the preceding weeks, he had a plurality that has to be described as overwhelming, surpassing any even of that magnificent campaigner, Al Smith. This is the kind of answer politicians make to their detractors. To them it seems a blindingly effective reply. They rest on it as the justification for every maneuver, every trade, and every compromise. It serves also as a reward for every effort. For Franklin it represented the crumbling of the last visible barrier between himself and the presidency. He had done well and his appointment had been confirmed.

He soon came down to reality. There was still work to be done, enemies to be defeated, nets to be thrown out for support. But the tide of approval and success now ran strong. He was in midstream.

The campaign of 1930 had had its difficulties. A kind of side light is thrown on one of them by a letter written to Professor J. C. Bonbright of Columbia, who has been mentioned as one of those he depended on for advice on the power issue. The letter is dated March 11, 1930, as the maneuvering began. It not only illuminates an issue and displays Franklin in an irritated mood, but it catches him in the act of formulating a realistic political principle, something he usually avoided in favor of the graceless clichés that are so much more acceptable to the layman and, it must be said, so much more satisfactorily deceptive:

My Dear Bonbright:

I am mighty glad to see that correspondence between Felix and you and Walter Lippmann. Of course, I have never been able to understand the editorial policy of the New York *World*. For instance, it was the *World* which literally drove Al Smith into sending that fool telegram after the Houston convention telling how wet he was. Al had every wet vote in the country but he needed a good many of the middle of the road votes to elect him President. A very wise elder statesman was right when he told me that the *World* did more harm to Al Smith's candidacy than all the Republican newspapers in the United States put together. . . .

I may be a little sore because a week ago I made a short radio speech on a national hook-up on the broad subject of State or Federal Constitutional Rights. I talked about broad principles and did not emphasize the Prohibition angle, but merely stated the fact of the Eighteenth Amendment. Therefore Walter hopped all over me the next morning, relegated all the rest of the speech to the discard and cursed me for not having made a speech on Prohibition alone!

If Walter would stick to the fundamentals, fewer people would feel that the *World* first blows hot and then blows cold. Perhaps you and Felix will have some effect. I hope so.[1]

Two other letters close to this in time (May 1930) are helpful in understanding Franklin's pre-campaign mood. One, to Archibald McNeil (national Democratic committeeman from Connecticut), who had

---

[1] *Personal Letters: 1928–1945*, Vol. I, pp. 109–10. The correspondence which evoked these letters can be imagined well enough. Franklin in this, as in other public pronouncements, was doing precisely what Lippmann accused him of—straddling. He had referred to prohibition as a matter on which the states had "wisely or unwisely" ceded their powers of control to the federal government. But it can be seen that evasion was wise as well as expedient. Prohibition was not a vital matter in 1930; also, it was in process of settling itself. Franklin was right to avoid becoming involved. He was forthright enough later on, when he was clear how things were going.

been having conversations with various prominent Democrats and had discovered that Franklin was the most likely candidate for 1932, asked Mr. McNeil to get it out of his head that he was "in any shape, manner, or form thinking about 1932." He was desperately anxious at that juncture, it can be understood, not to be the object of a conspiracy by other aspirants. They might very well see, as clearly as he saw, that the way to choke him off from 1932 was to choke him off in New York in 1930.

The other illuminating remark was an offhand one in a letter of thanks to John A. Kingsbury, indefatigable doer of good works, who at that time was secretary of the Milbank Fund and who had sent him J. Allen Smith's disillusioned *Growth and Decadence of Constitutional Government*. Franklin had not yet read the book; whether he ever did is questionable, though I am sure he got the gist of it and that it lent support to an already well-shaped opinion about the Constitution; but what he said to Kingsbury was this: "There is no question in my mind that it is time for the country to become fairly radical for a generation. History shows that where this occurs occasionally, nations are saved from revolution."[2]

This echo of Jeffersonianism in the spring of 1930 is, or rather would be if we had not heard Franklin saying things of this sort again and again, surprising in an aspiring politician. Potential candidates usually avoid such phrases with obvious care. It calls sharply to mind what the situation was just then and how the then President was reacting to the troubles that had so unexpectedly beset him. Herbert Hoover stands in almost classic contrast to Franklin, however he is looked at; but in his characteristic reaction to economic disaster the contrast is at its very sharpest. To Franklin, depression offered a lesson. The economic system must be reorganized to avoid such happenings in the future. It was a challenge to action. To Hoover, it was a cross to be borne, one he had not deserved. He saw belatedly that there had been wickedness afoot. But if he had seen it he did nothing about it until it had caused disaster. He turned to "shocks from abroad" for his official explanation. It was "the aftermath of war"; it was anything but natural to the business system.

Hoover, in 1930, was desperately trying to overcome the crisis and at the same time belittling it. He was entangled in the Republican claims, repeated so many times in the twenties, that the party policies

[2] Ibid., p. 118. In this letter he made another remark that probably reflected a concern about his own deficiencies. "One of the penalties of being Governor," he said, "is that one has little time to think of broader national problems." He had the depression on his mind. "It would be misunderstood," he said, "if I were to tell the public that I regard the present business slump as a great blessing, for while a nation goes speculation crazy and everybody is employed, the average citizen simply declines to think of fundamental principles." But that is the way he did regard it, especially at first.

were responsible for prosperity. The conclusion was only too logical that if prosperity belonged to the Republicans the depression did too, since the Democrats had been out of power for a decade. Hoover never fought loose from this entanglement. His administration—even he himself—was repeatedly guilty of minimizing the number of unemployed. Frances Perkins, Franklin's commissioner of labor, exposed the fraud. He could hardly meet with adequate measures a crisis whose depth and extent he stubbornly refused to recognize.

Between 1930 and 1932 Hoover would struggle convulsively with the monster which had fastened itself on the economy; in 1930 he was being sharply criticized because too little had been done, and that too late. This was even then a somewhat unfair allegation; it would be even more unfair in 1932. He did, in fact, exhaust every resource he could allow himself to meet the situation. Time after time he felt that enough had been done; repeatedly there seemed to be an upturn. But each of these illusory halts in the economy's vast sinking spell was followed by a further sickening decline. Industry after industry felt the clammy grip of fear as each in turn was invaded by the creeping paralysis. Each soon approached bankruptcy, and eventually the whole national network of credit was shaken by the spreading conviction that debts could not be paid.

Hoover had seen clearly enough that there was danger in the heavy foreign debts; he had also understood that the financial system was vulnerable to shock. But he had felt that a time of crisis was not one for reform. Confidence was the first need. It must be restored before anything else could be done. This was indeed the analysis and cure offered by all his advisers; it would continue to be the favorite depression remedy of businessmen for years to come. Franklin also would, in his time, be besieged by the same urgings for the "restoration of confidence." The argument ran that only when business venturers felt the future to be secure would they initiate and carry on those enterprises which, totaled together, made up the capitalist "system." Only when business was satisfied with its circumstances would employment be full. As could be seen clearly enough later, no more hollow and naïve theory ever established itself as an orthodoxy; it would amaze historians to see how anxiously, and at what pains, the theory was propagated.

That goods and services could not be bought by an impoverished people would seem so simple a fact as to be incontrovertible; but there were few—and those mostly intellectuals—who recognized it in the early years of the great depression. Everything, therefore, was done but the necessary thing. Only a few of the unorthodox talked about the restoration of purchasing power, and those few were smothered by dispraise. They were no more popular than radicals ever are. Hoover, out of humanity, organized some "relief" for the miserable unemployed millions;

he appointed a big-businessman committee which did in fact labor valiantly to check the flood of failures and shutdowns. It soon became evident that this finger in the dike was not enough, of course; but even then Hoover's retreat was reluctant. He resisted getting the federal government "into the relief business"; this would somehow destroy character and undermine local responsibility. So he allowed himself to be overwhelmed. Even in 1930 he had obviously lost control of the situation.

Franklin as governor could not accept the responsibilities Hoover refused. He saw only too clearly that no one state could meet the crisis, and that if it tried it would also be overwhelmed. Furthermore, he was caught, as he sometimes acknowledged, although not publicly, without any adequate explanation of what had happened. What he did understand was that the business system had broken down and that the search for causes ought to be concentrated on the system itself. He had no political necessity, such as Hoover had, for finding mysterious outside influences at work. He was inclined to think that Wall Street manipulation had had a good deal to do with it, but that hardly seemed to account for the vast consequences now visible. One thing he could do. He could claim that Hoover had not done anything effective to check the disaster. This was not wholly honest, perhaps, since he himself had no clear view of what it was that should have been done, but it was good politics; and, after all, the responsibility had been Hoover's.

Franklin offered some much-needed criticism in the 1930 campaign, when the depression was one year old, even if it did not go to the causes of the current trouble. He said, for instance, that everyone should understand from now on that prosperity and depression were not attributable to any partisan regime. Democrats could claim prosperity as logically as Republicans, and Republicans could obviously not prevent depression. But what he said about the depression was not so important as what he promised to do himself to cushion the shock and what he taunted Hoover for not having done. There ought, he said, to have been instituted at once a program of public works. He was far from clear about why these would be remedial, but he had no doubt that they would help, and he promised definitely to expand New York's program.[3]

That campaign was not wholly diverted to the issue of depression. Franklin had invested heavily in his other issues. He hammered his state opponents on power; he was by now expert in this field. Also, he had claims to make about assistance to agriculture, and he made them. He had offered a reorganization of local government and reform of the courts; he asked for support. There were enlarged and improved prisons

[3] This was in his speech of October 30, 1930, in Buffalo. Cf. *Public Papers*, Vol. I, pp. 404 ff.

and hospitals; there had been more welfare legislation. He let people know that these were to be credited to him. But it is impossible not to see behind all that went on a marshaling of the events that were moving the protagonists of their age into positions of opposition.

Hoover had entered politics not as a deep-dyed and tested conservative Republican but as an engineer in government. The professional politicians had not wanted him any more than they ever want one who is not one of their own. Hoover was definitely an outsider. They had accepted him because of public pressure and because important contributors to campaign funds wanted him. Even so, it could not be said that he had then represented business as later he was content to do; he represented efficiency, large-scale organization, the movement of American technology toward its apotheosis.

It has been noted that Franklin had known and admired the older man in Wilsonian days; now, in 1930, each was coming into the consciousness of the other as an almost inevitable enemy. Each was warily sizing up the other, and maneuvering for advantage beginning. This was the orientation of a rather cautious reference by Franklin to Hoover's claims of 1928 that poverty in America was practically at an end.[4]

Hoover was not the antagonist Franklin would have chosen if he had been allowed a preference. And until now it had not occurred to him that Hoover might be his opponent in the final struggle for the presidency. He had been thinking that Hoover would have the normal two terms and be retired in 1936. That, rather than 1932, would be the year of his own assault. If he had thought about his likely opponent definitely at all, he may well have guessed that it might be his upriver neighbor Ogden Mills, Undersecretary of the Treasury, who was rising rapidly in Republican regard; but it was even more likely that some as yet unnoticed governor might be chosen. It was not yet altogether plain that the sequence was to be interrupted.

Events, in other words, were arranging themselves but had not yet assumed a pattern. Franklin must have looked with some dread at a contest with so greatly respected a person as Hoover—that is, respected by him; others were rapidly losing their regard for the Great Engineer

---

[4] In the Buffalo speech already referred to. The paragraph from Hoover's 1928 speech, cited by Franklin, read as follows:

We in America are nearer to the financial triumph over poverty than ever before in the history of any land. The poor man is vanishing from among us. Under these impulses, and the Republican protective system, our industrial output has increased as never before, and our wages have grown steadily in buying power. Our workers, with their average weekly wages, can today buy two and even three times more bread and butter than any wage-earner in Europe. At one time we demanded for our workers a full dinner pail. We have now gone far beyond that conception. Today we demand a larger comfort and a greater participation in life and leisure.

who was proving so futile in the White House. The erosion of Hoover's reputation was one of the most striking phenomena of those years.

Franklin had as yet no equipment for meeting Hoover on his own ground. But instantly, when the gubernatorial election was over, it was plain that he would have to do so. For the next two years protestations of disinterest in the presidency would be out of order, and no more of them were forthcoming, although it was not until late in January 1932 that an open avowal of candidacy was made. Judge Rosenman tells of the return trip to Albany on the morning after the election of 1930. The company, which included Missy LeHand, Grace Tully, Doc O'Connor, and Louis Howe, as well as Sam himself, talked freely in Franklin's presence of the coming campaign. This was the first time that this had been permitted. Franklin said nothing, but he could be expressive without words, and it was understood that the years of dissimulation were over. Now the planning and managing would be open.

It was, however, much more than a merely political affair. Louis Howe and Jim Farley were out of their depth in the prevailing sea of economic troubles, much more so than Franklin. He was by now alert to every reasonable suggestion. And that morning, after his decisive victory, he must have given serious thought to the double task he faced—that of capturing the nomination in 1932 and, when that was over, finding a remedy for the economic crisis. For it was already plain to him that the depression would not resolve itself in the next two years. This, in fact, was to become the most marked difference between the two antagonists who this day entered the still dim dueling ground and began to search memories and seek advice about the emerging champion on the other side.

Hoover's attempts to check the debacle, strenuous though they were, rested on the theory that there were cycles of prosperity and depression and that what went down would come up whether anything was done or not. That was the orthodoxy of the time, supported by academic opinion and by businessmen's conviction. There were processes at work which had to be allowed to complete themselves. Deflation and bankruptcy would wash out bad debts, prices would fall, good debts would be paid, and activity would resume. At best the injury to individuals could only be mitigated. Individuals could go through bankruptcy; businesses could be supported through failure and reorganizations into calmer days; the unemployed could be cautiously helped to feed their families until jobs would again be available. But the federal government must not act directly; at most it could assist local and voluntary efforts.

There is no evidence that Franklin had any better explanations of the crisis than the going one. In all probability he had not yet questioned the orthodox view. But temperamentally he could not accept the implied consequences. His disposition was to take some action. Mani-

201

Social Darwin

festly he did not know of anything to do that would restore prosperity. But what is certain is that he thought a good deal about whether there might not be some governmental action that would do just that. He was in a position—being the challenger—to insist more strongly on irregularities among financiers as contributing to the weakness in the system now being revealed. But although this could be played up to a certain extent, he knew that it was not actually a cause.

It is probable that about this time he began to listen to the whispering that came to him from Cornell by way of Henry Morgenthau. Warren's suggestions that monetary fluctuations were the causes of economic stability and that monetary measures would restore prosperity seemed to offer at once an explanation and a remedy.[5]

These doctrines had been well publicized. They were essentially those held by the well-known Irving Fisher of Yale. But they horrified the creditor classes generally as well as the orthodox among academicians. Farmers were mostly debtors and they had always listened hopefully to such views; politicians were now being attracted. Variations on the cheap-money theme were, in fact, as old as agrarianism, and that meant that they went back to American beginnings. There were echoes of Ignatius Donnelly, William Jennings Bryan, the Farmer-Laborites, and many other persons and organizations in what Warren had to say. Franklin probably felt that he ought not to listen to Warren's suggestions, but they were persuasive. Without acknowledging the attraction, he began to wonder whether some magic might not be found to which the orthodox were blind.

He had already in 1930 begun some modest action. It was an orthodox one, a public works program. Even Hoover, as Secretary of Commerce, had agreed that an expansion of government expenditures in times of depression would be helpful.[6] And a Federal Stabilization

[5] Warren was associated with a strangely assorted company which called itself The Committee for the Nation, among whose members were General Wood of Sears, Roebuck and Company; James Rand, promoter of the vast Remington Rand concern; and various other individuals whose orientation was definitely fascist. All of them would turn up in the future, as they had in the past, as America First organizers, xenophobe isolationists, and as supporters of MacArthur and McCarthy. They were proponents of monetary measures because they seemed to be an alternative to planning. They were essentially a company of economic buccaneers to whom the worst of fates would be what they called "regimentation." The association with them of farm leaders was an indication of the reactionary leanings among all the agricultural interests. There will be occasion to mention them again later on.

[6] Among Hoover's genuine contributions was his sponsorship of a series of economic and social studies during the 1920s, exploring more thoroughly than had ever been done before the industrial and business systems as well as the social institutions of the time. The two names most prominently identified with these studies were those of Wesley C. Mitchell and William F. Ogburn, who were respected contemporary scholars. Their studies were invaluable probings of the system. One of their recommendations was the use of public works as a

Board to set up a "shelf of public works" had been provided for. This, like so many other of Hoover's measures, was, in principle, correct; but it was done stintedly and belatedly, perhaps because for the wrong reason. It might as well not have been done at all, for all the effect it had. In fact, the impression the country had was that Hoover's efforts were confined to claims that recovery was about to occur. Things had begun to go against him so badly that nothing he could do was right and everything he tried to do was belittled.

Franklin's most effective action in this crucial matter was taken late in August of 1931. It followed a good deal of talk and maneuvering about the unemployment problem. He had appointed a Commission on Industrial Stabilization during the spring and had repeatedly advocated a system of unemployment insurance. But by the summer of 1931 the depression had deepened to the proportions of genuine disaster, and it was the general impression that nothing was to come out of Washington.[7] The fact was that Hoover was struggling with a Congress now controlled by Democrats and Progressives. Wagner, La Follette, Costigan, Cutting, Wheeler, La Guardia, and others were making what seemed to him fantastic demands for planning councils, programs of public work, unemployment relief, and the like; and they were heartily damning his one vigorous gesture—the Reconstruction Finance Corporation—as "relief for business but not for the worker." Currently the struggle was whether public works should be "self-liquidating," as Hoover demanded. He was so afraid that people's characters would be undermined by doles that he seemed immune to their suffering. Humanitarian that he was, he was an even more stubborn moralist.

Franklin was opportunely asked in August to call a special session of his legislature to correct a deficiency in a law governing the inquiries of one of his commissions. Special sessions of the New York legislature could consider only those matters submitted to it by the governor. He resolved on a surprise recommendation along with the expected one. He saw that he now had an opportunity to seize the initiative in the matter of deepest interest to the whole nation. He had been thinking of some-

---

stimulant in depression. Hoover's Stabilization Board owed its origin to this recommendation. It was the forerunner of the Public Works Administration of the New Deal.

[7] One of Franklin's actions in this matter was to call a conference of the governors of several neighboring states. Some recommendations resulted, but the chief result was to create the impression of leadership. Making a show of action was a device he used afterward with telling effect—for instance, in 1936 when Landon, governor of Kansas and his Republican presidential opponent, was summoned to a "non-political" drought conference in Des Moines (to be described later); this was the most effective move in that year's campaign. This was when he was in full career, but at the very beginning we have seen that he used a similar tactic when he started the revolt over the election of Sheehan to the United States Senate.

thing of the sort for a long time; he had discussed it with Sam Rosenman and perhaps with others. What bothered him about what he felt he must do, however, was precisely what bothered Hoover: he felt that doles were deleterious to character and must at all costs be avoided. He could think of only one acceptable device—a dramatic expansion of "made" work, with temporary reliance on direct relief. He asked the legislature for a startling sum, so bringing the whole matter into focus. He may still not have known what to do about recovery, but he could offer a contrast to Hoover's inaction. It was, in fact, the deathblow in the still blind duel between the two, although at the time no one recognized it as such. The reaction would be delayed, but it would be sure.

The message to the legislature deserves careful study because it shows Franklin's instinct for directness when his mind was made up and also because it shows that he had no idea that what he was proposing had an economic significance. It was purely humanitarian—and, of course, political:

What is the State? It is the duly constituted representative of an organized society of human beings, created by them for their mutual protection and well-being. . . . Our Government is not the master but the creature of the people. The duty of the State toward the citizens is the duty of the servant to its master. The people have created it; the people, by common consent, permit its continual existence.

One of these duties of the State is that of caring for those of its citizens who find themselves the victims of such adverse circumstances as makes them unable to obtain even the necessities for mere existence without the aid of others. . . .

While it is true that we have hitherto principally considered those who through accident or old age were permanently incapacitated, the same responsibility of the State undoubtedly applies when widespread economic conditions render large numbers of men and women incapable of supporting either themselves or their families because of circumstances beyond their control which make it impossible for them to find remunerative labor. To these unfortunate citizens aid must be extended by Government, not as a matter of charity, but as a matter of *social duty*.[8]

He said, in concluding, that neither voluntary contributions nor the resources of local governments were adequate to the current need. He asked that the legislature join him in providing $20,000,000 at once, to be raised by new taxes. The funds would be used for useful work projects where they were feasible; but where work projects could not be arranged, the funds would be used for "food against starvation and clothing and shelter against suffering."

It can be imagined how the announcement of this venture rang across a stricken land whose workers (by now some ten or twelve millions of

---

[8] Rosenman, op. cit., pp. 50–51.

them) had neither work nor income, and who, moreover, until they heard these words, had had no visible prospect of either. The workers of New York, at least, now had renewed hope; workers elsewhere could wish they were New Yorkers—or, better yet, that the governor of New York had an enlarged jurisdiction. There was none of the implication here that unemployment was an individual responsibility; on the contrary, the conclusion was that the system had broken down, that it was incapable of carrying out its elementary responsibilities, and that the state must assume, even if only temporarily, the burden of providing relief.

Those who in retrospect look for Franklin's theory of government, for his conception of the state, will find it here. They will recognize, too, that, behind the occasion for defining the state as having a responsibility to the individuals who created and who own it, there was a latent challenge to those at home and abroad who conceived it in authoritarian terms as above and beyond the individual. Franklin was well aware that a totalitarian state was asserting itself in Italy, using individuals but owing them nothing in return. This, being an individualist, he rejected condignly. We can see now that democracy in his person was preparing a contrast to authoritarianism. There was a faint presentiment of world struggle in this summer message.

This was nearly a year after Franklin's re-election in 1930; by then not only Hoover but the whole Republican party was sensitized to the potentialities of his mere existence as governor in New York. Everything he said and did was watched and analyzed; all his actions had the inflated value of political potentiality. This particular pronouncement had a weighty impact. It caused a gathering together and a taking of counsel among Republicans in a way they had not had to do in many years. The reverberations and the disturbed twitterings were even more audible in Washington than in Albany. The party men did not pause over the allusion to Mussolini behind Franklin's words; they recognized themselves, their conception of the state, and their theory of its responsibilities in his forthright statement. They were at the moment forced to fight on his own ground—in New York State, where his advantage was overwhelming, even though the legislature had a Republican majority.

Franklin was at home in struggles with the legislature. He used his knowledge this time to enormous advantage. His message began with dissimulation—an invitation to co-operate. He knew they could not accept. He went on confidently to the next position. When, as he expected, the legislative leaders rejected his bill and offered a delusionary substitute, Franklin "went to the people." What happened then frightened the opposition so thoroughly that they immediately capitulated. Thus they made him the gift of an issue and proved their own

lack of confidence. They—and with them Republicanism in the nation
—were defeated in advance.

This establishment of leadership did not mean that the other contenders among the Democrats were ready to concede Franklin's nomination for the presidency. He had prepared the way; they were all the
more anxious for the privilege of capitalizing on his success. From then
on his double objective was to embarrass Republicans on national issues and to close his contract with the Democratic electorate. This was
now his task and his duty.

Meanwhile, it should be recalled, there was unfinished business in
New York. For, as I have noted, Franklin had been seized with a pro-
prietary interest, which called for the satisfaction to be found only in
really extensive improvement. How fortunate that a program of public
works to relieve unemployment resulted also in much-needed improvements. This was a thought that was to rest in Franklin's mind for
many years—a source of immense gratification. For it would not be difficult to extend the feeling of ownership beyond one state to the sisters
of the Union. All of them would be different—and better—because he
had worked on them.

It is pleasant to think of Franklin as governor going about the Empire
State seeking openings for good works and having the wherewithal to
initiate them. Summers he journeyed characteristically, in a kind of re-
gal progress, by way of the Erie Canal (Clinton's ditch) across the state,
living on the *Inspector*, which was an official barge. He and his party—
a large one—went slowly and stopped often. Everything that belonged
to the state came under his scrutiny. He noted deficiencies, marked
down evidences of inefficiency, and consulted with everyone who
wanted his ear about what more was needed. Cars waited at landings
for daily excursions ashore. Eleanor visited dormitories and kitchens in
long-neglected state institutions and told Franklin in the evenings what
she had seen. He looked over the state's wood lots, lingered over its
eroded hills, inspected the remedial work then beginning, and saw with
satisfaction the parks and forests which had been multiplying since his
days in the legislature. He estimated and discussed crops, watercourses,
roads, bridges, and power sites. No part of the state escaped. It was all
equally his, and all equally worthy of attention.

He felt that a good beginning had been made as he studied the
Tompkins County experiments being made by the Cornellians. Much of
the hill country around the university was exhausted; the new name for
it was "submarginal." In fact, as has been noted, the whole "southern
tier" of the state, from Sullivan County to Chautauqua, had a large proportion of farms that could no longer support their operators and were
best returned to trees and grass. It was as beautiful as any stretch of
country in the world, Franklin thought and said as he motored during

long summer days over its hills and, from their crests, viewed the lovely reaches of its valleys. But its people had fallen into the poverty characteristic of regions where the land was unsuitable for cropping. This Allegany country would again, as it once had, make magnificent forests and parks. But the people stranded on the eroded farms had to be resettled in the valleys before the hills could be reclaimed. This was the Tompkins County idea.

But Franklin went farther. As he looked at rural life in depression times, even after a decade of agricultural disadvantage, it seemed to him a far more secure and rewarding existence than that of city workers, who, when unemployment came, had no resources at all. He saw no reason why millions of such families might not have subsistence farms. He persisted, even, in contending that urban workers could succeed in part-time farming, thus relieving city congestion (from which he recoiled instinctively), curing, at least partially, unemployment, and making what he fully believed to be a better environment for family life and for the raising of children. There are more words in the public papers of his governorship devoted to this and allied problems than to any other general issue. Of nothing else did he feel so competent to speak. These were matters on which he needed no instruction. When he sat down to discuss them he had no need to force an interest or to find his way cautiously into the heart of the matter. It was his own province.

He felt, with reason, as he journeyed westward on the *Inspector,* that he had been, and was being, responsible for genuine improvements all over the state. He could see that results were already coming. Farmers were being helped by the reorganization of local government and by the state's assumption of many expenses and duties formerly borne locally (he advised them, if their taxes had not been reduced, to find out why); communications were improved, utility charges lowered, markets were supervised—in a hundred such practical ways he was working to better their lot. But not only farmers were within his area of concern; urban workers, too, had gone on making gains as they had in Smith's time. And all citizens were better off with the enlargement of welfare institutions, better public health measures, and, lately, special provisions to assist the unemployed. New York, in his regime, was beginning to be a functioning illustration of the state he had spoken of in his August message to the legislature, created by the people "for their mutual protection and well-being."

It could now be seen—and he saw clearly—how fortunate it was that he had been forced to assume the governorship, that he was not to make his bid for the presidency from a long retirement. Added now to all his former qualifications was the assurance that clothed a successful practicing executive, one, moreover, who had shown his political capabilities in the one convincing way—by overwhelming re-election. As he traveled

Commissions

slowly westward along the canal's pleasant reaches and back along Ontario's shores, he entertained on board the *Inspector* local notables—of all parties, because he persisted in assuming that the rank and file of Republicans, as distinguished from the tools of the interests he dealt with in Albany, were for him. He saw the fruits of his planning and his efforts coming into being; he noted the approval of the local men of influence; and he felt himself ready for what he had known would come someday but what he had not until now regarded as imminent. Whatever its demands, he would be equal to them.

There were times when he was momentarily at a loss, when he saw that necessary ranges of knowledge were completely unknown to him. As to these he allowed himself no despair; he noted the equal uncertainty of others and the serious disagreements among those who pretended to expertness. And, as we have seen, he had a practical device to be used in these dilemmas. This was the commission—which not only gained time but marshaled consent. He had used commissions very freely and by now was as skillful in their management as any politician who ever lived. Then, as we have also seen, he had an extraordinary gift for sorting out sane but realistic experts in whom to put his trust. He knew how to exploit their knowledge. For the new and more complex problems he saw descending upon him, he felt that those experts would be found on whom he could lean with confidence. While deliberations went on and he brought new problems into focus, commissions could be appointed and their work could be publicized. When his mind was made up he would act.

There was no doubt, however, that vast changes had to be contemplated. The easy relief for farmers in reducing their taxes and improving their roads, the help for city workers from welfare legislation—all this, lately so controversial, was rapidly becoming obsolete as an issue. These were picayune answers to the questions raised by the deepening depression. What public men were being faced with now was a new order of problems. The industrial system itself, and its interacting political system, was strained to the breaking point. There were signs of collapse. Anyone not part of the system itself—and Franklin was singularly free in this respect—could see behind all the pumped-up optimism flooding the nation that something was inherently wrong. There was a weakness, if not a rottenness, that went to the very nature of the institutions at the heart of industrial civilization. And their very existence was being challenged on the one hand by a Communist alternative and on the other by a National Socialist one. Both had pretensions to a world hegemony.

To Franklin these were as yet vaguely repugnant conceptions. The trouble was one that he must explore and master, untutored as he was and given to simple and politic remedies set out by the rather ordinary minds of those he set to work on his commissions. But he was by now a resourceful individual with more powerful motives than anyone knew. He was, moreover, freer than most of those of his generation from orthodoxies and dogmas. His mind was not only free to inquire and discover, it was not incapacitated by limitations on the running of his thought toward remedies. In this new technological world, which had relegated the simple schemes of his governorship to the storehouse, he readied himself to function on a level he had not known existed until he began to glimpse belatedly what a catastrophe the events of 1929 really had been. A whole people was preparing to endow him with leadership; they would expect him to know what was wrong and to provide remedies. He must not fail them.

The first essay into this new area of responsibility was the midsummer message of 1931. What was the state? The state was something created by them for their well-being. It must and would act in their behalf.

There was omitted—but everyone understood—the implication that implementation was necessary and that it could be supplied only by one who understood, and who had the political power to capture and use the state's institutions. Who was that individual? No one needed to be told. And after the engagement of the ensuing weeks with the Republican legislature, the lesson was too plain for anyone to miss. And anyone could understand, too, that such a power wielded in Washington rather than Albany was what a frightened and long-suffering people had been awaiting. Hoover and the Republicans might as well start packing. They were, in principle, through.

11.

Religion for Franklin was never again so creative a force in his life as it had been during his difficult adolescence at Groton. He must then make an adjustment to the mysterious changes within himself—almost explosive ones when they arrived—which are the one experience of that sort in the life of a man. To grow an inch a month, to add in the same time several pounds to body weight, to enter on the endless miseries of early sexual life, and with all this to have opening out the forbidding realms of knowledge from which selection must be made for the limited explorations anyone may make—all this creates a need for touch with the supreme giver of sympathy which never again will be so urgent.

Just at that time Franklin had the added problem—enough if he had had no other to keep him in torment—of placating the Groton circle to which he came so late. Added to this, moreover, his revered father was retreating into an invalidism which made him inaccessible. It is no wonder that the boy sought and found, with Headmaster Peabody's help, support and comfort in a heavenly father, established in a respected ceremonial, and represented by a concurrent earthly authority in Peabody's person.

The only other crisis of comparable depth and magnitude in Franklin's life before the presidency was that represented by his encounter with crippling disease. But by then he had reached mid-life; his resources and his communications were well established, his role in life had been well worked out, and the accommodations incidental to it had been running for a long time in the well-worn grooves of habit. He almost fitted the sketch he had outlined long ago as the person he would become—not quite, of course, for the completion of that picture required a position of power; and power required conquest. From one stage to another he moved with growing confidence. The possible interruption of this foreseen progress represented by his illness had been an agonizing prospect. It was this, and not the decision whether he

God was giving trials for FDR

should make a change in his whole direction, which must have unnerved him during those weeks while the doctors temporized and
yielded him only the uncertainties of their ignorance. There was, I feel,
never any question but that he would go on with his accepted career
if he could. The question was whether he could. That was the question
only God could answer.

It must be recalled that only a year before his illness he had had the
setback of electoral defeat. His bid for the vice-presidency, in the pattern of the other Roosevelt, had met with a complete check. He had
not at the time taken this as anything more than the fortune of politics.
It was not he who had been responsible for that Democratic debacle.
It had been, if anyone, Wilson; and, beyond Wilson, the war. Franklin
might have dissociated himself from it, but he had decided to run in
the interest of his future, although he would probably lose. He had not
been a confirmed Wilsonian for very long, anyway, and was certainly
not one whom Wilson would have chosen for succession. This may have
irked him; he must sometimes have inquired of himself whether he had
not undertaken the 1920 venture, so certain to fail, just to show that
one so undervalued by Wilson and all Wilson's official family (except,
perhaps, his chief, Daniels, who was so shrewd a politician and could
see around a corner) was, after all, more effective and consequential
than they had judged. If this had influenced him it was an ignoble motive, one, moreover, that he had no right to allow himself in the line of
his duty. He ought—as he knew very well—to keep strictly to the tactics
dictated by the grand objective which was large in him. Departure from
it was a kind of wickedness that deserved to be punished.

When he was immobilized—all but his mind—by polio, he must have
endured many an hour of tormented wonder as he asked over and over
to be shown whether that event in 1920 had to be put together with
this one in 1921. Perhaps he was so willful that one sharp lesson had
not been enough, and another and more decisive one had been supplied. He could only know when life returned to his paralyzed body
that this fear was not a justified apprehension. But would he have any
sign short of that? What if life came back only partially? What if he
could go on only by accepting a heavier burden and a far more trying
regime?

It seems to me quite evident what happened. The God in whom he
had rested so long bore him up, gave him reassurance, confirmed his
confidence. These were trials—defeat and disability; but they were not
warnings. Like other servants, he was being tested; he could find the
courage and resolution to emerge from his ordeal; he could be more
certain than ever that the course he was sailing was a true one, leading
to a harbor well prepared.

An ordinary observer would have judged that there was no reason why, in times that were completely—and seemingly permanently—Republican, Franklin Roosevelt, defeated vice-presidential candidate, paralyzed sufferer from crippling disease, should have been justified in looking beyond a long, humiliating, and painful convalescence, and beyond a "new era" in industrial civilization, to a time when his capability would return and when also the need for a leader would be urgent. That he did so look forward, almost at once, we know. A sign had been given.

The sign he saw was the vision of the objective, clearer now than ever before, with the way to it marked plainly. He was never a man of little faith; after his sickness he was a man of unassailable confidence. If so terrible a disease had not stopped his progress, if he had been allowed to go on, surely nothing else could stop him, and surely the means he had perfected were justified. How fortunate it was that the fallow years of politics for him ran concurrently with his disablement. He must recover and, recovering, he must prepare himself. Meanwhile events would be turning toward the time when his restored strength and his new wisdom would be put to use.

All this being far behind him by 1932, and the turning years having brought about the favoring situations, one after the other, it can be understood why Franklin, encountering them as the now-experienced governor of the Empire State, was a man expectant and serene as well as busy with good works. No prospect of responsibility could really daunt a man who had suffered both defeat and humiliation as he had suffered them and who had emerged as victorious as he.

One of the characteristics most puzzling to those who met him first as late as 1932 was the completeness of his assurance, especially since it seemed to proceed from a less than sufficient competence. There were many matters about which his lack of knowledge was total. There were issues about which even the groundwork had not been laid. Even his general attitude of liberal progressivism, sufficient until now for expedients, was suddenly irrelevant and obsolete. A national technological complex, come to its first total breakdown, was something that was not in the progressive book. It took a really durable faith to believe that at fifty a man could expect that this sort of knowledge—knowledge suited to the shaping of national policy—would be added unto him. But there was no sign of discontented wavering. There was only a calm probing for the missing theory and a searching for the required devices. He had no doubts, no qualms about asking for power and then more power.

When I first met him, in the early spring of 1932, I met the product of the environment and the experiences I have heretofore described. I should have been a strange young man had I not been instantly fascinated.[1] I had been brought to Albany by Raymond Moley, who had worked for him in the past on one of these exploratory commissions of which I have spoken. Ray's specialty was the administration of justice, but he was a well-trained political scientist and, as a whole generation of political comment has now shown, set no limits to the scope of his political and economic judgments. In those days he seemed to be a progressive out of the purest City of Cleveland tradition.[2] Progressivism was also Franklin's recognized inheritance from Uncle Ted. Ray felt and said that both these strains of American political thought came together in Franklin. Moreover, Ray was certain he was going to be President.

I was taken out of myself. I had been indulging, to the point of immoderacy, in public comment both about Hoover and about the business leaders who had presided so pretentiously and so blindly over the miseries of the depression as it had spread across the land. I now could turn to a more constructive kind of activity. I was not so sure that Franklin was to be President, not knowing all the planning and maneuvering in the background, and not having been aware of the position assumed by the political chessmen. As I was allowed to see the operations at first hand I became more optimistic, and this led, if possible, to more enthusiastic co-operation in all that I was allowed to do. As a result I did become an insider, and I did go on to Washington for four years of official life.

That my inquiring has gone on since that spring day in 1932 is my credential for writing this account. It will be understood, since I have said this, that meeting him was somewhat like coming into contact with destiny itself. It was a tremendous, an unnerving experience, only to be realized and assimilated over a long time.

Nevertheless, either the impact of this meeting did not prevent me from expressing myself or Franklin was extraordinarily patient about extracting from me what I so badly wanted to say. Perhaps my exposition by then was so well rehearsed that it could be repeated almost automatically. What I said to him I had been saying to anyone who would listen. At any rate, it sank in. He wanted more and I supplied it. What I intended was that he should understand the futility of the old approaches. What had happened was a breakdown not contemplated in any of the received explanations. Therefore, none of the approaches to remedial action was of any use.

I now think that he had come to some such conclusion himself. It may have been a mostly unconscious one, since he had available to

---

[1] Actually I was forty-one, not so young, but nine years younger than he.

[2] By this I mean to associate him with Tom Johnson, Frederic C. Howe, Brand Whitlock, Golden Rule Jones, and all the crusading righteousness of their generation.

him few leads into the new territory and only elementary equipment for such a journey. But he was certainly receptive. And he found in what I had to say, I believe, an adequacy of explanation he had not theretofore been able to find. He knew that he had to have something to rely on. He was about to enter on the final testing of his competence. And in these matters, now certain to be the center of controversy, he found himself unlettered. His instinct held him back; he found it hard to get outside the logic of laissez faire or to think in any reforming terms except those of the progressives in which he had been schooled.

His instinct may have held him back and may have caused a later reversion when he found, as he did, that even in crisis the terms of a revised theory were politically unacceptable, but he felt then that what was needed was opening out to him and he explored it eagerly. Later, as the resistance of politicians to disturbance was made manifest and as Brandeis from on high handed down the obiter dicta of orthodox progressivism, he would retreat. His measures in the long run would be confused because partly they would have their origin in the old thought and partly they would stem from the new. But we had an exciting time in Albany.

The campaign had already got well under way before the Brains Trust got to work. It began, if any beginning date can be assigned, on January 22, when Franklin entered his first primary campaign (in North Dakota) for the presidency. In formal terms this was a campaign for the nomination, with the battle for the presidency to come later. But such a separation is unreal. Franklin's opposition was not now the other Democrats nearly so much as it was Hoover and Republicanism. Perhaps I say this too flatly. Franklin was sure of the nomination, but others were not so confident, not even those close to him; besides, they were intent on the nomination and thought very little of the election to come. The Democrats in the West were largely favorable, although there was McAdoo in California, who was in an uncertain mood; but in the East the re-entry of Smith into the competition had complicated matters. Massachusetts' Governor Ely was a Smith man, so was Hague in Jersey City, and there might be others. So there was no letdown from over-confidence. By March a majority of the delegates to the convention had been corralled. But by an old rule it took two thirds to nominate, and two thirds was unattainable before the convention met. There would be a fight in Chicago, which was what Howe and Farley had striven so mightily to forestall.

Franklin fired his first broadside on April 7. This was what is known in political annals as the "Forgotten Man" speech—a phrase for which Ray Moley is better known than for anything else he ever invented—

and that was a borrowing from William Graham Sumner.[3] This is too bad, because Ray's labors during this year and the one that followed helped enormously in shaping the series of pronouncements, measures, and actions which as a whole are known as the New Deal.

[handwritten marginalia: Gives impression that Brain Trust formed FDR]

Ray's first contribution was to take charge of the Brains Trust. This informal group of mostly academic people may have been thought of first by Sam Rosenman or by Ray himself. Each has made a kind of claim. At any rate, as the first choice of the board of selection I broke the ice with Franklin. He found it possible to communicate with me, and I understand that this made it easier for others who followed, notably Adolf Berle, who was the only other, besides Ray and myself, who was regularly present at those unique meetings in the red plush surroundings of the Executive Mansion that spring.

Those meetings, we can claim, contributed to the fitting of Franklin for the presidency. We were able, Berle and I, with Ray abetting and Sam and Doc O'Connor looking on approvingly, to lead an exceptionally agile mind to a level of discussion adequate to the circumstances.

That level, of course, was theoretical. We pressed him to grapple with the complex realities of industrial life, to move beyond his reasonable but oversimple reactions which were obviously insufficient as guides to policy. He went with us toward a comprehension of large-scale technology, the forces it had created and the consequences of allowing it to escape regulation—or rather of allowing its management to be gathered into a few privately controlled ganglia. This we linked up with the price system, the network of credits, and the handling of commodities and services. Everywhere we probed for weaknesses and dangers and felt for such possibilities as there might be for leverage. We exposed for him the private wars going on among the titans of industrial society. *[handwritten marginalia: competition]* Each strove to exploit the other. Some succeeded and, in doing so, overbalanced the system. That, essentially, was our explanation of the current trouble. It was one he seemed to accept. I say that we led Franklin into these discussions. That is strictly true. Yet he was as eager as a boy intent on an exploration that has caught his imagination. He was often ahead of us. And none of our discussion was forced. Adolf had one of the most scintillant minds of his generation; that Franklin could come into contact with it and furnish the appreciation it required for sustained functioning proved to me once for all the quality of his thinking processes, once they were engaged.

I have tried to explain what it was that engaged them. It was the need of a man coming into responsibilities he must meet. I suppose it

[3] Sumner had used it in quite a different way. By the forgotten man he had meant the middle class, not those of whom Franklin spoke—the one third who were at a disadvantage of some sort—the aged, the unemployed, the incapacitated, the workers on submarginal land, and their dependents.

could be said—as I often thought, even at the time—that all the time and energy Franklin put into this rigorous Brains Trust course in socioeconomics was a measure of his amazing confidence in the future. It was obvious that none of it had anything whatever to do with the nomination which was now the immediate objective.

The operations of the political committee—if I may call it that, although outside of Louis Howe and Jim Farley it was almost as amorphous as our Brains Trust; that is to say, there were comings and goings of personnel, uncertainty of assignment, and frequent crossing of wires —were going on concurrently and had a natural priority. But we were not overconscious, in our sector, of this urgency. We were expected to deal with matters about as far removed from such pressures as could be conceived. Our subject matter was not timeless, but it was general. It had to do with social forces, concurrent ones, and their impact on each other. Politics came within our purview only as it had to do with grasping and keeping power. So for me it was no more than one of the recalcitrant variables with which an analyst must deal.

But none of us was a child. We were not so unsophisticated that we could remain unmoved by the drama with which we were now in touch. Besides, we often had to come down to earth as Franklin made contact with one or another issue that forced, or threatened to force, his hand. This, we could see, would often be necessary when the campaign came on after the nomination. Almost unconsciously we adapted ourselves. We began to approach the general problem through specific issues. We learned to see each in terms of an exposition that would fit into the public policy a President must have, a candidate must propose, and a prospective candidate must study.

The sectors of the economy most obviously in distress offered us ways into the heart of the system. Agriculture, banking, railroads, foreign trade, utilities, investments—these offered topical categories of such initial interest that they easily led into discussion of remedial action and public policy.

It is no more than a statement of fact to say that Franklin's progress in gaining an understanding of matters about which he had heretofore thought only in the oversimple way of an educated and well-informed amateur was so remarkable that by June a notable weakness was transformed into an all-round competence. He knew what it was he expected to say about most of the issues he was likely to have to meet in the campaign, and he was well on the way to shaping a system of policy to be used when the presidency was attained. This was an intellectual feat that would have been remarkable if he had had no other occupation. But he was governor of New York and an active contender for the presidential nomination at the same time. As academic observers, we

216

Formulated his platform

Refusing to obey authority

could be excused if we were amazed and even, perhaps, if we found ourselves, quite without wishing it, enlisted in a cause.

The Albany of that spring can only be described as given over to euphoria. Immense changes were in prospect and readiness for them was being established with satisfying success. It tried the capabilities, but it was getting done, and it would be done in time. There was no longer need to worry lest the confusion of the house and the office under the gathering pressure should make the work to be done impossible. The more the complexities multiplied, the more easily Franklin got through his days. It was as though the crowding, the insistence, and the centering of attention were no more than pleasant stimuli. The sensitivity of politicians to the probable sources of influence is extreme. It is part of what makes them politicians. The heady aroma of power being gathered for a new blooming was scented from afar, and crowds of applicants came to ask membership in the now-forming entourage. The old members of Franklin's team were inclined to be supercilious about late-comers. At this stage they were welcome as evidence of what was about to be and as workers for it—just to make sure; but the tendency was to assign them the most clerklike duties of preparation. The humility with which these jobs were undertaken amazed those of us who were amateurs. To the old professionals it seemed as matter of course as assigning a new boy at school the menial tasks of a dormitory.

We were also somewhat amazed to find ourselves regarded by the ingathering crowd of prospective co-workers as more important than we had been thinking ourselves to be. The politicians felt that anyone close to a candidate must have the one kind of influence they understood. It took some of us a good while to learn what went on in the minds of these professionals as they watched us at work and wondered what we were up to. We were embarrassed; we knew how little we counted.

One thing the politicians could understand: speeches had to be written. They were part of the ritual of campaigning, a necessary part, and they had to be done with care. A mistake in a speech was something too horrible to contemplate. But a speech was more than an opportunity to make mistakes. It represented the outward face of the grand strategy being worked up into a policy by the candidate and his circle of co-workers. In the spring of 1932 the politicians felt particularly inferior in these matters. The old clichés and shibboleths of Democracy, even of its progressive wing, were so obsolete that even they could perceive it; something novel had to be devised. The electorate that year was likely to vote against something, true; but its opposite had to be formulated. If the Brains Trust could do that, its members had at least to be tolerated. The best the politicians knew how to do for us was to treat us as a respected member of their own trade union. We came to, appreciate the compliment.

The truth was, however—and we never for a moment forgot it—that we, like the others, were being used by the principal in this grand political venture. Our first real lesson came to us as we worked on, and saw delivered, the "Forgotten Man" address. Others followed, but this was our baptism.[4]

The "Forgotten Man" speech could be regarded as Ray Moley's child; my own firstborn was the "Concert of Interests" speech in St. Paul on April 18.[5] It was a Jefferson Day dinner and as such was two months before the convention: in place, Floyd Olson's Minnesota, and in auspices, Jeffersonian. It was thus suitable for a major stroke. I consider that a major stroke was in fact delivered. But I admit, even at this remove, that I may be prejudiced. In all honesty, also, I must admit to no more real authorship than any but a very few of the numerous speeches of that year allowed anyone to claim. Franklin was almost always the real author. I wrote, but he rewrote, in the manner Sam Rosenman has so elaborately and faithfully described in *Working with Roosevelt*. As I read this speech in later years, only the last paragraph seems to me to come out clearly as a statement of the collectivism Berle and I represented—as against the atomism of the Brandeis school. And even this is not too satisfactory, except that the phrase was used and reiterated which I had labored to invent as representative of the new thought. By "the concert of interests" I intended to convey the necessity for encompassing in a system, subject to control, all the forces and functions of our society, each contributing its due part. I still like the phrase. And Franklin was willing to use it many times. Very evidently he liked it too.

But it was not until the next speech was made that all the implications of this point of view we had been developing were brought to commitment. And none of us in the academic sector of the Brains Trust had anything directly to do with that address. It was made at Oglethorpe University on May 22, and it was written by Ernest K. Lindley. There are complicated, and to me interesting, reasons why

---

[4] The speeches referred to here are to be found in full in *Public Papers*, Vol. I, in a special section devoted to pre-convention addresses.

[5] For the last two years Franklin had been making speeches, concocting statements, and turning on his fireside manner over the radio. But he had been carefully non-specific about various issues and definite only about those that were almost non-controversial. The time was coming, as he himself said, when "getting down to cases" was indicated. It may be objected that public power, for instance, was a controversial issue. But it illustrates the definition rather well. It was not controversial among progressive Democrats. It did not divide any of Franklin's potential supporters. His avoidance of many issues had been guided by this principle. He now proposed to gather in those who would follow him into reasonably new territory.

none of us from Columbia was on hand for its preparation, but I shall not repeat them here; it was done at Warm Springs, and the fact is that it was produced by Ernest, with some critical comment by James M. Kieran,[6] because he had not thought the "Concert of Interests" speech adequate, because he had been challenged by Franklin to produce a better one, and because he understood what we were trying to say as well as we did. For more of his language survived than survived in any speech any of us wrote—with some unusual exceptions which I shall note.

I mention this to make the important point that the Oglethorpe speech represented the high tide of collectivism. In fact, it presented the last of it in the campaign. Beginning with the next speech, which was, in fact, the acceptance address, Franklin reverted to the familiar atomism, and he kept pretty well to it from then on. He said not what he believed but what he believed people wanted to hear. He had made up his mind that all of us were pressing too hard. The nation was not ready to hear what must be done. He still considered that it would have to be done but that it would be better not to speak of it in advance. This was one kind of strategy, the kind the politicians had uneasily pressed for all along—uneasily, because even they could see its insufficiency. They simply gave way to fear—and a fear they imputed to the electorate—of the strange, the unknown, and the complicated.

I am still inclined to regard the Oglethorpe speech as the best of all the public addresses Franklin made in his long career. I mean "best" in the sense of representing the sincerest, most unpolitical statement of his real attitudes and convictions. I have said that it came in May and that it was prepared in the rather removed intimacy of Warm Springs by newspapermen who knew Franklin better, almost, than he knew himself. They thought it was what he ought to say because it was what he believed. No politician saw the draft or expressed his doubts or advised modification. None of them was around at the moment. It horrified them when they read it in the newspapers; it horrified Brandeis, the self-appointed progressive archangel, too. Bob La Follette

[6] James M. Kieran was the inventor of the Brains Trust appellation. He was the Albany correspondent of the New York *Times* as Ernest K. Lindley was of the New York *Herald Tribune*. Both of these newspapermen had a closer relationship to the effort of those days than is usually appreciated. The fact that between them they wrote the Oglethorpe speech is only one evidence of the concern with which they watched our work. Their public comment on it was not unfriendly, but it reflected very little of the intimacy with which they followed our discussions, or their own contributions to them. They were never actually present in the more formal sessions, when we discussed policy from prepared memoranda, but we had even longer discussions with them at other times. Ernest, of course, was the author already of one account of Franklin's life. He would later write two others. Cf. *Personal Letters: 1928–1945*, Vol. I, p. 193, in which Franklin told Ernest he could not use two anecdotes, one having to do with Hoover in 1920.

Oglethorpe speech Truly rep. FDR's feelings

and Bob Wagner congratulated me and refused to believe I had not had a hand in it.

The waters were troubled now, and the convention was upon us. Louis Howe was up in arms. What were we trying to do, make all his work useless? He would not have Franklin frightening people with strange talk about planning. It sounded like socialism, and there was too much suspicion already that Franklin had such leanings. Attacking businessmen was all right. It focused nowhere, pointed out no one. But this reaching out into theory had to stop. Brandeis let Franklin know, through the mysterious channels he used, that he disapproved. This collectivism must be abandoned. Franklin must go back to the safe advocacy of controlling business through the re-establishment of competition. The only safe business was a little one: make them all little and all would be safe. Also, they would never be in conspiracy against society if trust-busting was sincerely pursued as the Republicans, even T.R., had never pursued it. This was a voice from a high place; it spoke a traditional tongue. It gave Franklin pause, and presently he bowed to the dictate—to Bob La Follette's disgust, who recognized at once what had happened.

Bob La Follette, of all the progressives of that time, had made the most complete transition to modernism. He had become a collectivist by hard thinking and in the course of political experience in a tough school. He had been his father's secretary for years. Old Bob had been the kind of fighter who wears himself out in the eternal struggle with evil. Like George Norris, he was pure in heart and simple in mind. But industrial technology had created what Tawney called the Great Society under his eyes without his ever seeing it. Young Bob saw it. He had the mind for it, but the fighting blood of his father was in his veins too. He was as tough as they come. More than anyone else, for two years now he had made Hoover's nights hideous with stinging criticism. But he had also tormented him with alternatives to the policy of inaction. His were the bills for planning, for economic councils, for massive attacks on unemployment through public works and relief, which had lain so conspicuously on the congressional table throughout the economy's sinking spell.

As a historian of sorts, writing of events already far in the past, I do not speak of the decision Franklin made in this matter quite as I did earlier when my disappointment was freshly upon me. I do not even think at this remove that he made as basic a decision as I concluded then that he had. What he decided was only that he must be expedient; and expediency, he judged, called for the application of a political principle with which I afterward became familiar. I recall its statement and restatement in the nasal Tennessee locutions of Cordell Hull. He used to argue with those of us younger men in the administration who survived beyond the Moley period that we must learn discretion. "You don't," he said, "tell a man about it when you are about to cut off his leg. If you do you scare him half to death before his real trouble comes upon him." So, he would have had us agree, if you have to do some social reorganizing, you do it as quietly as possible. You play down its implications. You give no advance notice. You pretend that nothing unusual is happening. I heard this so often that I labeled it, for my own amusement, the "principle of secret amputation."

Cordell Hull was an old and experienced politician, and I, at least, listened to him with deference. He took some pains with me because of my obvious respect—usually in company with Charles Taussig, who regarded him as a prophet and haunted his office for years. But I also learned of another principle—not from him, but from young Bob, and perhaps because it was temperamentally more agreeable, it seemed to me a more practical guide. This was the rule of the mandate. It was Bob's contention—and it had obviously always been a La Follette practice from the very first—that nothing of importance could be done without support, and support could be had only by painstaking education of potential supporters. If important policies were sprung on an unprepared public, Bob said, there would always be a reaction which, if it did not entirely defeat the effort, would so attenuate it that its effect would be seriously modified.

Bob pushed aside the objections often made, which in argument I repeated to him, that to say in advance what was intended was to notify the enemy—those whose interests would be adversely affected—and allow the organization of opposition. It was his conviction that if the measure was good, if it "made sense," any competent politician could arouse his constituency to its support and hold their loyalty through the subsequent battles.

Franklin had to choose among these political principles—not that he did it consciously. He did not choose, as I at first thought, between one or the other socio-economic policy. He was not won back to atomism. He simply concluded that atomism was so traditional, so accepted, so widely believed to be the economic reform most needed, that it would be impossible to win a mandate for the collectivist policies he had been contemplating as campaign material. They would be necessary, but it would be better to come up with them when the time for action came, one after another, without any general labeling.

So the Oglethorpe speech was the last collectivist one. But it did not, as it might logically have done, represent the final essay of the Brains Trust. As Franklin drifted back toward orthodox progressivism he did not dismiss us. In fact our conversations went on, becoming now more detailed, and so less theoretical, but, even so, moving very rapidly through a range that would be amazing in any other circumstance than that of a political campaign. But there were no more major efforts in the last month.

Before leaving the matter of Franklin's expedient decision concerning social policy I must refer to one penalty it drew on him and, Bob La Follette would have said, always draws on an expedient decider. This was the more critical appraisal of acute commentators who understood what was being done. The most critical and the most disgusted of them was Walter Lippmann; but he was representative of liberal opinion, a matter that Franklin, as I have said, did not accept with equanimity and was not inclined to regard as justified. Walter wrote what later became a famous column dealing with the matter as early as January 8, 1932. This was the column in which he accused Franklin of carrying water on both shoulders. He was supplementing "two-faced platitudes" with private assurances in order to hold onto both right-wing and left-wing support. In Lippmann's forthrightly expressed opinion, Franklin lacked a firm grasp of public affairs and was altogether without strong convictions of any sort. He was "an amiable man, with many philanthropic impulses." But he was not the "dangerous enemy of anything." He was "no crusader . . . no tribune of the people . . . no enemy of entrenched privilege." He was "a pleasant man, who, without any important qualifications for the office, would very much like to be President."

Franklin resented this, and was not disposed to consider it deserved. Also, he did not allow it to change his course, unless the Oglethorpe speech can be considered a momentary change. On the whole, expediency in the persons of Howe, Farley, et al., among the politicians, and Brandeis among the angelic host, prevailed. The patient was not to be notified of the coming amputation. It was even worse than that. There was still to come an argument among the doctors at the bedside of the patient. Brandeis was going to prevent the amputation if he could.

The political situation in that last month was rather more worrisome than it had been since the victories of 1930. The stop-Roosevelt movement seems to have had more strength than Farley, Howe, and Flynn[7] had allowed for. They were, in fact, face to face with the necessity of making a deal, and it was not easily apparent with whom it might be

[7] It ought to be noted that Ed Flynn, who was the political boss of the Bronx, was playing an increasingly useful role. He was, it will be remembered, New York's Secretary of State, in which job he had replaced Robert Moses. This gave him reason for being in Albany much of the time. Franklin learned to depend on his clever, devious, and utterly quiet methods. He ran his organization with less friction than any other city boss; there was seldom any suspicion of corruption; and he had judged that Franklin's star was rising. He stuck to Franklin throughout this difficult year when the rest of the New York leaders defected to Smith. He would even stick to him at a future crisis when Farley—incredible as it seems—deserted. At this time he had probably taken over most of the liaison duties with the other bosses.

made. This was distasteful, but it was not at all a strange procedure in politics. Practical people make these accommodations as a matter of course. The thing is to give as little and get as much as possible, just as in any other bargain, but it was apparent that in this one something valuable would have to be given. Franklin's team, although it had accumulated a majority of the delegates, was all too conscious that Champ Clark had had a majority in 1912 and that McAdoo had had one in 1924. They were conscious, also, that it had been Smith who had held out unreasonably against McAdoo and had defeated him in spite of his majority. Evidently Smith had an unforgiving, a self-centered nature. He could not be dealt with.

Relations between Al Smith and Franklin had reached the stage of recrimination long before the convention. Al's good-soldier pose during the 1930 campaign had evaporated when the galling fact of Franklin's huge majority became known. Also, he had listened to Belle Moskowitz and Bob Moses when they brought him the various estimates of Democratic chances in 1932. The prospect of Democratic victory was more and more favorable, and he allowed himself to become more and more convinced that he was entitled to the better opportunity of 1932 after what he now regarded as his sacrificial effort in 1928. He was encouraged by Ely in Massachusetts and Hague in New Jersey. These would be Smith provinces, he was assured. So, following Franklin's announcement of candidacy on January 22, Smith made one on February 7, and the fight was out in the open.

It was the "Forgotten Man" speech in April, however, that precipitated the bitterness in Smith's heart. Concerning it, Smith released to the press his "class war" statement:

I will take off my coat and vest and fight to the end any candidate who persists in any demagogic appeal to the masses of the working people of this country to destroy themselves by setting class against class and rich against poor.

Franklin did not reply. In fact, from then on he gave Smith the silent treatment which so often infuriated his opponents. But it seems to me likely that Smith's imputation of radicalism was taken as a warning and was partly responsible for Franklin's deviation toward greater caution. It was urged on him by the Brains Trust—part of it, anyway—that this, if ever, was a time when radicalism would be politically desirable. They could cite a good many of his own statements in support. But the deluge of opposite advice was overwhelming. The politicians wanted to work on their nomination problem in secret, with no disturbance in the political atmosphere. As for the election, that was in the bag for a Democrat, whoever he might be; they simply wanted their candidate to make no mistakes that would prevent Hoover from defeating himself. The de-

Howe & Farley

sirability of a mandate made no impression on them whatever. Politicians never have a program for anything beyond election. That event to them is a kind of apocalypse beyond which the future is a blank.

Smith, at this late date, when the enemy had captured most of the South and most of the West as well, could not run on an outright "nominate-Smith" plan; it had to be a "stop-Roosevelt" movement. His supporters urged that if Franklin's nomination was prevented the way would be opened for someone else, not necessarily Smith—perhaps Ritchie, Byrd, Baker, or Garner. There were several direct clashes. In early March, Franklin won the primary in New Hampshire. In early April there were battles on the same day in Wisconsin and New York. Franklin won in Wisconsin, but the cards were down now in New York and all the compromising did not pay off. He won only one third of the delegates, all of whom were from upstate or from Flynn's Bronx. This was disappointing, but there was one thing about it that would be helpful at Chicago: Franklin no longer had any relations with Tammany, and this would please the Westerners.

Howe and Farley did not always use good judgment. They ought to have avoided a test in Massachusetts, where the warnings were clear. But they were intent on piling up delegates and would not concede. The primary was lost by three to one late in April. This was only partly compensated for by winning Pennsylvania two days later; it was not, in fact, an impressive win. In California in May something interesting, even if at the moment disconcerting, happened. Garner won, with Franklin second and Smith a bad third.

Taken altogether, out of six direct clashes, Franklin won four and Smith two. Smith could not himself be nominated. Franklin had the delegates of thirty-four states and six territories. They were pledged and safe—on the first ballot. But impressive as this showing was, the majority could very quickly break up. The vindictive Smith crowd set themselves, in a black rage, to defeat the man they now hated with an unreasoning hatred. The infighting during the last pre-convention weeks was far from pretty. It involved, among other maneuverings, the organization of the convention itself and the seating of contested delegations from Minnesota and Louisiana.

Since the convention was to be the scene of further struggle, its organization might be important in some crisis. A ruling, a recognition, an adjournment might be favorable or the reverse. Franklin's people were faced with the fact that Smith's friends were in an almost dictatorial position. Raskob was still national chairman, and since 1930 Jouett Shouse had been in charge of the executive committee, which really ran things. Shouse had made a good record during the past two years; he and his director of publicity, Charles Michelson, had done a good deal to expedite the disintegration of the Hoover forces. At least they had taken advantage of every opening. Until lately Franklin had not been certain of Shouse's affiliation with Smith, but presently it became as plain as that of Raskob, with whom there had been several undercover brushes.[8]

Shouse tried to effect a change in the convention rules which would increase the number of uninstructed delegates. Howe alerted Franklin's supporters on the National Committee to the danger, and the change was not made. But from then on it was quite clear that Shouse could not be trusted. When the other side proposed him for permanent chairman there was an embarrassing moment. Shouse had deserved well of the party. Franklin could not oppose him outright. He said to those who urged his support that he would "commend" him. When the time came to choose, all of Franklin's supporters voted for Senator Thomas J. Walsh. Franklin had been less than frank, and there were howls of anguished rage from the Smith camp. But Walsh was elected.

Another embarrassment arose over the two-thirds rule. About this Jim Farley nervously took too much on himself. He had a majority; he would use it to abrogate the rule. It illustrated his provincialism. The Southerners valued its veto power; by using it they could prevent the selection of anyone they disapproved. Howe had a tantrum and Franklin repudiated Farley in a press release.[9]

When the convention opened on June 27 there was no member of Franklin's entourage who was not overcome by the fears of the moment; only Franklin himself was sure. His confidence amazed everyone who was in touch with him during that period, but then none of them was aware of its source. Even Louis Howe, who ought to have kept his head now of all times, allowed anxiety to distort his judgment. He was as full of schemes as a gypsy and incapable of implementing any one of them. Jim Farley and Ed Flynn would have to do the actual work; Louis seemed worn down to a wisp as he journeyed westward. But Franklin in Albany, with Sam at his side and Missy close by, was never cooler in his appraisals, never surer of touch, never more certain that success was imminent. The delegates and assorted hangers-on gathered in Chicago on a sparkling summer day. Between the old Congress Hotel, where Franklin's henchmen had their headquarters, and the east-stretching lake, the world's most magnificent fountain tossed its showers

---

[8] The most notable of which was Raskob's manipulation of the wet-dry issue to force Franklin's hand. Cf. numerous accounts of the pre-convention maneuvers in Farley, Flynn, etc. I might mention again that the best account of the 1932 campaign—an indispensable one to the serious student of politics—is that of Roy V. Peel and Thomas Donnelly, *The 1932 Campaign* (New York: Farrar & Rinehart, 1935).

[9] It was Huey P. Long who, in complicated circumstances, began the move. Farley went along; but it may have been with Franklin's consent. His later reversal is not conclusive.

into the sun; and boss Ed Kelly's hoodlums passed the word to pack the convention galleries and shout for Smith.[10] Hague, Kelly, and Curry—Jersey City, Chicago, and New York—all against him! It made Farley shudder but not despair. There were professionals in Texas too. He eyed them speculatively as Franklin pointed them out.

I will only say generally about the convention that the stop-Roosevelt movement, engineered by the Smith people and abetted by Ritchie, Byrd, and others, had momentum enough to last through the first three ballots and to prevent Franklin's vote from reaching the necessary two-thirds majority. A simple majority was reached, which put Franklin well ahead. But when, after the third ballot, adjournment was taken, disintegration could have set in and a turn to Newton D. Baker, the leading dark horse, might have begun.

But this was not allowed to happen. A deal was made for the Texas and California votes, and Garner was given the second place on the ticket. The man behind Garner was William R. Hearst, an old man now, his vitality fading amid the extravagances of his San Simeon estate, but still a power in the party. He was a tired dictator, but he still had his newspaper chain and commanded its policies arbitrarily. He rather favored Franklin because of his criticisms of Hoover and because of his apparent moderation. His agent in the bargain for nomination was McAdoo, who was now a resident in California and a delegate to the convention. When on the fourth ballot McAdoo began to speak for California, everyone knew that a deal had been made and that the stop-Roosevelt campaign had failed.

Garner was not hard for Franklin, in the optimistic mood of the moment, to accept. He was a confused Texan who, as the most prominent congressional Democrat, had had the responsibility for shaping alternatives to the Hoover policies. He was, however, so conservative and so lacking in imagination that nothing had occurred to him that Hoover had not thought of first. He had thus endangered his standing with his fellow Democrats, but he had won it back by sponsoring three inflationary measures—to pay the veterans an immediate $2,400,000 by issuing Treasury certificates, to add a billion dollars to the capital of the Reconstruction Finance Corporation, and to issue bonds for another billion to be used in public works. This was pure demagoguery. Two of the measures passed the House, but only one passed the Senate, in a form satisfactory to Hoover. And anyway Garner was known to be more worried about balancing the budget than about unemployment. He was hopelessly sterile as a leader and his candidacy would have been absurd even if he had not been from the South.

Franklin was not looking for a running mate with ideas. He would

[10] Kelly was then chief engineer of the Chicago Sanitary District, but he was already a power in politics, more so than Mayor Cermak.

furnish those. But he was glad to have a Southerner. The time would come when he would see that his optimism about handling Southerners was unjustified, but at the moment he was confident. So the deal was made. Franklin could now be certain that there would be no conservative defection. What he would do with his allies was a deferred problem.

Franklin's agent in these negotiations was Farley, and their success gave him a start on his later reputation for political shrewdness. His prestige would be useful during the first administration, until the Southerners got completely out of hand. Ultimately he would team up with Garner and other conservatives against Franklin. But that was still far in the future, and Franklin was not one to worry about the future. As he flew out toward Chicago to make his acceptance speech, his certainty of victory was complete. The real problem, as so often, had been the nomination. That gained, nothing could stop his progress toward the presidency.[11]

---

[11] There will be other conventions, as there will be other campaigns, in Franklin's career. The scope here does not allow me to pause overlong at any one of them. I must just note, as to the gallery-packing at Chicago, how heady the shouts from there can be, even when it is known what the mechanics are. There is, for instance, an almost ecstatic column written by Heywood Broun about this Chicago performance of Kelly's henchmen. It is printed in *It Seems to Me* (New York: Harcourt, Brace, 1935), pp. 167 ff. Heywood was a Smith man. He began his column, "I'd rather be right than be Roosevelt," and pictured Smith as a marytred liberal. He had to retract in 1936, but in 1932 he so far forgot his newspaperman's detachment that he grabbed a banner and marched in a Smith demonstration.

Very Imp. — Tug. felt
economy should be dealt w/
as a whole & not specifically
Not FDR

12

The agricultural problem may serve as well as any to illustrate Franklin's movement from one to another level of understanding. I have noted how remarkably his public papers as governor anticipate his policies as President. This has to be modified by noting that the anticipation was more a matter of identification than an actual outlining of solutions. But even that is remarkable. I have also said that he found new reserves of energy and intelligence as the deepening problems of a sick society thrust themselves into public discussion while he was governor. Both these are true statements even though they may at first seem inconsistent. His instinct was to find quickly, and to use at once, some remedy whenever an abuse or a difficulty became apparent. He took much advice and selected more and more skillfully what seemed appropriate.

Very little that he proposed or did after this process was harmful. Most of it was helpful. But for the repair of the crumpled economic complex in 1932 none of the proposals—and not all of them together—appeared to be adequate. What was needed was a visualization of the whole economy, an understanding of the relations among its parts, and a knowledge of what had happened to disrupt its functioning. This was the level to which Franklin, as a national rather than a state leader, had to move. That this move had to be made shows the superficiality of the generalization that a governorship is the best training for a prospective President. That saying is not altogether false, but neither is it altogether true. There is a certain betraying simplicity about local problems that can be serious if carried over naïvely into national policy-making. Governorships help to develop executives, but they contribute remarkably little to the developing of statesmen.

To take the instance of agriculture: As governor, Franklin had made what he considered an outstanding record in assisting farmers. He could claim, when he reviewed it with pride in his comprehensive agricultural speech at Topeka in September, that he had done a good deal;

but he acknowledged that for meeting the deepening crisis a wholly new approach had to be made, one that would affect fundamentally the relations between agriculture and the rest of the economy. Farmers would have to join in adjusting their production of food and fiber to the effective market for it. The federal government would have to devise a mechanism which they could use for this purpose. They could not do it for and by themselves, and it could not be done on any smaller scale.

There was a reason for such an agricultural program which went beyond the claims of farmers themselves to a better life than they had been having; it was necessary to the health of the whole economy. It was a far more economically sophisticated Franklin who made the following remarks than the one who, in the preceding years, had thought enough accomplished if rural roads and schools were improved, local government reorganized, and taxes reduced:

> Our economic life today is a seamless web . . . we cannot have independence . . . unless we take full account of our interdependence in order to provide a balanced economic well-being for every citizen . . . This Nation cannot endure if it is half "boom" and half "broke". . . .[1]

This acknowledged a central responsibility, a need for general direction. The "seamless web" must be kept intact, the balance must be restored. This was the duty of the government, not of farmers alone for agriculture, nor of industrialists alone for industry. The interest of all, the public interest, was paramount. If any group, he seemed to say, was at a disadvantage, by so much the whole was less efficient than it should be. None—no individual and no group—could live in isolation; each individual was his brother's responsibility; all were in this together. Whether it was liked or not, no one could exploit his neighbor without himself suffering penalty. And nowadays penalty would not be long delayed.

It does not need to be insisted that this was precisely the reverse of laissez faire, the philosophy (but not, let it be said, the practice) of American business. The tenets of laissez faire required government abstention from interference except to prevent conspiracy leading to monopoly. There could be no central responsibility; there could only be mechanisms for the maintenance of fairness. Franklin had come to see, although he did not go so far as to acknowledge it publicly, that there was an inner contradiction in a *system* of free enterprise. If it was free it would develop centers of control, since the most efficient or the most ruthless would best their competitors and grow large. The fact of bigness was a self-enlarging advantage. There need not be a conspiracy to monopolize; monopoly could result from natural growth.

This was the reason why half a century of progressive agitation, the

[1] *Public Papers*, Vol. I, p. 697.

imp!

passage of anti-trust laws, and repeated efforts at enforcement had not succeeded in preventing concentrations of economic power, which, wholly out of social control, had finally unbalanced the system in their own favor to the extent of destroying their own markets. Those who were not allowed sufficient income to do it could not buy the goods issuing from the magnificent farms and factories of America. Conspicuous among those who were thus starved of income—although the stricture applied to urban workers as well—were the farmers of America.

The solution of the "agricultural problem" did not lie in agriculture alone or even primarily among farmers; it lay in redressing the balance between farmers and others. But it was also true that many of these "others" were sunk in a similar distress. It was almost as necessary that a redressing should take place that would restore the power to buy of many urban industries as it was that farmers' disadvantages should be corrected.

This concept, described several times as a "concert of interests" and referred to sometimes as "interdependence" and finally worked into legal language as "parity" or "fair trade practice," would be one idea brought to Franklin by the Brains Trust which he would never quite let go. It was responsible for agricultural "adjustment," and also for the "codes of fair practice" of the NRA. He would always be under pressure to abandon this concept or, if he would not give it up, not to attempt its implementation at any given time. Its outraged enemies would include the progressives with their heavy investment in the restoration of competition through the enforcement of the anti-trust acts, but these would be joined by all those who benefited under the going rules because they knew how to escape their application. Both big businessmen and their progressive enemies set themselves to prevent the application of a principle that would establish the government as planner, arbiter, balancer, in the economic system.

Franklin heard them. During the campaign he spoke for the organismic philosophy (after his nomination) only when appealing to some disadvantaged group whose members would gain from the change. Of these, the farmers were the most conspicuous. But even if he modified his public statements he did not lose the conviction that bigness had come to stay and that control was its concomitant.

It is interesting to note, however, in what spirit the agricultural forces accepted the proffered program. As we shall see, they were no more actuated by concern for the whole than any big businessman who exploits the whole by monopolizing a part. They very grudgingly accepted the necessity for a reduction of their own production or, indeed, any change in traditional practice. The politics of agriculture during the whole of Franklin's presidency would be marked by the farmers' struggles to get high prices and, at the same time, to avoid any of the self-disciplines necessary to their maintenance in the market.

In essence this would be no different from the selfishness and indiscipline which was to break down NRA almost before it got well under way. Franklin was trying to tell Americans that they must live together as co-operators and not as competitors, but he was not finding them receptive. A political leader, appealing for election, can push his ideas only a little way beyond those of his constituents. He has always to balance the risk of alienating support against his conviction about what must be done and his desire to put it into practice. It is a nice calculation. Any advance will always be against advice, too, because the professional politicians around him will not, for one thing, understand, and, for another, because they will always be overcautious concerning any but strictly political tactics. Strategies make them nervous. They will therefore always oppose departure from traditional solutions. They never want their candidates to appear unorthodox. They want them, above all, to be—and they put it just this way—safe and sane.

It was this way in the campaign of 1932. Louis Howe had a good deal to say of this sort. So did many local leaders, who were always, according to his custom, asked by Franklin about appeal to their constituencies. They counseled him to promise the voters what they wanted, not what they could have. They also wanted plenty said about benefits but nothing at all about the obligations necessary to their getting. So the public papers of the campaign, read in retrospect, exhibit a dichotomy hard to understand without knowing how Franklin was thus torn between what he knew was necessary and what he was told so urgently it would be popular to say. It was the same dichotomy that would torment all the New Deal years.

It began in the acceptance speech. That document was somewhat battered and not a little confusing as it was delivered; and no wonder, considering how it was done. But it had in it the approaches to some novel solutions. One version of it was made ready some time in advance of the convention, and everyone directly concerned was fairly well satisfied. There were a few passages that would have to be revised to fit such circumstances as turned up. It was not known for certain what the platform would say on all subjects, but it was not likely to contain any surprises. One difficulty was sure to be Cordell Hull's uncompromising international laissez faire; no old-line Democrat could go back on so traditional a doctrine, even if hardly anyone wanted to see it implemented. A compromise of some sort—perhaps a reciprocal trade proposal—might be worked out.

About agriculture itself, which all in Franklin's crowd recognized as of the first importance since it was hoped to win the Midwest, there were the differences that had developed in a decade of political dis-

All this done w/o govt. discipline

Restrict prod. of farmers — only alternative

cussion. The politicians—and the interests represented by George Peek, who has been noticed as Smith's adviser in 1928 and who was still around with his satellite Hugh Johnson—wanted to avoid any commitment to the "adjustment of production," which every realist knew to be necessary. The alternative was the sale abroad of something like twice the volume of farm products sold in recent years. That this was a hopeless dream was all too apparent.

In this matter Franklin had taken the position that the farm leaders must agree. This had been to them an excruciatingly painful demand since they themselves were politicians whose appeal to their constituencies depended on furious work to get farmers what they wanted without having to accept any limitation on their freedom of action. But the impatience of farmers with leaders who failed to affect policy was by now so great as to induce panic. Something must be done, even if faces could not be saved. Franklin's hope was that they would settle on some scheme that would make the now enormous surpluses manageable, raise prices, and thus approach a rebalancing with industry. He was determined to make them accept the responsibility.

The exploratory work of the Brains Trust in this matter had been extensive. I had had direct charge of it, and I had concluded that the best available scheme was one worked out by a committee of experts, of whom the intellectual leaders seemed to be M. L. Wilson and Henry Wallace, although others were also involved—Beardsley Ruml, for instance, recently dean of the Social Sciences Division at the University of Chicago, and, strangely enough, Henry I. Harriman, currently president of the United States Chamber of Commerce. This scheme was called by its proponents "the domestic allotment plan" and its attraction was that it accepted the necessity for limitation of production but depended on elected county committees for the enforcement of generally agreed crop quotas. Keeping the government largely out of disciplinary duties was, I thought, a remarkable contribution. I wanted Franklin to accept the principle at once.

The timing in this matter, however, was such that the convention was imminent before the scheme was fairly worked out and could be generally understood. The week before the convention I was attending a meeting in Chicago of agricultural leaders and conferring especially with Wilson and Wallace. It was with considerable enthusiasm that I reported about the scheme and its reception to Franklin and counseled commitment to it in the acceptance. I was conscious that to ask him, in the midst of the uncertainties of those days, to attempt the understanding of so complex a social mechanism was to expect the impossible. But I did hope that it would be recognized in the acceptance, if for no other reason than that it would end digressions and concentrate further discussion during the campaign.

232

Even in the midst of the delicate negotiation that held the committed majority of delegates through three long roll calls, and the even more important ones with Hearst, McAdoo, and Rayburn that resulted in making Garner the vice-presidential candidate, we had several telephone conferences. He could see my point; as in other issues, however, he wanted to be assured first of wide consent and second of practicability. I could not satisfy him on the first. Actually public discussion had not taken place at all, and farm leaders had not taken any position. Their approval was at best problematical. What was really being asked of him was that he should modify his principle of demanding preliminary agreement among all concerned. I wanted him, now that we had found a workable formula, to espouse it and to coerce the farm leaders into its acceptance by going over their heads to the farmers themselves. This was too much to ask. And to an extent my demand went unsatisfied.[2] Nor was it really satisfied during the campaign, although the formal agricultural address in Topeka went farther toward it than the acceptance. When everything was over and we were installed in Washington, agreement would even yet not have been reached. The Agricultural Adjustment Act would authorize several ways of meeting the current crisis. The necessity for choosing among them would devolve on the new administration. The quarrel, deferred, did not disappear. Presently it would disrupt the whole New Deal apparatus.

I should naturally feel that this history, which I syncopate here, tended to prove what I had from the first contended, that it was possible and desirable to go much farther than the professionals ever wanted to go toward establishing commitments which then turned into mandates. But I never won my point, in agriculture or anything else. Frank-

[2] What the acceptance speech actually said was this—which may or may not be taken to represent something of an achievement for my efforts:

. . . *The practical way to help the farmer is by an arrangement that will, in addition to lightening some of the impoverishing burdens from his back, do something toward the reduction of surpluses of staple commodities that hang on the market. It should be our aim to add to the world prices of staple products the amount of a reasonable tariff protection, to give agriculture the same protection that industry has today.*

And in exchange for this immediately increased return I am sure that the farmers of this Nation would agree ultimately to such planning of their production as would reduce the surpluses and make it unnecessary in later years to depend on dumping those surpluses abroad in order to support domestic prices. . . .

Farm leaders and farm economists, generally, agree that a plan based on that principle is a desirable first step in the reconstruction of agriculture. It does not in itself furnish a complete program, but it will serve in great measure in the long run to remove the pall of a surplus without the continued perpetual threat of world dumping. Final voluntary reduction of surplus is a part of our objective, but the long continuance and the present burden of existing surpluses make it necessary to repair great damage of the present by immediate emergency measures. . . . [Ibid., pp. 654-55.]

lin took the advice which, as a politician, I suppose his instinct also approved. He left everything fluid, general, and discursive. He said as little as he could in controversial situations and left to the ministrations of time and his own mediating talents the issues thus remaining unresolved.

There were other issues of a similar sort. There was the whole matter of a theory of recovery, for example, about which there was so much controversy. When Franklin in 1931 had decided to challenge the theory of the supine state and had said that government must not be indifferent to citizens' welfare, it had been done, not out of the conviction that an unemployed person was deprived of the buying power necessary to absorb the goods issuing from the industrial machine, but for humanitarian reasons. Only very gradually was the concept of income deficiency making its way, and the ideas associated with a compensating budget were yet to have any general acceptance. Those of us who were economists were familiar with them, and we spent many an hour —Berle and I—transmitting to Franklin the considerable body of material known to us for many years. Berle was an original worker in the field of corporate organization; I had long been familiar with the ideas of J. A. Hobson and other economists who held generally that depressions were the result of deficits in buying power. I was also a student of my elder at Columbia, W. C. Mitchell, who was a leader in exploring all the phenomena of the business cycle. After several decades the acceptance seems to me not so feeble an attempt. Unfortunately the excellent analysis of depression was not followed by the statement of a remedial program that was at all adequate. There was what seemed to me an unfortunate digression into simple reformism—reform of the financial system. To this in itself there could be no objection; it was long overdue. But I, at least, was tormented with the realization that it had nothing to do with recovery. This was a persistent fault all through the campaign. The cures offered seemed irrelevant to the diagnosis of the disease. The draft I had prepared had passages following the one I have quoted which spoke of economic planning, the control of prices, and the social management of investments, as well as an emergency attack by way of public works and relief. All that was, to my great disappointment, left out.

Rosenman has described how the draft actually used was finally shaped up. It was done on the plane traveling from Albany to Chicago, a trip unprecedented in those days for an important public man. As they flew over lake and hill, one page after another was reread, cut, redrafted, and even then perhaps discarded and a new beginning made. Sam worked most of the way on it, not conscious that Louis Howe had somehow summoned the energy to write one which he intended to insist that Franklin read. Louis' draft was a strictly party document, untainted with the theories of the Brains Trust and expressing merely courage and party spirit without any commitment to means. When Ray discovered Louis' intention he was understandably worried.

During those Chicago days—and nights—there were moments when it seemed that no speech at all was to be needed. Not until the Hearst-McAdoo-Garner deal had been completed were we sure. Finally Franklin took the draft thrust into his hand by Louis as he stepped off the plane, shuffled its first page onto the draft worked out during the journey, and made the connection as he read. This is why it deserves to be spoken of as a rather battered speech. But of course its status as a state paper is one thing, and the air of hearty elation and high optimism with which it was delivered is another. Regardless of the words, the meaning was plain. And since victory was in the air, words already mattered less than the appearance of competence and stability.

Franklin began his campaign with the usefully spectacular gesture of a plane flight to Chicago for an obvious reason. It was an initial note of vigor to forestall any comment on his disability. The appearance of a nominated candidate before a convention still in session was unprecedented. The nominee was, by tradition, supposed to stay at home in feigned ignorance until, after a suitable time, a committee of the convention called to notify him of his nomination. His flight to Chicago suggested that there was to be a strenuous campaign. For this there were the same reasons he had had for his seemingly overactive New York campaigns. Others close to him might forget, being used to the vigor of his daily life, that he was a cripple; but he never forgot that there would always be doubt whether all his faculties were intact.[3]

A great deal has been said about the apparent gusto with which he went into political battle. And it is true that he exploited to the limit all its incidents. The sights and sounds of travel in the circumstances of campaigning seemed to be savored during every hour. He had a train of his own, loaded with all the personnel and apparatus pertinent to political appeal. At least one car, and usually more, filled with newspapermen went along. There were assistants and secretaries equipped with typewriters and mimeograph machines; there were telephone and telegraph attachments. And then there were all the politicians. Several such went on the whole trip, arranging for local leaders and candidates to ride for an hour or a day, enjoying precious moments in Franklin's special car at the rear. With him they shared momentarily the unique American experience of looking out at gatherings all along the way and being seen with the "head of the ticket." They were "riding the coat-

[3] It may be that Franklin overcompensated for his helpless legs by working the rest of his body mercilessly; this may even have had something to do with his early death although he came from a long-lived family on both sides, but it was a duty he never shirked. And its relevancy to leadership is obvious.

tails" of a man with more appeal than they. There was no shame in this; it was part of the game.

Several times on most days the slow-running train would pull into switching tracks. Franklin would lock his braces, take the arm of his son Jim or of Gus Gennerich, Fred Willis, or Earl Miller, the New York state troopers who were his bodyguards (and, as well, almost "family"), and step out onto the little back platform of the *Pioneer*. He waved and smiled. Candidates always wave and smile, but none within recent memory had had Franklin's projective charm. Presently he said a few words to the hundreds or thousands gathered there. He always knew where he was; he usually knew some person to speak to or of; he mentioned the last time he had been there; and sometimes he spoke of some local issue or problem. This was partly the result of careful and continuous briefing, but only partly. He had a prodigious memory for such trivia, the very stuff of political appeal. Besides, he was journeying in his nation and among his people. The calls and cheers of the crowd came up to him and he seemed to absorb the good will as a thirsty man drinks, capaciously and eagerly. The sealing of the leader and the crowd was a kind of mystic rite whose ceremony was celebrated in these gatherings.

In spite of the strain, with its attendant exhaustion, of being pleasant through the long days to a demanding succession of local candidates and ruling bosses, of keeping informed across the states, one after the other, concerning every likely regional reaction and every special interest, Franklin did carry off his campaigning with an *éclat* unmatched in American annals except by Uncle Ted in his day, and perhaps Bryan in his. He got ready for these journeys with considerable care. When he started he knew pretty well where he would stop, whom he would see, and what he would say. He spent long hours over the itinerary, perfecting it with the care of the professional for the minutiae of his work. There was plenty of scope for ad-libbing, but the whole effect was visualized quite clearly in advance, and he seldom failed to achieve the effect he intended. There was a set speech every few days that had to be carefully prepared, but there were numerous informal ones that he took in his stride. It often seemed to me that at the end of one of those traveling days Franklin must have longed for the quiet of Hyde Park with an almost irresistible nostalgia. No man ought to be asked, I thought, to do what, day after day, he was required to do. Then I thought that no one had required it of him. It was a self-imposed duty. Studying this, I came to have the conviction that he was merely carrying out a contract with honest vigor. There was ample confirmation that such a contract, even if an implied and unspoken one, was coming into existence between himself and the national electorate in the first journey of 1932; later it became more and more obvious that the agreement was unassailably binding. It was to last as long as his life lasted.

It can be said that in campaigning as well as in all the ritualistic functions of becoming and being President of the United States there was the satisfaction of carrying out a particular and consequential designated task. Franklin had had to bear in his life distressing humiliations of a punishing sort, beginning with his difficulties at Groton and at least continuing in the loss of the superb physical equipment he had originally possessed for attaining political success. But humiliation had not made him a humble man. He was obviously conscious of having political talents of the first order. As he put them to use, he did it with the sure ease of a master. And by now, of course, the awkwardnesses of apprenticeship had all been worked off. In this sense the governorship had been wonderfully apt training.

When Franklin started on the first of his long swings across the country we could see that he was as well conditioned as the most careful contender in a foot race. It was not surprising that the exercise of his talent began to register at once and that when he left California, the place most feared as the scene of probable gaffes, the most skeptical opinion was that such finesse, such natural and easy expertise had never before been seen in contemporary times.

Ray Moley, who was with him on this and other trips of this campaign, has spoken in faintly sardonic vein of this political travel:

> To Roosevelt a good cause does not justify any trip; a good trip justifies any cause. Campaigning, for him, was unadulterated joy. It was broad rivers, green forests, waving corn, and undulating wheat; it was crowds of friends, from the half dozen who waved to the cheery face at the speeding window, to perspiring thousands at a race track or a fair ground; it was hands extended in welcome, voices warm with greeting, faces reflecting his smile along the interminable wayside. These are the things that ever and ever renew the life of a troubadour. What has "learning" to do with friendship and happiness? Travel is to make friends and influence people. And travel is in the blood of the *Reise*-Roosevelts.[4]

This tells something about the central figure of the 1932 drama; perhaps it tells even more about Ray Moley. In doing so it illustrates what happens to those in a leader's train who do not yield him the ultimate loyalty demanded by his position vis-à-vis the electorate: that nothing he does can be unacceptable. It may be wrong in a follower's judgment, he may argue against it and harbor reservations afterward, but he must accept it in all good faith and go on with the work there is to do.

Ray could not find the kind of loyalty in his heart that survives presumption on good nature and persists beyond the loss of personal pres-

[4] *After Seven Years* (New York: Harper, 1939), p. 52.

tige. He turned sour. And his reminiscences were sown with a bitter comment. *After Seven Years* is, in fact, one of the cruelest books I know of—for which I am deeply sorry because of the fondness between us. I could not say how many times since 1939 I have been asked: "What happened to Ray Moley?" I do not yet know how to answer. It is incredible still that the faithful servant who worried and sweated across the country and back on that trip, and on all the others of that year, could have displayed so deliberately shallow a caricature as his considered portrayal of the personality he then served.

I can say, of course, that it happened to others—to Joseph Kennedy, to William C. Bullitt, to any number of politicians, including Jim Farley, Bronson Cutting, and Burt Wheeler. But those defections do not explain Ray Moley's. For Ray, to an extent not matched by any of the others, had sunk himself in the service he had assumed. I conclude that this kind of moral conversion under the strain of political service is one of the hazards of the trade. Franklin must have felt after Ray's departure that no one could quite ultimately be depended on. It was not true. Harry Hopkins is the refutation, if there were no other. But after Ray's going, I imagine, he must have lost some part of his willingness to rely on others' loyalty; and it must have been a costly deprivation.

This has nothing to do with any sense of guilt a leader must have about exploiting others. That, he feels, he may do—even must do—with the utmost ruthlessness. All his co-workers are subordinate and they are expendable. But that, he assumes, they must expect. It is a hazard they must accept in taking the King's shilling. The sovereign is not required to explain or to regret the sacrifice of his servants. It is for the nation and therefore in a cause not to be compromised because of any man's pride or convenience.

Ray could not pass the test when the time came, as some others could and did. His natural kindness soured, his loyalty turned to hatred, and his progressivism turned to reaction. He even joined the opposition and this is the ultimate political apostasy.

But at the moment Ray's activities were important—as much, certainly, as those of the politicians at whose center Howe, Farley, and Flynn functioned. That was in the Biltmore Hotel in New York City. The headquarters of the Brains Trust was just around the corner at the Roosevelt Hotel. The political headquarters had all the duties usual to the operation of a campaign; the Brains Trust went on writing drafts for speeches, doing hasty research, and occasionally still having sessions with Franklin as well as among themselves. Its numbers had been somewhat added to after the convention, as it became more and more apparent how likely Franklin was to win. The most arduous worker among the newcomers was Hugh Johnson, who for a year or two would furnish much of the New Deal's color, if not its stability. Hugh had been until recently rather indeterminately attached to Baruch; farther back, as I have noted, he had been an associate of George Peek in the farm-equipment business. Both Baruch and Johnson had been active subterraneously in promoting Smith's interests and in attempting to injure Franklin's. But after the manner of politics all this was forgotten once the nomination had been made. Baruch wanted power; it was to be had by associating with the prospective victor, not by sulking as Smith and Belle Moskowitz were doing. So he sent Johnson to join our ranks. We found him fascinating if not welcome. In any case, we could not reject him, since Franklin had made known his wish that we agree to his accession.

None of us quite understood the acceptance of Baruch at the time, not being, like Howe and Farley, old hands at the business. I afterward learned something, even if not very much. Baruch was a successful speculator and a very rich man. He pleased himself by placing enough of his funds strategically in the political poker game so that a good many politicians, especially those in the Congress, owed him a certain return. There was nothing corrupt about it, except as any influence, not strictly a public one, is inimical to democracy. He was one of those who were able "to pass the word" concerning legislation, appointments, and policies. It was an influence with which Franklin thought it wise to temporize at least. Baruch had been chairman of Wilson's War Industries Board, and so Franklin knew all about him from old Washington associations. Perhaps he now wished to become Secretary of State; if he did, he was to be disappointed. Franklin would play him for the big fish he was, but what he would give to land him stopped short of a secretaryship. Franklin did not expect loyalty in his cabinet; no President ever does. But he knew all too well that he could expect so little from Baruch that constant intrigue to offset his machinations would be necessary.

It would be judged expedient to enlist Johnson in an emergency agency, but it turned out to be not so expedient to accept the Baruch formula for recovery which Johnson brought with him to the Brains Trust. This was the simple thesis that the depression would end when businessmen got back their confidence. When they could look ahead with optimism they would risk their capital; that would set the system going again, furnishing employment and making a market for goods. The confidence of businessmen, according to Baruch and Johnson, depended on their belief that the government's budget was to be balanced, that monetary experimentation would not be undertaken, and that taxes would be reduced. It was in pursuit of confidence that Johnson wrote and argued for the one disastrously unwise speech of the campaign—that on fiscal policy, made at Pittsburgh. It was this address that Sam Rosenman humorously advised Franklin, in 1936, to deny he had ever made. At the moment, even to those who were more realistic about the future need for relief and public works, fiscal conservatism did not seem an impossible policy. To me, for instance, it seemed in order to pay for these expanded programs from increased taxation. I was against inflation. My concert-of-interests theory required that, in the interest of parity, some prices come down as others went up. I had not yet understood that the far greater ease with which inflation could be induced would make any downward pressure so impolitic that, in fact, none would ever be exercised.

As it was, with inflation in prospect, which none of us was aware of at the time but which Franklin should have known would be necessary if he was unwilling to undertake a real balancing program, nothing could have been more irresponsible than the Pittsburgh speech.

It was in this field that Franklin was most uncertain even after all our discussions. His uncertainty was both economic and political—or, rather, involved both at once. He could see that recovery would be hastened by distributing income to prospective customers through relief and public works, but he had no realistic view of the probable cost and so thought it could be paid for out of revenues much more easily than it could. Those of us who were more realistic were mistaken only in our underestimation either of political difficulties in raising revenue or of Franklin's toughness about demanding the necessary discipline. Even at a long remove from those days of decision, the error can be said to have been of either sort. But there was an error.

Similarly, and connectedly, there was uncertainty about price policy. I was under the impression that stabilizing was to be undertaken. But Franklin was to shrink from the incidental harshness in such a policy and was to succumb to urgings of the inflationists—although he would never have a good conscience about it. Instead of causing some prices to fall and others to rise, some were merely to be encouraged not to rise as fast as others. Even this broke down and degenerated into a race among all economic groups to see whose prices could be raised first and fastest.

So the economic policy would never have the straightforwardness and simplicity it should have had. And it would never achieve recovery, either, during strictly New Deal times—until the war was imminent, unemployment would never be nearly cured, nor would industrial activity nearly reach the levels of capacity. But all during this period there would be unbalanced budgets and a more or less uncontrolled inflation. Rising prices would bear almost as unevenly on the economic groups of 1936 as on those of 1928. And there would be a depression in 1937— soon checked by more inflation—as there had been in 1929, but of course without the panic symptoms of the earlier disturbance.

Even for campaign purposes, Franklin was vulnerable in these matters. He spoke of recovery through increased consumer income; he had now begun to understand the possibilities of what we called "pump priming," a homely phrase that unluckily concealed more than it revealed; but he also spoke of reduced government expenditures and balanced budgets. He ignored the inconsistency; and it was the opposition's one effective talking point.

This talking point was to run on into the contention that Franklin was responsible for the depression—or rather for its continuation. Hoover would outlive Franklin by many years. During all of them he would be contending that his measures had turned the tide, only to have it reversed again by Franklin's indecisions. The business community, he would say, had been so frightened by Franklin's obvious tendency toward inflation—together with softness toward labor and other similar policies feared by businessmen—that the sinking spell had begun all over again and would not be exorcised by his own most strenuous incantations—especially since Franklin would refuse to join in reassurance that no harm to enterprise was intended.

It would forever be Republican doctrine that the events of 1932–33 constituted a "Roosevelt depression" for which Hoover and Republican policies could not be blamed.

This is perhaps to place too much emphasis on concepts and arguments as features of that campaign. Actually the contention of Louis Howe that the less Franklin said the better, except to endorse the platform and embrace all good party workers, was entirely correct so far as winning the election was concerned. It is to be doubted whether all Franklin's traveling and talking influenced more than a scattering of votes; certainly no such activity accounted for the multiplying signs of success which appeared week by week from July to November. It might much more accurately be put the other way, as Louis would have put it; Franklin *lost* no potential votes. Very few voters reversed their intention of casting their ballots against Hoover because of anything they learned about Franklin. The Republicans tried hard to belittle him; there were potentially dangerous rumors about his invalidism, there were even more about his weakness and incompetence, but obviously none of them was widely believed. The vigor of his appearance and the actuality of his record as governor refuted all such efforts.[5]

[5] As these pages were being written another Franklin Roosevelt, our Franklin's son, was making a serious bid for the governorship of New York after serving two terms in the Congress. His cousins, Joseph and Stewart Alsop, writing about him, as Ernest Lindley more than twenty years before had written about his father, had things to say that reminded all who read them, and were old enough, of the campaigns of '28, '30, and '32. Their reference was to his congressional campaign in 1949:

Day after day, Roosevelt strode through the streets, a huge, handsome man with a huge grin, towering over the crowds and infecting them with the Roosevelt vitality—what an embittered Republican has called "that damned extra Roose-

For a suspected leftist Franklin had some strange political friends. Not only Baruch, but some more solid industrialists and businessmen were in his corner—among them Frank Walker, Jesse Straus, William Woodin, R. W. Morrison, M. L. Benedum, Vincent Astor, W. R. Hearst, D. H. Morris, and Joseph Kennedy. Jesse Straus, who was director of relief for New York State under the 1931 act, formed a Roosevelt Business and Professional League which served as an incitement to rebellion among those whose leanings would otherwise be Republican. This, again, was part of Franklin's familiar technique. On the hustings he persistently made a distinction between Republican voters and Republican leaders. It was always assumed that stupid leaders were betraying the wiser voters. Their recourse was to rebuke their betrayers by voting for him. In this campaign, as in subsequent ones—and as in preceding ones in New York—the appeal was effective. Many Republicans must have voted for him, doubtful as it may be whether many of them were important businessmen. There had not been a genuine Democratic majority in the nation since Cleveland,[6] and Franklin ended with more than 57 per cent. Nothing like it had happened since the Civil War. No wonder Ernest Lindley felt justified in speaking of it as "The Roosevelt Revolution!" Franklin had, in fact, carried all but six states; outside New England, only Pennsylvania and Delaware went Republican. But there was something else about this election that would furnish material for immediate as well as future speculation and would be even more marked in the election of 1936. Franklin, everywhere except in the South, where often there were no Republican candidates, and in New England, where changes come slowly, had won by considerably larger margins than had the congressional candidates. It was a personal triumph.

More could be made than was really warranted of the presence in Franklin's camp of a few businessmen. They were, after all, quite few. Mostly the more influential among the tycoons—and of course Wall Street as a whole—suspected him of devilish intentions. He had nominated a set of villains in the second speech of his campaign, and they were the fallen heroes of the "New Era." They had been beaten to a pulp by the time it was over. It was the "moneylenders," perpetrators

---

velt gland." *It was a sight, it is said, to freeze the heart of the staunchest member of the Union Club. Towards the end, Roosevelt had an almost hypnotic effect on the crowds which followed him through the streets of the Twentieth District.* [*The Saturday Evening Post*, Sept. 4, 1954, p. 19.]

The younger Franklin lost this campaign, but no one thought his career ended.

[6] Wilson's two victories were won with a minority of the total votes, the first time because the Republicans were split by T.R.'s defection, and the second time because the majority in the Electoral College did not represent a majority of the total votes cast in the election, something which had happened several times in the nation's history.

of frauds and evils, who now served conveniently as whipping boys, just as the utility interests had served in his gubernatorial campaigns. After the last three years their pretensions were hollow; no one did them honor any more; their once haughty behavior had collapsed into helpless whining. They were already convicted in the minds of Americans of every possible fiscal crime. Those who had speculated and lost —and this included millions of once safe-and-sound investors—were only too ready to project their own guilt onto those few who had been guilty on a larger scale; they thus achieved a kind of vicarious innocence.

The Hoover regime, Franklin said at Columbus in August, had been:

the heyday of promoters, sloganeers, mushroom millionaires, opportunists, adventurers of all kinds. In this mad whirl was launched Mr. Hoover's campaign. . . .[7]

When the crash had come the Republicans had consistently lied about the extent of its consequences. *Now* Mr. Hoover said that commercial and investment banking ought to be separated; *now* he advocated a stronger banking system which would not "permit the credit of the country to be made available without check for wholesale speculation in securities." But actually what did the observer find?

We find two-thirds of American industry concentrated in a few hundred corporations, and actually managed by not more than five human individuals.
We find more than half of the savings of the country invested in corporate stocks and bonds, and made the sport of the American stock market.
We find fewer than three dozen private banking houses, and stock-selling adjuncts of commercial banks, directing the flow of American capital. . . .
We find a great part of our working population with no chance of earning a living except by grace of this concentrated industrial machine; and we find that millions and millions of Americans are out of work, throwing upon the already burdened Government the necessity of relief. . . .[8]

This was the pointing out of the devil. He was chased mercilessly around the stump. He ran, half defiantly, half in fear of the wrath to come.

It was a program that flushed progressive cheeks with vindictive emotion. And it was certainly true that banking reforms were as badly needed as reformers had long been saying. But the breaking up of managerial concentrations without the substitution for them of some other means of planning and controlling was something only the orthodox old progressives any longer believed was desirable. There was a good many of these, of course, but there were many more who only listened indifferently to the indictment.

[7] *Public Papers*, Vol. I, p. 672.
[8] Ibid., p. 679.

Still, politically, it was an excellent start. And the next pronouncement a week later concerned prohibition, another issue on which American minds were by now clear after years of controversy. Franklin had been tormented about this as about the League and about Tammany corruption during the past two years. Actually it was a matter of emphasis; and, judged by the political rules, it must be said that both his emphasis and timing were correct. Opinion about prohibition had now developed into a preponderant opposition. Franklin's position, when he took it, was forthright enough, but by his handling of the matter he offended neither side too greatly. He made a wet pronouncement, but those who were on the other side could see well enough that he was less than fanatic, and that was about all they could hope for as things were.

It was the same way about the League of Nations. Time had made differences. Isolationism had softened, but it was also apparent that the League had turned into a tool of European imperialists. It was only reasonable to ask even of the old Wilsonians that they seek the substance of international co-operation rather than its obsolete embodiment in the League. Colonel House was satisfied; and so, after a personal explanation, was Wilson's daughter, who was now Mrs. Francis B. Sayre.[9]

So everything went as smoothly as the most optimistic supporter could have hoped. If it sometimes seemed not to be going well, that was because in the midst of such hurly-burly it was impossible to attain much perspective. Crises did follow one another rapidly, and some seemed not to resolve themselves at all; they lingered on indeterminately, leaving an almost unassessable residue of favorable and unfavorable comment. Typical of this last was the holdover matter of corruption in New York.

Nothing illustrates so well Franklin's steadiness in real difficulty, it seems to me, as the handling of the Walker case. The last phase of this embarrassing contretemps reached its height in May, when Judge Seabury pilloried Mayor Jimmy Walker in a widely publicized series of hearings—widely noticed because the eyes of the whole nation were on New York. At their close Seabury said that he was turning the evidence over to the governor to dispose of as he saw fit. Franklin, definitely on the spot, replied that if the legislative committee had charges they were under obligation to submit them. What he said was, in effect, that they should put up or shut up. This smoked out Seabury, and on June 8 he did file charges. Franklin, after having them checked, forwarded them to Walker for answer on June 24, a date, it must be recalled, just three days before the convention in Chicago was to meet.

It would have been naïve to suppose that this timing was not in-

[9] Incidentally, she was now secretary of the Democratic State Committee in Massachusetts. Cf. *Personal Letters: 1928–1945*, Vol. I, p. 264.

tended to create the maximum embarrassment, and Franklin was not naïve. He said to Colonel House, who was much disturbed: "This fellow Seabury is merely trying to perpetrate another political play to embarrass me." Considering that Franklin was, from then on for many years, to be considered the very embodiment of reformism, it is something of a surprise to later investigators to discover how many of Seabury's sort—or Walter Lippmann's, for another example—were furiously concerned with stopping Franklin's progress toward the presidency on the ground that he was soft on corruption.

After the nomination, and after Franklin's own hearings, which were even more spectacular than Seabury's had been—he was, after all, a presidential candidate—Walker resigned, obviously now trying to escape actual punishment. This happened on September 1, just as the campaign was getting really warm. For a moment it seemed to settle things; the issue had contributed to rather than detracted from Franklin's prestige. It had been, in fact, just what was needed to offset the persistent "wishy-washy" characterization of him that was still rather prevalent. But then Curry showed his hand. About that time (late in September) Franklin's request that Tammany endorse Sam Rosenman for election to the Supreme Court was refused. Even the stinging defeat at Chicago, which had tamed Raskob, Shouse, Byrd, Ritchie, and other stop-Roosevelt conspirators, had not brought Tammany around. It was now proposed that Walker should be renominated to succeed himself in the special election following his resignation.[10] But even worse, Tammany had proceeded to line up all the county organizations in New York to block Herbert Lehman's nomination to succeed Franklin as governor. The spectacle of Franklin running for the presidency on the same ticket with some Tammany nominee for the governorship seemed in prospect.

It did not happen. Al Smith prevented it. Together Al and Franklin succeeded in nominating Lehman. This not only scotched Tammany's last effort to injure Franklin but brought about a reconciliation—at least of sorts—at the October state convention, which had been much desired by Franklin's political associates. They were made happy by the public handshake between the two which it was arranged that the newspaper photographers should record at the convention. Louis Howe and Jim Farley, "running scared," as Jim put it, were overjoyed. They need no longer fear that the Irish Catholics would defect.

As a matter of fact, the coalition which came together to give Franklin the unprecedented victory of that November was the most miscellaneous—and uneasy—one that had ever been assembled by combined

---

[10] Ed Flynn in *You're the Boss* (New York: Viking, 1947) relates the fascinating story of this Tammany defiance and tells how it failed and how the Lehman nomination was arranged.

strategy and good luck. It would be impossible to hold it together for very long; the conflicts among the factions were too acute. Nevertheless, although some of the supporters dropped away by 1936, a still more powerful combination would have been built by then. The Liberty League and Al Smith would "take a walk," Huey Long's radicals would go their way; so would Father Coughlin's followers and those of Milo Reno. But organized labor would by then be a mighty force. And the city machine would be coming around. These two would form the basic coalition for the future.

Historians still are very apt to regard Franklin's visit in San Francisco and his speech there at the Commonwealth Club as the high point of the 1932 campaign. There is something to be said for this so far as the conquest of Hiram Johnson, the legendary western progressive, is concerned. That was important; so, perhaps, was the speech. But it did not come, as so many seemed to think it did, straight out of Franklin's heart. For once he was caught without even a moment for revision. He never saw that speech until he opened it on the lectern before his expectant western audience. It was written by Adolf Berle with some assistance from me, although it was not altogether congenial, so far as I was concerned, nor, as I thought, was it an accurate representation of Franklin's attitude. He was much more an optimist than he appeared to be in that speech. Its argument proceeded from the thesis of maturity; being mature, we ought to recognize what our policies called for—consolidation, conservation, sharing of product, and the like. I was more inclined to feel that we were on the verge of a vast expansion if we recognized our collective nature and socialized our product. There was a deep difference here, but we all agreed well enough that collectivism was by now a commitment. This was a kind of reversion to the philosophy of the Oglethorpe speech. The trouble was that Franklin did not write it and that he was actually, no matter what that speech said, in retreat from this position.

It was easy to feel, with everything going so well, with the "breaks" coming one after another, that a strategy of non-disturbance was called for. At any rate, that was the one Franklin accepted. There were a good many speeches dealing with more or less specific subjects. Franklin capitalized very effectively on his gubernatorial record in a fiery speech attacking the utilities and especially the power companies. The old villains joined the new ones in the pillory. That was in Portland, the center of agitation for public power. It was enormously effective. In other speeches, utilizing Adolf's knowledge, he spoke learnedly of what might be done to reorganize the railroads and other concerns whose paper was held by so many insurance companies and savings banks. This spoke to the heart of many people who had begun to fear for the solvency of these vast agglomerations to whose care their savings had

Didn't appeal for a mandate

been entrusted. It appeared afterward that this, too, had been **effective**.

Nevertheless, looking back, it is plain enough that nothing said or done made any great difference except in that negative way I have spoken of. Vitality, charm, a sense of confidence in the midst of spreading fear—these were what Franklin had to offer. No one who voted for him did it because he presented himself as learned or competent in all the matters he talked about. In so far as the voters were not simply casting a ballot against a regime that had tolerated an economic system in which they themselves believed—something Americans had again and again demonstrated that they were capable of—they voted for the big, easy, smiling man who had no fear of failing at anything, who seemed capable even of saving sinners from themselves. Somehow, with the help he evidently knew how to get together and use, he would put things right. It was certainly as vague as that, but it was pervasive and strong. It was the way of democracy.

In view of Franklin's personal majority it seemed too bad that he had not appealed for a mandate instead of retreating to a safe, general, and discursive strategy. The professional politicians naturally claimed that it was this strategy that was responsible for the victory. But it was hardly a supportable claim; the fact was that Franklin was continually accused, by Hoover and others on the Republican side, of intentions that were precisely those he should have proclaimed; he denied these accusations, only to reverse himself embarrassingly later on. And then he had no mandate for support; he had, on the contrary, denials to overcome. His most difficult problem—one that would prove insoluble—was that of persuading southern reactionaries in the Congress to accept national plans, a genuine concert of interests, and government interference to redress the disadvantages that bore so hard on so many Americans. If he could have rested on a campaign appeal for such measures, he might have defeated the coalition, which formed immediately after the honeymoon period, between these Southerners and the Republicans.

But at the moment this seemed an irrelevancy. With such a magnificent victory behind him there seemed to be nothing he could not do. It was he who had won. He could appeal over the heads of any recalcitrant groups to those who had elected him. That this would not shake those senators and representatives from the South who came from "safe" districts, where by hook or crook the electorate was restricted to a homogeneous and stubborn few, no one was in the mood to consider. There was consternation in the business community and jubilation among the Democrats. Farmers thought they would now get some action on long-postponed measures for their relief; wets expected an end to the long dry spell; the unemployed hoped for assistance, perhaps even jobs; and others hard hit by various manifestations of the depres-

247

sion hoped that something would be done to relieve their distresses. Franklin beamed upon a friendly electorate and, without saying anything specific, gave everyone to hope.

Actually the newly elected President, dealing with the incredible pressures of prospective power and still for the moment governor of New York—he would hand over to his chosen successor, Herbert Lehman, on January 1—was concerned with bringing order out of the confusions of campaigning. The country had to be put in the way of recovery; measures to that effect had actually to be decided on. There was some time, but not too much. The new Congress was not expected to meet until the January following inauguration; before then everything must be ready.

13

As we look back through the intervening mists to the campaign of 1932, Franklin can be seen, already larger than life, riding a flood of approval bearing him on to authority far greater even than a President's formal writ. As he stood on election night, when it was all over but the statistical reckoning, high at one end of the huge crowded room in the Biltmore Hotel, Louis Howe on one side and Jim Farley on the other, the dreams and hopes of all Americans centered in his person. Anyone who was not blind and deaf sensed this as the returns came in. He stood there knowing it, accepting centrality, radiating response; he promised, without saying it, never to abandon his responsibilities; between those who had supported him and the hostile forces they had been learning to dread, he would always intervene. He would do more; he would exorcise the depression and secure them against such dangers in the future as they had just been so miserably living through.

They were the more certain of his ability to accomplish all this because he stood there—to be photographed over and over—in the company of genuine professionals in politics. He was one among these earthy and practical men, not thought to be too scrupulous, perhaps, but accepted as knowledgeable in worldly affairs. They knew their way around. They were contrivers. He would require them to contrive into being those measures he had spoken of during the campaign and any others needed for the welfare of his people. He would have the power and he had the means to use it.[1]

[1] He had been definite about this at Baltimore: "It seems . . . fairly obvious that the next Congress of the United States will have a majority of Democrats in both its branches. Any child can understand that it will be easier for a Democratic President to cooperate with the next Congress than it would be if the present Chief Executive were re-elected. But, let me at the same time add this in all seriousness and from my heart. I honestly believe that even if the Congress of the United States were to be Republican in one or both of its branches I could get along with it better than the gentleman who is running for President on the other ticket. . . ."

The last weeks of the campaign had indeed been hectic. St. Louis, Baltimore, Boston, and then the traditional speech in Madison Square Garden in New York City—these had been the high points. In these centers of population, the furor whenever he appeared had been a much-magnified example of something with which he was sufficiently familiar; but the magnification had been such that it astonished even the most hardened observers. Boston, where Smith had been much preferred for the nomination, had taken him to its Irish heart, and Governor Ely had presided at his meeting. He had spoken here again of unemployment and of "long-range planning," an address the Brains Trust had labored over faithfully. It was considered a kind of *coup de grâce* for Hoover—he was convicted, as it were, out of his own mouth:

The American people are a heart-sick people for "hope deferred maketh the heart sick."

Let me offer you an example. In 1921 and 1922 there was a depression . . . President Harding . . . called what was known as the "President's Conference on Unemployment," the first, my friends, of a long and distinguished series of President's conferences. . . . The report was published in 1923, six years before the present depression began.

It said many sound things. It proposed the control of credit expansion by the banks; it proposed the prevention of over-expansion of industry; it proposed the control of public and private construction in boom periods, and it proposed security against the suffering that might come from unemployment.

It was a good report, my friends. Sound and intelligent people . . . contributed to it.

The Chairman of that Unemployment Conference in 1921 was the then Secretary of Commerce . . . Herbert Hoover.

The President complains, President Herbert Hoover, because I have charged that he did nothing for a long time after the depression began. . . . It is true . . . from the time this report . . . was published . . . he did nothing to put into effect the provisions . . . against . . . future depression.

Instead of doing something during these six years . . . he participated in encouraging speculation . . .[2]

This was an effective attack, but Franklin went farther. He had learned by now that relief was not only good for those who received it when they were in personal difficulty but was also indispensable to the economy. Our high-geared industrial machine simply could not function in a system in which its customers could not buy. This again was the economic interdependence the Brains Trust had labored so hard to drive home. Because he was now thoroughly convinced on this point, he consented to suggest a constructive program—referring again to Hoover's conference for authority. First, he said, public works expenditures should be used as a balancer, but there must also be safeguards

[2] *Public Papers*, Vol. I, pp. 848–49.

against such credit inflation as had preceded 1929. Further, there must be unemployment insurance. These were long-run measures. Immediately there must be relief and emergency public works. Finishing this part of his address, he came out plainly for restored purchasing power:

There is one final objective of my policy which is more vital and more basic than all else. I seek to restore the purchasing power of the American people. . . .

John Maynard Keynes, over in England, cocked an ear when he read this speech, or an excerpt from it, in *The Times*. He was not fond of America and he had no great respect for Americans; he paid little attention to theorists among them; but this sounded like the doctrine for which he stood. He made a note to watch this man if he became President. But people—not only leaders but ordinary folk—all over the world were now listening. Not much is made of any American campaign anywhere abroad, and especially not its political oratory. But the masses everywhere were in misery, deeper misery even than they had been in customarily, and no one seemed to have any intention of doing anything about their sufferings. There was a good deal of talk coming from their politicians about business, about finance, about trade, but nothing effective was being done to put people to work or to give them hope of betterment.

The Germans and the British had done most. Indeed they had led the way into social insurance, something the Brains Trust discovered that Franklin knew a great deal about although he had not connected it at first with a recovery program. The "dole" was a minimum, as were the other insurance provisions; all of them had been undermined by inflation, but they did prevent the complete collapse of the economies. This was one lesson Franklin learned well and clung to. The Social Security System he would engineer into being would be a contribution to his nation whose spreading effect would grow through the generations. Presently it would become so much an accepted part of economic life that no one would be able to imagine a civilization without it. For Europe, in spite of social insurance, as for America, recovery would not come without radical measures. But there was no real intention anywhere of taking them.

Hoover knew before Franklin did that depressions could be controlled. But Hoover was a moral man fundamentally and he felt much more strongly than Franklin did—although it was a belief Franklin shared—that to receive income as a governmental gift was wicked. It was wicked because it "undermined character." It destroyed incentive to work; it taught people that they might get something for nothing. It tended to reward laziness, shirking, and shiftlessness. The truth was that Hoover believed this so firmly that he could not consent to adequate recovery measures that depended on relief of this sort. Only with the greatest reluctance had he given way at all. His feud with La Follette, Wagner, Costigan, Wheeler, Cutting, Norris, and other progressives, who were convinced advocates of recovery through the restoration of purchasing power, was as old as the depression. They had pressed him hard and he had countered with alternatives, with half measures, and with excuses. To all these, Franklin's espousal of their doctrine was a welcome contrast. They awaited his accession with impatience.

As the realization spread throughout the nation that new ideas had been chosen along with a new President, and as it spread beyond the United States to the rest of the world, the prospective adjustments to what was coming inevitably began. There were those who hoped, but there were also those who feared. And those who feared were powerful. They were already uncertain of themselves. Their slogans had proved to be empty; their measures had been ineffective; but they had not been threatened with discharge from responsibility. As long as they occupied the seats of authority they could pretend, while they experimented, that they knew what they were doing. The worst trouble was that they had fallen into the bad habit of pretending to themselves. Now all their pretensions were exposed and they were to be stripped of authority. Such was the businessmen's interpretation of Franklin's victory. It was what Hoover in his campaign jeremiads had said would happen, and their bad consciences refused them any hope that the new President would relent. They were bound to try, however, and possibly they might succeed in softening him. After all, Franklin belonged, they told themselves, to their "class."

It was true that there was no very definite mandate to govern the new President. It was not, as I have pointed out, the campaign strategy to ask for one. Franklin was not committed absolutely to anything. But he had talked about immediate relief for the unemployed and about long-range controls to prevent future depressions. Along with these promises there had gone, on a number of now well-remembered occasions, severe attacks on those who managed the financial affairs of the nation. Financiers had been denounced for speculating with funds entrusted to them, for inflating credit to be used in stock gambling, and for various other practices exposed by the depression. These practices they knew to be wrong. And they fully expected to be punished. They had ample reason to expect that some drastic change in the overhead management of the economy would deprive them of their monopoly of power. And the relief measures promised would cost them higher taxes. This seemed much more likely than that the inconsistent promises of recovery and an "honest dollar" would be kept.

There was no mandate; but the unemployed considered that there

252

was, and so did the nervous financiers. Franklin gazed at the scene his victory had created and was seized not exactly with panic—his sense of appointment was by now very strong—but with a conviction that there were urgent matters to be settled. There was indeed work to do, but who was there to do it? Until January he would be governor of New York; from then until March 4 he would be a man without place or income, presumed to be sitting at home and waiting for inauguration. He was not supposed to have any duties until then, and certainly there was no public provision for readying a new administration. He must do with what he had. What he had was what he had had before, minus the apparatus furnished by the State of New York, used so freely for the past year or two for extra-state purposes. For the next few months Ray Moley and I did major non-political chores. He himself did the rest, with some minor help from others.

Of course he could have had any number of volunteers. But most of those who would be of any use were disqualified by having an interest that made them ineligible. The need was for those who had capabilities but who would make no demands. Even now the impression, to which reference has so often been made, of Franklin's weakness and instability, of his readiness to be influenced, and of his liking to be liked had not been dissipated. There were some heroes of finance, not yet in panic, who thought that the new man, in spite of everything, was vulnerable in these ways. They had been fighting him, but now they would join him. He obviously needed advice. The measures that must be taken would be very intricate and he had no technical knowledge of any account. The effects of whatever was done would be far-reaching and must obviously be done with care. Who could advise him as well as those who knew all about finance and commerce from being in it, from having succeeded, as a matter of fact, in its fierce competitions? Wall Street, in effect, fantastic as it seems, offered itself now as Franklin's mentor.

He was amused, but he was not taken in. He listened patiently to all the important people: he cheerfully said "Yes" and "Thanks," and they went away with some hope. But they did not hear from him again. And presently something very like hysteria took hold of those who constituted the inner circle: they too began to understand the toughness of the reputedly weak fellow from Hyde Park. They discovered too late that he was elusive and hard to handle; that he was not impressed by their prestige; also, that he might be developing ideas of his own. This was frightening for more reasons than that there would very probably be a comprehensive reform during the forthcoming administration, and for more reasons than the prospect of an inflation that would force creditors to accept payment in cheapened dollars from their debtors. There was immediately the problem of international indebtedness, both public and private. And it made an enormous difference whether Franklin saw the issues involved in this as the bankers saw them. They were in for ruinous losses unless he proved tractable. To explain why this was so it is necessary to look backward briefly to the war loans and the post-war debt settlements.

Foreign affairs had hardly been mentioned during the campaign. Foreign affairs are hardly ever mentioned in any campaign, unless there is an entanglement to be liquidated. People have more immediate interests, as every politician knows; the nation's relationships with other nations seem to them remote and unimportant. That these undiscussed matters may involve, at the most serious, war or peace, and even at a minimum, important trade relations, is true enough; but there is seldom a time when people can be convinced that it is so. The strategists of the just-closed campaign had seriously considered dealing with several such issues. They were aware of them as specters haunting the domestic scene; they would someday have to be dealt with. They even came to have ideas about policy. These were put into speeches, but they were not used largely because of the professional objections. Franklin did speak in Seattle about reciprocal tariffs, using a formula the Brains Trust was rather proud to have worked out. But that was all, except for a reference or two to what afterward became famous as the Good-Neighbor Policy but which at this time was left very general.

Hoover had attempted to turn the Democratic flank by attributing the whole depression to "blows from abroad," but this explanation Franklin had flatly rejected; his contention had been that the causes were to be found in Republican policies. It had been left at that. But now that the campaign was over, the realities of the situation forced themselves on everyone's attention, Franklin's no less than others'. There was an immediate decision to be made about the intergovernmental debts, and Hoover sought to draw his successor into consultation.

It had been so flamboyant a decade, with first a boom and then an unprecedented bust, that looking back across it at the war and the settlements reached by the various negotiations concerning the vast debts seemed like looking back a century. What had been done had been done. It had been a settlement. And it had been expected that all the parties to it would carry out their undertakings without further palaver.[3] But the Europeans who had to pay the debts had found themselves in trouble almost at once, and they had irritated Americans by constant complaint about the hardships involved. This had risen to an embarrassing heat at times. Uncle Sam was called Uncle Shylock. Americans were booed in Paris streets. And politicians on both sides

---

[3] Except by the more realistic economists, of whom J. M. Keynes was one. It was about this that he had written his first famous book, *The Economic Consequences of the Peace.*

had made capital of the situation—especially the Europeans, who found it popular to promise that they would find ways to get the debts forgiven and that if forgiveness was refused they would decline to pay. Since the oncoming of the world-wide depression this kind of talk had become more and more popular. French politicians, and British ones to a less degree, had come to depend on blaming Uncle Sam for everything they might otherwise find it hard to explain to their constituents. If only the debts could be canceled, budgets could be balanced, inflation checked, taxes lowered, and industry restored to activity. It was a kind of cure-all. But if the stubborn Americans refused, they—the Europeans—had at least done their best.

Coolidge, in his time, had listened sardonically to the uproar abroad and had dismissed it with contempt. Hoover, being far more experienced, knew the dangers involved. He knew that the settlements, apparently so generous, were still ones that probably would not be carried out. What he must have known but did not admit was that the best reason they were unlikely to be carried out was an unwise action in which he had concurred. He had signed the ultra-protectionist Smoot-Hawley Tariff Bill. And that had shut off any possibility that other nations could export to the United States goods enough to build up the balances necessary for meeting the heavy debts. The alternatives were lower tariffs, greater imports, and possible payment, as against total or partial repudiation.

This had not been Hoover's campaign story. That had emphasized a Europe struggling in the aftermath of war. Europe had declined into disaster, and depression in the United States was a direct result. This, however, was a temporary shock and could be overcome by gradual liquidation of foreign debts and expansion at home, except that fears of what the Democrats were likely to do were making all his efforts futile. Expansion could not take place in an atmosphere of prospective oppression for business. Now that the campaign was over, it might still be possible to check the fatal decline. It would have to be begun by eliminating the intergovernmental debts: in other words—forgiveness. The situation would be clarified by making permanent the moratorium in effect since the previous year, but an immediate decision had to be made concerning the payments due to be resumed in December. The British, particularly, were protesting their inability to pay; but the other debtors had likewise indicated that they would not meet their obligations.

The specter of repudiation materialized immediately after the election. On November 12 Hoover, on his way back to Washington from voting in California, addressed a message to his successor-to-be. Franklin and those of us he consulted knew well enough what was coming.

We had discussed it over and over. Our conclusions were quite different from those which seemed to Hoover so axiomatic.

In the first place, we were convinced that the private debts which never got discussed were what lay behind the pressures for forgiveness of the governmental debts. These were of a size which, if paid regularly according to schedule, would exhaust foreigners' ability to get dollars.[4] The bankers therefore wanted the governmental debts out of the way. On the other hand, it could be argued—as we were inclined to argue—that if the private debts were got out of the way through default, the governmental debts could be paid. It was not true, as it had been put about by propagandists, that payment was impossible. It was just inconvenient for the bankers. And the Republican position was, as always, the bankers' position.

Franklin was therefore not too much disturbed by Hoover's message. Furthermore, something politically difficult was being asked of him. The American annoyance with European war debtors was widespread. There was a feeling that the settlements had been generous and that refusal to pay amounted to breaking faith. Altogether Franklin would have trouble with many supporters if he should join in recommending forgiveness. Allies like Hiram Johnson, for instance, would be likely to desert him if he should agree.

The temper of the country had been well enough expressed when the Congress, in consenting to Hoover's 1931 moratorium, had rejected his suggestion that a commission be established to review the whole question yet again. A resolution had in fact said:

It is hereby expressly declared to be against the policy of the Congress that any of the indebtedness of foreign countries to the United States should be in any manner canceled or reduced.

Hoover was caught in a real dilemma. The debts, in his opinion, must be canceled; on the other hand, if the Congress refused consent, cancelation was impossible. To persist in collection would be to set back European recovery and thus recovery at home. But he had no influence any more that could be brought to bear to modify the congressional intransigence. Franklin did have influence; he must therefore be appealed to for a joint effort.

While he was doing it, Hoover also called attention to certain other foreign questions that needed attention. Delegates were already meeting in Geneva to fix the agenda for the World Monetary and Economic Conference to be held in the spring, and negotiations for disarmament were going on. Concerning these matters, too, the old administration could do nothing. They would come to settlement after March. He

---

[4] Assuming no change in the tariff structure which would make dollars easier for Europeans to get. Any change would actually take time.

thought that Franklin ought to join him in establishing a common policy.

Franklin, however, thought not. It was his view that as a private citizen he could not be responsible for policy. And as prospective President he would develop policies to which Hoover and Mills would never agree.[5] Under the compulsion of pressing events Franklin's mind, even in the circumstances of a campaign in which it seemed to him best not to speak of foreign issues, had begun to grapple with them. He was therefore not so unready as his responses to Hoover's suggestions of co-operation might suggest. He was being wary; he was also keeping himself free for a reformulation of policy which he could not very well carry out under Hoover's supervision and with Mills' concurrence. He therefore merely agreed to a meeting. It was held on November 22.

Meanwhile Franklin was having some long thoughts, shared with no one, which only long afterward would issue in policy. Rising in Europe and in the Far East was a sinister public philosophy, anti-democratic and devoted to violence. Hoover's pacifism was well known, but it was not shared by Franklin. How soon, exactly, the President-elect formulated his position vis-à-vis the dictators is not known. Before inauguration one part of it would become plain when he joined the retiring Secretary of State, Henry L. Stimson (who years later would become his Secretary of War), in active opposition to Japanese expansionism in Manchuria. Hoover had refused to do this. It was one sign of new policy that Franklin acquiesced in Stimson's doctrine. The same doctrine would in time appear as that which was also to be applied to European aggressors. At the moment it was not explicit, but it lay back of the refusal to co-operate with the outgoing administration.

Franklin took Ray Moley with him to the White House meeting, a choice that annoyed the conferees on the other side, since they doubted Ray's competence to discuss international finance. In this they were justified. Ray's opinions in the matters under examination were recent and superficial. But the choice emphasized Franklin's determination not to be drawn into expert exchanges. He was there, as he said, to be informed of matters about which he would need to know. He was on his way to Warm Springs for his autumn vacation; Democratic leaders would visit him there; they would confer at length about what their

[5] Ogden Mills, Franklin's Hudson Valley neighbor, was now Secretary of the Treasury. Andrew Mellon, inherited by Hoover from the Coolidge administration, had been sent as Ambassador to the Court of St. James's. Mills was an extremely able man of wealth and a thorough reactionary. Franklin understood him well. He always knew exactly what "Oggie's" reactions would be. Mills had once been a candidate for governor and in the 1930 campaign had been among those sent from Washington—Stimson and Hurley being the others—to check Franklin's threatening progress. He was now Hoover's closest adviser and was considered to be the coming man in the Republican party.

policy would be. So, as Ray described it to me afterward, he listened, most of the talking being done by Mills.[6]

The scene in the White House on that dreary November day had all the elements of high tragedy. The cheerful fire crackling under the classic mantle in the red-hung room did something toward providing a cozy setting for a statesmen's meeting. But nothing could really relieve the chill. Hoover was a desperately tired and beaten man; Franklin was bland and impenetrable. Mills raged inwardly at the irony of a fate that was taking such decisions out of his competent control and entrusting them to his amiable but superficial neighbor, flanked by the most obvious of amateurs, Moley. Ray himself was embarrassed, but a little defiant too. He knew himself out of his depth, but he was sure, nevertheless, that he and his colleagues had developed more correct alternatives than Mills and Hoover, with their circumscribed principles, could ever evolve.

This was the first time Franklin had come face to face with Hoover since he had been a rival. The last time they had seen each other—which was after a Governors' Conference in 1931, when the governors were guests at the White House—their identification of each other as principals in the coming struggle was just becoming certain. Now it was over. It had been a swift and dramatic joust in which Hoover had heavy-handedly proved to his own satisfaction that he ought to be reelected and that, in any case, Franklin was a fantastically irresponsible alternative, and in which Franklin had smitten Hoover lustily, sometimes not above the belt, as Hoover thought. Now in the interlude before the handing over of power, which he was morally certain would

[6] Ray's firsthand account of the meeting is to be found in *After Seven Years.* It necessarily made a lasting impression and is vividly described. But Ray's view of Hoover and Hoover's policy was different in 1939—when his book was published—than it had been immediately after the meeting when he related the experience to me. In fact, his view went on changing. By 1954 it was just about reversed. In that year, on Hoover's eightieth birthday, his *Newsweek* column of August 16 had this to say:

Shortly after the election of 1932, President Hoover invited his successful rival to the White House to discuss the unpaid debts of various European nations. Mr. Roosevelt asked me to brief him on the subject and to accompany him to the conference. The briefing consisted of a collection of typed cards, which, held in the ample palm of the Roosevelt hand, provided the ammunition for a series of questions addressed to Mr. Hoover.

It is not a compliment to the quality of my prepared questions that Mr. Hoover after a few minutes confined his remarks to me. Perhaps this was in part because there was no love between the two recent candidates. Mr. Hoover himself in his Memoirs says that he thought he might thus educate me. At any rate, he did exactly that. For I sat enchanted by his wealth of detailed knowledge on the complex history of the debts and the cogent manner in which he explained it. It was a mark of his immense industry and his self-dependence that never once did he fall back on his Secretary of the Treasury, the competent Ogden Mills, who was also present. . . .

be fatal to the nation, Hoover had to choke down his revulsion and as best he could to perpetuate his policies. It was like punching a low. Hoover, pasty-faced, exhausted, despairing, went on to the end of it. Franklin took smiling leave. Nothing had changed.

But on December 17 Hoover was again writing to Franklin. This time he was mostly concerned about the preliminaries for the World Monetary and Economic Conference, about which something would have to be done in the way of preparation. It was to be held in April, and already conferences on the agenda had taken place at Geneva. The United States had been represented by E. E. Day and J. H. Williams.[7] Hoover believed—and said in this letter—that the large general questions then under discussion must be considered together: the debts, disarmament, the stabilization of prices and rates of exchange, and such obstacles to trade as tariffs, quotas, blocked currencies, and similar devices. Specifically he asked whether Franklin cared to join him in the selection of a delegation. He realized, he said, that "it would be normal to let the whole matter rest until after the change in administration." His reason for not doing so was that "in an emergency such as exists at the moment" he would be negligent if he "did not facilitate in every way the earliest possible dealing with these questions."

Franklin's people took a long, hard look at this communication. Their reasoning began by deducing the position from which Hoover argued. He felt deeply his responsibility and desired to clear away as early as possible all the uncertainties in the economic world so that reconstruction could begin. Among these uncertainties were the debts, which, if forgiven, would relieve other governments of a burden and would make possible a resumption of trade because foreigners could then accumulate dollars, now mostly needed for debt payments, with which to buy American products. With debts out of the way, stability of exchanges might be brought about by international monetary agreements, the basis of which would be a return to the gold standard. Going along with this, the heavy burden of expenditure for armaments could be lifted if the American proposals at Geneva were accepted.

This was a program that was typical of Hoover; it was orderly and systematic. It was typical of him also that he believed any alternative to be unthinkable; any reasonable person would want to co-operate in carrying it out. That there might be alternative policies he could not conceive. He may have recognized that it did leave out of account the Republican protective tariffs, but on that subject the party was split. The financier wing would have reduced and rationalized all barriers of this sort. It was the manufacturers who wanted them. This difference about tariffs seemed to Franklin's people important. They thought that

[7] Day was director of social sciences for the Rockefeller Foundation, and Williams was a professor at Harvard. Both were highly competent for the task.

trade could not resume, even if the debts were out of the way, unless foreigners could sell as well as buy in the United States. But also they felt that the forgiveness of the debts was largely a banker's idea. Moreover, they felt that the stabilizing of exchange was something that would have to follow, rather than precede, stability of economic conditions. If prices in the United States, they reasoned, were tied to those abroad, they could not be managed in such a way as to bring about the fair relations they had in mind. The point about this was, they were certain, that the international financiers wanted to manage prices and exchanges; they did not want it done by governments. What they intended was that all the nations should be tied to a gold standard which, in fact, was no standard at all, since under it the purchasing power of currencies would fluctuate as widely as the price of gold itself. Speculation in gold was a specialty with several European groups.

As a result of these considerations, as well as of deeper ones he was not yet ready to formulate, Franklin again refused to co-operate. It was his view, he said in his reply to Hoover, that disarmament, intergovernmental debts, and permanent economic arrangements would be found to require selective treatment. They could not be lumped together. Hoover answered this (on December 19) by saying that he was asking only that the preliminary studies should be undertaken, not that policies should be agreed to. At the end of the communication, in a rather tactless slap at the Brains Trust, he suggested that "Mr. Owen D. Young, Colonel House, or any other men of your party possessed of your views and your confidence and at the same time familiar with these problems" should be selected to sit with his own people in an endeavor to see what steps could be taken to "avoid delays of precious time."

Franklin replied again, saying that co-operation was possible only about exploratory work. He would, he said, gladly receive any and all information and expressions of opinions. But, he said, "the designation of a man or men of such eminence as your telegram suggests would imply not mere fact finding: it would suggest that . . . such representatives were empowered to exchange views on matters of large and binding policy." He "respectfully suggested" that Hoover proceed with the selection of representatives to conduct preliminary explorations both about the debts and the agenda for the World Economic Conference. This was supererogatory, of course; the debts would be discussed by Treasury officials; Day and Williams were already acting for the administration on the agenda for the conference; and Norman Davis was deep in the discussions then current concerning disarmament.

Franklin saw Day and Williams, and a little later he saw Norman Davis. He conveyed to Day and Williams his opposition to an early meeting at London—June at the earliest, he said. He talked at length to Davis, who was not only a diplomat but a banker. He got no advice

Franklin refused to cooperate concerning H.H.'s World Econ. Conf.

he could use, but Davis was asked to continue negotiations.[8] He had a distinct feeling that he was being rushed by the combined urgings of Hoover, the foreign governments, and the Wall Street bankers. He wanted time to find co-workers he could trust and to shape a policy. At the moment he had only the amateurs of the Brains Trust to lean on.

By Christmas, Franklin was taking advice about the members of his new administration; but as to any single cabinet position he had not yet come to a decision. He saw a multitude of important people. His door was open to politicians, of course, all of whom had pleas to make; they wanted not to be left out in the distribution of the rewards for victory. But others had the same or a similar idea. Every interest that had set itself up in Washington and, over the past twelve years, had established and perfected liaisons with the Republicans was presented with the problem of establishing the same cordialities with the Democrats. They were well enough entrenched in the bureaucracy—it had become overwhelmingly Republican—so that they anticipated no immediate difficulty about the continuing of those small favors from the administrative organization which mean so much to any business regulated by government or subject to the inconveniences of overzealous supervision. Every department had numerous regulatory acts to enforce, most of them important to some such interest—the Department of Agriculture, for instance, had forty-seven—and it was important that administering officials should not turn hostile. Even with a bureaucracy entrenched in Civil Service there might be embarrassing changes. These must be prevented.

Franklin, and everyone even remotely connected with him, was now the center of a vast confusion created by the more and more urgent attempts to gain assurances of this sort. So it was not only bankers who wanted to share the new power; it was every interest in the country with something to gain from governmental favor. Add to these all the politicians seeking something for themselves or their friends, and the situation may be faintly imagined. In the midst of these trials it was necessary to shape a policy. The detachment desirable for this was hard to come by. Franklin was grateful now for the foresight that had resulted in last spring's discussions. He was not yet clear about all the program. He had no settled financial plan, for instance, having promised both governmental economies, a balanced budget, a sound dollar, and so on; and having also promised recovery through the restoration of purchasing power, which, if it meant anything, meant spending. He

[8] The earnest between-wars disarmament efforts came to little more than earlier ones had. The so-called Preparatory Commission for the Disarmament Conference had been appointed in 1925, had met in 1926, and continued preparatory work until 1930. These extended discussions produced nothing of much consequence. The main Disarmament Conference met in 1932 and would come finally to a stop in 1934 without any tying up of threads. Its work would merely stop and be abandoned.

was reconciling these in his own mind by minimizing the funds needed for relief and public works and by hoping for economies by cutting down other government activities. He was amply warned by the Brains Trust that he was exaggerating both. But these were by that time—January running into February—very nearly moot questions.

Almost at once after the holidays a new sinking spell began that quickly assumed the proportions of prospective disaster. As the weeks passed, anxiety turned to something like hysteria. And a few weeks before inauguration it became evident that that ceremony would take place with the whole nation locked in the grip of a fiscal rigor mortis. Paralysis, it appeared, would be nearly complete. The first problem would not be how to recover from depression; it would be how to unlock any motor impulses at all and set the economy going again. So great was this panic that Hoover again addressed a letter to Franklin in February, warning him of the peril. There has been some criticism because this letter simply went without an answer while Hoover agonized over the onrushing disaster. No one knows whether Franklin's excuse, when he made it just before inauguration, was an actual explanation or not; what he said was that it had been overlooked by a secretary. It did seem strange that a communication from the President of the United States should simply get itself lost; but, anyway, it was not a warning that was needed. What was happening was apparent to everyone.

The whole financial system of the nation was collapsing. It was a question of time—and very little time at that—before banks everywhere would have to close their doors. The demands of depositors that they be allowed to withdraw their funds were increasing daily. No one believed any more that deposits were protected, and everyone wanted his own share made safe. He wanted to take it home in cash and keep it himself. Since the system was based on a use of depositors' funds that necessarily made them unavailable if they were all—or any large share of them—demanded at once, the banks would soon run out of currency to meet the rising demands.

Furthermore, the banks themselves, in an effort to get the cash their depositors were demanding, were calling loans as fast as they fell due. Also, they were refusing to make more. This constricted business. A business that could not borrow could not buy. The resultant cutting down of operations was a disaster piled on old disasters. A business constricted was one that fired its employees. Since this was going on everywhere, workers had less and less wages with which to buy goods. They were reduced to a misery that stood in flagrant contrast to American pretensions to high standards and made a mockery of Republican prosperity. And their misery was reflected in further factory closings.

The nation was in collapse on Franklin's inauguration day. There was a certain tendency to humility; there were even some admissions of guilt; but the striking mood was one of fear—mixed with a little hope that the new crowd would think of something to do. This was strongest among farmers and workers. To the one a promise of action had been given, if not one that was specific; to the other the promise of a new deal at least held out the hope that starvation and dispossession would be averted. To these minimal hopes had the magnificent pretensions of industrialism dropped. This was the end of the "New Era."

In the midst of the rising panic the Republican rationalization was almost lost; only Hoover and a few others kept it alive. As soon as recovery began to be apparent, it would grow, along with the expanding economy, until a decade later, or even before, it would come to full bloom. It would be vindicated in the election of 1952—just twenty years later. Franklin had *caused* the depression, the thesis ran, because of fear of what he might do. The system rested on confidence. Businessmen who had no confidence would not make ventures. The paralysis had spread because Franklin had declined to collaborate with Hoover and because reassurance to business had been refused. He had made it worse by threatening punishment of the "moneylenders," and moneylenders were very close to the heart of the system. It would not work without them.

Franklin was especially acute about political matters, of course, and he was not unaware that if he persisted in refusing collaboration he would in some way be blamed for whatever occurred, whether or not it might have been eased by his complaisance. He may well have been willing to see a long debate of this sort center in himself. It was well, as he had often proved, to have enemies who were also regarded as enemies of the people. He may well have thought that in such a debate he could always win. He would be right.

Other differences than the bitterness about economic policy at home were in the making; the issues that in years to come would refuse to be settled short of war were in their first stages. Fascism was already in being and Nazism was emerging; but they were hardly further identified than as "totalitarian" and opposed to democracy. Franklin at the moment was more interested in machinations in which the international bankers were deeply involved. There were Republican reactionaries at home; there were Tories in Britain, there were Nazis in Germany, and there were Fascists in Italy. So it went. A progressive American policy had to be thought out and implemented, one that would take account of these inimical forces, that would oppose and checkmate them. It was a hostile world for a progressive Democrat.

There was an immediate decision to be made about the banking crisis. The first trial of Franklin's administration would be precipitated by the collapse of the system. Would he re-establish the old or set up a new one? If a new one, what would its structure be, and where was the personnel to run it? The hectic conferences in the weeks before inauguration, and especially in the last few days, did not produce any really reconstructive policy. Franklin found no one among those who crowded his Hyde Park library and the second-floor study of his house on Sixty-fifth Street who could, he judged, carry through a reorganization. There were some who agreed that there had been abuses—curiously enough, one of these was a Morgan partner brought to him by Vincent Astor—but a new banking system that would take out of private hands the creation of a nation's vital medium of exchange, the setting up of deposit banks that would be merely that, and the establishing of a capital issues system with some kind of relation to national need—all of which the Brains Trust had discussed with him in a theoretical way—seemed so fantastic to those by whom he realized any system would have to be run that he gave up any hope of substitution.

The best Franklin could expect was that trustworthy financiers might be found who would carry out a liquidation of the existing banks, getting them going again as soon as responsible management could be secured. It was obvious that confidence in resumed operations would be hard to establish. The banks would be the same banks and the bankers the same bankers. Some, however, would not be allowed to reopen. There must be tests for resumption which would prove the safety of those institutions that did resume. When activity had been set going again and panic had been quieted, it might be possible to achieve substantial reforms. The pressures of the present, however, called imperatively for simple restoration of a system people understood under conditions that would assure them of future safety.

In the financial emergency Franklin found a calm and cheerful friend in Will Woodin. Will was one of those men of large affairs—like Frank Walker and Jesse Straus—who had supported Franklin's candidacy from the first.[9] When Carter Glass was asked to assume the secretaryship of the Treasury and refused, Franklin turned to Woodin. And it was he who presided so urbanely over the hectic doings of the pre- and post-inaugural banking crisis. He was a man of charm and serenity, with inner resources that gave him a certain immunity to surroundings characterized by disagreement, clacking fears, and exacerbated emotions. He was not exactly an expert, but he had a clear mind, and he gave Franklin comfort.

The Congress was meeting in lame-duck session from January on as Franklin worked over his program for the future, sorted out the claims on him for attention and place, and tried to find intervals for recuperation. The legislative leaders naturally expected direction from the

[9] None of this group went unrewarded; most of them had honorific recognition of one or another sort; but, most important, they represented a section of conservative opinion on which Franklin could rely.

Active executive

President-elect. Some were prepared to receive it, and some were ҏ
There were, among the old-timers, hints of that resentment all legislators harbor against the executive. There was even some rebellion. Franklin finally had to squash publicly a determined démarche by Garner,
who used his new prestige to advance the idea of a sales tax to substitute for progressive levies on incomes. Nothing could have been more
antipathetic to Franklin's principles. That Garner had no hesitation in
sponsoring it showed how deep a difference there was. The South was
unreconstructed, no matter what kind of program the party had put
forward in the campaign. Moreover, the principle of seniority had
operated to put Southerners at the head of all the important congressional committees. If Franklin really believed that he would "get along"
with the Congress, he had a confidence in his abilities to conciliate
which few of his close associates shared.

But how much that confidence was a public pose was revealed by
the arrangements he made to assure himself the leverage he would
need. He began by asking Lewis Douglas, on whom he early settled
as his Director of the Budget, to draft for him a measure giving him
powers of reorganization no other President had ever been able to
wangle from reluctant Congresses. This touched their controls over the
administrative establishment in so intimate a way that only the most
extraordinary conditions could possibly persuade them to concede it.
But those extraordinary conditions were impending and Franklin was
determined to have the freedom of action he needed. If his proposal
should be approved he could reduce or halt any operation and transfer
funds to enlarge others. The excuse could be economy, or efficiency, or
even merely "crisis." Douglas was more than agreeable. He was an ardent economizer who agreed thoroughly with Baruch that the first need
of the moment was the restoration of business confidence. Franklin did
not at first assess his stubborn determination at its true value. Since he
came from Arizona, he must be a sort of progressive, and he was so
personable and so charming that the stiff intransigency of his mind was
not at once apparent.

Franklin may not have thought it a bad thing to have such an
economy-minded Director of the Budget. He had, after all, pledged
himself to a reduction of governmental expense, and he had a balanced
budget very much in mind to achieve. But also, Douglas, having been a
congressman, ought to be a help in getting the important concession of
powers he wanted. The Economy Act would be, in fact, one of the first
of the New Deal measures; and the Douglas appointment would be to
that extent justified, whatever difficulties it might afterward cause.

The concession from the Congress was, however, not attributable to
the influence of any one person. It was the result of panic. With matters in complete chaos, the congressmen ran from responsibility. If any-

one else wanted to accept it under such circumstances, let him. But this giving way was not immediate or wholesale; it did not happen until the crisis actually arrived in late February. All during the preceding weeks the attempts of the New Dealers to anticipate some of the necessary actions of the new administration were frustrated by jealous or bargaining legislators. An illustration of this was the effort—unsuccessful in the end—to pass the bill for agricultural relief and get it out of the way.

It might have been thought that, after all the argument and with substantial agreement on all sides that something drastic must be done, such a bill would have been easy to pass. It was approved in the House in mutilated form and not at all in the Senate. The agreements turned out to be illusory, and the processors, with a strong hold on the lame-duck Congress, were able to prevail. Instead of getting agricultural relief out of the way, its proponents only found themselves much deeper in old quarrels. It looked as though it would be a long time before the agricultural distress would be met by any adequate measures for relief. The final check was furnished by Senator Ellison (Cotton Ed) Smith of South Carolina, chairman of the Senate Agricultural Committee. He simply was not letting any newcomer to the White House tell him what to do. And he had relations among the speculators in farm products which had to be protected. Franklin's charm broke down completely when he tried to force the issue. Cotton Ed squirted a stream of tobacco juice at the nearest receptacle and emitted a concurrent stream of words that smothered Franklin's reasoning.

Cotton Ed was only a worse example of the whole congressional prospect. A lot of new people would arrive in Washington on March 4. They would be amenable to leadership, at least at first, but with southern old hands in firm control of all the committees, it was they who would have the power. Some way must be devised to deal with them realistically. Obviously it could be done only by force, and the force at Franklin's disposal in this instance was patronage. Public pressure would not go far; the southern constituencies were "safe." He must simply refuse any jobs without a *quid pro quo*. He had a talk with Farley as soon as Jim was designated for the cabinet. They devised a simple scheme, old as politics, but understood by every practitioner. It worked. Combined with the panic of March, it gave Franklin the freedom to act without which the depression's sinking spell would not have been checked and the first items of the New Deal written into law.

The circumstances in which any new President must choose his cabinet are, to a certain extent, harried. He is pushed and advised, and there is little disinterested advice available. But Franklin's situation was much worse than usual. He had to work with a kind of rule, however, which enabled him to get through this task without too much difficulty.

266

It would be hard to say whether this controlling formula was present in his mind or whether—as with so much else—it is something to be inferred in retrospect, seeing to what actions it led. I am inclined, as always, to the latter view. Political leaders do not allow themselves to be governed by rote. They owe much of their success to originality—a limited, not too startling originality. This does not often result in anything very new to political mores; but, not having come out of a book, it carries a conviction, has a force and freshness, which are important. A political leader with genuine talents is far better for not knowing any rules—or, if he does know them, for having the courage to treat them with disrespect.

The gathering together of Franklin's official family thus seems to have followed a rule, but not to have followed it slavishly. It was departed from just enough to establish about it an atmosphere of personal determination. Once the line-up was complete, none of the trite remarks of the experienced commentators seemed to apply. The rule was well hidden. Still, it was there. In the making of his cabinet Franklin sought to further, as he was now to do in all else, the creation of a powerful presidency capable of furnishing leadership and implementing a policy. Everything was directed toward this end, even the negative, or seemingly negative, actions.

Positively, he surrounded himself with representatives of southern Democracy and western progressivism; he yielded nothing to business; he steered between the warring factions of labor; and, for agriculture, he settled on none of the heads of the farm organizations but on the one acknowledged intellectual among all those who had a right to be considered.

From among the Southerners there were Cordell Hull and Claude Swanson, and there would have been Carter Glass if he had not refused. Both Hull and Swanson were senators carrying the respect of seniority; and Hull, of course, had been very nearly the ranking Democrat during the years of exile. Representing the West, he had Ickes—who was designated by Johnson, Cutting, and other senatorial progressives—and George Dern, who had been governor of Utah. Ickes served to emphasize the welcoming of the Bull Moosers into the administration corral. Dern and Douglas (almost of cabinet rank) were Democrats, but they were considered to be liberal ones. To these progressives would have been added Senator Thomas Walsh of Montana if he had not died just before inauguration. Walsh, of course, would have brought with him all the prestige of the Teapot Dome exposures and would have emphasized the gathering up of all that was best in the Democratic tradition. At the last moment Homer Cummings, who supposed that he was destined to the governor-generalship of the Philippines, was substituted for Walsh. This was not at once regarded as a worthy appointment;

Cummings was best known as a professional politician. But his attorney-generalship, if it conceded too much to party claims, was notable for good judgment and for the kind of unexpected courage that would issue in 1937 in the scheme for reorganizing the Supreme Court, which brought Franklin such a fanatic support in the midst of apparently unanimous denunciation.

Daniel C. Roper as Secretary of Commerce was an ironic touch which most of Franklin's supporters missed. Roper was a South Carolina politician who had held jobs in the federal government running upward to the commissionership of internal revenue. He was, like Josephus Daniels, a party "wheel horse." His appointment pleased the Southerners, and it was a marked insult to business. The secretaryship of commerce had just furnished a President in Hoover, something no other cabinet position had done for a very long time. It was now deflated to match the deflation of business in the national regard.

Frances Perkins, who came with Franklin from New York State, had no claim whatever, in the going regard, to become Secretary of Labor. Presidents had until then allowed themselves to be guided by organized labor in making this appointment and had usually discovered that they lost by it both the regard of labor and the respect of ordinary citizens. The semi-official representative seemed like a betrayer of the workers, but at the same time he was not trusted as a representative of the public. Frances had demonstrated her competence; as much as anyone, she was responsible for the advancement of New York's labor laws and the excellence of their administration. But she was not identified with any of labor's warring factions. Her appointment was accepted as a perhaps necessary evasion of a choice between competitive leaders. Actually, it illustrated a principle Franklin felt and acted on whenever he could, although he would not acknowledge it any more than he ever would any other limitation.

Franklin understood that, whatever the Congress had intended in authorizing the enlargement of the executive establishment to include departments designated as "Agriculture," "Commerce," and "Labor," these must not be allowed to become, within the government, enclaves managed by special interests. That had been the tendency; probably it had been the intention of the Congress, always devoted to the additive concept of government. What Franklin got was three Secretaries who devoted themselves to the national interest, in one way or another, and not to the exclusive interest of the group whose label their department wore. All three came under fierce fire for this attitude, mostly from those who wanted to control the departments as they had been used to doing, but Franklin never gave way.

The usual comment at the time was that it was a rather mediocre group. Walter Lippmann intimated that he had expected nothing more from the "pleasant gentleman" who, without any competence for it, had wanted to be President. Others had much the same reaction. But Franklin was far from dissatisfied. He could not see how the Southerners could very quickly or very readily escape, however much they might dislike all that was about to happen. And all the power of the new West would support him. If he had misgivings about administrative competence, no one knew it. Indeed there is not the slightest reason to think that such talents were sought or considered. Cabinet building was a political job. It built power. If it succeeded in operating the governmental machine, that would be fortunate—but it would also be an accident.

14

His familiars afterward often heard Franklin tell how his first day as President began. He awoke a little earlier than usual in the still strange bedroom; breakfast came, but the newspapers were late and the assortment not just what he wanted.[1] After he was shaved and dressed, McDuffie, his valet, wheeled him out to the long wide corridor and they went down to the terrace level. Rolling along the flagstones this first time, he looked out across the lawns at the old trees—and especially the big magnolia he recalled from years before—and, bumping on the stone slabs, came to the office Hoover had left only yesterday. Its curving walls were bare, waiting for his choice of pictures; and when he sat at the large brown desk, his back to the windows, he faced the bareness and shuddered a little; a blank wall always annoyed him. There was nothing on the desk but an incoming tray on one side, an outgoing one on the other, a pad with leather corners, a pen set, and a lamp. An empty desk annoyed him too.

McDuffie left and there he was, he used to say, in a big empty room, completely alone; there was nothing to be seen and nothing to be heard. The nation, he supposed, was waiting breathlessly for the following up of his brave words of yesterday. There was a financial crisis, activity

[1] He seems to have forgotten that the fifth of March was a Sunday, but that is not strange, considering the crowded events of those days. He probably did go to his office on that morning. At any rate, there was a meeting of the cabinet on Sunday afternoon. There is a paragraph in *On Our Way* (New York: John Day, 1934), p. 4, which refers to this: "The first meeting of the new cabinet was on Sunday afternoon. Secretary Woodin had been in almost continuous conferences with the outgoing officials of the Treasury Department for three days. They had unselfishly rendered every possible help to him. By Sunday he and I were convinced that the drastic action of closing the banks was necessary to prevent complete chaos on Monday morning. At the cabinet meeting I turned to Attorney General Cummings and asked him for his report on the constitutionality of the proposed action. He replied that he had examined the statutes and was ready to assure me of the complete validity of the proposed proclamation."

of all sorts was congealed, and he was expected to find the means for bringing the nation's dying economy back to life. Here he was, without even the wherewithal to make a note—if he had had a note to make. And for a few dreadful minutes he hadn't a thought. He knew that the stimulus of human contact would break the spell; but where was everybody? There must be buttons to push, but he couldn't see them. He pulled out a drawer or two; they had been cleaned out.

Presently he sat back in his chair and simply shouted. That brought Missy LeHand from her office on the one side and Marvin McIntyre from the reception room on the other. The day's work then began. But it had been a bad moment, one that he spoke of often. It called up reflections, among those who heard it, of his physical helplessness; but that was not what he meant to emphasize. What seemed appalling to him in retrospect was the implication that the national paralysis had struck so nearly to the center and, for that short time, had reached the vital organ of direction. What would have happened if at that instant he had been permanently immobilized? Would the nation have broken up and its activities rebegun little by little in scattered places; or would some strong man or group of men have moved smoothly into control and set things going from the center outward?

This last would have been in the pattern of what had happened nearly everywhere else in the world except Britain, France, the Low Countries, and Scandinavia. Even the rest of Europe was locked in dictators' embraces, and no American republic actually had representative democracy. There were not lacking signs that persons who knew how to use the instruments of violence were more than ready to check the degeneration of the American society. Big businessmen and military commanders whispered among themselves about "the restoration of order." And their readiness was the same readiness that had been demonstrated in the "battle of Anacostia Flats" less than a year ago.

The fact was, however, that, lost though the new President might feel at that first instant, events were already in train that would make such an alteration in feeling as would amount to revolution. Indeed hope, just since yesterday, when he had spoken so challengingly, had visibly begun to displace fear. All that was necessary to consolidate the change was to see that action—the action he had called for—followed at once. And in several places in Washington at the moment action was being prepared. The legislative drafts authorizing it would soon occupy the empty acreage of that presidential desk.

The first two were ready. The one called the Congress into special session on March 9—the following Thursday. This was issued on Sunday evening. The other was the one that dealt with the banking crisis.[2] This

---

[2] It was actually the second one issued, but it was the first one prepared. It was the result of all that conferring at the Mayflower Hotel, in the Treasury, and

closed the banks officially, but it also went farther, forbidding any transactions in gold, including export. This last was the real objective. Speculation on foreign exchanges, as well as withdrawal and hoarding at home, had drastically reduced gold reserves and had consequently impaired the position of the banks. This, together with depositors' withdrawals, had made the doing of business all but impossible. The proclamation of the holiday was issued at one o'clock in the morning of Monday, March 6, and so was effective before business began that day. The "holiday" was to continue until Thursday, when the Congress would meet.

When the Congress met, Franklin was ready with a proposed Emergency Banking Act, the effect of which was (1) to validate the actions taken under the proclamation, (2) to give the President further powers to prevent transactions in gold, (3) to give the Comptroller of the Currency power to appoint conservators to handle the assets of closed banks, (4) to make it possible for banks to reopen as they were found to be solvent.[3]

Two other events of the first week following the inaugural tended to reinforce its bracing effect. The first was the Governors' Conference, for which Franklin had sent out invitations in February, not realizing in what circumstances the governors would converge on the White House. He meant to back up his demands on the Congress by judiciously creating a certain pressure for co-operation from back home. Governors are often, perhaps normally, rivals of senators and representatives, even when they belong to the same party. Franklin was wholly aware of all such political nuances and was prepared to exploit them. But he was caught in such a tangle of events that when he was wheeled into the East Room on Monday and faced the assembly of state executives, he had no prepared address and was not ready to discuss the several matters mentioned in his invitation.[4] But the meeting gave him a chance to reassure them concerning federal aid and to show them that a firm hand was on the wheel. They responded.

They passed resolutions recognizing that he was "ready to lead" if they were "ready to follow" and urging co-operation on everyone's part.

in offices on Capitol Hill, which had been going on since Franklin's arrival on March 2. But for a month before, there had been much discussion and taking of advice. The passage in the Trading with the Enemy Act, which was relied on, was the result of a suggestion of Mr. René Leon and had been carefully considered by a number of people—including outgoing officials. The Cummings opinion was by no means as confident as was implied by Franklin's later accounts. But all doubts were resolved by the immediate action of the Congress when it met.

[3] For descriptive note concerning these events, together with copies of the proclamations, see *Public Papers*, Vol. II, pp. 24 ff.

[4] These included principally conflicts in taxation and joint responsibility for relief.

This reflected the mood of the whole people. A leader had arisen who not only chided them for succumbing to fear but was beginning to show the way out of trouble. Two days later the first press conference was held, precursor of the hundreds that were to follow. And four days after this, the first fireside chat finished what the press conference had begun.[5] The President and the people were at one.

The press conference began with an announcement that the rule of written questions resorted to by Hoover would be abolished. The new President said that he saw no reason why he should not do as he had always done in Albany. He would talk about any public issue. He might not answer every question, either because it would be impolitic or because he was not prepared, but he saw no harm in saying so. There would have to be an understanding about what was "off the record," but certainly, he implied, it would be advantageous for publicists to be informed and he intended to see that they were.

His appeal for co-operation at the governors' meeting, his announced policy of sharing information with the press, and then his "fireside chat" made a remarkable cumulative impression. This was partly because of the feeling that it was a complete reversal of Hoover's secretiveness and withdrawal, but more because the instant deduction was that he knew what had to be done and so could be quite frank. The better feeling spread like a wave of sunlight over the whole country. There was a kind of euphoric flush that even the most pessimistic shared to some degree. Thus the first battle with fear was won with talk. The fireside chat was so simple, so lucid, so matter-of-fact that there was an unmistakable response to its appeal for confidence. And when the banks began to reopen, redepositing, to the bankers' amazement, began almost as though nothing had happened; and presently business was going on at the old stands.[6]

Seeing what his position was, and realizing that for the moment the Congress would deny him nothing, Franklin began at once to wonder whether what he had until now regarded as next year's business might not be got through at once—some part of it, anyway. But not much of it was in passable shape; it existed mostly as ideas, fairly inchoate. There were some few measures which, in a matter of days or weeks, with intensive work, might be brought into draft form. These could be gone on with. As to the rest, he would see.

Some of his collaborators were ahead of him. Before he could even

---

[5] Altogether there would be 998 press conferences. In itself this number is some measure of the continuous burden a President carries.

[6] A few statistics: 4,507 national and 567 state member banks were reopened within three days after the end of the banking holiday; the reduction of hoarding during March amounted to about one and a quarter billion dollars. Cf. *Public Papers*, Vol. II, pp. 65–66.

mention the matter, those of us who were going to be responsible for agriculture laid on his desk an urgent memorandum. Under the compulsion of farmers' woes, and with spring coming on, it might be possible, the memorandum suggested, to whip through the bill for agricultural relief or, hopefully, an improved version of it, which Senator Smith had blocked in the lame-duck session just expired. Franklin said "Yes" and started a frantic few weeks of activity. This quick request for action was encouraged by our observation of the congressional reaction to Franklin's first measures, but especially his message concerning the so-called "Economy Act."[7] It looked as though this was the time to ask for all the authority that might be needed for what would have to be done.

In the message proposing the Economy Act it was suggested that the Congress fix the amount and the general principles of expenditure, and then let the President arrange all the details. It was quickly seen that Franklin meant to reduce veterans' pensions and the salaries of government employees. He was pursuing confidence. This was the implementation of the Democratic platform and the Pittsburgh speech which had so self-righteously condemned Hoover and the Republicans for maintaining an unbalanced budget. The act was passed.[8]

There was some dissent to these measures among Franklin's own official family. This economy drive, in fact, caused the first serious schism —which would end in the defeat of economy a year later, involving then the resignation of Lewis Douglas as Budget Director. The dissenters doubted—aloud, as was the habit in those careless days—that savings and economy would be salutary. What would make more sense, they said, was an *enlargement* of expenditures, especially for relief and public works; the situation would only be made worse by reducing veterans' benefits and the salaries of civil servants.

Franklin was fairly soon caught in this contradiction of his own making: that he was trying to reduce and expand simultaneously. He was let off to a certain extent by the mention of a novel budgetary concept —one that set up "ordinary" and "emergency" categories. The savings were in the "ordinary" items. The expansion was in the "emergency" ones. Those who wanted expenditures increased had little concern for justification; but those who objected refused to be fooled. And criticism on this score would become more and more acute until a showdown was precipitated.

Franklin professed to believe right along that his economy measures

---

[7] Formally titled "An Act to Maintain the Credit of the United States Government," approved March 20, 1933, Pub. No. 2, 73 Congress; 48 Stat. 8.

[8] The "economies" were effected. Most of them were afterward lost, but the immediate effect was gained. The matter can be pursued by studying various items in *Public Papers*, Vol. II.

had served a good purpose, even after his understanding of the "compensatory budget" had obviously advanced in subsequent years and relieved him of the guilt he felt all during his first term over the budgetary deficit.[9]

But it was not the issue involved in this that so interested the agricultural people; it was the unprecedented willingness of the Congress to delegate precious powers. If they were in a mood to accede in the one instance, they might be willing in others. The point was that the quarrels still tormenting the movement for farm relief might just possibly be evaded by allowing the Congress to shift them to the executive branch. The Congress could escape the necessity for choosing among the "plans" so dogmatically held by various organizations and leaders by passing on to the President and the Secretary of Agriculture the duty of reconciliation and choice.[10] It was worth trying, they argued; and Franklin, laughing, said, "Well, we can try."

So the Agricultural Adjustment Act was conceived. It will be recalled that the differences among the proponents of agricultural relief had gradually crystallized into four roughly recognizable positions; there were (1) those who would fix prices by legislation or regulation, (2) those who would dispose of surpluses abroad, if necessary by "dumping," (3) those who would charge processors with the responsibility of increasing prices and would proceed through "marketing agreements," and (4) those who would increase farmers' incomes by reducing acreages and so limiting supply.

The last was the preferred plan of Wallace and most of the department's experts, and they had pretty well convinced Franklin that nothing else would do. The specific scheme for reducing acreage and limiting supplies was the voluntary "domestic allotment" device. This, for understandable reasons, was anathema to the processors of agricultural products; and it was only a last resort with many others who for some reason had objection to limiting production. There were those who would say, for instance, that it was absurd to cut down the growing of food and fiber when so many people were hungry and ill clothed. That this was an argument with force was admitted by those who advocated the domestic allotment plan. But, they argued, there were now huge surpluses of the staple crops which were doing no one any good. To go on with unlimited production would only add to them. Until there was an effective demand, until cold and hungry people could buy or

[9] There is even a note in the *Public Papers,* written in the forties, which justifies it. Cf. Vol. II, pp. 51 ff.

[10] This worked fairly well. It allowed the bill to be passed, even though delayed until after the planting and farrowing seasons. It worked less well at the other end. The unresolved issues, when they came to be fought out in the department, caused some embarrassing incidents.

Peekism   All could be used

otherwise possess themselves of the products, reducing was the only practical procedure. To allow surpluses to accumulate was to penalize farmers without doing consumers any good.[11]

It was not, as a matter of fact, this difference that caused the immediate difficulty or the quarrels that later would be so embarrassing. Consumers never seem to have any political power. Processors, however, do. And the millers, the packers, and the middlemen had a preference. They wanted legislation to center on marketing agreements in combination with the dumping of surpluses in foreign markets. Their idea was that the agreements, in return for their promise of higher prices for farmers, might give them—the processors—exemption from the anti-trust statutes. They would pay farmers more, but they would get it back from consumers. And they were not unmindful of the possibility that, in the process, their own profits could be enlarged. It was George Peek who most prominently represented this point of view; Henry Wallace and M. L. Wilson were committed to domestic allotment; John Simpson, of the radical Farmers' Union, shouted for price fixing and no nonsense about managing markets or reducing production; many of those who had for years been working on the successive McNary-Haugen acts still professed to believe that the surpluses could somehow be exported in spite of the known resistance in European markets.

Secretary Wallace had not much hope that these quarrels could be resolved in the Congress. What he would have liked to have was a bill to administer which embodied only the domestic allotment scheme. But he admitted the possibility that some surpluses might be disposed of abroad in spite of the growing resistance in Europe to dumping; also, there might be some gain from working with the processors without, of course, allowing them the latitude they hoped to gain. What he proposed to Franklin was that a kind of omnibus bill be framed, one that would permit any of the four hotly disputed methods to be followed. In the more calculating and less heated atmosphere of the Department of Agriculture, selective use could be made of any or all devices. Besides, if anything at all was to be done, there was no time to lose. Planting time was advancing.

Over a weekend a bill was drafted, and within a few days it was approved and sponsored by a hastily convened meeting of farm leaders.

[11] The force of this argument was recognized in another way—by the setting up of the Surplus Relief Corporation. By this device emergency funds were used to purchase surplus commodities which were then given to various relief organizations for free distribution. This public corporation functioned for many years and handled millions of tons of produce. But it might as well have existed so far as the New Deal critics were concerned; they preferred to pretend that the paradox of hungry people and crop controls remained unresolved.

276

Franklin sent it with a persuasive message to the Congress. What became the Agricultural Adjustment Act was thus started on its way. There was more delay than Wallace and his people had anticipated; the bill was not signed until May 12, almost two months after its submission to the Congress. The processors had tried to kill it, then to amend it out of all recognition, and had only given way to presidential pressure used to the limit. By this time much planting had been done, especially of cotton, almost the worst problem of all.[12] And in order to accomplish anything remedial during that year, cotton already planted had to be plowed up. That plowing up, and the subsequent slaughter of little pigs, with the same idea in mind with regard to hogs and corn, was the basis for a campaign of belittlement started by the Chicago *Tribune* and joined in by the Hearst press, which worried administration leaders but which—as would be made clear by the 1934 congressional elections—had no political effect. Nevertheless, for years afterward it remained a favorite taunt of the opposition.

While the agricultural administrators were laboring to get their program under way and trying to resolve the quarrels among the farm leaders which had been left open by the passage of the omnibus bill, much else was happening. It had not been forgotten that the most pressing national business—even before recovery—was the relief of the unemployed. It says something for the enterprise of the agricultural administrators that they were so quick to take advantage of the irresistible presidential prestige of the moment. And farmers were showing an angry temper that demanded attention. But also to be considered were the urban unemployed whose ills multiplied with every passing day.

To be sure, some relief was now being given. The states had had loans, inadequate in amount, for the purpose,[13] but enough to establish everywhere an easily expansible organization. Franklin proposed in effect to take a new start in a familiar pattern, but with an interesting variation. The new advances should be grants rather than loans. This would be an acknowledgment of national responsibility for economic disaster, a complete reversal of Hoover's insistence that this responsibility should be rejected and that all relief should be a local charge. But in Franklin's fertile mind this thought was joining itself to others and gradually forming the concept that disaster could be turned to

[12] There was a whole year's supply in storage; the price was around six cents a pound. It will be noticed how similar the histories of the twin New Deal measures—NRA and AAA—were.

[13] These loans were made under the Emergency Relief and Construction Act of 1932, about which Hoover had haggled with the Congress and left himself open to such severe criticism. He had insisted that the advances be loans, not grants, and that they be repaid by deduction from future highway grants. He had insisted also that public works should be "self-liquidating." Only about eighty million of the three hundred million authorization had been disbursed by the end of 1932.

constructive uses. Idle men could be put to work improving the national plant. They would have income; the nation would have the equipment they created.

This was not an overnight thought; it was something he had even experimented with in New York, as we have seen; moreover, he had by now joined to it a special scheme of which he thought better and better as he considered it. He would cause to be set up a kind of civilian army of young men who would work in the forests and parks, doing the many jobs forest managers never seemed able to get done—planting, cutting, trimming, making roads and trails, providing for recreation, preventing and fighting fire. He had a kind of vision, born, no doubt, of his long love for the forests as well as his concern for people, of youths taken from the street corners and poolrooms where they had been idling hopelessly and given the experience of working with and for the most valuable and most neglected of all the national resources. It would benefit them and it would benefit the forests.

So the message of March 21 concerning unemployment relief spoke of "three essentials": grants to the states for relief, a system of public works, and a "Civilian Conservation Corps." Among them, these agencies and their successors were to fulfill much of the New Deal promise. The Democratic platform had said, "We advocate the continuous responsibility of government for human welfare," and had gone on to speak of "the extension of Federal credit to the states wherever diminished resources make it impossible for them to provide for the needy." It had also spoken of public works. What actually happened could therefore be justified by Democratic writ. But the New Dealers enlarged the concept almost out of all recognition—for instance, by making grants instead of "extending credit." Franklin brought Harry Hopkins from New York in the late spring to administer relief. Hopkins called on the social workers all over the country, and they proceeded to "assist the needy" as they had hardly dared hope to be assisted; also, they would scandalize all those whose bent was conservative by the generosity of the New Deal government. But this was still in the future then. The Hopkins operations did not get under way until summer, and meanwhile things actually continued to get worse even though that was hard to believe because the *feeling* everywhere was so much better.

During the late spring the Civilian Conservation Corps also got under way with some awkwardness. What had begun as a simple notion that the experienced foresters would take under their care and direction a certain number of idle young men turned out in practice to be not so simple. There were problems of recruiting; who was to be chosen? There were problems of housing; who was to build the camps? There were problems of morale; who would look after health, recreation, and so on? There were complicated negotiations concerning these matters. The new administration had, in this, its first experience of establishing a novel agency that touched on many diverse interests. It was finally decided that all those sent to camps should come from families on relief. It was also decided, when pacifying the unions had become something of an issue, that the boys would not build their own camps but that union labor would do it.[14] It was further determined that the rangers and technicians would be responsible only for works; for all the other activities, as well as the management of the camps, reserve officers of the Army would be assigned. It all worked out very well after the initial confusion, and the Corps was politically popular as well as extremely useful. Certainly Franklin would regard its creation as one of his best ventures.

It was arranged that the young men should be paid, but less than going wages, and that a certain part should be sent home. This helped a good deal toward establishing an income for every family—which was an avowed New Deal objective.

There may have been as many as fifteen million of the unemployed at the beginning of March, a figure not agreed on by everyone. There were at the least twelve million—and this was a very large percentage of the working force. Franklin would never find a way in peacetime to reduce unemployment below five or six million, but there would in the end be some income to be counted on by every family. It would come in various ways—most importantly by way of the Social Security System, which was, even in the midst of this springtime rush to find stopgaps, firmly establishing itself in Franklin's mind as his most important objective. That so much was done in an emergency way seems in retrospect almost a miracle. But the fact was that by the end of summer there was hardly a family living in the same dread of the coming fall and winter as had been true a year before. This in itself was in such complete contrast to the last few oncomings of the cold season that good will for the author of this change spread like a benison over the land. And when there was added to this the prospect of real social security, his place in people's hearts became impregnable.

The stimulation given to relief organizations in the various states, when it was finally understood that the federal government was now committed to responsibility for welfare, was remarkable. The effectiveness of all these social workers, under encouragement from Washington rather than the reverse, altered the attitude of millions and millions of underprivileged people not only toward their President but toward their government and toward society. Sullen resentment was changed

[14] Furthermore, the director of the program was taken from a union—Robert Fechner of Boston. He was executive officer of the International Association of Machinists.

to hope and confidence. Something was happening that would turn out to be good; people felt that it was coming.

Franklin from the first was prejudiced against relief as such. He consented to it as a temporary measure. But he was just as much convinced as Hoover had been that unearned income eroded character. This was not something he would ever argue about. He was just certain that it was true. He was, because of this, aiming from the first at jobs rather than grants. He wanted people put to work. Like most others in those inexperienced days, he was far more optimistic about public works as a remedy for depressive unemployment than was realistic. When a bill was passed as a result of his recommendation and a Public Works Administration set up, he hoped that its operations would very soon eliminate the need for relief. In his message of May 17 about this he recommended the appropriation of $3,300,000,000, a sum that in those days seemed almost astronomical. He thought and said that prompt and vigorous action would override "the obstructions which in the past had delayed" such programs.

But even this proposal, endorsed by all those who were most learned in the ways of depression, was not the chief reliance. By then he had been seduced by another scheme, which, as it shaped itself in his mind, was a kind of twin to the outright inflation toward which he was edging under the euphemistic heading of "restoring the price level." He had become convinced that it was possible to stage a grand spectacular attack on the paralysis of the economy by way of a "re-employment agreement." If every factory, mine, and shop started up at once, it was argued, each would turn out to be working for the other. The wages paid would be income; they would purchase the ultimate products.

The argument he used in his message was direct, almost naïve; but it sufficed. A Congress that had been getting ready to pass the "thirty-hour" bill, which was the American Federation of Labor's favorite remedy for unemployment, was glad to accept the suggested substitute.[15] There was a good deal more in the proposed National Recovery Act than met the eye, however, and it will be necessary to explore its origins with some care.[16] Converging in it were several streams of thought developed by individuals or groups who hoped to serve one or another interest, not all of which were by any means public. For instance, the contribution of the business economists was the idea that association to obviate "unfair competition" ought to be legitimized. This was the idea behind the processors' marketing agreements mentioned earlier. These trade associations had, in fact, been developing for a

[15] The argument here rested on the old share-the-work fallacy that, since there is only so much work to be done, it—and the income from it—should be shared among the greatest possible number.
[16] Cf. *Public Papers*, Vol. II, pp. 202 ff. and 251 ff.

280

long time in a kind of shadowland. They were a pale if vigorous growth for this reason. The shadow was that cast by the anti-trust acts, so long the resort of all those who had a grievance against "big business."

Since 1890 there had been a continuous struggle, with advances, retreats, successes, failures, and ever renewed attempts at regulation (and evasions of it) between a growing and expanding system of big business and a determined progressive and orthodox opposition. Politically, the opposition was rooted in the West and South among rural constituencies. Progressives had often been Republican—La Follette, Theodore Roosevelt, and Hiram Johnson, for instance. But Wilson had stolen the progressive label and had had Bryan and Daniels in his cabinet to guarantee it; since he had been President for eight years and had had the blessing of the old-time rural Protestant progressives, his Democratic party was entitled to at least part ownership in the tradition. Besides, the progressives had always been mavericks among the Republicans. They had never captured the party, and with Harding, Coolidge, and Hoover leading, whatever reforming tinge Republicanism had once had was now gone. The line-up was fairly marked. Big business was Republican; those who wanted business made small, or wanted it restrained or regulated, were Democratic.

Any such hard-and-fast categories tended frequently to blur in American practice. During campaigns the leading candidates, seeking not to offend, moved toward central rather than extreme positions. And, for their own reasons, many who would be thought to belong in one camp or the other would be found in illogical company. There had been capitalists, and big ones, among the business leaders recruited by Jesse Straus for the campaign just past. There were progressives in the Republican party—young Bob La Follette, Senators Norris and Nye, for instance. And La Guardia, so far as he was anything, was Republican too.

Franklin's own position had been, as we have seen, somewhat equivocal and inconsistent. He sometimes seemed to be a latent trust buster in the most typical form. But sometimes, also, he seemed to feel that some alternative to this approach was necessary. He had, for instance, made the Oglethorpe address in which he had spoken out for planning and co-operation. Moreover, it would be recalled that he had been, during his fallow years, head of the Construction Council.

The Construction Council had belonged to an attitude or approach that stood in complete contrast to trust busting. It was one of the trade associations, and association is by definition the opposite of competition. Its function was to establish co-operation among its constituent businesses and to put an end to "cutthroat" practices. (Notice the semantic sophistication implied in the adjective.) The profession was that co-operation and competition were not the antonyms they appeared to be. But where the line was to be drawn was always escaping definition. Once organized, trade associations inevitably expanded and moved toward more and more extensive limitations on freedom. They were, in fact, the expression of an inherent business impulse to escape competition.

It was claimed, in their defense, that their function was to limit or eliminate unfairness, and the question of their legitimacy turned more and more, as they developed, on what was fair and what was unfair. It was certainly true that it was one of the sorest and most humiliating principles of the system that bad business tended to drive out good. Those who cut costs through low wages, child labor, sweatshop conditions, and the like, could undersell those who did not resort to these practices; they therefore tended to get the market for themselves. Regulation to prevent these abuses put all competitors on the same level. But the question often was where illegitimacy began. It was one thing to hire children and pay low wages; it was another to shift toward low-quality output under a once respected label, to give dealers' discounts, or to arrange for privileged rebates from railroads. The matter could, indeed, become very complicated. It would, moreover, be quite different for each industry.

Trade associations, under the aegis of Hoover's Commerce Department, had had an expansive development. Not a few industries had developed "codes" of fair practice which those who belonged to the association voluntarily engaged themselves to observe. But lurking in the background all the time there had been the threat of the anti-trust acts. What seemed to businessmen a legitimate organizing effort to escape from anti-social behavior might seem, at any time, to the lawyers in the Department of Justice a conspiracy in restraint of trade. Then there was the Federal Trade Commission, the favorite agency of the progressives for supervising business transactions. It supposedly had the duty of preventing unfairness. It ought to do everything that trade associations were organized to do. But its procedures were clumsy and long drawn out. There were many practices, also, which it could not reach. It could not, for instance, prevent the payment of hopelessly low wages. Such control among businesses would have to be voluntary unless the government was to go much farther than anyone had hitherto suggested toward detailed regulation.

There was good reason, in the tradition of Franklin's thinking, for considering that a large percentage of the unfair practices of business could be got rid of by voluntary standard setting, and for considering that only in the area beyond the reach of voluntary action ought the government to interfere. The government might well set wage minima, outlaw child labor, and require that consumers not be misled as to quality of products. And why should not the government both establish these standards and legitimize the voluntary organizations which would take care of the other unfair practices? The progressives of the old sort were ready with an answer to this. Because, they said, trade associations organized for these purposes would turn to sharing out markets, limiting production, and maintaining high prices. They would, in effect, be monopolies against which consumers had no effective weapon. Much better keep the Federal Trade Commission and widen its powers to establish standards, but otherwise vigorously enforce free competition in the interest of fair trading.

This is the gist of an argument that had been going on for more than half a century. Businessmen like Henry I. Harriman, president of the United States Chamber of Commerce; Gerard Swope, president of General Electric Company, and numerous others believed that more organization was needed in American industry, more planning, more attempt to estimate needs and set production goals. From this they argued that when this had been done, investment to secure the needed production could be encouraged. They did not stress the reverse, that other investments ought to be prohibited, but that was inherent in the argument. All this was, so far, in accord with the thought of the collectivists in Franklin's Brains Trust who tended to think of the economy in organic terms. They could see that a national collectivism would, however, make it necessary for government rather than business to make final determinations and ultimately to regulate the process of conjuncture in the public interest.

A few new officials watched with interest the reaction of the businessmen and their legal advisers to the atmosphere and the events of the beginning administration. And presently among them discussions began to take place that explored the common ground for a new approach to government-business relations. It can be seen now that there were unresolved reservations on each side. Businesses still hoped to determine production and price policies in their own interest, regardless of the fact that a merging would require subordination of individual interests to the whole; and the new officials estimated that the conjunctural function could be more strictly administered than they ought to have expected, knowing businesses and politicians as they did—not to mention the offended progressives.

But at any rate businessmen and administration got together, with labor interests hovering about and confusing the issues—the labor people were interested only in establishing once and for all collective bargaining and minimum wages and, of course, limitation on the hours of work.[17]

---

[17] In December, Senator Black had introduced labor's bill, and William Green of the AFL had testified that labor intended to force the adoption of the thirty-hour week—by a general strike, if necessary. The Senate passed this bill on

The National Industrial Recovery Act which emerged from several weeks of discussion and drafting was the product of these labors. The collaborators soon came to the drafting stage under Franklin's approving eye. There were really three groups whose ideas had to be reconciled: those of Senator Wagner, Frances Perkins, and others who were interested in labor's demands; those of the U. S. Chamber of Commerce and other businessmen who wanted mostly to escape the restrictions of the anti-trust acts; and those of people who were concerned to see a new start made in the relations of government and industry, substituting partnership for trust busting.

The individuals involved were Hugh Johnson, John Dickinson (Assistant Secretary of Commerce), Donald R. Richberg, and myself, with Jerome Frank as my second. When we failed to agree, Franklin told us to go somewhere, lock the door, and come out only when agreement had been reached. We were to do it under the chairmanship of Lewis Douglas, Director of the Budget. And of course reconciliations were made.

The bill, even after these compromises, was extensively amended. But its essentials were kept. In effect, it legitimized the trade association, provided for the drawing up of codes of fair practice and for their enforcement by licensing. The codes could be very comprehensive, including all sorts of rules for trade and provisions regulating wages and working conditions.[18]

There was again a very wide delegation of power to the President. He could approve or disapprove the codes and was free to set up the organization for administration. But this delegation, which would provide the excuse for the Supreme Court's rejection, was not what wor-

---

April 6, and Chairman Connery of the House Labor Committee showed signs of bringing it up at once in the House, adding a provision for prohibiting the import of goods produced by working more than a thirty-hour week. Franklin, under pressure, appointed a cabinet committee to consider what ought to be done. Frances Perkins, its chairman, carried its findings to the hearings on the Black-Connery bill. She suggested that a minimum-wage provision be added, that the government be given power to restrict production, to prevent it from exceeding purchasing power and forcing cutthroat competition which would make wages-and-hours regulations ineffective. This raised a storm among industrialists. A hundred of them met in Philadelphia on April 11 to protest, and there were other meetings of a similar sort. It was at this juncture that Franklin began to think seriously of a new approach to the whole matter and asked Moley to get together those who were interested so that new legislation could be shaped.

[18] These were later embodied in the Wages and Hours Act and were thus the only significant survivals of the original Recovery Act. It is sometimes argued that the act might have passed the scrutiny of the Supreme Court if it had not attempted so much. The most controversial of its provisions were those relating to labor. It might have been better to allow the Black-Connery bill to pass, minus its rigid thirty-hour limitation on working hours, and to keep the Recovery Act to a narrower scope. But that may have been politically impossible. Franklin thought so at the time.

ried anyone at the time. What did worry many legislators from the fi
was the implication of an unacceptable collectivism. Senator King of
Utah asked Senator Wagner, who appeared for the administration in
the hearings of the Senate Finance Committee, whether the bill was
not "drawn largely from the philosophy of Mussolini or the old German
cartel system." Senator Wagner answered that it was not; but Donald
Richberg, appearing at the hearings before the House Committee on
Ways and Means, admitted that the bill might encourage manufacturers
to fix prices and so achieve the same objectives as those of the European
cartels. This was damaging. It was not what the Brains Trust had intended or hoped to see in administration. They hoped the industrialists had given up such ambitions for the wider ones of planning and
co-operation. From then they began to have some doubt whether a
Frankenstein was not being created. But Franklin was inclined, as always, to think that if he was given enough leeway, if the bill gave him
wide powers, he could see to it that conjuncture and not restriction
would be the result. Nevertheless, Henry Harriman as a businessman
confirmed Richberg in saying that price fixing was contemplated.

On May 4, Franklin faced a meeting of the Chamber of Commerce
and spoke of parts and wholes:

. . . It is human nature to view a problem in terms of the particular existence and interest of the company or the business with which one is personally associated. . . . It is ultimately of little avail to any of you to be
temporarily prosperous while others are permanently depressed. I ask that
you translate your welfare into the welfare of the whole . . .[19]

He said something a little harsher and more realistic in a radio talk
a few days later:

. . . Government ought to have the right and will have the right, after
surveying and planning for an industry, to prevent, with the assistance of the
overwhelming majority of that industry, unfair practices and to enforce this
agreement by the authority of Government.[20]

He continued to speak in this vein, building up support for a fundamental change. The bill did not pass as easily as it seemed in retrospect.
There was a kind of ganging up of those who did not at once see how
they could use it to advantage, and they did not like the power government seemed to have. Talk of licensing was horrifying to businessmen
who had always done just what they liked. In fact there were a hundred amendments to the original text as it passed the Senate. But it
did pass, and final action was completed by its signing on June 16.

Labor was fairly well satisfied, although the thirty-hour week was not

[19] *Public Papers,* Vol. II, p. 157.
[20] Ibid.

Radical

made obligatory; it would be possible to write into the codes limitations on hours appropriate to each industry, along with other provisions such as collective bargaining. In fact Section 7A, which subsequently became so opprobrious in employer circles, left the way open for many changes; and labor hoped suddenly to achieve the goals of many years. If these gains had to be traded for concessions to business in the way of price fixing, they were prepared not to worry overmuch about that. This, too, caused the Brains Trust twinges of apprehension. Big labor and big business had always had the possibility of conspiring to further a mutual interest which would be far from coincidental with the public good.

Anyway, the act, even if voluminously amended, was passed with a large majority in both Houses, its Title II being really a separate bill providing an appropriation for public works and for an agency to administer it. Franklin said of the act, in a public statement, that "history would probably record it as the most important and far-reaching legislation ever enacted by the American Congress." He was ready with an administrator—Hugh Johnson, whose bluff and ready personality had fascinated him. Johnson had done much of the bill's drafting and, moreover, would keep Baruch pacific, something Franklin was anxious about. Richberg was made chief counsel, and they set up shop in the Commerce Building Hoover had built and occupied so pridefully under the aegis of a Recovery Board, of which Secretary Roper was chairman and which included several cabinet members and, paradoxically, the chairman of the Federal Trade Commission.

While this was going on Franklin had been busy with quite different matters. One of these was TVA (signed on May 18). Another was the Securities Act (signed on May 27); still another was the Glass-Steagall Banking Act (signed on June 16). But also the preliminaries which were to clear the way for the World Economic Conference in June and July were busily proceeding. Each of these was a demanding task in itself.

The Tennessee Valley Authority, as an agency to produce power, was related, in Franklin's regard, to other general objectives. These were conservation and the improvement of rural life. The opportunity was furnished by the long-standing controversy over the disposal of the facilities at Muscle Shoals on the Tennessee which had been the product of a World War venture in nitrogen fixation for fertilizer. Several Republican attempts had been made to turn these facilities over to private interests, and Senator Norris was as famous for opposing these as for any of his other efforts to oppose the plunder of the nation's resources. Franklin enlarged the Norris proposals and encouraged conservationists everywhere by talking in terms of river-basin development. This was a dream that none of its sharers had dared hope would become reality during their lifetimes. Franklin proposed to put it in hand at once. It was as thrilling to his supporters as any of the hopes he opened out.

His scheme had been broadly outlined in a spectacular trip through the Tennessee country just after election on which Senator Norris was invited to go along. This honor for the old progressive was notice that Franklin knew who his real friends were, as well as the fulfillment of hopes for a new start on grand works projects. The measure, when it was signed, promised all that Franklin had hinted at and more—for conservation as well as power; and it proposed, moreover, that the Authority it authorized should have it as a duty to improve the lot of all the people in the area. This it would do only in part by furnishing cheap electricity; it would also contribute to their welfare by improving the soil, enlarging the forests and recreation areas, preventing floods and erosion, and assisting them economically. Arthur Morgan, an engineer of repute and president of Antioch College, was made chairman of a three-man board, of which Harcourt Morgan, an agricultural leader, and David Lilienthal, a progressive lawyer with a midwest background, were other members. Under such auspices a modern miracle might be wrought; and that, seriously, was what was widely expected.

This brilliant first move of Franklin's was immediately recognized by the power companies and their related financiers for what it was—a preliminary experiment in public river-basin development, more than likely to be followed by others even more extensive. This would furnish yardstick power on a scale their worst dreams had never pictured. They prepared to fight under the leadership of Wendell Willkie, of whom more would be heard later. But at the moment they were handicapped by the recent exposures of their holding-company complexes as well as the collapse of the Insull empire with its vast losses to stockholders; they were neither so well heeled nor so well entrenched in Washington as they had been accustomed to being.

The vision of vast river valleys brought under multiple management to conserve water, turn it into power, and use the energy not for profit but for public use caught people's interest at once. It was the kind of thing Americans recognized as congruent with their conception of themselves. They at last had a leader who could show them the way to realize their potentialities. Taken together, the Civilian Conservation Corps and the Tennessee Valley Authority, if there had been no other achievements in the first New Deal days, would have established Franklin in the regard of Americans as the fulfillment of their ideal in the presidency. This was no compromiser who, when great matters were afoot, thought first of their effect on one interest or another, who cautioned against the dangers of growing governmental responsibility and found reasons for delay. This leader proposed that government should be deliberately strengthened and expanded to meet the necessities of a whole people. He was more afraid of what it might *not* do than what it might. Even those who would have been shocked at the suggestion of a leaning toward "creeping socialism"—which presently became the Republican slogan—responded to the challenge Franklin flung at them. His was an invitation to action. They were ready to support him in any action he proposed.[21]

This swelling approval was confirmed by the "Truth in Securities" Act, which was passed and signed shortly before the special session adjourned. This measure was aimed at the frauds and misrepresentations in issuing and selling stocks and bonds which had been so conspicuously revealed when the boom of the twenties had burst. Many an investor who, true enough, had himself been bent on speculation and actuated by a desire to get in on the prevailing "easy money" had found, when the market began to deflate, that what he owned were worthless pieces of paper. Perhaps they represented imaginary properties, perhaps they were simply vastly overvalued. In any case, the investment bankers who had sold them had made large profits and had made no guarantees of worth. Such a speculator, small or large, might not be entitled to his anger, but he harbored it and was in a mood to see the promoters and underwriters of such schemes punished, no matter how respectable they pretended to be.

The bill was an emergency one and did not go as far as Franklin intended. He meant to reach the Stock Exchange, which had so nearly resembled a gambling establishment. This latter objective went over to another session. The present measure provided only that securities would have to be registered with the Federal Trade Commission, accompanied by a full revelation of the financial affairs of the issuing concern. As Franklin put it, to a chorus of approval from a press which would be much more equivocal about the reforms of 1934, the new *caveat vendor* was now substituted for the old *caveat emptor*. Misrepresentation would henceforth be subject to prosecution.

This "blue-sky" law for securities was an old progressive aim now fulfilled. It had also been advocated in the Democratic platform, and Franklin, as is true of all innovators, liked to make much of such traditional objectives as he was faithful to. Anticipating, he had said a good deal in the campaign about "transgressors of a moral code" which might have been difficult to prove had ever existed in business. And he had

---

[21] It was amazing that this impression should root itself in American belief even while Franklin and his Budget Director, Douglas, were cutting government salaries, reducing staffs, applying stop orders to public projects, and cutting down veterans' benefits. Both warring policies were being effected at once. The public approval for the one so overwhelmed that for the other that presently the economy efforts died away and Douglas resigned in favor of a more amenable spender. But Franklin's embarrassment—in private if not in public—at not balancing his budget would be acute.

reiterated the theme in his inaugural. If it seemed a little exaggerated to speak of "money-changers in the temple," and if there were those who were inclined to ask what temple was meant, these were not questions that occurred at all to Franklin. And his policy is not to be understood unless this is recognized. He might be a strong government man, almost a state socialist of a modified sort, but he was not a communist. He never dreamed of a situation in which private business was not the main reliance of economic life. But modern economic life was complex and far-reaching, all had become dependent on it, and those who were its operators could not act like savages. They had responsibilities and they must carry them honorably. Franklin was a sharp reminder to businessmen that they had duties as well as privileges. They did not enjoy the pointed reference. But most others did.

The Glass-Steagall Act was really more of the same. It carried out other progressive ideas, long delayed but now irresistible. It was indeed a way, many progressives thought, of avoiding in future the troubles that now beset the economy. The Federal Reserve Board's powers were strengthened to prevent excessive speculation with borrowed funds. Further to accomplish this, investment and commercial banking were separated so that bankers could no longer use depositors' funds for such purposes as they had been in the habit of doing. Then, too, this act established the Federal Bank Deposit Insurance Corporation to guarantee the safety of depositors' funds. They were covered up to five thousand dollars; and this, it was believed, would obviate the phenomenon of such "runs" on banks as had recently resulted in the shutting down of the whole banking system.

These last three acts were all to be challenged and upheld in the same Supreme Court which would invalidate the Agricultural Adjustment Act and the National Industrial Recovery Act. And even a moment's reflection will reveal the reason. Reform, in the American system, however strenuously those affected by it might object, was traditional. It was within the accepted pattern. It was the application of righteousness to the practice of the going arts. But AAA and NRA reached out into new unexplored territory. They intended to manage some part of the economy, not merely to regulate it; they meant to plan collectively, through government, the direction it should take and the functions it should perform. They meant also to impose the disciplines necessary to the established objectives.

Those were powers not explicitly given to the government either in the Constitution or in the American tradition. They were reserved to individuals and to their creations, the corporations. Both the initiative and the functioning of the economic system were matters for private enterprise. The Constitution did not say they *might not* be controlled by a public agency; but there was no doubt that the judges were

Prep. for Radicalism paper

shocked by the idea that they might be, just as the old progressives were. And the Constitution was what the judges said it was. Franklin was enough of a lawyer—and, if he was not, Attorney General Cummings was—to know that he walked here in a no man's land of doubtful legality; and he must rely on recognition, even in judges' minds, of contemporary reality. The old world of private enterprise was gone; there actually existed a collectivity that society could not afford to entrust to private management. The public concern was obviously paramount. Simple good sense determined that a new approach be made. He would sell it to the people, but he must hope that the judges would give way. So he proceeded, and for the moment the acclaim drowned out the mutterings of dissent.

Thus was the first spate of New Deal measures improvised and enacted into law, long ahead of schedule, but to the undoubted satisfaction of the majority who had elected Franklin. They watched, with far less interest than they had in these domestic matters, the development of other measures which ultimately would be of even greater concern for them and theirs.

The boys who were now going to the CCC camps in the forests and parks, and many others who were pursuing, eagerly or reluctantly as the case might be, the prescribed educational courses for young Americans, would, when time had run for a decade, be called on to fight, and perhaps to die, for policies now taking their first tentative rough cast. A procession of foreign statesmen was making its way to Washington and being received with imperturbable urbanity by a completely composed Franklin. He did not forget that, after all, he was in the creditor position.

The foreign statesmen—among them MacDonald of Britain, Herriot of France, and Schacht of Germany—were, even if first of all interested in the debts, also interested in recovery. They tended to think in terms of monetary stabilization because it would presumably lead to an expansion of trade. For the same reason tariffs were important, and some reduction of the extremely high post-war barriers (among which the American Smoot-Hawley law was one of the worst) was sought. Franklin also thought of these approaches, and the experts who discussed matters with the advisers to the foreign statesmen talked in terms of such changes. Stabilization was a first consideration of the American monetary experts, and Cordell Hull and his entourage were low-tariff advocates of long standing.

As the foreigners came and went, optimistic joint statements issued from the White House; and when Franklin made his second fireside chat on May 7 he himself said that it was his purpose to stabilize currencies as well as to cut down trade barriers. The future of the world demanded, he said a little grandiloquently, that the impending con-

BUT

ference succeed, and everyone had pledged his best joint efforts to that end. Yet his first concern was recovery at home, no matter what he said; and he knew very well that foreign trade was likely to play a very small part in that, especially in any immediate future. Also, he knew that not stabilization but an increase in the price level was needed. If all the nations' prices could go up, that would be fine; but the heavy internal debts could be got rid of only by a dramatic increase, and he was determined on it. Stabilization could take place after the rise had been achieved.

Evidently Franklin hoped for more results than actually came from his first monetary measures—freeing the dollar from gold so that its price would fall, forbidding the hoarding and export of the metal and taking ownership of it in exchange for certificates, and abrogating the gold-payment clauses in all public and private contracts. It had obviously been expected that gold would fall and other prices rise. Actually this was happening. On the international exchanges the dollar fell and American prices began a rapid increase. If Franklin had expected more he must have been looking for a magical change.

Actually he was elated by the effect of the new measures; but since the American rise in prices was not paralleled by a rise elsewhere, the American position in the world's markets was not improved but worsened. And there were all those agricultural surpluses to be thought of. Both the AAA and NRA drafters had provided countervailing clauses to prevent the entry of cheap foreign goods. This had the effect of new tariffs, and such dams were obviously more and more necessary if a flood of foreign products was not to swamp domestic markets. Yet they were inconsistent with all the talk about reduced barriers and more trade. Franklin, sometime in the month of May, had some second thoughts. Hull's free trade would tie American recovery to that of all other nations, and monetary stabilization would do the same thing. Unless the other nations would take the same emergency measures for recovery as were being taken in Washington, they would be a drag on the American efforts. They might well defeat the whole program.

Suddenly Franklin decided not to submit the bill Hull's people had so optimistically prepared to provide the presidential powers necessary for lowering the whole system of tariffs through reciprocal agreements. Also, rather significantly, he spoke of "international action to raise price levels." But the enthusiasm about this among the foreigners was obviously assumed. What they wanted was stabilization at approximately present levels. They wanted to use the conference for such arrangements as would enable them to sell in American markets without making it easier for American products to be exported. Franklin was perhaps a little slow to grasp this intention. He obviously had not thought it out when he instructed the heterogeneous company of dele-

FDR now seeing time w/ in prices wouldn't submit to internatl stabilization

Plight of workers

gates to the conference. And this accounts for the embarrassing contretemps which would occur in July. It is not impossible to explain, but it was unfortunate. The conference ought to have been postponed, perhaps to the next year; Franklin did not see in time the trap that had been laid for him; when he did, however, he backed away from it with a violence that naturally annoyed those who had laid it.

When the special session of Congress came to an end on June 16, Franklin was being given premature credit by much of the press for having ended the depression. Only a little more of what was going on, it was said, and the trouble would have been surmounted.[22]

It was strange and paradoxical that a sudden bull market in Wall Street occurred. It looked rather as though Wall Street had benefited first and most from the emergency actions. Purchasing power was lagging far behind the rise in prices, and the increased production must be going to inventory; consumers could not be buying it. Actually, there was a vast movement to get rid of money, which was falling in value, and to acquire goods, which were rising. Consumers were worse off than before, with prices rising and their incomes remaining stable. There was, in other words, a time lag. Businessmen saw what was happening and anticipated it. They went too far, and there was a minor crash in July. This, and the evidence, which at once became noticed, that the NRA codes were going to be exploited by business and not be dominated by a government policy of expanded investment and price control, led to a wave of discouragement among the very people who had until then had such strong hopes.

There was, in fact, almost at once a new emergency. Franklin met it in the way he had for some time had in mind. Just when he was sending his "bombshell" message to the London conference, he was also launching his re-employment agreement. The Blue Eagle was being loosed for its short and disastrous flight.

[22] The index of production rose from 56 in March to 101 in July, according to the *Statistical Abstract* of 1934 (p. 70); more particularly, the index of farm prices had risen from 55 to 83. Food prices (retail) had risen some ten points, no comfort to the unemployed, but a sign, nevertheless, of recovery.

15

Franklin, moved to Washington and established in the White House, was not quite the same individual he had been in Albany. How could he have been? The worst strains and pressures of the ambitious years were now relieved; there was still posterity to think of, but time was given for that. Furthermore, the doubts he may secretly have had about his ability to meet and master the degenerative forces working at the foundations of the economy were now fairly resolved. He was on the way to succeeding. If not much had actually been achieved in the way of recovery during the first weeks, he knew roughly what was the matter. And many of the difficult measures for attack had been worked out. Some of the agencies he believed would reverse the trend had been authorized and were being set up. He had only to wait a little for results and make adjustments in a complex of machinery he thought sufficient—not sufficient for reform but for a beginning recovery.

While the attack on depression was being devised and people's spirits lifted, Franklin, as has been noted, had met and estimated numerous contemporary foreign statesmen with whom he would have to deal. He had not found himself or his entourage as inferior as their amateur rating might have determined. The dealing with other nations which had so worried his predecessor did not promise to escape from his competence. He already had an awareness of matters abroad that had very generally been overlooked. And anyway, diplomacy was like other problems. It existed. He became conscious of it. He sized it up. Something occurred to him. After a cautious interval he began to broach ideas to this or that associate or to someone called in for the purpose. His understanding broadened and deepened satisfactorily, and policy began actually to shape itself. He put someone or a group to work on detail or on verification, and presently there it was, ready for action.

This was not very different from his method of procedure as governor, but he had naturally not been quite certain that in the vaster field f federal policy-making it would be sufficient. It might expose him at worst to ridicule, and even this side of ridicule, to the verdict of mediocrity, and so he proceeded in a gingerly way at first. Yet the exigency was such that he could not experiment at any length, except as all novel governmental arrangements are experimental. He had to go ahead. The banking crisis was probably the worst to handle. He dealt in this with unfamiliar materials, with people he did not altogether trust, and was exposed to the criticism of those who had lately been the most powerful people in the nation. He was extremely cautious and conservative, so that even the most alert critic could find little to say except to deplore the tendency, largely imaginary as yet, toward inflation and punitive measures.

As to inflation, he could now see his way ahead. He did not, in the first place, regard it as inflation to restore prices to the levels at which the bulk of people's debts had been incurred. Inflation resulted from unbalanced budgets, and he intended to balance his. If prices could be raised by monetary management, he would do it; and he was, at odd moments, letting his mind play with various suggestions for a managed dollar, particularly that which had been so often urged by Warren of Cornell, abetted by Henry Morgenthau, who was now administrator of the newly reorganized and consolidated Farm Credit Administration.[1]

He was being pressed already to "do something about silver" and he could see that ultimately he would have to.[2] But he was fairly satisfied at the moment with the monetary measures he had taken.

He was fairly satisfied in general; considering the boiling disturbances all around the New Deal periphery, the center at the White House was remarkably tranquil and easy. It was Franklin who made it so. He was master in this house out of which lines of direction radiated to the whole nation. When the NRA had become law, succeeding a half dozen other recovery measures, it was as though a quiet shift of gears had taken place and new power had flowed into and filled the man who sat at the brown desk in the pleasant office room in the west wing. He looked now at walls crowded with naval prints; the flat expanse of desk before him had begun to accumulate that collection of small objects which were brought to him by followers—junk, all of it, to an observer who did not know the origin of each or what it meant; precious to giver and receiver, who did know.

Franklin had a fondness for "junk." He had no artistic sense, just as he had no musical or literary feeling. He could not tell a good sculpture or a good picture from a bad one, as George Biddle was later to remark

---

[1] Authorized as Title II of the Agricultural Adjustment Act.
[2] This agitation was the more embarrassing because it came from Westerners to whom he owed so much—Wheeler, Pittman, and Cutting, for instance, senators from Montana, Nevada, and New Mexico, respectively.

as he looked around at the products of WPA artists on the walls of the executive offices. But George also would go on, rather thoughtfully, to add that no one in all history had ever done so much for art and artists. And something of the same sort could by then have been said for musicians and writers. They were inclined to forgive his lack of discrimination and his preference for the banal and sentimental. They had anyway been treated like human beings, and that was enough even for a poet or a novelist, used traditionally to hardship, when for years mere deprivation had become sheer starvation.

The only time Franklin himself regretted his artistic incapacities, so far as anyone knew, was when it came to writing speeches, proclamations, and messages. He would have liked them to be eloquent as Wilson's had been, to be vivid as Uncle Ted's had always managed to be, and to compete with his contemporary statesmen—especially Churchill—a little later.[3]

As to this last, he sometimes outdid himself. Close study of the occasions when his eloquence was most assured, restrained, and adequate shows something of a pattern. He was at his best when he saw the issue clearly, had time to choose his words, and was really moved by the need for appeal. It was his leadership to which words and phrases gathered as though in a kind of service. Sometimes then he really would achieve a kind of eloquence. It is interesting that when he had most to do with one of these documents—they were not often from his hand even in major part—the language echoed the St. James version. Consider, for instance, certain sentences which he himself wrote to accompany the submission of the AAA to the Congress:

Deep study and the joint counsel of many points of view have produced a measure which offers great promise of good results. I tell you frankly that it is a new and untrod path . . . if a fair . . . trial of it is made and it does not produce the hoped-for results I shall be the first to acknowledge it and advise you. . . .[4]

And there was one of the less quoted passages in the inaugural, which, in view of all that followed, can be understood to be packed with meaning. It too was classically simple:

The people of the United States have not failed. In their need they have registered a mandate that they want direct, vigorous action. They have asked for discipline and direction under leadership. They have made me the present instrument of their wishes. In the spirit of the gift I take it.[5]

[3] Harry Hopkins told me, just after he had come back from his first mission to Churchill for Franklin, that the first question he was asked did not concern the mission at all. "Who writes Winston's speeches?" Franklin had demanded. Harry said: "I hated like hell to tell him that Winston wrote them himself."

[4] *Public Papers*, Vol. II, p. 74.

[5] Ibid., pp. 15–16.

This was a rather free interpretation of an election which had certainly gone far more *against* Hoover than *for* Franklin. But it was the kind of expression Franklin could achieve on occasion. Discipline was what people now wished they had possessed rather than the speculative fever that had betrayed them. The words came welling upward from some hidden spring, carrying with them an interpretation only externalized when they had been spoken. It is to be supposed that all first-rate political artists possess this access to the as yet unexpressed feelings of their people; certainly Franklin possessed it to a degree that sometimes seemed incredible. It is this sure touch that is so easily missed in the chilly exposition of policy.

Some students of the New Deal are quite rightly inclined to belittle this first attack on the nation's ills—for that matter, they belittle the second and third attacks and are inclined to say that only preparation for war rescued Franklin from the results of incompetent policy-making and administration. They underweigh the judgments he had to make concerning what he could do and when he could do it. These were influenced very strongly by his insight, his sense of the public mind, his gift for knowing what was latent and acceptable. All these are imponderables, and it is, I think, impossible to conclude that his judgment was wrong.

Just now as he began his relatively long career in the presidency he was acting presidentially, not consciously, any more than he produced biblical language for his messages consciously, but nevertheless with talent and with the painstaking care that accompanies a serious effort. What I mean about this can be understood by recalling that there have been Presidents who never seemed to act the role. The office requires its occupant to be both heroic and human, not an easy combination to put together and maintain, day in and day out. And failing at it may not be any measure, really, of intelligence or competence. But failing at it does indicate a lack essential to a successful democratic leader. Very different kinds of people have it and do not have it. Among recent Presidents, Cleveland, Taft, Coolidge, and Hoover had not "taken hold"; but McKinley, Theodore Roosevelt, and Wilson had. Perhaps, also, strangest of all, it must be believed that Harding would have measured up had he lived.

Presidential success has nothing to do with experience, education, or competence. It is wholly mysterious. But that it is recognizable everyone admits. Franklin used to size up his rival candidates with it in view. Of all of them, only one, to the end, would seem to have the gift—that would be Willkie, some way yet in the future. And of all Franklin's present contemporaries, only two were really generously outfitted; those were La Guardia, who at the moment was out of office, and Olson, the Farmer-Laborite who was governor of Minnesota but who was marked for death. There was no such person in the cabinet, none in the Congress. There was none anywhere on the horizon who might be a rival. Neither La Guardia nor Olson would ever be that. One of them might be a successor, but this was too early for either to be anything but a follower.[6]

There were some demagogues. Father Coughlin was spreading poison but was still not yet wholly off the New Deal reservation. Milo Reno was not yet silenced among the midwestern farmers. And Huey Long sometimes seemed a threat to the established order. Just what kind of threat Huey offered, no one seemed to know; but he had conquered Louisiana and spread his influence into Mississippi. He was now starting on Washington from a Senate seat. He wanted power, and his ambitions would naturally have centered in the presidency. His "share the wealth" and "every man a king" slogans, like those of some minor demagogues in California—the "ham 'n' eggs" group and the Townsend old-age-pension agitators—had a cruel appeal for those whose careers had ended in shabby cul-de-sacs of poverty and no longer had any dreams except those of lavish handouts.

Franklin was not unmindful that thunders from the left had a certain utility. His special forte was that of estimating and playing against one another, to his own advantage, the forces and movements that were stirring, still almost unrecognized, in people's minds. There would always be strong and sometimes rabid opposition from the right. Those who had power and wanted no inroads made on it would resort to every possible preventive. And they were sufficiently long-sighted to expect the worst. They maintained "legislative representatives" with adequate expense accounts to stave off or divert threats from "the Hill." But they could never be sure that something untoward would not emanate from the White House; Presidents had a way of breaking out, even the safest of them, under the urging of responsibility. So great pains were taken with the executive establishment too.

For what Franklin would have to do, this was serious. Amendment and delay can sometimes defeat the most vigorous executive. To have opposition working also among his close associates can be even more serious. And there was a swarm of "fixers" in Washington from the first. They were Democrats, and they displaced a similar lot among the Republicans. They were smooth talkers, able to mention a good connection, usually political—sometimes they had party posts—and often they

[6] I omit from the list of potential rivals two individuals who *were* respected as possibilities, although not for the presidency, unless the New Deal should prove a pretty complete failure. In that case either the far left or the far right would provide a formidable contender. Franklin was settled in his own mind as to who each of these would probably be: in the one case Huey P. Long, in the other Douglas MacArthur. This rivalry at the moment was latent rather than active.

succeeded in interposing between Franklin and his objectives a soft and good-humored barrier that was hard to locate but was incontestably there. Even in the rush of the first days they were on the job. They were responsible for most of the hundred amendments to NRA; they were able to hold up AAA for weeks while spring planting was going on; they looked out for the bankers' interests as the new credit and monetary machinery was set up.

Franklin knew about Huey Long and "the demagogues." He assigned aides to pacify and pet the madman from Louisiana and from time to time had him in—after all, Huey was a Democrat, and he had been useful at Chicago. But Huey soon wanted more than could be given, and after having said at first that he "was goin' to do what Frank told him to do," he was soon saying that he "could not be bought." He was the all-or-nothing sort. So were the lesser Hueys. They had no place in a peaceable movement. They lived on trouble. And if things got better, as they now seemed likely to do, they would be returned to the obscurity from which they had emerged.

Their one chance was to propagate impossible goals and to condemn Franklin not for having done nothing but for not having done enough. In such ways they might hang on or make progress toward power. The most interesting figure among all of them, and the only one about whom Franklin had curiosity, was Upton Sinclair, who was apparently riding the wave of unrest in California but who was himself not of the Long-Coughlin breed. Nothing would come of his belated career, but Franklin at least took pains to see that he should be kept friendly and should not escape into the prevailing raucous chorus.

Looking back, the fixers and the demagogues of 1933 do not seem so important as they did at some dangerous moments then. They disappeared, one after another, as Franklin's hold on the people spread and deepened. They would not be heard of again after the overwhelming and unprecedented victories of 1934 and 1936. Neither, unfortunately, would some others whose role in American life was a different one and who were regarded by Franklin with a respect that was often tinged with affection. There were, of course, Norris of Nebraska, and La Guardia of New York; there was Olson in Minnesota, regarded at one moment as a most likely successor; and there were the Wisconsin La Follettes, Philip, the governor, and Bob Jr., now senator. These were the true breed. If Franklin had not been a Roosevelt I am quite certain he would have liked to be a La Follette.

It was not a calm season, however equably Franklin, in the White House, went about his business. The strange possession that had seemed to freeze the nation until March was shaken off as the New Deal began to function. The loosed demagogues denounced the New Dealers (not the Old Dealers); the frantic lobbyists and fixers moved every source of influence they could reach to shape the fast-emerging legislation in their own favor; the progressives denounced the regular Democrats; and the Democrats clamored for jobs. As AAA and NRA were legislated and then organized, businessmen in the thousands descended on Washington like the proverbial locusts. They emerged in the morning from their hotels and spread into every corner of the town, going about their influencing trade. They held innumerable meetings with their permanent Washington staffs; they negotiated and entertained and went home, only to be sent for again in a hurry. Even in the first months of World War I, Washington had seen nothing like it. It was at this time that the city lost its last resemblance to the old southern town of earlier accounts.

The turmoil in Washington—and even elsewhere in the country—was indeed spectacular; and, naturally, a long-starved press, which had subsisted far too long on a diet of Hoover depreciation, made the most of renewing life. The capital coverage of the newspapers expanded and a new business of inside advice and prediction grew up, trading on businessmen's greed and gullibility.

The hungry Democrats were no problem to Franklin. He knew exactly what to do about them. He held them off until he had got what he asked for. He used them against the lobbyists and the demagogues. Only the most necessary appointments were made. The thousands of subsidiary jobs were withheld until the job seekers' principals had "delivered." Farley's talents were stretched to capacity, but they proved adequate to their tasks. His formidable organization spread throughout the government, and its first assignment, the unpleasant one of standing fast until the emergency laws were on the books, making promises but making no deliveries, was efficiently carried out. By June matters had cleared so that the job-giving could begin. There was a feast to follow the fast. And Democrats in streams entered Washington's marble doors to disperse into the clerkships among the desks of the offices where the assistants to the assistants worked.

However well such a task is done, not everyone will be happy as the first spate slows down, and it was true in this case. Added to those who were unhappy, there were those who were now free because they had been paid off. They no longer had to behave. Farley paid too high a price; he left himself too little to bargain with and next year would find himself falling back on the politically futile device of calling attention to past favors. But still the pay-off had been in the tradition and done in good order. The Republican hordes departed and Washington settled down to living with the Democrats. They were surprisingly little different.

But the White House was different. Nothing any occupants could do to it would alter much the appearance of this home of Presidents.

Its air of having been set here on its lawn and among its trees for some benign use, its withdrawn and dimly glowing dignity had not been destroyed by the political meannesses it had seen so often. The urgent job seekers, the seekers of other sorts for advantages bestowable by its master—all this had been absorbed and transmuted, somehow, into something finer. It was as though the Presidents here had been patient with graspingness, understanding of human weakness, and had, decade by decade, created a tradition of centrality which the house reflected. The mansion sat within the eye of the political storms, but their whirling destruction was always beyond the gates of the park.

Dwelling here, a President could be conscious of all that went to make up the United States, ignoble as well as noble; but he himself, in this place, was withdrawn to be everyone's surrogate but no one's servant, not even those who had put him there.

It is a remarkable comment on the presidency that the processes of party politics, so often corrupt, boss-managed, and infiltrated with venial arts, have never deposited a man in the White House who was wholly unworthy. There have been those who were ignorant, weak, unwise, or overkind to friends; there have been many who were slow to understand their essential duties; but there never has been one who did not grow better, wiser, more dedicated to the public interest. Even Grant and Harding, usually cited as lazy and inept and subject to corrupt influence, grew toward presidentiality. Harding, it was said, turned the Oval Room into a hangout, a saloon; but Harding, when he died, was a man convicted of sin and doing penance. And Grant rose to near greatness before he departed.

Franklin's immediate predecessor, Hoover, had been austere but demanding. The White House had seen little gaiety in his time, few of the occasions its great rooms demanded, when the froth and glitter of women's finery and men's uniformed glory invaded it to symbolize the side of life which was one of its rewards. Hoover's had been solemn occasions; he had suffered through state dinners, boring musicales, and tiring receptions. During his term the mansion underwent no indignities, but neither did it gather any charm. In his way, so different from Franklin's, he had been a worthy President.

It can hardly be imagined how changed the atmosphere was at once when the Roosevelt family moved in. It was very much, someone said, as though the house had sat there enduring patiently since the days of Uncle Ted, waiting for something like this to happen, for life and living to return.

It was not, it must be recalled, either a strange or an awesome place to Franklin or Eleanor or their children. All of them were accustomed to great houses at home and abroad, to the smells of furniture polish, floor wax, and hothouse flowers, to spacious views from richly draped windows, and to the quiet care of dignified servants. And Franklin and Eleanor, at least, had known the White House itself from childhood. This did not mean that they came to it with less respect, merely that they came to it with ease and familiarity, as though they had come home. The home would be a place of public duty; its occasions would be, many of them, stated and demanding; but these were not to be resisted and suffered through; they were to be experienced and enjoyed. This was because ceremonials had a reason for being; they were part of a tradition of which the Roosevelts, too, were a part. The White House and the Roosevelts could go on together very naturally.

Eleanor was a little reluctant. She had been enjoying the outlets for energy she had developed in New York, and she disliked giving up the independence she had so belatedly won. She exaggerated, perhaps, the restrictions of presidential wifehood, having observed the narrow activities of such capable ladies as Mrs. Coolidge and Mrs. Hoover. She would find ways to escape—at some cost in criticism—just as she had in Albany; but at first she could not see how it could be managed. She has said that this was how she felt, but no one would have known it. She complied with the formalities in her specially graceful way and at once began to establish herself as a great lady in her own right. She would not be immune, exactly, to the shafts of satire aimed at her, but her air of superiority to all such meannesses would be so unaffected and her geniality would be so genuine that all the critics would in the end retire defeated.

A good deal of Franklin's life now centered in the second-story Oval Room. On one side of it he had a great working desk, and all about it were scattered overstuffed chairs and sofas into which visitors sank helplessly. Tall windows, like those of his office, looked out to a south prospect that seemed alien indeed to an industrial civilization; there was nothing to be seen but rural arrangements. Many an evening Franklin was to spend in this room, endlessly conferring, or sitting over the piles of his correspondence, quickly disposing of sheet after sheet until the basket was emptied and Missy LeHand or Grace Tully was stiff-fingered and heavy-eyed.

His bedroom was next door. And after a while it was so much like his bedroom at Hyde Park that they could almost have been interchanged—something that could hardly have been accidental. This room was larger, but the prints on the walls, the bed with its table beside it, the odd books everywhere, and the little mementos—more junk—gave it the same air. And just as his bed was fixed at Hyde Park so that when he sat up first in the morning he looked out at a landscape of trees and hills and the river, so here he at least looked out the same way at trees and hills toward the southwest. There was about it an amplitude that was completely unostentatious. It was a workingman's bedroom, where he slept but never abandoned the job which was his life.

There had not been children in the old house for a good while—since Uncle Ted's day, really. But now they sometimes seemed to take over the premises for their own uses and there was nothing inappropriate in the change. Large boys racing up and down stairs shouting loudly to each other, Anna and her friends, young married women and their small children, made the place lively. Often during school holidays there were not enough bedrooms to accommodate all the Harvard lads and the girls who were house guests. And the East Room heard music at late hours, not provided by classical artists. When the cave dwellers of Washington heard that at one early dance there had been beer barrels on tap in the corners, the eyebrows were lifted higher even than they had been before. They were already high; Alice Roosevelt Longworth, widow now for two years and arbiter in her arrogant way of capital customs, had let it be known that these were the wrong Roosevelts. Franklin, she implied, was an upstart, thus echoing her half brother Theodore Jr. The Oyster Bay family was not forgiving toward the Hyde Park branch for taking over; there had been plenty of sons in direct descent; the Hyde Park collaterals need not have been turned to.

There was a prevalent disposition in Washington society, therefore, to deplore the Roosevelt doings. They were held to be more disgrace to the White House than Harding's tobacco-chewing hoodlums from Ohio. Those tough birds had been at least Republican and, if no ornament to society, not subversive. Franklin demeaned the Roosevelt name in the first place by being a northern Democrat, and in the second place by "betraying his class." The cave dwellers had their incomes from the sources Franklin seemed likely to dry up. They found it easy to believe of him and his family that their unfitness in the White House need only be called attention to to have something done about it. Their indignation, they felt, must necessarily be widely shared.

This kind of exchange traveling about Washington by way of whispered talk between dinner partners and over the teacups in the dark stiff rooms of old mansions tended, as reactionaries can never understand, to confirm the Roosevelts in their position, just as it was of advantage to Franklin that the press of the country, the columnists, and the radio commentators should be nastily critical most of the time. It was an advantage, too, that his "class" should regard him as a traitor. Just what the electorate wanted was someone whom the Hearst-McCormick-Scripps-Howard-Gannett newspaper axis regarded as unfavorable to business interests. And they felt a kind of oneness with Roosevelts who were rejected by a "society" which natural democrats regarded anyway with a certain suspicious scorn.

It is true that Franklin and Eleanor were society of a slightly different strain from the cliff dwellers or the Long Island country-house set. So had Theodore been, for that matter. They wore their ancestries easily. They had the idiosyncrasies of the true aristocrat who conforms only when he likes to. Franklin and Eleanor showed their good training, but they knew when they were bored; and both of them would rather work and make their way than rest on place and wealth, and both seemed to have urges that welled up from very deep springs.

Eleanor was more matter-of-fact, more earnest, and more unswervingly moral than Franklin. She understood the necessities of politics, but she had many moments of doubt whether Franklin's compromises were worth the price. Sometimes she was seized with the conviction that they were wicked, and then she protested to him. He met her objections sometimes with explanation. Their long-common background made elaboration unnecessary and he could usually convince her—when he himself was convinced. When he was less sure that he had done the right and essential thing, he retreated into evasions. Even Eleanor had to grant a President some leeway. She had done her duty by protesting. She let it go at that. There were no high words. She was a quiet woman whose indignations, however sharp, were still understanding.

So far as conduct went, the Roosevelts did not conform even in small things if it did not suit them—they were that independent. But as to most customs, of course, they went the familiar ways of the socially assured and the wealthy, because these ways had become familiar and convenient. Eleanor was amused when it came to her ears that Alice disapproved of her behavior, doubted her sense of humor, questioned her intelligence; she was probably hurt when the father[7] whose alcoholism had so saddened Eleanor's girlhood was mentioned. But she understood how hard it was for the other Roosevelts (to whom she belonged by birth) to accept Franklin's rise as a Democrat. She never responded in kind. Her bland refusal to listen to gossip or to show hurt probably infuriated Alice more than any other conduct could have done. What was hard for many people to learn was that Eleanor was pure and good and kind to a degree that few human beings ever are, and that forgiveness and understanding did not necessarily imply lack of intelligence or a deficiency of courage.

Eleanor was intelligent enough, and she probably knew her own capabilities and limitations better than anyone else. She knew that the years had not made her more beautiful in the physical sense. She was, indeed, an almost ugly woman, big, still ungainly, her face falling into

---

[7] Elliott, Theodore's brother. Someone should have reminded Alice that her father's *Hunting Trips of a Ranchman*, 1885, had been dedicated to "that keenest of sportsmen and truest of friends, my brother Elliott Roosevelt." Also that Elliott had written competently himself of his African adventures.

ruin, her prominent teeth more than ever prominent. But she had poise and dignity and a grace of manner that went far to overcome the lack of beauty. Those who sat with her and talked, or rode with her as she drove her own car, or listened to her as she spoke from a platform, tended very quickly to surrender to her sincerity and her sympathy. For Franklin she was a definite asset. She had a shrewdness, not apparent on the surface, which was the product of an active and wide-ranging interest.

Moreover, lacking other activities so necessary to her existence, Eleanor at once began that reporting service which as time went on became almost a career in itself. Of such sources, she was only one, even if perhaps the most important. Franklin had many legs to substitute for his own withered ones. A good part of his every day was spent in collecting miscellaneous information that sorted itself out in his mind as the need for it arose. The people who came to him were mostly unaware that they were furnishing the materials for decision-making; usually they had the impression that Franklin himself did most of the talking; yet every one of them left something his capacious memory stored away.

A good part of a President's usefulness depends on his ability to gather from entirely unorganized sources, however many other formal ones he may have, the materials of this sort he needs. He has not only to have a kind of impulse receiver that gathers out of the air true impressions of public opinion, but he has to have the kind of mind that classifies it effortlessly, puts it together with other impressions, attaches weights and significances, and lays it away ready for application to relevant judgments. Presidents who do not have these sixth and seventh senses may be principal characters of an age just because of their position, but they never become the kind of first-rate politician-statesman who understands and leads a people into and through the crises of national life.

It was being recognized by now that Franklin possessed political finesse to an extraordinary degree. Those sentimental but rather skeptical persons who made up the White House press corps were the first to become aware that they were dealing with a master of the arts they knew so well from long observation. Because they appreciated political potency they gave Franklin a respect no President had had in the lifetime of any member. Mark Sullivan, David Lawrence, and Frank Kent could have remembered Uncle Ted and made comparisons, but they were hardened old-timers now, turned fearful and reactionary; the comparisons they made were shaped by prejudice. They wrote voluminously, Sullivan for the New York *Herald Tribune*, Kent for the *Sun* papers of Baltimore, and Lawrence for his own syndicated column. They expressed alarm; they probed their vocabularies for expressive

Imp.

invective; their voices seemed to break with more and more labored satire directed at the New Deal and the New Dealers. Their worst words were withheld as yet from Franklin, as is customary in the case of a popular public figure, but they were tuning up for attacks to come as they practiced on lesser figures around him.

But the younger men, not having become pundits as yet, whose stories were often the anonymous ones of mere reporters and even when written under a by-line had not the dignity of syndication, were free to admire the technique now in operation at the White House and even to enjoy the pleasantness of the association with its occupants. They were not compelled to deplore, as their publishers were, who carried the weight of an institution dedicated to the support of policy. They had a policy—the protection of business—because the production of newspapers was a business and because they shared, even to a heightened degree, the prejudices of businessmen. The reporters were their employees and so were far from free to express their opinions. But no one knew better than Franklin how much difference it made, even so, to have the respect and admiration of those who were in immediate contact with him. It soon became well known how the reporters felt; and if their stories were rewritten to another slant in their home offices, still something of their own feelings came through. Nor did the substitution of one reporter for another accomplish much for the publishers; in a short while the new man was as partial as the old had been.

On infrequent occasions—usually when they were having meetings—Franklin met the publishers en masse. On such occasions they had an opportunity to see for themselves the influence that subverted their minions. Whatever pull they may have felt in the same direction, the institutional influence was too strong; never during his long incumbency would Franklin have a friendly press. Usually three quarters of the newspapers and practically all of the slick-paper periodicals would be hostile to the degree—and even past it—judged to be tolerable by readers.

Whether or not he became reconciled to living in this atmosphere of active hostility, evident in every edition of almost every paper, Franklin never gave up trying. It was characteristic that he did not conclude from this—as he might have done, since a good press would have smoothed his way immeasurably—that the press ought to be gagged or in some way controlled. Even when later he would feel and say that the courts must be disciplined to the acceptance of the public will for change, he would not question the right of the publishers to oppose the same measures the courts were objecting to. He might not like it. It might irritate him mightily, even sometimes to the point of protesting, but he would never consider the sterner measures that had

...en almost the first recourse of his contemporaries, Mussolini and
...itler.

There was this one thing that the newspapermen had in common
with the American people generally as regarded Franklin: they knew
that he was entirely and instinctively a democrat. No totalitarian
measure entered his mind even when it would have seemed most relevant. Many enemies found it convenient to shout about dictatorship
when their privileges were in question, but the allegation fell flat. The
evidence was too strong. There would be times—had already been
times—when dictatorial powers would seem appropriate to the tasks
to be done. To some the delegations made in the NRA and AAA acts
and the currency measures during this year seemed dictatorial; they
were not, and were never so used. Looking back, even those closest to
the events of those years would have some wonder about Franklin.
They need not. He knew how to manage in the democratic way. He was
a leader, a persuader, a people's man. He had no need, really, for the
violent resorts of the current demagogues. And even when he seemed
to need them, he always found an alternative that was in the democratic tradition. One of the items he was proudest of in his governorship
of New York was that he had never called out the state militia. He
expected never to resort to force now that he was President. Historians
would sometimes be faintly surprised when he was gone from that
office to realize that he never had. Domestic tranquillity was more real
than the wordy uproar in the newspapers would indicate.[8]

What are usually spoken of as "the masses"—meaning large numbers
of ordinary uninstructed folk not interested professionally in public affairs and having opinions deriving more largely from impression than
from consideration—had, by the end of the Hundred Days, accepted
Franklin. It would be an exaggeration to say that they understood him.
Theirs was not that kind of loyalty. They rather simply had concluded
that by and large they had a man in the White House who was for
them and against their enemies. Americans seldom use the words of
class conflict. Franklin's masses did not think themselves oppressed, exploited, or enslaved. But they did think that a good many businessmen
had gathered more power than they ought to have and had used it in

[8] But there was much industrial unrest, especially in 1934 and 1935, when
unions were establishing their right to bargain collectively. Union recognition was
at issue in fully half the strikes of this period. It has to be noted that military
forces were called out in nineteen states in 1934. The most publicized strike was
the so-called general strike in the San Francisco Bay area in summer while
Franklin was at sea in the Pacific. In his absence there was some talk of federal
intervention. General Johnson denounced the strikers in a Berkeley speech. But
Franklin, at long range, pacified the more violent of those who felt that American
institutions were in danger, and the incident passed without unusual difficulty.
Even if the state officials resorted to force, and perhaps because of his policy,
his own record was clear.

Very good point

ways that ought not to be allowed. Some of this, they felt—and Franklin reflected precisely their feeling—had been wicked in the sense that rules, customs, commandments, understandings had been violated. Such people ought to be punished and ought to understand that they would be punished in future. But there was some comprehension—which Franklin was trying to enlarge—that the old rules were not adequate to the new system, that modernization was in order. Involved in this was the resistance to change which always has to be reckoned with. People did want to avoid future depressions, they did want abuses stopped, they did want higher living standards; but they would hardly have been human if they had not wanted all these without any really disturbing new ideas or arrangements, or even without changing their obsolete conceptions of the industrial system as having the simple face-to-face structure it formerly had had.

NRA was an expression of Franklin's belief that he could create an acceptance of change in conceptions and causes as well as effects. It would turn out that even he, shrewd politician that he was, had either overestimated his ability or underestimated the resistance. As prosperity returned, people tended to forget; their willingness to accept reforms quickly diminished.

This willingness has to be understood as a matter of a little more or a little less; also it is complicated by the means democracy possesses for expressing consent. It is a fact that the Congress usually represents minority feelings in the country. Representatives, especially, under the continual pressure of biennial election, with its necessity for maintaining support at home while serving in Washington, are responsive more to the wishes of the activists who will support them than to those of inarticulate people at large. The secretary of the chamber of commerce, judges who are also politicians, businessmen who contribute funds, trade-union representatives—the demands and attitudes of such interested individuals and groups count most. The inchoate popular feeling for Franklin expressed itself through congressmen only with difficulty. The fright of the past months had stifled many voices which in most circumstances would have been strident in opposition. The Congress, with such pressures released and, moreover, wanting patronage, had been relatively complaisant. But that would quickly change. From now on Franklin's problem would be that of most Presidents for most of their time—to respond to, and shape into useful measures, the popular demand for governmental action, and to do it largely in spite of local and special interests violently opposed and strongly influential in the Congress.

At the moment he had reason to be optimistic. He had prevailed to an extraordinary degree in the special session. And, as has been said before, he was inclined to optimism anyway in those matters that fell within the category of things for him to do. He had reason for confidence in his powers to persuade, in his inventiveness, in his assessment of situations to be remedied, and in his powers of analysis. Was he overconfident in these respects? Certainly there were those who said so, and there are historians who still say so even more emphatically.

I myself feel that the more critical appraisers rely overmuch on a hindsight to which appeal is hardly fair. Also, they are apt not to sense the transient elements in the political world. In rising from its nadir the American economy went through some astonishing variations within short periods of time. For instance, there was the false period of speculative prosperity in the spring as manufacturers produced for inventory, anticipating higher costs and price increases as the codes became effective; then the minor panic in July. As months passed and the first excitements of the re-employment agreement and the making of the longer codes were superseded by disappointment as the indexes of genuine recovery failed to support earlier hopes, it became clear that neither NRA nor AAA was enough. AAA was thwarted by so favorable a crop season that the reductions from the plowing-up campaigns were offset, and the bigger businesses were cynically exploiting the code-making process. Small businesses were finding the rules made by their larger competitors hard to comply with; labor found that NRA was being used to prevent strikes but not to raise wages. Worst of all, prices were rising at the same time that consumers' incomes were falling. This result was due partly to AAA's processing taxes, partly to manufacturers' fixing of prices, and partly to lowered total wages. From week to week many varying factors assumed different relations with each other. Franklin had to deal *de novo* with more and more complicated situations. Some of his decisions seemed unwise to some people at the time —in other words, there was disagreement. But for none of them is it true that there was no reason or that there was no authority to lean on.

There are two particularly relevant matters that illustrate the nature of his then problems and his method of meeting them. Let us look briefly at the NRA complex and at the series of developments that culminated in the "bombshell" message to the London conference.

We know that from his years in Wall Street, and particularly from his work with the Construction Council, Franklin was familiar with the conjunctural difficulties of industry. There were matters that most industrialists would have preferred to withdraw altogether from competitive influence. This was not only because the competition was unprofitable but because it gave an advantage to the least scrupulous. There were always those who would exploit labor and consumers; and as long as they were unchecked, others were under compulsion to use the same methods. But it was not only to eliminate this kind of "unfair practice" that trade associations (like the Construction Council) had grown up; there were positive advantages in exchanging information concerning standards, methods for attaining efficiency, the general conditions governing manufacture and sale, statistics covering the industry, and so on. None of these came under the prohibitions of the anti-trust acts. But they did easily merge into prohibited practices, such as division of markets and agreements about prices. These were conspiratorial and in restraint of trade. In the half century during which this kind of control had been exercised in various ways, elaborate investigations and many court cases had defined the permitted and prohibited practices. But there was always an uncertain area into which escape was continually being made. And even prohibited practices would be resorted to if there was little or no enforcement—as tended to be the case in Republican regimes.

Franklin, in common with a good many others, felt that the negative regulatory philosophy was obsolete, and that a more positive approach ought to be substituted for it. Industry ought to accept the responsibility for decent social behavior, and it ought to be allowed to develop those common standards of practice which, if enforced, would eliminate the nonconforming few who persisted in "unfairness." NRA, understood in this way, was a logical further extension of the trade-association development sponsored by Hoover in his Department of Commerce days and has since become a pervasive and recognized institution, usually with headquarters in Washington and often with a numerous staff, including "legislative representatives" and publicity men.

Applied to the recovery problem, a system of codes embodying practices agreed on by those associations would, it was conceived, tend to raise wages, increase efficiency, reduce costs of production, make marketing more orderly, and, by granting businessmen privileges they had long sought, encourage expansion. At best the departure might lead to industry planning—that is, the estimation of needs and the adjustment to them of investment; this in turn would provide a basis for national planning, thus reducing waste, raising standards, and increasing real incomes. So the argument ran. But there were two impinging influences which took no account of the national interest in rationalization. These were the businessmen and organized labor. Each saw in NRA an opportunity for aggrandizement. And each proceeded to exploit the code-making process in so wholly unrestrained a way that reaction was made inevitable.

Franklin presided over these activities in a characteristic way, and it proved to be not a good way. General Johnson, his administrator, had less capacity for administration than for demagoguery. He was very soon lost in exhortations and florid posing as the flood of businessmen and labor leaders rushed in on the organization. The codes were presented and processed in such great numbers and with such detail that

NRA exploited by Labor & bus.

no general rules could be formulated and applied. And many of them contained, as Franklin was repeatedly warned by his more cautious associates, those very provisions that had always been the center of the progressive contention. There could be no doubt, as the rush slowed up, that many industries had been given permission to raise and control prices, arrange and divide markets, and make it impossible for small competitors to continue. That this was fatal, Franklin ought to have known out of his own experience; and if he did not, he was amply warned.

Partly because much of the impetus for NRA had come from the same pressures that had almost forced through the Black-Connery thirty-hour bill, labor had insisted on the insertion of the so-called 7A provisions. These had all sorts of possibilities; at the least, labor intended to get into the codes as "fair practices," collective bargaining, limitation of hours, and improved conditions of work, as well as higher wages. Added to this was an ambition on Franklin's part to put an end to child labor, especially in the South. Management and labor, in effect, adjourned at least some old quarrels and shifted the costs to the consumers of their products. And Franklin, again exercising judgment, felt that these gains, too, were an important offset to any concessions there might be in the way of freedom from anti-trust prosecutions. A businessman who agreed to enlarge his labor force at once, recognize the union in his plants, raise wages, and renounce child labor could, for the moment at least, be allowed the privilege of restraining trade and increasing prices. It was a good bargain for the public.

It is an interesting inquiry to ask why Franklin got himself into what can only be described as an impossible dilemma when he must have known better. Whether or not any answers can be substantiated, the inquiry itself reveals significant characteristics of his mind.

What suggests itself to me as having happened is that Franklin totted up, in the subjective way he had, the utility of giving something to get something else—the alternative being something, naturally, that he felt to be worth more—and that his calculation turned out to be mistaken. In this case it was badly out, and the consequences would be damaging. To appreciate what he went through, rather more description has to be resorted to.

When the codes were at flood—that is, during the summer and fall of 1933—the demanding problem that conditioned everything else was recovery. Recovery, Franklin conceived, could be had by the combination of "reflation" (the restoration of the price level to that, say, of 1928, so that debt adjustment could take place and the issuance of credit be resumed) and the direct inducement of industrial activity. This last could be approached through relief and public works, which would restore purchasing power; and this method was authorized and under way.

NRA
rather naive

But both relief and public works were to an extent unsatisfactory. Relief was bad for people, and public works were, as Franklin quickly saw, so slow as to be ineffective as an immediate stimulant. Something else was needed.

One suggestion made to him was that public works could be vastly expanded and expedited by a general loaning of funds to local governments at no interest. And there were the beginnings of the discussions which led, after a while, to the kinds of projects the Civil Works Administration used when it succeeded the Federal Emergency Relief Administration and which went farther in the Works Progress Administration. But at this juncture Franklin found neither of these resorts sufficiently dramatic. Neither seemed to him adequate to the need. He found what he wanted—in a way, the intellectual counterpart of inflation—in the re-employment agreement suggested by the imagination of General Johnson.

It was unfortunate that this necessarily got itself inextricably mixed up with code-making and that it interfered with the elaboration of uniformities and working rules to govern the various industries now hurrying to put through their agreements with each other. What was most fatal of all, it led also to neglecting the setting up of an enforcement organization. It even omitted the irreducibly necessary governmental representation on the code authorities to see to it that industry behaved in the civilized manner envisioned in the self-government theory. The public must necessarily be and remain the senior in any partnership-with-industry arrangement. But nothing was done to establish this principle. And presently even to suggest it was to raise a storm of protest from those who had taken leave to use the new institution in their own interest.

All these neglects were the result of a kind of bargain. This bargain on Franklin's side was that the re-employment agreement would be carried out. If business would do that, the aggressions of other sorts known to be going on would simply be overlooked. I have no doubt that Franklin intended to come back to all these violators of the spirit in which NRA had been undertaken and coerce them into decent behavior. But at the moment he felt it expedient not to insist on restrictions or compulsions to which there would be any such stiff opposition as would cause resistance to the re-employment idea. He was certainly enamored of this scheme. He was willing to sacrifice much to see it through.

The attitude toward the re-employment campaign of various local officials and of the press can only be described as enthusiastic. The hint of magical transformation that attended the launching of the drive was most agreeable to all those who still hoped to escape from depression without changing the institutions to which they were accustomed. If all that was needed was to get together in a kind of Rotarian hoopla, that was an enormous relief. Parades and meetings were reassuring; so much action must have some result. The idea had been spreading insidiously that something vital had failed in the capitalistic system and that a serious overhauling would have to be undergone. To be assured that what had been to blame was, in the first place, the misbehavior of a few financiers who would be punished and, in the second place, a fortuitous paralysis that could be remedied simply by everyone starting activity again simultaneously, appealed to naïve hopes for painless restoration of accustomed conditions.

Following a familiar formula, General Johnson, with public clamor of unprecedented intensity, sought and found a symbol. The Blue Eagle, he called it; actually it was the Navajo thunderbird, conventionalized symbol of a culture as far from industrialism as the imagination could conceive. But oceans of ink and forests of wood pulp carried it into the whole nation's consciousness. It was supposed to be displayed only by those who had joined the crusade for recovery. They were to expand their labor force while maintaining wages and keeping prices stable. The theory was that if all employers did this at once, the resultant wages would buy the enlarged total product. A recovery "spiral" would be started which, once under way, would support itself.

It failed miserably. Later analysis seemed to show that from the first it had been sabotaged by those who were its most enthusiastic supporters. What businessmen in large numbers had calculated was that each could take advantage of the compliance of all the rest. He would restrict, raise prices, bear down on wages; and because others were doing the reverse, he would make a nice profit. General Johnson began almost at once to denounce these "chiselers." But the size of the undertaking made any real enforcement impossible, and the campaign gradually fizzled out. It was a deep disappointment to Franklin, and although the pyrotechnics and exhortations of the general had had his approval —he had even reinforced them with appeals of his own—it was soon apparent that he would have to resort to other measures. These must be of a sort that would create a diversion. The much-publicized Blue Eagle must be forgotten.

The resort was found in new measures for inflation. Late in autumn of 1933 he adopted the Warren plan for raising the price level by increasing the market price of gold. This made each dollar less valuable but also much more serviceable in discharging debt. Also, it put the United States in a more favorable position for expanding foreign markets. Altogether Franklin hoped it would give that fillip to recovery which still eluded him.

The truth was that although there had been some reduction in unemployment it had not been nearly as considerable as had been hoped.

312

The index of production had risen, then had dropped. Retail prices had recovered more than had wholesale prices—which meant that the standard of living was lower rather than higher. Farmers, especially, were complaining bitterly that the prices of products they must buy were going up much faster than those of the products they had to sell.

The optimism of last spring had vanished by autumn. The situation in the Agricultural Adjustment Administration grew very tense. George Peek was refusing to agree with Secretary Wallace that anything more was necessary than marketing agreements with processors. The processors would promise to raise farmers' prices, he said. Yes, said the economists, but at the expense of consumers. And that would be no contribution to recovery. The split on policy became so serious, finally, that Peek forced the issue and had to resign. This incident, as would be expected, caused much discussion, a good deal of it caustic. Franklin ought not to have postponed deciding on a policy to the point of allowing the quarrel a public airing. A choice had to be made finally, anyway, and it might better have been made much earlier. But Franklin, still exhibiting political caution and with a wary eye on Baruch, sought to ease Peek's departure by giving him a post in the Department of State. He was to be a consultant on foreign trade. But since his scheme for selling more products abroad was totally antithetical to Hull's determined sponsorship of most-favored-nation treaties, it could be seen that presently more trouble would erupt.

By late autumn Franklin badly needed a diversion. And the Warren scheme was such another magical formula as would at least monopolize attention for some time. It would infuriate the financial community and start a heated controversy in which the agricultural West would feel its old anti-Wall Street sentiments rising again. The Blue Eagle could be abandoned, the more careful processing of individual industrial codes could replace the "shotgun" agreements, and NRA could retreat from its splurge of publicity into more practical organization.

Such a respite was badly needed. The travels and exhortations of Johnson, together with his faults as an administrator, had created a chaotic situation in the organization. In spite of this, many codes were being shaped and approved. The difficulty was that no general principles infused the process. Johnson's predilection for allowing businessmen to have their way when they seemed determined led to many freedoms they could not safely be allowed. Close reading of the first extensive codes scandalized those who from the first had been skeptical of the partnership theory. There arose a difference between Johnson and the Recovery Board—presumably his superior authority—which was liquidated by dissolution of the Board. This action of Franklin's left him completely responsible for Johnson's administration. It was done for a political reason. Franklin was intent on getting from businessmen compliance with the re-employment arrangements as well as the agreements wanted so much by labor. The unwise codes were bribes.

The search for easy, politically desirable, hopefully inoffensive means for recovery must have been regarded by Franklin as a political imperative. He had a formerly demoralized nation now transformed into a hopeful and willing one. What he had to capitalize on was a temporary good will which, as he knew very well, stopped short of willingness on anyone's part to make any real sacrifices. We can imagine him judging that he must find expedients that would not require any severe disciplines but that would nevertheless keep hope alive and ensure at least a minimum of co-operation. If they also contributed to recovery, that was an added gain. He undoubtedly hoped they would, but his real reliance for recovery was on inflation and the expansion of purchasing power. Time was required, however, for these to become effective. He must play his cards, meanwhile, so that confidence did not evaporate.

One of the incidents most criticized by contemporary economists was his handling of the World Monetary and Economic Conference to which the "bombshell" message came out of an apparently clearing sky. But most of his critics seem not to have understood either the policy to which he was really committed—without saying so too emphatically—or the majority attitude in the country toward foreign financiers. Nevertheless, it can hardly be argued that he appeared to advantage in his conduct of the proceedings.

His policy was nationalistic, necessarily so, as it came belatedly to be defined. He could not raise prices for all the world; he could do it only for a United States isolated from a world which would oppose such an effort with every means that could be devised. He could not initiate a public works program or an NRA for all the world—though he had tried to interest visiting European statesmen in a program to run concurrently with that of the United States. Neither monetary measures nor others necessary to recovery could be taken successfully unless a fairly impermeable wall could be built around the economy. That such a separation should be suggested infuriated the Europeans, particularly the French. Their intransigence ran to an indignation that sounded almost moral, a position it would have been easier to sustain if Franklin's monetary measures had not been used against the United States repeatedly in the past, and especially by the French. He was not impressed. He was, in fact, annoyed. We were through with standing stupidly still to be exploited.

There was some ineptness in the conduct of the affair. That has to be admitted. It will be recalled that Franklin had required Day and Williams, Hoover's delegates to the agenda meetings in Geneva, to reverse some of the Hoover commitments, particularly that which would have allowed the intergovernmental war debts to be discussed in the same context as currency stabilization, exchange restrictions, and tariffs. Franklin was forced to be very cautious about the debts; they were a highly sensitized subject. The exigencies of politics would not permit their forgiveness, but it could be foreseen that if they were discussed at London nothing else would get done until the debtors were satisfied; it was a sensitive subject with them too. So debts, at his insistence, had been omitted from the agenda.

This omission angered the debtors; but what angered them even more, if possible, was Franklin's leaving the gold standard and entering on devaluation even before the visits of the statesmen who came to Washington in the spring. That, in fact, was what they had started for Washington to prevent. The Frenchman Charles Rist was actually at sea when devaluation was announced, and he nearly turned around and went home without seeing Franklin. And on neither of these matters—the debts or currency stabilization—had the Europeans really given up; politically, perhaps, they could not. What they failed to grasp was that if they could not Franklin would not. There was, as the conference began, an unrecognized impasse. Neither side had the requisite leeway for bargaining.

Most of the misunderstanding arose, probably, because of the disagreement and confusion in the American delegation, and this went back to the conversations with the visiting statesmen in Washington during the preceding months. Those talks were conducted by people who disagreed. Messrs. Feis and Lindsay, economic advisers to the Department of State, shared Hull's laissez-faire bias; and James P. Warburg thought he understood the President's mind when he gave the foreign experts reason to hope that some stabilization arrangement could be arrived at. Others, disagreeing, and believing that the recovery program required temporary isolation, counseled caution in these matters; but because of wishful thinking these last were not taken too seriously.[9]

The delegation was neither carefully chosen nor well briefed. At the last moment Franklin was constrained to appoint Hull head of it, even though the Secretary had had almost no part in the preliminaries. He had intended to appease Baruch with the chairmanship. Senator Pittman, another delegate, could be expected to interest himself in nothing

---

[9] Perhaps I should say that this was my own role in the talks. Although I was disturbed at the manner of its doing, I agreed with Franklin's final position. It had, in fact, been the one I had taken all along.

The account here of the London affair is not intended as a serious analysis. There have been discussions of it in Moley's *After Seven Years*, in Hull's *Memoirs* (New York: Macmillan, 1948), Lindley's *Half Way with Roosevelt* (New York: Viking, 1937), and in numerous other places. My purpose is only to comment on Franklin's relation to it as exhibiting his presidential method.

but silver and to confuse everything with his insistence. Senator Couzens obviously had little knowledge of the issues or understanding of Franklin's intention. The Texas financier, Morrison, had only the credentials of a campaign contributor. On the whole they were neither united on a policy nor in a position to shape one. In fact Hull opened the proceedings with a long speech advocating free trade, or something vaguely like it, in direct contravention of such instructions as there were. And when the Europeans determinedly opened the subject of stabilization, the confused Americans were inclined to give way.

Franklin, on vacation in New England waters, watched from a distance and realized his mistake. After the conference had got started, with Hull bumbling about free trade, and the whole delegation had allowed itself to get out of its depth in bargaining about stabilization rates, Franklin dispatched Moley to London with a message of caution.

Moley's journey turned into one of those inflated affairs the world press builds up when all its resources are marshaled. He made a spectacular airplane trip to meet Franklin, who was cruising off the coast; then he caught a liner for Southampton, accompanied by Herbert Bayard Swope. During the week of his trip the tension mounted. He was carrying presidential instructions. The conference waited. The whole world waited. Obviously another miracle was expected. Meanwhile Hull, realizing belatedly that he had blundered, and with his Tennessee choler rising higher and higher as the press hinted that Moley was to supersede him, waited to receive his Assistant Secretary with a fury he hardly bothered to conceal.

Moley could not have carried any instructions except those of caution. Franklin could hardly rebuke his Secretary of State through the Assistant Secretary. Nor could he stop the talk about stabilization without knowing more than he could know at a distance about how far it had gone. Moley had talked with him about this and he understood, as he says, that a cautious and flexible arrangement would be agreeable to Franklin. It must not tie the currency of the United States to gold again, as the French wanted, but it might form a framework within which a gradual approach to stable and agreed relationships could be arrived at. It would be desirable, Moley understood, to move toward stopping the international competition in devaluations for advantage. When he got to London he succeeded in turning the negotiations toward this, and presently he had what he believed to be a workable formula. It was not what the Europeans wanted, but they understood that Moley spoke for authority and that what he offered was all they were going to get.

As it turned out, it was more than they were going to get. When Franklin got Moley's proposal he was on a battleship at sea; with him were Morgenthau and Warren; among them they finally came to the policy determination which should have been made before the conference met and should have been embodied clearly in the instructions of the delegates. What Franklin said was:

I would regard it as a catastrophe amounting to a world tragedy if the great Conference of Nations, called to bring about a more real and permanent financial stability and a greater prosperity to the masses of all Nations, should, in advance of any serious effort to consider these broader problems, allow itself to be diverted by the proposal of a purely artificial and temporary experiment affecting the monetary exchange of a few Nations only. . . .[10]

Hull was furious and almost resigned out of hand; Moley, too, felt, although unnecessarily and mostly because the press said so, that he had been repudiated; the rest of the delegation were merely flabbergasted. The conference limped along for some weeks longer, getting nowhere, then adjourned to a later date which never came. One result was that Moley left the Department of State at Hull's insistence and presently would be lost altogether to Franklin. Only those who felt all along that isolation for recovery purposes was necessary saw in Franklin's action a statesmanlike decision, and even they could hardly explain away the method of his arrival at it and its conveyance to his own representatives as a kind of reprimand.

The end was reached, but Franklin reached it in a most awkward and embarrassing way. His capacity for finesse was nowhere evident. Making up his mind as he went along, doing what had to be done, was the more or less public rationalization of his method. It was, he said, the way a quarterback would run a football team. But there was much to be desired in the method. It lacked firmness and consistency. He seemed not to have administrative control over the processes of his government. His enemies had been given an opening; soon they were busily at work exploiting the advantage. But little political good it did them!

The historian returning to this period and reading the newspapers and magazines is bound to note that each of these incidents I have dwelt on made spectacular news and remained for a prolonged time the center of national attention. He will recognize also that although Franklin came in for some severe haulings over the coals there was no serious undermining of his leadership position. NRA would presently be liquidated and forgotten; the London conference would be put down as a little-understood attempt of foreign governments to take advantage of

[10] *Public Papers,* Vol. II, p. 264. There is an interesting comment on this appended as a note in the *Public Papers* (p. 266):

It is true that my radio message to the London Conference fell upon it like a bombshell. This was because the message was realistic at a time when the gold-bloc Nations were seeking a purely limited objective, and were unwilling to go to the root of national and international problems. The immediate result was a somewhat petulant outcry that I had wrecked the Conference.

the new administration. Criticism from the economists, the editorial writers, the conservative columnists, and others of that sort might be embarrassing. But Franklin soon learned, if he did not already know, that it did not count against him with the public; rather the reverse. A situation was rapidly being created in which he could do no wrong, in which his ineptness would be explained away, and in which his mistakes would be forgiven.

There were a number of very good reasons for this, aside from the need people had, after their years of continual insecurity, to find a leader they could trust. Those reasons were to be found in the help that was reaching almost every family that had before been without the means of meeting its adversities. As the autumn passed and winter approached, concern might be—and was—felt in administration circles because recovery was insufficient and because new evidences of unrest could be discovered. John Simpson, Milo Reno, Father Coughlin, and the rest were at it again; and Huey Long was threatening. But people knew that even if they were not put back to work they would be taken care of. The care might be insufficient and they might prefer the job they could not find. But a father no longer had to face possible starvation or freezing for his family when cold weather came. From a quarter of a million families a son or two had gone to CCC camp. He was off the streets and was sending money home. Farmers, too, might gripe about rising prices for the goods they had to buy, but AAA checks were nevertheless tangible evidence of concern in Washington. Home owners no longer feared dispossession, and even bankrupts began to chirk up and conclude that the world had not come to an end.

The press, besides the meaner and more florid stories, had accounts to print of a White House rather gay than sad, of a President who was full of action and confident that he would find a way to make things better. He was a man who could laugh, who loved sights and sounds of the countryside as the American millions loved them, who was no great shakes at economics, maybe, who had no taste in art or music and who read detective stories rather than "literature," who had a big appetite for plain food, who exchanged repartee with reporters cheerfully and openly, who meant to do a lot of rebuilding about the country—roads, public buildings, sewers, power plants, parks—and who had a wife he called "the missus" whose distress for the unemployed and their families was open and notorious. He was a man they could feel was their own, and they loved him with a fondness nothing—then or ever—could diminish.

16

Toward the end of 1933, a lot of experience seems to have been crowded into the months since early March, some of it both embarrassing and valuable for the new administration.

The various busy departments and emergency agencies had already begun to think of a returning Congress to be dealt with. Estimates for the fiscal year to come (which, in the federal government, begins on July 1) must be ready for the Congress in January, already having been scrutinized by the Bureau of the Budget and incorporated in the President's message. There had been some hard feeling because of the economy drive. As the department heads came to understand their work they found that the cuts demanded by Douglas were unrealistic. In an emergency, when every agency was being asked to carry heavy responsibilities, a reduction of personnel seemed more and more unreasonable. Some shifts were possible, and cuts in obsolete activities could certainly be made; but expansions totaling more than the reductions were necessary for the new activities. The irritation and controversy within the official family over this issue were considerable. The new estimates would certainly not be less than Hoover's had been.

In matters of administration Franklin began to have what might be called a graduate course almost immediately after the Economy Act had been passed and Douglas had begun to apply it. It was something of a shock for him to learn, for instance, that just when he was pressing the Congress to make a large appropriation for public works, he had brought to an arbitrary stop all those works that had been going on under the old Hoover program. A stop order put before him by Douglas, and signed without realization of its effect, had paralyzed such public building as there was. This embarrassment was temporary, but it furnished a lesson. And when, under Ickes (who, in addition to being Secretary of the Interior, was made Administrator of Public Works[1]), the

---

[1] To the disgust of General Johnson, who had wanted to include not only the code-making for business within the NRA but all the "recovery" activities. His

allocation of funds for his own program began, he very soon had a further lesson concerning something he already knew in an elementary way. This was that the estimate of time in all social arrangements is an essential. To induce the government departments and then lesser public agencies—such as states, counties, cities, irrigation or power districts, and various other administrations—to submit workable projects, to scrutinize them and allocate the funds before doing the planning and before acquiring the necessary property and materials, was to enter on no short and casual enterprise. The building of a power or sewage-treatment plant for a city in Nebraska or Nevada could scarcely get well under way, with the best will in the world, for two years. There were some projects, as Ickes' engineers found, that could be undertaken more quickly because the planning and land acquisition had already been done. The building of highways by the states, supervised by the Bureau of Public Roads, was an instance. This was because it was a continuing project, planned far ahead, needing only to be expanded; but there were not many such. Most had to begin *de novo*. Very little immediate employment resulted.

Inevitable delays of this sort led to the establishment, during the fall, of the Civil Works Administration to give employment on quick and easy projects. This infuriated Ickes, who was developing that empire-building compulsion which infects so many public administrators and which can be seen so clearly in his published *Diary* to have had an extreme development in his case. Ickes had worked hard, and he had many projects under way; he objected bitterly to the setting up of what he considered a rival establishment. Nevertheless, Franklin subtracted part of his funds for the alternative administration and entrusted Harry Hopkins with its running.

The ingenuity and courage with which the task of providing employment was undertaken by Hopkins and his group startled the whole country. There had been a tendency to estimate the New Deal as failing in what it had set out to do. Ickes' performance was under criticism for being too slow—an unjust estimate because delays were inevitable when projects required planning and preparation. Hopkins' Civil Works Administration would be criticized for the reverse reason. It would fall inevitably under the scrutiny of those carping critics who wanted it not only to give work and so increase income but to produce permanent improvements as well.[2] Presently "leaf-rakers" would become a generic

---

first organization charts had a works division and a relief division as corollary agencies to that for fair trade practices. It is suggested by Frances Perkins that his pique at being confined to code-making was largely responsible for embarking on the re-employment agreement. The whole Blue Eagle campaign, she intimates, was an attempt on his part to monopolize the recovery effort.

[2] Or said they did. Actually the criticism was largely an expression of the attitude of those who were simply and emphatically against the acceptance by

Too active.   Ickes felt as Admin. of Pub. wks. the CWA was an infringement on him.

term for groups of men leaning on hand tools around sociable bon
and wasting government funds. But the criticism was irrelevant.
kins got the results Franklin wanted. Together with the gold purchase
"shot in the arm" and the benefit payments to farmers, Civil Works
made the winter of 1933–34 tolerable.

But as the budgets began to be put together for the incoming Congress it was obvious that they would not show that "economy" which
Franklin had promised and which Douglas had tried his best to enforce.
And this was soon another item in the enlarging conservative indictment of the New Deal. Even the distinction between "ordinary" and
"emergency" expenditure did not carry any considerable conviction. It
was clear that the budget was not going to be balanced; and if "confidence" depended on this test, there would not be much confidence.
On this particular issue, however, not only Franklin but the business
community was being educated. It is true that this was the seed time
of the Liberty League, that strange grouping of rabid reactionaries,
financiers, big businessmen, and corporation lawyers, which would
come into the open in August to oppose the New Deal for the next
few years. This group would naturally have more than adequate representation in the press and would be lavishly financed for propaganda
purposes. But it was an extremely small coterie and, as it soon appeared,
its policies were not those approved by all business leaders. Business
was not agreed on policy, and there were those whose objectives were
just the reverse, on many points, of the League. All agreed, of course,
on criticizing the government.

A new strain began to appear this time in the pronouncements of the
pundits of the press. Many of them began to see that it was much more
important to balance the economy than to balance the budget. Consumer income was needed, they had learned, to create a market for
goods and services. They began to understand the stimulating effect of
government spending when private spending fell off. Franklin was himself making notable progress in this kind of understanding. He seems
never to have grasped the concept fully until now.

This was something Bob La Follette and his progressive friends already knew. They had been insisting for the past two years that a spending program was needed. La Follette—nominally a Republican—had

the government of any responsibility for welfare. Civil Works was one among
many targets for this kind of sniping. The Civilian Conservation Corps quickly
became too popular for criticism; so did the Home Owners Loan Corporation.
The RFC had always been exempt: it helped business, not people. But AAA
was from the first subjected to a barrage from the urban press, which always
deplored assistance to farmers; and NRA came under fire as soon as it became
plain that its exploitation by private interests was no longer to be tolerated. But
the favorite butts of heavy-handed humor and ill-tempered carping were the
welfare agencies. The attack was never on the principle, only on the performance;
this was safer.

Liberty & the Comm
Leaguers & for the Nation.

embarrassed Hoover by his insistence. He could cite Hoover's own experts. The Mitchell conclusions about the business cycle, in *Recent Economic Trends,* had been tentative; not too much was known about the incidence of economic behavior, but some remedies seemed obvious. Hoover had been aware of Mitchell's findings, as he had been aware of most knowledge in the economic field. Franklin had only to adapt and enlarge policies already recommended.

Al Smith's defection to the Liberty League, under the influence of his friends Shouse and Raskob, and even his dangerous—because characteristically apt—shaft in which he spoke of "the baloney dollar" were offset by the contrary activities of The Committee for the Nation, as amply financed and as well equipped with slogans and newspaper sympathy.

It was the idea of The Committee for the Nation that most of the New Deal was unnecessary for recovery. Its businessman members regarded most of the new measures as "radical," and, for publicity purposes, tagged them as "socialistic" if not something worse. The Committee recommended giving up AAA, NRA, and all the other "adjustment" measures requiring any social discipline and would have relied altogether on currency manipulation.

The Liberty Leaguers made their way into public consciousness by using Al Smith as a stalking horse—effective, as they felt, because of his old reputation as a Democratic liberal—and by circulating a solemn round-robin, signed by many famous lawyers, assuring the country that most of the New Deal measures were unconstitutional.[3] The Committee for the Nation got itself most prominently noticed as a result of what came to be called "The Great Wirt Incident," thus getting the jump on the Liberty League by some months.

Wirt, like Warren, was a hired propagandist for the Committee, who wrote pamphlets and made lectures. During the spring several Committeemen came to Washington for the purpose of testifying against the New Deal measures, among them Wirt, who, in his home capacity, was superintendent of schools in Gary, Indiana. He had an acquaintance with one of the obscure but enthusiastic New Dealers and was, in this way, introduced to a circle in which, as was the fashion then, much talking was done about national affairs. It was a time when received ideas were being questioned; when, along with the decline in businessmen's prestige, there went a decline of conservative prestige in general. And the widest-ranging discussions broke out whenever young intel-

---

[3] They would doubtless think themselves fully justified by later Supreme Court decisions. I should note that the Liberty League did not achieve nationwide notice until a few weeks before election in November. The most prominent members were John W. Davis, Frank Polk, Jouett Shouse, the du Ponts, and Al Smith.

322

lectuals got together. Not all of it was gloomy; much of it was fanciful. A new crowd had got a chance to work and express itself after years of smothered fulmination, and some irresponsibly high spirits were shown whenever there were gatherings.

Such a group in an Alexandria home one evening saw in Wirt a foil almost too good to be credible, and those present seem to have had a lot of fun with the scary old gentleman. He came away with the impression that they were probably revolutionists and in any case were a threat to the country's institutions. He was especially struck with an analogy, developed lightheartedly in the course of the conversation, picturing Roosevelt as the Kerensky of the New Deal revolution, with its Stalin yet to come. This development was a managed one, they told Wirt, and Roosevelt was behaving according to plan.

Wirt made all this public in a solemn warning to the American people. The Democrats, who had had enough of this kind of thing, summoned Wirt to a congressional hearing. He was made to look a fool. Several of the young people denied any other purpose than the exercise of high spirits on a credulous conservative. They said, moreover, that the Kerensky theme may have been developed but that actually it would have been a kind of defense against boredom. Wirt had monopolized all the early discussions with Committee for the Nation propaganda, and they had got tired of it.

The publicity this trivial farce commanded can hardly be imagined at a distance in time. What is hard to credit is the prevalence of fear in the minds of most of the nation's pundits and former decision-makers. It was upon this near hysteria that such silly allegations as Wirt's fed. This kind of susceptibility tended to disappear as the Democratic administration steadied down and a certain recovery became established. But oppositionist propaganda was put out in great quantities throughout Franklin's first two terms, and every once in a while some one of the inventions would take hold and become, for the time being, a *cause célèbre*.

The passing from the scene of Ray Moley was everywhere pictured as a defection from the New Deal. Actually Franklin's "bombshell" message to the World Conference in London had been a rebuke to Hull rather than Moley, but circumstances made it appear otherwise. Moley, attempting conciliation, had negotiated what he believed a harmless compromise, and it was this that Franklin rejected so abruptly. So the press, glad to bear down on a Roosevelt intimate, exacerbated Moley's feelings until the smart became unbearable. It was illogical for Franklin to keep Hull as Secretary of State.[4] Moley reflected Franklin's point

---

[4] From the ideological point of view. Actually it illustrates the predominance in presidential strategy of political support. Hull, as a conservative Southerner, was indispensable; Moley was an expendable.

Reversal

of view, and Hull ignored and blandly opposed it. Nevertheless, Moley was eased out and Hull was kept.[5] Moreover, within a year Franklin would have consented to the submission of legislation on foreign trade, got up by Hull, which completely reversed the stand taken in July of 1933.

This reversal was complete. Franklin not only sponsored the Trade Agreements Act which looked to free trade—the same one he had refused to submit to the Congress in 1933—but after months of the dollar manipulation so annoying to the European politicians, he came round to fixing the value of the dollar and thus prepared the way for the stabilization he had so emphatically rejected just a year before.

There is something in this to be accounted for. But the historian who deals with it is also confronted with similar reversals of several other policies at the same time. One of these had to do with NRA. That organization during 1934 evaded by a narrow margin a congressional investigation threatened by disaffected progressives. It would have disclosed that in the organization there was favoritism to big business, tolerance of restrictive practices, including price controls, and a favoring of employers as against employees in spite of the writing into codes of rights to collective bargaining. There was a turn to company unions, dominated, as labor leaders alleged, largely by employers, which nullified the collective bargaining provisions. This had been condoned not only by General Johnson but by Franklin himself. All this seemed not only inconsistent with New Deal professions but intolerable to the progressives. Added to these criticisms was that coming from farmers. High prices for industrial products were, they said, more than offsetting their own gains from AAA. And, at least temporarily, what they said was true. It was an unhappy moment.

The congressional forum was an excellent one for the country's assorted demagogues, more rampant now than ever. But there were others on the outside, dominated on a rising note by Father Coughlin, who had a strange fix on inflation, which, it was maliciously suggested, was not unrelated to silver investments. Inflation was indeed a favorite theme with many others. Senator Wheeler was fulminating, which was understandable in the representative of a silver state. But he was only somewhat more insistent than other Westerners. And it was obvious that a silver-buying program, similar to that for gold, would have to be undertaken.

Finally the silver people prevailed. But by this time Woodin was gone from the Treasury and Morgenthau had succeeded him, first as

---

[5] Moley became immediately an adviser to the Department of Justice; within a few months, however, he departed to become editor of *Today*, a magazine founded by Vincent Astor and Averell Harriman. It was the forerunner of *Newsweek*. Its initial New Deal orientation was soon lost.

Acting Secretary and then as Secretary. He was glad to carry out gold and silver purchase programs under the direction of Warren.

But the monetary experiment ended as abruptly as it had begun. In January, Franklin, with fine disregard for consistency, asked the new Congress to set limits within which he might determine the dollar's value in gold from time to time. The Congress passed the legislation he asked for, and on January 31 he fixed the dollar at 59.06 per cent of its former gold value. It was a disappointment to the Warren theorists—including Franklin—that commodity prices had not risen in proportion to the devaluation established by manipulating the price of gold. The chief result of the policy actually was to import quantities of gold at a high price in dollars.

But the Gold Reserve Act had still another provision that indicated a change of policy from one of devaluation to one of stability. It allowed the Treasury to use two billions of the profit from the new dollar value of its gold, and of the gold turned in by its owners at the old price, as a stabilization fund. It would be used, it was explained, to deal in government securities. They would thus be held in steady relationship to the new value of the dollar. The fall in the dollar had raised the pound to about five dollars and the franc to a corresponding high level. This was just what the Europeans had wanted to avoid. It put them at a disadvantage in world markets. So now it was they who rejected suggestions for formal stabilization. They would come around to it in a few years, but at the moment they were still not reconciled to the American advantage.

If stabilization was a reversal of policy, the Reciprocal Trade Agreements Act, signed by Franklin in June, represented another and even more startling about-face. This was the fulfillment of a long-held dream of Hull's: he had preached free-trade doctrine month in and month out for most of his political life. It was taken also as a sign of his ability to prevail in this administration even over the President. This was the often-repeated interpretation. But something more general than any one or two incidents was obviously developing. If Franklin appeared to have given in to Hull, the giving-in appearance was for political effect—to appease the Southerners so powerful on the Hill—and was not fatal to his general purpose.[6]

[6] The policy of the Reciprocal Trade Agreements Act was far from being the free trade of the theorists. It represented Franklin's modification in the direction of favoring those nations that would grant favors in return. It was thus not so considerable a departure from the nationalism of the early New Deal as was sometimes represented. The ensuing negotiations with various nations in subsequent years were very realistic exchanges and were based on careful study of American interests to be aggrandized or injured by the specific proposals. There was, however, a struggle over the adoption of the most-favored-nation principle, and on this Hull and his group prevailed. This went a long way toward negating the realism of bilateral negotiations.

Reciprocal Trade agreement
Another inconsistency.

The developments of 1934 led to the position Franklin had begun to assume during the campaign under the pressures of politics. It may be best to put it another way: he was returning to an accepted version of the progressive position in all these matters. This was the result, I think, of a number of combined estimates on his part. One of these was that the weight of the movement still lay with the older orthodox progressives. They believed in bearing down on big business and encouraging little business; in the development of foreign trade outlets by reducing barriers and even by subsidizing exports; in the favoring of farmers in their perennial contest with processors; and in the development of extensive welfare measures. Going along with this was probably a judgment that, if these policies were developed in all their ramifications, the likely defection of reactionaries in the South and their linking up with the Republicans in the Congress would be offset by strength among urban workers and the city machines, which he had not hitherto been able to rely on.

The progressive orthodoxy was simple. It was regarded as having been reinforced by the occurrence of the depression. Big business and big finance had been responsible. The admission of these very persons and interests to governmental partnership in the NRA had set up a kind of unnatural union. General Johnson became with the progressives a kind of *bête noire*, and their disapproval was made known in emphatic terms. Then, too, the many representatives around him of the Brandeis philosophy were annoyed, and in Franklin's Valhalla no figure loomed larger than the old justice. His disciples, beginning with Frankfurter, had infiltrated the administrative organization to an almost incredible extent, and this was a movement that tended to enlarge. The partnership theory was one they refused to accept.

This year is spoken of by one New Deal historian—Professor Rauch —as a year of transition, and this is a just comment. Franklin was in process of making a complete turn-around. It is no exaggeration to speak of the situation after the legislation of 1934 as a Second New Deal. It not only had new objectives, it had a new personnel. This is not evident at the higher levels. There were no cabinet changes except at the Treasury. But the first group of secondary helpers, beginning with Moley, were by year's end almost wholly replaced with Frankfurter nominees. This was achieved through two of his energetic lieutenants—Corcoran and Cohen—who personify this Second New Deal as the Brains Trust personifies the First.[7]

General Johnson departed from the scene in October and was replaced by a board whose policies were obviously going to be very different from his. This change was carried out in a storm of publicity

---

[7] Thomas Corcoran and Benjamin V. Cohen.

Gen Johnson leaves

which, in his subsequent years as a pungent newspaper columnist, turned him into a sharp critic of Franklin and all his helpers.[8] Franklin seldom succeeded in getting rid of people gracefully. But the going of Peek and Johnson, the Baruch twins, was particularly embarrassing. However, it was finally done, and the Brandeis influence came uppermost. From this time on, collectivism and planning would have no place in Franklin's policy. Whatever he secretly believed, he had now publicly placed himself squarely in the older progressive tradition, and there he would stay.

It must never be forgotten that Franklin was first of all a practicing politician. There were to be mid-term elections in the fall of 1934, and the prospects were not altogether favorable. Recovery had not been sufficient to justify any considerable claims; there were still perhaps ten million unemployed; spending was outrunning receipts; prices had gone up, but in such ways as to favor middlemen rather than producers or consumers; and there was still bitter complaint about the cost of living. Then, too, the press had by now begun to relax the restraints of the first few months; Franklin was not yet a direct target, but his less conservative associates were no longer pictured as merely interesting figures; they were fast becoming menaces.

Every phase and many persons in the New Deal entourage were by now under intensive watch for critical possibilities, and slips were exploited to the full. There were exceptions. The more conservative officials apparently could do no wrong. Immunity was more or less complete for Hull and Jesse Jones; on the other hand, the constant criticism of Ickes, Frances Perkins, Harry Hopkins, and myself made working very difficult. This barrage of adverse comment laid down on his left wing was becoming harder for Franklin to tolerate; his irritation showed once in a while in press conferences or in conversations. But, more important, he can be seen in retrospect to have allowed his policy to be shaped by a desire first to escape from the continual manifestations of ill will, and second to find among the multiplying signs of opposition some real haven of political friendship.

[8] The tremendous build-up of the Blue Eagle campaign and the publicity attendant on all Johnson's activities during the first year of the New Deal made his going much more embarrassing than it would otherwise have been. When the reaction to business policies in NRA became so violent that a congressional investigation had to be headed off, Johnson himself suggested a critical review of policy to be carried out by an independent group. As chairman, in what he afterward described as "a moment of total aberration" he consented to the appointment of the famous radical lawyer, Clarence Darrow. Darrow's prejudices took command at once. He reinforced the claims of the congressional progressives that big business had run away with the codes, that labor was at a hopeless disadvantage, and that restriction and price fixing were the chief activities of the organization. The report was circulated but never printed, and obviously Franklin wished to play it down. It had a good deal to do with Johnson's rapid decline in prestige and his replacement a few months later.

Franklin's natural affiliation was with the progressives, whether Republican or Democratic; this had been true, as we have seen, since 1912 when he had made his choice for Wilson. He very probably was surprised and was certainly disconcerted to find himself in the bad graces of those he regarded as closest to him in political faith. Reactionary opposition he expected, but progressives he had thought would be his fast friends and uncritical supporters. He may well have felt that if he really lost them it would be fatal. He could really count on no other support. The conservative Democrats could be kept in a posture of nominal acquiescence in his leadership only by constant cultivation and costly realistic trading. Sooner or later their permanent sentiments would come uppermost and he would not possess the means to buy consent. He would then face a coalition of reactionaries in both parties and come to that same stalemate in the inevitable contest with the Congress which had tormented many of his predecessors. He must have the support of the leading progressives. But the fact was that in this 1934 session his worst critics were Senators Borah, Nye, Wheeler, and Cutting, all progressives out of the West. It is clear that he felt he had made a fundamental error which he should at once try to correct. He never got back the support of the older men—except Norris; but the voters they represented accepted him, and that was enough.

This was not the kind of difficulty Franklin ever asked for advice about. He did on occasion, as he was considering a problem, talk with those around him rather as though he were thinking out loud. But he came to his conclusions and made his dispositions without saying what it was he was trying to do. Anyone was free to draw his own inferences; but as for himself, he would not admit that any change had taken place. Even his thinking out loud was usually a justifying soliloquy. He was merely pursuing his experimental way toward recovery and reform; he ought to be allowed some leeway by his supporters. But he must keep them. And this he thought he could do by being progressively orthodox.

The result was the shaping of those policies which came to be called the Second New Deal, the kind of thing the old gentleman on the Supreme Court approved. Relief could be given, welfare measures could be enlarged, public works could be undertaken, but he must abandon his leaning toward collectivism. He must support free enterprise and keep the government out of it. The Court, when it came to judge, would find no fault with any spending he wanted to do, but he would not be allowed to plan or to make any arrangements for social management. So far as this was a warning from the Court, Franklin had a first impulse to resist, much as he venerated Brandeis. The judges were adherents of an obsolete social philosophy, and he would, if he could, have refused to conform; but unfortunately his natural allies in the Congress were even more convinced that the old ways were best. He gave in.

The question whether in these compromises Franklin allowed expediency to overcome his duty to press for the policy the nation should have been persuaded to adopt is one it is not possible to answer. How can anyone after the event so closely analyze the imponderables of political support as to say whether Franklin was right at this juncture in concluding that he had to give way? Much less, how can anyone measure how far he should have given way? It was, at any rate, his judgment; and the judgment was his to make. Besides, this was not the first time he had resorted to compromise. From the Oglethorpe speech to the campaign's end there was a marked retreat. In taking up collectivism again, in AAA and in NRA, he had obviously hoped he had found ways to reconcile the progressive objectives with more realistic modern means for their attainment. The character and volume of the critical attacks from the progressives showed him that he was too far ahead.

He had hoped to satisfy everyone and had used all his political arts in the attempt. He was not succeeding. Month by month the signs were becoming more ominous. The bitterest and most concentrated criticisms were now centering in NRA. And this was unfortunately the fire he was least able to return effectively. For the truth was that, in this instance, he had alienated practically every interest that might have given him support. This had been unnecessary. He had been warned against it repeatedly, and now he had no adequate answer for any of the critics. He would go on toward defeat ungracefully and without alternatives.

For instance, to show how stubborn he had been, I, as one of the authors of the act, had been aware that its objectives—as I conceived them—were being perverted from the very first. I had registered the most active concern. I had protested, vigorously detailing my complaint. I had also warned Franklin that complaisance concerning the running away with the codes by big business was certain to alienate all the progressives. I knew this because he had asked me to be in touch with these natural allies and had indeed given me the task of holding them together if I could. Their disaffection was important, but it was even more important that the policy would result not in a general reduction of retail prices and a wider market for goods—thus creating employment—but in restriction, higher prices, and more unemployment. Even when I brought in Bob La Follette and Burt Wheeler to reinforce my argument, he had not been won over. He had traded the privileges wanted by business for the re-employment agreement and for certain other objectives that did not belong, I thought, in the codes and ought to be legislated separately—as they later were—such as minimum wages, the abolition of child labor, and the like.

Now he was up against it. The businessmen had betrayed him and the re-employment drive was a failure; the expected economic results had arrived, and the political results were just as had been predicted.

nd the course followed throughout had been calculated to maximize
e bad results and minimize the good ones—for NRA was far from
having fallen into irrecoverable ways if policy was sharply changed and
new management installed.

As I have noted, the executive order setting up NRA had vested top
management in a Recovery Board made up of cabinet members and
certain other interested officials such as the chairman of the Federal
Trade Commission. This Board really deliberated, explored the possibilities, and followed the administrative activities critically but, as was
thought, helpfully. Almost from the beginning it began to dissent from
Johnson's policies; and when he insisted that they were the President's
own, the Board still persisted in calling attention to their danger. This
annoyed Johnson, who by then had an incredibly expanded ego from
having become the cynosure of all eyes, and he persuaded Franklin to
advise Secretary Roper, the Board's chairman, that the Board had better cease to meet. It was in effect abolished. It was presently merged
into the Executive Council (an invention of Franklin's, made up of the
cabinet plus the heads of the new emergency agencies), and no more
was heard of it. A reading of the transcript of its meetings reveals very
clearly the amplitude of the warnings Franklin was given and the perverseness with which he delivered himself to his worst enemies.

His recovery after this serious error of judgment was not easy. As a
matter of fact, it was not successful. He never again had united progressive support and never again could expect the Congress to pass any
measure that did not have conservative approval. Even in this session
he would have trouble with legislation having to do with labor disputes
and regulation of the Stock Exchange, and these were not controversial
in the same way that NRA had been. Seeing these troubles coming up,
and knowing by then that they centered in NRA, he made his first
conciliatory move in January by way of an executive order. It provided,
as he said,

a practical and rapid way for making effective those provisions of the National Industrial Recovery Act that were designed to prevent persons, under
the guise of purported sanctions contained in codes . . . from engaging in
monopolistic practices or practices tending to eliminate, oppress or discriminate against small enterprises.[9]

This was the policy he had disbanded the Recovery Board for insisting on. The big businessmen had every right to think its adoption an
act of bad faith. They considered that there had been a deal. They had
not carried out their part, but they had not been penalized or even
chided for that. Now their privileges were to be curtailed. And this was
only the start. At the time the Darrow review machinery was set up

⁹ *Public Papers*, Vol. III, p. 55.

in March, Franklin told the assembled code authorities of some six hundred industries that "balanced recovery" was possible only if policies looking toward lowered prices, more moderate profits, and higher wages were pursued. He went farther. He went all the way back to trust busting. The anti-trust laws, he said,

must continue in their major purpose of retaining competition and preventing monopoly; it is only where these laws have prevented the cooperation to eliminate things like child labor and sweat shops, starvation wages and other unfair practices that there is justification in modifying them.[10]

Gone were industrial planning and partnership with industry. The businessmen had begun to think that partnership was accepted; moreover, that they were to be senior, not junior, partners. Now everything was changed. Suddenly the emphasis was on welfare measures and partnership was ignored. It might never have been mentioned. They felt betrayed. They—or most of them—had been willing to make cautious concessions about child labor, hours of work, and minimum wages. Now they were to get nothing in return. When the Johnson resignation had been awkwardly secured and a board had been substituted, Franklin, in another fireside chat, redefined the objectives of NRA:

Let me call your attention to the fact that the National Industrial Recovery Act gave business men the opportunity they had sought for years to improve business conditions through what has been called self-government in industry. If the codes which have been written have been too complicated, if they have gone too far in such matters as price fixing and limitation of production, let it be remembered that so far as possible, consistent with the immediate public interest of this past year and the vital necessity of improving labor conditions, the representatives of trade and industry were permitted to write their ideas into the codes. It is now time to review these actions as a whole to determine . . . whether the methods and policies adopted in the emergency have been best calculated to promote industrial recovery and a permanent improvement of business and labor conditions. There may be a serious question as to the wisdom of many of those devices to control production, or to prevent destructive price cutting which many business organizations have insisted were necessary, or whether their effect may have been to prevent that volume of production which would make possible lower prices and increased employment.[11]

The object had been to present to the electorate in November nothing but the most orthodox of institutions. The businessmen may have felt betrayed, but the voters were reassured. During the campaign the press did its best on the theme of socialism and departure from "the American way." But when the returns were in, Franklin must have felt

[10] Ibid., p. 129.
[11] Ibid., pp. 417–18.

that his sudden pulling up and reversing had been justified. That the representation of the party in power should be increased rather than diminished in an off-year election was unprecedented; in the non-presidential years control of one or both Houses had often gone to the opposition. The triumph of 1934 was a political coup of enormous importance. Such a ratification of policy was unmistakable evidence of approval.

It was indeed unusual. The loss of congressional control had made Hoover's last two years singularly futile, but it had happened to many Presidents before Hoover and would happen to many after him. Sometimes Presidents can themselves be re-elected without leading a corollary congressional victory; or if they do, they might lose it again in the succeeding off-year. Consequently, changes of Presidents in Washington result in a burst of legislation during the first two years of a term and very small accomplishments thereafter. At the worst, the six years succeeding the first two might be ones of political degeneration, characterized by bickering, irritation, and but little attention to national needs.

There was little about politics Franklin did not know, and he had no intention of allowing the usual pattern to imprison him. He was not starting on two years of accomplishment with six years of futility to follow—not if he could help it. He had in mind vast changes for the United States and even for the world; they could not be approached successfully except by the leadership method—at least by him—and he had utter confidence in his capability. But he could press only gently, and whenever he pressed he waited for reaction to register on his sensitive apparatus for the reception of mass impressions. This method of his had been in course of being perfected for some time; it would become habitual—rather complex and so not readily recognized, but nevertheless fixed.

Franklin's method involved a separation of objectives and means which, following his instinct for obscuring his ways of working, he never allowed to become obvious. There never was a prominent leader who was more determined about his objectives, and never one who was more flexible about his means. Others were always supposing that what were actually only means to him were his objectives. They therefore could not judge what battles he would fight and what ones he would run away from. They thought him vacillating, even cowardly, when actually he was following an elaborate strategy. His strategy was based on the manipulation, or the nice balancing, of the vast imponderables of democratic life. It was calculated in the end to bring about the conditions he judged worth working for and sacrificing to establish.

All this went on in his most secret mind. Others got glimpses of the process. A few familiars came to understand something of its basic procedures; but there were not many of these. It sometimes seems that

332

those who were closest to him for the longest time were kept there because they did not probe or try to understand but rather because they gave an unquestioning service. It was a delicate matter to find people like Steve Early, Marvin McIntyre, Pa Watson, Missy LeHand, Grace Tully, Bill Hassett, and others of shorter tenure, who never really knew what was going on, no matter how intimately they might be concerned with it. And it was far more difficult to find people who could write speeches about policy without discovering what the intent was, whether he was advancing or retreating, what public effect he hoped for, what was to be committed to and what left essentially open, what were means and what were ends.

He found such people. Moley had been an excellent workman, as good as Rosenman while he was around, but Moley had been pitchforked into fame as a presidential second and so had lost his usefulness as a ghost. Franklin's way of using his helpers was indeed well illustrated by Moley's embarrassing repudiation at London. If anyone was ever in a position to know Franklin through and through, it was Moley, for reasons that we have seen. But how little presumed intimates were really intimates was shown by Moley's complete misconception of what to Franklin were ends and what means. Whether the international bankers and the European statesmen who lent themselves to the bankers' schemes approved his policies or not was a matter of indifference. Those whose approval Franklin must have—at almost any cost—were those American voters who had elected him. Within their approval he hoped to find means for recovery and reform, but these must above all not be beyond the range of their tolerance.

Moley knew about politics. But in the course of duty he had been intimate for months with bankers as well as with Franklin. His eye wandered and he somehow considered opinions important which were only loud. He was sharply reminded by the "bombshell" message of what actually had been a policy he himself had approved—a nationalism that amounted to isolationism, temporary but actual. Moley was gone now, in 1934, except for infrequent visits when he worked at the writing of speeches in the old way and with the old skill, without mistaking himself for a statesman. But there was a rankling in his heart, and he was slowly persuading himself that the man he once had served so well and so unquestioningly was not only ungrateful but also a species of charlatan. That elaborate adjustment to public tolerance, that delicate, almost mincing approach to departure from the accustomed, that devious hinting at and suggesting of something new and needed—all this technique became repugnant to Moley. But that was politics—its very essence. Franklin was a master in its practice. And Moleys were useful but replaceable.

An election like that of 1934 washes out everything that has gone before, proves or disproves everything that has been said, and puts everyone in his place. This election was a glorious ratification for Franklin; it hitched congressmen more definitely to his coattails and served as a caution to them against declaring independence. Furthermore, although it was not done as spectacularly as many other moves, Franklin had produced the issue of whose overwhelming approval there would never be the least doubt. This was social security. Just as the Congress was departing in June to get ready for elections, Franklin stated his intention and announced a study group charged with producing a measure. It was understood that the terms of reference were comprehensive, and it spoke straight to the heart of uneasy, still-frightened Americans.

Franklin had become convinced, after a little more than a year in Washington, that the shaking up people had experienced repeatedly during the past five years had induced a longing for certainty that transcended all other desires. He had concluded that the satisfaction of this wish was the most potent of all the possible political issues still waiting to be used. The timing was perfect; the issue was latent but real; the conservatives were committed to condemnation; and it remained only to produce a practical scheme. Casual exploration convinced him that not only was such a program feasible but that the opposition was off balance from opposing the crackpot pension schemes so prevalent just then. They had spent so much time and energy repelling the threat to their pocketbooks furnished by Townsend, Long, Coughlin, and others that they could scarcely turn around and accept any alternative suggestion. They were certain to oppose, and certain to be immoderate in opposition. This, politically, was perfect.

But Franklin had long known about the European experience with insurance against the hazards of industrial life, even with that against unemployment, although this was the most doubtful of the insurances he had in mind. Actuarial figures about old age, accidents, illnesses, and the like, were dependable. He had determined on a contributory scheme. Deductions from pay envelopes and enforced contributions from employers would carry all these costs. Unemployment was the real social risk because it was unpredictable. It was, moreover, so massive in the downsweep of the depression cycle—such as was still lingering—that it might overwhelm any attempt to build up reserves for benefits. A little exploration convinced him that there were several sorts of unemployment, however, and that at least two sorts were of such a nature as to be susceptible of prediction—that caused by movement from job to job, and that caused by the obsolescence of processes and the starting up of new ones. There was a constant idleness in the United States of a discoverable percentage of the working force which was thus temporarily displaced. This was an insurable risk. It was the mass un-

Possibly most imp. Political strategy

employment of depression that offered the real difficulty. But even with this, something could be done. Benefits might have to be limited to a certain period (perhaps a few months), but even if this left the worst risk uninsured, it would still offer automatic assistance until something could be devised to meet the large-scale emergency of depression.

When Franklin began to think about this conception, it took hold of his imagination and he proliferated ideas so rapidly—and for once so openly—that none of those about him could keep up with him. Washington for weeks was devoted to speculation about the various possibilities after the infection began to spread. And the talk spread out to wider and wider circles. Franklin did nothing to check it. And the reason, presently, was obvious even to those of his associates who had been slow to catch his enthusiasm. Most of them had their own preoccupations; all of them were overworked, and another vast new scheme added to all those just getting under way inclined them to indifference if not opposition. It was not long, however, until social security had a hold on people's minds that demanded attention.

Very possibly the putting forward of this issue was the most potent political stratagem of Franklin's whole career. For one thing, it diverted attention from his change-over to an internationalist position that would involve freer trade, stabilization, and arrangements to scale down the debts—all likely to be unpopular if they were allowed to become issues. It served also to smother the acute dissatisfaction with the catering to business represented by the operations of NRA—the price fixing in the codes, the failure of NRA's subsidiary Labor Board to satisfy workers, and the extreme discontent of those who had been charged to watch out for consumers' interests—Mary Rumsey, Leon Henderson, and W. F. Ogburn were disaffected and likely to become an active embarrassment.[12] It also diverted attention from the turn-around in the whole NRA matter. It drew attention that otherwise might have centered embarrassingly on the giving up of the old policy and the adoption of the new.

For progressives of all sorts, social security was an article of agreement not matched by any other item in their agenda. All of them felt that such a program was long overdue, that it had been deferred only

[12] Both AAA and NRA had an advisory group, supposedly to watch out for consumers' interests as policy was shaped. Both were considered nuisances by the administrators, and they were quickly reduced to little more than window dressing. They were the subject of vitriolic attacks by the business interests, and that of NRA was treated with contempt by labor. In the consequential bargaining going on among the vast powers of industry, it was a small but irritating matter to have a consumers' counsel speaking up against high prices, poor qualities, and insufficient services. Frederic C. Howe in AAA was soon being pictured as a "Red." The same could hardly be said of Mary Harriman Rumsey in NRA, but she was treated with gentle condescension and excluded from all real policy-making activities.

because businessmen, who thought they would have to pay for it, were opposed, and that European experience had demonstrated beyond any doubt its complete feasibility. They joined at once in a chorus of approval. Then there was labor—and this was important. Because Franklin's potential political support was shifting, it was necessary to have labor and the city machines on his side—which neither had been hitherto. Farley had done something with the machines, but labor was more skeptical and distant than ever after early NRA experiences.

The events of 1934 and 1935 changed all this, and before the elections of 1936 labor was fairly committed to the New Deal. The Labor Relations Act of 1935 was hardly responsible for the change; its provisions were not such as to win labor's loyalty. It was social security that was overwhelmingly convincing to the working population. Franklin might not show any great favor to labor's tycoons; indeed, in a way he rather took their place in the worker's regard; and this not unnaturally alienated such dictatorial officials as John L. Lewis and the whole AFL hierarchy. Politically, social security consolidated a support that from then on could be counted on. There was nothing labor leaders could do but go along.

Labor's good and true friend in the Washington of that time was Senator Wagner. He had done the unprecedented thing for a legislator of accepting an executive responsibility; he had been chairman of the National Labor Board during the first half year of NRA. During that service he had seen how little could be accomplished without powers to enforce the principles that were supposed to be those of all New Dealers. Such intractable employer corporations as Weirton Steel, Budd Manufacturing, and Ford Motor were either refusing compliance or were making use of company unions to evade collective bargaining. In February 1934, Senator Wagner induced Franklin to issue two executive orders authorizing the Board to hold elections for determining bargaining agents and to present violations to the Department of Justice for prosecution. But Wagner was convinced that more was necessary and on March 1 he introduced a Labor Disputes Bill.[13]

Senator Wagner's bill enumerated several "unfair practices" to be prohibited, such as the sponsoring by employers of company unions, interfering with employees' choice of bargaining representatives, and refusal to bargain with elected agents. Under the bill a new labor board

[13] There was a section of the National Industrial Recovery Act, numbered 7A, which defined labor clauses to be incorporated in the codes. It was on the authority of this section that the Board was set up over which Senator Wagner presided. It was this experience that led to the writing of a separate Labor Disputes Act to ensure that collective bargaining should become legal. In fact so much attention went to the settling of labor disputes that the other—and in the long run more important—features of the codes were neglected. This was true of Franklin as well as others.

336

would be set up, fully equipped with staff to investigate and powers to enforce the provisions of the act. The subsequent history of this proposed legislation presents Franklin in a very equivocal role, to be understood only, I think, by assuming—because he did not explain—that he distrusted labor leaders and was appealing over their heads to the workers on issues other than those having to do with organization. Such matters were absorbing to leaders but not to the rank and file, and Franklin could take advantage of this. It is also essential to keep in mind the problem he was having with NRA. Furthermore, it must not be forgotten that he needed to maintain a middle position as the elections of the fall approached, even apparently at some risk to his progressive credentials, and that very delicate balances were involved in this.

As to the first of these, the most effective appeal by a long way was social security. How powerful an attraction this issue would furnish, none of the politicians appreciated at first. Most of them were inclined to belittle it, and not a few were frightened by the "radical" tag instantly attached to it by the press. The associations called up by Franklin's announcement in June that this was to be his next important objective were with the "crackpot" schemes already spoken of, but specifically at the moment with EPIC,[14] which Upton Sinclair in California was promoting. As it turned out, the study committee, under the chairmanship of Frances Perkins and with Professor Edwin Witte of Wisconsin as research director, was the center of absorbed attention until it reported. That was not until after the elections; but, even so, social security was the broadly appealing issue which, in spite of disappointments with NRA, AAA, and PWA, carried conviction that Franklin would keep trying until he found the means for ensuring permanent well-being for the people of the United States.

Political technicians—speaking now of national politics—often allow themselves to become confused because of the necessity they feel to persuade people that what is good for the special interests to whom they are indebted is good for everybody. They attempt this because the special interests will be their genuinely active allies and supporters as long as the politicians co-operate. It is these interests which organize support, which maintain a favorable home climate, which give expert advice and, above all, furnish funds. Just plain voters without axes to grind do not go out and ring doorbells, work on committees, or give money—not as a rule. Generally they must be urged even to vote. So it is hard to keep in mind that, after all, they do possess the ballots of democracy and that they will give or withhold them for very simple reasons. These reasons, apart from local issues and sheer caprice, either of which may interfere and establish exceptions, can be enumerated on

[14] The initials stand for End Poverty in California.

the fingers of a hand. They are economic well-being, security, peace, and freedom. The order of importance among these will change. Peace, for instance, displaced well-being at the head of the list along about 1939, but in 1934 and on to 1936, well-being and security were the matters people cared about above all others.

The generation then at voting age had been through a war, but even the veterans had withdrawn into indifference to the issues they had fought for. This was strange, perhaps, but even more true of those who had not been directly engaged. Beginning with a disillusion expressed even in 1920, when Franklin himself had as a candidate encountered it, an active hostility had grown up as Europe repudiated the debts owed to the United States and went on in more or less the old imperial fashion to appropriate German territory and exploit colonial peoples. Americans said bitterly that never would they allow themselves to be drawn into another European war, and they could not see any threat developing to modify this resolution. They were therefore so determined on peace that it was a sterile issue. They were even indifferent to disarmament. Hoover's, and later Franklin's, efforts to carry this movement farther had to be made without political credit, a penalty calculated to dampen a leader's enthusiasm in spite of the strongest convictions.

Nor was freedom an issue of any importance. There had been a period just after the war when Wilson's Attorney General, A. Mitchell Palmer, had made himself notorious as a Red-hunter; but this had happened before in American history. It was the result of fright. When people felt the need for cohesion and discipline, they tended to forget that it was of the essence of democracy that there should be tolerated differences. The processes of arriving at majority decision are sometimes heated and majorities are often narrow. Dissenters do not always give way gracefully; there are usually some who would appeal to force when persuasion fails, after the pattern so well marked out in Latin America and elsewhere. But crazes and waves, affecting a small or large minority, were passing matters, and attempts at coercion died out in a prevailing climate of indifference, preoccupation with daily concerns, tolerance, or just plain common sense. Besides, there was no real threat to American institutions from any convincingly subversive source. Socialism had long since passed its maximum domestic strength. There had been some fright over the I.W.W. during and just after World War I; and there was a ready market for fearsome tales about Communists, but party members were so few that only the hysterical could believe them capable of becoming an actual threat. Nor were even the more immoderate attempts to suppress or punish them so extensive or frequently repeated as to rouse any general feeling. Civil liberties are a viable political issue only when their violation is a clear, present threat

—as, for instance, when the Alien and Sedition Laws were being enforced. Violations in the twenties had offended vigilant liberals of all sorts, but the voters had not reacted.

The moving and dependable issues of the early and middle thirties had to do with well-being and security, provoked by the resentment against the rising cost of living and unemployment. This was the result of the disasters that had affected every home and every individual in the land; no one but had felt the impact of the war and of the depression; no one but wanted to recover his position and be given some assurance of permanence in it. Franklin knew this. He knew that the "movements"—like EPIC in California—however irresponsible and unrealistic, came out of a deep source. The thing a politician must do was not to belittle that source or attempt to dam back the flow of political sentiment from it; what he must do was to divert it to his own uses.

It was fortunate indeed that social security had this appeal, because Franklin seemed to do his best all through spring and summer to offend, if not to alienate, labor leaders and progressive allies alike. The Securities Exchange Act and the Communications Act, both signed in June, were progressive measures, but much more the center of attention was the Labor Disputes Act. This was partly because NRA was in such disrepute with progressives and partly because of the numerous strikes which were being savagely suppressed by the use of company police and National Guard troops. Employers, spoiled by labor's compliant attitude during the depression years, were reluctant to surrender their advantage; they simply refused, in large numbers, to bargain fairly. When the Wagner bill was introduced there was a protest of tremendous volume from chambers of commerce and other businessmen's organizations. The ensuing campaign of opposition was abetted by the press. It became fashionable to suggest that code authorities be allowed to settle all labor disputes, and Franklin himself seemed to think this an adequate court. Code authorities were dominated by the trade associations, of course, and this, therefore, amounted to abandoning the principle of equality in bargaining.

Senator Wagner was so discouraged by Franklin's equivocation and had so little hope of his bill being passed that he agreed to amendments having the effect of legitimizing the disputed company unions. This followed Franklin's intervention in a serious automobile-industry strike in which he arranged a settlement favoring employer-dominated unions. He subsequently made the same kind of settlement in a steel-industry dispute. On the same day this was done his representative in the Senate, Majority Leader Robinson, prevented a vote on the Wagner bill and substituted for it a resolution giving the force of law to executive orders modifying but recognizing the NRA machinery. The progressive senators were enraged, but the resolution passed and sub-sequently also passed the House. On the strength of this authorization Franklin, late in June, established by executive order a new National Labor Relations Board. It was this Board that Lloyd Garrison was appointed to head later that summer. Senator Wagner's efforts had come to discouragingly little.

The meaning of all this strange behavior was to be found in political necessity. How serious Franklin calculated that necessity to be can be judged by what he risked. Senator Bronson Cutting, old friend and most loyal of senatorial supporters, said in a bitter speech that the New Deal was being strangled in the house of its friends. And he and Frank-lin entered on an estrangement that lasted until Cutting's death some-what later in a plane crash. Robert Wagner was more philosophical, being a thoroughly experienced professional and probably having a shrewd understanding of the pressure to which Franklin was bending. The other progressives protested more or less emphatically and could not again be counted as certain allies, only ones of convenience. They considered—and said—that they had been betrayed. These defections were a high price to pay for business confidence.

Franklin was moving defensively toward the political center—per-haps past it, because of all the storm over his "leftist" and "radical" as-sociates. He seemed determined at any cost to placate business and to win over businessmen. He not only defended NRA from the aspersions in Darrow's report and gave the employers' their way about bargaining with workers, but in October, a month after the reorganization of NRA —when he had announced a "specific trial period of industrial peace"— he addressed the American Bankers Association in terms calculated to dampen down the smoldering resentment of its members. He was evi-dently convinced that his progressive friends had no alternative to his policies. They would not oppose him because they could not.

The functioning President, appealing for electoral support, was show-ing no faction favor, was neither rightist nor leftist; he was intent on national well-being and the maintenance of the traditional ways. Every-one, if he could manage it, was to co-operate, to work together in har-mony. There was no recognition of a weighing of institutions against the underprivileged, no suggestion for drastic revision of any law or custom. "Gather to me all of you," he said, "and we shall go forward together."

Of course it was different when the elections were over. Almost at once the address to the new Congress had to be prepared. The theme was a very different one from the campaign tactic of keeping to the middle. This was the way the message went:

We find our population suffering from old inequalities, little changed by past sporadic remedies. In spite of our efforts and in spite of our talk, we have not weeded out the overprivileged and we have not effectively lifted up the underprivileged. . . .

We have, however, a clear mandate . . . that Americans must forswear that conception of the acquisition of wealth which, through excessive profits, creates undue private power over private affairs and, to our misfortune, over public affairs as well. In building toward this end we do not destroy ambition, nor do we seek to divide our wealth into equal shares on stated occasions. We continue to recognize the greater ability of some to earn more than others. But we do assert that the ambition of the individual to obtain for him and his a proper security, a reasonable leisure, and a decent living throughout life, is an ambition to be preferred to the appetite for great wealth and great power.[15]

Progressivism had returned to the White House—an orthodox brand, but authentic. The old progressives might be furious—and many of them were; the businessmen might feel a curious uncertainty—and most of them did. But the people and their President had reached an understanding. They would trust him; he would get for them what he could.

[15] *Public Papers,* Vol. IV, pp. 16–17.

17

To one studying Franklin's progress through life, his early years as President are among the most difficult of all to bring within the canons of order. They seem to be characterized by more confusion and contradiction than progress toward consistent objectives. There was, for instance, indecision concerning the adoption of a progressive line. This has been mentioned. Then there was the shift from an isolationist to an internationalist trade policy. And there was the gradual change from isolationism to collective security in foreign affairs. There were others, as well. The "partnership with business" represented by NRA was given up for renewed regulation; and efforts at monetary management ended in the stabilization that had been so dramatically rejected at the London conference. Everything done in 1934, almost, seems to have been reversed in 1935. Even assistance to the unemployed turned from home relief to work projects. It had seemed in 1934 that the divorce of work from income, as an economic principle, had been firmly adopted; but in 1935 people's self-respect, Franklin said, demanded that their livings should be *earned*.

These and many other reversals are cited by Franklin's critics. They seem to show that most of the time he knew neither what he was doing nor why he was doing it. He could not possibly be right in so many instances when he was on both sides at once.

But if the whole change is studied carefully a pattern does emerge. And it can be understood if reference is maintained not to any economic or social theory but to political necessity and to Franklin's larger objectives. What he meant to do came within a very general intention; how it could be done was a matter of expedience. If it involved seeming contradictions, that was because, within what he intended, he was feeling for the most appropriate means.

He had to find a broad base of support, and he had to have the specific consent of the powerful groups he must work with. He must persuade the people that he meant well, and he must carry with him a congressional majority. Further than this, he must not alienate dangerous non-governmental groups—businessmen, the newspapers, the lobbyists, the immigrant conglomeration, the Catholic Church. Or, rather, he must not alienate enough of them at once to give real trouble. He must have the balance of consent necessary to allow him the tolerance he needed. But at the same time he must maintain enemies—convenient enemies such as he had always cultivated.

So, it can be seen, what went on can be understood only by first comprehending what he wanted to do as an American leader and then by looking closely at the institutions, the forces, and the people who could, if they wanted to, withhold consent and obstruct his plans, as well as the others who could be made to appear as obstructors. It can, of course, be said that this is what any political leader who rises to the presidency must do. But what distinguishes Franklin so markedly is his single-mindedness, his persistence, and his success. Nothing stood in his way, no person, no group, and especially no theory. Furthermore, he did not hesitate to risk what most leaders decline to put in jeopardy, his reputation for consistency. To be spoken of as inconsistent seems to most men a charge of incompetence, of infirmity of purpose, and they find it intolerable. It must be said that Franklin, too, found it disagreeable; the elaborate explanations he often made to his associates showed this, and the later analyst can find the same sophistical arguments in notes prepared for the volumes of his public papers.

But it must be said that Franklin never hesitated to run even this risk, repugnant as it must have been. And the way to penetrate his motivation is to understand his aims and to watch him as he adopts the means appropriate to these aims. Neither ways nor means may be approved by biographers equipped with hindsight. But a President accepts responsibility; he has things to do, and he proceeds, using his best judgment, to do them. A curious quality of Franklin's proceeding, perhaps, is the confidence he had in it. But this went back, again, to the fixation of his objectives and to his sense of appointment as the one charged with their attainment. Armed with such an inner confidence, he could not really be shaken by any criticism or attack. He might resent them—and in fact he did—and they might affect his method. If they seemed to represent strength, they would cause him to feint, or maneuver, or change his timing. But they did not change his objectives —the larger ones—those he had determined to gain.[1]

---

[1] A listing of the major actions taken and the measures approved during 1935 indicates a year of intense activity. It cannot, of course, convey the sense of energy radiating from the White House, but by inference the inquirer will know that leadership was largely responsible: Social Security, the Wagner-Connery Labor Relations Act, Fair Labor Standards, $4,000,000,000 for relief, etc. (under this last act there were established by executive order the Resettlement Administration, the Works Progress Administration, and the National Youth Administra-

In only one instance in all his presidency—one not yet clearly indicated—is there a probability that he gave away more than his judgment warranted. And even in this instance he must have felt at the time that the bargain was necessary. This was the inclusive heartbreaking trade he would be forced to make of various New Deal measures for the support of preparations for war. This sacrifice was far ahead still; just now he was feeling for the strength to rehabilitate a stubbornly sick economy so that he could get on with more fundamental changes. But it should be noted that war was even so early in his mind, something still only faintly anticipated but yet requiring a certain consideration.

The economy was still far from healthy in spite of the efforts of the past two years and in spite of a much better morale than had prevailed in Hoover's time. There was still unemployment. It had been reduced by a few million, but there were still many other millions without jobs. And business activity had not been resumed in the hoped-for volume. The NRA had failed as a stimulus. Most important, the induced rise in the price level had been a rise mostly of the wrong prices. The cost of living had gone up faster than wages or than farmers' receipts or wholesale prices. Buying power had consequently not increased for those who needed it most or whose spending would most affect the economy. There were many who were actually worse off than ever.

So when Franklin got down to the preparation of his message for 1935 on the State of the Union, he had behind him the ratifying victory of 1934 which had actually increased the Democratic majority; but also he had some worrying critical appraisals from those whose respect he valued. The first policies had not succeeded too well. He would now discard them. About all the large issues likely to confront him, however, he had done much thinking. The social insurance proposal had been threshed out; his determination to substitute employment on public projects for relief in money or kind had been made clear; the policy changes concerning currency, foreign trade, and NRA were completed; he had decided to maintain and defend AAA; the disciplining of the financial community would continue; something remained to be done for the rural distressed (AAA had operated to favor the large and more prosperous farmers); and more attention must be given to foreign relations. This last began to bulk larger and larger in his regard, though how it must be handled politically, he was far from clear.

The dictators were displaying an intolerable arrogance; at the very least they must be civilized, but the means for such an effort were not

---

tion; also this appropriation extended the work of the Public Works Administration), the so-called Wealth Tax Act, the Public Utility Holding Company Act (containing the "death sentence"), the Motor Carrier Act, the Air Mail Act, the Banking Act of 1935, the act amending the Tennessee Valley Authority, and the Gold Clause Act.

344

easy to visualize, considering the monumental American determination never again to interfere in Europe. Franklin had seen for some time that co-operation with those nations not yet subdued by dictators would have to be undertaken. The signs of this attitude had been made manifest much earlier—in his endorsement of the Stimson Doctrine, in fact, even before inauguration. But foreign policy was far from first in the regard of Americans in these times. Even the dramatic Good-Neighbor Policy was only apathetically approved.

This last, however, in the total context of Franklin's progress, has considerable significance. Consider in what contrast it stands to the attitudes of the younger Assistant Secretary of the Navy who inspected the marines in Haiti so approvingly in 1917, who boasted in the campaign of 1920 that he had had some experience in writing constitutions for backward countries, and who, even farther back, as a student, had been so excited by Uncle Ted's tremendous imperial achievement in Panama.

The change in his view of the relations that ought to exist between a large nation and its smaller neighbors did not develop suddenly. There were already signs of it when he assumed the governorship. In 1928 there had appeared under his name an article in *Foreign Affairs* which, in effect, repudiated one of Uncle Ted's definitions—the "Roosevelt Corollary" to the Monroe Doctrine.[2] It was consistent with this change that he should evolve a new European policy as well.

The new approach had two distinct sides. There was good-neighborliness for the weaker nations within the American orbit, but there was determined opposition for all those who could be called "aggressors," and this applied both within and without the hemisphere. The first ran on into the policy of "collective security" or group action among those peoples who could be called "free" in the sense that they were democracies resting on a sovereignty of the people; and the second became collective action against the "totalitarians," whose philosophy was inimical to individual freedom, in whose book the democracies

[2] The Monroe Doctrine, it will be recalled, asserted the paramount interest of the United States in the Western Hemisphere and warned other powers that they might not acquire new territory in South, Central, or North America. The "Corollary," added by Theodore Roosevelt, asserted the right and duty of the United States to control the conduct of lesser nations, since it was forbidden that other powers should discipline them. Franklin's *Foreign Affairs* article stated a revised Democratic view. This was that there should be no unilateral action. All nations, large and small, he said, had equal rights and equal responsibilities; all should join in any necessary action concerning one. It might be pointed out here that Franklin's successor, Harry S. Truman, carried this policy still a step farther by accepting responsibility not only for acting with others but for assisting such of them as were seriously in need of expert advice or of capital. Some discussion of this developing policy may be found in the author's "Caribbean Obligations" in the volume of conference reports issued by the University of Florida, 1953.

were rotten and decadent, and whose ambition was to assert the superiority of a personal or class dictatorship.

This polarization is a kind of guide for one trying to understand Franklin's foreign policy. He would from now on seize every opportunity to speak or act in accordance with his fundamental belief that the opposition of the two principles was complete and final and that it implied an antagonism to be resolved only by the surrender of one to the other—it did not always seem to him clear which would prevail—and a suppression that would amount to eradication.

From the first he was reluctant to temporize with aggressors, and he was equally eager to co-operate with their enemies. There is a seeming inconsistency in his rapid recognition of the Communist regime in Russia. The Communists were undoubtedly totalitarian, but they seemed to him a different breed; moreover, they had sometime since adopted a policy of collaborating with liberals against the Nazis, whom they feared. Their success could be attributed to reaction from the conditions all liberals were pledged to oppose, and it must be remembered that Franklin exacted from Litvinov, the Russian negotiator, written promises to respect certain liberties. Among these was an undertaking to establish religious freedom, something Franklin felt very strongly about. This promise also eased the annoyance of the Roman Catholics, who had been so much opposed to recognition. There was, in fact, only a very slight adverse public reaction, thus justifying Franklin's action.

It must be said in this connection that in these first years Mussolini was regarded as much less offensive than Hitler. To Franklin he seemed to have risen for much the same reasons as Stalin and had not used measures as repulsive as those of Hitler. Mussolini did not seem to contend that Italians were a super-race entitled by innate qualities to rule the world; he did aspire to some pieces of Africa, but it was not yet the savage demand it later became as Hitler inflamed his ambitions.

Hitler was the real enemy in Europe—he and his Germans. No Italian military venture could be very greatly feared, and Mussolini's claims to the Mediterranean as "an Italian lake" were not taken very seriously. But no one with a memory reaching back to the World War could minimize the German potential. Germans made the world's best soldiers, and their General Staff was a closed group of the most respected officers since the Romans. Such a nation rearmed and led by a fanatic was indeed something to be feared, and Franklin feared it.

It was certainly not widely realized at the time how important for the future of the United States were the decisions of 1933–35. But as the historian can see, practically every important phase of foreign policy for the next decade—until the end of World War II—had its origin during this period; no more than an enumeration of the more important decisions is needed to show this: the endorsement of the Stimson non-recognition doctrine; the recognition of Soviet Russia; the repudiation of the "Roosevelt Corollary" and the renunciation of unilateral action (at the Montevideo Conference in 1933); the refusal to intervene in Cuba and the abrogation of the Platt Amendment permitting interference; the termination of the Haitian protectorate and the liquidation of bankers' control over Haitian finances; the passage of the Tydings-McDuffie Act looking to Philippine independence; the long struggle with the Congress over the principle of collective security which ultimately yielded the authority to impose an arms embargo on belligerents, even if not on the aggressor alone; and the effort at Geneva toward further disarmament, which, however, came to nothing because of Senate opposition and Hitler's withdrawal from the conference and from the League of Nations.

That all of these commitments should have been made during a period of domestic difficulty, when most people's thoughts were necessarily directed to the problems of recovery, seems a really remarkable achievement.

The course followed by the administration's foreign policy was at least partly attributable to the public concentration on recovery. The Good-Neighbor Policy could be established because there was no dissent; and Philippine independence was as much determined by cynical sugar and fats-and-oils lobbies (who wanted to handicap Philippine competition, and who succeeded in obtaining several limiting measures within weeks of the independence measure) as by any pursuit of principle. The Stimson non-recognition doctrine needed no congressional authorization, but there were mutters of dissent. And when it came to showing outright disapproval of aggression by refusing to trade with the aggressors, the hackles of the isolationists lifted. They were joined by those who for one reason or another approved of Italian or German policies. These might merely be the familiar immigrant blocs who objected to discrimination against the parent country on any grounds, or they might be those Americans—and there were a considerable number —who favored the Nazi-Fascist policies. These last were those reactionaries who under one or another guise had been opposing progressivism all along and very likely were members of the Liberty League. In any case, they lined up against Franklin's policy and for the moment they prevailed.

It might be thought that the election of 1934 would have killed the Liberty League. It seemed at the time to be thoroughly discredited, and members of the administration presumed on the defeat. But they forgot that, like a deeply rooted weed, such groupings persist beyond all calculation in a democracy. They are never really eradicated, however often they may be rebuffed. Among their number are most of those who are really potent and powerful in the industrial and financial world.

347

They possess money, they have power, and they are indispensable to the operations of a capitalist economy. Since they continue to have influence and possessions, they are bound, from time to time, especially in periods of disorder or when their prerogatives are threatened by reform, to reach out for political power. For some time now they had been aware that people like themselves in Italy and Germany were supporting Fascism and National Socialism and were being honored in the councils of state; it was natural that they should long for such status at home.

To an extent they found this kind of recognition in NRA and hoped for more. But they had no moderation. They proceeded to abuse their privileges and to subvert the intention of the organization. Self-interest became unintelligent and destructive. They were not only defeated at the polls, they were struck a heavy blow by the Supreme Court. That many of them were jubilant about the Court's decision does not affect this generalization. Many of them did not recognize NRA as their own because it was linked with the hated New Deal.

If 1934 was a year when the reactionaries made the most noise, 1935 was dominated, in the same sense, by thunder on the left—a circumstance Franklin did not much appreciate at the time but which he would miss when its loudest voice was stilled. Huey Long seemed a dangerous individual, and some maneuvering had to be arranged to contain his spreading influence, but actually his extremism made possible actions that otherwise could not have been undertaken. He helped in his way, for instance, to pass the Social Security Act, the bill for an increase in corporate taxes, and the huge (as it was then regarded) appropriation to combat unemployment. He inveighed against all of these, but that he denounced them as insufficient, along with his fellow demagogues, certainly contributed to their passage.

Long, for this reason, deserves somewhat more than mere passing notice in Franklin's story. He had had a boisterous part in the nomination proceedings at Chicago.[3] Because of this, as well as because he was entirely conscious of his power in Louisiana spreading out into neighboring states, he felt that he ought to be consulted about many matters. He wanted the exclusive control of Louisiana patronage, of course, but this was only a beginning. He also wanted to be consulted on party policy and have it known that he was listened to.

I can speak of Franklin's experience with him because I was involved in a small part of it. One day just after the convention and before active campaigning had begun I was sitting at table with Franklin and a few others—mostly family—in Albany. The phone rang; the steward answered and then said to Franklin that it was Governor Long of Louisi-

---

[3] Told about in Farley's *Behind the Ballots* as well as other accounts of the convention.

348

ana. Franklin indicated that he would speak, and the phone was brought to the table. The crackling voice at the other end could be heard distinctly. "God damn it, Frank," he said, "don't you know who nominated you? Why do you have Baruch and Young and all those Wall Street blankety blanks up there to see you? How do you think it looks to the country? How can I explain it to my people?" This was not the end of it. The tirade went on in an uncheckable stream for several minutes. Franklin answered with a quip. Baruch and Young were people too, he said, and old Democrats. This provoked more invective. These were Smith men, Huey said, and "would have scuttled your boom if they could." Now they seemed to be the fair-haired boys; no "real" Democrats had a chance.

Franklin soothed him, saying that he knew well enough who his friends were. He knew specifically how much he owed to Huey too; and Huey ought to know that, whatever it looked like, the two of them stood for the same thing. He was only trying to hold the whole party together, to heal wounds, and so on. There was a considerable expenditure of charm before Huey was pacified. It occurred to me, listening— as Franklin signaled me to do—that Huey had not been asked to visit Albany, although many others were appearing by invitation. And I wondered how long after he rang off it would be before he realized that he still had not been asked to come.

My meditation was interrupted by Franklin, who, looking at the phone and replacing it in its cradle, said, "It's all very well for us to laugh over Huey. But actually we have to remember all the time that he really is one of the two most dangerous men in the country." He spoke further of this, referring to Hitler and his haranguing method, his unscrupulous use of specious appeals, his arousing of hate, envy, fear, and all the animal passions. Our demagogues had learned their lessons very well, he said, and spoke of the others, Father Coughlin leading, who were rampaging up and down the land.

I had the wit presently to say that he had spoken of *two* dangerous men. I supposed the other was Father Coughlin. "Oh no," he said to my surprise, "the other is Douglas MacArthur." This required some explanation. And we discussed it at length. There was latent, he thought, not far below the uneasy surface of our disrupted society, an impulse among a good many "strong" men, men used to having their way, mostly industrialists who directed affairs without being questioned, a feeling that democracy had run its course and that the totalitarians had grasped the necessities of the time. People wanted strong leadership; they were sick of uncertainty, anxious for security, and willing to trade liberty for it. This was the thesis.

Talk of this kind, Franklin said, had been passing around in clubs and business gatherings for some time as the depression ran on and as disorder threatened. What was lacking was the familiar symbolic figure—the man on horseback—to give it realism. Just as the French people, in a moment of disillusion with the disorders of democracy, had voted Emperor Napoleon III into power, and as the legislatures in Germany and Italy were even now voting themselves out of office, so it might happen in the United States if the symbolic man appeared. There was none so well endowed with charm, tradition, and majestic appearance as MacArthur; and the Nazi-minded among American leaders recalled with approval the incident that had seemed to all liberals so reprehensible—that, of course, was "the battle of Anacostia Flats," in which the unemployed veterans had been dispersed with tanks and tear gas when they had organized a protest march to impress President Hoover and the Congress.

This rightist threat was only latent, something requiring an appropriate opportunity to be brought into the open. A Nazi coup was not yet a realizable possibility in the United States. Except among certain susceptible folk such as those in the German Bunds, its advocacy was disguised as super-patriotism of various sorts. The leftist, or presumed leftist, appeals, in which everything was promised that anyone had ever longed for without the slightest acceptance of responsibility or acknowledgment of cost, was a clearer present danger. That it might have its uses, he already saw. "We must tame these fellows," he said, "and make them useful to us."

And as time passed he did try. He made something of Father Coughlin, and so did others in his behalf. And as to Huey, we all treated him at first with softness and consideration. In Washington I had been definitely assigned to "keeping him happy" for a while. But it was impossible. He wanted power, and he could get it only at Franklin's expense.

In 1935 there was a battle on. Huey was dominating the Senate and the press with his raucous speeches. He was rousing the rabble tirelessly. But Farley was using federal patronage against him in Louisiana, and all of us who had responsibilities were under instruction to shut him out of all participation. The battle came to a tragic end with his assassination,[4] but while it lasted it was epic. When he was gone it seemed that a beneficent peace had fallen on the land. Father Coughlin, Reno, Townsend, et al., were after all pygmies compared with Huey. He had been a major phenomenon.

I think he had really given Franklin concern for a bit. It has to be recalled that the recovery hoped for after the brave beginning in 1933 did not come very rapidly. And when an almost complete turn-around was made in 1935, after the confusions and failures of 1934, it was not a happy circumstance that one of the most effective demagogues the

[4] In September 1935.

country had ever known should be attacking with spectacular effect every move and every measure devised to meet the situation. It did get on Franklin's nerves. He must have regarded Huey's removal as something of a providential occurrence—one more sign that he himself moved under a star.

None of Franklin's uneasiness or concern in any of these situations was allowed to show. All through this period of turn-around he presented an imperturbably serene countenance to the nation. Americans were watching with an intensity never before known—partly because never before possible—every act, even every mood, of the man in the White House. Never can there have been a closer, a more intense union of leader and led. And he behaved in wholly appropriate fashion. He used the press—hostile though it meant to be—and his mastery of radio was something never before known. His stature increased. He glowed and gave out light. The people responded.

Such a phenomenon is not measurable except in the grossest terms. To say that the White House correspondence multiplied so that it nearly swamped the available facilities is to mention only one evidence, although an important one. The letters were, many of them, very personal, asking for assistance in some trouble, or reporting some difficulty about relief or employment on public work. But many also undertook to give advice, sometimes elaborately worked out, showing long concern for the nation's plight. It was impossible from the first for Franklin to answer all this mail or even to read it. This had been true even during the campaign, and one of the most onerous tasks of Moley and myself had been to scrutinize the more serious of the many suggestions for governmental action in the crisis. Now that action was being taken, much of the correspondence centered on the desirability or undesirability of New Deal policy. And it furnished one important indicator of public opinion.

This touch with the people was not the only guide of this kind Franklin had. There was Eleanor, who traveled much and brought him news of the country. And Harry Hopkins had observers everywhere whose business it was to report the reaction of the communities they served to the administration's program as it unfolded locally. There is a priceless social document, written day by day by Miss Lorena Hickok as she traveled for Hopkins, with specific instructions to gather up and report on the national health.[5] These reports were passed on to Eleanor, who kept very close track of Hopkins' work, and she showed many of them to Franklin. But also he saw many people of diverse sorts and from various places every day, and from each he extracted some item of information, often without their knowing it; then, too, the newspaper

[5] To be found among the Hyde Park papers. Miss Hickok had been a skilled newspaper reporter in Minneapolis and elsewhere.

reporters assigned to the White House were, as they said, using a boxing term, "in his corner," regardless of their publishers' preferences, and often were able to give a warning or a suggestion of considerable use.

One of the favorite mysteries of the time, and a baffling one to his enemies, was the completeness and precision of Franklin's knowledge of public opinion. They granted it, but they could never understand it, and they never were able to believe that it issued from a persistent digesting that had the permanence of a system. They both under- and overestimated him. They underestimated his industry and determination, and they overestimated his talents. They tended to think him a miracle man instead of a tough, persistent, and responsible one. And his advantage from this was enormous.

Besides, it has to be said that some part of the awe with which Franklin came to be regarded as a political wonder-worker was due to the extremely bad judgment and the incredible ineptness of the conservative opposition. These American leaders were so uniformly wrong, and the measures they undertook so invariably reacted in Franklin's favor, that some general explanation has to be looked for. Franklin himself was inclined to think it was to be found in the capacity of such people to delude themselves. The big businessman, the financier, and the corporate lawyer were the people in a capitalist society most susceptible to self-deception. This was not only because of their intense desire to have things one way and not another, but also because they were so effectively insulated from reality. They carried this to an absurd extreme, surrounding themselves with sycophants, exposing themselves only to favorable opinion—no conservative would for a moment consider the regular reading of an opposition newspaper—and generally taking care that no estimate of future happenings reached them that was not in accord with their preconceptions.

This habit of the conservatives, and their consequent inability ever to produce a positive suggestion for any social difficulty, gave Franklin a tremendous advantage. He always had better information and reached sounder conclusions than those who were so persistently his enemies. They never knew what people wanted or what they would accept. Franklin, on the contrary, although he shared the nervousness of most politicians who are dependent on recurrent referendums, was infinitely more realistic. His judgments of people's reactions, his sense of timing, and his conception of the precise appeal necessary to gain support for his objectives were, by contrast at least, remarkable.

The consequence was that before he had gone far in his first administration his political reputation had become one to match that of the best of his predecessors. After the elections of 1934 and the even more remarkable one in 1936, he would be given credit for having surpassed them all. When Wendell Willkie, aspiring to the Republican nomination in 1940, would be asked about the third-term problem, his reply would be that he hoped Franklin would run. He wanted, he would say, to defeat "the old champ himself." And that was an accurate attribution. Franklin did become the champion. But not all his political reputation was due to his own genius; much of it was conferred on him by an unusually stupid opposition. As he said to me one time, speaking of a particularly bad mistake he himself had made: "Oh well, I always have one comfort. The opposition will come up with a worse boner tomorrow or next day—soon enough to blanket mine."

The attitude represented by this remark is sometimes inaccurately called "philosophical." If by that is meant a mood or disposition for accepting the occurrences of life without deep disturbance, then Franklin was indeed a philosophical President. We have followed his development long enough to understand why that should be. He was now—at somewhat long last—mature. He had found his way. Concerning all the large problems he would ever meet, the critical choice had been taken. The lesser decisions, having to do with tactics, were not ones to agitate the depths, to pray over, to suffer from. They were implementing ones, in a sense routine, although it is not meant to imply that some were not more worrisome than others. Especially when they turned out to be inept or even mistaken, they could return to annoy him. But this is quite a different matter from working out those controlling conclusions that do create far-down disturbances and are far worse than annoying.

Perhaps it could be said that these determinations or governances were arrived at long before his presidency began. It may have been during his earliest years that the influences were exerted that made him a sympathetic neighbor rather than an exacting one, a progressive rather than a reactionary, a conservationist rather than a despoiler, a democrat rather than a totalitarian. No one, I think, can say or ever will be able to say when each of these bents was firmly fixed. All we can say is that at some time an overt act, a public decision, revealed one of them. And in many such instances the revelation was very gradually unfolded as though the conviction were a growing one being tested for public acceptance.

This, I think, was not the case. My interpretation is that this gradualism was only seeming, that the tentativeness of the putting forward *was* a trial of public acceptance, but that this was only a necessary feeling-out process to determine how much objection there was likely to be. The acquiring of this knowledge was not so that the determination could be withdrawn from. It was so that there could be a gauge of the persuading that would be necessary. This is something that is profoundly political, the most delicate task, indeed, of the dedicated technician. It is the distinction between great and small. It is the difference between leader and follower.

One of Franklin's special aptitudes, one for which he was given as much credit as for his political finesse by contemporary observers, was his ingenuity in creating devices of all sorts to gain his ends. He dazzled and bewildered the confused conservatives by the multiplication of governmental agencies, by the many projects he sponsored, and by the expedients he adopted. The conservative defense was ridicule, an old and well-tried defense against innovation. And sometimes Franklin had to meet these attacks head on. I recall very well how, on some of his "nonpolitical" journeys and on some campaign trips as well, he would say to a listening crowd, "How do you like your new power station?" (Or bridge, or schoolhouse, or post office, or park, or sewer and water project.) Invariably there was a chorus of approval. Then he drove the lesson home: "It's always the power station in another town," he said, "that constitutes a boondoggle. Over there in the next county the doubters say that building *your* powerhouse was a waste of government money."

The attacks on some of his administrative group had become severe by election time in 1934. The intellectuals, especially, were considered by the conservatives to be a profitable target. Day after day the Chicago *Tribune* carried on its front page the caricature of a college teacher in mortar board and flapping gown offering ridiculous advice to wiser and more experienced men than he. The Hearst papers, very powerful still in those days, and presently the Scripps-Howard chain, joined in the gibing chorus. Ickes, Wallace, and Frances Perkins were only lesser instances; it was convenient to picture them too as "theorists"—a favorite ridicule word. But until the election of '36 the college men got overwhelmingly the most attention.

So far as Franklin himself was concerned, the attitude of the press, of radio commentators, and generally of the organs of opinion was minatory. They said terrible things about him in private or in those semipublic places where they gathered; but at Rotary luncheons, businessmen's conventions, and like occasions, they attacked everyone around him but not him. They advised him strongly, however—with dire predictions and hidden threats—to get rid of the fools he was trusting and find some "practical people." They never seemed to realize that they were talking to themselves, that only those already convinced were impressed, and that the whole effort was futile. The fact was that this very opposition was just what Franklin needed to convince his majority that he belonged permanently to them and not to their enemies. His detractors had been responsible for that "new era" which had ended in disaster. Franklin and his group represented the reversal of all those policies that people had learned from experience to distrust.

Being President in those circumstances was no very comfortable occupation. But it has to be observed that Franklin was almost ideally suited for it. He had long ago learned to conceal from friend and enemy alike his thinking and deciding processes and even many of his convictions—such, for instance, as his clear belief that a showdown with the dictators would have to come, or his preference for a planned and disciplined business system. The way to these eventual developments would be long and difficult. There would be much dissembling, many maneuvers. But neither the native American Nazis nor the business dictators must be allowed in the end to triumph. It was his job to establish the conditions for their disciplining.

But that job was one that required a long time and much finesse. It required sudden emergences from the ambush of equivocation. If he had been an admitted socialist, say, committed to a doctrine, the opposition would always have known where to have him, how to attack, how to prevent what he was committed to do. With his comparative freedom from commitment to means, with his half-hidden objectives, they were deprived of a definite target until the last moment.

Yet when it is considered what a weight of responsibility this imposed, the burden seems appalling. That he could carry it at all indicates an inner adjustment to its peculiar requirements; that he could carry it with serenity and even gaiety betrays a statistically miraculous concurrence of a man and the need for him.

The White House days each had their problems, sometimes instant and demanding, sometimes not so instant but, in the long run, equally demanding. They had to do with both personnel and policy. Decisions about all of them—even the decision to postpone decision—had to be reached with the most delicate discretion, bringing into use knowledge of complex situations and judgment of men and events. The opportunities to make mistakes were varied, but the opportunities to bring off successful coups were equally varied. Day by day a President's reputation for leadership can grow or decline. Franklin's grew.

The compulsions began early in his day—before he was out of his bed in the comfortable, pleasantly ugly room whose windows looked off to the south. When he woke he hauled himself up on the pillows, reached for his old gray sweater, and with a breakfast that grew more and more frugal—his paunch seemed to be getting entirely out of control—he read several newspapers with a kind of grim eagerness. He saw in them the results of much plotting and conspiring. It was constantly necessary to use the columns of hostile sheets to gain the effects he desired. On the whole, he had remarkable success in this, but the care and concern about it imposed a daily study appreciated by only a few of his helpers. It seemed artless and effortless; that it seemed like this was the best evidence that it was not.

Presently, on a typical morning, there came to his bedside Marvin McIntyre, his appointments secretary; Ross McIntire, his doctor; Steve

Early, his press secretary—these three and sometimes others: Harry Hopkins, Frank Walker, or myself, quite often; and, less frequently, some other administrator who had to be briefed without anyone knowing he had seen the President.

Sometime after this the transfer to the White House office in the west wing—rebuilt now and a good deal more commodious than it had been at first—was carried out. There was a bit of ceremony even about this accustomed journey, as there is about every movement of the chief of state. He can never forget—is never allowed to forget—his position. The Secret Service signals his intentions, the way is surveyed and prepared, various agents take up their positions until he has passed, and when he has arrived, wherever it is, it is the government's central ganglion, from which impulses of power pass outward to the nation's peripheries as long as its occupant remains.

At the White House this center was a brown desk with a swivel chair facing north away from the floor-length southern windows. There were eastward-looking windows on his right, however, which yielded some sense of the outdoors. They opened on a piece of lawn and the terrace along the south front of the mansion. The office bulged out into the lawn, however, and Franklin had only to swing around to command the whole pleasant prospect of grass and trees and seasonal blooms, a thing he did a hundred times in every day. As a countryman he found the scene pleasing, as well in drizzle, fog, or heavy cloud as when the sun lay warmly on the earth.

There came to him at his desk men and women of many sorts, almost all of whom wanted something. Sometimes what they wanted was what he wanted too, but often it was not. They seldom went away certain of success, but they always went away proud to have had contact with the knowledgeable and equable man behind the big desk in the lovely room. He personified almost to perfection—even if the person who came there was not predisposed to impression—the dignities, responsibilities, and restraints of a nation's chosen head.

Interstitially there came in from one or another door Louis Howe, as long as he was there, with some acid advice, less and less relevant to the exigencies of the day; he was fading now, a wheezing wisp of a man, presently to be confined almost wholly to his White House room, then to the naval hospital, and then to the narrow room of his grave. Franklin was kind to him now and not elusive as in other days. Missy LeHand's own small office adjoined on the same side as the cabinet room, and often she came in with some garnered intelligence or, being called, to take instructions. Some sort of co-ordination had to be maintained in Franklin's multifarious affairs, and mostly Missy had to do it. She knew more than anyone else what was outstanding, but even she could not keep everything straight, and untanglings were chronically necessary, not infrequently with applications of balm for irritated egos. For Franklin, in search of knowledge, or feeling out reactions, or just moving people about and influencing events, set many of his visitors in motion one way or another; and many brief, cryptic chits Missy had to type, on which the initials FDR appeared, were the directives. When Franklin's presidency was over, there were thousands of those slips of paper in hundreds of files, some carrying the boldly inked initials, some with the letters only typed. Very few could be explained without reference to a frame that was usually missing.

The need for some modernization of the presidency was apparent to Franklin from the first. Among the assignments given to several of his co-workers—me among them—was one to study the reorganization of the executive establishment and of the presidential office itself. Nothing much came of this at once—although much could have been done under the terms of the Economy Act of 1933—and reorganization hung fire throughout the first four years. By that time there were so many suggestions and there was so much confusion that in desperation the famous Committee on Administrative Management was set up and on the basis of its report actual changes began to be made. Until then Franklin seems not to have been confident that conflicting advice about reorganization came out at a defensible whole.[6]

He was working under handicaps to be relieved gradually as time passed. He brought about changes with such gingerly care, however, that no considerable controversy was kicked up at any time about the matter. Once in a while some disgruntled or overvigilant legislator would speechify on the subject; and it came up occasionally in connection with the favorite taunt of gored oxen among the lobbyists, that the

[6] The members of this committee were Professor Charles E. Merriam, Louis Brownlow, and Luther Gulick. Besides many detailed recommendations for transfers and regroupings of the executive establishment, two passages in their report achieved immediate notoriety. One of these was a scathing objection to the activities of the Comptroller General. He was responsible to the Congress, not to the President; and by assuming the right to pre-audit expenditures, he was constantly interfering in the functions which, in the theory of separated powers, belonged exclusively to the President. Nothing came of this attack, but it called attention sharply to the growing aggressiveness of the legislative branch. Another evidence of this was the tendency to set up independent commissions, patterned after the first of them, the Interstate Commerce Commission. These were supposed to be regulatory, but, by their elaboration of administrative law and their interferences in economic affairs, they tended to invade more and more deeply the executive territory.

The other much-noticed suggestion of the committee—one that was carried out—was for a number of presidential assistants to expand the presidency into a genuine institution. These assistants, the report said, should not be officials in their own right, but part, almost, of the President's person; for this reason they should have as one characteristic "a passion for anonymity." The resulting discussion of this phrase contributed measurably to public education concerning the functions of the executive office.

Congress was a "rubber stamp for the President." They preferred the legislature to be a rubber stamp for themselves, and usually, it must be admitted, congressmen were more amenable as individuals to lobbyists' influence than to the President's; if they took orders from the White House, their compliance was less than cheerful.

Franklin's relations with the Congress, considering his demands, had not yet degenerated notably. That things were going this way, as in the case of other Presidents, could be seen. The dissenters became vocal as soon as their first appetites for patronage had been satisfied. They felt themselves at once to be in a better bargaining position, and their price began to go up. This was especially true of Democrats from safe constituencies in the South who had been in Washington long before the New Deal, who now had positions of power in the Congress and probably had an extensive infiltration of henchmen in the executive departments. The southern constituencies had an especially restricted electorate, one heavily weighted with business and professional men, planters, and other members of the upper middle class. They were hostile to the New Deal except as it favored the South and particularly their own class in the South. Their most active hostility was aroused by measures likely to favor Negroes, or workers, or sharecroppers; and they suspected the whole New Deal of tending to this favoritism. They were vigilant to counter it, and on the whole they were very successful.[7]

Franklin resented the distortions and misuse of relief measures, of emergency credits, of agricultural benefits, and of the allocation of public works into this class pattern. He spoke feelingly of the unfortunate, yet he understood and did not expect any rapid change in the existing class relationships. But he did mean to raise the minimum levels. He thought every child ought to have opportunity; he interpreted the profit system as fair pay for honest effort; he believed that minima ought to be established and protected, and he thought that the helpless members of the community—children, mothers, the aged, the crippled, and the unemployed—should be public charges. This noblesse was an integral part of his system of intentions. A large portion of his time and energy during the earlier years of his presidency was given to planning, intrigue, maneuver, and bargaining in the interest of these ends.

He sat in the Oval Room in the executive suite most of the day, talking, considering, figuring, starting up here and there movements and explorations, sending out directing chits to his associates. And what was it all about? It was about the well-being of Americans, in good part; and it was also about the nation's security; and somehow, in spite of the outcries and the maneuvering of those more fortunate and com-

[7] There are always exceptions to any political generalization. The South produced Senators Hugo Black and Lister Hill, as well as Congressman Maury Maverick, for instance. But these were not the rule.

fortable people who had to give something up, who had to conform to some change, or who had a different ideology, he made progress. Those for whom the product of all this activity was intended somehow knew and appreciated the effort.

This knowing and appreciating were not so much because he was a good explainer—although his enemies, to excuse their own losses, attributed to him a kind of genius for persuasion—as because, on the whole, he had some success in what he was trying to do. The unfortunates, the disenfranchised, in spite of attempts to sabotage Franklin's efforts, or to misinterpret and to deflect them, were year by year better off. They had no interest in charges of inconsistency; they were not worried about a balanced budget or inflation, and they were even less worried about the Constitution; they had, moreover, almost no concern at all about accusations of "dictatorship" and "domination of the Congress." They probably considered vaguely that leadership and discipline were necessary to the results they wanted.

Franklin lunched at his desk, and never alone. Usually this was a time when one of his official family was invited, but seldom more than one. No one knew better than he the uses of consideration and even of prestige. The big men in Washington are very small about some things. They listen eagerly for gossip, especially if it involves themselves. They very quickly surround themselves with sycophants just as businessmen do, and usually they set up a spying organization to protect their empires from the inroads of rivals. They invariably have another organization to maintain their trading relations with congressmen, and they treat with the tenderest care their "information" services —those subordinates who maintain press contacts and strive to paint an approved picture of themselves for the public.

A President who knows his business watches these operations of his subordinates with tolerance and sometimes with amusement; he also makes use of it for his own purposes. He can do this very well because of his powerful central position. He can further or obstruct the ambitions of those about him without ever showing his intentions. He can smother their news, blur their picture, and worsen their relations. If they "get a little above themselves" he *must* do it, especially if their inflation threatens his own prestige in some way.

No President ever had a more intimate understanding than Franklin of these complex matters. He watched his subordinates at their games, checked them when necessary, contributed to their build-up when it was convenient, reprimanded them effectively by non-recognition, rewarded them by intimacies. Asking them to lunch occasionally was one of these rewards. Every other member of the official family knew that Harold Ickes, Henry Wallace, or Jesse Jones was lunching alone with the President; and everyone spent a little time considering what it meant for his interests. How this system worked under Franklin's management can best be understood by reading such a document as Ickes' *Diary*,[8] those unhappy revelations of a perpetually sore heart. There was one period of more than a year when Ickes never saw his chief alone. On the other hand, very often Franklin had to tell him, or write a note and say, that he was indispensable. It depended on the circumstances.

Ickes was useful to Franklin in several ways, especially at first. He had been designated by the progressives, and they watched his progress with some vigilance. Later most of them were lost to Franklin anyway —Hiram Johnson, Bronson Cutting, Bert Wheeler, Gerald Nye, Ned Costigan, and even Bob La Follette were all in one or another way alienated by the beginning of the second term, but by then Ickes had a reputation as an administrator which gave him some protection, and he had an unchallenged regard for the trust of his office which was not to be taken lightly, considering some of the unhappy experiences Presidents have had with Secretaries of the Interior. But he was a whiner, an egotist, and an incorrigible empire builder. He had to be kept in his place. But it had to be done without allowing his pique to overcome his ambitions so that he would quit. He was always resigning and taking it back when reassured of Franklin's affection.

Some other members of his official family gave Franklin even more trouble. Henry Wallace, presiding over the agricultural sector, was a difficult inward-turning individual, but he had the best intelligence of anyone around and in a sense was the most loyal. He very early came down with the presidential virus, and this handicapped him in his office; but Franklin treated him very differently from Ickes, sensing his loyalty, his affection, and his genuine worth. He drew Wallace out, encouraged him, and, until Wallace's services had been rewarded by the vice-presidency, never punished him as he was always punishing Ickes. His later annoyance with Wallace—of which Jesse Jones was an equal recipient—was an unusual outburst, a kind of exception, and shows how far Franklin's powers had declined in the later days of the war.

The others in the cabinet and in the emergency agencies were men of convenience. Sometimes they turned out fairly well. In any case, Washington understood politics, and there would have been much more criticism if senatorial recommendations or the claims of weighty organizations had been ignored. The two members of the cabinet who still had no political backing were Frances Perkins and Henry Morgenthau. Frances was always bitterly resented by organized labor, and John L. Lewis' heaviest sarcasms were directed at her. Henry could not be criticized at the moment because it was hardly to be expected that a banker

[8] *The Secret Diary of Harold L. Ickes*, edited by Jane D. Ickes, 3 vols. (New York: Simon & Schuster, 1953–54).

would be taken into the cabinet after the performances of the past few years. Marriner Eccles might have been selected had he turned up earlier, but no other person with a financial background was even considered.

Such people as Roper, Dern, and Swanson (as well as their successors), if not exactly nonentities, were far from outstanding personalities, however useful their connection may have been. And so far as Franklin's semi-private life is concerned, they might as well not have existed. A President—and especially one who was seized with his office as Franklin was—has very little privacy, and what little he has is apt to be very precious. Franklin is a curious case in this respect. He—and Eleanor—lived without much resentment as an exhibit, perhaps because of long schooling. Stories about most Presidents illustrate their unhappy adjustment to public life. They attempt to outwit the Secret Service, they steal hours to themselves, and they complain bitterly of the restrictions imposed by protocol. None of this was true of Franklin or Eleanor. Franklin sometimes ran away from his escort in the Hyde Park woods or on back roads near Warm Springs, but this was attributable to a kind of puckish playfulness. He was always mildly addicted to practical joking and to a kind of involved humor of expression not always in good taste. But it was not carried far. He was known to the Secret Service as a good President. And this, of course, was because he felt naturally suited to all its demands. He belonged to the public. Eleanor was more intractable. She drove her own car and came finally to a kind of understanding with the Secret Service which allowed her a certain freedom.

Conversely, it could be said of Franklin that the public belonged to him, and others did not matter too much. Those around him were not expected to furnish leadership. They were expected to smooth his way in getting what he had decided on. A few he valued as generators of ideas or inventors of devices. But their novel proposals were for his exclusive use, and his adaptations of them were frequently so bizarre that their authors found them unrecognizable. But it was the interesting people of this sort that he found it congenial to relax with. At the cocktail hour just before dinner, on a Saturday night or a Sunday afternoon, late on a summer day at Hyde Park or in the crisp autumn at Warm Springs, he liked to have those about him with whom he could exchange quips and who would respect his need for release. These could be people who were interesting but not ambitious. Those who cared about him were the best. But he could relax to an extent even with those he did not fully regard as disinterested if they were amusing and did not presume. It was these with whom the President had mostly to content himself. The others tended to escape from the presidential ambit.

It is a tragic fact that a President can hardly ever have a friend. There are enough, always, of those who aspire to his intimacy; but even those he has known longest will often betray him, sometimes without realizing how serious the breach of confidence has been. Then, too, he will have outgrown others—as Franklin had outgrown all those of the Groton-Harvard circle. They will not understand, as a friend must, the casual allusion in conversation, the reference to this or that which it would be tiresome to explain. They will not grant him his right to decide, to choose. Sometimes they will get on a moral high horse and ride away from a man who must always be guided by political possibilities.

So Franklin's days now were a President's days; only moments were snatched from his people. Yet I recall going with him and a few others on weekends at Hyde Park, at Warm Springs, or on the Potomac when whole days passed without one statesmanlike exchange. We shared the amusement of reading in the papers—perhaps delivered to the *Sequoia* by seaplane as she lay at anchor in the Severn or off some point in Chesapeake Bay—about what we must have been discussing. What we had been doing was visiting onshore, playing a game, studying maps, or just sitting looking out over the water and talking of the most remote and pleasant matters. This seemed to both of us—as I am sure it did to others, like Harry Hopkins—a privilege earned by carrying a heavy load. But no one apparently wanted to believe that a President had moments of vacancy.

When Franklin was in the White House and committed to the daily regime, he sometimes gathered friends to dine and see a movie or to play poker in the Oval Room. But as the pressures tightened down and his responsibilities widened out, there was less and less of this. When the war came there was almost none of it. By then I was no longer in Washington, but I often spoke to him of the need to relax, a need he knew about but would not always admit.

On one of the ordinary days in the first term, as the afternoon wore on and visitors came and went, Franklin, seeing people and signing papers, flagged a little, reviving to charm each new person, but tiring more and more quickly. About four-thirty or five he saw the last of them go, signed a pile of urgent papers for Missy, and called for his chair. He went then to have tea and to swim and be rubbed. Afterward, those in the house who were dining, or intimates asked to come a little early, shared the cocktail hour in the oval study, most precious moment of the presidential day, unmarred by responsible talk, wholly given to persiflage and the mild stimulation of a little alcohol in a good deal of fruit juice. Dinner came all too soon. But even dinner did not end the presidential day.

Very often, and oftener as the years passed and the presidency became more and more the world's center, there was business after dinner, and sometimes a basket of papers to be disposed of while Missy or Grace worked each in turn. Not until midnight or later did he settle back on his pillows with a detective story. But when he slept it was invariably a long, deep, and restorative oblivion. There was no deep disturbance in his mind. Even when he could not get away to rest, he could sleep. It was a fortunate habit.

18

Franklin's quarrel with the power companies, extending over many years, outmeasures any others of similar usefulness—except, of course, the one with the totalitarians that ended in war. Yet there were two domestic "enemies" of only slightly less importance. Account must be taken of them here. These were the money and banking interests and the Supreme Court. During the first term—until 1936—recurrent battles over the New Deal banking laws, the demands for and against inflation, the search for ways to influence prices, the separation of investment from deposit banking, and the regulation of the exchanges—all these and other subsidiary issues caused a most satisfactory furor. They were the center of attention for long periods of time and were the cause of heated recriminations. Financiers are influential men; they do not surrender easily and there was always furor when they were attacked. Altogether the controversies surrounding them formed a consistent background for the man who sat in the White House and pushed, insisted, denounced, and maneuvered in the effort to get his way.

It was all done with the kind of publicity a politician can best use, furnished paradoxically by a press increasingly hostile and denunciatory. The newspaper publishers seemed no longer able to control their fear and hate. It had escaped all reason. They bore down more and more on New Deal wickedness, but it was done with a bitter bias very well understood by people in general. "That man in the White House" became a favorite phrase in places where powerful people forgathered. Polemists took the texts for their expositions of foreboding from the daily and weekly press, but what they never seemed to realize, and what none of the denouncers realized, was that those texts had a reverse side. The same actions they thought horrendous, millions of others thought courageous. The man they denounced as a "traitor to his class" was rated as a great and good friend by other and far more numerous classes.

Franklin operating at the topmost level in peculiar circumstances can be seen in retrospect to have shaped his general strategy with almost perfect relevance to his intentions. He sensed what people wanted; he learned what they could be got to approve, and he knew how to convince them that he was determined to get for them what they should have. People very often did not themselves identify their objectives. He did it for them. He had few ways to reach them except through hostile media, so he arranged to use those media in spite of hostility. He got the same effect from daily diatribes directed at himself and his helpers that a Mussolini or a Hitler got from ownership and operation of the entire machinery of publicity throughout their nations.

The denunciations of the first year or two could be traced mostly to financial interests of one or another sort. The feud between Franklin and the bankers broke out again and again, even after conciliation seemed to have succeeded. But only less furious was the quarrel with the courts, beginning as soon as the New Deal laws began to be tested by litigants who were in some way adversely affected. This was a much more delicate matter than the quarreling with the bankers, and for obvious reasons. After the troubles of the past few years the bankers were discredited. Their opprobrium had been self-inflicted. Franklin had only to take advantage of it. But the courts, to Americans, were sacred institutions, connected in many people's minds with some very precious concepts such as liberty, justice, and order. That there was about this more sanctimoniousness than genuine respect, the most active American leaders had always seen. There had been quarrels between Presidents and courts—the executive and the judiciary—as long as there had been a government of separated powers. It was not so endemic a trouble as that between the Congress and the presidency, but it had broken into the open on numerous occasions; for instance, when Chief Justice Marshall had established, by a famous tour de force, the Court's right to the determination of constitutionality. There were other famous instances too, in one of which the redoubtable Jackson had reportedly said of the Court, "They've made their ruling, now let them enforce it." Uncle Ted Roosevelt had quarreled loudly with the judges. And, as seemed to be almost forgotten when Franklin proposed it anew, the Supreme Court had been "packed" by one of the most revered of Presidents—Lincoln.

Nevertheless, to use the courts as a foil was a much more chancy matter than the public castigation of bankers who were in bad public odor anyhow and whose every indignant defense recalled their behavior during the booming twenties. But Franklin accomplished exactly what he intended by his use of the issues presented to him by the courts. This is not always understood, because it is written that he "lost the Supreme Court fight" in 1937. This is true, and it riled him at the moment. But he gained more politically by losing than he would have gained by winning, something even he tended to overlook in the pique of the moment. All the conservatives felt and said that a dastardly attack on judicial institutions had been repulsed; but Franklin went on, as the people's champion, not the courts', to more victories because of his attack. On the whole, it was almost as useful a quarrel as that with the bankers.

But the row with the bankers began first, and among such devices it certainly ranks next to that with the power interests, which had been so dramatic during his governorship and would go on through TVA, through quarrels over utility-holding-company legislation (involving the marvelously apt "death sentence"), to dramatic battles with the utilities' champion, Wendell Willkie, and, as well, to the wonderful prospects opened up by Bonneville, Grand Coulee, Passamaquoddy, and all the other publicly owned sources of hydroelectric power. The utility fight did not stop, but for long periods it was obscured by the epic battles with the bankers and with the judges. These were hammer-and-tongs affairs capable of raising the temperature of the most lethargic voter. Taken as a whole and in political terms, the performance was magnificent.

The fight with the financiers was not so appealing on the positive as on the negative side. If he won, Franklin could promise only a rather technical fair regulation of a very intricate business, understood only in broadest outline by most people—even those who used the banks constantly. But he reduced the issues to the broadest and plainest terms, understandable by anyone who listened carefully; and somehow the division became a moral one and stayed that way. Perhaps that was the effect of those biblical allusions in his inaugural, when the outgoing Hoover, seated near him, had so visibly shuddered at the demagoguery of his successor. "Money-changers in the temple" was really a rouser; and there was no one who did not recall who had been the champion on that occasion. The comparison was daring, but it was not challenged.

Leading up to this highly charged passage, there had been others in other speeches; and especially there had been that campaign speech[1] when he had used the word "oligarchy" and had laid down a program of enforced "truth telling" and "regulated honesty."

This speech at the time surprised me. After its first part, which had been a recital of the fatal events during the years just past, I had expected a broad approach to the causes of depression. When instead Franklin presented a seven-point program for reform of banking and security selling it seemed to me an avoidance of the real issues, a kind of anticlimax. But anyone could see, looking back, how excellently it

[1] At Columbus on August 20, 1932, *Public Papers*, Vol. I, p. 680.

had fitted the campaign needs. It had prepared the way for the most spectacular events of the three years to follow. It had pointed to the dragon most useful in the circumstances because of his wickedness and the fierce light already beating upon him from every side.

The campaign promises were followed by more promises in the inaugural. And then came the spate of legislation. It has to be recalled, in considering the measures of 1933–35, how complicated was the situation to be changed. Almost the whole range of finance had to be dealt with. Something had to be done at once about the closed banks, and emergency measures were taken. These succeeded to the extent of reopening most of the solvent institutions. There followed presently a system of insurance for deposits.[2] Then the relation of the banks to the Federal Reserve System had to be revised. About this there was much controversy. It was Franklin's position that the banking system occupied too central a position to remain essentially independent; the government must have a say about general policies, and especially those affecting the expansion and contraction of credit. These were directly connected with economic activity.

But this was not all. There was the problem of prices, obviously involved in the issuance of currency and the manufacture of credit.[3] This was essentially a private transaction, subject to a certain governmental control. It seemed to Franklin that this was too vital a function to be left to purely self-interested motivation. He was sure that it had been abused—that the banks were run for private, not for public purposes. This neglect of the public's interests had been responsible for the collapse of the system as soon as difficulties arose. The banks, in their

[2] Concerning deposit insurance, there was an involved series of negotiations not gone into here. It seems strange, but Franklin was clearly against this measure when it was first put forward, and agreed only reluctantly to its approval. Before long, of course, he was claiming it as one of the most creditable of New Deal measures. The reasons for this turnabout have to do with the quarrels among the bankers themselves, some of whom did and some of whom did not want it. Cf. R. H. Myers' "The Politics of the Dual American Banking System," University of Chicago doctoral dissertation, 1955.

[3] Both these were functions of the deposit banks. The banks got currency to pay out over their counters from the District Federal Reserve Banks (of which there were twelve) by rediscounting "commercial paper." This "paper" represented loans made to borrowers, sometimes with collateral, sometimes not. But the theory was that the amount of currency would expand or contract as business activity expanded or contracted. It was this function which involved bankers' judgments—many bankers and many judgments. The Federal Reserve could affect the policies governing loans by raising or lowering the rediscount rate and so encouraging or discouraging loans; also by other policies having to do with the acquisition of securities and the fixing of the amount of gold held in reserve to protect the currency in circulation. All these were fixed within limits by law but were subject to a certain manipulation. It must be remembered that the Federal Reserve Banks were owned by the member banks, although the government had representation on their boards.

desire to make money, had neglected to protect depositors and had considered the general effect of their activities very little, if at all. This must be corrected by more control from the center.

Added to this was the confusion of investment with deposit banking. So long as bankers accepted deposits and dealt in securities, they could use depositors' funds for what were essentially speculative purposes. Many of them had got caught in the market decline with heavy commitments of this sort. They could not be liquidated easily, even if the paper was valid, and so depositors could not get their funds. If there had been a profit the depositors would not have shared in it, but they shared in the losses; sometimes "innocent investors" bore all of them.

It was to this sort of practice that Franklin referred indignantly when he spoke of the "money-changers." From the first, one of his clear intentions had been to separate these two functions. Speculators were no longer to be able to use other people's money without their consent, risking not only deposits, but the stability of the whole system.

As it unfolded, then, the group of New Deal policies having to do with money and banking had these long-run objectives:

1. To reform banking (a) by making deposits safe, (b) by separating deposits from investments so that bankers could not speculate with the depositors' funds.

2. To raise and then to stabilize the price level.

3. To strengthen central management so that governmental influence could be brought to bear on business activity.

These purposes are to be thought of as apart from the emergency measures intended to restore the functioning of the system and to encourage the resumption of business activity. For this purpose the banks had to be reopened, after being appraised as to solvency, and emergency credit had to be extended where liquidity had disappeared but where there was actually solvency. This was one responsibility of the Reconstruction Finance Corporation, already in existence but needing to be strengthened and enlarged.

It must be remembered that this whole task, so important to an industrial economy, had to be undertaken in the difficult conditions imposed by deep depression with all its attendant need for haste and all its accumulated irritation and impatience. It had worn out Franklin's predecessor, and in fact Hoover had failed at it although he had known well enough what had to be done.[4] Bit by bit, measure by measure, Franklin got all of it done during his first four years, climaxing the emergency measures with the establishment of the Securities and Exchange Commission to supervise dealing in securities, and with the Banking

---

[4] As is clearly revealed in his *Memoirs* (New York: Macmillan, 1951–52), 3 vols.

Act of 1935. This last settled once for all the quarrel concerning government control of banking policy.[5] The Securities Exchange Act brought into play the principle Franklin had enunciated, that *caveat vendor* should be substituted for *caveat emptor*. When he finished with all this in 1935, the change in the financial system was enormous. There was still not a government-owned central bank as other nations knew it, but the control of credit and of dealing in securities had been brought under strict regulation. It was made quite unlikely that bankers in partnership with speculators could again bring on such a debacle as had occurred in 1929.

The government still could only regulate; it could not initiate. It had no part, actually, in the running of the business system. It could prevent abuses and check unwise policies, but it could only indirectly stimulate activity or ensure expansion. It could affect credit policies and the price level, but it could not direct investment or substitute its judgment for that of the bankers who were in contact with borrowers.

Yet Franklin was fairly well satisfied with what had been done. Obviously it was not yet enough. Unemployment still persisted, showing that business activity was still restricted or unwisely directed. But confidence had been re-established and the system was running. The rest could await accommodation to what had already been done.

The din of the battles involved in these changes had sometimes been loud and the struggle had indeed been furious. No group of Americans had always been so certain of their judgment, so set in their ways, and so indignant at any suggestion of invasion as the financiers. They had been pretty well deflated during the banking crisis, but their recovery was quick, and they offered the usual stubborn opposition to all the measures of reform, most of all to those reorganizing their own affairs. That these were largely in their own interest, and calculated to rehabilitate their lost prestige, no one could have guessed from their behavior. They denounced, they subverted any and all of the individuals concerned if they could be reached, they spent money recklessly in propaganda; but in the end they were reformed in spite of themselves. They had not convinced the nation that Franklin was a Communist or his

[5] This was accomplished: (1) by reorganizing the Federal Reserve Board into a Board of Governors, appointed by the President; (2) by authorizing this Board to manage the open market operations of the system, fix the rediscount rates of all the District Reserve Banks, and determine (within limits) the reserves to be held by member banks; by providing that the Board should appoint the presidents and vice-presidents of the District Reserve Banks and should fix the salaries of all officers; by allowing this Board to set stock market margins and prescribe the conditions for the extension of consumer credit; by providing that the Board should appoint three of the nine directors of each District Bank, one of whom should be designated chairman and Federal Reserve agent (representative of the Treasury Department), and one vice-chairman, and should have the power to remove any officer of any Federal Reserve Bank.

associates traitors, as they tried to do; they had only convinced the majority that he was right to bring them under effective discipline. It was the financiers and their allies in opposition who brought about the unprecedented electoral victories of 1934 and 1936. They thus served Franklin very well as a necessary foil.

He would not have had it quite this way if he had had any choice. He did not enjoy opprobrium any more than anyone else; and although he was quite certain that the measures he was being denounced for insisting on were popular with the people, there were times when the unpleasantness got entirely out of hand. The fury of the conservatives at some moments approached the revolutionary. And after all the distresses of the past few years it could be guessed that the public temper might be short. It was fortunate indeed that expression at the polls was possible. The overwhelming rebuke to the conservatives in 1934 was accepted sullenly, but it was accepted. When the election of 1936 was past, the reforms were fixed. The accomplishment was written into law and had been ratified. The disgruntled could only seethe and mutter. They no longer had any hope of stirring up an opposition strong enough to cause an overturn.

The difficulties Franklin encountered as he felt his way toward these changes were not altogether those of a determined opposition. They were partly in his own mind. The ambivalence of a political reformer seeking to bring about serious changes while maintaining his own sources of strength was never better illustrated. Franklin did accomplish it. And he found ways, with much tentative exploration, with some false starts and retreats, to come out at the end with both ends substantially achieved. He had got his reforms, even if severely watered down, some of them; and the getting of them had immensely increased his power.

Who can say what his motives were? Like those of all of us, they were undoubtedly mixed. Because of this he sometimes seemed bold and courageous, and sometimes weak and indecisive. With any leader of this sort, the critical judgment must necessarily be in the large and after the event. What the contemporary opinions were is important only as representing his secondary achievement—that of getting and maintaining electoral approval. Looking back, we consider the success or failure in operation of the measures he sponsored; we forget that at the time it was very necessary that they should simply be approved by ordinary people. If it seems now that he was more concerned that they should be popular than that they should be effective, that is because he was a good politician. He was going on to other things. He could not leave behind him too large a residue of disapproval. He had to compromise often, and sometimes just next to disastrously.

On the other hand, if he was likely to be on the scene for some time his policies would have to meet the administrative test. If they proved to be unworkable or if they had unexpectedly bad effects, they would return to torment their sponsor. Franklin's opponents made a continuing effort to show that their opposition when the measures were being discussed had been correct. The program of belittlement and ridicule was formidable and persistent. It involved nearly every one of the new measures. Each was tested out in this way, seriatim, for possible use as items in the propaganda barrage. The newspapers and the magazines of those years seem, as they are looked at now, to have in them very little else but these carpings. Some of these attacks made use of legitimate material; they were not wholly inventions. The new agencies, and the expanded old ones, were nationwide in scope; their staffs quickly grew from very small to very large. Their undertakings were often novel, and this meant that there was no experienced personnel and no previous knowledge of the acceptance or rejection the program was likely to encounter. Such an organization as AAA depended largely on the existing network of agricultural services—the state colleges and research stations, the Extension Service, and so on—and as a consequence could go to work very quickly. But even that most fortunate of all the New Deal organizations had seemingly almost insurmountable problems. Where, in Washington, could there be found housing for a new staff or some five thousand employees? The old department was already crowded and would be hostile to sacrifices of space. And out in the field there had to be a considerable staff in every state and county; in these centers the same problems on a smaller scale had to be met. This, moreover, is to say nothing of the indisputable fact that some proportion of those who would inevitably be drawn into administration would not approve what they were doing—in New York State, for instance, the disapproval in the air was almost palpable.

To pursue the AAA illustration a little farther: the whole matter was complicated still more by the disagreements at the top already forecast here. George N. Peek, who was made administrator at first, was induced to take the job because he thought the domestic allotment plan of the "theorists" would prove to be a failure and that his own preference for giving responsibility to the processors and subsidizing exports would be returned to. Before the first year was out the quarrels about policy had become acute and Peek, proved wrong, was forced to resign. It was some time before the organization could recover its morale and go on to do its job. Even then the processors did all they could to disrupt administration, and the legislative struggle to amend the act during its second year so that it would operate better was about as difficult a one as that over passage of the original act.

In the long run Franklin was saved by the opposition from such legitimate embarrassments. The struggle was so intense over principle that matters of confusion and inefficiency were given very little attention. Then the Supreme Court was kind enough to say of this, as of NRA, that it was unconstitutional, thus rallying to its support even its most lukewarm beneficiaries. The new bill, the Soil Conservation Act of 1936, passed after the Court's action, was better than the old one in every sense. Its operations, using a now-experienced organization, were subjected to far less criticism. It passed into the category of accepted change. The parity principle—that there should be an equality between agricultural and industrial incomes—was one it would not again be revolutionary to support.

The experience of the AAA was bad enough, but few of the other new organizations had as good a one. The object of most intense attack during the early months was, as might be expected, the relief organization, so hastily put together, and so loosely administered by Harry Hopkins and his assistants. The spending of unprecedented millions for such purposes offended many thrifty or more fortunate souls who had escaped the worst rigors of the depression and had managed to keep job or income. Work projects seemed—and were—inefficient to a degree. They were offensive to all orderly individuals. It was impossible for better citizens to be persuaded that even wasteful relief and fantastic inefficiency had to be overlooked. Most of them could not understand the economics involved. They could only see that waste and sloth were being paid for by the government. They thought of their taxes and of inflation. And they damned the whole program.

There proved to be not so many of these people as would have been thought by any observer at the time. They were loudly vocal, they were supported and reinforced by press and pundit, and they seemed to constitute the nation's judgment. They even frightened Franklin from time to time. The recipients of assistance had no voice; perhaps most of them did not even read, except casually, what was being said. Their sentiments had to be ferreted out or guessed at—which is where such investigators as Miss Hickok came in, where Eleanor tended to steady the President's nerve, and where progressive support was most useful when it was available.

Besides this kind of criticism directed at the assistance programs, there were such downright debacles as that of NRA. From these Franklin could not escape. By the end of 1935 the echoes of this disaster had very nearly died out, but not before Franklin had made a serious point about the Supreme Court, the first of a series destined to end in the epic battle of 1937. The Court was already the "Nine Old Men," in the columnists' phrase, and was earning the enmity of all those with a stake in New Deal legislation. The whole program stood in jeopardy and Franklin was preparing the ground for a post-election showdown.

The Court gradually moved front and center to become the cynosure of all eyes. This happens periodically in the United States, but it had never happened more opportunely than on this occasion. Nor had it ever been used to more effect. The Court's turn did not come, however, until the bankers had faded into the obscurity out of which they had come.

The dramatization of the fiscal struggle was effective. It was described as a process of "moving the financial capital from New York to Washington," and this was something the progressives had been wanting done for a long time. They thought they had done it when in Wilson's presidency the Federal Reserve Act had been passed, setting up twelve regional centers to replace Wall Street. It was the fashion for Senator Carter Glass, Professor H. Parker Willis, and Edwin W. Kemmerer, who had had much to do with its conception and drafting, to speak of that act as "democratizing" the banking system. But the Reserve Bank in New York had remained much the most powerful among the twelve.[6]

These old defenders of the Federal Reserve System were inclined to view New Deal changes with suspicion, and especially after Senator Glass was offered the secretaryship of the Treasury and refused it because of Franklin's reluctance to promise that there would be no inflation. There was a new hero in New Deal days. He came out of the West—from Salt Lake City, in fact. This was Marriner Eccles, who became chairman of the Board of Governors of the strengthened system and who, in fact, was the most active worker for the amendments under which he was appointed. He was to remain in that post throughout Franklin's presidency. He, more than any other individual, impressed his personality on the new system.

Franklin counted himself lucky to find Eccles. He had the two qualifications most needed. He was a successful banker (and financier), and he did not come from New York. No one could say of him that he was an inexperienced theorist, and no one could connect him with Wall Street. Eccles long afterward wrote one of those "assisted" books detailing his experiences.[7] In that account one of the recollections that seemed to intrigue him was that he had been accused of being a "Keynesian," but that, in fact, he had never read a word of Keynes'

[6] The New York bank performed two important central bank functions: it executed the open market operations for the whole system, and it acted as the fiscal agent for the system and for the government in dealings with other central banks and with foreign governments. The New York bank in consequence was in many ways more powerful than the Board in Washington, and sometimes more powerful than the government, a situation ended by the changes of 1935.

[7] *Beckoning Frontiers: Public and Personal Recollections* (New York: Knopf, 1951). It was Mr. Sidney Hyman who did the assisting, the same Mr. Hyman who had also assisted Robert E. Sherwood in writing *Roosevelt and Hopkins* and who wrote, on his own, *The American President*.

writings—had never even heard of the British theorist until after his own ideas had been worked out. Eccles' case was not an unusual one. It became fashionable in the later thirties to attribute the financial aspect of the New Deal to Keynes' influence, a generalization most agreeable to the British and repeated in the official *Life* of Keynes.[8]

What truth there is in the Keynesian myth is that Franklin behaved in what later came to be called the Keynesian manner—that is to say, he kept feeling for a "balanced economy rather than a balanced budget," and that he had shrewd notions about the means needed to attain that end. These included the management of money, of price levels, and of industrial activity. These could not always be approached directly. Money and prices could be affected by banking policy; and business activity responded in a degree to an expansion of purchasing power (through relief and public works), the manipulation of taxes, and other similar devices. But Franklin, too, had arrived at these notions before he ever heard of Keynes. Like Eccles, he never in his life had read anything Keynes wrote, except perhaps some newspaper pieces commenting on his own actions. The first of these—and probably the first time he became conscious of Keynes, except as one of the Brains Trust may have mentioned him—was the Englishman's favorable comment about the "bombshell" message to the London conference in 1933. This remark was startling because it was unique. Almost everyone, and especially everyone abroad, professed to be shocked by the message. Condemnation was so universal that a word of praise from such an authority was by contrast a marked occurrence.

The explanation of what seems to students a causal relationship between Keynes' theories and Franklin's policies is that Franklin lived in an intellectual climate created not by Keynes alone but by many others as well who were considering the same problems. They were all unorthodox together, pioneers in this respect. Their thinking resulted from study of the special problems created by an industrial and commercial system now coming to its technological maturity in a climate of obsolete ideologies. Wesley C. Mitchell and his colleagues were the explorers of the business cycle. Their patient work and their tentative conclusions were spreading throughout the intellectual world, and orthodox economics and political science were gradually giving way before the weight of new fact. Franklin was sensitive to such changes, although he did not read the original literature; and his sensitivity had been increased by his explorations of the depression with the Brains Trust.

Keynes had many times refused opportunities for visits to the United States, but he did come across the water in 1934 to be given an honorary

[8] *The Life of John Maynard Keynes,* by R. F. Harrod (New York: Harcourt, Brace, 1951).

degree at Columbia University and to satisfy a certain curiosity about the happenings in Washington. Not unnaturally, perhaps, I was more or less host to him among the New Dealers. He was entertained at my home, I introduced him around, and altogether his visit was a mutually valuable interlude. Someone remarked after he left that for the first time, after long talks with Keynes, the President knew what he was doing. But I was present at some of those interchanges, and Keynes' attitude was more that of an admiring observer than that of an instructor. How much Franklin opened to him that extraordinarily secretive mind of his, I do not know. I was not present at all their talks. But it was true that his frankness was unusual. This, I judged, was because he was talking to an outsider who could neither obstruct nor further any designs he might have.

At that time Franklin was in process of making transition from what I have called the First New Deal to the Second New Deal. He talked to Keynes about this, and it was the first confirmation I had of what theretofore I had only suspected about the change. The earlier clue had been the acceptance of unemployment insurance at a time when both Hopkins and I were inclined to argue for the more flexible method of a permanent relief and public works system. But Franklin thought of social security as the necessary floor for the laissez faire to which he was reverting, and he wanted it to be comprehensive. He wanted to assure everyone of a minimum; above this, the system could operate without more regulation than would assure fairness in competition. He still thought that a good deal of planning and even of directing would be possible, but it would not be formidable. It would consist of strategic pressures used at focal points where there was leverage. But this concept was still hazy in his mind.

A Planning Board was emerging from Ickes' Public Works Administration. Franklin would adopt it as his own and it would go on until killed by the Congress in 1943. It had been at first thought of as a guide to public works. In that role it was undertaking comprehensive studies of national resources and their utilization. It would afterward be moved to Franklin's office, with perhaps some idea that it might select the levers most useful for influencing the economy. But about the time it was becoming useful it began to have the fight for its life with an increasingly anti-executive Congress, which would end in its abolition. It never became the kind of agency Franklin seemed to think it might become.

So that while Franklin was from time to time having spectacular battles with the bankers, leading up to the Banking Act of 1935, there was going on behind the deceivingly careless façade a search for new policy. This had to be acceptable in a majority sense; it had to be capable of managing indirectly to maintain a stabilized and expanding economy;

and it had to seem—although this was perhaps part of the first requirement—a development, not a replacement, of the business system. The Second New Deal, apparently so characteristically a season of battles with the financiers, was actually an attempt to find a rapprochement with business, but one not stultifying to government.

There are two incidents in this general unpleasantness that seem to me illuminating. The first is the so-called "breathing spell" so artfully publicized in 1935, and the other is the quarrel with the American Bankers Association—and specifically with Jackson Reynolds of the First National Bank of New York. Mr. Reynolds was to introduce him at the Washington meeting of the association in October 1934, and it was Mr. Reynolds' remarks that caused the outburst. The whole incident reveals how little the bankers understood, still, their role in the deployment of national forces, and how easy it was for Franklin, with his political talents, to make use of their obtuseness. But first the "breathing spell."

Roy Howard was at that time in charge of the Scripps-Howard newspapers and a very enterprising publisher, not quite so violently antagonistic to the New Deal as some others among the publishers. After the passage and signing of the Wealth Tax Act on August 30, 1935, Mr. Howard wrote to Franklin. Businessmen, he said, believed that this act and others recently passed were intentionally hostile. The tax law in particular was regarded not as a revenue measure but as a punitive one, part of a general attitude. Business, he said, needed to have its fears quieted; there ought to be a "breathing spell"; during it "experimentation" ought to stop.

Franklin, having got on the books most of the items of the Second New Deal, surprised Mr. Howard and, for that matter, everyone else by seizing on the letter as an opportunity to declare an armistice. What he said was that the administration's program had now been substantially carried out and that "the breathing spell of which you speak is here—very decidedly so."

Preceding this declaration were several paragraphs explaining the theory of the tax bill. This was an effective statement of the progressive attitude. The Wealth Tax Act, he said, together with the Social Security Act and the reforms imposed on the banks and utility concerns, constituted a whole governmental economic policy. And it did. Bob La Follette, for instance, began to see now that it was emerging as an alternative to the collectivism in which he believed. I recall his talking to me about it in a disappointed way. He thought the new policy hopelessly insufficient. Insufficient or not, it was obviously what Franklin had determined on. And he felt, moreover, that he had now reached a safe position. His letter to Roy Howard showed that:

The tax program of which you speak is based upon a broad and just

social and economic purpose. Such a purpose, it goes without saying, is
to destroy wealth, but to create broader range of opportunity, to restrain
growth of unwholesome and sterile accumulations and to lay the burdens of
Government where they can best be carried . . .

Congress declined to broaden the tax base because it was recognized that
the tax base had already been broadened to a very considerable extent during
the past five years. . . .[9]

What Franklin had fallen back on as a policy was what Justice
Brandeis had said he could have. The old justice had told him that he
could not have a collectivism in which the government made and enforced policy; that he must rely on regulation to establish fairness among
competing enterprises. Competing was a policy in itself. On the other
hand, there was no limit to the regulating, provided that it was necessary to fairness. The harsh measures of the 1935 session would be in no
such danger from the Court as had been encountered by NRA, AAA,
and other laws of the First New Deal. Also, Franklin had been told,
there was no limit to the taxing power, and there could be no interference with spending for welfare purposes the funds raised by taxation. There were, therefore, three basic items in a national economic
policy: regulation, taxation, and spending. It was to this dictum that
Franklin was conforming.

When he wrote to Mr. Howard, Franklin was telling the unperceptive businessmen that their own theory had prevailed. They could have
no objection, in principle, to what was now being done. It was all in
conformity with the laissez faire they so strongly professed. They must,
of course, concede the subtractions from their incomes necessary to
maintain purchasing power (and, incidentally, welfare), and they must
accept the regulation necessary to the success of a system of competition. But this was nothing to get excited about; it was not revolutionary.
It was, indeed, in the most realistic sense, reactionary. It went back.
It was the necessary corollary to their own theory. They ought to be
supporting, not opposing, it. Besides, he now could tell them, the essential conditions had been established: the regulations had been set
up, the taxes had been imposed; there was nothing more to fear.

It is perhaps not surprising that the breathing spell was not accepted
as meant. It had been unilateral. There had been no negotiations looking toward peace between Franklin and the businessmen. It was part
of his deepest conviction that there could not be. Neither negotiation
nor peace was thinkable. How could the representative of the state
negotiate with business as an equal? Could the whole allow the part to
determine policy? It was repugnant to his every instinct. He was also
not unaware, probably, that it would be bad politics; but that was not

    [9] *Public Papers*, Vol. IV, pp. 355–56.

what primarily actuated him. The actuating and controlling impulse was well illustrated in the Reynolds incident already mentioned.

There were involved in this occurrence several of the characters who had now moved toward the center of the stage—and one who was moving away from the center. Those who were moving in were Henry Morgenthau, now Secretary of the Treasury, a post of dignity beyond his legitimate expectation; and Harry Hopkins, just assuming that confidential role as Franklin's Friday which was to be confirmed by the years. The one who was moving out was Ray Moley, whose place was being taken by Brandeis believers.

In the wings was Jesse Jones, the redoubtable chairman of the Reconstruction Finance Corporation. Jesse had come to Washington in Hoover's time, appointed to the Corporation's directorate at Garner's request. He had been promoted to chairman by Franklin when the RFC's powers and authorizations had been so vastly expanded in the 1933 crisis. He was big, thick, tough, and ruthless—a Texas speculator. He owned real estate, a newspaper, and much else. His poker playing was legendary. But much more legendary, especially among New Dealers who were mostly despised by the older politicos, was his ability "to get away with murder." He escaped criticism in the Congress for actions others would have shuddered to contemplate. Because of it he could operate among the tottering ruins of the financial system with practically unlimited funds, bolstering here, pushing over there, spending to rehabilitate, to re-establish liquidity, to "get things going again."

Jones would have a later career as Franklin's war financier, preparing the nation for its ordeal with the totalitarians; at the moment he was up to his neck in rescue work, some of it successful, some not. When it was, he bragged a little about the profits to the Corporation; when it was not, he simply wrote off the loss. Every once in a while he told a committee of the Congress about it. There was seldom a murmur. There can never have been, in all the history of our government, practically unsupervised financial operations on such a scale; and there never have been operations on a much smaller scale that were not questioned by disgruntled interests with congressional connections. Big Jesse was, indeed, the miracle man of the administration.

Franklin's ability to use all kinds of people was responsible for his delegation of power to Jesse. For Jesse despised Franklin, just as Garner did, and lost no opportunity to implement that deepest of all disloyalties, the undercutting of a chief of state by a trusted subordinate. The Southerners—with exceptions such as Senator Black, soon to become a Supreme Court justice; Lister Hill, who would succeed him; and good Sam Rayburn, so different from the malicious little man from Uvalde—all hated Franklin. They hardly bothered to conceal it, and certainly Franklin knew all about it in his wary way. But his bland pretense that no such antagonism existed was one of the anomalies of those times. They were tied together, but mutual dislike was not allowed to interfere with the interests of each in a collaboration they must maintain. When either could injure the other with impunity, it was done; but the struggle was one carried on in the dark with knives. There were no gunshots to disturb the apparent friendliness.

Jones, as representative of the administration, had made a tough talk to the bankers' meeting in 1933. And he had proceeded to a policy the bankers feared above all. As the price of "bailing them out" he demanded equities. The end of that could have been, as the alarmed bankers urged, government ownership of their institutions. Where was this powerful Texan headed? they wanted to know. He seemed to have been given his head by both the President and the Congress.

This of course came on top of a general development that seemed to the bankers almost equally threatening: the government had gone wholesale into the business of extending credit. Agricultural credit, especially, had been enormously expanded under the 1933 Farm Credit Act. Then there were the loans to home owners by the Home Owners Loan Corporation. Others were in the making. It really seemed as though the lending of credit might become a government monopoly. Lewis Douglas was known to be protesting, but by now he was a defeated man and was leaving his directorship of the budget. The "lenders and spenders" seemed to have everything their own way. Worst of all, the antagonists in Washington—the New Dealers and the southern reactionaries—agreed on a hate of Wall Street and, the bankers believed, had a common weakness for inflation. Morgenthau, now in the Treasury, had set up the new Farm Credit machinery and had been its first administrator; he could be judged to be in favor of the indefinite extension of government credit.

As the bankers gathered for their Washington meeting in 1934, however, Jones addressed them without rancor, and this seemed to set the tone for a policy of reconciliation on both sides. After the acerbities of the past months the bankers were chastened. They hoped for an end to their punishment. There was a "harmony" group in the administration. It included that friend of all men, Frank C. Walker, who never saw hurt inflicted if he could prevent it. He had not liked the pillorying of the financiers by Senator Black's committee preceding the New Deal punitive legislation. He had watched Ferdinand Pecora, committee counsel, operate on the bankers, and he had not liked it. It seemed to run far beyond its purpose, and merely to express a malice that had got out of hand.[10]

Walker was close to Franklin. He was, in fact, now director of the

[10] Cf. Pecora's own account, *Wall Street under Oath* (New York: Simon & Schuster, 1939).

Executive Council, a sort of expanded cabinet, taking in the heads of agencies as well as the old departments. As such, he occupied a central position. Everyone trusted and liked him. He was one character in the New Deal cast without taint of self-interest, of ambition, or of vindictiveness. All this, of course, did not mean that he was always wise or that he understood what Franklin must do. He merely wanted no one to be unkind. He was a businessman, but he loved Franklin and he really hoped that eventually other big businessmen would come to love him too. They must, in the long run, see that their chastising had been for their own good. Now he wanted the punishment to end. A good place to start was with the bankers, who had been treated most harshly of all.

These issues came to their climax as Franklin prepared to write the speech he had agreed to make to the bankers. *The Wall Street Journal* noted that the pre-convention atmosphere was "hopefully conciliatory" and that since the meeting would be dominated by the "larger bankers" conciliation could be expected. It was, it seemed, the smaller bankers now who were least disposed to forgive and forget. But one of the big ones, Jackson Reynolds, president of the First National Bank of New York, had been chosen to introduce the President. He had prepared a little speech for that purpose. Let Moley tell of the conflict in the upstairs Oval Room of the White House as the ghost writers got down to their task:

At once Hopkins and Morgenthau began what has come to be known in political jargon as the "needling" process—that is, the process of recounting information or suspicions in a way likely to irritate or vex a man with respect to others. For over an hour they regaled F.D.R. with stories of business antagonism to him. The President listened, his face stiffening. I broke in from time to time, of course, but without being able to deflect the torrent.[11]

What Moley broke in to say was that emissaries of the Bankers Association had asked the President to make the occasion a "hatchet-burying ceremony." He also reminded the President, he says, that it was he—Franklin—who had asked that Reynolds be his introducer, a request the bankers had gladly granted. Moley goes on:

At this point Morgenthau shifted to the edge of his chair and announced with a look of triumph that he had a copy of the Reynolds speech and that it was enough to make a man's blood boil. The copy was then handed to me, and I was asked to read it aloud.

Obviously, it was designed as a friendly greeting. But there were two passages to which Morgenthau and Hopkins took particular exception. The first one was an allusion to a clash between Scipio and Hannibal in Africa, before which unsuccessful peace efforts were made and in which one army was de-

[11] *After Seven Years*, p. 296.

stroyed and the other decimated. There was a good deal of confusion among those present as to whether the passage meant to suggest that Mr. Roosevelt was the brilliant Carthaginian or the victorious Roman . . . the objection made was that this passage implied that, in meeting the bankers, the President, representing the government, was put on an equal plane with them.

The second passage referred to the fact that when the President was a student at the Columbia Law School Reynolds had been his teacher. I was about to ask Morgenthau whether he didn't perceive that the reference was intended as a humorous one when I noticed the expression on F.D.R.'s face. He had a baleful look. It was obvious that public reference to his law studies wasn't calculated to improve his good humor.[12]

As the Moley account goes on, he persuaded Morgenthau to see whether Reynolds would not delete the objectionable passages. The President calmed down, but the "needlers" had been so effective that the draft he began to dictate showed his irritation. Moley revised it and next morning Franklin approved his friendlier draft. But meanwhile Morgenthau had to carry out his agreement. Reynolds was summoned to his office in the Treasury Department:

He found Morgenthau sitting in state in his office, the central figure in a half-circle of co-inquisitors and aides. There were Undersecretary Coolidge, General Counsel Oliphant, the Treasury public-relations director, Mr. Gaston, and a stenographer with a poised pencil. Facing this formidable array was a vacant chair. Reynolds was directed to be seated. Without any preliminaries Morgenthau announced that if Reynolds should deliver his speech as it then read he would be "mobbed"—"torn limb from limb." Morgenthau's remarks were hardly calculated to elicit a calm answer from a man of spirit. Reynolds rose, remarked that it would probably be best if he did not make his speech at all, and made for the door. Ultimately Morgenthau was forced to change the tone of his comment, and Reynolds agreed to delete the two references to which the President had come to object the night before.[13]

This little glimpse of life among the New Deal officials is slightly colored by Moley's disaffection. No doubt Morgenthau and Hopkins were indignant; but Franklin was indignant too, quite on his own. He spoke to me about it. "Imagine," he said, "referring to a representative of the American Bankers Association and the President of the United States as equals! And," he went on, "imagine what national policy would be like if, instead of requiring such groups to conform to the public interest, they were free to bargain about what they would or would not consent to accept. Outrageous!"

Perhaps Franklin cannot be understood by anyone who does not sympathize with this impulse to reject the pretensions of social groups so impressed with their own importance that they feel they may bargain

[12] Ibid., pp. 296–97.
[13] Ibid., pp. 297–98.

with society about their place in it. Franklin was a holist. He was now the defender of the American whole; that he should reject the suggestion that it was not paramount seems to me not at all strange. Whether or not Moley wrote most of that speech, there are some passages in it that Franklin must himself have written:

> You will recognize, I think, that a true function of the head of the Government of the United States is to find among many discordant elements that unity of purpose that is best for the Nation as a whole. This is necessary because government is not merely one of many coordinate groups in the community or the Nation, but government is essentially the outward expression of the unity and the leadership of all groups. Consequently the old fallacious notion of the bankers on one side and the Government on the other side as being more or less equal and independent units, has passed away. Government by the necessity of things must be the leader, must be the judge of the conflicting interests of all groups in the community, including bankers. The Government is the outward expression of the common life of all citizens.[14]

This preachment was lost on Franklin's hearers; and no one else at the time commented on it, although there was widespread interest in what was usually spoken of as the administration's "quarrel" with the bankers. The body of the speech recounted some recent history. It seemed to indicate that the punishment was past, but some other indications were more frank than conciliatory. Immediate balancing of the budget was impossible, Franklin said, and a publicly proclaimed final valuation of the dollar "inadvisable." He did, however, hope that the coming business expansion would be financed with bank credit, and he anticipated that expansion would reduce the need for relief expenditures.

The New York *Times* said of it that it was "reassuring," and even spoke of a "dramatic reconciliation." But the *Times* was more optimistic than the press generally. The *Chicago Journal of Commerce* said that the speech could not be read "with much real satisfaction." And *The American Banker,* although it reported the Wall Street view that the speech had been promising, was skeptical. The whole affair, it said, showing how little it noticed the presidential warning, was "a complete victory for the administration." The New York *Times* reported:

> There were many, particularly among the country bankers, who felt that Mr. Reynolds . . . had gone further in his public confession of the bankers' failings than the occasion called for, and that the President had not advanced nearly so far as had the bankers' spokesmen in the ceremony of exchanging olive branches.

The idea of equality was one Franklin had not eradicated with one speech. Nor would he in many others. The additive attitude among

[14] *Public Papers,* Vol. III, p. 436.

Americans had very deep roots—and they were as deep among progressives as among such others as bankers. Whatever Franklin might feel, he would find himself temporizing with it, perhaps in the end giving up any attempt to loose its strangling hold on government.

Franklin may have felt at this time that the bankers' day had passed. They had been subdued and returned to civilized functioning. They had not altogether lost their political utility; there would be further references, on suitable occasions, to their sins. But at the end of this speech he again returned to a favorite theme of the 1932 campaign—the concert of interests:

> It is not in the spirit of partisans, but it is in the spirit of partners, that America has progressed. The time is ripe for an alliance of all forces intent upon the business of recovery. In such an alliance will be found business and banking, agriculture and industry, and labor and capital. What an all-America team that would be! The possibilities of such a team kindle the imagination. . . . They make easier the tasks of those in your Government who are leading it.[15]

But Moley, writing his memoirs seven years later, was sourish about the address whose peroration he himself had penned:

> The newspapers of the country hailed the . . . speech as a laudable gesture of cooperation with business. But the atmospheric conditions in which the speech was perfunctorily delivered approached the frigid. The President was scarcely pleasant either to his audience or to Reynolds.[16]

There was no "armistice" in the "war." The bankers were still eligible as a political foil. They had missed their chance to understand their position in civilization and to be dismissed into the anonymity of good co-operators. Nevertheless, they had soon served their political purpose and were less and less often referred to in New Deal diatribes. The Court gradually moved to the center of attention. But the spotlight which later would fall on the dignified justices was directed with fine discretion until after that most remarkable of electoral occurrences, the presidential victory of 1936.

---

[15] Ibid., p. 439.
[16] Op. cit., p. 298.

19

It has been noted that several Presidents before Franklin had had open differences with the Supreme Court —on a few occasions critical enough to be fought over in public and even to become electoral issues. These disputes had never done Presidents any harm; they had, in fact, often had favorable outcomes. In the nature of the case the courts had to conduct themselves in a restrained manner. Their dignity would not permit open controversy joined in by the justices themselves. The President could agitate, but they could not. On the other hand, they could wrap their robes about themselves and retreat into injured silence while the interests they sheltered complained loudly that the Constitution was endangered. And this was sometimes a very effective tactic.

Leadership, in other words, was a natural function of the presidency but repugnant to the nature of the judiciary. Several times justices had stood for a disputed principle, but they had had to stand for it in embattled silence except for oblique pronouncements from the bench. These, however much they might owe to prejudice or predilection, had to be clothed in a pompous simulacrum of disinterest.

The first skirmishes in the presidential-judiciary war of 1937 occurred in 1935 when the "Nine Old Men" gave an adverse decision in the "hot-oil" case.[1]

Soon after the Court said that the oil business could not be regulated

---

[1] *Nine Old Men* was the title of a contemporary book by two indefatigable and unabashed columnists, Drew Pearson and Robert Allen. The "hot-oil" case had a special legal interest because the declared unconstitutionality consisted in an undue delegation of legislative authority to the President, a principle afterward important in the NRA case. This was the first time a statute had been invalidated for this reason, but it was understood at once that it would not be the last. A new hazard had been added to the "due process" clause and the narrowing interstate commerce clause, hitherto the chief obstacles to regulatory legislation. All advocates of government attempts to enhance welfare and to establish stability were alerted at once. It was clear that the principle could not be abandoned by the administration without losing its claim of progressive advance.

Big Mistake

by the federal government, the "gold-clause cases" came up. Immense interests were involved in these; indeed the whole of the monetary program was jeopardized. Franklin thought for a time that everything he had done to affect prices might be called illegal. Anticipating it, he prepared a fighting statement; he was "going to the country." But the Court did not accommodate him. It held the gold clause legal as to private contracts. As to public obligations, the statute was held inadmissible; but since no damage had been proved, this reverse had no practical effect. And Franklin decided against immediate challenge of the Court.

But presently the Railroad Retirement Act was declared unconstitutional. This had set up a scheme for paying pensions to railroad employees. And not only was NRA invalidated, but two other adverse decisions were handed down. One of these declared the Frazier-Lemke Act, designed to ease the paying of farm mortgages, unconstitutional; and the other held—this time unanimously—that the President could not remove a Federal Trade Commissioner.[2]

These decisions, taken together, constituted an intolerable rejection of Franklin's leadership and an open affront to the executive. But the judges had gone too far. From this time on there was very wide acknowledgment that it would have to be made impossible for the conservative prejudices to base themselves on the Constitution. Indeed, the liberal minority of the Court was already protesting what they regarded as a perversion of the judicial powers.

For some kind of Court reform Franklin felt, after this, he had very general support. He indicated that a proposal would be forthcoming. And using the NRA decision as a text, he spoke of "horse-and-buggy" ideas, a phrase so apt that it immediately gained the currency of a popular aphorism. Yet it does have to be said that this particular decision was opportune and that it was a relief to have NRA terminated. That he was rescued from an embarrassment was something Franklin himself could not acknowledge. Nevertheless, it was probably this that prevented his immediate declaration of war on the Court.

If open battle was not at once joined, a kind of twilight war did begin. Unfortunately, as it began differences over strategy were tormenting Franklin's staff. These would not resolve themselves easily. Franklin would have to choose among alternatives, and his choice for once would be very wrong. His defeat in 1937 on this issue would be traceable directly to his own mistakes. He decided against the honest method of asking for a constitutional amendment and consented to a court-packing scheme devised by Homer Cummings, the Attorney General. He also decided not to go to the country during the campaign but to spring a

[2] Although in an earlier case the Court had held that the President had the power to remove any officer he appointed.

385

surprise reform bill on the Congress after election. To make the list of errors complete, he decided—although this was not until 1937—that he would appeal for his bill by contending not that the justices opposed progress but that they were too old to carry out their duties and needed younger coadjutors. All three of these decisions were so abhorrent to moderate minds that they must be held responsible for widespread defection among his supporters; on strictly professional grounds he deserved to lose his battle.

It should be added at once, however, that all the disappointments involved in the failure of the proposed bill and his undoubted chagrin should not obscure the usefulness of the fight as a political incident. It is impossible to determine after the fact how calculatingly the Court was used as a foil. I myself find it impossible to believe that Franklin developed the issue without fully realizing that its long-run consequences must in a sense be favorable, however its immediate phase might be decided. He may have been angered by failure to impose his will on the Congress. He undoubtedly was. Yet if he had won, a valuable issue would have been lost to him.

The dramatic episodes of the Court controversy occurred in two series, so to speak, with an interval between. The first series consisted of Court opinions nullifying New Deal acts with some dark objecting by Franklin but no specific reprisal. The second series reversed the initiative. It began with Franklin's message to the Congress on February 5, 1937, which was accompanied by a proposed reorganization act which would have reduced the Court's powers to obstruct social change.

There followed scenes in three locales—the Court itself, the Congress, and the White House. When the second series began, all other interests were, for a matter of months, adjourned. The drama had the nation's full attention. Franklin's tactics called for minimizing the significance of his proposal, but actually his most intense interest was engaged. The Court had injured his *amour propre* even more than his sense of presidential dignity, and he was not the man to retreat from such a test. As usual, he chose his own time and his own methods. It was necessary, as he knew very well, to prepare carefully. But to those who recognized the signs it was clear from the first that this was a matter he meant to pursue. And, as it developed, it became apparent that he had more in mind than a rebuke to the justices.

The minor actors in the drama were not the same from scene to scene; but, as they would in any well-constructed play, the protagonists continued in their respective parts throughout. First among them, playing opposite Franklin, were the Court's members. The reading of most interest in a catalogue of the justices would be from right to left. At the far right were the four hard Tories: Willis J. Van Devanter, Pierce Butler, James Clark McReynolds, and George Sutherland. At the far left were the three liberals: Harlan Fiske Stone, Louis Dembitz Brandeis, and Benjamin N. Cardozo. In the center were Owen J. Roberts and, above all, the Chief Justice, Charles Evans Hughes.

The President's opposite number, the Chief Justice, was a worthy opponent. He had once lost the presidency by the slightest of margins (in 1916, when Wilson, for the second time, had become a minority President); he had been so successful a politician that he had become governor of New York, and he had been such a notable governor that he was still recalled as one of New York's best. He had become famous first for the exposure of doubtful practices among insurance companies, and so ranked as one of the nation's crusaders. Beyond all this, he had been the outstanding character in Harding's cabinet, and as Secretary of State had made contributions to peace considered worthy of any professional diplomat. Now he was an elder statesman, a man of integrity and weight, whose character was unassailable and whose appearance alone sufficed to impress beholders. Comparison with Jove was often made in his later years, and it seemed wholly appropriate. He was distant, reserved, and dignified; his beard and his robes became him; he was very nearly the embodiment of that judicial image the conservatives were at such pains to propagate.

Similarly, it must be said that to those who regarded the Court as the protector of the privileged, the Chief Justice was the very symbol of all they detested. But what those who calculated the probable outcome of the struggle often missed was that under the heavy disguise there operated one of the shrewdest of political intelligences. And these underestimators included Franklin. Hughes was a match even for the experienced tactician in the White House—and not only in experience but in wiliness as well. The combination of Hughes and Wheeler[3] would prove too much for Franklin.

There was, in the struggle between President and Court, a third party at interest. This was the Congress. It was impossible for the legislators to be indifferent when the governmental balance of power was in question. They had traditional differences with both the executive and the judiciary. It might be thought that their strongest impulse would be to hold the Court in check; it was, after all, their acts which the Court had assumed the right to review. The fact was, however, that the differences between the executive and the legislature had grown so acute in recent decades that the Court and the Congress had developed a tacit liaison. And this crucially affected the course of the battle in 1937.

[3] Burton K. Wheeler, Democratic senator from Montana, so old a progressive that he had been the vice-presidential running mate of the elder La Follette in 1924. He really enters this drama in its second act, but he was already antagonistic to Franklin and ready to do him harm if he could.

An explanation of this alliance is to be found not only in the nature of the respective institutions but also in the preference of the legislative branch for conservative policies. And doubtless the preponderance of lawyers in both Houses had its effect. It was often said that senators who failed to become President—as most of them felt was their due—thought that the least recognition their talents should have was a federal judgeship, preferably on the Supreme Court. Gradually the prestige and the emoluments of the courts had been enhanced until there was no position in public life to rival judgeships in compensation, security, or prestige—not even, in all these respects, the presidency. An attack on the Supreme Court was felt vicariously by every prospective member of the judiciary; and most of these were in one or the other House.

All this is said to explain why Franklin's aggression, when it developed, could be so easily deflected. Within a few days of the sending of his message, a group of senators—Borah, Burke, McNary, Vandenberg, and Wheeler operating as a steering committee—assumed active leadership of the opposition. It was most discouraging that it should be preponderantly progressive; and it was most depressing that Wheeler, so hung about with progressive credentials, should be the chosen captain. It was something Franklin would never forget or forgive. How could he keep it clear that the opposition was reactionary when so many progressives were standing against him? He did, of course, have young Bob La Follette and that rock of integrity, George Norris. These were as authentically liberal as Wheeler. But for the rest he was dependent on dragooning Democrats into service, most of whom were very reluctant indeed, and who had a constant tendency to succumb as pressures and blandishments developed.

It may have been that Franklin decided against opening the fight in 1936 because of apprehension that just such a line-up would occur. There was sufficient reaction to certain of his less temperate statements to furnish such a preview of what actually happened. But if in 1936 he temporized, it was only to select his own time and his own device. The better time would be when his power had been renewed. The device would be a procedural law to be passed by a newly elected Congress. Meanwhile he prepared the way.

When the Court, in its now irrational determination to check his presumption, went on into the campaign months unchanged and unrepentant, he considered that it was preparing its own chastisement. For nothing could be clearer than that the tide of approval for himself and for his policies was gathering for a mighty demonstration. Court and Court supporters would be swamped in its flood.

As so stirring an account of this incident as that of Alsop and Catledge is read, it is well to keep in mind that after the curtain fell on their drama there were consequences they did not record.[4] The conservatives would believe, when it was all over, that they had won; and so they had if only the congressional battle is considered, but this is not the important consideration for after years. The significant result is that Franklin had engaged a classic enemy of the people, had fought a good fight, and had made his way deeper into the affections of his supporters. Americans appreciate their champions even if they register their approval only on stated electoral occasions and are drowned out in the intervals by louder voices of denunciation.

Between the first and second acts of the drama there occurred the election of 1936, and one of the interesting phases of the action is how the Court's perverseness was made to count for electoral purposes. It shows Franklin at his tactical best, as the post-election strategy shows him at his worst. After the outlawing of NRA, the equivocal gold-clause decisions, the decisions concerning oil and coal, and the AAA opinion, Franklin was in a position to say that the Court had made it impossible for either the federal government or the states to protect the public interest by regulating business. Any attempted limitation on industrial or commercial activity was either not "interstate commerce" or it was the taking of property "without due process of law." By the first test, federal regulation was prohibited; by the second, the states were unable to act. Between the two nothing could be done.

A sharp distinction has to be made between the two kinds of regulation sought to be imposed by either or both governments: the one had to do with welfare; the other had to do with business competition. If the same constitutional principles had not been necessary to both, the line-up of antagonists would have been different. Businessmen wanted regulations limiting unfair competitive practices; many others—notably labor organizations—were interested in other regulations protecting welfare. For a long time business lawyers had sought ways of achieving the one without bringing about the other. And labor's lawyers had always contended that union activities were not among those prohibited as conspiracies in restraint of trade. Each group sought the assistance of the Constitution for its own purposes, but each resisted the application of constitutional principles when its interests might be adversely affected.

Unfortunately the Constitution was a pre-industrial instrument. It

[4] The book referred to here is *The 168 Days* (New York: Doubleday, 1938), surely one of the most brilliant accounts of a complex political occurrence ever written. The authors' characterizations of the actors were sharp and just, but they had to guess at a good deal of the hidden maneuvering, and they were free with attributions of motive. Still theirs was an almost unprecedented contemporary performance. That they were mostly mistaken about the long-run consequences detracts only slightly from the interest of the essay. A more detached and scholarly discussion of the issues involved is to be found in *The Supreme Court Issue and the Constitution*, by W. R. Barnes and A. W. Littlefield (New York: Barnes & Noble, 1937).

contained no specific references to such issues as had now arisen. Its authors would have needed to be prophets to have furnished the guidance needed now. This lack made it possible for those who had one or another view of the most desirable interpretation to argue that the general clauses it did contain supported their contention. To the conservatives the "due process" clause meant that the regulation of wages and hours illegally deprived them of property. To the unionist the mention of welfare meant that it was the duty of the government to establish and protect a minimum well-being; regulation of business, they contended, *was* due process.

This difference, as much as any other, divided conservatives from progressives in the United States. Because the division grew sharper as industrialism advanced, the difficulty for justices who must decide what the Constitution did mean in these respects grew greater. It became a regular thing for such liberals as Holmes and Stone to protest that the conservative justices were deciding as their social and economic preferences disposed them to do. Since the Constitution was equivocal, the liberals would not have pretended that the Constitution furnished direction; they would have allowed the lawmaking branches to decide.

This, as a matter of fact, was the position taken by Franklin. He wanted the Court to stop obstructing merely because the justices did not approve what the other two branches had decided on as policy. His differences with the legislature he was prepared to handle by political means, and in any case he and they were tied together in lawmaking. The legislature passed bills, and the executive approved or rejected them. Both had to submit to election. But—and here was an enormous difference—the Court did not. It was sheltered behind life appointments. Only in an indirect and long-run sense did it need to consider public opinion. Franklin proposed to reduce this remoteness.

There were two possible approaches to Court reform. The Constitution could be amended to provide for social and economic regulation, or something violent could be done to change the make-up of the Court so that it would agree to regulation. An amendment would take some time and require a good deal of manipulation even after the Congress had been persuaded to approve it. Getting it through three quarters of the state legislatures, aside from the effort involved, might require years. To shorten the time would involve extraordinary efforts. It was, of course, the forthright and permanent cure. If it was done carefully it could establish the missing principles by which the Court could be guided as it judged legislation in the industrial age. It need not present the legislative or the executive branches with fundamental powers they did not now possess. It could merely extend the power to regulate into the new areas of technology.

There were those among Franklin's people who argued strongly for amendment. When it became evident that he was turning toward another method, they were, in various ways, disturbed and disappointed. Among some of them this amounted to shock as they slowly came to understand Franklin's real purpose. The progressives generally felt more or less deeply this way. Of these, I may say I was one. But my protests, like those of others, were ineffective.

All progressives and liberals had been antagonized by the Court. It could not be allowed to go on prohibiting necessary regulation. This was true whether or not the kinds of changes Franklin sponsored were approved. That matter could be settled appropriately in legislative battles. This preponderance of opinion among liberals that "something must be done" had not been reached until in 1936 the Women's Minimum Wage Law of New York was struck down. Opinion had been shaping even before this decision, but only slowly; and even then the feeling was far from unanimous; those who did not share it, however, were those few who were far rightists in political philosophy. As the situation was now, workers had been refused labor legislation, farmers had been denied relief, and the Social Security System had been put in jeopardy by the prohibition against compulsory pension schemes. The justices had become heroes to members of the National Manufacturers Association and perhaps to most upper-bracket lawyers, but to almost no one else.

The question still remained: What was it best to do? Franklin, considering it and listening to conflicting advice, refused premature commitment. Even in the famous "horse-and-buggy" press conference he shut off discussion when reporters pressed him about a course of action.[5]

Being a politician and having an election to face in 1936, he followed

---

[5] The phrase, abstracted from Franklin's statement on the occasion of the NRA decision, was cleverly spotted by Francis Stephenson, an experienced White House reporter. It did symbolize what was, in effect, a lecture of some length exploring the issue posed by the Court's action. The point was made that if the Court's view of interstate commerce prevailed it would reverse what had until then been a uniform tendency to "view the interstate commerce clause in the light of present-day civilization." He enlarged on the changes hitherto recognized by the justices as necessitating "an evolution in interstate commerce." He then listed four "major human activities," which the decision said were out of reach of federal regulatory powers: construction, mining, manufacturing, and agriculture. The absurdity of depending on state regulation to establish fair competition and protect workers and consumers was argued. "We are," he said, "facing a very, very great national non-partisan issue. We have got to decide one way or the other . . . whether in some way we are going to restore to the Federal Government the powers which exist in the national governments of every other Nation in the world to enact and administer laws that have a hearing on, and general control over, national economic problems and national social problems."

It was an impressive performance for one who was not a legal expert, and the reporters were responsive. The attention he got in the press was very wide; if most of it was unfavorable that, perhaps, was what he expected at the opening of what was obviously to be a long campaign.

the normal rule. He evaded a decision that would have divided his party. He allowed the campaign to develop rather as a general referendum on the New Deal. The Republicans tried to press the Court issue. He refused the gambit, but naturally proceeded to extract every drop of credit coming to him for his efforts to promote well-being. That was the paramount issue of the New Deal years.

He was attacked for inconsistency, which, on the facts, might have been damaging if anyone was interested, but apparently hardly anyone was. He had tried to improve people's condition; the "economic royalists" had opposed and sometimes prevented him from achieving what he had intended. That their chief instrument was the Court, most people knew; and if they did not, the Republicans saw to it that they did. The Court, as they represented it, was the bulwark of liberty; in Franklin's reference it was the protector of privilege. The third branch of government was unreformed. It was, Franklin had said, "out of step." But it was not he who insisted on the issue during the campaign.

When the election had been won, Franklin occupied a position no President in recent history had attained. If he felt that the overwhelming approval was a mandate to press on toward those objectives he had defined as necessary, it is hard to see how he could have felt otherwise. And if he felt himself free to proceed in the way that seemed to him best, it is hard to see how he could have anticipated a check. Even if he went beyond what he had intimated was his goal, who now could stop him? Those who had opposed him would recognize his power; they would understand that he could always "go to the country" and that his support would rally swiftly and overpoweringly.

If Franklin, who not only had a vivid sense of presidential prerogatives but who by election and re-election was the chosen leader of the American people, felt that the obstructions of the Court constituted an impertinent denial of his right to act as leader, there was certainly justification. It has been suggested that the Humphries case constituted an affront to the presidency. It may very well have been that case, even more than the other decisions of 1935, which provided the motive for the post-election attempt to humiliate the Court in turn; for of all the ways open to him, Franklin does seem to have chosen the one most upsetting to judicial dignity. And it was this more than anything else—more even than the attempt to reduce the judicial power—which created reaction of a violence he hardly anticipated. Most of those who wanted to eliminate the interferences of the Court with progress still had a deep concern for its dignity. Senators who were lawyers, particularly, found that in the end they could not condone such an affront as was proposed.[6]

[6] Removal from the Federal Trade Commission in the Humphries case was justified on the simple ground of lack of confidence. Franklin wanted to appoint

Alsop and Catledge, in a few paragraphs of *The 168 Days*,[7] penetrated the bland surface Franklin presented to the world except on
those few occasions when he momentarily gave way to irritation, as he
did several times during the Court fight. Speaking of him, they said
(and it is perhaps well to recall that the Alsop understanding had its
beginning in a distant cousinship, also that the account was written
immediately after the events they described):

The Court's conservative decisions not only outraged his love of power;
more important still, they frustrated his good intentions. Indeed, they virtually
denied their existence, although the most obvious thing about Franklin
Delano Roosevelt is that his intentions are good. Where his intellectual response to a given situation may be inadequate, where his administrative habits
are often strikingly peculiar, his emotions are generally deep and true. He is
so evidently a man of good will that the voters, accustomed to politicians of
a very different sort, have sometimes been ready to take his wish for his deed.
To him the lot of the underprivileged and distressed is an ever-present problem. To him the great dilemmas of modern society are always at hand, calling
for solutions which will usher in an era of greater security and fuller living.
To him the whole future is a challenge, a time to be conquered by fore-
thought in the present. It was this emotional quality in the President which
gave him his splendid aptness to a troubled moment of 1933.

His excellent intentions are only reinforced by his unusual awareness of
his own historic role—best expressed in his celebrated remark at the time of
his first inauguration, that if he proved a bad president, he was also likely to
prove the last president. Such an awareness would oppress most other men
to the point of stultification; not so the President. . . . Once he vouchsafed
the explanation that he knew more about psychology, and especially mass
psychology, than any expert or professor in the business, and that his knowledge always permitted him to reach his objectives in time. As a former White
House intimate has pointed out, he has an almost mystical belief in his own
ability to perform his role with perfect adequacy.

No man of such self-confident good will could have knuckled under to the
Court forever. Least of all could the President, in whom the Court's reactionary decisions aroused all the vindictiveness and obstinacy which are as
strongly his as good intentions or love of power. He wanted to pay off his
score with the Court as well as to make his good will effective.

It is true that his remarks about the Court at the time of the NRA
decision (in May 1935) roused an impassioned protest from the press.
The extent and violence of this reaction did not frighten the reformer,
but they spoke to the politician. The time to act had not yet come. He

---

someone else. Humphries sued to regain his place but died before the suit
was settled. His widow continued the action. The Court directed that his salary
be paid to the time of his death. It also—and this was the irritant—forbade future
dismissals of the duly appointed and confirmed members of such commissions.
It seemed vital to Franklin that the executive powers extensively employed by
these "semi-judicial" agencies should not remain beyond presidential control.

[7] Pp. 14–15.

would wait until the election was over and the flood of his power had gathered its greatest strength. If there were those who thought the noisy attacks had changed his intentions, they did not know him very well. He felt securely based not only in his union with the electorate but also in presidential tradition. The outburst of indignation in an already prejudiced press might make him more cautious, but it could not change his mind. He had never in his life considered himself to be so right on any issue, and he was certain that popular opinion, however the press might distort its appearance, was with him.

It may seem strange that a lawyer would permit himself so frank an appraisal of the Court's position and, if his status as a lawyer did not restrain him, that he should not treat more respectfully one of the sacred cows of politics. For however much politicians knew of the way judges came to the bench and their habitual bias in favor of their sponsors, they assiduously protected the illusion that mere men were transformed by putting on the robes of judicial office. That Franklin was not so restrained, in spite of the caution he used in other respects, shows how thoroughly he belonged to the executive branch of government even before he became President. And this identification had, since then, been reinforced not only by natural presidential self-consciousness but by having the Court behave in a violently unwise manner. The provocation offered by the 1935 cases, therefore, reinforced an already alert prejudice. His determination to act was both personal and official. Something would have to be done or he himself would be written down as incapable of achieving for Americans what he was deeply committed to bring about. And the presidency would have received more severe injury during his incumbency than during that of any of his predecessors. It can be imagined how intolerable such a thought must have been.

But if he seemed to abandon caution in the "horse-and-buggy" press conference after the NRA decision, and if, indeed, he did arouse passionate protest from the conservatives, his daring was only seeming. At the end of the conference, when he said that decision one way or the other was imperative, he hedged about time: "I don't mean this summer or winter or next fall, but over a period, perhaps, of five or ten years . . ." Also, he refused to suggest, for the benefit of the opponents he expected to have, what he intended to do. This may have been because he did not actually know; on the other hand, it is too much in the pattern of his usual presidential method not to have about it the suggestion of deliberateness. What happened on that day and during the subsequent weeks indicates to me his gratification that his enemy was now out in the open. He would establish that enemy's wickedness firmly in as many other minds as possible, and then he would choose his own method, his own time, and his own allies as he proceeded to the attack.

394

The Court made an ideal opponent in many ways, especially as it was then constituted. Its conservative majority was blindly determined to have its own way. These outright Tories had abandoned the flexibility which, through many crises, had protected the judiciary from reprisals originating in other branches. They were now opposing measures of change which, if not individually wise, still were possible and reasonable ways of attacking the vital problem of institutional accommodation which had been far too long delayed. They had allowed themselves —had indeed volunteered—to become the defenders of groups and classes whose prestige had drastically diminished during the depression. The Court had on its side only dignity; and this a President, with all the weapons he commanded, might easily undermine. The Nine Old Men were close to the danger of ridicule; and once ridicule began, dignity would melt away.

The worst weakness of the Court was somewhat like the worst weakness of the presidency: it had to be supported by legislative action. This was not only because funds had to be voted by the Congress; it was also because the Congress could reshape the Court on any model it chose, just as the Congress could revamp the executive establishment.[8] The Constitution said a good deal about jurisdiction but nothing at all about organization. It was not specified that the Congress should determine the Court's numbers or its rules; but who else could possess that power?

That daring Federalist Chief Justice, John Marshall, who had asserted the right to determine the constitutionality of laws, had been operating in a no man's land; his tour de force was good only if the other branches either concurred or were unable to overrule him. Such an arbiter of constitutional questions was undoubtedly necessary, which accounted for long acquiescence in the Court's bold occupation of such high ground; but the ability to hold it, as most justices—including Marshall—had recognized, depended very considerably on discretion. The Court must not allow itself to be maneuvered into untenable positions. It was a certain flexibility in Uncle Ted's time that had led the caustic humorist Mr. Dooley to remark that the Supreme Court followed the election returns. The justices, in the larger strategic sense, must be politicians. They were vulnerable. And the continuance of their prerogatives depended upon their holding the substantial confidence of the country.

Franklin obviously believed that the Tory majority had, by its intemperance, created an exploitable situation; they had become vulnerable. And obviously he proposed to enhance the presidency at the Court's expense, much as Marshall had enhanced the Court at the expense of

[8] The Court was actually more vulnerable; legislative acts at least needed the President's signature.

the lawmaking branches. He did in fact intend to end the Court's simple and sole prerogative of interpretation. That he would have no compunction about this had been shown by his Baltimore remark in 1932. Ousting the reactionary justices would be no more a moral matter than ousting Hoover from the White House. They were servants of the people too; their obligation to serve impartially had been abandoned; they must be recalled to their duties.

Considering what must have been in Franklin's mind from the first, a biographer is struck by the way the campaign of attrition was handled. Long after this controversy had been superseded by others and Franklin had come to the editing of his public papers, it still haunted him. The very titles of the volumes are revealing. That for 1935 was headed *The Court Disapproves;* that for 1936, *The People Approve;* and that for 1937, *The Constitution Prevails.* The plain inference of this sequence is that the Court had been wrong from the first about the Constitution and that he had been right. This had been established in the election, when the people had approved. And the picture is that of the Constitution being upheld by President and people against a Court determined to destroy it by interpretation. This is undoubtedly the view posterity was intended to accept.

There are a very few lawyers who would approve this statement of the issue. It is a politician's approach. Yet there is no way to interpret the change in the Court's attitude in 1937 as contrasted with 1935 except by attributing precisely the same reasoning to Chief Justice Hughes and Mr. Justice Roberts. Without admitting openly that it was being done, they solemnly, and with all the paraphernalia of legal exposition, reversed themselves. Going over to the liberal minority, they made it a majority. What had in 1935 been the reasoning of dissent now became the rule of law. It was now the elderly who deplored and deprecated; the government's third branch had given way to the New Deal. There is no sophistical argument capable of making this change anything but what it was—a political decision. The Chief Justice—and one of his associates—had decided not that the contentions of the President had a new force but that the Court as an institution must be removed from a looming danger.

That danger to the Court was made definite in the plan submitted to the Congress on a February day while a sitting was in process. Alsop and Catledge, in a realistic passage,[9] describe the arrival of the news among the justices. This may be taken as the opening of the second act of the drama:

Shortly before 1 P.M. on February 5, 1937, the lawyers and sightseers crowding the benches of the Supreme Court room observed a curious phe-

[9] *Op. cit.,* p. 135.

nomenon. A page slipped through the curtains behind the justices' dais. Quietly, very quietly he hurried down the row of justices, handing a paper to each of the nine. Each glanced at what he had been given; Cardozo read most of it, and Sutherland and Stone took the trouble to read it through to the end. A tiny incident it would have been anywhere else, but that strange chamber, so like the interior of a classical icebox decorated by an insane upholsterer, has a routine which seems to have been fixed at the moment of the creation of the world. The justices' brief inattention was as striking as a small noise in a very large, very silent empty space. The lawyer at the rostrum, disconcerted, paused for a second in his exposition. A murmur ran down the benches. What could these documents be which so interested the justices? What were these papers?

What so interested the justices was soon made evident. The court attendant had brought the documents from the Senate chamber where they had just been read. There were three: the President's message, a letter from the Attorney General to the President, and a proposed judiciary bill. The bill itself had four proposals: (1) that when any judge of any federal court who had served ten years and become seventy and had not resigned within six months, the President might appoint a coadjutor to the same bench; (2) that the numbers of any bench should be increased permanently by coadjutors, but that the Supreme Court should not have more than six additional justices, nor any lower court more than two, nor the total federal judiciary more than fifty; (3) that circuit judges might be assigned as extras to any unusually busy circuit court of appeal, and that district judges might be added to any district court; (4) that the Supreme Court, through a proctor, should supervise the lower courts, watching litigation and recommending to the Chief Justice the assignment of extra judges.

It is not too much to say that many of Franklin's most loyal supporters, including those convinced that some reform was needed, were depressed by his choice of methods; but if the bill seemed to them unwise, they were positively horrified by the wording of the message. It had to be described as tricky; and in such a serious matter as this, affecting the very structure of government, anything less than the most earnest and high-minded argument seemed to them out of place. Instead of addressing himself to the constitutional question in everyone's mind, Franklin had chosen to dwell on the inefficiency of the courts, on injustices caused by delays, and on the inability of the aged judges to understand modern issues.[10] To have said this to a Court which only

[10] On this matter the message said: "Modern complexities call also for a constant infusion of new blood into the courts, just as it is needed in executive functions of the Government and in private business. A lowered mental or physical vigor leads men to avoid an examination of complicated and changed conditions. Little by little, new facts become blurred through old glasses fitted, as it were, for the needs of another generation; older men, assuming that the

recently had included Holmes and which now included Brandeis and Cardozo was insulting. It was also contrary to fact. Age was no criterion of liberalism, and certainly years did not detract from experience or wisdom. The argument was on its face specious and was at once recognized as such by all who read the message.

How did Franklin conclude that this evasive approach to so serious an issue for the nation could possibly be effective? First, I think the message has to be understood as no more than a bad example of a habitual method. There had been and would be others almost equally illustrative of his usual indirection even if none so doubtfully scrupulous. It should be said at once—as I have said before—that this sort of thing was inherent in the method practiced by Franklin. This was well enough understood by everyone. It had nothing to do with ends, only with means. And the judgment of a politician's worth was not whether he resorted to such means but whether he got statesmanlike results.

There is a kind of distinction to be made between those practitioners of the political arts who know what they are doing and those who do not. There have been in the American past some supreme hypocrites who never allowed themselves to understand the depravity of many resorts to which they were forced. There have been others who understood and faced reality, accepting the immolations of conscience as inseparable from the getting and keeping of position. The justification even those have had was that their attaining of power resulted in good. This may seem to the critic an unjustified claim, but the critic has the advantage of hindsight. Many a politician has intended more than he could deliver. And this was as true of Franklin as of any. What he would have done cannot be measured against his accomplishments; it can rightly be measured only against his intentions, and in such a comparison it would only be possible to guess at the disparity. Yet a study of the record shows it to be indisputably impressive. Superb as his talent was and well controlled as his scruples were, still the reactionaries in Congress kept him far distant from his goals. It may be guessed that he was satisfied that he could have done no more, but that is a guess.

Franklin would in the end gain something from this affair even though he would lose the current battle, but his method of dissimulation amounting almost to deceit would in this instance be inappropriate. He would lose the immediate battle not because he misjudged public opinion but because he was careless in his choice of method, perhaps made so by an electoral victory that would have inflated any leader's opinion of his own power. He obviously felt that the Congress would not resist a leader with so tremendous a proved following. But about

scene is the same as it was in the past, cease to explore or inquire into the present or the future." The reader might here be reminded that Justice Brandeis was now eighty. *Public Papers,* 1937 vol., p. 55.

the necessity for bringing such weight to bear specifically where it would result in legal approval for his program, even Franklin still had much to learn. It was taught him in the months subsequent to February 1937. He would not take the lesson too kindly; he would find it hard to believe that the Congress could resist needs and demands he himself felt to be compelling, however they were presented. In 1938, in another mid-term congressional election, he would attempt the famous "purge" of legislators who had stubbornly opposed his—and the people's —desires and who were up for re-election. His score would not be very high.

If Franklin learned from his defeat, he never admitted that he had made at least a tactical error if not one of principle. As he saw it—or sought to have others see it—he was simply defeated by recalcitrant reactionaries. At any rate, he handled the thing badly from the first, and when it was over he had so little capital remaining that in 1939 he could hardly buy from the hard bargainers in the Congress what he began to feel was vital to national survival. They were harder bargainers —the congressmen—because they had measured him for defeat in 1937 and because in spite of his hold on the American electorate they had not been rebuked. Their relative immunity taught them independence. They felt free to consort with the company they preferred.[11]

---

[11] When the Court fight was going on, Robert H. Jackson of the Chautauqua County (N.Y.) bar was an Assistant Attorney General, having been promoted from the Treasury, where he had been special counsel since 1934. (In 1938 he would become Solicitor General and in 1941 a justice of the Supreme Court.) He was a junior, of course, but accepted as a member of the White House team. He would die in 1954, but not before he had published his reflections on the Court's position in the national scheme. To him it would seem, more than a decade later, that "not one of the basic power conflicts which precipitated the Roosevelt struggle against the judiciary has been eliminated or settled." He would still be uneasy about checks and balances. "The old conflict between the branches of government," he would say, "is ready to break out again whenever the provocation becomes significant." But he would be able to offer by way of advice only the suggestion that the Court should use restraint. The judges ought to be careful not to limit unreasonably the Congress's constitutional powers to regulate, and chary about jurisdiction when it could be avoided. (These observations occur in *The Supreme Court in the American System of Government,* Cambridge: Harvard University Press, 1955.)

One of the reviewers of Mr. Justice Jackson's book (Professor Edmond Cahn of the New York University School of Law, writing in the New York *Times Book Review,* July 10, 1955) would remark of the Court struggle that it was one "in which Roosevelt lost the battle but won the war." In this, he would say, "It was like every other American war in one respect: when the conflict was over and victory emerged, the victors could not agree on what they had been fighting for. . . ." And it is true that retrospective judgments of the issues in 1937 would be thoroughly confused. The lawyers did realize, however, even if only dimly, that Franklin's intention was to shift the balance of governmental power. He intended that the President and the Congress, as the policy-forming and lawmaking branches, should be made immune to judicial check or, at the least, that their immunity should be widened. He did not say this. He never

399

The liberals who, as he felt, failed him sensed a sinister intention, although they had nothing definite to go on; and it was because of this that they were opposed. They feared an indefinitely strengthened executive. They were highly sensitized to dictatorship by Hitler and Mussolini; and Franklin had showed signs, they thought, of suggestive impatience. Nevertheless, they did "want something done," and when they defined it, what they wanted was freedom for the legislative branch to regulate business in the interest of public welfare. They felt the same frustration that Franklin felt about the no man's land in which neither the federal nor the state governments could touch business enterprise. But they did not want, as Franklin did, to reconstitute the Court so that on no issue could it oppose the other branches. Decidedly, this was too much. They felt, for instance, that the Court was right in the matter of Humphries, which had so incensed Franklin. This fear of theirs was why they much preferred an amendment that would have brought business within the regulatory scope of the government but would not have taken from the Court its power to interpret the Constitution. That power they regarded as an invaluable protection of many precious liberties. It was why they had committed the party firmly to amendment in its judicial plank last June in Philadelphia.

Franklin, as we have seen, argued that this would take too long, but what he meant was that it would not give him what he wanted. Actually he felt that the Court's power to interpret the Constitution was one that had been seized by a doubtful tour de force. He rather more than hinted at this in the introduction to the first volume of *Public Papers* which referred to the struggle,[12] saying that it was "academic now to discuss whether it was originally intended that the Courts should exercise this power" and going on to remark that the Supreme Court's own restraint had been all that had made the judicial assumption tolerable.[13] The gravamen of his present complaint was that this self-imposed rule of restraint had had only lip service from the courts "during the last fifty years." For this there was good authority—for instance, Mr. Justice Holmes, who had said in 1930 that it seemed to him incredible that the Fourteenth Amendment "was intended to give us *carte blanche* to embody our moral or political beliefs in its prohibitions."

If the Court had not always been restrained, neither had the execu-

---

approached it except by inference, as when he spoke disparagingly of aged judges' views of "modern matters"; he came closer in after-battle comment. But even this was equivocal.

[12] Vol. IV, p. 3.

[13] As illustrated by Mr. Justice Washington's remarks in Ogden *vs.* Saunders in 1827 (12 Wheat. 213, 217): "It is but a decent respect due to the wisdom, integrity, and the patriotism of the legislative body, by which any law is passed, to presume in favor of its validity, until its violation of the Constitution is proved beyond any reasonable doubt." This sort of remark had many times been repeated by other justices. Franklin had studied them all.

tive or the legislative. And there were those who, in the time when Franklin was making up his mind, argued with some vehemence that restraint would cover the present case; it was, they said, essential to the maintenance of a structure so delicately balanced as that of government under the Constitution. It may not have been intended so by the founders, who evidently had some illusions about automatism, but actually the balance was very easily upset if one branch was given the least added power to compel the acquiescence of the others. Self-restraint was not only the safest reliance, it was the only one.

Franklin heard so much of this point of view but was so unconvinced by it that its effect was not to deflect his intention, but rather to induce resort to much more than usual indirection. And he appears to have been genuinely surprised that the liberals of all schools and degrees saw through his subterfuge instantly and, unless they had the strongest reasons for not doing so, promptly joined the opposition. He seems to have thought that they would approve.

What resulted was a line-up after a week or two, and before any open moves had been made in either House, in which the far right and the far left were joined in a common cause. This was easier because the objective was purely negative—the defeat of a presidential proposal. But it proved to be an extremely effective coalition.

On Franklin's side in the congressional engagement the captain was Senator Joseph T. Robinson, the majority leader. Robinson was a bulky, bull-voiced man with limited sensitivity but used to the kind of leadership demanded by party discipline. He was accustomed to taking and giving orders, and he expected to obey and to be obeyed. When he had to buy support, he paid the usual price and demanded the usual return. He did not like the Court bill when he understood it; he belonged, after all, to the southern conservative bloc. But the President and Farley had treated him with due deference, and it was not in his book to go against the head of the party.[14] Others of his clique were roughly of the same disposition; but whereas their loyalty was unequal to the strain put on it by Franklin's demands in the present instance—particularly after they heard from home—his had the added buttressing of official position.

During the ensuing months of almost indescribably complicated bargaining and maneuvering, Robinson sat in his mahogany and plush Capitol office, summoning colleagues and listening to their demands, arranging payment and then disposing their efforts to suit his tactical sense. When the Senate was in session he often spoke and oftener buttonholed the reluctant in the lobbies. The trouble was that, contrary to rule, they did not stay persuaded. Even after he had lined them up

[14] It is not irrelevant that he was promised the first available appointment to the Court.

they tended to stray. Only after several months of such labor did he get down to a hard core of Senate votes, and when he did it was short of a majority. He redoubled his efforts, but the situation did not improve.

The opposition was ably led throughout by Wheeler and a few others. Wheeler was a natural Irish rebel who had fought the copper interests in his state without gloves and had escaped their punishment at last. He was not a trusted leader in the Senate; he was too individualistic to be predictable or to accept discipline. But he was agile and determined. He did not like Franklin, for reasons of his own. These were never clear to me, but that they had originated in resentment that Franklin had seized the progressive leadership I was fairly certain. Resentment was, however, compounded with distrust; he simply did not believe that Franklin meant well and would not accept his leadership.[15] When he read the message accompanying the reorganization act, he was so outraged at its implications of unintelligence among legislators that he repudiated his already tenuous affiliation. In this fight he took or was given the lead. But after several months, when he counted his certain votes, he lacked a majority, just as Robinson did. It was time then for compromise—or so the two practical politicians thought.

Franklin, when he should have agreed to compromise, would not. And his refusal was of a piece with his management of the affair from the start. There were several ready suggestions. Since there were many more legislators who wanted some change than there were who would accept Franklin's version of what that change ought to be, the compromisers at a certain stage held the balance of power. A large majority could have been mustered for some such suggestion as that laws should be declared unconstitutional only by a vote of seven to two—that is, by more than a majority—or that two permanent additions should be made to the Court. But Franklin was simply unavailable for bargaining.

The real difficulties were two. The first was the hidden intention to

[15] There was one obvious contributing affront; how much it counted, it is hard to say, but with senators some matters loom larger than they do with others. J. Bruce Kremer was national committeeman from Montana. He was an ally of the copper crowd—in their employ, Wheeler would say—and he was certainly bitterly opposed to Wheeler. In New Deal days he was one of the most notorious of the fixers who battened on the New Deal. He was an intimate of Cummings, and his influence in the Department of Justice was, to say the least, considerable. All the departmental patronage and as much other as could be arranged was used to feed his Montana machine. All of this was a danger to Wheeler, and his resentment can well be understood. Whether or not it influenced him materially in his enthusiastic fight against what he felt was a Cummings bill, it is impossible to say. But certainly his outrage may well have disposed him to opposition. One of the small ironies of this battle was the prominence Wheeler had had as a presidential supporter in the just-finished campaign, but so had Senator O'Mahoney, who was now similarly in opposition. Both had appeared often with Franklin on campaign trips and were supposed to be his loyal friends.

cripple the Court permanently in its dealings with the presidency. This, Franklin conceived, could be done only by allowing him to appoint co-adjutors as fast as the judges reached the age of seventy; the second was that he had expected the legislators to be far more respectful of his recent electoral victory than they were. This expectation made him overconfident and stubborn, emotions he usually had under control. All his sagacity seemed to desert him; he was arrogant to those who counseled caution, disbelieving when they warned him of defeat, and neglectful until too late of their alternative suggestions. Besides, although they knew well enough what it was, and although he knew that they knew, he would never admit his real purpose. The strain he put on simple party loyalty was far too great.

Among other things, he forgot that even though he had been re-elected so triumphantly he was now a second-term incumbent; or, if he did remember it, he acted as though he did not. He did not deign to suggest that such popularity as his might break the two-term tradition. If he had he might have influenced such a waverer as Ashurst of Arizona, chairman of the Senate Judiciary Committee, who had the bill in charge. The senator was a fence-sitter. It was his method to please everyone. In this instance he neither wanted to report the bill nor to refuse action until it became apparent which side would win. His skillful evasion defeated even Robinson's gross bellowings.

The Senate had been the scene of many oratorical contests. The vocal capacities of elderly legislators are just next to infinite; and this bill, once they had chosen sides, gave them ample scope. The speeches were endless. Whatever their intent, it became clear that after the bill reached the floor without committee approval, the effect would be to strangle the presidential scheme. Time worked implacably against it. This was contrary to Franklin's forecast, since he judged the interests on his side to be far more committed to any cause he designated as his own than they proved to be. Nearly every one of them turned against him. This included farmers, organized labor, and city machines.

The farm organizations had a treaty with the New Deal, but it was a very limited one; it turned out, actually, not to run beyond the farmers' own interests. No political return could ever be counted on, and in this case the opposition was active. The so-called farm leaders, actually lobbyists, either appeared against the bill or let their representatives and senators know how they felt. Organized labor was represented by several prominent figures, among them William Green of the AFL, John L. Lewis of the CIO, and such others as Sidney Hillman and David Dubinsky. The larger constituencies by far were those of Green and Lewis. Green was a comfortable figurehead. He did his duty in this case with an absolute minimum of enthusiasm, knowing that his conservative colleagues disapproved. Lewis, although he owed his recent

Purge

rise in power to the New Deal, was disposed to credit Franklin with none of it; on the contrary, he intensely disliked the author of his present prosperity and refused in the present instance to acknowledge any obligation. The city machines, which had played so great a part in the recent election and would be even more important in that of 1940, were listening now to the powerful voices behind their popular façades. And their representatives among the legislators had at best confusing instructions. On not one of the power groups he had thought he controlled could Franklin actually count.

It took him an unconscionable time to discover his weakness. This must be charged mostly to overconfidence. He thought himself stronger and his enemies weaker than was true. But part of the difficulty arose because the White House staff entrusted with congressional liaison was utterly incapable of carrying the weight he put upon it. Those depended on in the Court battle were Joseph Keenan, an assistant to Cummings in the Department of Justice, and Charles West, who had been placed in Ickes' department, much to that irascible administrator's disgust, in addition to the ubiquitous Corcoran, who was everywhere. West, assigned to the House, had no one really to work through since Representative Hatton Sumners of the Judiciary Committee was bitter in opposition. Keenan, who worked in the Senate, was a happier lobbyist than Corcoran; he looked the part, and professional politicians were comfortable with him. He was a help to Robinson, a help largely offset, however, by Corcoran's irritating effect on most of those he sought to influence.

This group—Corcoran, Keenan, West, and Jackson—met frequently —in fact, daily—in the White House to assess their progress and to devise strategy. At this time James Roosevelt was having one of his spells of duty at the White House and acted as a kind of co-ordinator. As it became apparent that things were going badly, these individuals fell to backbiting, and the recriminations became less and less restrained. The tendency at first was to blame others. Farley, it was said, was "lying down on the job"—which he certainly was. He did, however, make a series of speeches to Democratic groups in various places, speaking mostly of party loyalty. These efforts, the White House familiars thought and said, were weak and even silly. This infuriated Charles Michelson, the publicity genius of the National Committee, who had written the speeches, and Edward L. Roddan, his assistant, who was writing other speeches for any Democrat who could be persuaded to deliver them.

It was no very happy family which gathered daily at the White House that spring. Corcoran's command of the accordion and his repertory of popular songs still entertained Franklin in his off hours, but they began to be regarded sourly by the others. Homer Cummings, who was responsible for the specific plan, was away a good deal of the time. At the height of the pressure he was enjoying the southern sunshine on a prolonged vacation, and Jackson represented the Department of Justice. Franklin went fishing too, in the Gulf, as he liked to do in spring, and appeared not to be carrying any heavier burdens than usual.

Beneath the surface, however, he was thoroughly annoyed. He would never forgive Wheeler for his leadership of the opposition; and for the "regular" Democrats—George, Gillette, Bailey, McCarran, Tydings, Clark, Ashurst, Harrison, O'Mahoney, King, Burke, Walsh, Copeland, and others—he afterward carried a resentment it was difficult to conceal.[16]

The struggle prolonged itself into late spring and early summer. There was endless talk, and the party seemed to be tearing itself apart in internecine bitterness. Robinson could not enlarge his list of supporters; his efforts finally resulted in such exhaustion that on the morning of July 14 he was found dead in his bedroom of a heart attack. The fight then was left to Barkley, Logan, Minton, Schwellenbach, and Guffey—Democrats—and Bob La Follette—progressive Republican.[17] Garner, who had not concealed his distaste for the bill, repeatedly tried for compromises. They were always more than Franklin would concede, however, and nothing came of them until, when Washington was deep in summer heat, when tempers were high and enmities exacerbated, it was obvious that defeat was imminent. Franklin then had no face left to save.

Several contributing causes for defeat besides Robinson's death had injected themselves along the way. One of the recalcitrant four of the older justices, Van Devanter, had retired in June, persuaded, it was said, by the Chief Justice; and from then it was obvious that a more amenable Court would be constituted. But this was not the most telling blow; that was a letter Wheeler persuaded the Chief Justice to write and allow him to make public. The lucid exposition of this statement so conclusively refuted the arguments Franklin had made in his message concerning the Court's work that it ended any chance for passage the bill may have had. Hughes proved that the justices were entirely competent, however much they might be disagreed with.

But besides this—just a week after Wheeler had read the Hughes

---

[16] Secretly he must have admired the tactics of Charles McNary, the Republican leader, who with some difficulty kept his minority colleagues quiet while the Democrats fought among themselves. He and McNary always had an understanding. McNary could often get favors for Oregon that his colleagues envied. McNary in this case was only doing his job and Franklin harbored no resentment.

[17] Bob had failed to convert any others of the progressives. Nye, Frazier, and Shipstead, for instance, joined with Wheeler almost at the beginning, and Bob was unable to detach them from the opposition. Norris was only passive in support.

communication to the Judiciary Committee—the Court entered on its famous series of reversals. On the decision day of Monday, March 29, the Railway Labor Act and the Frazier-Lemke Farm Mortgage Moratorium were unanimously upheld. Then, on April 12, the Wagner Labor Relations Act was sustained. The argument in this case turned on an interpretation of the commerce clause. The Court once again was forced to say whether manufacture (and so agriculture, mining, etc.) was a local matter not affecting interstate commerce. Stanley Reed, the Solicitor General, arguing the case weeks before, had had to ask—with what reluctance can be imagined—that the Court reverse itself. And, contrary to all expectation, that was what the Court did. Such matters now were brought within the meaning of the Fourteenth Amendment. Regulatory power was restored to the federal government.

This could be said to be a victory of sorts for Franklin. It would be regarded as such in after years. But it was not the victory he wanted in 1937. And as long as he lived he was not likely to forget the report of the Judiciary Committee of the Senate. It was the worst public humiliation he had ever had. Moreover, it went to the realities which he had sought to evade. He was thoroughly exposed and, in effect, denounced. The Constitution, said the report:

was carefully planned and deliberately framed to establish three coordinate branches of government, every one of them to be independent of the others. For the protection of the people, for the preservation of the rights of the individual, for the maintenance of the liberties of minorities, for maintaining the checks and balances of our dual system, the three branches of government were so constituted that the independent expression of honest difference could never be restrained in the people's servants and no one branch could over-awe or subjugate the others. That is the American system. It is immeasurably more important, immeasurably more sacred to the people of America, indeed to the people of the world, than the immediate adoption of any legislation, however beneficial. . . .

There was a good deal more of this effective eloquence in the report, all of it laid like a whiplash on the presidential back. With the Court's retreat and the exposure of Franklin's real intention there was no longer the slightest chance that his bill might pass. At the end he did try for a compromise, but what happened was that the bill was recommitted, and for it there was substituted a bill to reform judicial procedure, omitting entirely the Supreme Court itself.

Franklin might be said to have had a kind of revenge a little later when he appointed Hugo Black to Van Devanter's place on the Court. Black was a genuine liberal and would for years to come uphold the principles of liberalism from the bench. But when the Congress adjourned late in summer Franklin found it difficult, as it had never been before, to retain his presidential aplomb—how difficult would be demonstrated when he allowed himself the luxury of the purge attempt in 1938.

It should be noted that the committee's judiciary bill was finally passed, one that made some minor changes in the lower courts. Franklin signed it, but with bad grace. It could perhaps be said that he had the last word. When he came to write the note for his *Public Papers* about the matter, he could claim that the 1937 defeat had been only temporary and that ultimately all the changes he had advocated had been accepted.[18] But he certainly knew that the vital one had been refused; and I have often wondered whether, if he had lived on into the post-war period, he would have tried again.

[18] 1936 vol., pp. 338 ff.

20 I have allowed my narrative to run beyond the events of the 1936 campaign. It seemed easier to follow the Court fight to its conclusion without the interference involved in considering concurrent problems. But, as I noted, there were two distinct series of events—two acts, if you like—in this drama; they were separated by a year, and between them there came the quadrennial election. This has to be told about if my account is to be at all complete: not that the campaign of 1936 was at all unusual. It was not. There were the traditional appeals to the voters, the familiar attributions of responsibility for old disasters, and the equally familiar forebodings of more disasters to come if the other party was chosen. There were rather more than the usual whisperings of a malicious sort about Franklin and the family, and dark forecasts of happenings sure to occur if he was continued in office. But mostly this was within the ordinary expectation. The significance of the event lay in the extensiveness of the victory. It could not be said that the Republicans had merely been defeated. They had been overwhelmed. It was an affirmative ratification. In 1932 it could be said that the voters had been against Hoover. This time they were for Franklin.

As in most such contests, the principals and their immediate circles showed at one or another time the capacity for fright which is so characteristic of candidate-politicians, but the professionals on both sides sensed a Democratic victory well before election day. I was assured by Ernest K. Lindley, a representative of the New York *Herald Tribune*, who much of the time was with the Republican contender, that Mr. Landon seriously believed himself to have a good chance of winning. I doubt whether Franklin ever thought he would lose, but certainly he thought he *might* lose, and he took no chances. His canvass was as carefully planned and as faithfully executed as any in his whole career.

The situation he had to deal with was fairly simple, and there were few alternatives. He had to stand on the record. He might improve it by interpretation; he might explain why it was deficient; but it was *his* record and it could not be escaped. If he had wanted to conceal or exaggerate beyond reason, the opposition could be expected to cite the account. He chose the bland line, as he had in 1932. He apologized for nothing, explained nothing, and promised nothing.[1] He merely said, in effect, "If you agree that I am trying to make things better in America for the common man, I deserve your support." He ignored Republican criticisms and the needling of his opponents; he assumed throughout an air of serene and cheerful confidence; he was, he implied, above and apart from purely partisan affairs. He wanted the support of everyone, not just that of Democrats.

This technique of his was not new, as we know. He had always propagated the myth of non-partisanship and implied that good and thoughtful people were on his side, whatever their party. There was some basis for it in this instance. He still had progressive support—that of the La Follettes of Wisconsin, for instance, of La Guardia of New York City, of Hiram Johnson of California, and so on through a fairly long list. None of these was a Democrat. And, at a carefully calculated moment in mid-campaign, he even repudiated the Democrat who was opposing Senator Norris in Nebraska, called the old man "one of our major prophets," and asked Nebraskans to send him back to the Senate. Those progressives who were alienated were not yet openly opposed.

Franklin had certainly seen for years that he must make use of the Democratic party without becoming its prisoner, but during the first term this necessity had grown into something of an obsession. It was more and more obvious that even his talents would not be equal to the task of making the party securely progressive. He was still pretending that such a transformation was happening; he even pictured liberalism

[1] Except that in the traditional Madison Square Garden speech winding up the campaign he spoke of "our visions for the future" containing "prophecies rather than promises." That vision, he said, included the improvement of working conditions, the ending of monopoly in business, the abolishing of unfair trade practices, the attaining of cheaper electricity and transportation, the lowering of interest rates, the improvement of home financing, the assurance of honest banking, the regulation of security issues, the maintenance of reciprocal international trade relations, and the wiping out of the slums.

Efforts would continue, he said, in behalf of farmers, for better land use, for conservation, for drought and flood control.

And, "Of course we will continue our efforts for young men and women . . . and help for the crippled, for the blind, for the mothers, our insurance for the unemployed, our security for the aged. Of course we will continue to protect the consumer against unnecessary price spreads, against the costs added by monopoly and speculation. We will continue our successful efforts to increase his purchasing power and to keep it constant."

But all this was not an election promise; it was merely a calling of attention to what was going on. The "of course" was stressed.

as the tradition of Democracy. But the illusion was becoming almost impossible to sustain.

He saw no alternative, in the long run, to creating a new force. A new progressivism must be shaped—one capable of succeeding where that of Bryan, of Wilson, of La Follette the elder, and of Uncle Ted had failed. He would be its founder as Jefferson had been the founder of the Democracy. The campaign of 1936 was not so much an election contest as an appeal for ratification of a progressivism quite as much Republican as Democratic.

In this direction there had been significant developments, and these would continue until the necessity for war preparations gave the congressional conservatives renewed bargaining power. They would occupy that position and use it ruthlessly all during the latter part of Franklin's second term and through his third. But he was stubborn, even if the stubbornness seldom showed. As the war was ending, and when post-war international organization was fully planned, he would return to his progressive project. We shall see him opening negotiations with Wendell Willkie during his fourth campaign. If he had lived to run for a fifth term, I am convinced that it would not have been as a Democrat, but as a Progressive. If a war had not been in prospect, this might very possibly have happened in 1940.

This project of Franklin's to steal or abandon the Democracy may not easily be credited and, even if credited, may appear an unrealistic expectation on his part. But it seems to me to have been the strictly logical answer to his dilemma. He was conscious long before anyone else that he had been crowded into a corner from which there was no other escape. The sources of his power to shape and carry out a program lay among groups implacably hostile to the program with which he had identified himself in his own mind. He had either to give up his dreams of a transformed nation, of new and higher levels of well-being, of an economy managed in the general interest, or he must gather behind them a political support sufficient for the purpose. The coalition he now headed—the Democratic party—was so deeply divided that to hold it together he would be compelled to go on compromising and temporizing. He was growing tired of it. He was also completely aware that if he did not somehow get more substantial control it would escape from his leadership. The risk of this was so considerable that the alternative of a new party, in spite of the failure of new parties in the past, can well have seemed more practical.

Even now, object as he was of adulation from supporters and of respect from political opponents, he felt himself the prisoner of essentially unfriendly groups. He could never say what he thought; he could never advocate what he really believed; he could not use his power as a democratic leader must. He was checked and defeated in every instance by the determined and skillful undercover maneuvering of those who pretended to be his partisans. In order to make any progress he had to conciliate them, to pretend an agreement that both sides knew false; he had even to admit them to his official family, a humiliation he deeply resented. Old Jack Garner, representative of that hard-shell Texas vigilante spirit he so distrusted; Hull, the Tennessee mountain politician, bumbling free-trade advocate; Joe Robinson, Senate leader, a southern reactionary of the most typical sort; Jesse Jones, who conspired with the congressional conservatives to thwart his will—these and numerous others he had to dissemble before every day of his life as they sat at his council table. It was worth doing only if it came out somewhere, had some profitable end. He knew even as early as 1935 what that end was, and the 1936 campaign was designed to bring it measurably nearer. This, at least, is what I conclude.

I knew what the intention was; so did Harry Hopkins, Bob La Follette, and Fiorello La Guardia. So must Sam Rosenman have known. How many others were told of it or speculated about it I do not know. There must have been many who guessed even if none was told. Such a project had explosive possibilities in those years, and we were very careful with our information and our deductions. Even Harry, Bob, and I, intimate as we were, did not very often speculate among ourselves. And only a few times did we discuss it with La Guardia, although later, when I had moved into his administration in New York, he and I talked together about his own chances. The difficulty with Fiorello vis-à-vis Franklin was that of any potential successor. Since his election to the mayoralty in 1933 his ambitions had enlarged. It would be an exaggeration to say that he ever became a rival; his attitude was colored by his sense of Franklin's superiority; but he definitely had expectations —with every right—later on, after Franklin's re-election, when a third term was still to most people a prohibited idea. And he regarded himself as ideal vice-presidential material. But he could advance only as a progressive. This could not happen unless Franklin made a commitment, and this, as we know, he would not bring himself to do until too late, for himself as well as for La Guardia.

There was some of this difficulty with Bob La Follette, although Bob was a curious kind of unambitious politician. There can hardly ever have been a more selfless individual, and as a senator he was almost unique. But there was another member of his family—Philip, the governor of Wisconsin, who had obvious expectations. Phil was the scintillant brother whose career Bob cared more about than his own. It could be anticipated that Phil might be a potential presidential successor too. Franklin was sensitive to such possibilities, more so because of the special circumstances and because of his particular ambitions. He wanted the progressives as allies, but those who might be rivals had to be kept at a distance. They must not know of matters that might be important as their rivalry developed. He had a wary eye on Phil La Follette from the first.

I did not make too much of this, especially at this time. It became important, however, later on in the case of each. La Guardia would be expectant in 1940 and would be bitterly disappointed when Franklin decided to run for a third term. And, as will be recalled, Phil La Follette tried in most inauspicious circumstances, aided by Bob, to set up a new party. It was premature, and Phil, anyway, was not so widely accepted a leader that he could succeed in his attempt. But it does show that in his own mind he was actually the rival that Franklin suspected him to be.

When in these early days Harry Hopkins, Bob La Follette, and I did explore the possibilities, we had enough to go on so that we were certain of Franklin's intention, but not enough particulars to enlarge our conversations very materially. It was only in the most intimate circumstances, and only once, that I can recall Franklin speaking to us of it. Even then it was not much more than to reiterate what he had said to me in Albany: "We'll have eight years in Washington. By that time there may not be a Democratic party, but there will be a Progressive one."

In quoting this remark, I still am not certain—as neither Harry nor Bob could be certain—whether that word "progressive" was meant to be capitalized, although it seemed to me the obvious inference. Did he mean to transform the Democracy so that it would become progressive, sloughing off its reactionaries; or did he mean following Uncle Ted's example but improving on it, to found a Progressive party under that name? After all, he *had* implied the disappearance of the Democratic label. This might serve to enfold the liberal Republicans who would only reluctantly become Democrats. He had made his remark to me when he was obviously just beginning to develop the idea, and I feel sure that what he said was what he meant. But of course either kind of evolution would answer the purpose he had in mind, and of either he seemed prepared to be the activating leader. It depended largely on resistance in the old party and on the accretion of new forces under his, rather than the other politicians', leadership.

The three of us chewed over the related ideas, at any rate, and felt that we were more realistic than most of those around us. We at least possessed some knowledge that others had to guess at. We could, we thought, because of what we knew, interpret more intelligently the confusing events going on about us. It was with particularly sardonic humor that we watched Farley in this and succeeding years move toward his immolation. He was busy building an impregnable Democratic machine. He had no present interest—although he was obviously conservative—in the ideology of its various members and agents. He meant to make it strong. His view of Franklin was still unperceptive. He felt that he and his fellow professionals had "made" Franklin; after a second term they would "make" another President, and he too would be a good and amenable Democrat, useful for keeping other Democrats in power. It had not yet occurred to him that Franklin was a Democrat of convenience. At this time he would have been horrified, I think, at such a suggestion and would have entertained it only with the utmost reluctance. He must have had a bad moment over the Norris matter and over Franklin's open friendship with the La Follettes. The curious fact is that apparently Franklin never gave him notice of these divergences and did not explain them to him afterward with any care. The vast victory probably buried his doubts, but he must have had some premonitions of trouble even in 1936, and must afterward have wondered why they had not been stronger.

On several occasions Franklin spoke to me of this possible Progressive organization. One was when I was protesting the course NRA was taking under Johnson's administration. He promised then that he would not let the blanket codes go too far in the direction I feared. My protest had been that the more powerful industrialists were using them to restrict production and raise prices, when what we wanted was just the opposite effect. But he answered that once he had substantially all industries under the blanket the job of revising would begin. They would have conceded much, and especially the principle of coordination; they could hardly resist revision if resistance would jeopardize their investment in partnership. He thought it ought not to be too difficult to establish a new rule about the matters worrying me.

I was not at all satisfied with his explanation, or optimistic about the reform he suggested. I anticipated that returning prosperity would encourage an aggressive refusal to accept discipline, which was already noticeable. Besides, I said, it was this very tendency that was alienating the progressives. They were reluctant to see big business strengthened and were turning against NRA. They would hold him responsible. He might well lose the whole scheme because it had been badly administered.

It was then that he spoke of his Woodrow Wilson recollection. Wilson, on one occasion, it seemed, was annoyed by the propensity of the progressives with whom he had had dealings to refuse him their loyalty. They not only insisted on thinking for themselves but were determined to act on their thoughts. It was not possible to develop leadership, because they would not follow. The conservatives, said Wilson to young Franklin standing before his desk, have the striking power of a closed fist; the progressives are like a man trying to strike with his fingers spread out stiffly. He would accomplish nothing and would very likely break his fingers. This was so useful a parable that I expect Franklin used it on other occasions, although none to my knowledge has been reported. I talked it over with my friends, as I was undoubtedly meant to do. To all of them it meant the same thing; they ought to be more willing than they were to believe that Franklin's intentions were the same as their own and that his tactics and his timing ought to be accepted as essential to the common end.

To me, to Harry, and to Bob it meant more than that. It was as if he had said, "I am the progressive way; only through me can the common intention be realized." That was not necessary to say to me; I had long ago granted him leadership without reserve. When I could not sustain that loyalty I would not stay in his service. I would continue to differ and to protest, but only in private. And this he very well knew. Yet I had become notorious. And during the 1936 campaign the professional politicians were so certain I was a burden to the party that I resolved to stay in office no longer. Farley was pleasant to me, but he was firm to others about my being a detriment. No one ever spoke to me directly, but I knew how I stood. I shall say only one more word about this. I had another reason for going when the campaign was over. The Brandeis-Frankfurter-Corcoran influence had prevailed. Franklin did not doubt my loyalty any more than he ever had, I am sure, but he had been half persuaded—and Eleanor even more than he—that I had totalitarian leanings. I had spoken too highly of planning and had not succeeded in persuading those who heard me that it was, as I believed it to be, an essential device for democratic government.

My ideas concerning the necessity for co-ordination and conjunction were interpreted over and over as similar to those which underlay the corporative state. Franklin never argued this with me. He must have understood that this was a misinterpretation; but he was a politician. He could support only so much disapproval of an intimate; when the tolerance was exceeded, friendship must not be put before expediency.

Before I went, however, I had another glimpse of the grand conception. It was when I was arguing, concerning the adverse Court, for a constitutional amendment to ensure the federal regulatory power, and conversely arguing against any change in the Court to be brought about by legislation—on the ground that this would constitute a successful aggression against one co-ordinate branch of government by the other two branches.

Franklin was inclined even then toward legislation and against amendment. I made the usual progressive argument that the Court was on occasion a bulwark against encroachments on precious liberties. These were safe neither with the Congress, responsive as it tended to be to pressure groups and to reactionary influences, nor with the presidency, which was often entrusted to indifferent or weak individuals.

414

We needed, I said, the kind of specific authorization for the regulation of business that we had in the Bill of Rights for the protection of our liberties.

I warned him that I spoke for most of the progressives, but I think that many of them had already spoken for themselves; he knew well enough, without my insisting, what the argument was. But he rejected it, and on the ground that in American life, and with our traditions and institutions, such protections had to be ensured by political means. Only if power was massed behind ideas did they have any validity. I ought to know—no one better—that he was massing weight behind the principles of progressivism. It would be a delusion of certainty to have an amendment. It could be interpreted out of existence at any time by a hostile court, just as other liberties had. "Look," he said, "at what has happened in the case of the Fourteenth Amendment." I thought he was not on too safe ground there, but I saw his main point. He drove it home.

"We are exactly as safe," he said, "as we have the political strength to be. If we do not have a winning party, standing for the objectives we are developing, those objectives will never be gained. If my leadership is to have any effect it will be because I have mustered strength to overcome those who are against what we are trying to do. You—and the others—are deluded. There is no easy way, no quick way. I spoke in my press conference about the next five or ten years. I meant that. This is a struggle which must go on and on. We may never quite win it, but we ought not to lose it. Either way it goes from time to time, its success will be measured in votes. If people will elect a leader who is determined to go forward, they will go forward. Otherwise it won't happen."[2]

It is mistaken to think that Franklin's grand conception of a new political alignment was ever at any time absent from his mind. Only to meet emergencies did he invent or consent to the devising of programs or agencies not somehow, even if remotely, contributory to this end. The vast maneuver changing the whole tenor of the New Deal in 1935 was made necessary by this large intention. He would put himself in the main stream of progressivism before trying to harness and transform it. NRA and AAA, resting as they did on concepts of holism, must be abandoned. The progressivism of America was additive, atomistic. And Franklin had been working toward a holism congenial, fundamentally, only to big business. Traditional progressivism rested on littleness and was bitterly opposed to mergers, to integration, to large-scale operation, to centralized planning and management. He had not been able to re-

[2] I do not pretend to have quoted literally what was said in this conversation. But I am certain that the attribution is not an inaccurate representation of several conversations at the time of the NRA decision and during the next two years.

Viewing aspects as unconnected or antagonistic fragments

Viewing aspects in their relationship to the whole.

fine and reorient the movement. He must swallow its orthodox tenets, even if he choked a little.

The retrogression went all the way back to atomism, hanging onto the holistic conception only in a few accepted fields, such as natural-resource development, conservation, and the provision of social minima.[3] In these fields the European pioneering, combined with fright from depression years, made planned intervention acceptable. Aside from this, the federal government must confine itself to breaking-up activities. But these led inevitably to interventions calculated to ensure freedom in competition after the breaking up. This was not strictly logical, but it had grown to be an orthodox item of the progressive creed. Sometimes it seemed to pre-empt most of the progressives' attention.

To make use of hostility to bigness was one way, Franklin conceived, of approaching, by indirection, the planning necessary to a high-energy economy. Fair competition could be expanded, as a concept, to include such an intimate knowledge of industry and such circulation of that knowledge as would make strategic control obviously necessary. Progressivism itself might eventually evolve, or be made to evolve, into an adequate social philosophy.

NRA might have come out this way if the pattern of partnership had been carefully established and if it had not been used by faithless businessmen to gain advantages they might have known they would not be allowed to maintain. It was a relief to everyone, including Franklin —although he covered his relief with a careful camouflage of indignation—to have NRA disapproved by the Court. In a way it was ironic that he should have been able to use so fortunate a reverse as a club with which to beat the reactionary justices. Looking back, it would be seen that it was not very clever of the old plotters to give him such an opportunity. They would be much smarter when they allowed Chief Justice Hughes to diminish Franklin—and the presidency—by giving him what he asked for in 1937. The reversal in the hot-oil cases would constitute a marvelous start that would develop without effort on his part right up to election time in 1936; but the favorable decision concerning the Wagner Act in 1937 would stop him cold. The Supreme Court would never again be an issue he could use. The justices would retreat into the shadows now occupied by the financiers; other dragons would emerge to replace them.

On the other hand, he wanted from the very first to win the Court battle because of the need to enhance the presidency and because, by winning, he would have brought measurably nearer a progressive grouping about himself and his office. As it was, the tremendous gain of the election would be lost in the humiliations of the next nine months.

---

[3] And even this was carried out in an awkward progressive way, conceding much to states' righters and sacrificing uniformity to local prejudice.

Such a check to the careful plan he had worked out for advancing toward his goal would enrage him, experienced politician though he was —so much so that, until too late, he would fail to give the struggle the close attention needed for even a respectable result.

But if he was to turn careless after the returns were in, he showed no such lapses in the months preceding the election. In fact the campaign of 1936 was as remarkable for efficiency as any in our history. There was evident in it a supremely professional management; there was no concession to the opposition and as little evidence of "running scared" as it is possible to find in any such contest. There was confident assurance throughout that his presidential course would be approved. There was a kind of welcoming approach to the reaffirmation of popular support. But besides this, a suitable aggressiveness confused and divided the enemy. Franklin occupied the whole of a widened center, pushing his opponents far out toward right and left. Splinter groups, seemingly so noisy and successful, came off very badly; and the other great party, forced to accept the reactionary label, was so badly beaten as to occasion wonder whether it may not have been permanently destroyed.

Most remarkable of all was Franklin's use of his opportunities. There was evident familiarity with all the best conventional devices, but beyond that there was the imagination which made the most of the advantages peculiar to this one occasion—advantages that might well have been fatal handicaps. One of these opportunities was presented by nature: it was the terrible drought during the spring and summer months; the other was the fatal blunder of the Republicans in attacking social security. In both these instances, so different yet so alike in presenting an opportunity, Franklin exploited the openings to the fullest extent.

At the end of the campaign, when he was detailing a "vision of the future," it was his own personal vision, not that of the Democrats as a collectivity. It was less agreeable to about half the Democratic professionals than to more than half the Republicans. Whether or not they might approve, there were few voters who would not have recognized this if asked. As Franklin conducted it, the campaign was a kind of exercise in personal leadership. And to see how true this is, it is only necessary to ask whether there was another politician among all the Democrats who would have made the same appeal. It is not only impossible to think of such a one, but it is impossible not to think of a dozen who would have made a very different one. The party was set so far along the path of Franklin's intention that when 1940 came it would be obvious what had happened. There would be no acceptable Rooseveltian candidate, and only such a candidate could be elected. There would be no alternative to choosing Franklin for yet another term —that third one which smashed so old a precedent. That he was elected

1940 as well as 1936 is the proof of the strategy. It worked. It began to work in 1936.

So confident had he become toward the end that he grasped several nettles a less experienced or less confident politician would have avoided like poison. He turned Republican attempts to use ridicule into claims of Democratic virtue. We have seen him do this before in his state campaigns; in 1936 it emerged as a full-blown tour de force, and a highly successful one. He adopted the very words of the opposition; and when he was through, "boondoggling," for instance, was a claim to virtue rather than an epithet to cower away from; and "spendthrift government" was one not afraid to use its resources to create welfare.

Before the campaign ended, most of the Democratic politicians had begun to understand, even if only dimly as yet, what was happening. Their party was being taken away from them. They were at the beginning of a wonder, destined to grow, concerning their own blindness and complacency; and the really hard-shelled oldsters, who had all along been skeptical, savagely resolved not to give another inch. The Supreme Court fight, beginning almost at once, would not be one for defense of the Court nearly so much as one for the return of the party to their control. The Republicans, as we have seen, would have the wit to keep out of the way; there would not be much left of their prestige anyway after the election, and the Democrats would battle it out among themselves. When it was over Franklin would have been checked, but he would not have been defeated. His course would be deflected but not altered. This was somewhat as Hitler would check but not defeat him. And, indeed, the two kinds of opposition did not seem to Franklin so very different. They often merged in his mind.

He was speaking of and to the reactionaries in his own party as much as in the opposing one when he assailed the "economic royalists" in his acceptance speech at Philadelphia; but he had already opened the attack months before in his January address at the opening of Congress. In that speech he had definitely linked the autocrats abroad with those at home. Big business, he had said, was actually fascist. Its representatives constituted a small but powerful minority which, under Republican administrations, had dominated the government. They had abdicated in confusion in 1933; "but now with the passing of danger they forget," he said, "their damaging admissions and withdraw their abdication . . . They steal the livery of great national constitutional ideals to serve discredited special interests. These individuals exhibit autocracy toward labor, toward stockholders, toward consumers, toward public sentiment." They threaten something more menacing than a return to the past. "Our resplendent economic autocracy does not want to return to the individualism of which they prate." They want control

418

of the instruments of power which are safe only in the hands of a people's government.

There were in these allusions not the first but so far the plainest intimations of things to come. The totalitarians were being ushered onto the American stage. The ensuing conversion of a people impervious to suggestions that they must resist aggressions in Europe was to take a long time, much effort, and serious sacrifice. It would be the most fateful of all Franklin's essays, leading as it did to war and a new balance of power in the world. Before very long we shall see it become the center of his interest, taking first place in public discussion and engaging all his powers of persuasion. Resistance to it will be formidable and stubborn. In maneuvering to outwit the isolationists and to establish his own policy he will use all the arts he has learned, and he will use all the credit accumulated in his political bank. The nation will come to its final decision late; and it may seem sometimes that it may never be taken. It will end as Franklin willed it to end; but the negotiations with public opinion will seem endless. They were now at their earliest stages.

The Congress which listened to his message on the state of the nation in January 1936 had a suddenly diminished enthusiasm about the Roosevelt leadership as compared with the year before. Then it had accepted a new New Deal and eventually turned much of it into law. There had been some disaffection then, but now the disaffection was no longer confined to a recalcitrant few; it had spread to a much larger number. It was only the progressives who approved the castigation of their ancient enemies. There were more, both Democrats and Republicans, who listened with a misgiving rising slowly toward the resentment that would express itself explosively in another year—more explosively because of Franklin's electoral success. He was now no longer merely a threat; he was a menace.

After election many a Democrat asked himself why he had agreed in Philadelphia to the abolition of the two-thirds rule—which had slipped through the convention so easily.[4] Even Farley must have begun to wonder shortly how this foresight had failed. With him, at this time, repeal of the rule was an item of unfinished business; he had got himself into trouble by pushing such a resolution prematurely in Chicago in 1932, and it was a kind of vindication to have something done so easily that had once caused such a violent reaction and brought him such discredit. It is easier to explain why Farley asked for the action than to explain why the southern delegations did not oppose it more strenuously. But whatever the explanation, the Southerners would find

---

[4] This, it will be remembered, was an old Democratic device by which southern delegations, unable ever to nominate one of their number, still kept a veto over the convention's choice.

that they had walked into a trap. That trap would be seen waiting for them too late, when in 1940 Garner, Hull, and their coterie would choose Farley for their champion. When he had been led to a high place and shown the promised political land, simple majority rule would effectively bar the way.

But Philadelphia at the beginning of summer in 1936 belonged to the incumbent President. He was renominated by acclamation, and it was to a wildly cheering audience at Franklin Field that he made his acceptance speech. That occasion did not differ in kind from many other political appearances, but there was in his greeting from the enormous crowd none of that synthetic enthusiasm so familiar in canvassing appearances. As he came forward to the rostrum on the arm of his tall son James the shouts carried an adulation seldom extended to any leader.[5]

And he was ready to ride the wave of approval. A recast team of ghost writers had prepared a rather new kind of speech, an aggressive, indeed a provocative, one, and one that made more definite the trend already evident in several pre-convention addresses. Big businessmen, no longer partners of government, had replaced the financiers as public enemies. It was no longer just Wall Street he was to castigate. He was to attack the citadels, wherever they might be—in Detroit, in San Francisco, in Boston as well as in New York, and right here in Philadelphia —of autocratic monopoly. He had indeed come all the way back to the orthodox progressive line. It was a speech Bryan might have made, or La Follette, or Uncle Ted in 1912. Their shades seemed to hover over the spotlit crowds in and around the vast spaces of the stadium. The voices of a hundred predecessors rampaging up and down the prairie states joined themselves with his as it went out over the air to millions upon millions of listeners. But something was added now—an appeal to city folk in all the fast-growing industrial centers.

To many an oldster these were words he had waited long to hear, and to the younger generation they spoke of hope. It was a familiar American theme, and it was irresistible. Many a hearer realized for the first time as he heard this address that the original New Deal was now definitely abandoned. In that effort, farmers, workers, and businessmen had formed a triad with whom the government was to work. Each was

[5] It was on this occasion that the most serious mishap of his career, owing to his disability, occurred. As he came forward from the back of the stage he lost his balance and fell, helpless as James' support slipped away. Quick-thinking Secret Service men surrounded him and lifted him quickly to his feet. Only a few had seen what had happened or, in fact, were aware that anything was amiss. He was at his confident and smiling best as he grasped the desk and spread out his papers. And it was then that he made one of the most buoyant of all his speeches. The reminder of his physical fallibility affected his delivery not at all.

to have its strength built up until each could claim from the others its fair share of the national income and equality in other respects as well. Each was to be furnished a method and devices to make good its claims; all were then to join, under government auspices, in that "concert of interests" which had been so frequent a theme of Franklin's in 1932 and after.

That phase was now over. Big business, maker of the NRA codes, was now dropped from the triad. Workers and farmers were still to have their governmental affiliations. But big business was to be thrust out. From now on it would have only the protection of tightened regulations to ensure fair competition.

Yet the point has most emphatically to be made that only *big* business was read out of favor; there was a reaching out to embrace the small enterpriser, which was in some ways the most remarkable phase of the campaign. The small businessman had not hitherto been the object of New Deal consideration; the codes of NRA and the marketing agreements of AAA had been allowed to be framed to a pattern that was most distinctly weighted in favor of the larger units of all the industries. Yet Franklin now claimed to be the friend of the little businessman; almost, it might be said, a fawning one. This was a Second New Deal; he wanted the First to be forgotten.

The truth was, however, as could be seen well enough when it was all over, that the formal campaign—which opened on September 29 and continued until November 2—made very little difference to the outcome. The decision was already foregone before the proceedings began. Franklin had already won when his "non-political" journey to the drought-stricken prairies was over in September. And if any clincher was needed, it was furnished not by his own rather specious appeal to the little businessmen but, as has been suggested, by the Republicans' attack on social security.

This is the perfect model for a campaign—to have victory "in the bag" before the canvass starts because the candidate's leadership has become unassailable, not to make any mistakes so that what has been gained is lost, and then to have the enemy make all complete by committing the most fatal of all errors—an attack on the most popular of the candidate's achievements. The Republicans actually threatened, as people understood it, to repeal the social security laws. This was an intolerable threat.

I must tell something, at least, about both these phases of the campaign. They show a working politician at his professional apogee.

I have emphasized at other times Franklin's interest in conservation, in farming, and in the state of the land. To a person with such a sensitivity, a natural disaster such as the drought of 1936 rapidly became was something that ought to have been anticipated but, once having happened, could at least be used as a lesson for the future. No one knew better than he how vulnerable the United States was to such occurrences. Much of the land affected by this terrible ordeal should never have been brought into cultivation, especially that in the short-grass country. The old cover should have been undisturbed. The rainfall there was insufficient in most years to make a good crop, and periodically it fell below even that level. When it did, the plowed land was little better than a desert. Franklin had preached many a sermon on this theme, and many beginnings of corrective practices had been begun since he had become President, but they had not gone far enough.

Until World War I, farming had not seriously invaded the really dangerous areas, although as long as there had been homesteading on their fringes there had been a kind of rhythmic moving in and out of homesteaders. They would be tempted by a cycle of years when the prairies were green, and just when they had got settled and well started in farming, the cycle of dryness would begin. They would find themselves unable, after a year or two, to continue. Their land would be baked, their wells would give out, and they would have to find some way to retreat or to move on toward the West.

It had happened that the need for increased food supplies during the war had coincided with a wet cycle, and a really formidable migration into the danger areas had taken place. When a crop was made at wartime prices there were large profits. And this encouraged more venturesome farmers to move in. But in the thirties the inevitable occurred. In 1934 rainfall had been so short that severe damage had been done. Speaking nationally, that drought had been an ironic blessing—it had helped to reduce embarrassing surpluses of wheat—but for the individuals and families involved it had been disastrous. At that time there had been improvised various relief measures carried out with emergency funds. Most of the livestock had been moved out and slaughtered, and the people had been given relief. Somehow they had survived. Some families had read the signs and moved, ill prepared as they were to finance the journey; others had determined to stick it out.

But in 1936 when the rains did not come at all and when week after week the sun blazed down on the thousands of square miles once green but now dun-colored and grassless even where they were not covered with dunes of dust, many more families, discouraged and beaten, began to load their few possessions into trucks or trailers and go east or west, anywhere to escape the disaster. It was then that a careless nation, which had not made a policy to meet nature's imperatives in spite of pleas and warnings from those who knew what must happen, began to realize how foolish this neglect had been.

Dust clouds darkened the skies even as far east as Washington. And one incredibly apt storm of this sort actually occurred as hearings got

422

started at long last on Capitol Hill concerning a proposal to establish a soil-conservation service. But also the tide of migrants began to flow into surrounding areas with better climates. And especially, following the American impulse, the thousands of "jalopies" creaking under loads far beyond their capacity rolled toward the Pacific Coast states. Soon the nation began to hear about the "Okies." They camped along the ditchbanks in California; they overwhelmed the little towns in Oregon and Washington; their children, and they themselves, were wholly dependent on casual labor or some sort of relief. The local facilities were quite unequal to the task, even when the funds were provided by the federal government, and before long there was a kind of crisis arising from the social problems they created.[6]

The drought was worst in the southern reaches of the short-grass plains, and this area was dramatized as "the dust bowl." All Americans began to accept as a problem what only a few more foresighted conservationists—among them Franklin—had always known was a threat to the national well-being. By 1936 the Resettlement Administration had come into being, however, and there could be far more prompt and effective action on everyone's part. The worst effects were mitigated. And especially migration was better handled and somewhat moderated. Families were encouraged to stay where they were until there was some place for them to go, and meanwhile they were given relief or emergency work near their homes. Many water-conservation projects were carried out, for instance, and road and school building were expanded. Altogether 1936, although it was a much worse drought year than 1934, was a far less difficult one for those who were caught in its burning blast.

The Resettlement Administration had been set up in the spring of 1935 by executive order. Its job was to be a multiple one. It was to assume the same responsibility for indigent rural folk as Hopkins' Works Projects Administration (set up at the same time) was to assume for the urban unemployed. Beyond this, it was to take people off unproductive land and resettle them where the possibilities of making a living were better. And it was to turn the submarginal land, now abandoned, into forests, grasslands, parks, wildlife districts, or any other public reserve which seemed appropriate. These areas were henceforth to be kept from being farmed. Such lands made people poor, and poor people made such lands so much worse that they became a national problem.

Of this whole sequence there had never been a better illustration than was forced on American attention in 1936. RA was not yet ready

[6] It was out of this material that Steinbeck fashioned *The Grapes of Wrath*. This novel served to fix the portrait of those years in the American memory and assisted mightily in keeping the problem focused until some action was taken.

to tackle on any large scale the rehabilitation of millions of families now being starved off their homesteaded farms. The planning for and provision of resettlement areas were extremely difficult technical problems. First the land had to be found and acquired, then farmstead facilities had to be provided, and usually the demoralized family had to be guided and helped over a considerable period. To carry out such a task on any large scale with a quickly assembled organization was impossible. It had been hoped that the problem could be approached slowly and carefully and that the scale of operations could be increased by decades rather than by years. The condition had been growing worse for half a century at least; it might well take an equal time to reverse the trend and carry out gradually the relocation of the millions of misplaced families who were doomed to a failure as certain as the succession of seasons and the cycles of weather.

The organization was thus faced with a task it could not possibly do well. It had to put aside for the moment its long-range plans and plunge into the emergency job of helping those who had been demoralized by the implacable hostility of nature. This it did. By late spring and early summer some two thirds to three quarters of the farm families throughout the whole drought-struck area had been reached by some kind of assistance. They had been given cash grants for supplies; they had been given emergency jobs; their livestock had been cared for in one way or another; schools and other social agencies had been kept functioning and civilization had at least been supplied at a minimum everywhere. It was all done awkwardly and wastefully but it was done.

No one in the short-grass country was happy. The worst of the region's problems had not been solved. But there was a general gratefulness that in their extremity no money or effort had been spared to bring the affected families assistance. There had been a minimum of red tape; plans for permanent arrangement had not been much discussed. Help had simply been brought, and not too many questions asked.

Franklin had watched this successful succoring effort from Washington with some satisfaction. This was the stronger because he saw that the present trouble out in the plains would inevitably contribute to deeper understanding of what must be done to avoid its happening again in the future. Conservation had suddenly become a practical and pressing necessity. He capitalized on it immediately by appointing a Great Plains Drought Committee to study and report, and sent its members out to tour the devastated areas. Also, he resolved to dramatize the problem by himself going to meet his committee there, thus using to the full nature's lesson.

At the same time, being a politician, he saw that the emergency must not only be used for education generally but must actually contribute to remedial action. It could do this only through his leadership, and his leadership would be continued through the years only if he was re-elected. This, he was continually aware, and more so as summer approached, was an election year. If his subordinates had done a good job among the distressed farmers, and if there were worth-while plans for future betterment, national attention, already alerted, could be focused intensively on the dust bowl with great profit—profit to conservation and profit to the coming campaign.

So on a summer morning a special train bearing the President of the United States and a full corps of correspondents rested in the railroad yards of Bismarck, North Dakota, after its trip from Washington. And that morning it rained. As Franklin's Great Plains Drought Committee climbed the steps of the *Pioneer* to report, shining pools of water reflected the blue sky. The dust bowl was wet for the first time in seven months, it was said wonderingly by the Dakotans. It was impossible for the most skeptical oppositionist not to conclude that Franklin was blessed with luck. His followers were inclined to rate his good fortune even higher. It seemed to many of them that a providential arranger was at work.

I shall not pursue the account of this journey unduly; it is, after all, meant only to illustrate how a gifted candidate allows opportunism to take charge of his destiny when fate seems to be developing favorably. I must, however, go on to say that the national spotlight, at its highest candle power, followed Franklin through the next ten days as he went about consolidating his good fortune. It was climaxed by a governors' meeting in Des Moines, the capital of Iowa, to which all the chief executives of the drought states were invited. Alfred M. Landon, being the governor of Kansas as well as the Republican nominee for President, had to come. His state was as badly damaged as any, and he could not refuse to participate in talks having to do with relief for Kansas. In his person he represented the essential negativeness of Republican policy as contrasted with Democratic energy. To him Franklin was affable and generous. But Landon left the conference a beaten candidate. How could he hope to challenge successfully the great man who had brought such benefits to the nation and was now just coming into full career?

The correspondents enjoyed the "non-political" illusion Franklin insisted on for all this journeying, and for this and other meetings. They played the game. The opposition politicians fumed in fury; the Democratic professionals relaxed. They had now only to make no mistakes in order to stay in power for another four years. And it was not the Democrats but the Republicans—as has been hinted—who made the really notable mistake of that campaign by attacking social security. Fatuously, it now seems, they thought they could enlarge their own resentment into a social cause. Landon himself was not so much involved as

425

the many industrialists who caused anti-security tracts to be put in their workers' pay envelopes. Not all employers fell into line, but there were enough so that it had the appearance of a concerted scheme to influence workers' votes.

In Wilkes Barre on October 29, Franklin accepted this Republican gift. "No employer," he said, "has a right to put his political preferences in the pay envelope. That is coercion even if he tells the whole truth. But this propaganda misrepresents by telling only half the truth. . . ." And he went on to explain that under the federal act employers were required to contribute three dollars to the workers' one for protection during unemployment and old age. "Three for one! There's the rub . . . their purpose has always been to compel the workers alone to put up all the premiums." He drove it home:

These propagandists—with allies whom I do not have to describe to you who know them—are driven in their desperation to the contemptible, unpatriotic suggestion that some future Congress will steal these insurance funds for other purposes. If they really believe what they say in the pay envelopes, they have no confidence in our form of government. . . . It might be well for them to move to some other Nation in which they have greater faith.[7]

This opportunity and the appeal it made possible were especially created for the circumstances of 1936. It was a most effective vote getter; but, much more important, it contributed to his deeper purpose of party realignment. But then, the whole Republican strategy contributed to that, consisting very largely, as it did, of appeals to propertied folk. Moreover, the bias of these appeals was to slide upward rather than downward on the income scale. This upper group Franklin had determined to slough off, along with its sycophants and its apparatus. If he tried to hold onto any part of it, his compromises would have to be such that he would be unable to consolidate the gains he was making among the lower-income groups. And these he must cement to himself if he was to have a really firm base from which to make further moves.

Besides, as we have seen so often, he must have a foil, some group to pillory as anti-social, dangerous to the economy and to the nation. The Supreme Court was for the moment ineligible for this role. The financiers had had their forced dose of reform. He returned, therefore, to the old progressive devil, big business, and coincidentally, as we shall see, to the equally old progressive angel, little business. Up and down the land, he beat the "economic royalists" until the dust obscured all other issues. In doing this, he accomplished just what he hoped for— he attracted the millions of ordinary folk who saw no evil in their tradesmen but much in their manufacturers, more in their "middlemen," and

[7] This and the quotations following will be found in *Public Papers*, 1936 vol.

most in "Wall Street." Also, he so infuriated those he attacked that their tempers escaped control and with their tempers went their judgments. Presently they were wildly flailing the air.

Those who were now being drawn to Franklin were the many voters who were not good party members. They much more easily gave their loyalty to a man than to an organization; and, once given, it was difficult to disturb because difficult to reach. Such people were unmoved—as the Republicans seemed unable to learn—by newspaper exhortations; and this was almost as true of radio propaganda. Once they had finally made up their minds who could and could not be trusted, the strongest possible bond was fixed between themselves and their man. All the events of the 1936 campaign seemed to contribute to this result.

It was part of this skillfully managed alignment to appeal for the support of what Franklin called the "independent" businessmen. Again and again he developed the theme that the New Deal had saved the system of private enterprise. If, as was now being claimed, the administration was hostile to business, if anyone in it had had the slightest inclination to change the system, "all that it would have had to do was to fold its hands and wait."

Instead we did what the previous Administration had declined to do through all the years of the depression—we acted quickly and drastically to save it. It was because of our belief in private enterprise that we acted. . . .

Along with this, he repeatedly reminded Americans that they were inescapably interdependent. There could not be one program for farmers, one for workers, and one for small business. Each needed the other; if one suffered, all suffered. This was something, he said, that the Republicans had never learned.

Holism?

The simple fact of our dependence upon each other was either unknown or entirely ignored by the Republican leaders of the post-war period. Their doctrine was to give definite help at the top and to utter pious hopes for the bottom. Twelve years of that brought the inevitable crash.

For the Republicans—and the Democrats who were, as Al Smith put it, "taking a walk"—to argue that Franklin was fomenting "class war," that he was stirring up hatred certain to end in violence, was such obvious nonsense, in view of his appeals for interdependence and tolerance, that it alienated far more support than it gained.

There was a visible gathering of strength about Franklin's center position, an adherence to his doctrine of concerted interests, all through the campaign. And it was not checked by his more aggressive speeches, those denouncing the "economic royalists" and warning against their return to power. The depression was still a lively recollection in millions of minds. The Republican appeal to put the businessmen back in

427

power was hopeless. It was they who had used their position to protect their own privileges while the country bled itself white. They were linked with Hoover; they were reminders of depression.

Franklin never acknowledged that he was running against a new man. Landon's name was never mentioned. The specter of Hoover was often raised—not by name, because that was not necessary, but by implication. And finally, the Republicans fell into the wide-thrown net. They brought Hoover out of retirement and fairly allowed him to take over the campaign—with assistance from the renegade Al Smith.

Speaking of the latter part of the canvass, Basil Rauch remarks[8] that the overshadowing of Landon in the last weeks was "as if the party leadership had regretted . . . the strategy of compromise with the New Deal. . . ."

Ex-President Hoover in Philadelphia on 16 October delivered a sharp analysis of the administration's budget practices. . . . This was the first of a series of vigorous assaults which ended on 30 October when the former President asked whether the administration intended to "stuff" the Supreme Court and called the Statue of Liberty the forgotten woman. Alfred E. Smith's contribution was chiefly invective. The irony of his approval of the Party and policies he had fought all his life was complete. He made his last effort to discredit his former friend when he associated the President with communism, atheism, and crackpots.

Franklin accepted with hardly concealed delight these Republican gifts. He had only to coast home to win, as anyone could see; but far more important, his hidden objectives were being massively forwarded by every move of the enemy. Still he could help, and naturally he did. He ought not to owe everything to the opposition.

It was really an exquisite touch that he should choose Wilmington, Delaware, as the locus for a speech on liberty. This was the headquarters of the du Ponts who had financed the Liberty League, and of John Raskob, the du Pont official who had been Smith's campaign manager in 1928. The speech was a kind of aside in the campaign; yet it illustrates the professional acumen so evident throughout. He quoted an amazingly apt passage from Lincoln, and except for a few short sentences, this was his whole speech. It was one of Lincoln's parables—the one about the sheep, the shepherd, and the wolf:

The shepherd drives the wolf from the sheep's throat, for which the sheep thanks the shepherd as his liberator, while the wolf denounces him for the same act, as the destroyer of liberty . . . Plainly, the sheep and the wolf are not agreed upon a definition of the word liberty; and precisely the same difference prevails today among us human creatures . . .

Recently, as it seems, the people . . . have been doing something to define liberty, and . . . the wolf's dictionary has been repudiated.

[8] In his *History of the New Deal* (New York: Creative Age, 1944), pp. 260–61.

To this homely story of Lincoln's Franklin only added:

What Abraham Lincoln said three-quarters of a century ago applies today as it did then. The people, men and women, of the City of Wilmington and the State of Delaware will, I think, appreciate their significance in the same measure as men and women in every other part of the Union.

An added fillip to the proceedings of that late summer and fall was provided by the demagogues of the splinter groups—notably Father Coughlin, Gerald L. K. Smith, Dr. Francis E. Townsend, and Congressman Lemke. Huey Long, who might have organized a really formidable third party, was now dead, and the Long machine in Louisiana had come to terms with Farley. But Smith, a minister from Shreveport, who had been a Long organizer, saw an opportunity and grasped it. He refused peace and put himself forward as the inheritor of Huey's Share-Our-Wealth movement. He was an authentic backwoods ranter, fanatic, reckless, and driven by ambition. He could always draw a crowd to hear his excoriations of the New Dealers. Dr. Townsend, growing old and tired, allowed himself to be drawn into Smith's wake. His scheme for universal old-age pensions had lost much of its appeal when the Social Security Act had been passed, and he thought some of his movement might be salvaged in a merger with Share-Our-Wealth.[9] For Smith this was less important than his natural merger with the fellow demagogue from Detroit, Father Coughlin, who was approaching a climax of abuse for all Rooseveltians, including, finally, Franklin himself.

Father Coughlin was one of those phenomena a democracy throws up once in a while and, because of its devotion to the principle of free speech, must tolerate until the appeal wears out. This union of Smith, a Protestant minister, and Coughlin, a Catholic priest, both devoted to the stirring up of hatred, intolerance, and civil disturbance, might seem strange in other lands; in America it was not unfamiliar. It was another "know-nothing" movement, anti-intellectual and completely irresponsible. And, as usual, there soon developed a following of the ignorant and malicious, always latent in any population, but given latitude only in a democracy.

In 1934 Father Coughlin had developed a radio audience of impressive size and had begun the publication of a propaganda newspaper. These fed his National Union for Social Justice; and the headquarters of that organization in Royal Oak (a suburb of Detroit) was one of the busiest spots in the nation. As the New Deal progressed and welfare legislation was adopted, he—like the other demagogues—was

[9] This resulted in loss of identity for Townsend's movement. Smith's current scheme was a "transactions tax" to pay for a minimum income of $5000 a year for everyone, which each would be compelled to spend. But the particular plan was of less importance than the fomenting of hatred which was Smith's stock in trade. His harangues approached the limit of allowable public speech.

forced to become more and more extreme. This allowed Franklin, as a national leader, to occupy more and more of the area left of center. The ranters were really desperate as the election of 1936 approached. Franklin, who had been obviously apprehensive while Huey was alive, and who had tried at first to take Father Coughlin into White House counsel, was now independent of them. They had worked themselves out to what was recognized by all but their most fanatic followers as the "lunatic fringe."

Anyway, they had never had an intelligible program. They seemed to agree only on a nonsensical enlargement of an inflation that was already one of the most criticized phases of the New Deal. To say of Franklin and his group that they were "antichrist," "Communists," and "godless capitalists," as Father Coughlin and Smith repeatedly did, was to try the credulity of even their blindest devotees. They made their final essay when they announced in June (of 1936) that they would support Representative William Lemke of North Dakota for President. They set up a "Union party" and made a bid, finally, for support. Lemke himself and his associated demagogues garnered less than nine hundred thousand votes. This was the virtual end of all the rightist radicals as a force in politics. No leader afterward gave them the slightest attention.

The Lemke *détente* enlivened the campaign, but it was the desperation of the Republicans that gave the proceedings real color. For the reactionaries, who "wouldn't be caught dead" in the company of Coughlin, Smith, Lemke, et al., finally retreated into a fanatical maze almost as incoherent as Lemke's,[10] and no more calculated to attract the voters. Al Smith's diatribes were especially violent, and Hoover had not made more palatable the sour and sullen comment that was his specialty. But the most savage of the Roosevelt-baiters was John D. M. Hamilton, Landon's campaign manager, who, as Ickes said—developing that vein of sardonic humor that would be so devastating when used on Willkie and Dewey—"was making a good run for President." Landon, the candidate, was the most moderate of the lot, but he was lost sight of as the election approached and the genuine reactionaries—those who had written, as the opening words of the Republican platform, "The nation is in peril"—swarmed out of their big homes and spacious offices to clamor that disaster would follow at once if the Democrats should win.

But the Democrats not only won, they won so overwhelmingly as to constitute a humiliating rebuke to the hate-and-fear campaigners. The

[10] It should be noted that only in appeal to violence were the demagogues "radical." They advocated inflation; but Socialism or Communism, the usual conservative *bête noires,* were anathema to them as they were to Landon, Hoover, or Al Smith. This sort of confusion is also a characteristic of democracy. Free people are incorrigibly unamenable to classification.

voters made it very plain that they approved of Franklin and of his policies and that they had no intention of authorizing the conservatives' program, Republican or Democratic. Franklin had gone a long way toward the realignment he was preparing.

If Franklin's intention had not been made clear during the early campaign, it was unmistakably so after his closing speech in Madison Square Garden. He then asked every voter to examine the record and said that the New Deal had not come so far without a struggle and could not go farther without more of the same.

For twelve years this Nation was afflicted with hear-nothing, see-nothing, do-nothing Government. The Nation looked to Government but the Government looked away. Nine mocking years with the golden calf and three long years of the scourge! Nine crazy years at the ticker and three long years in the breadlines! Nine mad years of mirage and three long years of despair! Powerful influences strive today to restore that kind of government with its doctrine that that Government is best which is most indifferent.

For nearly four years you have had a government which instead of twirling its thumbs has rolled up its sleeves. We will keep our sleeves rolled up.

We had to struggle with the old enemies of peace—business and financial monopoly, speculation, reckless banking, class antagonism, sectionalism, war profiteering.

They had begun to consider the Government of the United States as a mere appendage of their own affairs. We know now that Government by organized money is just as dangerous as Government by organized mob.

Never before have these forces been so united against one candidate as they stand today. They are unanimous in their hate for me—and I welcome their hatred.

I should like to have it said of my first Administration that in it the forces of selfishness and of lust for power met their match. I should like to have it said of my second Administration that in it these forces met their master. . . .

All over Washington on election day small groups made arrangements for getting together that night. Almost before they could gather after dinner, the family radios they surrounded were telling the news of victory. It came from everywhere, and as the count went on it only became more evident that a vast affirmation was taking place. Roosevelt supporters toasted their leader and made new resolves of loyalty. They were almost as elated at the discomfiture of the Democratic conservatives as at the humiliation of the Republicans. Now the New Deal—in abeyance during the last congressional session—could resume. They themselves would have revenge for the ridicule they had been treated to on Capitol Hill. It was their victory, as the conservatives had better learn.

The White House was silent and deserted. Its master and mistress, with all the entourage, were where they always were at election time —at Hyde Park. On the eve of the election Franklin had made a radio speech to the nation. Its tone was as different from that of the Madison Square Garden speech two days before as it is possible to imagine. He was calm and confident; he spoke of common things, of Americans going to the polls, making their free choice after having thought things through, and also of what an experience it was in responsibility and humility to be allowed, as he had been, "to know and share the hopes and the difficulties, the patience and the courage, the victories and defeats" of a great people. And, he said, "whoever is elected tomorrow will become the President of all the people."

Almost twenty-eight million Americans voted for Franklin next day; he carried every state but two. Riding on his coattails were the Democratic congressional candidates, so that three quarters of the senators and four fifths of the congressmen would be Democrats when the Congress convened again. If he felt in the after-election interval that now the way was opened to his further objectives, it is hard to see how he could have felt otherwise.

21

That mythical detached observer who has from time to time been referred to would have been baffled by a contrast now to be recorded. As the election returns of 1936 came in he would have seen a leader completely vindicated, victorious in a free election as few political leaders have ever been. Clearly he possessed the confidence of the American people; clearly they had expressed the wish that he should go forward in the way he had pointed out.

Just one year later, however, our observer would see that leader defeated, his program rejected, and he himself subjected to furious abuse. He would be unable to influence the legislature although the majority of its members would owe their election to his leadership. He would be reduced to protesting that, even if frustrated, he was right, an extraordinary come-down from his apparently impregnable prestige of last year. The interests he had excoriated in the late campaign would be back in control; depression would be threatening again; agricultural surpluses would be building up with all the sinister implications of former years; unemployment would be returning, and he—the leader—would be calling into extraordinary session during the autumn the Congress he had been unable to manage during the spring and summer. He would be hoping that he might now get from that hostile body a few measures out of the large number he had requested and which had been rejected.

Franklin's November hope would have had its origin—like that of January—in another unmistakable expression of popular support. The enthusiasm he had aroused on a journey among the people had rekindled his energies. His appeal, however, would again be diffused into the confusion of congressional procedures, and the extraordinary session would grant him no more than the regular session had granted.

When in October Franklin addressed the nation directly, a month in advance of the special session he was calling, he was just back from his journey—another "non-political" trip, similar to that of the summer

I MP.

His efforts to show congress
his pub. support had no
effect.

before. This time he had gone all the way to the Pacific Coast, stopping on the way at many cities and visiting numerous projects conceived and executed by himself and his administrators. The focus this time was on conservation, as before it had been on drought relief. Among the exhibits now readying were some that were admired everywhere in the world, and much attention centered in his visits. The great projects at Fort Peck, Grand Coulee, and Bonneville were now in being; everywhere the forests, the parks, and the grazing lands had been improved by the various measures and agencies he had fought for; the cultivation of the public domain by the Civilian Conservation Corps had begun to show. He was moved by what he had seen and very proud of the achievement. He asked the nation to share his pride.

Everywhere he had gone there had been a welling up of emotion only to be described as grateful loyalty. The crowds had been larger, if that was possible, than those during the campaign of last summer; and there had been that change I have spoken of, from a weighing, almost persuaded doubt, to complete surrender. He had won people's hearts. In every congressional district the politicians who had just refused him the support he asked, who had checked and cheated him through the bitter months of the regular session, had crowded and jostled each other to appear by his side before their constituents. Our observer would have found it an amazing performance. But he would have been still more amazed to see an instant return, when the legislators were back in Washington, to the same jealous hostility, the same refusal to co-operate, which had defeated the proposals whose passage Franklin regarded as his and their commitment to the electorate.

That is how it was. Franklin now had a place in people's affections which was secure. They had demonstrated in the only ways open to them their approval of his objectives; yet the representatives elected by the same people, who eagerly claimed to be his supporters, fell at once to obstructing and frustrating his every effort to make progress. How could there be a dichotomy like this in a representative democracy?

Part of the answer to this is that he represented a different constituency than they. The American system tended always to set the locally elected representatives against the nationally elected President. The jealousy, the refusal of co-operation, and the deep difference in objectives were built-in characteristics of the system. The President sought the general good; the representatives sought the good of those on whom they depended for direct support. These, they considered, although they protested in public that they shared the aims of the head of the ticket, were the men, the groups, the interests in their localities who kept them in office.

This structural fact went some way toward explaining why Franklin stood both victorious and defeated at the end of 1937 and on in even more distressing year that followed. And there seemed no that he could do about it, at least nothing he could think of. The Court fight had largely exhausted such resources as he could muster in assembling a majority for his measures. During the whole session, aside from obtaining renewals of several earlier measures which had had time limits, only two considerable accomplishments are usually marked up to his account, and both of these were very severely compromised.[1] These were the Farm Tenant Act and the Housing Act, the one setting up the Farm Security Administration in place of the Resettlement Administration, and the other making possible for the first time a formidable attack on the slum problem. But to one of these there was no great objection, and to the other there could be brought very strong lobby support. Neither really tried Franklin's leadership.

The events of 1937–38 form a well-delineated period in Franklin's career which offers certain real difficulties to the inquiring biographer. He can plead the structural difficulty I have mentioned, he can refer to already exhausted resources of political credit, and he can suggest the weakness inherent in a second—as contrasted with a first—presidential term. But none is sufficient, really, to account for the ineffectiveness and the continuous defeat of so thoroughly experienced and originally talented a politician as Franklin had become. Here he was, high in the popular regard, with years of success behind him in overcoming resistance—and he was able to get from Congress only those measures to which no one could find much objection or to which a fortunate concurrence of lobbyists brought enough support for passage. He lacked the force to get or keep the really remedial projects he knew to be necessary.

Explanation, it seems to me, must be looked for in two of the existing conditions (besides those already mentioned): one was Franklin's growing preoccupation with events abroad, and the other was the incredible ineptitude of the White House management in that period. The one diverted Franklin's attention from the domestic scene some time before his preoccupation was generally realized, and this left the

[1] The setting of automatic expiry dates on measures they did not quite dare kill and which they still secretly opposed was one of the favorite conservative devices of these years. Franklin caused much trouble for himself by good-naturedly allowing such provisions to be written into some early emergency bills, only to find that the aggressive conservatives demanded that such provisions be attached to all or nearly all his measures. This necessitated bitter fights all over again about the same issues every year or two. One of the worst battles of this sort was that in 1937 over the reciprocal trade treaties. The lobbyists for special interests very nearly prevailed, but the trouble need not have been brought on if at the first Franklin had objected to this procedure. The effect was that Franklin found himself struggling desperately every year just to stay where he was.

shaping of a domestic program, as well as the day-to-day management of congressional relations, to the current White House staff.

When Franklin made commitment to the Second New Deal he made his last basic policy decision until he made the fateful one that totalitarianism and democracy were so incompatible that the nation must prepare for war. This embracing of orthodox progressivism, requiring the turn-around begun in 1934, involved many more specific changes than ever were got into law. They still hung fire as Franklin turned away from their embarrassing demands to the more exigent struggle against dangers from abroad. Some of the problems were temporarily solved by the expansion involved in preparedness so that they could be at least postponed without penalty. Such, for instance, were the problems of unemployment, of conservation, of farm surpluses, and, indeed, of business regulation. In such an uprush of forced production as was brought on by the coming of war, demands for food and clothing became insatiable, unemployment turned quickly into labor shortages, and business abuses were overlooked or even excused as a necessary corollary to expanding activity.

This kind of explanation runs on into one of the important subsidiary decisions inherent in Franklin's determination to oppose rather than conciliate the dictatorships. This was that the existing competitive capitalism should be entrusted with the mobilization. He would not attempt to organize and socialize industry; he would leave it all to the businessmen. It would have been illogical at this point had he chosen otherwise, but of course this following of logic ran on to other consequences. There would be much encouragement by way of profits and induced, but not directed, expansions; and there would be tolerance for practices otherwise forbidden in the progressive book.

The worst of these practices was the open suppression of small competitors. Thus, as will be seen, the dilemma of laissez faire finally posed itself. Freedom became monopoly—but *private* rather than *public* monopoly. And the virtues claimed for free competition were sacrificed by strict adherence to its tenets. Grappling with this problem would be put off until the war was over—and until Franklin himself was dead.

What Franklin finally felt about the probable outcome of the choices he was making at the apparent nadir of his presidential life in 1937–38, no one can say. There are no signs of recognition anywhere in the record. But then he had not emerged into the victorious after years of war before he died. He would be put down as Commander-in-Chief of a powerful nation and the ruling spirit of a victorious coalition. The problems left unsolved by the rush of preparedness would again disclose themselves as the disillusions of peace returned. But Franklin would be resting then in the final peace of the high-hedged rose garden at Hyde

Park. It would be others who would have to face and solve the recurring issues of normal times.[2]

That Franklin's concentration on events abroad was deepening all through the 1937–38 period is evident in all that has since come to light. We can now understand the full meaning of his repeated essays into explanation and warnings several times repeated in his public speeches. These warnings invariably annoyed those in the Department of State who had prepared the innocuous first drafts. They were thought by the foreign service officers to be provocative. They were doubtless meant to test American opinion. It is by studying them that we can best understand his intentions toward the "aggressors" and his desire to reassure and support the other "democracies" and Russia, and we can see the urgency of his wish to create the greatest possible friendliness among closer neighbors. The speeches, the actions, and the private correspondence all contribute to the conclusion that these attitudes were all the time deepening and hardening and that long before his associates—Hull, for instance—were allowed to know it, Franklin had decided on active struggle against what he regarded as an implacable menace.

That he regarded this menace as held over from 1918 is very likely. It will be recalled that he had been dissatisfied with the ending of World War I. The indignation he had felt when the Germans escaped the penalties of their crimes had lain dormant for a long time; it was roused again by the Hitlerian political victories of 1933. Very quickly he decided on opposition. From the very first he refused friendship or compromise. That this might run on into war, he must always have known; but this is not to say that he was reconciled to such an outcome. On the contrary, the best chance to tame the dictators, short of war, was to build up the national strength and use it inexorably in every crisis. Perhaps the megalomaniacs would be taught caution. There was no other way, but of course even this might not succeed. It would certainly not be sufficient unless the strength were real and the will to exert it obvious.

At any rate, whether or not the aggressors would recall the lessons

[2] These difficulties for his successors would be much aggravated by the consolidations of corporate power gained during the war. I mention here something I have noted before (in "The Compromising Roosevelt," *Western Political Quarterly*, 1953), that his old mentor, Josephus Daniels, now Ambassador to Mexico, warned him about this. Daniels cited to Franklin something Wilson had said to him as World War I was beginning. This was to the effect that if the United States did enter the war, the interests controlling steel, oil, shipping, munitions, and mines would of necessity become dominant. When the war is over, Wilson had said, the government would be in their hands. Daniels said to Roosevelt that Wilson had been right. You have done something to reduce the privileges, he told Franklin, but the big interests will get them all back and more if we go to war and allow them to run it. Who will say that Daniels was not as right as Wilson had been?

of 1918 and stop short of such provocation as would bring the United States to a declaration of war, a build-up of the armed forces was indicated. So, for that matter, were related endeavors to strengthen the nation and to weaken the potential enemies. Of these measures, the most important was what came to be called collective security. This amounted to an alliance with those nations whose territories or interests were in some way threatened: principally Britain, France, Scandinavia, and the Low Countries. There could be various degrees of commitment to such a group. Franklin had in his mind's eye from a very early time a fast agreement to oppose aggression. Considering the nature of Nazism, he felt that nothing but the threat of force used by a powerful alliance would serve as a check.

It was to the double task of establishing collective security and rearming—the most urgent, to his mind, that he had ever undertaken—that he sacrificed everything else in the years before the actual outbreak of war in Europe.

There are complicated reasons why Franklin failed to mobilize the nation against the dictators, both materially and spiritually, in time to put them on notice that the United States would oppose by force any attempt of theirs to break out of their boundaries. It is enough to recall at this point that he did fail, that a war did come, and that it might have been prevented had he succeeded. So, at least, he, along with many others, would always believe. The sacrifice of the New Deal bit by bit proved not to be enough to buy support for a strong policy. The most he could persuade a divided Congress to give him, until war was actually imminent, was one grudging compromise after another. And he never could get, in anticipation of trouble, permission to discriminate between belligerents. The Congress would only consent to an equal embargo on both. And this, naturally, was taken by the dictators as a kind of assurance that there would be no interference with their designs for the United States.

One important early event was evidently discounted or overlooked by Il Duce and Der Führer. This was Franklin's successful change of relationship with the Russians. It must have seemed to the dictators—as to most Americans—a policy with purely domestic implications. Nonrecognition had become absurd; it was, besides, attributed mostly to Republican reaction; liberals were apt to have certain sympathy with the Russian revolutionists who were at least trying to improve matters for their people even if in an abhorrent way, and this was a liberal administration. There was, besides, a desire to resume trading. All this sufficed for explanation. It was not necessary to look to the balance-of-power implications of Russian rapprochement. Looking back, it can be seen that the central states of Europe could hardly have been defeated in the war which was to begin in 1939 if Russia had not exerted pressure

438

on one side until the United States could exert it on the other. But no one credited Franklin with such foresight. And even in later years, those who did not know of his very early determination to oppose Hitler paid little attention to this anticipatory move.

The year 1937 was the very beginning of the long intermittent attempt to show the American people where danger lay and what must be done to avoid war if it could be avoided. It was, unfortunately, also the year in which, for other reasons, Franklin's power to influence events was diminished. The Court fight demoralized his forces and weakened his hold on the party. What strength he had must be used against the gathering menace of totalitarianism. Even that soon appeared to be insufficient. The remaining items of his domestic program were simply shelved. He would not risk the provocation involved in asking for them.

How early he saw that what was coming would be a global engagement, and therefore much more hazardous than it seemed at first, when there was only the fanatic in Germany to worry about, it is again hard to say. But that the time must be set far earlier than it usually is, I am certain. For one thing, such considerations had tiny beginnings in his mind and grew to maturity without much outward manifestation. This was in accordance with the rule we have often observed. It was only after the certainty had crystallized that he began that other process which is so large a part of the art of politics. This is the fitting out of what-must-be-done with acceptability. Only when a widespread opinion has arisen that will support a public policy can it be formulated as a program. The business of creating that opinion, of coaxing it into being by argument, by the pointing up of lessons, by taking full advantage of illustrative incident, is a matter for experiment and is apt to be prolonged. It may well fail.

We should recall, in considering this, that Franklin was in full process of equipping the nation with a New Deal outfit when he ran into the difficulties we have noted: the resurgence of legislative enmity for the executive, conveniently centered in the Court fight, following the shift from the First to the Second New Deal. When he considered in his heart what he wanted most for the American people, as he must have done again and again in this period of attenuating power, he clearly concluded that what came first was survival; the world must be rid of the active menace to democracy. Nothing, really, was of any use if survival and freedom were not ensured.

It cannot have been difficult to give this interest priority in any weighing process. Totalitarianism was a kind of activist philosophy that could not tolerate the competition of democracy. A struggle to the death was inherent in the coexistence of the two views. Nazism and Fascism were linked with imperialism and aggressive expansion. The philosophy they represented was evident and growing in Europe and in Japan. The

United States, it was entirely possible, if preparedness did not go forward, might be crushed by attack from two sides at once. So Franklin must have reasoned. And, however sadly, he must have resigned himself to the price he must pay.

The old lessons from Mahan were always in Franklin's mind. Pressure from East and West must be kept away from the coasts. The logic of dividing and so weakening American strength by simultaneous pressure at points separated by four thousand miles of land must have occurred to the military and naval strategists of the aggressor nations. They must indeed be calculating the necessary force and planning its use. For that purpose the airplane borne to its taking-off place by ships was ideal. The development of airplane carriers and of suitable planes must be watched. The United States must have a shield extending out into the Pacific or across it, and the British Isles as a bastion and staging base must be utilized to the full, with the nations on the continent as buffers.[3]

Spain entered into these calculations, and perhaps Africa. Spain behind the Pyrenees offered the only practical buffer, at all comparable with Britain, to Nazi expansion. Accommodation with the Spanish was important. The best way of arranging this was to ensure a friendly government. Britain would always be our ally. It was part of democratic nature that it should be so, even if geopolitics had not so determined; and the British fleet was a precious asset, just as the islands themselves were indispensable forward bases. But there was trouble of a most embarrassing kind in Spain. And with the situation at home as it was, Franklin must have despaired of getting a free hand to deal with it. If only he could liberate himself so that he could discriminate between belligerents, he could support with various invaluable kinds of aid the forces friendly to the United States and to democracy. It was the tragedy of 1937–38 that he could not win this struggle. He was annoyed by the outcome of the Court fight, but he was dismayed and frightened by his inability to achieve any freedom to act in shaping foreign policy.

Thinking about his problem in this way, it is much easier to understand the events of this period. Consider the burden of his annual state-of-the-nation addresses in 1936, 1937, and 1938, together with the Chautauqua speech in August 1936 and the "quarantine" speech at Chicago in October 1937. Consider how far he had come by 1940, when his "dagger-in-the-back" speech was made at Charlottesville in June. It was a long, hazardous road. There was always stiff opposition. The speeches I have mentioned are only the better-known incidents in what

---

[3] In a memorandum for his son James, intended for Richard Neuberger, then a Pacific Coast writer and much later a senator, he called attention to the obvious consideration that any real defense of the coast must be "between three and four thousand miles" at sea. Cf. *Personal Letters: 1928–1945*, Vol. II, pp. 750–52.

actually was a persistent and anxiously conducted siege of American minds by the nation's President.

Franklin had had imposed on him by the isolationists a neutrality law.[4] But there can hardly have been anyone who did not know that the least neutral of all Americans was the man in the White House. He never neglected an opportunity to draw a lesson, and he pushed as hard as he dared against the opposition, often having to dissemble or retreat because he had gone too far and was in danger of bringing on a reaction. But he never swerved from his determination. And, what is important at this point in our narrative, he sacrificed all else to one overmastering objective: the checking of the dictators.

I have said that 1937 was not a fruitful year for either of Franklin's great purposes. Domestically, the Congress refused him a new agricultural act to replace the Soil Conservation and Domestic Allotment Act, which had proved insufficient; also, it rejected his proposal for seven new regional authorities to develop natural resources.[5] This proposal did not even emerge from committee. And the Executive Reorganization Bill, based on the findings of the Merriam-Brownlow-Gulick committee, quickly lost itself in shrill charges of dictatorship—a holdover from the Court fight.[6]

Perhaps worse than these defeats was the economic recession beginning in mid-1937 and running on through 1938. In this setback much of the ground gained so painfully during the preceding four years was lost and Franklin was open to the same charges he had made against Hoover—that he should have prevented trouble and, when it arrived, should have moved more quickly than he did to combat it. It could now be said that he had been slack and careless. It was easy to explain afterward what had happened, but not so easy to understand Franklin's inaction—not easy, but not impossible.

The slow recovery from the low of 1933 had gained a certain momentum by late 1936. And Franklin now had in the Treasury not only

[4] Signed on August 31, 1935; renewed by resolution, May 1937, to run for two years, after a strenuous unsuccessful effort on Franklin's part to secure changes that would free his hands.

[5] These were not, as he explained over and over, seven TVA's. They were merely planning organizations to receive and collate the proposals of their regions. These would again be sorted out and recommended for action at the national level. Franklin started out by wanting seven TVA's all right, but found himself opposed by many administrators (including Ickes) as well as many interests. This watered-down version was confused because of the mixed counsel. Nothing would come of it, and the dispute would last for a long time. Later it would settle into the hands of two protagonists—Ickes, who wanted his Interior Department to control resources; and Lilienthal, who thought regional authorities better than a national one. Like so many such disputes, this one ended merely in acrimony and stalemate.

[6] As we shall see, something was salvaged from this proposal in later attempts. The new Agricultural Act would also pass, much mutilated, in 1938.

Henry Morgenthau, always a gloomy viewer of the economic scene, but a collection of equally gloomy economists assembled by Morgenthau, who regarded all the proceedings of the past few years with a kind of horrified revulsion. It is not to be supposed that Franklin viewed the Morgenthau advice as anything more than amateur maunderings. But the fact is that no one in the whole administration was oftener in the White House. It was a matter for humor among all the others around Franklin. There was some feeling back of this wry acknowledgment of intimacy. For one thing, everyone else by contrast felt himself neglected; for another, no one could understand it. The dealings of others with the Secretary of the Treasury uniformly left them puzzled by his mentality, and they found it hard to imagine that the President could find either profit or amusement in the frequent and often prolonged conferrings that went on.

The secret of this curious relationship between the political genius and the inarticulate and unoriginal co-worker is not one that is easily penetrated. Part of it was Morgenthau's sheer doglike devotion, although the jealous manifestations of that worship sometimes amused but often visibly annoyed their object. Henry was always there, asking for attention, offering his services, viewing darkly any proposal not channeled by way of himself—but, above all, making his services, so far as he could, indispensable. Part of his hold on Franklin was personal and social. There was nothing Franklin could not ask of him, and I conclude that out of sheer convenience he did ask more and more. For often his private affairs were tangled and difficult—he had so little time for them, and perhaps so little competence even if he had had the time! How much of this kind of service he got, no one will ever know. The records will certainly not be allowed to survive. But I should guess that it was substantial and that it tied him to the Secretary with a certain bond that strengthened as his needs grew more compelling and as his debt increased.

On no other hypothesis does the long and intimate relationship seem explicable. But the relevance here is that, however the monopolization of Franklin's time and attention was made possible, something important to the public business must have gone on between the two. Morgenthau was, after all, Secretary of the Treasury, and he did have such people about him as Jacob Viner, whose economic predilections were well enough known. They were at complete variance with Franklin's views and with the advice to which he still seemed most susceptible. Day in and day out, over a long period, Morgenthau must have channeled dour and orthodox forebodings into the White House.

The policies that caused the embarrassing depression of 1937–38 are too similar to those Morgenthau was pleading for not to be tagged as almost certainly causal. Somehow Franklin made up his mind that expansion must be checked, that "pump-priming" must be contracted sharply, and that the budget must be brought quickly into balance. Advice of this sort must have come to him from the financial community by way of the Treasury and have been reinforced by the old-line Democrats. And if the historian, admittedly with too few facts to lean on, guesses that Morgenthau for months and years gloomed and objected, argued and begged for a conservative policy, there is the justification of almost inescapable inference. No one else in Franklin's confidence would have argued for such a change. And Harry Hopkins, for instance, as well as Henry Wallace with all his group—much respected by Franklin—must have anticipated trouble and must have felt thoroughly justified when depression set in so promptly.

Morgenthau's arguments, I should guess, were at first received with that quizzical negligence Franklin reserved for presuming intimates. But there were reinforcements. Politically it would be a fine thing to balance the budget. If this could be done and the recovery movement be kept going too, the trick would represent legerdemain of first-rate competence. Morgenthau's constant exhibition of demands for retrenchment and for "soundness" must have seemed to Franklin finally to have a really formidable substance.

On the other hand, Marriner Eccles was now regarded with respect and he felt that fiscal management should work both ways—should help to contract, when that was indicated, as well as to expand, so that at the moment he may have been uncertain but was generally reluctant to jeopardize recovery. He was, as has been noted, the unconscious Keynesian of the administration and, since the passage of the Banking Act of 1935, chairman of the Board of Governors of the Federal Reserve. From this very powerful position he used all his influence to sustain the recovery he felt was now gaining momentum. The difficulty was that as that movement progressed, the number multiplied of those who, in spite of the plain lesson being unfolded before their eyes, refused to believe that it had been induced by governmental measures. Indeed, they claimed the contrary with more and more effect.

Reaction is not perhaps a whole, but its fabric has a certain integrity. That the orthodox economists would refuse to believe what they saw, was expected by those who knew them; but Franklin was undoubtedly somewhat taken aback by the weight of concurrence. It was, for instance, one of the grievances of the Byrd-Hull-Harrison-Garner axis that the budget continued to be unbalanced. There was also objection to the nature of the spending program; it tended to help the disadvantaged. But in the conservative vocabulary this was the wrong appellation: "shiftless" was their preferred descriptive word. Any attempt to assist such people was a waste. It was worse than that, although the conservatives did not always admit the reason. It upset the class dis-

443

tinctions and the economic cleavages that were fundaments of their world.[7]

In Marriner Eccles' account of his government service[8] there is a chapter describing the economic events of 1937–38. Everyone in the administration was disconcerted, and there was a certain tension arising from the general attempt to escape responsibility as well as acute differences about what ought to be done. Franklin seems to have been rather ingloriously uncertain. He had made many moves that only a believer in a compensating budget would make; on the other hand, he had a secret longing to balance the national accounts. On the one side was Eccles telling him that the contraction of government spending was precipitating the trouble; on the other side Henry Morgenthau was agitatedly wringing his hands and denying that his policy of "soundness" had anything to do with the reversal. The truth was, Morgenthau contended, that Eccles and his crowd had caused such a loss of business confidence—the old "confidence" again—that enterprisers had all diminished their operations at once.

Eccles naturally argued otherwise. In his book it is put this way:

The . . . recession . . . was due principally to a rapid and speculative building up of business inventories at a time when government spending was curtailed and when consumer income was further reduced by the inauguration of the Social Security law. . . .

He goes on further to explain that the heavy speculation in inventories occurred for various reasons, including the approach of war in Europe with heavy influxes here of foreign gold at the same time that the government was reducing consumers' disposable income. The Social Security Law's taxes went into effect in 1937, but there were no outpayments. Then there was no soldiers' bonus in 1937. That had been paid out and had stimulated the demand for goods. The whole result was that in 1936 there had been a budget deficit with the outpayments going to consumers, but that in 1937 the budget was in balance and consumer income was reduced. It was, in fact, reduced by roughly the amount of inventory overaccumulation. Spending had not been enough to keep the economy going.

This is now the generally accepted explanation for the recession. At the time, however, conflict within the administration concerning the

---

[7] "I know what's the matter with Harry Byrd," Franklin said to me one time when Byrd was objecting to a resettlement project in Virginia. "He's afraid you'll force him to pay more than ten cents an hour for his apple pickers." Harry Byrd was the apple king of the Shenandoah and so his interest was direct. Others, like Jim Farley, who was turning his coat, wanted to think like the wealthy men they most admired. So it went. There were fewer all the time, instead of more, who really supported government action to stabilize the economy, much less to improve the lot of the lower-income receivers.

[8] *Beckoning Frontiers.* The chapter referred to here is Chapter 30, Part V.

FDR asked for continuance of spending

cause—and therefore the cure—was bitter. Eccles, thinking that government contraction was to blame, wanted to resume spending. Morgenthau, pressed by those on whom he relied, was almost hysterically defensive. Eccles wanted to embark at once on a vast housing program; Morgenthau, presuming on Franklin's ambivalence—which shows how excited he was—made a speech in November at the Academy of Political Science in New York which amounted to a declaration in favor of a balanced budget. It was presumed that the Secretary of the Treasury spoke the President's mind.[9] Yet during the special session of that fall Franklin was espousing Eccles' bill for an expansion of building.

The housing bill passed in January, but it was not until the middle of April in 1938 that Franklin really got off the fence and asked the Congress, in a special message, for a resumption of large-scale spending. Morgenthau's cohorts were routed, but it was not Eccles who was directly responsible; it was Harry Hopkins.

Harry for months had been desperately ill. His trouble had finally resulted in the removal of some two thirds of his stomach at the Mayo Clinic in Rochester, an operation so severe that his convalescence had been a long and trying one. Actually he would never be a well man again. But his physical weakness did not kill his spirit; and, as is known to everyone, his most important services to Franklin and to his country were still to come. That they should have been performed by one who half the time was in hospital or in bed, who never had the energy he needed to get through a normal day, and whose nutritional deficiencies were never to be quite understood, makes his subsequent career almost inexplicable. Heroic is the only term that seems adequate.

Franklin seemed to have more fondness for Harry as these disabilities increased. Harry was not the only individual, in these years, over whom he yearned in friendship. His own boys were all big, vigorous, even obstreperous men. About them—and about his womenfolk, for that matter—he had little cause for concern.[10] They went their ways with an independence and energy which were a kind of Roosevelt characteristic. But Missy LeHand was fragile and marked for early death, and Marvin McIntyre was by now so faded as to be almost transparent. They

[9] Morgenthau was disconcerted and, when he thought it over, indignant at the reception he got from the assembled pundits and financiers. To put it bluntly, they laughed at him. It seemed to them excruciatingly funny that a Secretary of the Treasury in Franklin's cabinet should be advocating a sound-money policy, especially since that Secretary was known to have been involved in what the financial community regarded as the childish attempt to manage prices by manipulating the market for gold in 1933–34. Morgenthau was actually hooted, and he naturally felt aggrieved. His enthusiasm for "confidence" was notably diminished by this experience—the more so since it had represented an unusual breaking of discipline on his part.

[10] Except for matters other than health, to which some reference will be made; and except for James' trials with his ulcers.

were to leave him, as Louis Howe had done, with unfillable gaps in his loyal surroundings. But dearest of all to him was Harry. He had him live in his house, finally, to be by him inseparably.

It happened that Harry awakened to responsibility again in March, just when he was most needed, and, leaving the ease he loved, headed back to Washington by way of Warm Springs, where Franklin was. It seemed to Harry, who had heard distressing reports from Bob La Follette and Bob Wagner, as well as from his own people in WPA, that Franklin must abandon Morgenthau and all his theories and act at once. He resolved to undertake the task of conversion.

Eccles tells what happened:

Harry Hopkins, who had been most active in earlier months in urging a resumption of deficit spending, was in Florida at this time, recuperating . . . While there, he seemed to sense that if he once again pressed the President for action . . . he might get a favorable answer. He was to join the President at Warm Springs, and en route there he stopped off at Atlanta and summoned to his side Leon Henderson, Aubrey W. Williams and Beardsley Ruml. Together they worked out once again the whole case for planned deficit spending. Armed with this memorandum, Hopkins proceeded to Warm Springs . . . By April 2, when the Presidential train was headed back to Washington, with Hopkins aboard, the whole of the budget-balancing program had been scrapped. . . .

The nation was informed of that fact on April 14, 1938, when Roosevelt sent a message to Congress [asking] for a resumption of large-scale spending.[11]

So the recession of 1937–38 was finally overcome, but not until vast damage had been done to the economy and much hardship had been visited upon low-income families. The stubborn opposition to government action, the obstinate refusal to learn were not yet abandoned. Even after this new lesson there was no more than a sullen retreat. In 1939, indeed, Eccles was to have the most open of the engagements in his long struggle for the principle of compensatory spending. He would have a public radio debate with Byrd. It would be a fierce difference. Byrd had a really fanatical concern for economy, but old Mormon missionary Eccles would carry the day for spending.

Eccles may not have convinced his opponents; but he won the battle for Franklin's mind. Something occurred, in fact, that was so rare as to be almost without precedent. On the morning after his earnest radio effort Eccles had a phone call:

I at once recognized the President's voice.
"Hello," he said. "How are you this morning, Marriner?"
"Fine," I said.

[11] Op. cit., p. 311.

"Well, I just called to condemn you and commend you. I condemn you because you kept me up last night . . . But now I want to commend you. I think your address was excellent. You made the problem so simple that even I was able to understand it."[12]

This was intended as persiflage. As the old saying goes, however, there may have been more truth in it than poetry.

Yet if Franklin seemed not to be certain of the means for recovery even though he had been using various of them for several years now from the White House, it was a time when he had reason to doubt everything. For all his philosophies as well as his abilities seemed to be failing him. He was no longer able to be certain of what he ought to do because nothing he did seemed to have the old magical habit of producing the effect he wanted.

It will be recalled what was concurrently happening. When the recession's first signs became unmistakable in the summer of 1937 the Court fight was just coming to its inglorious end. As trouble deepened during the autumn Franklin was again struggling with a Congress reluctant to grant him anything. He did nothing then about the economic situation, and he said nothing about it when the adjourned session opened in January of 1938. In February he recognized the growing problem of unemployment by asking for a supplemental appropriation. During the three months before that some three million workers had lost their jobs. Such a disaster could not be ignored, but it was not until April 14 that his "Recommendations to the Congress Designed to Stimulate Further Recovery" was sent.

To be sure, in his State of the Union message Franklin had spoken of the increase of purchasing power as an "underlying necessity." But it was made plain that he expected that increase to come from private enterprise. Economic recovery was connected with most of the measures he asked for, even the governmental reorganization hitherto rejected by the Congress as "dictatorial." He spoke of taxes and of the public attitude, generally, toward business. If this seemed hostile, it was because abuses had generated hostility. But the government sought, he said, to prevent or to regulate such matters so that co-operation could be more complete. Such a measure as a wages-and-hours law, for which he was asking, was definitely one of these. But he finished by saying that co-operation was something government could not conscript:

. . . no government can help the destinies of people who insist in putting sectional and class-consciousness ahead of general weal. . . . We have improved some matters by way of remedial legislation. But where . . . that legislation has failed we cannot be sure whether it fails because some of its details are unwise or because it is being sabotaged. At any rate, we hold our

[12] Ibid.

objectives and our principles to be sound. We will never go back on them.[13]

These were not the words of a defeated man. They were, indeed, a kind of renewed challenge to his chosen enemies, the big businessmen. They were complaining about taxes; they wept publicly every day over the unbalanced budget; they detailed the wastes of WPA; they said that Franklin himself was a dictator because he wanted a more effective presidency, and that he was a demagogue because he appealed for wages-and-hours legislation and for farm relief; he had undermined character, first with relief and then with social security; beyond all this, he was taking the nation into war—on the wrong side! It was an unending wail. And these sentiments could be read as often in the columns of the *Congressional Record* as in the newspapers and magazines.

It was certainly hard luck that just when the justification of his policies depended on their results, those results should turn unfavorable. There was no disposition to recognize that the conservatives were making a phony argument. The economic facts, as they gradually became known, supported Franklin and refuted his opponents. The "spending and wasting" they complained of were largely unreal. There might be wasteful spending, but there was too little, not too much if the economy was to be sustained. And so far as the economy was concerned, wasteful spending was as helpful as the most careful kind. In spite of his later protestations it seems quite clear that Franklin had intended to balance the budget even, if necessary, by liquidating WPA. He had hoped so much that he had refused to recognize signs of trouble and had waited too long when he did. When finally he acted in mid-April the situation had become desperate. It must be said, however, that when he was convinced, he was emphatic. A special message to the Congress opened with these words:

The prosperity of the United States is of necessity a primary concern of Government. . . . It is because the course of our economics has run adversely for half a year that we owe it to ourselves to turn it in the other direction . . .[14]

And he recommended appropriations he judged commensurate with the need. They would go to the Works Progress Administration, the Farm Security Administration, the National Youth Administration, and the Civilian Conservation Corps. The Reconstruction Finance Corporation had recently been authorized to expand its loans; now the bank reserve requirements were lowered. In addition, Eccles' housing expansion was asked for, and a new appropriation was requested for public roads and for flood control and reclamation projects. To make the attack complete, large sums were demanded for public works both by grant

[13] *Public Papers*, 1938 vol., pp. 13–14.
[14] Ibid., pp. 221–22.

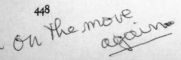
on the move again

and by loan. Speaking generally, he got what he asked for. The position in the Congress melted before the attractions of pu spending.

From this time on, with some few improvements, this would be the accepted pattern of response by government to signs of business recession. Never again, even in Republican times, would there be effective objection. There would, in fact, be less opposition in Republican times than there was at the moment. For just now the bipartisan Tories were in control. Also, they had a theory, and they intended to make it stick.

The theory was that what was proposed was just the reverse of what should be done. This new expenditure, they contended, would cause inflation; inflation would cause a loss of confidence; and that loss of confidence would stifle enterprise and decrease employment. Franklin, they contended, had stepped into the vicious circle again.

Of course recovery came, and once again the Tory theory was refuted; but once again, also, evidence was invented to explain the reversal. The last-ditch champion, Harry Byrd, was appropriately enough a southern Democrat. So were most of his allies. Franklin's determination to try for a political realignment was confirmed. The reactionaries would never change.

The struggle in and around the White House while Franklin hesitated to accept the advice of Bob La Follette, Bob Wagner, Harry Hopkins, Harold Ickes, and Henry Wallace was a strangely bitter affair, considering Franklin's former commitments. But his revulsion against inflation and an unbalanced budget was strong. He tended always to consider them evidences of incapacity; and whenever he surrendered to the necessity for using them he was under compulsion to explain away or camouflage the action. This was the first time—after four years—that he appears to have accepted, not only theoretically but, as a matter of positive governmental virtue, the management of income and outgo as a regulator of the economy.

This genuine conversion can be credited to Harry Hopkins as much as to anyone. Harry, in the circumstances of that dreadful winter—almost as bad, again, as that of 1933–34—put aside his habit of accepting Franklin's views. If Henry Morgenthau, on the other side, so far forgot himself as to make a public appeal while the matter was undecided, Harry managed so that the pressure of events should bear hard and unremittingly on his principal. Franklin was spared nothing. If he saw Harry at all, he was reminded of returning soup lines, of Hoovervilles, of apple peddling, and of despairing social workers. And in the end Harry's Augusta memorandum was the text for Franklin's April message to the Congress.

What a terrible season that was! The dictators were becoming more aggressive, the depression was worsening visibly week by week, and

449

his enemies seemed to be entrenched in the Congress elected to support him. He was denied the right to discriminate against the aggressors abroad; the isolationists were impregnable. There was such a row about the spending policy that he might be able to do nothing about the recession, even if he was sure what he should do. He was denied wages-and-hours legislation. And his proposed administrative reorganization was being treated with contempt.

Finally some of what he asked for was granted. Besides the Congress's inability to withstand the urge to appropriate funds for works projects in an election year, the advocates of wages-and-hours legislation finally overcame the businessmen's lobbyists. The Fair Labor Standards Act[15] had been under consideration during three congressional sessions; seventy-two amendments had been argued about, most of them broadening the exemptions for certain industries. The businessmen's demands and the Congress's vulnerability to their appeals had very nearly resulted in no action at all. And this was, as I see it, the last of the measures to be classified as belonging to the Second New Deal. Such regulations and standards as could be achieved were now on the books. There would be nothing more. Rather there would presently begin a reversal. If the lobbies were powerful in 1937 and 1938, they would be far more so in 1939. And Franklin's leverage would be far weaker.

It was not only the Congress that Franklin had to struggle with; he had a more and more difficult problem with the press. An illustration of this is furnished by an incident he himself related at a special conference with newspaper editors. It shows Franklin, I believe, in his best light. He was meeting hostility not with suppression or the least hint of it, but with arguments and with appeal to an ethical standard he believed to exist. He was arguing from his knowledge of operations, part of that store which always seemed incredible to those who were introduced to it for the first time:

Q: Mr. President, do you think the American press—we are newspapermen here and not stock market speculators—do you think the American newspapers have been unfair?

The President: I do not think they have been unfair, but I think they have been more responsible for the inciting of fear in the community than any other factor.

Q: I would like to ask you, Mr. President, in what particular?

The President: . . . Here is an example: The other night . . . there was an A.P. story. Well, I never expect an A.P. story to give my side the lead. I have not for years . . .

Q: Do you think the A.P. is unfair to you?

The President: I am not saying it is unfair. Listen, let me finish: Every time . . . there is a debate in the Senate—well, you have got, what is it, 11,

[15] Approved June 25, 1938. Cf. note, *Public Papers,* 1937 vol., p. 215.

12, 13, 14 Republican Senators, 3 or 4 Progressives like George Norris and La Follette, and you have got, oh, a half dozen, 6 or 8, old-line Democratic Senators who, if they lived in the North, would not be Democrats anyway. All the rest are Democrats.

Now, what happens? You have got a very small minority, less than a third who are not Democrats. Arthur Vandenberg gets up, or somebody else gets up, Carter Glass gets up, and makes a speech. Then the majority of the Senate hops all over him and makes some speeches on the other side.

Now, what is your lead? I know the mechanics of the thing. Your lead is based on speeches coming from less than a third of the Senators every time.

Now, your Press associations, especially the A.P., will, in their second or third paragraph, mention the fact that Alben Barkley or somebody else replied, and they will give them space, but your lead and the headlines of 85 per cent of the larger papers of the country will feature the speech of the Minority Member of the House or the Senate.

The other day, there was a party on the air. There was Vandenberg, and on the Democratic side there was Senator Hill of Alabama. Well, they each, I think, had—whatever it was—half an hour on the air. The first I knew about this fact—I very rarely listen on the radio and I had not arranged it in any way—was the next afternoon when I got the first edition of the New York *Sun*. I read the headline, "Huge Recovery Plan Attacked by Republicans; Vandenberg Denounces Roosevelt Relief Program; Says Pump Priming Means Bigger Debts, Bigger Deficits." Then there is the Washington headline, A.P., and it goes on. First the main story, right-hand column. And it goes on, "continued on page 7," and talks all about what Vandenberg said. And then it goes on and talks about what John Hamilton gave out.

"Well," I said to myself, "that is funny for the A.P. I do not believe it left out what Mr. Hill said, but there is not a peep, there is not a mention of Lister Hill in the *Sun*.

So—it happened to be on my bed that night—I picked up another New York paper and this story carried the whole of the A.P. story. Now, this A.P. story in its lead mentions the anti-New Deal attacks of the Republicans, it mentions Hamilton in the second paragraph and eventually, in the third paragraph, it talks about the feeling in the Congress. In the fourth paragraph it talks about the Administration side. That was left out of the *Sun* story. In the fifth paragraph, it talks about my weekly conference with the Congressional people—that was left out in the *Sun*. The sixth paragraph [reading] "The Vandenberg speech was made during a broadcast with Senator Hill of Alabama. Hill said——" And then Hill's remarks were carried in the seventh, eighth and ninth paragraphs. In other words, outside of the lead, the A.P. did give you a truthful story . . . the *Sun* deliberately cut out what the A.P. had said to them. If you people think that is fair newspaper editing, I do not. Now, you find hundreds of cases of that kind.

Then, there are papers that have their special bureaus in Washington. You know perfectly well that the special bureau chiefs down here write what the owner of the newspaper tells them to write, and they leave out half of the truth. . . .[16]

[16] Ibid., 1938 vol., pp. 278–80.

This incident seems to me significant because it is of a type. One who reads the documents, the newspapers, and the other commentaries of these years, as well as Franklin's letters, must see how deep his concern was with the obstacles to his leadership. He thought of these as denials of democracy, and no day passed without some manifestation of his uneasiness. There were the lobbies affecting the Congress and either blocking or compromising the measures he asked for. There was growing uneasiness because of infiltration by these same insidious termites of the administrative agencies where they influenced the writing of regulations and influenced even more their application.

Worst of all, there was the constant poisoning of the public mind by the press and the radio. This caused a special indignation on his part because it complicated so much his own corrective efforts. These, he had good reason to feel, were not succeeding. He was unable to bring the real pressure of public opinion to bear on the Congress, partly because he lacked the means to create that opinion, and partly because, even when it existed, it was deliberately distorted and misrepresented. There did not exist, he contended, a free or a fair press. Its owners, like the Supreme Court, had predilections; and, to them, their properties were organs for propagating their views.

There is no evidence whatever that Franklin's constant efforts changed this situation in the slightest degree. He protested publicly sometimes; he frequently wrote to publishers and others about specific unfairnesses. But the press and the radio were agencies of business; and business was allergic to him. The treatment he continued to get was hostile and unforgiving. There were a few exceptions among the organs of opinion, but the usual estimate was that 85 per cent of the press was against him. It must be understood, however, that this was not the gravamen of his complaint. What concerned him most was the unscrupulous doctoring of the news columns. The rationale of a press free from governmental interference, he often said, was that it reported the news so that public opinion could shape itself in accord with the facts. The owners of press and radio, in typically unscrupulous fashion, maintained the pretense of non-partisan reporting; but actually it was a fraud. They deliberately and studiously managed reportage to create the opinion they favored, and they refused to register opposition to their views.

This same sensitiveness and indignation show in Franklin's letters during these years. He complained to Baruch about the newspapers:

> But I hope that this experience of yours will enable you to understand a little better the kind of misrepresentation—unfortunately deliberate—to which I am subjected almost every day.[17]

[17] *Personal Letters: 1928–1945*, Vol. II, p. 777.

But that this was a matter running far beyond merely the misbehavior of the press was made clear in other letters. He seized one opportunity in particular to read Fred I. Kent a lesson sharper than can ever have been ventured before by one in his position. Mr. Kent was a prominent banker and a member of Secretary Roper's Business Advisory Council. He had been one of Wilson's wartime financial confidants. He let himself in for the following lecture by objecting to Franklin's advisers. They were, he said, impractical theorists intent on destroying business. Mr. Kent came in on this chorus a little late but quite full-throatedly. Franklin replied:

Dear Fred:

I am sorry that your letter of February seventh shows so little conception either of fundamental economic facts or of suggestions for remedying the fundamental causes of economic and social ills. . . .

In regard to your statement—typical of so many of your friends and mine —that I receive bad advice, I can only call your attention to the fact that like the Pharisee you assume that all advice which does not conform to your advice is bad advice. If occasionally you would give me advice on some subjects which relate to the deeper aspects of sound, national economics, you would be more helpful.

You remind me of a friend of yours and mine who came in the other day and to whom I said "What do you think should be done about the farm tenancy and share cropper problem?" This gentleman could see no relationship of that problem to his business until I pointed out to him that fifteen or twenty million Americans . . . have no purchasing power . . .

I see a greater number of the type of person you mention [the practical men] than any other group. I do not consider them dishonest and I do believe that they are in the process of learning many lessons which are fundamental in their relationship to the good of the country. You yourself are in that category. I think you are learning greatly. If you could sit in my office beside me for a week it would be very helpful to you, for you would be gaining in education in every line as greatly as I am gaining as each day passes. I am really sorry that you do not have opportunities of this kind, and I hope you will seek them on every possible occasion.[18]

This and other rebukes of the same sort had a deep origin. There was something he struggled against and felt that he must do something about, yet he was frustrated; and his frustration made him irritable. That the opposition to his efforts should be unremittingly and universally maintained was something he felt was unfair. He could not accommodate himself to what he regarded as a gross betrayal of democracy. He had a fundamental fear, I think, that the whole system to which he was committed was jeopardized by its apparent inability to cleave to a concept of fairness and to operate by its own acknowledged precepts. In spite of his apparent serenity and lack of tension there was

[18] Ibid., pp. 758–59.

453

growing in him an unease. Many times in the past few years he must have asked himself whether he had chosen well when he made the change from the First to the Second New Deal. That change had been made because when the First was tried it had proved politically unacceptable. He could not persuade the American people to redefine their progressivism. They would not go into partnership with big business and try to tame it in association. That was his conclusion. He felt justified, certainly, in this assessment by the approval he got from those whose good opinion he sought—the Brandeis school. And he allowed them, with their primitive philosophy, to staff his own office, to speak and act for him in liaison with the Congress, the courts, and the public.

Franklin and his "advisers" were building now a rigid containing framework for big business. This stood in contrast with the flexible partnership of earlier days. They would define what business must *not* do, never what it *must* do. There were admittedly exceptions. The banking and monetary arrangements were something more than this. But inconsistency was something that troubled the progressives very little except when it really affected their theories. They had to make an exception of fiscal policy in order to have the freedom they wanted in other fields. They thought the economy could be sufficiently balanced by fiscal manipulation so that laissez faire in industry and commerce could be enforced and would work. They had been unhappy ever since the dissolution of NRA because mere dissolution was not enough. They wanted to initiate an aggressive campaign to break up the big businesses. They wanted to implement Brandeis' faith that littleness was a cure-all. Given rigid and well-enforced negative rules and given a smallness among business units which kept power within bounds— given these, the competitive system would work, and work fairly.

It is doubtful, I think, that Franklin ever believed in this as a system. Certainly his ambivalence toward it was always marked. The Brandeis people were never really happy about him even after they had captured the White House. Their unhappiness probably had its center in the incontestable fact that they were unable to get their way even with Franklin's talents enlisted in the cause. The lobbies were too strong, the press was uncontrollably and persistently unfair, and public opinion was indifferent. The Congress perhaps believed in competition. But it persisted in writing the kinds of laws businessmen wanted. Monopolies were growing, but they were private. Matters were getting out of hand.

22 It has been remarked that Franklin's concern for Harry Hopkins' health and that of Missy LeHand and Marvin McIntyre was perhaps all the greater because his own and his family's health was so seldom worrisome. Eleanor was at her most vigorous in these years. She was expressing herself more satisfactorily than she had ever done before. She had discovered the government and its potentialities for good. Her reluctance to leave New York for Washington was quite overcome and, by now, forgotten. She seemed to be everywhere and in everything; and, although this did not suit her stuffy critics and annoyed self-centered administrators, it was approved by an enormous following, especially of women, who were grateful for her intervention in behalf of the causes they were sure men —and certainly men who were bureaucrats—tended to neglect.

The Roosevelt children, all five of them, were strong and extroverted. The boys had grown to be robust men, well over six feet tall, and handsomely put together. Anna, their sister, had corresponding looks and spirit. Eleanor said to me one time when I was suffering from hay fever that it must be terrible to have a chronic affliction. She sympathized with me, she said; and then, overcome by her incorrigible honesty, she went on to say that that wasn't really true. She couldn't *really* sympathize with anyone. She didn't know what it meant to be sick. She had had no sickness in her life, if her six confinements were excluded. She had never even had a headache. She looked at me as though she were trying to reach across an impassable gulf.

Aside from Franklin's illnesses—and he had had several, as we have seen, including a severe bout of typhoid, besides the polio—she had had no worries of this sort since the death of the first Franklin Jr. Both she and Franklin were to have one in 1938. James, the second boy, the one to whom Franklin was always trying to pass on his political knowhow, was to discover himself afflicted with stomach ulcers—much as Harry Hopkins was—and to have an extensive removal operation at the

Mayo Clinic—again like Harry, except that he made an altogether better recovery. But this aside, most of their worries about the children were of another kind.

The inability to stabilize at a normal family life, which in the end would afflict all but John, was already showing itself. Anna and Elliott had already been divorced and remarried—not the last time for either—and James' marriage to Betsy Cushing, who was so much beloved by Franklin, would soon break up. During this time both the younger boys would marry. Franklin's new wife would be Ethel du Pont, a venture most people thought ironic. Uniting the Roosevelts and the du Ponts was a kind of tour de force it would be hard for the young couple to sustain, and they would not succeed very long. John's marriage was more stable. He was inclined toward business and seemed likely to be the most settled and dependable of the boys.

The politicians in the family were to be James and Franklin, as could already be seen. James was working as a White House assistant. Franklin was exhibiting good looks and a charm of manner almost startlingly reminiscent of his father. Many a professional looked at Franklin, when he appeared in his father's company, with a thoughtful and speculative eye. Franklin was still only a boy. But Roosevelt boys could never be written off. They too often had futures.

There were other worries about the boys. Two of them had made embarrassing forays into business, and they exhibited a regrettable lack of sensitivity about using influence. All the Roosevelts were under the most intense surveillance, especially since the conservatives had recovered their aggressiveness. The publishers who detested Franklin were happy to make the most of the business deals into which the boys were led by older men of doubtful reputation or deficient scruple. But it must be said that neither of them resisted very strenuously. The Roosevelt vigor expressed itself in restless activity. And since neither could by any stretch be called an intellectual, the restlessness was not channeled off into professional activity. James had been revealed to be an insurance man with a large and lucrative clientele. And Elliott might be described as a miscellaneous speculator, since he was in and out of one deal after another. He seemed to have a weakness for real estate, the movies, radio, and airplane ventures; and all of them could be affected by White House influences.

There was not anything remotely resembling illegality about any of this. But all the same it left a good deal to be explained. It was well known—or became well known—that Franklin had aided some of his sons' ventures in various ways. There is nothing wrong, either, about a father assisting his sons to get a start in the world. But when the father is a President, it is arguable that he ought to be more cautious than Franklin was. If the boys had no discretion, Franklin should have instructed them. This is actually not a very nice passage in the family history. It has to be put down that there was less scruple evident than ought to be a minimum in so centrally situated a group.

The divorces went very badly with the religious communities in the United States. It was not that divorce, under provocative circumstances, would not be forgiven almost anyone; it was that among the younger Roosevelts there seemed to be a casual lack of respect for the matrimonies they contracted. Also, that these same children should seem to have a deficient sense of fitness which led them to exploit the presidential office made it possible for detractors to harp on the theme of a Roosevelt weakness which, at the extreme, became a broad inference of unethical conduct. That Franklin and Eleanor were faithful, that Eleanor was completely selfless, and that Franklin was devoting his talents to public work tended to be forgotten when the children's vagaries were commanding attention.

There was question whether these vulnerabilities might not be politically useful to the opposition, and actually several newspapermen, from about this time on, undertook a persecution of the family which had all the earmarks of a crusade. No opportunity was missed. In the long run, however, the malice and enmity intended in these attacks were neutralized by the parents' behavior. And most people wound up rather feeling sorry for a President and his wife who were—like other parents—having a difficult time with their children.

There was some wonder whether an upper-class childhood, followed by Groton and Harvard, had *caused* the aberrations among the boys. All the advantages in the world seemed to have been theirs. And the parents had been loving enough. The speculation tended to miss the point that public life defeats family care. Franklin had been, except for the interval of his convalescence from polio, immersed in political affairs, and Eleanor, in recent years, hardly less. And anyhow the Roosevelt ebullience had reached a kind of apogee in these children; it was bound to burst convention and spill over. Then, to put it plainly, few members of the other sex found it easy to ignore the virility and handsomeness of the Roosevelt boys. Restrictions tended to melt very easily in their presence.

Eleanor did not love them less because of their faults, nor did Franklin for that matter, although as parents they may well have wished that each would discover—what none of them had—an absorbing occupation. It seems strange that only one of the five became a professional of any kind. Franklin Jr. finally opted for the law, but his pursuit of it was rather like his father's—nothing to brag about. Still, it might do as a foundation for a political career. Up to the time his father died, however, Franklin Jr.'s foot would not have been planted on the ladder that so obviously awaited his tread. He was a fun-loving young man whose pursuit of pleasure was threatening to become an occupation.

During the second term all the children were in and out of the White House. None of them lived there, except for brief spells. They were growing up; they filled the guest rooms with undergraduates at vacation time, and there were entertainments for them—dances, usually, in the East Room to the music of lively bands. But the social life of the mansion could not actually be dominated by the younger people. It was fixed by protocol. Ceremonial, however, under Roosevelt auspices, had a way of escaping the appearance of routine. Both Franklin and Eleanor had the gift of infusing social duties with a warmth that transformed them into hospitality. Guests never forgot that he was the President and that she was the President's wife; yet the graciousness they radiated was so well practiced that it seemed informal. Franklin called an incredible number of acquaintances by their first names, and his surface cordiality was impervious to the most biting sarcasm of his critics. Eleanor was everyone's friend, and her warmth was tempered just enough by worldly wisdom to make it realistic. They were a presidential couple of classic competence, and even their enemies recognized their fitness.

The White House schedule is an exacting one. There are numerous set occasions, entertainments of various sorts for the Congress, receptions and dinners for the judiciary, for foreign diplomats, and for the cabinet. All must be carried out according to custom, and it was done with fine distinction. Even the glassware and china for state dining had been Franklin's choice. Then there were miscellaneous occasions when the press was entertained, when a mixed list of the socially eligible had to be received; and there were always the minor officials, far down in the social ranking of Washington, but still entitled to some attention. Several nights each week during the winter season there were formal dinners, receptions, or musicales. And even when the more magnificent affairs were not scheduled there were guests for dinner. The informal dinners in the family dining room could run to thirty guests, and there were seldom less than a dozen.

Those who had a claim to attention of this sort and were asked by Mrs. Helm, the social secretary,[1] to be present at one of these dinners felt that these were among their most precious memories. For all was done in order but with grace. Each guest was a guest indeed and made to feel not only welcome but somehow intimate with the presidential group.

[1] Edith Benham Helm, who became the author of *The Captains and the Kings* (New York: Putnam, 1954).

Visitors on these occasions were met at the door by the chief usher,[2] who began the process of easing the natural embarrassment among newcomers with a smile, but better still with explicit instruction. Even for most of the small dinners there was a seating list drawn up on a large cardboard, and the entering guest was told where to sit and how to get there. Then he was taken into the Green Room to wait. The other guests were there or came in presently; all were introduced. Then Missy came in with Mrs. Roosevelt and the two of them went around the circle, finding things to say. Presently all went along to the dining room. Franklin was already there, having come down in the elevator and been wheeled to table first. He transferred to his armchair, and as the guests came in he had a word for each, but especially for the lady who sat on his right.

That lady, unless she was very accustomed and sophisticated, was apt to be awed. If she was tongue-tied, Franklin had a way of leaning to her and calling up some subject within her competence to set her talking. It might be only a mutual recollection or a question about her family or her work. Presently she was looking into his face and exchanging animated remarks. It was a kind of magic he had. But Eleanor had it too. She, just as effortlessly, had engaged the man on her right. But before the meal had progressed very far the conversation was likely to have escaped the low-voiced exchange of neighbors. Franklin or Eleanor would have tossed a gambit into the circle, perhaps to draw out one or another of the guests, and not infrequently, then, Franklin would take command. Almost always those present felt when they left that they had been taken into the confidence of very important people and had discussed affairs of moment. Franklin sometimes appeared to be indiscreet. He told stories; he related incidents; he characterized public figures; he spoke of policy as though no one could possibly disagree.

These informal performances as Franklin sat in his big chair in his velvet dinner jacket, a large, almost flamboyantly handsome man, gesturing with his long cigarette holder, were among his very best. Even the most cynical and withdrawing skeptic was apt to find himself disarmed. But at these smaller unofficial occasions those who were unfriendly usually were not present. The small dining room was reserved for that "family" of Rooseveltians whose numbers grew and grew until there were thousands who were "friends" and felt themselves actually to share an intimacy with their President and his wife.

This was a useful art. But very few who saw it operate thought of it

<hr/>

[2] For a description of the usher's duties, see *Forty-Two Years in the White House* (Boston and New York: Houghton Mifflin, 1934), by I. H. (Ike) Hoover, who worked at the White House in one or another capacity from the Harrison administration to that of the second Roosevelt.

as an art. They saw a splendid public figure off duty, relaxing as his gentlemanly training required, among family and friends, at table and in the drawing room. It was an unconscious performance. I often wondered at the effort expended. Both Franklin and Eleanor had had long and tiring days, and it was not restful to be looking after comparative strangers, putting them at ease, skillfully guiding the conversation of twenty or thirty people at dinner and on into the evening, through two or more hours. Yet night after night, even when there were not more demanding dinners stretching out interminably through fixed courses in the state dining room, the same care was given to the conduct of the affair. In spite of the relaxed air it had, it must, I felt, have been a user of energy which could ill be spared from other duties.

When dinner came to its end, Franklin left first, swinging onto his wheel chair and going out gaily. There might then be conversation upstairs or there might be—often was—a movie. There was a projection room rigged in the second-floor hallway, and the long room could be turned into a kind of theater. For an hour or two then Franklin and Eleanor could be excused conversational duties. But more and more, as the pressures increased, Franklin disappeared after he left the dining room. One or two of the guests, or others who came in after dinner, were asked into the Oval Room. Matters of state were still to be discussed. And even when these visitors had gone, there was still an implacable pile of papers, the famous "wash" Franklin was always doing and never got done. Eleanor made nothing of these disappearances; her husband, she said simply, had work to do. She took charge until the guests departed.

For one who had a realistic view of the current situation, the outstanding characteristic of the White House regime was its serenity. That the grand and urbane gentleman who presided at table or stood to receive passing lines of guests, who chatted with ambassadors, secretaries, and senators without a hint of annoyance, and who talked freely to the press, answering calmly even the most "loaded" questions (though he sometimes let go in private)—that this paragon of presidential behavior was everywhere checked and harassed, that he was borne down with anxiety for the nation's future, no one could have guessed.

Yet the fact was that troubles had multiplied. His loss of leverage had gone disastrously far. And when it was seen that he could neither complete his domestic program nor persuade the Congress to grant him a free hand abroad, the watching totalitarians were quick to perceive and to take advantage of his weakness.

The businessmen no longer trembled when he threatened; he had no power to bear down on them. They even began to plot the recovery of their privileges. They would begin with taxes. They had been especially annoyed by the levy on undistributed profits. This was a favorite operating ground of the insiders in corporate management. Their first blow for freedom would be to strike at this restriction. But the dictators abroad also had precisely the same reactions and intentions. The foreign-language blocs—America's native Nazis and Fascists—operated more defiantly as the months passed. And abroad, the dictators themselves sneered at democracy and pointed to the helplessness of the leader of all the world's democrats.

The effect of Franklin's subsequent failure with the Congress of 1938 was to strengthen reaction both at home and abroad; and although the casual White House visitor would never have guessed it, the erosion at the center was serious. Franklin was aware of it; more so than anyone else. His journey through the nation in 1937 ought to have renewed his command of the situation; but it did not. What else was there that he could do? He waited through the early months of 1938. Things got worse rather than better. And this was the most serious period of the recession. In late summer he went off to southern seas. He came back by way of Georgia, and there, at Barnesville, he counterattacked by asking Georgians not to send Walter George back to the Senate. It was the beginning of "the purge."[3]

It was a serious matter for a President to interfere in local electoral contests, and Franklin knew what the risks were. But he felt driven to it. He was as nearly desperate as he had ever been in all his political life, which seems strange to say of a man who had such vast popular support and had won two presidential elections. It was nevertheless true. A brief review of the events between winter in 1938 and the succeeding autumn will show why this was so.

Take first the congressional session: In February the new Agricultural Adjustment Bill was passed; this could have been counted a success in other circumstances, since it was an advance over previous measures. But Franklin had very little to do with it. It was passed because the farm lobbyists had reached a kind of truce in their quarreling and agreed finally on a bill. It was so favorable to agriculture that they could hardly oppose it. It was the work, originally, of Henry Wallace and his group and included the new provisions for which he had been agitating. These were picturesquely described as an "ever-normal

[3] The incidents of this famous "mistake" of Franklin's will not be described at length. Reference to them can be found in Rosenman's and others' books. The emphasis here must be on the converging pressures that made such an attempt necessary. That the purge failed in its main purpose—that is, the securing of a liberal Democratic majority—should not blur the clear reasons for his undertaking it. Nor should the consequences of the failure, running on into the war, be obscured by its lack of success. From Franklin's point of view it was well worth trying; and afterward he could not have found excuses for himself if he had not made the attempt.

Henry Wallace

granary," which meant that the responsibility for surpluses was accepted by the government.[4]

The agricultural interests were well pleased, and the processors were not too annoyed—if they had been, the bill would not have passed—although they would have preferred to eliminate the government from the storage business. The credit went mostly to Henry Wallace, as it should, and his reputation was considerably enhanced. He was by now an active presidential candidate, one of several who relied on the assumption that Franklin would not run for a third term. But he was as unpopular as ever with the professional politicians, who said that he was "unreliable"—he had, after all, been a Republican until recently. They also distrusted what they heard about him personally—his mysticism, his lack of warmth, his awkwardness in public.

But Henry Wallace gave more real strength to Franklin's administration at this time than it got from any other source. The Department of Agriculture was an idea factory; more imagination used in the public interest was evident there than anywhere else in Washington. And it was a happy event to have a satisfactory comprehensive law written and actually passed when so much else was hopelessly lost in the congressional thickets. Moreover, as Franklin noted the signs of eroding loyalty everywhere around, it grew on him that Henry Wallace could be counted on to the limit. He might be maneuvering for the presidency—he undoubtedly was—but he was doing it within the accepted rules.

Franklin had now three possibilities for the succession in 1940. He had still not fixed on any one. He had not even given the slightest encouragement to any of them. But then no one knew better than he that the presidential virus grows lushly with no more encouragement than the absence of outright hostility. He was not telling anyone, any more than he ever did, what was going on deep down in his mind; but it can be seen now what were the elements of the general problem being formulated there. First, he would not run again. So he was telling himself and even broadly hinting to others. Second, the choice of successor would be difficult for him to determine because Tories at home and totalitarians abroad were a threat no liberal could ignore. All that he had worked for, and what so far he had achieved, might easily, very easily, be lost to such a combination. The domestic Tories would conciliate Hitler. That consuming monster, feeding on success, would re-

---

[4] The devices used were complicated. They consisted of loans to farmers if prices were below parity, with storage in government-owned or private facilities of produce withheld from market. Provisions for keeping supplies within bounds were also complicated. They rested on a consent ballot and, when consent was gained, a reduction of acreage, with penalties for overproduction. The "ever-normal granary" phrase was one Wallace had used when he had been editor of the family farm journal, *Wallace's Farmer*.

duce Britain first, and then America, to at least some degree of subservience.

If he was to have a successor he must be certain that whoever he was would and could stand off the enemy at home and meet, without shrinking, the threat from abroad. He looked, I am sure, with an appraising eye at his three possibilities. I think he ranked them at this time thus: Hopkins, La Guardia, and Wallace. That incorrigibly political mind must have played endlessly with the possibilities. But even if he told himself that he must not run again, he never let it be concluded that he had actually decided. It hung in the air. And whenever he thought of his new-party project and considered how slowly it was developing, he must have wondered whether the consummation was not fated to be postponed beyond 1940.

His progress was certainly so slow as to be almost nonexistent so far as actual achievement went. His hold on the Congress grew weaker rather than stronger, and this might very well mean that his hold on the party would not be sufficient for the needs of 1940. The Tories could very well nominate their own man—probably, he must have thought, Hull, who more and more was the center of reactionary praise. He was a good gray elder statesman, dull but vindictive. He was dear to the Southerners, but actually he came from a border state. He was no collectivist; he was not even a New Dealer of any sort. And he would move into war without compunction. They regarded him as the very ideal of the stuffed shirt they were looking for. Under him businessmen would run the country and generals would manage the forthcoming war. This was the conservative model of Utopia.

Hull, like Wallace, had got something from the Congress. His international laissez faire in a moderate version was so thoroughly in the Democratic tradition that his reciprocal trade treaties were authorized and reauthorized in spite of strong high-tariff lobbies. Of course the effect on the tariffs had not been noticeable and no considerable expansion of imports had occurred, but there was a lot of credit for the handsome Secretary of State in what had been accomplished.

Hull was probably less privy to presidential intentions concerning the crisis boiling up in Europe than anyone around. If Franklin was his own Secretary of the Treasury he was even more his own Secretary of State. He saw Sumner Welles, the Undersecretary, oftener than he saw Hull; he confided in the younger man and entrusted him with missions and maneuvers he would not allow Hull even to know about. Yet Hull's reputation, carefully fostered by the press, was growing formidably. What could happen if such a front for the Tories should be established in the White House, he must have shuddered to think. The old man was beginning to presume just a little on the tide of approval setting in his direction. It was manifested in small ways, but they were unmistakable. Franklin knew very well what they meant.

The Congress, approving of Hull—and of Jesse Jones, who also loomed larger and larger—turned its attention more to politicking than was normal. An election was again impending, only a congressional election, it was true, but it would be nationwide. In June the torment of two issues was allayed by the passage of attenuated bills, one better than the other, but neither being what Franklin had asked. The acceptable one was the Fair Labor Standards Bill; the inadequate one was the Food, Drug and Cosmetic Bill. To get the labor bill passed, Franklin used the last iota of his political credit. It established in law what the NRA had attempted to establish by codes—and Franklin was inclined to feel that, if nothing else, he was entitled to fame as the abolisher, finally and forever, of child labor. The act had other provisions, but they were no more—and even somewhat less—than had become accepted in the years just past. For there was no doubt about it, the employers of 1938 were chastened characters compared with those of five years earlier. They might not like the new conditions, but they were no longer inclined to risk everything in opposition.

The Food, Drug and Cosmetic Bill as it passed in 1938 was a discredit to everyone concerned in it. What had started out in 1933 on a tide of consumer approval to be a new charter of honesty and fair dealing in the manufacture and sale of products in everyday use had ended as a renewed permission to exploit the public. No standards, no grades, no penalties for fraud, no restriction on patent medicines of however dangerous a nature—there was nothing to take pride in. The proceedings had been disgraceful. The Congress had truckled to every shabby interest that had appeared, shamelessly and openly. And Franklin, who had begun by thinking he might make a record in this matter to compare with Uncle Ted's back in 1906, had long since lost interest. He had spent his political currency in other ways; consumers, so far as could be seen, had no votes. At least they had no voices.

The instance of the food-and-drug legislation is indeed an instructive one for the student of politics.[5] This was a matter high on the agenda of progressivism; it had to do with that most valued virtue, truth. What would have been asked by the original legislation was no more than business often acknowledged to be necessary, which was, of course, regulation in the interest of fairness. To say that exactly was being offered for sale and not to misrepresent it in advertising was all that was required. But business had become so entangled in adulterations and misrepresentations, so dependent on deluding the consumer, that

[5] Cf. Ruth de Forest Lamb, *American Chamber of Horrors* (New York: Farrar & Rinehart, 1936).

the requirement of truth would literally cause a revolution in ordinary practice.

The connections between businesses engaged in doubtful conduct and local politicians turned out to be very direct in many places. Every maker of nostrums and low-standard food products, of poisonous cosmetics and worthless health appliances, seemed to be a heavy campaign contributor. Nor were most of the "ethical" firms willing to support stringent regulation, even though they themselves would not be touched. The advertising industry handled their accounts as well as the fraudulent ones, and it was the advertisers who undertook the defense as a kind of crusade. They professed to believe that their profits were threatened and, along with them, good business as well as bad. They controlled newspaper policy, and they were able to do a typical public-relations job with newspapers and the radio as media. The game was to refuse discussion of the merits of what was proposed and to undermine the reputation of the proposers. Eventually, they had reason to believe, anything emanating from such sources would be anathema.

They were entirely justified in their cynical assessment of the possibilities. When the legislation failed to be adopted, as its sponsors had hoped, in the first rush of the Hundred Days, and was held over until the regular session, the advertisers were given time for the kind of campaign they knew so well how to conduct. By the time the bill came seriously under discussion again it had been labeled "Red"—an un-American attempt to destroy business and introduce Communism.

Since it was a thoroughly accepted progressive measure, Franklin at first committed himself to it without hesitation. But other matters were more pressing, and when the special session of 1933 wanted to adjourn without passing it, he consented. After all, such a measure had little to do with recovery, and recovery was his first objective. Then, as we have seen, there followed the turn-about. The Second New Deal had to be introduced and implemented. It was urged that the Food and Drug Bill was strictly in the line of the new philosophy—to regulate industry, but not to require of it planning or performance. If manufacturers were to be required to conform to wages-and-hours requirements and to treat each other fairly, they ought also to be asked to treat their consumers fairly.

This was unanswerable logic. But politics is not logical. There was organized labor to fight for wages-and-hours legislation; and not all businessmen were wholly averse to fair competition among themselves, but a requirement that they treat consumers fairly had no really powerful support. And since the notion had been successfully spread about that those who wanted such legislation were unpatriotic, no politician could afford association with it. Franklin quickly discovered that there was organized opposition and that the advertisers were succeeding in their campaign to discredit those of his associates who had been chosen to bear the responsibility for the bill. Again, he found that other matters were more important.

The legislation therefore existed in a kind of limbo from 1933 to 1938, periodically being used as an illustration of the New Deal's socialistic tendencies but actually never being pushed by any political sponsor. Because no one else wanted it, the bill very early fell into the hands of Senator Royal Copeland of New York. Senator Copeland was a physician, a Tammanyite, and a Hearst-paper health columnist. He at once rewrote the measure with the help of certain of the lobbyists who had been fighting it. This he conceived to be a clever ruse, and he was right. What was marked as a radical measure could actually be captured, emasculated, and passed. There would be credit in it for everyone concerned. He would be the author of important legislation; the food, cosmetics, and patent-medicine industries would have legislation of a sort that would not adversely affect their operations; and the Congress would have got an embarrassment out of the way. Franklin never felt that he could expose or seriously combat the conspiracy.

The process of turning the first effective bill into the subverted thing it became required all those five years. It was no small task to conciliate all those who must be satisfied that no clause affected them in any limiting way. But it was finally accomplished, and the Copeland bill became law. Franklin smilingly signed it with no outward sign that a cause had been betrayed to which many devoted people had given time, energy, and even their reputations.

The Food, Drug and Cosmetic Act was only a worse example of much else. Particularly after the disorganization caused by the Court battle, Franklin's ability to get anything from the Congress rapidly disappeared. There was another distressing example in 1938—taxes. This can be understood, as the handling of food-and-drug legislation can be understood, only by realizing the situation in which Franklin found himself as his political dispositions became more difficult and as his strength tended to evaporate. He could not take the strong position that there was a whole program and that commitment to it as a whole must be accepted. There were too many issues in which the opposition came from different sources, varied in its malignancy, and was held more or less in check by forces he could mobilize. Taxes were like the food-and-drug legislation in having no powerful friends. No legislature likes to impose taxes, but some kinds are resisted more than others. For how long a time an income tax of any sort was held off in the United States, after being adopted in many other countries, will be recalled.

In 1938 Franklin not only had an unbalanced budget which was bothering him, but he also had to propose an enlargement of expenditures to resuscitate a fading recovery. This enlargement would have to be paid for. Furthermore, he had learned, among other fiscal lessons, that the incidence of taxation was a potent influence in the economy. It was possible to stifle or to stimulate activity by managing imposts. And he had begun to experiment with these devices. To pay for his new program of works, he wanted to raise money but he wanted to do it in such ways as would contribute to equalization and stabilization. He would like, if he could, to enlarge the beginning made in 1936, when the first tax on undistributed profits had been laid. This would, as he thought, modify one of the worst contributing causes of such collapses as that of 1929. One of the phenomena of that time had been the retention by corporate managements of their earnings, using them for speculative purposes rather than for dividends. The tax on undistributed profits would stop this abuse.

But, as in the food-and-drug instance, it was the abuses become privileges which businessmen were most sensitive about and most determined not to permit the government to touch. He had nevertheless got such a tax in 1936; he wanted now at least to keep it while other taxes were renewed. The struggle over this issue in the 1938 session cannot be pursued here as it deserves. There is really no better illustration of conservative subservience to big business, of the deep split in the Democratic party, and of Franklin's tenacity and resourcefulness when something he regarded as vital was at stake. In this last it stood in complete contrast with the Food, Drug and Cosmetic Act.

He lost the fight, but he lost it with honor. It was the southern Democrats, led by Senator Pat Harrison of Mississippi, who in spite of Franklin's best efforts carried the bill to abolish the tax and to substitute for it a corporation levy which had the reverse effect. The senator, speaking for his fellow conservatives, but not at all on the defensive really, because there was so much expressed approval of Franklin's defeat, said that concessions to business had been necessary in order to encourage recovery; abolition of the tax would contribute to renewed activity.

This infuriated Franklin. He refused to sign the new measure, allowing it to go into effect, because he had to have revenue, without his signature. He denounced those who had voted for it. It was in the interest of long-run understanding that he said, in a speech about the Revenue Act, that it gave "an infinitely greater tax concession to the man who makes a very great profit than to the man who makes a comparatively small profit. It helps the very few, therefore, at the expense of the many."

This and the rejection of his Executive Reorganization Bill in usable form were severe setbacks. The reiterated charges that a dictatorship was being planned which accompanied the debate on this bill, repeated endlessly by the same organizations responsible for the defeat of the judiciary bill in 1937, created a situation new to Franklin. How disorganized he was can be seen by reading a letter of this period which denied that he had any inclination in this direction. He usually ignored such charges, but on this occasion he elaborated. He had, he said, none of the qualifications a dictator must have. Furthermore, he went on, "I have too much historical background and too much knowledge of existing dictatorships to make me desire any form of dictatorship for a democracy like the United States of America."[6]

This denial of what, after all, was no more than a fanciful suggestion would seem to suggest a leader in full retreat. There is even a hint of panic in the protests he made that he had no ambition to become another Hitler. It might not be guessed by those who sat at the White House table, spoke to him across his cluttered desk, or glimpsed him as he rode through the Washington streets, but there was an element almost of fear in his mind, as there must have been in Caesar's on the Ides of March. At a time when the economy was enfeebled, when sinister occurrences abroad were being reported daily, when he seemed unable to force or to persuade the Congress to give him the instruments necessary to combat either menace, he must have been disturbed to the depths, and his unconscious mind must have been furiously at work to preserve his leadership.

That the people were undoubtedly with him and willing at any time to follow his lead made his inability to make any progress with the Congress much more sinister. Would he be forced to some such resort, or some modified version of it, as he was being accused of seeking? It did begin to look as though, if well-being was to be re-established at home and if enemies from without were to be checked, he might need to have powers this Congress would never grant.

This was the season of his choosing—1938—and if he was beset by worry, it was in fear that a dictatorship he did not want would become inevitable. His whole theory, as we have seen, was that he knew how to operate the mechanics of democratic leadership. To become a dictator would be to acknowledge failure in his life's endeavor. Yet he cannot have been sure but that events were forcing something of the sort. There was no doubt that he could have greatly enlarged powers if he would strike for them at the right moment—a moment he could sense was not far ahead. Perhaps a year, perhaps two, were given for coming to a decision; but the issue was hardening very rapidly. He must very soon make up his mind what to do when the national peril should force him finally to act.

When it is recalled that 1938 was the year of Munich, that Mussolini was holding Ethiopia in subjection after a brutal conquest, that the

[6] *Public Papers*, 1938 vol., p. 179.

Japanese were ferociously settling themselves in China, that the Spanish loyalists were defending themselves from the treacherous clerical-militarist attack from within which was massively supported by an Italian army and German planes, the pressures building up in the American President's mind can be imagined.

There does seem ample excuse for the famous "purge" of that autumn. The provocation was intense; the need for influence with the Congress was pressing. He would try again, and more directly, to translate his hold on the people into a legislative majority that would accept the discipline of referendum. If this succeeded it would carry him through the present crisis. He could meet his economic troubles and warn the dictators that their present course would lead to conflict. Meanwhile, if any of the potential successors seemed able to capture the nomination and carry the country in 1940, he might be excused altogether from the choices he was afraid might be approaching. But the successors were not developing very rapidly, and the crisis was coming on at a frightening speed.

Franklin must often have exchanged persiflage with his dinner companions and with his office visitors without actually engaging his mind. Somewhere down underneath the level at which the day's affairs were conducted his shrewd but determined political intelligence was at work. He must assume that it would produce the right result in time. At least it usually did, even if the present constriction of his powers seemed to deny it.

The events of 1938, following the discouraging ones of 1937, were what made inevitable the complete reappraisal that occupied Franklin's mind at this time. Whether he reached any conclusions or not, we cannot tell. Events continued to dominate decisions. When the time came there would be no alternative he could see to running for a third term, and running as a Democrat. Why he did not do as Lincoln did in a former crisis and invent a Union party, inviting into it only the supporters of his policies, we shall see when we come to that year. In 1938 and 1939 it was something kept in mind along with several other possible moves.

The attempted purge taught him one lesson useful in his reappraisal and his charting of a future course: his own popularity would not always affect votes for legislation. But there were occurrences before this of almost equal importance. One was the rather unexpected struggle over the so-called "Ludlow Resolution." Ludlow was a midwestern congressman whose sentiments were isolationist. His suggested amendment to the Constitution was an obvious reaction to Franklin's inclination toward intervention and specifically, perhaps, to the "quarantine" speech in Chicago the preceding autumn. It would have required a popular

...endum before the Congress could consider a declaration of war.[7]

...e intention was to substitute this almost absolute prohibition for the system of collective security Franklin was attempting, so far as he was allowed, to develop. It could be seen that the sentiment for such a move was formidable when the Congress resumed in January of 1938, and Franklin met the threat by writing a letter to Speaker Bankhead denouncing it as impractical and as "incompatible with our representative form of government." He went on to point out, what was already obvious and was indeed the intention of its proposers, that "it would cripple any President in his conduct of our foreign relations, and it would encourage other nations to believe that they could violate American rights with impunity."

The isolationists, pacifists, and foreign sympathizers whose sympathies were engaged in this attempt proved to be dangerously strong. The vote on the resolution in the House was adverse by only a small margin,[8] but for a politician of Franklin's astuteness the total vote was not nearly so important as its composition. An analysis showed the kind of opposition he would have to deal with in all foreign policy matters from then on. The Republicans mostly voted for consideration. This was expected partisanship. But it was actually the southern Democrats who defeated it.[9] They had had a well-developed coalition with Republicans in opposition to all domestic administration measures—with a few exceptions—but on foreign policy they were to be counted on as solid support against isolationism.

If he had not sensed before that something like this was developing, Franklin knew it now. The chief strength of the opposition to his foreign policy came from the sources he counted on to uphold his domestic measures. It looked as though he might have to choose between them. It amounted to this: He could risk collective security to get domestic reform, or he could risk domestic reform to get an acceptable foreign policy. As the months passed and he considered this dilemma, he was gradually forced to the conclusion, especially after the Munich results became evident and Hitler was again on the move, that the world crisis was paramount. Reform must be sacrificed.

The shift required by this decision was not made suddenly; he still tried during the 1938 session to make some gains in domestic matters. And he denounced publicly the Southerners' joining of the Republicans to ruin his tax program. But actually he had accepted the unspoken ultimatum of the conservatives. The attempted purge of that summer and fall represented his last effort to find a way out of this dilemma

---

[7] Except in case of invasion.

[8] The actual vote was 209 to 188.

[9] Along with Franklin's small following from the northeastern states. These votes he could count on for the support of both foreign and domestic policies.

which would regain for him some freedom of action. If he could substitute, for even a few of the reactionaries, new members of the Congress who would support both his foreign and his domestic policies, he might be able to rescue the New Deal from what otherwise would be a process of agonizing attrition.

The active purge process began as soon as the Congress had gone home. On June 24 he made a fireside chat. He praised the departing legislators mildly, citing what legislation there was to cite as favorable: the agricultural law, the Fair Labor Standards Act, the setting up of the United States Housing Authority, and increased public works funds, especially. But he again let go with both barrels at "defeatists" who wanted liberalism to adjourn permanently, and at those who continued to demand "the restoration of confidence." To these last he addressed this charge:

From March 4, 1933, down, not a single week has passed without a cry from the opposition "to do something, to say something, to restore confidence." There is a very articulate group of people in this country, with plenty of ability to procure publicity for their views, who have consistently refused to cooperate with the mass of the people, whether things were going well or going badly, on the ground that they required more concessions to their point of view before they would admit having what they called "confidence."[10]

The important thing, he implied, was not that these people lacked confidence—they had demanded it when the banks were closed, when hungry people were thronging the streets, and when droughts had burnt half the country; and they had overplayed their plea. His belief was, he said, that there was plenty of confidence; only it was possessed by the mass of the people, and it had to do with their own ability, with the aid of their government, to solve their own problems. But that job was not yet done, he said, and "in simple frankness and honesty" he needed all the help he could get if it was to be completed.

He then spoke of the imminent primaries and of the elections to follow, in which there would be

many clashes between two schools of thought, generally classified as liberal and conservative. Roughly speaking, the liberal school of thought recognizes that the new conditions throughout the world call for new remedies. . . .

The opposing or conservative school of thought . . . does not recognize the need for Government itself to step in and take action to meet these new problems. . . .[11]

After making this elementary distinction, he ranged himself among the liberals or progressives and implied that, if he was to get on with the

[10] *Public Papers*, 1938 vol., pp. 396–97.
[11] Ibid., pp. 398–99.

program approved in his name, he must have supporters. This was the justification for his present appeal:

> As President of the United States, I am not asking the voters of the country to vote for Democrats next November as opposed to Republicans . . . Nor am I, as President, taking part in Democratic primaries.
>
> As the head of the Democratic Party, however, charged with the responsibility of carrying out the definitely liberal declaration of principles set forth in the 1936 Democratic platform, I feel that I have every right to speak in those few instances where there may be a clear issue between candidates for a Democratic nomination involving these principles, or involving a clear misuse of my own name. . . .[12]

Thus equipped with justification, he made his attempt to extricate himself from the dilemma closing around him.

There could be no doubt of the intransigent nature of southern reaction. There had been three startling evidences of it in the session just past: a fight over an anti-lynching bill, the crippling of the Farm Security Administration, and the defeat of the tax proposals. On the anti-lynching bill—which would have established federal jurisdiction over local officials who allowed lynchings—the Southerners had filibustered for more than a month, holding up all the work of the Senate. Tempers had risen and the antagonism between northern and western liberals and the southern conservatives had reached a bitterness not experienced for many years. The South had profited enormously from the New Deal, but gratitude had not run to softening on the race issue. Franklin had watched the fight but had not intervened. He had been urged again and again to exert his leadership, but he had turned his back. More than anything else, this had emphasized for his supporters his essential helplessness vis-à-vis the Southerners. It was from then on that the conservative veto over all measures had been recognized as nearly complete. And even the wages-and-hours legislation had been compromised to their satisfaction. The dictators had at least won a conservative victory in the United States.

A similar and almost as striking illustration of Franklin's inability to achieve purposes not consented to by the conservatives was the reduction of the appropriation for the Farm Security Administration to half of what had been authorized. Notice was thus given that the class structure of the South must not be disrupted by federal assistance to sharecroppers and tenants. From this time on the good intentions of the former Resettlement Administration, already watered down to suit southern preferences, were understood to have been abandoned. This agency was never to have the effect it might have had in recon-

[12] Ibid., p. 399.

structing southern agriculture. The sharecroppers were abandoned to the ancient customs of the landlord system.

Franklin's ability to affect congressional proceedings was not actually tested on these issues; he let them go by default. On the tax issue he did fight, however, and lost. It was a sad but revealing spectacle. The business lobbies were in complete control. And Democrats with seniority were their floor managers.

There was indeed ample reason for Franklin to take thought seriously concerning his position. If he did nothing, the chances were that degeneration would go farther. As his need for control grew, his ability to achieve it would lessen. He was getting consent to inflationary spending, and this might overcome the recession; but what position would a nation be in to meet a war crisis if its debt had already been rising for years? And it seemed to him that the dictators had begun to presume on his inability to oppose them as he wished. It was far from enough that an increase of naval expenditures had been allowed. That had been done only after the isolationists had loudly asserted that the administration had secretly made an arrangement with Britain to support that nation's aggressions.[13]

As these arguments went on, Hitler annexed Austria and began the campaign of vilification which was preliminary to the seizure of Czechoslovakia. The Chamberlain government in Britain, devoted to appeasement anyway, was further confirmed in its policy by the isolationist strength shown in American congressional debates. The President might indicate a preference for checking aggression, but he was bound by the Neutrality Act and, outside of naval enlargement, was evidently unable to get it modified.

In October, Hitler moved into Czechoslovakia. The Munich Agreement, which Franklin encouraged and which he as much as Chamberlain seemed to feel might establish "peace in our time," was seen within a matter of weeks to have deluded the democracies. To the aggressor such accords were no more than useful devices for quieting more scrupulous nations. It was becoming more and more clear that Hitler had no stopping place short of total European conquest—and perhaps not even there. The time of trial was fast approaching. Britain and France would soon be forced to fight if they were not to knuckle under completely. Would the great democracy, of which he was the responsible leader, look the other way while those nations faced up to the common enemy?

The attempt to liberalize the party was not a success. Some indi-

[13] The Naval Expansion Bill was signed on May 17. It provided for what its supporters had labeled a "two-ocean navy"; the reference being to Japanese violations of treaty limits on shipbuilding and the need for naval forces in the Pacific as well as the Atlantic.

viduals he had pointed to as not his kind of Democrat lost, but some others won. The balance in the party was not much changed. But also, there were notable Republican gains. Franklin's position, when the new Congress should meet, would be no better than during the disastrous two years just past. Very likely it would be worse. No Republican would vote for New Deal measures, and Republicans from the West were isolationist by nature. He would be more handicapped than ever in both his objectives—the increase of well-being and the security of the free world.

What way should he prepare to move?

23

The central event of 1939 was the outbreak of hostilities in Europe with its immediate preliminaries and consequences. This, for Franklin, as for others, was a separation point in history. Nothing was the same on the morning after Hitler's tanks began their sweep across the Polish plains.

The Soviet statesmen had demonstrated what Communist realism meant by signing in August a pact with the Third Reich. It was Hitler's assumption that after this Poland could be conquered before France or Britain could make an effective move, and, with Russia immobilized, he need not face a two-front war. Within a matter of weeks, if he was not attacked from the west, he would have most of his forces disengaged and free to meet any later assault.

Those forces, with the blitzkrieg technique he was about to employ for the first time, would, he was certain, subdue all Europe before the Americans could intervene—if they intervened at all.

The first part of the Nazi schedule worked out well enough. The blitzkrieg was finished before Britain and France could intervene. But if Hitler had correct reports from the United States, they must have reflected a change. In the elation of victory he probably paid no attention. And it is true that until this moment Franklin was fatally hampered in maneuver vis-à-vis the aggressors. There were few Americans who agreed with him that there were aggressors, and the isolationists used some rather heavy sarcasm on his "attempts to scare the American people about a fanciful menace."

Both 1937 and 1938 had been such disappointing years for Franklin that desperate thoughts can seldom have been absent from his mind. He would have been quite justified in giving way to a profound discouragement. He must have felt that all he could do might not be enough. So critical a situation might well develop that unprecedented resorts might be necessary. If it did—and as 1939 opened out, such a

475

Sectionalism   Yes   Purge failed

possibility seemed to be coming closer and closer—what he must do would, he hoped, be less than he feared he might have to do.

But if the crisis came he would be ready. The readiness with which one measure after another was prepared as the succeeding events ran on into war shows clearly how far ahead he had thought and planned.

His handicaps, however, were monumental; and considering in what regard he was obviously held by the electorate, they seem hard to credit, much less to explain. It is possible to understand them only by keeping always in mind the strange fact that Americans vote for their President for one reason and for their senators and representatives for others.

The purge of 1938 had failed in its main purpose—that of making a beginning at transforming the Democratic party into a liberal one. It was true that a few of the worst candidates had been rejected and more progressive ones substituted: Pepper in Florida was a real gain. But neither George of Georgia nor Tydings of Maryland had been displaced. At the election Republicans in the House had increased from 88 to 170, and they had gained eight seats in the Senate. This was a serious setback. As a result, the possibilities of transforming the party had disappeared, and Franklin was adjusting to this disappointment as the year opened.

If 1938 had been disappointing in domestic matters, 1939 threatened to be downright disastrous. Franklin would face his now familiar dilemma with its alternatives made more disagreeable. The North and West would support reform but not collective security. The South would support collective security but not reform. He would have to confirm the choice he had begun to make in 1938: sacrifice of the New Deal for foreign policy. And the price demanded would be higher, perhaps much higher than his most pessimistic calculations had forecast before the elections.

When the November returns had come in, Franklin had at first been annoyed and disconcerted; but presently, with characteristic resilience, he was interpreting them, or anyway picturing them to others, as not so bad as they seemed. Old Josephus Daniels down in Mexico wrote from his Embassy saying that he had lived through many defeats but that this one was "unexpected and depressing" beyond the others. Franklin sent him some comfort. It was not too much, but it was all that could be found:

Curley in Massachusetts is, I hope, finally out of the picture. Quinn and O'Hara in Rhode Island tried to murder each other and both are dead! Cross was too old a story in Connecticut and Lonergan was a reactionary. Hague was slapped down in New Jersey and the Pennsylvania row brought inevitable defeat. In Ohio, Davey, the worst of our Governors, wrecked the whole ticket.

Beside cleaning out some bad local situations, we have on the positive side eliminated Phil La Follette and the Farmer-Labor people in the Northwest as a standing Third Party threat. They must and will come to us *if* we remain definitely the liberal party.

Frankly, I think we will have less trouble with the next Congress than with the last. I think the idea is slowly getting through the heads of people like Tydings and George and Bennett Clark that even if they control the 1940 Convention they cannot elect their ticket without the support of this Administration—and I am sufficiently honest to decline to support any conservative Democrat.[1]

This was professional political talk between two old hands even if it was making the best interpretation of an ugly fact. Franklin was thinking out loud, so to speak. He had concluded, it can be guessed, that his sinking spell in 1938 was due to the circumstance that he was in his second term. He was on the way out, and therefore his reprisal threats need not be feared. But he had also concluded that the professionals would see, as 1940 approached, that he would have a deciding voice at the nominating convention. The new man would have to have his approval. But much more important, he would control the election— that is, he could defeat a conservative. Moreover, he might just do that, and his tormentors uneasily recognized that he might.

Why Franklin thought these circumstances would make for a more tractable session in 1939, it is a little hard to see. Surely he did not think the conservatives would bargain for his support of a conservative in return for legislative favor. They were still elated and were not yet in a trading mood. At any rate, his reasoning was too optimistic. For him 1939 was to be, if anything, worse than 1938.

There would be in the whole year of 1939 no gains for the administration. No new measures would even be suggested. His executive reorganization would get through after being savaged through several sessions, torn and tattered in every clause. And defeat for collective security—until the desperate special session after hostilities had broken out in Europe—would be even more humiliating and complete than in former years.

There was open water ahead, beyond the dividing day when Poland would be invaded by Hitler, but the fogs would be dispersed only by the big wind of war; nothing Franklin could manage would have any effect. Sailing into the mists after the elections, he made his first move. He appointed Harry Hopkins Secretary of Commerce. This was a suggestion concerning succession. Harry regarded it as such, and so did others.[2]

---

[1] *Personal Letters: 1928–1945*, Vol. II, p. 827.

[2] This seems to have been an almost inexplicable expectation to Hopkins' biographers, Robert E. Sherwood and Sidney Hyman. They walk all around the evidence of it in *Roosevelt and Hopkins*, viewing it with a puzzlement that

But the members of the Farley-Garner-Hull group were startled and angered by the implication. To them the verdict of 1938 had meant something very different from Franklin's interpretation. To meet its warnings by rushing Hopkins into the ring was just the reverse of what they figured must be done; preferences do often warp judgments. But they—and others like them—from this time on set out to control the events they were now certain Franklin was intending to mismanage, or anyway to manage in ways they would not like.

The conservatives had hitherto suffered in comparative silence, an enforced silence except in their own intimate confabs; they now considered that they were justified in believing Franklin's intentions politically unwise. Their reading of the 1938 elections was that American opinion had veered sharply to the right, and unless the Democratic party conformed it would go out of power. The wild men had had their day; it was time now for a return to sanity. They felt for every opening looking toward tightened party control.

Commenting on the background of the annual message to the new Congress, Rosenman, in *Working with Roosevelt*,[3] wrote equivocally concerning Franklin's intuitions at that time:

The President had come through a long series of setbacks in the domestic field in the last year and a half . . . His prestige at home and abroad had suffered a great deal. I do not know what course he would have taken in 1939 if events had not forced his major attention into international fields. I know of his feeling of frustration in pushing further reforms. I know that the fundamental solution he was thinking about was not a new third party of liberalism but a combination of the liberal forces then existing in each party. It may be that if international matters had not claimed his attention, he would have tried the task of realigning the two parties before his second term was over.

This is testimony that even after the failure of the purge and defeat in the elections Franklin still had it in mind to transform the Democratic party and to entice into it all the progressive elements so unhappily appended to Republicanism. But, says Rosenman, the necessities of the international situation were working against it. And it is true that many of the progressives were isolationist. A long list of them could be made, beginning with Bob La Follette of Wisconsin, running through Gerald Nye of North Dakota, and perhaps ending with the most intransigent

---

is never resolved. What they did not sufficiently consider, perhaps, was Franklin's situation at the moment. They were naturally preoccupied with Hopkins' apparent lack of realism. It was very clear afterward that his expectation of nomination had been fantastic, but it seems not to have been clear at this moment.

[3] P. 181. It is there recorded that this message was prepared, in the familiar sense, by Rosenman, Corcoran, and Cohen. This was now the White House triumvirate. Of this message, however, he says that Franklin spent on it many more hours and much more effort than was usual.

FDR couldn't count on progressives for his internal policy

of all, Hiram Johnson of California. For what Franklin saw coming from abroad he could not count on any help from these otherwise like-minded public men. It looked as though he had no alternative to bedding down for the duration with those southern conservatives who accepted his foreign policy. This precluded the formation of a third party for the duration too; and it does seem likely that, from the day after the 1938 elections, he shelved his third-party plans until the crisis should be over.

But even with this decision made for him, so to speak, all was not plain sailing toward a charted port. On the contrary, there was a delicate and complicated series of political considerations to confront. They were, in fact, the most difficult of his whole political career—even more difficult than the situation in 1928 when, against his judgment, he ran for governor of New York and so surprisingly won.

In this instance there were involved both his career and his intentions for the nation. Up to now there had never been any question about the identity of each with the other. He had been the link—the bridge, as he once described it to me—between a country dominated by old-style business privateers and a new one with built-in securities for common folk. The chief requisite for the new country as compared with the old was that the privileges of the few should be reduced whenever they limited the securities of the many. The few were entrenched, and especially in the Congress and in the realm of public administration. They must be routed out. He must, he said, "make Christians of them."

The old guard, among the Republicans and Democrats alike, were determined to oppose, with all the weapons they could command, any invasion of the areas of their privilege.

Franklin's struggle to capture enemy strongholds one after another without destroying them had been a strenuous and sometimes a bitter one. It had split both parties, but particularly the Democrats, a division which was worse just after elections but tended to be diminished as drawing together for campaigns became necessary. In 1936 Franklin had been nominated by acclamation. His hold on the people had forced the reactionaries to accept him.

But immediately in 1937 the Court battle had given them an issue. They could fight Franklin without doing it as a challenge to his progressive leadership. They could pose as friends of freedom. He, for once, was a devil on the run. The winning of this battle had emboldened them to carry on until 1938, and the elections of 1938 had further encouraged them to hope that in 1940 they might end the Roosevelt menace once and for all.

Franklin had the problem of setting himself against this resolution of the Democratic old guard. But they were now having an added advantage, a new ally as it were. That ally was Hitler. What they never would have dared attempt by themselves—kill the New Deal and rid

FDR had to forget the N.D. Hopkins couldn't succeed de

the party of Franklin—Hitler was offering to help them do. And not all of them saw that it was a fatal offer. The Republicans did not see it at all.

Franklin can thus be described as exchanging one cause for another —national security for social security would be one way of putting it. But his career had been identified with the one and it was not yet quite solidly equated with the other. He had led a domestic crusade with missionary confidence in rightness; there was growing in him the sense of a new identification. It was still not complete, yet it gathered in him with expanding power.

Hopkins as successor? That thought must have been very tentative indeed, and moreover very brief. That Harry could not carry the mission was at once evident. Health was one reason, but the other was his inability to establish himself politically. He could never wrest the nomination from the convention. But that was the handicap of every other potential successor. The old guard, if any irregular was pushed, would defeat him for the nomination. They did not control the electorate, but they very nearly did control the party. They could without doubt defeat La Guardia or Wallace, the best other bets now. If it was to be either it would have to be by way of a third party. But then if one of them should lose, having both old parties against him, what would become of the mission—that opposition to aggression called for more and more as the months passed and Hitler's effronteries multiplied?

Franklin was a man approaching inevitable commitment during 1939 and early 1940. There was no way out. But until the fusing of career and mission had been completed, he could not decide. And what kept him from deciding—the strongest influence—was the necessity of abandoning the New Deal. Or perhaps it should be put more delicately as the necessity for abandoning any further development of the New Deal —that and close figuring on what could be salvaged, by bargaining, of what had already been accomplished. The New Deal was part of himself. Could he tear it out and destroy it?

But that such a decision must be made was not yet clear—not altogether—in 1939. Franklin knew that he would have to compromise in the year to come because he must depend on the old guard for military appropriations. He was, after all, President in the present; and he must, at whatever necessary cost, implement his foreign policy. Whether he would have to trade himself as well as the New Deal to get what would be vital in the future was not yet determined. He would give as little as he could manage in order to get as much as he could bargain for.

But the conditions for bargaining were very much worsened from earlier days. He could get less and had to give more with every passing month and year. It is not strange if he was very unclear at the moment.

There might come a time when he would just have to give too much, or even when all he had would not be enough. There would be—and he could foresee them—some narrow escapes before national commitment to collective security was made complete.

There might even arise circumstances that called not for the assumption of dictatorial powers but for abdication. He might not care to preside over the course forced on him in spite of all his efforts. There may very well have strayed into his mind thoughts of escape. And once such a possibility was accepted, releases and pleasures would begin to enlarge in prospect. There was no existence so full and satisfactory in his mind—except the presidency, shall we say?—as that of the country gentleman. And added to the amenities of Springwood there now would be the library and museum, built to his own plans and maintained by an expert staff, where he could sort over his papers, prepare his memoirs, entertain his associates, and become gracefully an elder statesman.

The room in the library where he could visualize himself would be a thoroughly Roosevelt room—square, solid, well proportioned. There his furnishings would be those recalling historic occasions; there, and thereabouts, would be collected all the mementos and records of his life. The old trees he regarded as friends, the stretches of lawn, the gardens and fields, the view of the river and the country beyond, veiled in the hazes of autumn, whipped by the winds of winter, reviving in the varied greens of spring and expanding into summer—all this he would see from his windows. He could sink back into such a background and, as he thought, be content. He spoke of the possibility on several recorded occasions.

Many members of the administration were speaking out for a third term, Ickes and Hopkins loudest, Wallace following along as ambition for the vice-presidency gradually supplanted that for the presidency. La Guardia was incredulous. He thought the third-term talk fantastic and redoubled his efforts to suggest his own availability—though how he thought he might capture a nomination he did not say. Farley said to Franklin that a third-term nomination would be possible but that election would not be so easy; he spoke, however, from a self-interest that was now apparent.

Everyone who knew Franklin well sensed the reservation in his outspoken longing for retirement. And it was indeed only a momentary weakness; there was never much substance to the sentiment. Moreover, if he had been planning to retire he would not have said so—the diminution of his authority was already serious enough.

Yet Sam Rosenman, who was with him most of the time now—as was Harry Hopkins, who had come to live in the White House—says that he really concluded for a while that retirement had been decided upon. He thought this, he says, until the spring of 1940, when the "phony

... ended and the aggression, which so far as western Europe was concerned had until then been a threat, turned into reality. All the White House staff studied Franklin's mood as they would be bound to do in such a relationship. Their careers were dependent on his, wholly so, and naturally they read and discussed all the signs and circumstances.

They thought he was going to quit. So they later said. Perhaps pessimism influenced their interpretations, but my own conclusion was the same. I was not a familiar now of the household, I was an official of La Guardia's New York, but I was often around. To me as well as others Franklin spoke of 1940 as the year of his release, and I too misread the signs. It seemed very foolish of me afterward not to have sensed the depth of his antagonism to Hitler and the Hitlerian system. But for the moment I was convinced. So was Ernest Lindley, who was as shrewd an observer as any living person where Franklin was concerned. He went right out on a limb in his syndicated column.[4]

Rosenman says that when he and his wife Dorothy were visiting at Hyde Park one weekend a real estate man turned up who had been told by Franklin to show them an available place nearby. Harry Hopkins was also looking over the possibilities. The three of them—and perhaps a few others—were to congregate in the neighborhood, work in a leisurely way at the papers, and savor the joys of country living. It was a picture in the tradition of Mount Vernon, Monticello, Montpelier, and the Hermitage.

That this was literally true there is some collateral evidence. How else can one of Franklin's most appealing contemporary papers be read —his address celebrating the anniversary of the first presidential election? In it he spoke of Mount Vernon as the place where Washington's "heart was planted for all time," where he could

> talk with his neighbors about the improvement of navigation on the river, about grist mills on the creeks, about the improving of highways, about the dream of a canal to the western country, about saw mills and rotation of crops, about the top soil, which even then had begun to run off to the sea, about the planting of trees, new varieties of food and fodder crops, new breeds of horses and cattle and sheep. . . .
>
> Rightly he must have felt that his labors . . . had rounded out his contribution . . . [and] that he had earned the privilege of returning for all time to the private life which had been his dream. . . .[5]

But of course for him, as for Washington, such desires had only the substance of a wish; for him, as for Washington, there was more to come. The library and the room, with its furnishings, materialized. They

---

[4] To be found in various newspapers *circa* March 15, 1940. The one consulted here was the Washington *Post.*

[5] *Public Papers*, 1939 vol., pp. 207–8.

are there to be seen today. And it can be said that sometimes Franklin spent a day or a week where he had hoped to work for years. But he never was to have an instant there in the release of retirement. Neither Hitler nor the American isolationists would allow it.

His present opponents were provocative enough to call out his combativeness and not formidable enough to be unconquerable. As classic political antagonists they were more useful even than the power barons, the financiers, and the big businessmen. Franklin's struggle with them was just beginning. His whole career up to now had been identified with welfare objectives, and it was almost like putting on a new personality to become the leader in fighting foreign aggressors. It could not be done quickly or without adequate justification. The domestic crusade had been one of a missionary intensity; he had been entirely confident of its rightness. The new one was gradually exerting the same sort of domination. He was becoming identified with it and all question of its rightness was leaving his mind. This process was still not complete; its inevitability was not yet accepted; but, as we know, it had been for a long time deep in his mind.

Moreover, he still thought—and probably insisted for public purposes that he thought more than he really did—that the nation might escape from military intervention. This was the year of "measures short of war." He talked of these with a confidence it seems impossible to believe now that he really felt. And this has led to an interpretation of all his actions and pronouncements at this time as false. He was, it was said by a whole school of "revisionists," deliberately plotting war, leading the nation toward it step by step, each one making the next inevitable.[6]

It can be said that this was almost a familiar occurrence by now in the United States. There were those who thought that Lincoln might have avoided the Civil War, and there were many who condemned Wilson for leading the nation into World War I.[7] The significance of this is that in a democracy there is seldom unanimity on any question; and on one that engages intense national interest there are sure to be excited discussion and a residue of dissent. The revisionist bitterness represents a rejected policy. Such an opinion is not necessarily wrong; it may indeed prove to have been right. But such proof will never satisfy

[6] The most formidable and reputable of the "revisionists" was the historian Charles A. Beard, who devoted two volumes to the argument—*President Roosevelt and the Coming of the War, 1941: A Study in Appearances and Realities* (New Haven: Yale University Press, 1948); and *American Foreign Policy in the Making, 1932–1940: A Study in Responsibilities* (New Haven: Yale University Press, 1947). These were the first, but others followed as they did after World War I. For an examination of their efforts see Basil Rauch, *Roosevelt from Munich to Pearl Harbor* (New York: Creative Age, 1950).

[7] Not to mention the criticism of Madison for the War of 1812 and of McKinley for consenting to the Spanish-American War, often called the most useless conflict in American history.

everyone; and, at any rate, it represents a judgment that was not followed. Revisionism in this instance, as in the case of Wilson and his war, is the remnant of a strong opinion that Franklin followed a head-strong and mistaken course. The argument rests on the belief that he wanted war and maneuvered to engage the United States against the Axis powers. It goes further; it argues that the war should have been avoided because matters were worse following hostilities than they would have been if a policy of compromise had been adopted.

It can be seen that no conclusion can ever be reached in such a discussion. It is conceivable that, as far back as his first days in office, Franklin might have begun to cultivate liberal elements in Japan. He might also have cultivated his early rapport with Mussolini. And he might have dealt realistically with Hitler, allowing Germany the *Lebensraum* her energy entitled her to acquire. But just to state these possibilities is to reveal their inherent difficulties. The Japanese militarists were mystic obscurantists. How an American leader could have kept them from conspiring for power, the revisionists do not say. The alternative to opposing, finally, Japanese designs in Asia was to allow the complete subjection of China and other nations, perhaps including India. The revisionists must contend that a Japan based on such a source of power and subject to oligarchical rule would not have been an intolerable menace to the West.

Perhaps something might have been done with Japan and with Mussolini, but is it arguable that Hitler could have been dealt with? He was an irrational monster, and the mighty German Reich had given him absolute power. As for assisting the Germans to avoid Nazism, it must be remembered that Hitler came to office concurrently with Franklin. In 1933 it was already much too late. And the effect of conciliation on Hitler was demonstrated with some conclusiveness by his conduct after Munich.

In spite of developing events, there is reason to believe that Franklin did cling to the hope of compromise. And even when in 1939 Poland was invaded by both Germany and Russia, he seems still to have felt that somehow the United States might keep out. But about the course most likely to accomplish this there were differences of opinion too. The isolationist way was to keep entirely aloof, allowing the struggle to take its course. Franklin's way was to assist the nations opposing the aggression in every way possible. What, in the end, the controversy came down to was an interpretation of intentions. As Franklin saw it, the Nazis asserted an inherent superiority. They asserted further a right to rule the world. They believed in the total state and the subjection to it of individuals. The nations opposing them stood for democracy—rule by representative government resting on popular sovereignty.

This was the interpretation Franklin proceeded from. And because he saw no reason to modify it as events developed, he felt more and more strongly that the very life of the nation depended on the defeat of the Axis. How much actual hope he had by 1939–40 that Britain and France could accomplish that defeat with assistance from the United States "short of war," it is impossible to say. Those closest to him felt that he was still hopeful and that he meant exactly what he said in repeating that he "hated war," that if the nation was rearmed and resolute, and if all possible help was sent to Britain, our intervention might be avoided.[8] There is indeed reason to believe that the last vestige of this optimism was not squeezed out of his mind until the news from Pearl Harbor came over the White House wires. It must by then have been very slight, but it does not seem to have vanished completely.

What makes this credible is that Franklin was a politician and had complete faith in his political powers. Resort to force was an admission of failure which went to the sources of his confidence in himself. By instinct, if not by reason, he was told from within to deal and keep on dealing even with incorrigible antagonists. The hope was that they would have the sense to see where force led and, even at the last moment, to give in.

He was proud of never having called out the militia during his governorship. He had the same pride as President in his ability to negotiate, to avoid force, and arrive at some settlement in even the most acrimonious disputes. The international field was only an extension of the national one. The same arts were useful. He would never give up the effort to find a way to peace. It might be an uneasy, even an unjust, one. But if war was not resorted to, continued negotiation might bring even the most fatuous antagonist to the recognition that he could not win a war with the United States.

It is thus mistaken, I believe, to interpret Franklin's repeated warnings to the aggressors, his struggle for collective security, his building up of military strength, and his insistence on aid to the Allies as, in his mind, preliminaries to war. To him they were the essentials of a program for avoiding actual conflict. If afterward he could have commented on the revisionists' attacks, he might very well have said that if he had had his way with less disputation and delay, his hopes might have been justified. He might have argued that Hitler felt free to go on to his final aggressions because he judged the American President had no power to interfere and therefore no strength from which to issue warnings. This was the result of the isolationists' policy, not of his.

[8] Eleanor says so. In *This I Remember*, p. 207, she speaks of it again and again. Even when she had given up hope, she felt that Franklin had not: "I do not think Franklin ever felt that war was inevitable, and he always said he hoped we could avoid it, but I had a feeling that once war started, there was not much chance for any part of the world to escape it . . ."

It was at five in the morning on September 1, 1939, that Franklin in Washington called Eleanor in Hyde Park to tell her that Poland had been invaded in spite of all his—and other Allied statesmen's—efforts. We have a picture of Franklin in his narrow bed, awakened before dawn to hear the news, there to wait, realizing that now Britain and France would declare war.[9] A juggernaut was rolling which only force could stop. His arrangements for assistance might still so bolster the Allies that they could defeat the aggressors. But the help would have to be generous and prompt. He evidently said none of this to Eleanor; but, husband-like, he had the impulse to tell her the news and to hear her words of comfort—perhaps to the effect that he had done all he could. . . . As he hung up the phone by his bedside the words he would use in calling a special session of the Congress—now they *must* give him a free hand—may very well have been shaping themselves in his mind.

How Eleanor felt after that phone call she has told us in *This I Remember:*

I remember going over in my mind some of the things I had felt in World War I—my foreboding that my husband might leave the Navy Department in spite of being urged to stay; my anxiety when he actually did go across in the summer of 1918; my knowledge that if the war went on he would undoubtedly resign and get into active service; my thankfulness that my children were too young to be involved; and my desire to do all I could at home since I could not leave the children and yet could not help feeling I should be doing something in the actual danger zone. All the old conflicts and anxieties passed through my mind like the fragments in a kaleidoscope.[10]

Eleanor's feelings were similar to those of many Americans. It was already obvious to her that the United States would be involved. She speculated about her own role. It looked, she said, as though she would be "sitting out the war comfortably in Washington." And she felt a kind of rebellion when she realized that her sons would all be old enough this time to take an active part. But the rebellion was not against danger for her sons; it was against her own necessity for sitting "safely and idly by."

[9] It was long before dawn, in fact, as was noted in the next day's press conference. There was, in that conference, a satirical reference to Senator Borah, who had told Franklin at a White House meeting in the spring, called to negotiate revision of the Neutrality Act, that there would be no war in Europe. The senator's sources of information, he said, were more reliable than those of the administration; and they assured him that no war was in prospect. Now Franklin recalled the pompous senator's effrontery. To him it was a typical piece of isolationist irresponsibility. And how costly it was could now be seen. But Borah showed no sign of contrition. He would vote against repeal of the act even in the special session shortly to be called.

[10] P. 207.

Eleanor, it is quite apparent, accepted what was happening as inevitable. She had no reservation about the course of American policy; indeed, she seems to have drawn closer to Franklin in his ordeal because she believed his effort to avert American entanglement would be futile. Neither she nor he had any decision to make about what side to be on—only how much to be involved.

The family was rather more at Hyde Park this year than usual. But Sara went abroad in the summer and gave Franklin some anxiety by being caught, as were many other tourists, in the confusions of war's beginning. But John and his wife Anne were in Europe, too, and they shepherded the old lady safely home.[11]

The laying of the cornerstone for the library was at least one pleasant interlude in what otherwise was for all the family an anxious and melancholy time. But that did not happen until November, and by then war was well begun. In August, Russia and Germany had signed their non-aggression pact, and Franklin had returned hurriedly from a cruise in Canadian waters on the *Tuscaloosa*—which he had hoped would allow him to forget for a moment his bitterness over congressional defeats. He sent urgent appeals to Hitler, to King Victor Emmanuel of Italy, and to President Moscicki of Poland, imploring them to settle peaceably the Danzig corridor issue which was Hitler's ostensible issue. Next day he sent Hitler another message. But it had the same reception as earlier representations he had made in spring. It was ignored.

Hitler evidently thought the American President's appeal not worth considering. But it was just after this that Franklin called a special session and again requested that the embargo on arms shipments be repealed. This time Hitler had ensured the success of his appeal. Repeal went through, and during 1940, although it was an election year, Franklin would feel somewhat more free to support the Allied cause. It would always be done as a contribution to peaceful settlement, but it would be done.

He had little reason to feel much more comfortable about the national security. He was tormented by what seemed to him stupid refusals everywhere to comprehend the elements of strategy in an air age. The airplane, he was certain, had changed everything. Navies were not yet obsolete, but unless they discovered that planes had modified their modes of use they might easily be destroyed.[12] He was already turning over in his mind the elements of the "50,000 plane" speech he would make in May 1940.

[11] John and Anne had lost their first baby that spring, and this reminded Eleanor of losing the first Franklin Jr. long ago (in November 1909), "the biggest and most beautiful of all."

[12] It is ironic that the Navy Franklin had taken such pains to strengthen against this threat should have been caught defenseless in the debacle of Pearl Harbor, gathered in an anchorage as if inviting destruction.

prosperity

Looking back at that period of reluctant preparation for possible intervention—reluctant because the hope was so persistent that it might be avoided—we can feel with Franklin the anxiety and foreboding that must have been a constant torment. Unless he could have his way about preparedness, the nation would not be strong enough to be listened to by tough and ruthless dictators. And preparatory steps represented, to the timid, provocations which at all costs they would avoid. There were many appeasers. They would have talked softly to Hitler and to Mussolini, and each of Franklin's bolder essays threw them into panic. Even rearmament was accepted with fear and trembling. This attitude seemed even more prevalent after the invasion of Poland and entry on the year of the "phony war"; and it was clear from the first that it would have to be dealt with as an election issue. The opposition in 1940 would be largely the isolationists.

The appeasers, added to those numerous others who frankly wanted the Nazis and Fascists to prevail, made up a considerable part of the electorate, how large a part Franklin was almost afraid to estimate. One of his problems was to reduce their numbers, and much of his effort for the next year would be devoted to glorification of the Allied cause and to emphasizing the dangers of Axis conquest.

Affairs had been pretty much at a standstill until September had brought open hostilities. No actual changes were made in the domestic program; there was, indeed, a constant erosion, all through the executive establishment, of loyalty to the professed principles of the administration.[13] Certainly no advances could be made now until some crisis or change occurred to disturb the balance and set Franklin free. As for foreign policy, so long as the Neutrality Act governed his actions Franklin could do little but warn his countrymen of their dangers. No one knew better than he, however, that mere warnings were largely wasted. Not many wanted to hear. A reasonable return to prosperity was being registered after the recession of 1937-38. Americans liked things the way they were and had no intention of exercising themselves about Europe. No matter what Franklin said, they thought the repeated crises would settle themselves; and, even if there should be a war, they showed clearly a disposition against allowing it to interfere with their businesses and their amusements. The lethargy of this time would afterward seem inconceivable.

[13] This was perhaps natural as the second term wore on and the executive was more and more infiltrated by employees loyal to congressmen and the business interests they represented. There were only a few remaining centers of progressivism, mostly in the emergency agencies, but not by any means all of them. The Department of Agriculture had returned to its Republicanism and its solicitude for processors, and the RFC under Jesse Jones was unashamedly reactionary. Harry Hopkins' organization was the only emergency agency thoroughly faithful to the welfare ideal and even that, in many localities, was more political than faithful.

It was inconceivable to Franklin all along. He was tormented by previsions of what would come unless he could act. But it now began to seem to him a terrifying prospect whichever way Americans finally decided to go. If the present indifference remained unbroken and the Allies were defeated, he saw a world delivered to the savagery represented by Nazi purges, Italian massacres in Ethiopia, and Japanese atrocities in China. If finally there came an awakening, it now was so late that subjection even of the United States was not impossible. He knew the power of German efficiency. He studied it closely; and the more closely, the more it alarmed him.

His repeated thrusts at the dictators had disappointing repercussions. There were more reproaches than messages of support. He was stymied, but he was not in the least reconciled. He only grew more determined that the nation should awake to its responsibilities and stir itself. The liberties most precious to Americans were in jeopardy, but indifference to the threat was nearly universal.

The first shock to complacency with nationwide impact was the attack on Poland. The Munich arrangements had rather served to confirm indifference than otherwise; even the invasion of Czechoslovakia had not caused any very deep revulsion. But the Polish invasion and the ruthless success of the sweeping blitzkrieg did cause a wide awakening. With pained surprise many of those who had been inclined to favor German hegemony in eastern Europe watched the tank fleets and the Stuka planes smash Poland's old-fashioned armies. Something new had been added to the German armory. *Schrechlichkeit* had emerged as a weapon. From now on there would be much more disposition to listen when Franklin talked of national danger.

Until this crisis furnished an opening, however, Franklin was a giant in chains. No ordeal in his career can have been so frustrating. Not even the humiliations of 1937 and 1938 were comparable to those of 1939. They had—they must have had—a profound effect on his mind. It was during this time, I believe, that the politician began his rise to the stature of a statesmanship indifferent to self; above the level, finally, even of national concerns. He would emerge into the world at war a different man from the one who had fought so clever an electoral campaign in 1936, who had sought to enhance the presidency in 1937 at the expense of the Supreme Court, and who had played with the ambitions of potential successors while he planned retirement to the status of elder statesman. In the end he would belong to all humanity, not to Americans alone, much less to any faction, class, or sect in the nation.

Eleanor asked Franklin occasionally, she says, why he had not prepared a successor. She must have known she would get an equivocal answer; at least that was the kind she did get. Franklin merely said that Presidents could not be made, that they had to emerge because

489

of their own qualities. There was much truth in this. The talent and toughness necessary to the presidency, Franklin meant to say, are rare qualities and are best discovered in open competition. Successful Presidents are ones with the wide and solid support necessary to establish a policy. This cannot be bequeathed. It has to be earned.

On the other hand, what he neglected to say was that an incumbent President can stifle incipient booms for potential candidates with considerable ease. In the case of Garner and Farley the means used were direct and conscious. Farley's Catholicism was a handicap, and Garner never had any but southern support. Hull had to be given rope, but he had no way to use his opportunities unless Franklin would withdraw, and he never would. Robert H. Jackson was allowed to be killed off by Farley, who prevented him from running for the governorship of New York at the proper time. In the case of Paul McNutt, whose ambitions were obvious, more care was necessary. And McNutt would still have a real following at the Chicago convention in 1940. But it would be far from sufficient to stand against the third-term movement.

What the analyst has to deal with in this, as in so many other political matters, is a subtle and unacknowledged disposition in the presidential mind, one that would be denied by its possessor, and one that cannot be proved. Yet I suggest that Franklin, like others in a similar position, even if almost unconsciously, had managed, as 1940 had to be planned for, not to have any acceptable successor.[14] There probably was a time when he regretted this. That would have been just now, in 1939, when the nadir of his White House years was being passed through. But that soon changed. In the autumn of that year, as the blitzkrieg took hold on the American consciousness, he could feel returning pulses of response from public opinion.[15] Many an indifferent citizen, reading about the obliteration of opposing armies and the enslavement of civilians, suddenly realized that Franklin had all along been trying to tell him what was about to happen. He had a growing apprehension, moreover, that he was far from having heard the last of

---

[14] W. L. Chenery, in *So It Seemed* (New York: Harcourt, Brace, 1952), has commented on this (cf. p. 259). It occurred to him that negotiations he was having with Franklin concerning post-presidency employment (Chenery was offering a writing contract with *Collier's*) had a certain unreal quality. The elusiveness he sensed was, he thought, due to Franklin's perhaps subconscious intention to run a third time:

I was doubtful because on an occasion when he asked me in rhetorical fashion, not expecting an answer, who might be chosen to succeed him, I had ventured quite simply to mention the names of a few of the more eminent men associated with him. I quickly learned that every one had some fatal weakness . . .

[15] There even came a time when he was moved to complain of being pushed ahead too fast rather than of being held back. This irritation was expressed in a note to Harry Hopkins in December of 1939. Cf. *Personal Letters: 1928–1945*, Vol. II, p. 970.

Isolationists

it. If Poland, why not France? And if France, why not Britain? And all at once he stopped regarding Franklin as an Anglophile for wanting to support the British. He could see that if all Europe should become a base for Hitler, with no hostile Russia in the east, the interests of the United States were indeed jeopardized. The Atlantic seemed much narrower with Germany controlling the other side than it had when the British fleet had held it in sure control.

There was a difficult year yet to come, but never again would ridicule of Franklin's fears have so receptive an audience as in 1939. Returning support made itself manifest in various ways. And one of the immediate results of the turn in sentiment was the general discovery that a third term was not impossible. At about the same time it was discovered by Franklin that it was inevitable. From the day when Poland was invaded, the gradual conviction grew that no one else would do. The pleasant thoughts of retirement were laid aside.

With more than five years still to serve, he was, however, already a tired man. His burden had been weighty, his disappointments had been grievous, and he no longer had the resilience of his first term. He was fifty-seven, which was certainly no great age in a long-lived family, but the strain of the past two years had made them count for many. Whenever he set out now to find recreation in journeys or in stays at Hyde Park, the daily grind was hardly less than when he was in the White House.

It must be remembered to what extent Franklin himself had the responsibility for foreign policy. He must also take care, as no other President had felt forced to do, that national well-being was maintained. Economic prosperity or the lack of it now centered in the White House. There was no delegation. But added to these were the responsibilities that we have been speaking of for preparedness in all its phases. And this, it must be said, was peculiarly wearing because of the official circumstance that involvement in war was to be avoided, in his judgment, only by preparing for it at home and strengthening the Allies abroad. The elements of contradiction in the program he was evolving confused a good many people. Those who thought his policy cowardly were almost as troublesome as those who were certain that he was managing affairs to bring about intervention. He was a man weary and harassed.

But until the end of 1939 his worst troubles came from the isolationists. Perhaps Robert E. Wood of Chicago, president of Sears, Roebuck and Company, was as typical a member of this group as could be found.[16] Franklin was arguing with him about neutrality as he had ar-

---

[16] General Wood's participation in public affairs always had the kind of bizarre orientation that seems so often to develop in the Midwest. Wood had, in early New Deal days, been a member of The Committee for the Nation and so had stood sponsor for Wirt and Warren; just now he was aggressively isolationist;

491

gued earlier with Kent, the banker, about welfare measures. Wood had written to complain that the whole administration expected war and would welcome it. Franklin replied:

Dear Bob:

I really thought that at your age you would have learned to discriminate between newspaper interpretations on the one hand and facts on the other. I do not know anyone in official Washington who, as you say, "feels it inevitable that this country should be drawn into the European conflict." You make all kinds of wild and wholly incorrect statements. "The whole Department of State" is *not* permeated with this feeling . . . nor are "some of the Ambassadors," neither is "notably the Ambassador to France." Neither do I share this feeling. Neither does Mrs. Roosevelt share this feeling.

I think, too, that you are asking the impossible when you suggest that high officials of the Federal Government should be "neutral in thought." What you mean is, of course, that while they cannot humanly be neutral in thought, they ought not to let this affect their neutrality of action in any shape, manner or form.

So, my dear friend, stop being disturbed and get both of your feet back on the ground.[17]

Correspondence of this sort—and there was a good deal of it—shows what an anxious time this must have been. But it also shows what extreme pains Franklin was taking to bend opinion toward internationalism. He cannot really have expected to change Wood's attitude any more than he could hope to change that of Charles A. Lindbergh or Robert R. McCormick and his Chicago *Tribune.* But he was neglecting no possibility. The *Tribune* at the moment was extending itself to oppose, by the use of every conceivable device, legitimate or otherwise, the policy of support for Britain. It was not far from approving Hitler's design for the subjugation of Europe. It must be said that Franklin did get some—perhaps unexpected but certainly welcome—support from farther west. William Allen White, "the sage of Emporia," had organized a Non-Partisan Committee for Peace through the Revision of the Neutrality Law. The White committee helped to offset the denunciations of the *Tribune.* So also, it should be said, did Frank Knox's Chicago *Daily News.* The *Tribune* continued to be mostly a noisy nuisance, but it certainly represented a considerable Chicagoland opinion.

The special session was a turbulent one, reflecting in this the deep division of national opinion. But the isolationists could not stop the turn toward sympathy with the allies and revulsion from German ruthless-

---

in later circumstances he would be a member, along with McCormick of the Chicago *Tribune* and others, of America First; and still later he would sponsor For America. All these were related negativist and reactionary movements. They attracted the most die-hard of the isolationists who were also aggressive nationalists of a strongly in-turning sort.

[17] *Personal Letters: 1928–1945,* Vol. II, pp. 937–38.

ness. There was as yet no sign that fear for the national safety had taken hold on people's minds; the prevailing sentiment was rather that of sympathy for the victims of aggression and anger with Hitler. Franklin was given a "cash-and-carry" law. But he still was very much aware that he could not presume very far on the prevailing opinion. It would still not support a drastic policy.

To bring the nation as far as it had been brought, he had, during the past two years, not only traded away much that he had hated to let go but had also thrown a very wide net to gather in every possible kind of support. This included more than approval at home; extraordinary efforts were made to develop friendship in other nations. The time was coming when it would be needed. There was an unusual procession of invited foreign visitors, entertained in Washington with a maximum of publicity. The press was unable to resist the appeal of royalty. The journey of the King and Queen of England counted most, perhaps, but there were others, and so good was the management that the result was a strong counter to isolationism.

Eleanor devotes a charming chapter of *This I Remember* to the visit of British royalty. Reading this, and noting the letters and memoranda among Franklin's papers, it is impossible not to be impressed by the care given to these exhibitions. They are to be listed among the apparently irrelevant occurrences which could afterward be seen to have had an important effect on opinion.

The King and Queen were first brought to Washington with due formality, and every detail of the set program came under Franklin's scrutiny. He liked to tell afterward how he had reversed the protocol officers on seating arrangements at the state dinner—which was watched intently by the newsmen. He was told that the King must be seated at his right hand and must be served ahead of others. He insisted on what he said was the universal arrangement for entertaining in a gentleman's house. The Queen sat at his right and the King at Eleanor's right. The royal folk were delighted—and so was the American public. But the touch of finesse was added when at a Hyde Park picnic the spectacle was presented of a King and Queen sitting on the grass and eating hot dogs among a miscellany of guests, reporters included.

Visits of this sort served to reinforce Franklin's insistence that the European nations were democracies in danger from totalitarian aggression and that they were the first line of American defense. If their liberties were extinguished, he kept saying, those of our own people would at once come into jeopardy. Well-mannered and friendly visits from the heads of those states were intended to and did make that lesson more vivid in American minds.

The British visit was in 1939. Accompanying the King and Queen was the Premier of Canada, Mackenzie King. English-speaking people were united for all the world to see. And this, it must be recalled, was at a very difficult stage in Franklin's campaign for support. It was obvious that, defeated as he might be in congressional battles, and deep in economic trouble as well, he was not deflected from his intention that the democracies facing the dictators should have, at the least, friendly support from their powerful natural ally. It was a lesson meant for both the Americans and Europeans. He was still President of the United States, in charge of foreign policy. This might make the isolationists furious. And it did. But the calm determination with which he appeared to pursue his course was notable even in the worst days of 1938 and 1939. His worries were well hidden.

During this period, also, one of the striking evidences of his cautious preparation for what might come is to be found in his letters to the various ambassadors—MacVeagh in Athens, Cudahy in Dublin, Phillips in Rome, Bullitt in Paris, Davies in Brussels, Kennedy in London, Grew in Tokyo, Mrs. Harriman in Oslo, Steinhardt in Moscow; wherever they were, they must not forget that they were the President's own representatives, assumed to be as eager as he to forward a policy they understood together.

One of these communications may be selected as fairly typical. It was written to Phillips in Rome in June 1939. It was not hard to think of a hard-pressed President, with every reason for discouragement, sitting alone at night with a sleepy secretary at the big desk in the Oval Room, working to reduce the pile of correspondence before him. He came, we may guess, to a communication from Phillips, telling an old colleague about affairs within the purview of his chancellery. We can see the President reading it, fingering it thoughtfully for a moment, then dictating in a clear unhesitating voice, however tired he might be:

Dear Bill:

Many thanks for your grand letter of May twenty-sixth. You are right about telephones. The transatlantic service is probably listened to not only by London, Paris, Berlin and Rome but probably also by at least four or five other European capitals. That seems to be clearly established.

I hope and pray, every day, that the influence of Mussolini will be definitely against war. But on the other hand, I am worried by the fact that both Germany and Italy are maintaining such an enormous number of men under arms and continuing to spend such vast sums. It seems to me that if Germany visualizes a peaceful working out of the political and economic problems, common sense would require the starting of conversations as soon as possible in order to avoid an even worse financial situation.

I fear, too, that both dictators think their present methods are succeeding because of the gains they have made in Albania, Hungary and Yugoslavia.

The King and Queen arrive tomorrow and we look for a strenuous four days. I devoutly hope everything will go through without any upsets. We hope to see Caroline this summer. Take care of yourself.[18]

And we can, without straining, guess that Phillips, in his chancellery, tired too and getting old, but conscientious in his plodding way and secretly disgusted with Il Duce's posturing, but always polite in an especially polished, almost obtuse way, may have taken a little heart from such a letter written by his Chief of State. No one knew better than Phillips the routine of ambassadorial communication. He was an experienced career officer. But something of Franklin's vigilance and determination must have come through in this letter. He would have thought of their old days together, back in Wilson's presidency when Franklin and Bill, Eleanor and Caroline had been young together in a very different Washington. Perhaps with a sigh for the vanished days when things were less difficult, he may have held Franklin's letter in his hand as he thought of the next move in the maneuvering of that summer when so much depended—or seemed to—on the ability of the diplomats to check the wild men short of war.

I think that Phillips, so different from Franklin, may have been glad, in his career-officer way, that the leadership in this affair was Franklin's responsibility and not his. It had got to a level beyond his reach as a strategist; but he could do the work, and do it well, of representing a principal.

As a matter of fact, Franklin was well represented in this way everywhere except in London. Kennedy had more sympathies with the isolationists than with the interventionists; and when war began he would find himself unable to believe that the Allies could—or perhaps ought to—withstand the Nazi attack. His successor, John G. Winant, would, however, by his charm and steady resolution, help to link the two nations in ties of indissoluble strength.

Even this early, then, in the management of relations abroad, Franklin must be judged to have had a comprehensive conception of the American place in the world and to have conceived the devices necessary to the implementation of collective security. This would emerge eventually as the capability to command the most puissant force ever assembled to represent a nation's will. He would be perfectly certain about objectives and quite as certain about the means to reach them.

Franklin was in fact already functioning as Commander-in-Chief. This can be seen in the various public papers. Among them are memoranda, directives, and searching questions sent to the heads of the armed forces. Even with Franklin's known capacity for storing away detail and his strong inclination to direct physical affairs, some of these

[18] Ibid., p. 891.

495

indications of his foresight and technical capability are amazing. I quote only one of many:

October 9, 1939

MEMORANDUM FOR THE ACTING SECRETARY
OF THE NAVY: [CHARLES EDISON]

I have been disturbed by:

(a) The slowness of getting the East Coast, Caribbean and Gulf patrol under way.

(b) The lag between the making of contacts and the follow-up of the contacts.

(c) The weakness of liaison between Navy, Coast Guard and State Department.

It is, therefore, necessary to make the following orders clear!

(1) The patrol operations will be rushed to completion by the use of the 18 East Coast and 22 West Coast Priority No. 1 destroyers and by completing the aircraft patrol planes.

(2) When any aircraft or surface ship sights a submarine a report thereof will be rushed to the Navy Department for immediate action. The plane or surface ship sighting a submarine will remain in contact as long as possible. On the disappearance of the submarine, immediate steps will be taken by the Force Commander (in the absence of special orders from the Department) to try to pick up the submarine again at dawn next day and during the night to endeavor to patrol such area as the submarine might use for a refueling operation from tankers.

(3) On establishing contact with any suspicious craft of any nationality which might conceivably be carrying oil or supplies for a submarine, such surface craft will be followed day and night until such surface craft has proceeded to her port of destination or sufficiently far out to sea to preclude any possibility of her return to patrol area waters.

(4) Planes or Navy or Coast Guard ships may report the sighting of any submarine or suspicious surface ship in plain English to Force Commander or Department.

In this whole patrol business time is of the essence and loss of contact with surface ships cannot be tolerated.[19]

The establishment of the patrol area and its policing by the Navy would not have much direct effect on the fortunes of the Allies. But it did serve to put the Navy to work and to give an America suddenly impatient some sense of participation. This was a "measure short of war" which was not very far short.

Franklin spent a November weekend at Hyde Park in the fall weather he loved, then he went to Warm Springs for Thanksgiving. But by December 1 he was back in Washington, enraged over "the rape of Finland"[20] by Russia and calculating how he should proceed, now

---

[19] Ibid., pp. 936–37.
[20] Cf. letter to Lincoln MacVeagh in Athens, *Personal Letters: 1928–1945*, Vol. II, p. 961.

that he had more freedom to act, in the direction he had no more need to consider.

Eleanor could already see, even if Sam Rosenman could not, that the third-term issue was settled. Farley and his allies were afraid that they could see it too. But they had not yet given up.

24

The engagements during 1939 and 1940 were to be the last of Franklin's real political battles. He would go on after that in a different fashion—a fashion whose pattern was foreshadowed, more or less, by the Court reform attempt in 1937. The indifference displayed then to immediate results, so uncharacteristic theretofore, would be duplicated during the years when military strategy and geopolitics were dominant in his mind. He would then apparently assume—as he had in 1937—that he had support, that what he asked for must be given, and that maneuverings and machinations were unbecoming. It was as though he said: "Take it or leave it," knowing it must be taken. We have seen how this resulted in disaster once; we shall see how it resulted in steady dominance in the different circumstances of war.[1]

Isolationism would still possess a good many minds in the pre-war months. But as the arguments preceding Pearl Harbor went on, it could be seen how diverse were the attitudes brought under that label. It finally became a term used for all those who opposed American partici-

---

[1] Franklin mentioned this in a letter to Frank Knox, publisher of the Chicago *Daily News* (to be found in *Personal Letters: 1928–1945*, Vol. II, pp. 975–77) and Landon's running mate in 1936. He had spoken to Knox about coming into the cabinet. He now wrote to him (December 29, 1939) that it had better be put off. It would be called a political rather than a patriotic move. If, he said, a stalemate in Europe continued, there would probably be an old-fashioned hot and bitter campaign in 1940. On the other hand, if there should be an aggressor's victory, party government could be put aside. What he felt about such a campaign was this:

Such campaigns—viewing with alarm and pointing with pride—are a little stupid and a little out of date, and their appeal to prejudice does little to encourage a more intelligent electorate. But I suppose we have not grown up very much since the campaign of 1920 between Harding and Coolidge on the one side and Cox and Roosevelt on the other. I might add that I am neither bitter nor cynical—but I do wish there was less immaturity in political thinking.

Translated, this seems to mean that he was tired of using political arts for the mere purpose of continuance in office.

pation, to any degree, in the war. Some of these were people of German or Italian descent whose pride in their ancestry blinded them to the meaning of totalitarianism. But there were always those to whom Nazism and Fascism offered attractions. Then there were others who, although they opposed American participation on the side of the Allies and asserted that Franklin was an Anglophile, offered suggestions for aggressions of the most fantastic sort.[2]

All these individuals were thrown into the isolationist category along with those others who really wanted to ignore all the menacing developments beyond the nation's shores as well as those—and there were not a few—who simply felt that American policy was wrong and that resort to war would settle nothing.[3]

Franklin, at one or another time, had to deal with all these dissenters. His steady contention was that aid to the Allies was necessary because they were fighting for a cause that was also America's cause. There were some warm engagements with the opposition and some narrow victories. It was seen as soon as it was signed that the Neutrality Act repealer in 1939 did not carry an extensive commitment. Franklin, always sensitive in such matters, knew this very well; consequently, following its signing early in November, he entered a more rather than less cautious period.

Events now would have to finish what leadership had begun. Franklin pressed when he could, but he was less insistent than his supporters desired; he even seemed, for some time, to be holding back. This was a source of immense concern to the British and the French as they suffered the agonies of 1940. But Churchill, for instance, when he succeeded Chamberlain as Prime Minister, being a politician too, would have confidence that Franklin was going forward as rapidly as he could without creating reaction. He would be impatient, but he would not insist unduly on British needs.

As we study Franklin's activities during these months, we understand that, although it would only be apparent after the fact, vital preparations were being made. But while he seemed to wait, and while the nation hesitated, slowly stiffening for the onrushing crisis, terrible events were occurring one after the other across the Atlantic. There was a sinister pause after the fall of Poland, but in spring the Nazi fury fell on Denmark and Norway; then France was invaded and crushed; the debacle of Dunkirk occurred; and in June, Mussolini, a harpy feeding on a wounded body, invaded southern France.

These disasters penetrated the American mind with devastating ef-

[2] The United States should seize the West Indies, the Azores, or islands in the far Pacific, etc.

[3] Of these last, Robert Maynard Hutchins and Henry N. MacCracken were two; presidents, respectively, of the University of Chicago and Vassar College.

fect. They tended to exaggerate already deep divisions. But there were those who saw in them justification for not taking sides, or perhaps for not supporting those belligerents who had been—or seemed about to be —conquered. The German war machine was truly terrifying. It rolled over and crushed all opposition. Nothing could stand against it.

The facts, as they unrolled, were horrifying enough; but they were made worse by being exaggerated and distorted for American consumption, and there were not a few people who from being indifferent had now passed to being frightened. They said to themselves: "Unarmed as we are, we had best conciliate this monster before it crushes us." That this was cowardly made no difference. Fears cannot be argued with, and they were so prevalent that for a long time politicians treated them with respect.

Franklin, however, although he was somewhat circumspect, consistently and constantly opposed the various timidities and totalitarian preferences with appeals to courage and justice. He did it by speech, by example, and by action. He was far from standing as still as was maintained by those who now would have liked to move much faster. He was certainly not retreating from the advanced positions he had occupied. In fact from June to November the presidential campaign of 1940 would have as one of its issues the need for opposing the threat to liberty represented by totalitarianism. It must be done, he would say, first by supporting those who had undertaken to hold the lines, and then by rearming ourselves so that we should be ready if they failed. He would campaign against Hitler that fall as much as against his Republican opponent.

By election time there would be very little content to the professed expectation that the nation could still be kept out of the war by supporting the Allies. The Allies would soon be in agonizing straits, the smaller nations conquered, France disorganized and occupied, the British humiliated and disarmed, awaiting invasion, with only their frail air arm to defend their coasts. Franklin still would not give up the fiction of avoidance, but he would stress more and more the need for preparedness; and finally he would have the audacity, before the election, to demand really drastic measures. Nothing could have shown so well how his confidence had grown.

He could not even yet be entirely sure that supporters of his foreign policy were a majority. When the election year opened, public-opinion polls had seemed to show that sentiment for participation in the war was rather declining than rising. If he showed more discretion than boldness during the winter and spring, this is the reason. It was the reason, also, why he had not been certain, all during the debate on the neutrality resolution, that it would pass. Moreover, this uncertainty accounts for the tactics used in that fight. In similar circumstances, in

1937, he had allowed his White House emissaries to cajole, bargain, threaten, and otherwise try to influence votes against the Court. In this instance, showing perhaps that he was tired of cheap maneuverings, he threw the whole responsibility for carrying the repeal resolution on the legislative leaders and went about his business as though nothing of importance were going on.

This tactic had an interesting result. The resolution passed, even if by small margins, in both Houses. There were many professions of opposition, many bitter denunciatory speeches, both in the Congress and outside. The isolationist press did its worst. But Franklin used his tremendous influence on public opinion to play down the proceedings, and for so consequential a proposal there was remarkably little real furor. And this was in spite of an incident abroad that was extremely provocative: Russia presented demands to Finland whose severity obviously implied the complete subjection of the small nation to the larger one. When, as *Time* remarked:[4]

she presented demands to Finland's envoy to Moscow, she also presented President Roosevelt with a major problem in statecraft. It forced on him what correspondents did not hesitate to call "the most delicate and momentous decision of his career" . . . In blunt terms of domestic politics any blunder might have changed the situation in the Senate. Any bold and dramatic action would have given ammunition to critics. . . . Inaction was unthinkable on moral and political grounds—not only had Finland scrupulously paid her war debt installments to the U.S., but U.S.-Finnish relations have been an untroubled model of what international relations should be. . . .

What Franklin did in these circumstances was very circumspect indeed. He himself wrote a note to President Kalinin of Russia, saying only that he had "an earnest hope that nothing may occur to injure the peaceful relations of Finland and Russia." This somewhat mollified those who thought Finland badly treated but did not provoke the isolationist press. Incidentally, it seemed to cause no rancor in either Finland or Russia.

This was a sample of the light treading Franklin was for the time doing among his various problems while his congressional leaders pressed for the requested change in American foreign policy. But he made other contributions as well. They were not recognized as such, but they were very practical. He gave Americans a soul-filling exhibition of presidential confidence and serenity. He was ably abetted by Eleanor. Indeed, the whole Roosevelt clan, numerous now, performed unself-consciously its role of first family with happy aplomb. And most Americans—although there were a good many carpers—approved.

By Thanksgiving, 1939, the special session was over, the legislators

[4] October 23, 1939.

had gone home, and the proclamations banning belligerent submarines from U.S. ports and defining the combat areas had been issued; also, it had been announced that still another vast appropriation would be asked of the next Congress to pay for another hundred naval vessels—aircraft carriers, destroyers, and submarines. By Thanksgiving, also, Franklin had made two Hyde Park visits—to dedicate the library and to vote in local elections—and had gone from there to Warm Springs for the customary holiday celebration.[5] The whole country watched as these journeys were pursued. The endless detail supplied by special correspondents was consumed eagerly; its fascinations were irresistible. Franklin drove his small car about Hyde Park as usual and once got stuck in the mud; he caught cold and had to take it easy. He visited with the neighbors; he inspected his Christmas-tree plantations and sold his apples.

On October 30 *Time* said of Franklin's behavior:

For all the signs that President Roosevelt gave last week, he might not have known that the Senate was still engrossed in its Great Debate. Neither oblivious nor negligent, Mr. Roosevelt was simply complying with the admonition laid down by his Senate strategists, Key Pittman and Jimmy Byrnes: "Stay out of the neutrality fight." By staying out he exhibited a restraint remarkable for him, regrettable for Senate isolationists, who would welcome nothing more than a rousing White House scare to scare off Administration votes.

That week at Hyde Park, Franklin read the nation the second chapter of a lesson begun when the British King and Queen had been his conspicuous guests. They had gone with him on a Sunday to the St. James

---

[5] Franklin's dedication speech had a charming reminiscent passage:
Half a century ago a small boy took especial delight in climbing an old tree, now unhappily gone, to pick and eat ripe sickle pears. That was about one hundred feet to the west of where I am standing now. And just to the north he used to lie flat between the strawberry rows and eat sun-warmed strawberries—the best in the world. In the spring of the year, in hip rubber boots, he sailed his first toy boats in the surface water formed by the melting snow. In the summer with his dogs he dug into woodchuck holes in this same field, and some of you are standing on top of those holes at this minute. Indeed, the descendants of those same woodchucks still inhabit this field and I hope that, under the auspices of the National Archivist, they will continue to do so for all time.

It has, therefore, been my personal hope that this Library, and the use of it by scholars and visitors, will come to be an integral part of a country scene which the hand of man has not changed very greatly since the days of the Indians who dwelt here three hundred years ago.

We know from simple deduction that these fields were cultivated by the first inhabitants of America—for the oak trees in these fields were striplings three centuries ago, and grew up in open fields as is proved to us by their wide spreading lower branches. Therefore, they grew in open spaces, and the only open spaces in Dutchess County were the cornfields of the Indians. [Public Papers, 1939 vol., pp. 580–81.]

Church. Now Franklin, as senior warden, was attending a special service and presenting a Bible sent by Their Majesties to be a gift in commemoration of the occasion on which the chiefs of state had worshiped there together. No isolationist could miss the implications of this incident.

Franklin left Hyde Park for Warm Springs as the leaves were falling. There seemed just then to be a favorable turn of events. The Germans and Russians were disagreeing; they were evidently not such close allies as their rapprochement of the summer would indicate. The Comintern was denouncing the Nazis' philosophy, and trade-agreement negotiations were becoming more difficult. Furthermore, there were rumors that the German-Italian friendship was cooling. There was an attempt on Hitler's life by bombing in a Munich beer hall sacred to the Nazis, and this caused observers to conclude that internal strife in Germany might be serious. Chamberlain in Britain, encouraged by these indications and happy over the abandonment of embargo in the United States, said for publication that the position of the Allies had, "as the weeks have gone by, rather strengthened than deteriorated."

It was on this note of optimism that the year ran on to its conclusion. Franklin benefited from the Georgia sun. And Americans seemed to benefit from watching him. At Warm Springs there was another dedication—the long-awaited community center. He carved the Thanksgiving turkey, swam in the pool, and inspected—attended by the press—his twenty-five hundred acres of hilly land. On this occasion, as he had done before, he held a roadside press conference which turned into a sermon on conservation. It was complained that he gave the correspondents nothing to write about. But the truth was that they were perforce writing about what he wanted them to—which was his doings in the nation's interest.

It did no harm that it was reported how "pretty, yellow-headed patient, Ann Smithers, age six, who won the right to sit at the President's table, gnawed a drumstick despite the fact that her baby teeth are falling out." And most of the nation smiled when Franklin, making a little speech to Warm Springers, wondered, as any member of the Chamber of Commerce might have done, why the post office was so inadequate. "What have we got?" he asked. "We have got a little over a year left." This was a reference to the running out of his second term and was taken by everyone as having a humorous equivocal meaning.[6]

This oblique comment on the probable end of his White House service fell into the midst of what was becoming a tiresome insistence that he was "plotting" a third term. It was therefore linked with a series

[6] Somewhat later, in the interest of concentrating on defense, Franklin canceled an allocation of public works funds out of which the post office would have been built. It must have given him a twinge.

503

of conjectures reflecting intense interest of both friends and foes. The Gallup poll in December showed a slight decline in his popularity. Even his cautious handling of the neutrality issue had frightened a good many people. This was a sufficient answer to those supporters who considered that he had been going too slow. He had pressed as hard as he could. On the other hand, the same poll showed a rather startling increase among those voters who favored a third term. He must have judged that his conduct was about right. At any rate, he went on in the same way.

Christmas came to the White House in 1939 in splendid and heartwarming fashion. It was at once elegant and homely; it was also merry and sad. There were war and suffering abroad; there were grave decisions, affecting the lives of all Americans, in the making; and it seems likely that most of them by now could see, in spite of Franklin's continued protestations, how these decisions would have to be made. But, as Americans usually can, the sadness and apprehension were temporarily laid aside. Peace, good will, and even jollity descended on the nation. And, symbolically, these manifestations descended most conspicuously on the White House and its occupants. The whole country shared its first family's joys. Spirits, long weighed down by the gloomiest forebodings, seemed to lift for the season.

In many a home Christmas was brighter because the relations of people and their government had been radically changed in the past few years. There were still unemployed running into the millions, although many were being absorbed into the intensified "defense efforts."[7] More billions of public dollars were now becoming available for the expansion of industry than had been dreamed of in the early days of the works programs. There was a lesson in this. The appropriations now were rising to four and five times the old limits, and unemployment was at last beginning to disappear after seven years of halfhearted attempts to banish it. A high-energy free-enterprise society—to use terms then familiar—needed to have its government spend appreciable percentages of the national income for public purposes—whether of one

---

[7] Eight million were still without work, it was estimated toward the end of 1939. If this, to a later generation, indicates tolerance of a social disease not to be thought of in their time, it is a mark of the slowness of Americans to accept governmental responsibility for industrial activity. It ought to be recalled, at the same time, that the Social Security System by now operated to assist, in however small a way, the unemployed and their families. Within a matter of weeks old-age assistance would begin, as Franklin reminded the nation when he catalogued the nation's blessings at holiday time.

An additional note: the national income, reckoned in 1929 at eighty-two billions, was by 1939 only back to sixty-five billions. Recovery, in the ten years, had not been spectacular. The economy was only tolerably productive, and Americans stood it only because they had access to income from public sources so that what there was was shared more equitably than in earlier times.

sort or another. This was to ensure that capital expanded, plants were renewed, income was available to all, and activity was maintained. This was apparent now, though businessmen were still reluctant to accept the inevitable.

It was at this time that Franklin, with all his other worries, was thinking out his approach to the industrial expansion which would provide an unprecedentedly huge volume of munitions—and indeed of all sorts of other goods, including foods and fibers. How insatiable the demands of war would be he foresaw earlier than almost anyone else, perhaps recalling the onset of a former war when he had had responsibilities for naval procurement. Even if the United States was no more than a furnisher of goods and not a belligerent, the goods must be in dependable supply. How early he came to the decisions involved in this, we cannot tell. We can be sure, however, as in other instances, that it was long before there was any outward evidence that they had been made.

The transition to war status was facilitated, as the next year passed, by establishing a number of emergency agencies, the first of which was a War Resources Board, whose head was Edward R. Stettinius, chairman of the U. S. Steel Corporation. This Board was temporary. It reported, its report was accepted, and it disbanded. This had not been intended, but the whole matter had become involved in the policies Franklin was evolving and about which he would not be hurried. Besides, the issue was precipitated just when the Senate debate on neutrality was in full swing. For the moment he temporized. No one could tell yet what he intended even if there were many who thought they could guess.

The matter was peculiar because an equivocal situation existed in both the War and Navy departments. Everyone realized that there would have to be replacements of both secretaries as expansion went on. Neither was judged to be capable of meeting the new responsibilities. Such changes, however, were not easy, political considerations being what they were. And Franklin was cautious almost to the point of endangering the national interest. The Navy situation was not too complicated. Charles Edison, the incumbent, would give way gracefully when the time came in accord with an arrangement at his appointment, and his successor was already chosen in Franklin's mind. The more awkward situation was in the War Department. The Secretary was Harry H. Woodring, former governor of Kansas. He had been a misfit; moreover, he was not in sympathy with collective security. He would have to give way; yet to dismiss him would create a furor. He had friends among the isolationists and a political machine at home. Also, however, there was an extremely active and ambitious Assistant Secretary, Louis A. Johnson, who, if possible, was even more potent politically, having been national commander of the American Legion.

Johnson had put it about freely that he expected to succeed the departing Woodring. And he had proceeded to complicate matters by appointing in August, evidently with Franklin's rather absent-minded consent, the Board headed by Stettinius of U. S. Steel. In October he announced that this Board would, in wartime, become a War Resources Administration with vast powers of mobilization and management.

It was this announcement that created Franklin's policy crisis. To resolve it Franklin was widely expected to replace both the Secretary and the Assistant Secretary. And he did, in fact, offer the secretaryship to Frank Murphy, who was then Attorney General. Murphy refused. He had been governor of Michigan and governor general of the Philippines; he wanted to go to the Supreme Court—as he later did. Franklin was not ready to name anyone else. It was widely rumored that La Guardia was to be appointed. So indeed Franklin had intended. But there was political objection. And after almost committing himself (he told a number of people that La Guardia was his choice) he temporized and allowed the crisis to continue. It worsened as the months passed.[8]

When Franklin dismissed the War Resources Board he also left another policy crisis unresolved. He was not yet ready to take direction of the needed industrial expansion. More preparation of public opinion was necessary. And very possibly he was still struggling in his own mind with alternatives.

Probably the issue had already been settled in principle. He must have concluded, as his evolving policy would shortly begin to reveal, that the socialization of industry for war purposes was impractical. It was more than impractical; it was impolitic. Socialization of the sort that might have been carried out could well have been said to imitate the pattern of national socialism. When the NRA was given up and trust busting again undertaken, the return to traditional free enterprise (with regulation) became the American alternative to both Nazism and communism. Put in personal terms, it was the Roosevelt platform in contrast with the platforms of Mussolini, Hitler, and Stalin.

The gathering up of the nation's strength, its channeling toward the provision of needed goods and services, would in the end be turned over to businessmen, some of them working in government, some in their own industries. There would be general overhead direction; there would be moderate restrictions. But it would mostly be done for profit with vast government subsidies.

---

[8] La Guardia believed, until Stimson was appointed in June, that he would be given the post. By that time he knew that Franklin's third-term intentions had spoiled his chances for a presidential nomination. He aspired to—and perhaps rated—the nation's highest posts. That he never attained them was more because of being contemporary with an even cleverer politician than himself than because he lacked the necessary quality.

Capital would be made available for expansion and reconversion, markets would be guaranteed, and earnings would be high, sometimes fantastic. Inflation would follow, and so controls would have to be put on prices. This, in turn, would involve rationing. In the end, a tight system would evolve, with businessmen in control so firmly that in after-war years it would be utterly unrealistic to speak of a free-enterprise system. Monopoly would be institutionalized and recognized. Government controls would be disestablished with peace, but not the consolidated collectivism under private direction fostered by wartime government.

Franklin did not need the warning about this prospect that old Josephus Daniels felt impelled to send him. But obviously his dilemma was a deep one. To have attempted socialization of the industries basic to war production would have been to accept colossal responsibilities. Such a tour de force even in the circumstances of peace would have involved managerial duties beyond the competence of any corps of men, not now in charge of the same industries. It would therefore involve a change in ownership, but not in management. Would that personnel, deprived of its high salaries and its many privileges, have the incentives necessary to the exigent task ahead? Would he not risk indifference, if not outright sabotage, of a total effort in which the nation's security was risked?

There were, besides, the many commitments he had made in the years just past to the free enterprise of progressivism, together with the more rigorous controls of the Second New Deal. These had to be considered. He had given up his first essays in collectivism for this revised program. In its battles—to establish controls over the exchanges, to protect stockholders, to abolish "unfair" trade practices, to fix the minima of bargaining, and to set up the social security structure—he had risked much. To Franklin's mind it was, taken all together, responsible for giving free enterprise—capitalism, it could be called—a new term of life. If these reforms had not been made the system would have collapsed at its next self-induced crisis. He had saved the system. To be sure, he was not thanked for it by most of those who had been involved. They would even now, if they could, return to the old ways. And they blamed him for their inability to do so. He was reviled in their press. Daily he was castigated as something he was not—a socialist, for instance—with an irresponsible inaccuracy that was sometimes maddening.

Franklin had followed the eager willingness with which this thesis was accepted. It is always comforting to have a theory for the support of prejudice; and he knew that businessmen thought themselves thoroughly justified in their detestation of the New Deal and of himself as its author. He was more than just their enemy as individuals and as businessmen. He was a threat to what they averred was the source and

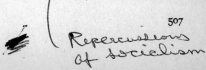

Repercussions of socialism

sustenance of American progress, the profit system. It was the repetition ad nauseum of this justification that enabled Republicanism to recover its morale and, even after the crushing electoral defeat of 1936, to become again a powerful party ready to contend for control of the presidency. And that control would be decided in 1940. What his opponents did not see until too late was the trap he had laid for them. In attacking him they would be leaguing themselves with Hitler.

Franklin could not judge that the coming contest would be one-sided. He knew that it would not. Even in his own party there was a recurrent weakness for accepting the Republican version of events. The conservatives were anti-welfare; they were budget balancers; and, withal, they were identified with business. They fully accepted the thesis that confidence was destroyed by such overregulation as Franklin had prescribed and that enterprisers, given more freedom, would return the nation to its former condition of prosperity.

There were, therefore, a whole series of policies that Franklin must think of in correlation with each other. They could not be separated. They need not be announced together or even announced at all, ever; but they must be clear in his mind as he prepared the nation to meet the tests ahead. They would be his guide in the ordeal to come.

There must be a system for mobilization and, along with it, a better way of procuring munitions. There must be improved military organization and management. And there must be such support for himself as national leader that he could act with confidence in crises—at least until he should finally make up his mind whether or not to continue beyond 1940.

Franklin, in whose mind so many matters were churning toward some issue, was, as we must see, a man distrait during this holiday season in 1939. But his dissembling was so successful that no one, except perhaps Eleanor, guessed his inner abstraction. As he carved the turkey at Warm Springs, as he created a diverting public interest in his forestry operations and his herd of beef cattle, as he picnicked with friends and newspapermen, and as he prepared to celebrate Christmas in traditional style, no more than the surface of his mind and the most facile of his emotions can have been engaged. Yet he gave a superb performance. Never before had the holiday spirit spread more pleasantly over the land; never had the blessings of peace seemed so sweet. And never had the nation's Chief of State more fittingly led his people in celebration. In all the ritual there was a piercing quality of jeopardy to make it doubly precious.

Eleanor and Franklin could now be rated as ancestors. They could reckon their grandchildren at eight. They hoped to have most of them at the White House for the holidays. There were some difficulties about divorced mates who had custody of children. So far as the grandparents *trouble w/ his children*

were concerned, they were equally fond of the separated children-in-law. Still, there were some discreet absences. In spite of these, there was a family gathering of impressive size and of more than impressive ebullience. Adulthood had not tamed the Roosevelt children. They were still irrepressible. Their doings, as well as those of the grandchildren, attracted national attention.

But it was the grandfather first and the grandmother second who held the center of interest, almost as royalty fascinates the British. Every detail of life was magnified and exclaimed over, and all the more so because the Roosevelts, of all others who might have been in the White House, represented so well, except for the divorces, what was traditionally acceptable. There were many small children to enjoy the exquisite pleasures of Santa Claus' visit, of the Christmas tree, of the feasts and all the other seasonal rites. There was a large and lovely house whose decorations were lavish. There was a sincerely religious reference all through—it was never forgotten that all the gaiety and bounty were in honor of the Christ child, who was, familiarly, the Prince of Peace. And that reference people everywhere cherished with desperation just then. The whole nation went around the square to St. Thomas' on Christmas morning with its first family.

The press, at holiday time, was recording hints of an intensified war to follow the "phony" one; there was concern over the brutal Finnish invasion by Russia; there were complaints that neutrality restrictions were hampering trade (American shippers were annoyed because the defined combat zone around Europe shut them off from ports they were accustomed to use); and there was a surprising concentration on the domestic issues to be dealt with by the incoming Congress—labor legislation, the unbalanced budget, taxes, and so on. And in Franklin's press conferences, there were, to his annoyance, because nothing could be less relevant, almost as many questions about "spending" as there had been in past years.

Yet when the obvious contrast with Europe was thought of, the country's blessings were an overwhelming cause for thankfulness. The *United States News* summarized the "gifts in the nation's stocking":

Industrial production as measured by the Federal Reserve Board index has been 22 per cent better on the average this year than during 1938;

Wages and salaries have increased more than 6 per cent;

There are 1,250,000 more people at work than a year ago;

Farmer income is up almost $300 million;

Approximately 450,000 families have moved into new homes and apartments built this year;

Railroad traffic is up 12 per cent over 1938;

932,000 more persons bought new automobiles in 1939 than in the previous 12 months.[9]

Besides this, the *News* went on to say, the economists generally agreed that 1940 would be "moderately better" in a business way. It was agreed also that the prospects were for a Congress unlikely "to enact new business reforms or controls . . ." But, above all, it was said, Americans rejoiced "over the preservation of peace for their country despite the spreading conflict in Europe and Asia. Over there 15 million men are under arms, families are separated, normal business is disrupted, and many peoples are living under alien rule."

There was a good deal of this kind of adding up and of thankfulness for the gifts of fortune. But mixed with it was a continuous and irritating apprehension. American immunity was fragile and temporary; hence it seemed, in such a world, almost too good to be true. In spite of determined optimism, the holidays were suffused with lurid reflections from a war those flames flared higher and higher as the months passed. Even those who muted their talk of such things betrayed an uncontrollable uneasiness.

It was a deceptively carefree grandfather whose grandchildren gathered about him, sitting in rows on the floor, the youngest on his lap, parents in a circle all about, to hear him read, as he did every year on the Eve, his own modified version of *A Christmas Carol*. But there was certainly no deception in his reiteration of the last line, as the children repeated with him the words of Tiny Tim, "God bless us, everyone."

When from a White House room, as the trees were being lighted across the land, he spoke to the nation (over the radio), this was his theme:

The old year draws to a close. It began with dread of evil things to come and it ends with the horror of another war adding its toll of anguish to a world already bowed under the burden of suffering laid on it by man's inhumanity to man. . . .

But, thank God for Christmas. This night is a night of joy and hope, and happiness and promise of better things to come. And so in the happiness of this Eve of the most blessed day in the year I give to all my country-men the old, old greeting—"Merry Christmas—Happy Christmas."

He went on to ask who, a generation ago, would have thought that one month hence (January 30, 1940) tens of thousands of elderly men

---

[9] December 18, 1939. When the *United States News* is quoted here it should be recalled that it was edited by David Lawrence, one of the most opinionated and perverse of all the reactionary Republican publishers. At the same time he was gifted with news sense and, if the bias is discounted, his paper's record of the early Roosevelt years is possibly the best available in any contemporary periodical.

would begin to receive insurance checks—and not only they themselves, but their wives or widows and their orphaned children. And who would have thought that the unemployed would, for an appreciable period, receive a certain income to take the place of pay. There were also, he reminded his hearers, millions of blind people, of crippled children, and others who were incapacitated, who would be protected. Our new neighborliness, he said, reaches down to all our own Bob Cratchits, our Marthas, and our Tiny Tims. He ended on a note of exhortation:

In these days of strife and sadness . . . let us in the nation which still lives at peace, forbear to give thanks only for our good fortune in our peace.

Let us rather pray that we may be given strength to live for others—to live more closely to the Sermon on the Mount and pray that peoples in the nations which are at war may also read, learn, and inwardly digest these deathless words.

He then intoned, for the whole nation to hear, the beatitude beginning "Blessed are the poor in spirit . . ." His words died away. He was wheeled to the elevator, went up to the hall where the family was gathered. The stockings now were hung, and the children went unwillingly to bed. Among them, I might note, was one small girl who was not a Roosevelt. She was the daughter of Harry Hopkins—and of his beloved wife Barbara who had died of cancer. Of all the gathering, she was the one most closely held in Eleanor's protective arms, and it was she who had the warmest grandfatherly kiss. Harry, gaunt and ill, was unnerved. On such occasions he was overcome by loneliness in spite of the kindness of his great friends. The rest of his life would be given to proving in his own way the depth and reach of his gratefulness.

Crowding the Christmas season were other occasions. There was, for instance, the annual dinner of the Gridiron Club.[10]

Far from being offended by such probings, Franklin enjoyed them, or anyway appeared to. He always responded on these occasions in his best light vein. In this instance the reference was, of course, to the anxiety of those whose fate was involved in his delayed decision to run or not to run for re-election in 1940.

[10] Made up of Washington correspondents. The annual dinner was a carefully worked-up affair, notable for its skits parodying public officials. Franklin always attended and always laughed heartily at the rather heavy humor concocted at his expense. This year he was portrayed as a Sphinx, and this gave Smegert, the cartoonist of the San Francisco *Chronicle,* the theme for a sketch of Franklin with prognathous jaw, prominent pince-nez, and firmly closed mouth, all pressed into the Sphinx stereotype. This sketch for years hung in the President's outer office at the White House, thus amazing visitors from lands where ridicule of persons in power was not allowable. It was reproduced in the *United States News* of February 9, 1940. Visitors can still see in the Hyde Park museum a papier-mâché bust carrying out this Sphinx idea.

Concerning this uncertainty, Farley was the unhappiest of all. He had become convinced that he could have the nomination if Franklin withdrew. And it was true that his hold on the party machinery was very tight, made so by seven years of earnest cultivation. He spoke to Franklin somewhat later and was told that there was "no objection." So old a hand as Farley should have noted how negative a statement this was, but ambition reduces the most experienced men to naïveté. And Farley proceeded, as though he were a complete neophyte, to court humiliation. Naturally he could not serve his own interests and those of Franklin at the same time; and Franklin, knowing very well what he would have to do, began to work through others—Frank Walker and Ed Flynn, most importantly, although Corcoran and Hopkins were already busily beating the bushes. But it should be emphasized that Franklin's diligent kind of professional attention was lacking in the preliminary politicking of 1940. Only sporadically and with casual carelessness did he make the moves necessary for control of the convention.[11]

Beyond warnings that he would oppose a conservative, he made no statement until after the situation in Europe had degenerated so that any alternative to his renomination was out of the question. As a matter of fact, it was not made until the convention had assembled; and even then, as will be noted, it would be made in equivocal terms. The convention was free, he would say, to nominate anyone it chose—but that presumably included him, as every delegate would instantly understand. So he remained a Sphinx during that winter and spring. Perhaps he himself was less certain now how the European struggle would go than he had been some months previously. This was the pause when Chamberlain's optimism increased, when Gamelin in France felt certain that the Maginot Line would hold off the Nazis, and when even the Belgians and the Dutch seemed to think their defensive measures not entirely futile.

It was during this period that Franklin made two moves of so ambiguous a sort that historians would always wonder why they had been made. No one could ever do more than guess, because no one was consulted and no one was given an explanation beyond bland and obviously inadequate ones. He appointed an emissary to the Vatican, and he sent

---

[11]At the annual Jackson Day dinner in January of 1940 he read his party a lesson on the theme of irregularity:

> . . . the future lies with those wise political leaders who realize that the great public is interested more in Government than in party politics; that the independent vote in this country has been on the increase, at least for the past generation. . . . Party regulars who want to win must hold their allies and supporters among those independent voters. And do not let us forget it.

Knowing what Franklin had in mind for the party, if and when the circumstances should ever be propitious, this seems a significant passage.

Sumner Welles[12] on the strangest of all missions to the belligerent governments. Both were sensations in a time of suspenseful waiting.

Of the mission to Pope Pius XII, I can do no better than quote the surprised account in *Time*:

> To the Vatican in Rome, as the President's personal representative to talk and work for peace in Europe before all hell breaks loose this spring, will go Myron Charles Taylor, 65-year-old retired head of United States Steel Corp. Mr. Taylor, who will have the rank of Ambassador, but without portfolio, will be the first U.S. envoy to visit the Vatican officially since Rufus King left Rome in 1868, after Congress refused to appropriate any more money for his salary . . . good, dead Cardinal William Mundelein of Chicago would be glad to know that the idea he planted with Franklin Roosevelt in 1936 has flourished thus solidly. . . .[13]

There was some adverse reaction; but it was not notable. Any suggestions of peace were being hailed with pathetic eagerness. The action had a somewhat disarming setting, coming as it did at Christmas; also, it had its publicity along with a letter sent not only to the Pope but also to the president of the Protestant association, the Federal Council of the Churches of Christ in America, and, as well, to the president of the Jewish Technological Seminary of America. I quote *Time* again:

> The big man in the rumpled suit scratched his pen steadily across the large white sheets. In the stillness of the Oval Room the two flags hung limp on the mahogany standards; blue smoke from his burning cigaret wavered up from the silver tray. On his desk were newspapers, staring headlines of bombings and battles; and a Bible open at Isaiah.
> *"Your country is desolate, your cities are burned with fire: your land, strangers devour it . . ."*
> The big man wrote on. Through the ceiling-high window, framing the long roll of grass, tired-green now with winter, came the faint honks of the cabs, rolling shoppers home with Christmas packages. Thousands of miles away,

---

[12] Then Undersecretary of State. He continued to work uneasily with Hull. He was, however, an old Grotonian and, although somewhat younger than Franklin, recalled attending the wedding on East Sixty-fifth Street in knee pants. This established an old-school-tie relationship which Hull viewed with sour distrust.

[13] January 1, 1940. This last was probably true, although *Time* can hardly have known the date of its first broaching between the two. Cardinal Mundelein was a constantly consulted adviser from governorship days. The understanding between the two was largely responsible for what seemed to many observers a strange enthusiasm among Catholics for a Protestant Episcopal President. That support was well earned. As readers of this account will recall, Franklin was always an enemy of religious intolerance; moreover, he had denounced those who refused to support Al Smith because of his Catholicism—something that might have been thought risky in upstate New York. Somewhat less happily, Franklin had tried to influence the appointment of Mundelein's successor but had failed, and was henceforth without any faithful friend among the hierarchs.

helmeted men squinted through bomb-sights; homeless families trudged despairingly through the snow.

"Come now, and let us reason together, saith the Lord; though your sins be as scarlet, they shall be as white as snow . . ."

The big man's face, rock-like when he is intent, the mouth sad and down-bitten when he isn't smiling, bent steadily over the pages scrawled in his bold vertical hand. Then he pressed a buzzer—the one that goes off like a small bomb under Steve Early's desk. Down the colonnade that is called the President's Walk, past the swimming pool and up the elevator, there awaited him a highball, a Christmas tree shiny with colored balls and tinsel, two soap-smelling, bediapered grandsons—warmth and relief from the crushing responsibility, the solemn loneliness that is a U.S. President's when he has to make a momentous decision. . . .

The letter being written so laboriously by Franklin to be sent to the religious leaders read (in part) as follows:

I take heart in remembering that in a similar time, Isaiah first prophesied the birth of Christ. Then, several centuries before His coming, the condition of the world was not unlike that which we see today. Then, as now, a conflagration had been set; and nations walked dangerously in the light of the fires they had themselves kindled.

But in that very moment a spiritual rebirth was foreseen—a new day which was to loose the captives and to consume the conquerors in the fire of their own kindling; and those who had taken the sword were to perish by the sword. . . .

In their hearts men decline to accept, for long, the law of destruction forced upon them by wielders of brute force. Always they seek, sometimes in silence, to find again the faith without which the welfare of nations and the peace of the world cannot be rebuilt.

I have the rare privilege of reading the letters and confidences of thousands of humble people, living in scores of different nations. . . . I know that these, and uncounted numbers like them in every country, are looking for a guiding light. We remember that the Christmas Star was first seen by shepherds in the hills, long before the leaders knew . . .

. . . while statesmen are considering a new order of things, the new order may well be at hand. I believe that it is even now being built, silently but inevitably, in the hearts of masses whose voices are not heard, but whose common faith will write the final history of our time. . . .

In the grief and terror of the hour, these quiet voices, if they can be heard, may yet tell of the rebuilding of the world. . . .

In these present moments, no spiritual leader, no civil leader, can move forward on a specific plan to terminate destruction and build anew. Yet the time for that will surely come. . . .[14]

The letter, written in such circumstances, with such ill-suppressed indignation and such certainty of guidance, is one to study. It tells much.

[14] *Public Papers*, 1939 vol., pp. 606–8.

There is frustration in it, and some patience, but not much. There is belief in democracy and detestation of dictatorship and aggression; there is faith in the future, against which time men of good will must be ready for the world's rebuilding.

Now that years have passed since this Christmas of 1939, we can see how Franklin's own prophecy was fulfilled. There were indeed sorrow and suffering without limit, but the conquerors were in the end conquered, and statesmen were given their chance at reconstruction. He would be gone, but he would have worked steadily even in the midst of war to lay the foundations for the rebuilding he knew must come. That it would be delayed, difficult, and tortured by selfishness, he probably would not have been surprised to know.

The student ought not to miss, either, the religious connotations of this letter, written in the rare solitude of that holiday. We are familiar by now with Franklin's unquestioning relationship with divinity. There is no reason for believing that it had in any way changed since his adolescence—except that it had become a broader reliance, matured by time and experience. Its most severe test—the ordeal of sickness and long-delayed recovery—was long in the past. In the contemporary years there were no comparable trials. He was reviled, but he was also revered. He must have felt at this time that he had brought the American people through their depression crisis with fair fortune. If the economic troubles had not been entirely overcome, their impact on individuals had anyway been mitigated. Now that there was a new crisis to be met he would meet it with a confidence reinforced by his other success and in the certainty of divine support.

In any case, as the days darkened toward deep winter and the sinister signs of further aggression became unmistakable, he did not at all feel that God had abandoned the Allies. On the contrary, the justness of their cause was emphasized by the temporary prevailing of evil forces. There was a course to be run. But in the end victory would come to the hosts of righteousness. There was a steadiness in Franklin's faith in the Allied future which allowed him to consign precious American matériel to Europe when most of those about him felt it would surely fall into enemy possession by conquest. This faith would have its fullest development in the magnificent conception of Lend-Lease and, even before that, in the so-called destroyer-bases deal—a device for putting at British disposal a fleet of much-needed lesser ships of war.

The loneliness in which the pattern for the coming year was worked out is illustrated by the testimony of those closest to him. They were not aware that the decisions had been made. It only became evident much later that the framework must have been taking shape when they were still speculating on his intentions. Afterward it could be seen how inevitable each determination was. Yet it is somehow impossible not to be affected by a retrospective pity to think of a man, alone with his God, wrestling in agony to discover what he must do to save his nation and even the world. Only one sustained by the belief that he rested on higher than mortal authority could have come through such an experience into the serenity exhibited by Franklin as he faced the new year.

For, as we examine his doings, and especially his public addresses, his private correspondence, and what was said about him by contemporaries, it is a strong and certain man, full of confidence, functioning vigorously, that we see. And this is perhaps more true just now than at any other time. The crushing burden he was carrying added hours to his daily task—although it seems impossible that he should have found them—and demanded of him incredible expenditures of energy. Yet his face, as we look at the Christmas pictures, is full and firm; there is humor latent in it, and more determination than ever in the set of the chin.

Franklin, God's servant, was about his Father's business with no doubts to torment him.

But it was a bad winter, and Franklin mentioned it in several letters. There was that peculiar combination of chill, dampness, and changeableness which Washington at its worst provides. And after weeks of it Franklin was doubtless very glad when he had got Sumner Welles started on his journey to Europe and could himself with good conscience go off on the *Tuscaloosa* to cruise the warm seas as he loved to do in February.

The Welles mission began and continued in that atmosphere of mystery I have mentioned. It was very evidently a project of Franklin's (although Welles may have suggested it originally), and it is obvious that he hoped it would develop into something much more significant than it did. Hull opposed it, but that made no difference one way or the other. The idea was to make direct contact with the heads of government. Franklin always believed that personal negotiations had much more chance of succeeding than those attended by formalities, prepared for by elaborate position papers, and conducted at arm's length with experts looking over the principals' shoulders. I think he wanted to know whether he could not say simply that fighting ought to stop and be replaced by negotiation. So Welles had a difficult and limited mission. He was only to ask about intentions. If, as he sized it up, Franklin could usefully suggest a top-level meeting, that would follow. Then the famous charm, backed by the mightily increasing power of the United States, would have its chance.

No one knows that Franklin intended such a meeting if Welles had been received more hospitably; it is merely my own belief that Franklin hoped to invite Hitler, Mussolini, and Chamberlain to confer on neutral soil or in some neutral sea. There were rumors about this time of such

516

plans. They developed an embarrassing prevalence as Franklin went off on the *Tuscaloosa* while Welles was touring Europe. The correspondents were certain that he was going to meet the belligerents. It was embarrassing, in fact, that nothing of the sort was possible.[15]

A combination of confinement, heavy work, and the frustration of his hopes for personal intervention in Europe had, by the time Franklin got away in late February, changed the healthy vigor of Christmas to a weariness apparent to anyone who saw him. But this had happened many times. Those who knew him best had seen him try his constitution beyond its limits repeatedly and sink into tiredness so profound that it showed in his gray and lined face. Yet in two weeks at sea he would bounce back to ruddy health, ready again to tackle the duties of his office.

His intimates—and his doctor, Ross McIntire—were so familiar with this phenomenon that they had a formula for the prevention of exhaustion. They knew his weakness for the Navy, for southern waters, and for the isolation of shipboard life; and they dangled its attractions before him at every opportunity. He knew, himself, well enough what he ought to do; but, as others have done, he allowed himself to be driven beyond the tolerance of his system, and often when he gave up and went away he appeared to be almost in collapse. It seemed that way this February to a Capital reporter.

Last week an unaccountable gloom settled over Washington, wrapping its marble palaces in melancholy thick as the wet grey fogs that float up from the Potomac. Congress seemed listless, disheartened, worried.

The flag came down from the White House staff; a haggard, grey-faced President was whisked over slush-bound streets to his special train on the lower concourse of echoing Union Station. Prying newspapermen had discovered Franklin Roosevelt was headed for Pensacola, guessed he would there board the cruiser *Tuscaloosa*. But every movement had been shrouded in gloomy mystery; trainmen acted as if they had sealed orders, knew only that they were headed south. For the first time since his Administration began, Franklin Roosevelt had not furnished the press with an exactly detailed itinerary . . . "Submarines," said an aide . . .

On the train the President spent hours over prison pardons; forced a tired

---

[15] Franklin told newsmen who were curious about intensified security measures that he was going to visit the Andeman Islands, the Celebes Islands, and the South Shetland Islands. For good measure he spoofingly added "the Cherable Isles."

Afterwards he himself was curious about this. He thought the name had popped into his head because he recalled it from Lear's *Nonsense Poems*. It bothered him so that he asked the librarian of Congress about it. The result was an amusing "voyage" among authors by David Mearns, superintendent of reading rooms. He never found the Cherable Isles, but he produced a delightful essay. Cf. *Personal Letters: 1928–1945*, Vol. II, p. 1082; and for the memorandum, the Hyde Park library.

smile for newsmen . . . Piped aboard the *Tuscaloosa,* he posed for the usual pictures, standing at the rail; soon tired, he rested in a chair, bundled against the damp, chill day . . .

Away from telephones, snow, gloom, pressure, rumors and Term III, Franklin Roosevelt could take off his coat, sit in the sun, nap, read a murder mystery, flip cigarets into the blue Gulf waters—perhaps smile at the revival of the 1939 rumor that he would meet heads of European governments in mid-ocean, there settle the world's hash. Last week he could have killed the rumor with a wink or a lifted eyebrow; but he did not . . .

This reticence was probably because he still hoped for just what was suspected. But let us see what the report was as he returned two weeks later:

Franklin Roosevelt jammed his broad-brimmed soft felt hat down over his thinning grey hair, hooked the top frog of his officer's boat-cloak, came ashore at Pensacola.

Behind him, in all probability, was his last real seagoing vacation before he and the U.S. people find out about Term III. Ahead of him were months of arduous labor in the White House: the burden of operating a vast, peaceable democracy in a war-gripped world, the problem of holding together the sagging New Deal. Tanned, re-toughened, in bounding spirits, his February melancholy and his barren fishing luck forgotten, he took train for Washington ready to fight the G.O.P. and the White House air-conditioning for at least eleven more months.[16]

The press of that day, however, recorded some business done on this trip. Franklin had gone through the Panama Canal and had been reminded of its vulnerability in an air age. He renewed a demand made previously that the Congress authorize a third set of locks; he also wanted to double the number of anti-aircraft installations and of defensive planes.[17]

Also, he took occasion to refer to hemispheric solidarity, something both he and Sumner Welles (who was still in Europe) had good reason to be proud of since it was largely their creation. Three countries near the Canal Zone, he said, had given him assurance that their airfields would be available to the United States for military use.

This reminded editorial writers of Welles' mission in late 1939 when, as the Neutrality Law was being debated, the American nations were meeting. That meeting had resulted in the Declaration of Panama. The collective security Franklin wanted among all the democracies first came into being in the Declaration as an inter-American policy. Welles

---

[16] Franklin hated the air conditioners installed in the White House and believed them largely responsible for his chronic sinusitis. Like all the modernizing of the old house, these units were makeshift and unsatisfactory. The quotations just above are from *Time.*

[17] Both requests were rejected.

was able to persuade the few reluctant members that their interests coincided with those of the United States.[18]

The Declaration was signed on October 3, and on November 4 the new neutrality proclamation was signed in Washington. The safety patrol, extending far out to sea from the American coast, was made an international affair, not just an action of the United States. This, together with the cash-and-carry policy, was an invaluable aid to the Allies, since only Allied shipping could penetrate to American ports.

During that fall Franklin had a serious influenza. But sick as he was, he avidly followed the course of affairs. None of the reports was good. Worst of all was the punitive peace following the short war Russia had imposed on little Finland. It foreshadowed worse things to come. Surmounting his weakness, he made an address[19] which, against the background of the cruel terms of the Finnish peace and the swirling dark rumors (engendered by the conferring of Mussolini and Hitler in an Alpine village) that Russia now was about to join the Axis, stated his own concept of the peace needed by the world:

> It cannot be a real peace if it fails to recognize brotherhood. It cannot be a lasting peace if the fruit of it is oppression . . . It cannot be a sound peace if small nations must live in fear of powerful neighbors. It cannot be a moral peace if freedom from invasion is sold for tribute. It cannot be a righteous peace if worship of God is denied.[20]

Presently Sumner Welles came home. And presently the hope died that somehow the aggressors may have been made to recognize reason. Time ran on toward the fateful April when all thought of conciliation would be destroyed by Hitler's furious spring onslaught, first to the north, then to the west and south.

---

[18] German shipping had stopped and goods were piling up in many ports; Welles offered to buy it all.

[19] To the Christian Foreign Service Convocation, representing 129 Protestant bodies with some 30,000 members, meeting at the Waldorf-Astoria in New York. This was notable for another reason: two chiefs of state spoke to the one gathering. Queen Wilhelmina as well as Franklin broadcast to this and other similar meetings in other cities.

[20] *Public Papers*, 1940 vol., p. 103.

25 There were not many people who, after April in 1940, were able to think much about politics until the national conventions came along in July. Farley, shut out of administration counsels, continued his hopeless attempt to check the rising tide of sentiment for a third term. But measured against the world's monstrously disorganized affairs, such small matters were little attended to. The war in Europe was the center of everyone's worried concern. For by now it had become total; and by now the totalitarian threat, even to the United States, no longer seemed to anyone a bogey invented by the President. There were, it was true, differences about ways of meeting the threat, but no one doubted its reality.

There were those who continued to believe (and even considered their belief to have been reinforced) that Nazism was "the wave of the future." The power they had said the Third Reich possessed, because of the abandonment of democracy and the gathering into a unified and centrally directed organization of the nation's potential, they held now to have been amply demonstrated. The way to meet such a development was to learn from it, to come to terms with it, and to treat it as a welcome force in the world for order and progress. Day in and day out Charles A. Lindbergh and others of like mind, backed by the Hearst press, the Chicago *Tribune*, the New York *Daily News*, and the other unfriendly newspapers, pressed their violent dissent.

Involved in this was the corollary theory that the nations now being overrun were weak and "rotten," made so by the wastes and tolerances of democracy. The United States, it was implied, was far gone on the same route to degeneracy. Reform was urgent, and the model for it could be seen in the Third Reich.

This was far from being a majority sentiment. There were many more at this time who were so shocked by the sudden bursting into their area of consciousness of the brutal and overwhelming power of the Wehrmacht as it smashed through the Low Countries and into France that reaction was confused and delayed. There was a good deal of frightened concern suddenly about the American military potential. Franklin's renewed pleas for appropriations were no longer denied. But this did not imply a taking of sides against the aggressors; it merely meant fear.

What had to be faced by May was the imminent possibility, rapidly turning into probability, that the Germans would have a quick and complete victory. It looked as though all Europe—including Britain—would be brought under subjection in a matter of months. The Atlantic, with Britain gone, would shrink to a lake. If the British fleet should go—and voices even of recent Anglophobes quivered as they talked of this—how could the Germans in the Atlantic and the Japanese in the Pacific be kept away from American coasts?

As Americans at last began to consider these problems—as Franklin had for years been urging them to do—he grew immensely in their regard. His old urgings were recalled. There was some humbleness, and even the irresponsible Congress was somewhat tamed. Its mood was more compliant than it had been since 1933.

The American situation in May was stated in his categorical fashion by Walter Lippmann in a *Herald-Tribune* column which, at the same time, offered Franklin some advice:

If the offensive which Hitler has now launched succeeds, we shall know no peace in our lifetime . . . our duty is to begin acting at once on the basic assumption that the Allies may lose the war this summer, and that before the snow flies again we may stand alone and isolated, the last great democracy on earth . . . The first thing that must be done only the President can do. He must tell the people the truth as he sees it, and trust to their patriotism and good sense . . . The disinterested people of this country are just about fed up with all this calculated insincerity . . . are aware of the extreme peril of this hour and they will respond to . . . leadership.

This dig and the tart Lippmann reference to "calculated insincerity" were intended as reproaches for Franklin's hesitancy and for his continued emphatic protestation that war could be kept away from the United States. But these self-righteous critics had very little justification for their attitudes. Isolationism was not yet argued down by events. It would turn up again with a certain strength even at the Democratic convention in July and be written into several clauses of the platform. What it would have been more accurate to say was that there existed sudden fright and anger, those unpredictable sentiments which must be reckoned with but which are as unstable as moving water. All over the country violent signs of change could be heard and seen, but that they would support a policy of all-out aid to the Allies was not yet clear. Franklin's barometer still registered "cloudy."

But it did seem to Franklin that the time had come when he could insist, without reservation, on arming the nation. The prevalent agitation would sustain an advance of this sort. On May 16, 1940, he went to the Capitol and made his move. The speech on that occasion shocked the nation. After the passage of a little time it would be hard to realize that this had been true, but that only indicates how determinedly Americans had refused to face their situation. It was a lesson in geopolitics that Franklin read his hearers on that day—an elementary one. It doubtless seemed very elementary, indeed, to Lippmann. But it was needed, and it had the calculated effect. Never again would this ground have to be covered by an American leader.

Americans, he said, must completely recast their thinking about national protection. It was now the day of the tank and the plane. Parachute troops could be dropped behind enemy lines and troops landed in open fields or on highways. Lightning attacks from the skies had become possible, carrying destruction to civilians as well as soldiers. Fifth columns had been adopted as a familiar new technique. All this had its immediate relevance to the American situation.

Attacks from the air on the American continent were now entirely possible:

From the fiords of Greenland it is four hours by air to Newfoundland; five hours to Nova Scotia, New Brunswick and to the Province of Quebec; and only six hours to New England.[1]

He went on to recall, in short sharp sentences, that the Azores were only two thousand miles away, that if Bermuda fell into hostile hands modern bombers could reach the seaboard in less than three hours, that from a base in the outer West Indies Florida was only two hundred minutes distant, that the islands off the coast of West Africa were fifteen hundred miles from Brazil, which made them seven hours distant, that Brazil was four flying hours from Caracas, Caracas two and a half hours from Cuba, Cuba and the Canal Zone two and a quarter hours from Tampico, and Tampico two and a quarter hours from St. Louis, Kansas City, or Omaha.

So much for the fancied remoteness of Midwesterners. As for the Pacific Coast, Alaska was within four or five hours of Vancouver, Seattle, Tacoma, and Portland.

To meet the possible threat, he went on to say, there were certain improved defenses; also, there was under way a large naval construction program. But every day since last September had offered lessons of vital significance. Battlecraft were no longer safe at sea without air cover. Planes adequate a year ago were now hopelessly obsolete. American production, it was true, had doubled in the last year (from six to

[1] *Public Papers*, 1940 vol., p. 199.

twelve thousand), but that was because of expansion to meet foreign orders; it was still grossly inadequate. Then he put it bluntly:

Our immediate problem is to superimpose on this production capacity a greatly increased additional production capacity. I should like to see this nation geared up to the ability to turn out at least 50,000 planes a year. . . .[2]

The Congress closed its eyes, held its breath, and authorized all he asked.

Almost at once he moved to shore up the government for the burdens it must carry. He reached back to two sources for authority and had good reasons for gratitude to his Committee on Administrative Management of 1937. Their report had recommended an Office of Emergency Management in the President's establishment which had seemed unnecessary at the time, but the Congress had somehow let it stay in the final reorganization bill, and now it seemed providential. All or most of the vast structure of agencies necessary to the war was brought under it. I say "most" because the Advisory Commission of the Council of National Defense, the first device used, rested on an old statute of 1916 which had never been repealed. The Council was a largely paper body of cabinet officers, but the Advisory Commission under it was an actual working body which would serve for planning and procurement until the Lend-Lease Act should come into effect a year later. Then the Office of Emergency Management would be activated, and under it the Office of Production Management, the Office of Economic Stabilization, the National Defense Mediation Board, the Office of Civilian Defense, and all the rest of the proliferating war agencies would be placed.

Reorganization under way, Franklin went still again to the Congress for appropriations—and again they were granted. He began to breathe more freely. His imagination began to exceed its old confines. But sober people soon saw that he must have his way. The immensity of the expansion that followed is almost beyond conception. Behind the demand for ships, planes, tanks, arms small and large, and provisions of all sorts for men in the services, there developed enormous secondary calls for raw materials, for transportation and communication, and for production facilities. The basic plant and facilities of the economy had to be expanded before the end products could be processed. And in order to start and sustain such an unprecedented growth the funds and authorizations had to be provided. This involved reversal of many attitudes and habits—for instance, those concerning governmental finance which had been so stubbornly held even during the depression. Fear releases inhibitions that not even misery will unlock.

There was only one possible source of funds. That was government. But the government did not have them and could not get them by taxa-

[2] Ibid., p. 202.

tion. They must be created by fiat. And that is what was done. The expansion of the public debt to finance production was of an order that would have seemed nightmarish only a short time before. And since the method was to proceed by the enlargement of industry under private auspices, the funds were simply made available as loans to those industries that would accept them.

An immense and complicated system of contracts at once came into existence, and since shortages at once appeared, controls and priorities soon became necessary. There was stiff bidding for scarce materials and so there had to be price regulation. Labor also was in demand, exceeding the supply for the first time in a generation, and it became necessary to set up a system to distribute manpower and mediate disputes over wages. So it went all through the system.

There was waste everywhere. Industry expanded unevenly. Co-ordination in a theoretically unco-ordinated system was achieved awkwardly. The controls imposed by government had to be operated, as were the industries, by those familiar with the processes they were to control. Dollar-a-year men again flocked to Washington. Often they forgot to leave their old affiliations at home. There was much favoritism and many near scandals.

There was one virtue in Franklin's lonely decision to entrust private industry with war production. This was the advantage of decentralization. Amateur planning, red tape, stupid controls, and favoritism, much as they hampered those who were actually in charge of production units, could not effectually suppress natural Yankee ingenuity and patriotic spirit. Factories began to turn out goods, railroads performed prodigies of transportation, ships were constructed, military camps came into being, and men were trained. Everything had to be fitted together after, rather than before, production and recruiting; but somehow energy and determination had their way. One who saw the immense stores of material clogging the ports, standing on railway sidings, and cluttering yards, warehouses, and piers; who saw the foundations of immense structures being laid at a time when the end product should have been issuing in volume; and who realized that it could not emerge from the new plant for months or years—such a one would not have been able to believe that this awkward, sprawling, amorphous nation could ever compete with German efficiency.

It would somehow or other assume a certain order, straighten itself out, produce munitions, train men, and deliver them to ships, planes, and battlefields overseas. Looked back on, it would even seem magnificent. In after years there would be the long grinding payment of inflation, redeployment, and all the unhappy readjustments to peace. But while it went on, there would be daily achievements, thought nothing of because there had to be more remarkable ones tomorrow, but actually almost miraculous. Only in the post-war period would it be known what the price was—as Wilson and Daniels had warned Franklin it would be—for yielding control of the economy to monopolists. They would have made a good thing out of war and would be set to make a better thing out of peace. But no alternative having seemed to him possible, he could at least have argued that the job, at whatever cost, had got done.

May of 1940 was not the actual beginning of expansion. As Franklin said, a start had already been made—indeed, an allocation for naval expansion had been extracted by presidential order from the first public works appropriation in 1933 (it now seemed admirably foresighted, whereas then it had been criticized as at least unethical and possibly illegal, and another such diversion had been provided against by an angry Congress in subsequent bills), and in more recent years other appropriations had been made. But this in 1940 was the real closing of eyes and stiffening of determination. It was when Franklin began to have his way, and the war machine began to roll.

When he could see that the Congress was subdued and likely to continue compliant he turned seriously to his problems of organization, and it was then that progress began to be made. In a matter of two months governmental agencies performed the prodigious feat of letting two billions of dollars' worth of contracts. Something had been started that would grow, however awkwardly, almost of its own momentum. It was only necessary to approximate a planning system and allow it to shape itself into adjustment. At any rate, to look forward a year, American and British orders would approximate by June 1, 1941, forty billions of dollars.[3] Even long afterward that would seem a superhuman feat.

Before the middle of July, when the Democratic convention met and politics became too demanding, there was time to set up a containing structure and to select men capable of handling the fantastic expansion. New faces began to appear in and around the White House and new names to dominate the headlines—such names, familiar to all those who recall or have read about the war, as Knudsen, Batt, Nelson, Hillman, Forrestal, Clayton, and other civilians, along with new military leaders. General Marshall had already become Chief of Staff, succeeding General Craig, who had been worn out by his efforts to get things done while his principals—Woodring and Johnson—quarreled. Admiral Hart was in the Far East, MacArthur was commanding in the Philippines, and a man trusted by the Commander-in-Chief—Admiral Husband Kimmel—had the naval command at Pearl Harbor. In the Navy, at least, Franklin began to feel some confidence. And Marshall needed only a

---

[3] A breakdown of this achievement, made by Franklin himself, is to be found in *Public Papers*, 1940 vol., pp. 207 ff.

new Secretary to straighten out the Army; his own organization was becoming adequate.

And that, in fact, was the next thing Franklin took care of. He appointed Henry L. Stimson to the Army and Frank Knox to the Navy. To shake himself free, he had to request Woodring's resignation, and Woodring did not retire gracefully;[4] but presently it was done and for an interval he could turn to politics. This matter of appointing two prominent Republicans to the service posts in his cabinet a few weeks before the party convention was naturally a shocker for the politicians. They thought he might have waited until after the election if it had to be done at all. It seemed to indicate that the crisis was not to be a Democratic one but, so far as Franklin could make it, bipartisan. It reinforced the fears of all those who suspected, or had reason to know of, Franklin's cavalier attitude toward the party. It was to be a Roosevelt war. The organization could adjust itself to that. The politicians began to wonder whether Garner—who had made his continuance in the vice-presidency impossible by offering himself for candidacy to replace Franklin—would not be asked to make way for a Republican too or, even worse, a progressive.

Whatever Franklin's intentions, he was not yet free from the party in 1940. It is truer to say that he was the prisoner of its worst element— the big-city bosses. It was these bosses who were going to renominate him. Harry Hopkins, the former social worker, and Corcoran, the White House fixer, were now the intimates of Flynn, Hague, Kelly, Pendergast, and the rest. And these hard bargainers would expect to be paid off.

When Franklin consulted Senator Harry S. Truman about La Guardia's appointment as Secretary of War, Truman is reported to have objected. This was going too far. The New York mayor kicked the bosses around too gaily. But Stimson was different. He was a Republican, but he had not fought the bosses for half a lifetime as La Guardia had. Knox had a similar immunity. The secretaryship was his first public office.

So the shock involved in the co-opting of two Republicans—and others in the emergency agencies—was felt by all good Democrats, but some of them could see the utility of taking hostages. And anyway, coming as it did less than a month before the convention, not much could be done about it. Franklin by then had all the delegates he needed for the nomination. And since he had a recent but smooth-working liaison with the city bosses and with certain labor men, the nomination was foregone. He need pay little attention to the convention except to

---

[4] Letters exchanged in this matter are to be found in *Personal Letters: 1928–1945*, Vol. II, pp. 1041 ff. This date was June 19, 1940, about one month before the Democratic convention.

maneuver for unanimity rather than a majority and to name his running mate. Who should run with him he did not greatly care, so long as the choice was made from a list of party progressives headed by Jackson, Douglas, Wallace, and a few others. That could go until the last moment.

During these months Eleanor became somewhat more a politician as Franklin became less so. It was in recognition of her importance that a weekly news magazine (*Time*) whose lead article every week was headed "The Presidency" devoted its first three columns under that heading (on April 15, 1940) to her instead of to Franklin. She was, indeed, a well-traveled and well-known person. She was supposed to have influence at the White House, and that endows any American with importance. She was not only supposed to have that influence, she did in fact have it. She never hesitated to speak to Franklin about any matter within her interest, and that included a multitude of affairs, especially, of course, those having to do with women. But she was in constant touch with her old friends, Mary (Molly) Dewson, Dorothy McAllister, and Lorena Hickok (now employed in the Women's Division of the Democratic National Committee), and the new group of amateur White House politicians, especially Hopkins and Corcoran.

Eleanor traveled constantly, lectured everywhere, presided at diverse ceremonies, and, as she traveled, dictated her daily column to her faithful friend and secretary, Malvina Thompson. "My Day" continued to be a success. It appeared even in hostile newspapers, and editors explained its incongruous presence very simply by saying that their readers demanded it. It gave Eleanor a vehicle for the expression of opinions which sat rather strangely on a President's wife. She was gentle in her comments, naïve about many things—after all, she had had a very defective education—she had, or showed, no sense of humor, and she was patiently sincere, earnest, and of encompassing good will. But she was definitely liberal and not infrequently she seemed to infuriate the reactionaries more than Franklin did.

In consequence of her lecturing, her daily column, and her frequent radio talks, she had an immense correspondence to which she attended conscientiously. Her correspondents often asked favors, and mostly she tried to grant them. She was a frequent caller at government offices and an even more frequent communicant by phone. She was likely to ask about anything under the sun, and her naïve probing into the affairs of various agencies could be embarrassing. Some members of the cabinet dreaded and resented them—Ickes did, as his *Diary* afterward showed—but some others had the wit to take advantage of her interest. Frances Perkins often conspired with her to the public advantage; but probably no one knew as well as Harry Hopkins how to use her influence.

Innumerable times Eleanor must have sat down in her gentle but determined way before Franklin and said what was in her mind or asked what were his intentions about relief or works projects or the incidence of regulations—a thousand matters that were strictly none of her business.

They were not her business, and yet no one could say so, and this included Franklin. So fine and disinterested were her motives, so genuine her puzzled inquiries, and so quick her intelligence, that an answer could no more be refused than could the questioning of a child just discovering the complexity and essential injustice of many of the world's accepted arrangements. Evidently Franklin did not discuss with her his large determinations of policy. The preliminaries to these took place as always in that secrecy I have described, and they emerged only in his own good time. Eleanor's participation was on a different level— that of action. She sometimes seemed to be making a career of easing the contacts of government and people. At any rate, she was touched by any injustice or hardship and could not rest until what she could do about it—if anything—had been done.

As we know, Eleanor was no stranger to politics. Since her induction by Louis Howe following Franklin's illness in 1921, she had done something in nearly every campaign. She had long ago graduated to the national scene and obviously considered herself an expert. But even she was puzzled by Franklin's intentions for 1940.

She made no secret of her preference for retirement. "My own personal opinion," she said in March, "not as the wife of a President, is that except in extraordinary circumstances we should stick to our tradition." That was what Farley thought too, except that his definition of "extraordinary circumstances" might have been a different one.

She was in California in April, visiting at the Beverly Hills apartment of her son James, who was now between divorce and remarriage and trying a new business—the movies. While she was there she made a characteristic gesture. To show her regard for Melvin and Helen Gahagan Douglas, she went with them to explore the "Okie" problem. She visited squatters' camps outside the squalid California towns, talked with the women, looked into their shacks and tents, and was appalled by the primitive sanitation and the condition of the children. She went on to the projects, begun years before by the Resettlement Administration and now of considerable size, for the housing of these migrants. This was one of those ventures which divided liberal and conservative, in the way described so vividly in Steinbeck's *Grapes of Wrath*. Eleanor was on the kindly side. She said so.

A little later in San Francisco she admitted to reporters that she was undertaking a new radio series, broadcasting for a soap company on Tuesdays and Thursdays. She could say what she pleased, politics aside, she said, and might have guests appearing with her. Her standard rate, it was reported, was three thousand dollars for fifteen minutes.

Later in the same month it was reported that she had signed a five-year contract for "My Day," whether or not there was a third term. She was not only the President's wife any more. She was beginning to be the great lady that still another generation would know so well.

After this long time it was plain that the lives of Eleanor and Franklin ran together rather less as the years passed. Eleanor traveled a great deal on her own occasions. Franklin was quite used to vacationing without her and, indeed, to being in the White House while she was away. She nevertheless assumed her share of the social duties, was present when necessary, and arranged her busy schedule in such a way that Franklin would not be embarrassed by her absence.

She was probably not privy to his thoughts, but there was nothing new about this; it is doubtful whether she had very often known what was in his mind. Moreover, as she made her many various pleas, she did so as a person arguing, not as one pleading.

There was the recollection between the two of shared experience, difficult and pleasant, and there were the sorrows and joys of common parenthood. But they were two equals now whose lives were joined in a common cause. She was no longer—had not been for a long time —the matron centered in husband and children. She looked abroad; she grew wiser; she sought to do what one woman could to mitigate the cruel circumstances of the unfortunates she knew so well.

Eleanor was aware that most alleviations of human misery on any considerable scale have to be reached by political means, and she was not averse to cultivating and using these means. She had indeed become adept at it. But just now she had one overmastering conviction. Of all the massive causes of misery in a disorganized world, the worst was the dictatorship in Germany. Her heart bled for the Jews and for all the people in Poland and the other nations being brought under the Nazi whip. She had no doubts about all this. It was America's business to intervene.

One of the keys to Eleanor's character was a wonderful indifference to distinctions others habitually made between people. To her a person was simply a person, whether he or she was of one or another color, or origin, or income group. All were equally entitled to life, to justice, and to happiness. It was the plain duty of everyone to interfere when injustice was being done, to help when suffering or disadvantage existed, and to create, as far as it was possible, some happiness to be shared by all. So direct and disarming were these beliefs of hers that no one could doubt her absolute sincerity.

It was from these standards that she judged the performance of Hitler, Mussolini, and their allies. They seemed to her monstrously wrong, and this was so patent as to be beyond discussion. If Franklin had to furnish the leadership to oppose the dictators, she would help, even though her judgment, on personal grounds as well as traditional ones, was against his going on in the presidency.

Looking back, anyone can see that by the end of April there was no longer any question that a majority of the delegates was available for a third term. What was known, therefore, was that Franklin could have the nomination if he wanted it. What was *not* known was whether he wanted it. That would not be revealed until the convention met.

Much credit for this result was awarded by the shrewdest of the newspapermen to Hopkins, Corcoran, and others operating out of the White House. They had been busy all over the country for months, rounding up delegates, sometimes by methods the professionals would have hesitated to use. Farley was in a kind of limbo. He was still nominally chairman of the National Committee, but every politician in the country knew that he had no authority. So his writ ran only in those areas—like Boston—which were for him and against Franklin for deep and bitter reasons. Farley must sometimes have wondered how he had got himself into such an impasse. He was quite conscious that a Catholic was severely handicapped; and after Franklin had broken precedent and sent an envoy to the Pope, he must have seen that even the Catholics had been won over to Franklin. As his support faded away, however, he found reasons for not believing the obvious. Finally he fell back on principle. He had been wronged; also, a third term was reprehensible. He was slipping toward oblivion, but he was doing it righteously.

Whatever credit was to be awarded the White House amateurs, it was plain all along that most of it ought to have gone to Hitler. It was he who made the third term really inevitable. He was in the process of reducing all Europe to subserviency. His tanks and planes were enforcing his will. His was no political victory. He used naked force by preference and sneered at the processes of politics. The man who was his implacable enemy could hardly be denied a continuation of his leadership.

Besides Hitler, of course, there were other reasons for the third-term demand. One of these was the change which had by now taken place in political groupings. It had been established that Franklin was a liberal-progressive;[5] this meant that businessmen, and conservatives generally, were alienated. But he had the support of a far more numerous group: this was labor. Until 1936 it had been doubtful whether workers could be counted on as a cohesive political force; after the

[5] Franklin had as much difficulty as others with terms describing political position. He spoke of himself as both liberal and progressive; but frequently he joined the two words. Neither, evidently, seemed to him adequate by itself.

gains of the first and second Democratic administrations there was no longer any such doubt. The labor movement itself was split. There was a Congress of Industrial Organizations recently set up which had broken away from the old American Federation of Labor. But however much these organizations might dislike each other, they agreed on support of the Democratic party and especially its leader. It was true that John L. Lewis, who had risen with the expanding movement, was in the process of departing the New Deal in pique, very possibly because Franklin had refused him favor, but that was a minor worry. It was obvious that he would not take many votes with him to the Republicans.

Even more important, perhaps, was the adherence of the big-city political machines, especially in New York and Chicago. They were extremely influential at conventions, and they delivered votes at election time. The administration had been very kind to them. Hopkins' relief and works projects had been used to reinforce their hold on their voters, and Corcoran had traded favors generously for legislative support. The bosses were not bothered by the principle which Farley respected so highly—the two-term limitation. They saw no harm in a third term if the voters did not object. And it was very apparent that they did not.

The more conservative Democrats yearned for a change, and for a while after 1937 and on through 1938 they had believed that the country's sentiment had turned to the right. But they had no really good candidate except Hull, and Hull was far from the young and vigorous man they would have liked. Farley was encouraged to place himself in this picture as second to Hull, but somehow he promoted himself from the vice-presidency to the presidency. So shrewd a politician as Garner knew that Farley was an impossible presidential candidate, if for no other reason than because of his religion, so he allowed his own name to be used for stalking-horse purposes and had some success among the out-and-out southern reactionaries.

Neither Farley nor Garner got very far with their insurrection in spite of Franklin's bland refusal to oppose them. This was not because of good management but because their bid was politically fantastic.

All the while Hopkins, Corcoran, Ed Flynn, and others, to Farley's fury and despair, were working hard and shrewdly anywhere and everywhere to ensure the third-term nomination which Hitler had made almost inevitable. But they knew that Franklin would be far from satisfied with a majority in the convention. He wanted a call—a unanimous or near-unanimous demand. Only that would really justify him in violating the two-term tradition. Farley, however, with his few hard votes from certain constituencies, would not give way. Garner with his reactionary delegates was almost as intransigent. Both were sore and vindictive. They were, moreover, dazed by having been outmaneuvered. The amateurs, Hopkins, Corcoran, and their subordinates, had cornered a majority, but that was far from the unanimity Franklin wanted. As a result even those closest to Franklin could not be absolutely certain that he would not at the last moment refuse.

It was a curious and disturbed political season—the spring of 1940. The fall of the Low Countries and of France took people's attention. The amateurs could operate without much danger of exposure. And at the same time they could feel that developing events were favorable. For Franklin was being proven right. He had said that Hitler was dangerous when saying it had seemed ridiculous to many people. Their eyes were opening now. His program of aid to the Allies and of an emergency build-up of military forces for defense was now approved by a good many more people than had been true a few weeks ago. Even many of the conservatives who were not isolationists were suddenly among his warmest supporters. Stimson and Knox were representative of this group. Everything indeed conspired to continue Franklin in office.

As to Franklin's behavior, there are two letters, one written in March to Governor Horner of Illinois, and one after the convention to old Senator Norris, which together explain most of his reluctance and his desires.

The March letter written to Horner acknowledged a message of support. You and I, Franklin said, are liberal Democrats and we realize how serious it would be if those "who put property ahead of human beings" should come into control in Washington. But it would be a pity if the continuance of liberalism depended on one man alone. Because of this, he said, "we should seek a platform and candidates who are progressive liberals at heart and not merely in lip service." A good many aspirants, he went on, were automatically eliminated by this criterion. But even more were eliminated when a second was applied—the liberal must be able to win. "It is silly," he said, "to put up, as we have several times in our lifetime, a ticket which is foreordained to defeat." It was still too early to make selections. "Several people who might be considered available may stub their toes in the next four months. . . ."

This kind of talk was not to be understood by laymen but was perfectly plain between professionals. Governor Horner was notified by it that Franklin had no other candidate than himself. In the first place, all the others who had been mentioned at all, or who had any chance to be nominated, were eliminated by the two criteria. In the second place, it was impossible to conceive that between the last of March and the middle of July any new person could become eligible. Franklin had, in effect, defined himself into third-term candidacy. And so the governor understood. All the other professionals were also made aware in one way or another. And if, coupled with his double talk, there were protestations that he wanted to retire, they understood that he could not; and this became more apparent with every event of those crowded months. For Europe was crumbling fast, and he was moving into the acknowledged leadership of the whole democratic world.

His situation finally became so obvious that he expected, in spite of the reactionary conspiracy, another nomination by acclamation like that of 1936—and he was capable of indignation at not receiving it. The letter to Senator Norris tells about this. It too was in answer to a message, one of congratulation on his having been nominated. It began by Franklin's saying that he would rather have had such a message from the senator than from anyone else in the country. It went on to confess that he had written his old friend a letter sometime before the convention and then had not sent it. The contents had been essentially the same as those of the acceptance speech. He had intended to send it on the convention's opening day, Franklin said, but, two days before, it had become evident that "the old-line conservative element" in the party had obtained a much larger share in the control of the convention than it "had any right to have from the point of view of public sentiment." He had therefore felt it best not to speak out until the permanent organization had been effected on the second day. He had, in fact, he said, been amazed by the conservatives' terrific drive. It had put the party back where it had been years before, and it had gained strength from the adherence of the "hater's club," who, as he said, consisted of "fellows like Wheeler and McCarran and Tydings and Glass and John J. O'Connor, and some of the wild Irishmen from Boston, etc. etc."

Essentially this line-up (except for Wheeler and one or two others) was the same as the one-third of the Chicago Convention of 1932. Obviously that crowd had no chance to make a fight in 1936. However, they were greatly heartened by the 1938 elections and thought that this would give them a fighting chance to put the control of the Democratic Party back where it was in 1920, 1924 and 1928.[6]

It had been, he went on to say finally, very stupid of them to make a final fight against Wallace, who was "a pure liberal," for the vice-presidential nomination. The row they had made might cost the ticket many votes in the election, and they must have known they could not have their way.

The letter to Norris, written but not sent, could have been used only if Farley and Garner had given up. But they insisted on a ballot, even when the hopelessness of their candidacies made it ridiculous. In a talk with Franklin over the phone just before the convention Farley reiterated his refusal. What Franklin wanted was to be able to say that a

[6] *Personal Letters: 1928–1945*, Vol. II, p. 1047.

generally recognized national crisis made it imperative that he give in to an overwhelming demand. But the rebels would not agree. They not only refused to make the vote unanimous, they sought to disrupt and confuse the convention in other ways.[7] It was a thoroughly irritating outcome. And it made Franklin's campaign prospect much more difficult than it would have been had he been "drafted." He had a split party behind him. And so he would once more be likely to have to fight a slugging campaign. His hoped-for above-the-battle pose would be hard to sustain.

So set had he been on this kind of approach that toward the end of the Chicago proceedings he began to write a speech refusing the nomination. It was, of course, not made; but the speech he did make in accepting was anything but conciliatory.[8]

He had had no intention of going on into a third term, he said, until the events of 1939 had jeopardized the whole future of the nation; and even then he had expected to declare himself out of consideration at some appropriate time. But that time had never come. It had been important not to lessen his authority as Chief of State during the crisis, and personal desires had had to be disregarded. There had never been a time until the convention had actually met when he could say to his fellow Democrats that they were free to select someone else. They had chosen him again. He, no more than others who had been asked to assume onerous duties, had a right to refuse service. If the people drafted him again he felt that he must comply.

The rest of his acceptance, besides that part which called attention to domestic gains during the eight years just past, was a challenge, not so much to the Republicans and their candidate, as to those antidemocrats—the totalitarians—who were now dominant in Europe. He spoke as though the Republican party were a branch of the National Socialist organization. It was a keynote. Wendell Willkie had, by an extraordinary tour de force, managed to capture the Republican nomination. He was eager to run against "the champ." Franklin affected to ignore this effrontery. He intended to run against Hitler.

The Government of the United States for the past seven years has had the courage openly to oppose by every peaceful means the spread of the dictator form of Government. If our Government should pass to other hands next January—untried hands, inexperienced hands—we can merely hope and pray

---

[7] For instance, by attempting to insert a plank into the platform which read: "We will not participate in foreign wars . . ." etc. The best Franklin's people could do about this proposal of Wheeler's was to secure the addition of the phrase "except in case of attack." The whole platform was, in fact, isolationist in tone. And the conservatives almost succeeded in putting the convention on record against third terms in principle.

[8] For the speech not made, cf. Rosenman, p. 216.

that they will not substitute appeasement and compromise with those who seek to destroy all democracies everywhere . . .[9]

Speaking in political terms, Franklin had now the most satisfactory enemy of all his career. No virtue need be allowed him; if he prevailed it would be a national catastrophe. He was fully in sight, completely on stage. He was appropriately belabored. If he, Franklin, was defeated, it would be Hitler who would win. This was made quite plain. Very early in the campaign he made a "non-political" appearance at the Norfolk Navy Yard in company with Secretary Knox. He was, it could be inferred, appearing as Commander-in-Chief of the armed forces. What civilian competitor could match that position? And when, in a press conference on August 20 at Hyde Park a member of the press tried to tie him down, the colloquy ran as follows:

Q. [Mr. Durno]: Mr. President, when are you going to start your debates with Wendell Willkie? The President: George, you had better reduce it [that question] to a mimeographed copy and give it to Bill [Mr. Hassett] every morning. . . . You know what the situation is on that just as well as I do, all of you. I told the people, told the Convention . . . that whether I like it or not, I happened to be the President of 130 million people, the United States and dependencies . . . and things are in such shape this year that it is, of course, perfectly obvious that I cannot do any campaigning . . .[10]

The politicians, and even the White House crowd, had not yet caught on, so there was much puzzlement. Did Franklin really mean that he would do no campaigning? They forgot his old "non-political" technique of which this was only another variety, a very advanced and sophisticated one, but not different in kind. Not a few of the more orthodox thought he had lost his senses. First, he had appointed two Republicans to the cabinet; then he had cooked up a deal to give Britain fifty naval craft; then, of all things, in the midst of a campaign he was demanding a draft law that would offend every parent in the land, not to mention the potential draftees. It was enough to make a politician's hair stand on end. They had the simple notion, still, that he was running against the Republican candidate and that a campaign was a campaign. It was only gradually that he turned everyone's eyes on Hitler. Franklin, of course, became the indispensable guardian of American security. The pending destroyer-bases deal and the draft act turned out to be politically favorable rather than otherwise.

At the opening of the Great Smoky Mountains National Park early in September, an apparently artless passage in his dedicatory speech referred to conscription in terms every American could understand:

[9] *Public Papers*, 1940 vol., p. 301.
[10] Ibid., p. 333.

The old frontier, that put the hard fibre in the American spirit and the long muscles on the American back, lives and will live in these untamed mountains . . .

Today we no longer face Indians and hard and lonely struggles with nature . . .

The earth has been so shrunk by the airplane and the radio that Europe is closer to America today than was one side of these mountains to the other side when the pioneers toiled through the primeval forest. . . . The arrow, the tomahawk, and the scalping knife have been replaced by the airplane, the bomb, the tank, and the machine gun. Their threat is as close to us today as was the threat to the frontiersmen when hostile Indians were lurking on the other side of the gap.

Therefore, to meet that threat—to ward off these dangers—the Congress . . . and the Chief Executive . . . are establishing by law the obligation inherent in our citizenship to serve our forces for defense . . .

It is not . . . easy or pleasant to ask men of the Nation to leave their homes, and women . . . to give their men . . . But the men and women of America have never held back even when it has meant personal sacrifice on their part if that sacrifice is for the common good. . . .

What shall we be defending? The good earth of this land, our homes, our families—yes, and far more. We shall be defending a way of life which has given more freedom to the soul and body of man than ever has been realized in the world before, a way of life that has let men scale whatever heights they could scale without hurting their fellows, a way of life that has let men hold up their heads and admit no master but God. . . .[11]

If Sam Rosenman had not said specifically that the first of the presidential speeches on which Robert E. Sherwood worked was in October of this year, it would certainly be thought that this Smoky Mountain address was his work. It had an unusual eloquence. But the fact is that even Rosenman, taking Franklin at his word when he said that he would do no campaigning, had gone off for a Montana vacation with his family. He was summoned back by Hopkins early in September. There would be speeches to write after all. This one has an authorship we cannot identify. Perhaps Franklin wrote it himself.

Willkie might not be recognized by Franklin as his opponent, but he was making a tremendous stir all across the land. He was that unusual combination, a conservative who was brilliant and colorful instead of dull and stodgy. He had not been wanted by the Republican old guard; he had been promoted by a curious element among the conservatives just now beginning to demand recognition. These were suburbanites, people in the executive class, not themselves primary producers, but facilitators of the business process. They were advertising specialists, investment counsel, customer's men, executives in the hierarchy of salesmanship, upper employees in the publishing trade,

[11] Ibid., pp. 370–71, 374.

and so on. The tone and policy for the group were set by such individuals as Luce of the Luce publications and Howard of Scripps-Howard. They were bright, shallow, sophistical, and thoroughly jesuitical. They were just now discovering that politics was a game wonderfully suited to their talents and their freedom from scruple. And it had the attraction of great power. It was the lever to move the nation.

This crowd went to battle with the old guard for the first time that year with a considerable advantage. The old guard had no candidate who could be imagined to be a match for Roosevelt. But Willkie could be thought of as a genuine rival. He had, in fact, set himself up, through well-publicized negotiations, as the champion of conservatism. He was known everywhere for his voluble indignation at the operations of the New Deal.

The old guard's hatred of the administration and of Franklin was mostly either inexpressible or had an obviously negative popular appeal. Its members were, in other words, protecting interests it had been customary for governments to let alone. But it was difficult to argue in public that they had any right to be let alone. When the rights and privileges of corporate wealth and of the individuals connected with it were argued for, it was better to do it behind legal curtains. When that sort of thing got out into the open, adverse opinion rapidly crystallized. The real animus in the hatred for Franklin was just this. There could be no "confidence" because no one could know that his privileges were secure. At any time Franklin might set off on further probing expeditions. During the New Deal years, one of the favorite methods of preparing for punitive legislation had been congressional investigations. They had invariably exposed business and businessmen to ridicule and eventually to restrictive regulation. From Pecora and his Wall Street probe to Nye and his munitions-maker investigations, the whole history was a frightening and repugnant one.

It was the argument of the new activists that the fight had to be a political one. The battle could and must be carried to the enemy. The government was a stronghold to be captured. Only when it was in friendly hands could business be certain of protection. This tactic ran against the deep instinct for covering up and keeping in the dark, which was so prevalent among the old guard. They always wanted a candidate who would discourse in platitudes but who had the bearing of a deacon. They had found and manipulated such puppets in the past with success. From McKinley to Coolidge they had managed to have their men in the White House much of the time.

The trouble in 1940 was that such a man could not win. They had tried with Landon in 1936 and had almost been wiped out. They had been encouraged by gains in 1938, but even the most optimistic among them knew that Taft or Vandenberg could not beat Roosevelt in 1940.

The case of Dewey was not so clear. He was less a stuffed shirt but, beside Willkie he was a cold, disagreeable, lawyer-like fellow. But Willkie was the kind that reactionaries distrust. He was, they felt, almost as bad as "that man in the White House." He was too voluble and flexible. He was unpredictable, and unpredictability is a major sin in the conservative book.

Willkie was a lawyer from Indiana who had never lost his midwestern manners. Even his speech flowed from his lips in the volume and with the intonations of debate in a fresh-water college. Harold Ickes made one of his memorable bon mots at Willkie's expense during the campaign when he spoke of "the barefoot lawyer from Wall Street." And that was Willkie's weakness. He *was* from Wall Street even if he did not look or sound as though he could be. Through the New Deal years he had fought ferociously for the private power interests he represented. Commonwealth and Southern, his concern, was caught in the TVA expansion and forced, eventually, to sell. Willkie shouted and protested throughout the long-drawn-out proceedings, the last of them face to face with Franklin himself.

No one in the country was so plainly and personally the ideological opposite of Franklin. He was indeed a logical opponent. But he had another advantage. His ideological oppositeness was purely domestic. He was not one of those who had secret leanings toward totalitarianism as so many of the old guard did. He was a thorough Democrat. That was why he had argued long and loudly against the New Deal legislation and against the taking of his holding company by TVA. He was not one to suffer in silence or to go underground with his resentment. His proposal now to erect this resentment into a campaign against the "creeping socialism" of the New Deal was the only attack that would have any chance of winning. The old guard hated it, but they took him.

During the early part of the campaign Franklin watched Willkie with growing uneasiness. His pose of unconcern had been shaken at the convention. He had been forced into the open as an avowed candidate; it looked as though Willkie might force him to fight openly and hard for electoral victory. Willkie was a very attractive fellow. His attack was making headway. And the identification Franklin had postulated for him with Hitler was hard to sustain. Willkie was very American and very democratic—more so, if you stopped to think about it, than Franklin himself. Indiana had no Dutchess County.

The problem was not easy. It required more concern than Franklin had been prepared to spare for politics that summer and fall.

26

The campaign of 1940 came out all right. Franklin's opponent was forced—or felt that he was forced—to champion the isolationist cause, becoming more and more extreme as election day approached. Finally he went the limit. If Franklin was elected, he said, we would "be in the war by April" and "plowing under every fourth American boy." Most of the later claims of the revisionists were anticipated by Willkie during that summer. The excuse was that he must present a simple alternative to Franklin's position—a compulsion often felt by presidential candidates whose parties lack striking differentiations of policy, either domestic or foreign.

Willkie's heart was not in this extremism, but it was demanded by his supporters—or many of them—and was obviously what the crowds he addressed wanted to hear. His audiences were so responsive and showed everywhere such whooping enthusiasm that, much as Landon had in 1936, he allowed himself to be persuaded that he was on the way to winning. He never seemed to realize that he had fallen into Franklin's trap. He, as well as others, was deceived by the arranged support. This estimate stimulated his energies and, at the same time, lowered his standards. The result was conduct that he was not proud to recall when the campaign was over. He had done what he knew he ought not to have done, in a way he did not approve.

Franklin, some weeks after the convention, when Willkie's barnstorming had got well under way and was apparently attracting many independent votes, allowed himself to be persuaded that Willkie had become dangerous. In mid-campaign he still held to his strategy of pillorying Hitler, but he judged that his tactic of aloofness was untenable. He did not go to the length of meeting Willkie head on—he never mentioned his name—but he referred freely to "Republican orators" and belabored them heartily. In doing this he necessarily shifted ground and talked of domestic issues as well as foreign policy. The war issue had certain risks, especially in isolationist territory, but people had not forgotten the depression, and it was good for yet another round. Hitler was not lost sight of. "Measures short of war" were defended as strictly self-interested for the United States. The furnishing of munitions, especially since they were being paid for, was the least contribution Americans could make, so Franklin contended. Yet there was a sizable dissent. And playing up the New Deal, so long neglected, as likely to be liquidated by the Republicans was actually a safer issue. Hoover was a less formidable opponent than Hitler.

Actually it was easier to identify Willkie with Hoover than with Hitler. He had been nominated from a dark-horse position and represented a defeat for the Republican old guard, but he unmistakably had behind him the business interests most distrusted by a disillusioned electorate. These had been the interests behind Hoover too, and his name was still a symbol for the reaction so feared since the depression. Most of the press not surprisingly favored the Republicans—including the New York *Times* in this campaign, something Franklin shrewdly made use of, knowing how deep was the popular distrust of newspapers. On one occasion he chided Republican orators and the editor of the *Times* together.

This part of his campaign had a slight tinge of panic, although the hysteria was more evident in those around him than in Franklin. When Willkie turned isolationist, thus, in effect, embracing Hitler, and seemed to be making headway, Franklin had some second thoughts. He may have made a mistake; Americans still shrank from war. The last part of his campaign was a recognition of this. As it turned out, his strategy was correct, but he had moments of doubt. He had guessed in August that he would have an electoral vote of 340. That figure represented confidence, but of a modified sort; he thought himself likely to win, even if not by a wide margin.

One incident of the campaign had some reference to Willkie's public-relations experts in association with those who had opposed the New Deal and were now opposing collective security. It was the fortuitous alliteration of three names—"Martin, Barton, and Fish"—which, before Franklin finished, had the currency of a popular song. The Barton of this trio was a partner of one of the best-known publicity enterprises who had got himself elected to Congress and had written a best-selling book about Jesus of Nazareth. Jesus was, in the Barton version, much the same sort as American businessmen. Martin was Republican minority leader in the House with an unblemished reactionary and isolationist voting record. And Fish was the Dutchess County congressman, known to Franklin from youth, who was most recently notable for having offered singlehanded to arrange matters in eastern Europe for Hitler. They were representative of the old guard, and as such they

540

Destroyer — bases exchange

were telling targets. The chant, "Martin, Barton, and Fish," was delightedly repeated by millions who found it a satisfactory expression of their deep suspicion of synthetic ballyhoo.

So Franklin beat the experts at their own game, as he had once boasted he could do. It was, in fact, one of his most impressive victories. Instead of the 340 electoral votes he had expected, the actual count was 449.[1] The only drawback was that he had allowed himself to be drawn into making some assertions of doubtful wisdom, even of doubtful validity—as when in Boston he said: "I have said this before, but I shall say it again and again and again: Your boys are not going to be sent into any foreign wars." Willkie had indeed smoked him out in true debater fashion. He had stormed up and down the land shouting imprecations, talking by the hour, rumpled, homely, and attractive. Americans enjoyed him. It was a good show.

Yet, although Franklin reacted to it, he probably was not overmuch excited and he probably did not doubt the correctness of his plan. Even before the election, in moves inconsistent with his more extreme protestations of peaceable intention, he had asked for and got the selective service system, America's first peacetime draft of men and boys, and he had consummated the destroyer-bases deal with Churchill. Both these strained the "measures short of war" formula almost beyond recognition. They were assumed by everyone to be answers to Hitler's aggressions in Europe. They were obviously part of a still-unfinished build-up. It would go on to further actions if there was continued provocation. Franklin's bland defense of them on other grounds was not taken seriously; it was afterward quoted against him, but it can be seen now to have been part of his demonstration of hostility to Hitler. And objectors to it were by inference on Hitler's side. Campaigns are not won by speeches alone.

There was an interesting exchange between Franklin and Churchill as the destroyer-bases exchange was worked out. Franklin was anxious to represent it to the country as a bargain, advantageous to the United States, and not as a gift to the British. Churchill thought and said that this was a rather low level of international dealing. He urged Franklin to be high-minded; he wanted to show his British people, who were inclined to think the worst of Americans, that Yankees could be generous. The two statesmen could not agree. So what actually happened was that the destroyers were traded for certain bases; but Churchill, to shame Franklin, made a gift of others.[2]

[1] From thirty-eight states; Willkie, in contrast, had only eighty-two from ten states. The total of Franklin's votes was a little more than twenty-seven million to Willkie's approximately twenty-two million.

[2] Not an actual gift; they were 99-year leases. The general arrangement was to trade fifty over-age but still useful destroyers for bases in the West Indies.

This deal had troubled Franklin in another way. He had supposed that he must have authorization from the Congress for it and was apprehensive about the debate over his request. But Robert Jackson, who was now Attorney General, persuaded him that no congressional authorization was needed—merely the same certification from the service departments as was needed for other munitions. So the papers were signed and the announcement made without preparatory talk—and nothing much happened!

This acceptance in the midst of the campaign was remarkable. Taken together with the ratification provided by the election, it undoubtedly emboldened Franklin to go on to the final measure short of war—Lend-Lease; but for this he did have to go to the Congress. And on it there would be a full-blown debate, the last, really, before Pearl Harbor shut off the isolationists until the war was over.

There were not many speeches during the 1940 campaign, but what there were had to be prepared in a hurry—Franklin changed his tactics, and there was rather more confusion than usual—as is related in *Working with Roosevelt*.[3] The speech writers were not too clear about the policy they were to defend. The New Deal's function of bringing business under discipline was not being stressed, since businessmen were now coming to Washington in great numbers to "co-operate" and since the erstwhile progressives, whose policy this was, were most of them isolationists and so were anti-administration. Then, too, there was the difficulty that what seemed to realists progress toward war had still to be represented as a succession of moves purely for defense. In these circumstances the speeches had to go through an unusually elaborate process, involving long preliminary conversations regarding content, the getting of suggestions and drafts from many sources, and a final weaving together. This, when submitted to Franklin, had invariably to be redone—ordinarily six or seven times, and sometimes more. It was wearing.

This burden fell mostly on Rosenman. The old helpers were gone. Stanley High had long since disappeared. Strangely enough, he was writing Republican propaganda now, as, for that matter, was Moley. But Rosenman had a new recruit, the best, he felt, that he had ever had. This was Robert E. Sherwood, who was a well-known writer of plays.[4] He was brought in by Hopkins, who, since his success at the Democratic convention, had become top man among the White House group, spoken of by the newsmen as "the Janizaries."[5]

[3] Rosenman, Chapters XIII and XIV.

[4] Afterward to become the author of *Roosevelt and Hopkins* (New York: Harper, 1948). Among his well-known plays were *The Petrified Forest* and *Idiot's Delight*.

[5] An invention of Hugh Johnson's in one of his rather bitter critical comments. He became a widely read columnist for a few years after ending his career as NRA administrator. He was as brilliant and mordant a one as ever set out to get

It is not apparent what contribution Sherwood made to earn Rosenman's high praise. The speeches of that year were not remarkably better than others; not, as a matter of fact, much different. This would seem to show that Franklin made them all alike by working them over and over. Perhaps Rosenman appreciated Sherwood's endurance. He needed someone who could and would sit all night working with him so that a draft could be taken to Franklin's bed by the White House usher on his first awakening in the morning. At any rate, Sherwood, from then on, was in and about the White House as a speech drafter, never on his own, always helping Rosenman, but willing.[6]

The playwright was a wide-eyed admirer of Franklin's. He had first become so because he was an ardent interventionist and an enthusiastic Anglophile, sentiments discovered by Hopkins. But he went on as a continually amazed watcher of the "great actor" in the White House. It was this, as much as anything, that held him, pure patriotism aside, for he had never seen or imagined anything like Franklin.[7]

Sherwood would never lose that fascinated wonder: the President had such a sense of fitness and of timing, he was so sensitive to possible complications from anything he said or did, his motives were so hard to uncover, his plans so calculatingly hidden. The whole complex was a studied pattern of deception. Sherwood would come to call him an "artful dodger," but there was meant in that phrase no disparagement; it expressed rather admiration for the determined carrying through of a

---

even with a former boss. He himself was given the picturesque appellation of "old iron-pants" by his colleagues in the writing fraternity.

[6] During the war he would become director of the overseas branch of the Office of War Information.

[7] Sherwood's being Anglophile was a guarantee of enthusiasm, but not necessarily a recommendation to Franklin, who had a curiously ambivalent attitude toward things British. He had some harmless jealousy of Churchill's superior eloquence, but he often disparaged the Prime Minister's reactionary imperialist attitudes. More than once he discoursed to me on his difficulties from this source. Just at this moment it was especially desirable that he should not be ticketed as a British devotee. His critics were saying it for their own purposes, but he insisted over and over that his support for British policy was purely in pursuit of American interests. Sometimes he went to curious lengths to repudiate any love for Europeans, as when he rebuked Ernest Lindley through Early, his press secretary, for having written an article saying that "from his earliest years Franklin D. Roosevelt had moved in a society . . . which was not conscious of any differentiation between the interests of the United States and those of Europe." This, Franklin said, was pure invention. He then rejected in detail all of the kindly argument. Among other things, he said, if Ernest would look into "family ties" he would realize that the Roosevelt family in the West Indian sugar business was compelled for many years to contend against the British and French interests. He also spoke of the Delanos and the China trade, which would have prejudiced the family against the British. There was a good deal more, including his own behavior in the previous war. It was indeed an elaborate denial. He felt strongly about it. The memorandum is to be found in *Personal Letters: 1928–1945,* Vol. II, pp. 942 ff.

trying task. The role of President was naturally one to engage the endless interest of a dramatist, and Sherwood was among the best of his generation. He made the most of opportunities he continually marveled at having. In the end no one understood Franklin better than he, unless it was Archibald MacLeish, the poet, who was also helping with the speeches. A playwright and a poet: between them they divined some of the hidden motives as none of the other familiars did.

Sherwood's other hero was Hopkins. This was natural, in a way, since Hopkins was his contact with the presidency; but it came to be something more. That a man who was so ill as to be out of commission half the time should be driven by such compelling urges was an irresistible study. Was he ambitious? He had been, but in a strange way. And anyway, by 1940 all that was given up. He had been Secretary of Commerce and had resigned because the burden was too heavy. He was living at the White House in the manner described so vividly in *Roosevelt and Hopkins.* He was, he said, "the office boy around here." He had managed the affair of the third nomination at Chicago and had sat in on the campaign conferences, although he was never useful in concocting speeches. He was as near to an alter ego as a President ever had, and because of this he would assume a role of unique importance as the war came on.

His own description of himself was far from being accurate, Franklin's curious relationship with those who served him being what it was. They had to guess what he intended. He almost never told them. When he did make some explanation it was in a moment of euphoria and it was not likely to go far; he almost never talked when he was worried or depressed. Those with whom he discussed his plans were not expected to argue about them or to ask many questions. He seldom wanted advice, although he sometimes wanted reassurance. Hopkins served better than anyone else ever did under these conditions. But he was intensely jealous and exclusive—much as Louis Howe had been. In a sense he took Howe's place, as Rosenman had occasion to note. Having been a helper both in Albany and in Washington, Rosenman had unique opportunities for comparison. But Howe had been a frequent objector to Franklin's schemes. Hopkins was not. What he existed for in his later years was to anticipate what Franklin wanted to do and to expedite its doing. That was what he had done in the third-term matter. It was what he would do as the central figure in the vast Lend-Lease operation.

It was true that sometimes Franklin thought out loud—as he seemed to be doing when he talked several times with Hopkins about possible successors in 1940. But Hopkins, even while he was being talked to, was going on with complicated machinations to see that none of those talked about succeeded. He conceived himself as an operator, not as

544

a statesman, and so he escaped the fate of most of those who, at one time or another, were made use of and then allowed to depart.

At this moment one of those painful separations was occurring. Corcoran was taking the same medicine he had in the past helped administer to others. He found it bitter, and perhaps more so because of his awareness that Hopkins had had a hand in preparing the mixture and would remain after he had gone. The two had been rivals for four or five years. Corcoran had been a lively member of the White House circle. His malice and vindictiveness were well hidden under a jolly red-faced exterior. But his intention had been to fill all the important posts surrounding the center of power with his own people, and for several years he had had amazing success. This was partly because he had had access to a reservoir of academic and legal talent ready and willing to serve. Most of his protégés were exceptionally able people, often reminded of their obligation to their sponsor. But Hopkins had the same intention. His selections were almost as numerous as Corcoran's and they were now moving into the higher echelons.

Corcoran had a partner whose connection with him was so intimate that they were seldom spoken of separately. This was Ben Cohen, who was as nearly his opposite in personality as he could possibly be—quiet and scholarly, an able draftsman, gentle-seeming in manner. In his way Cohen was as determined as Corcoran; his mild and disingenuous manner concealed a tough determination. The two, working together with such outside allies as Frankfurter, who had, in fact, been responsible for their original assignment,[8] were determined workers in a curious cause. They were infected with the malevolence of old Justice Brandeis. The old justice had a gentle manner, too, but no harder character ever played a part in the nation's public life. He preferred to persuade; but if he could not persuade, he was willing to use much harsher methods to dispose of dissenters. For this purpose he operated through numerous satellites, of whom Frankfurter, Corcoran and Cohen, and the New York lawyer, Morris Ernst, were only a few, but as able as any.

The influence of the Brandeis philosophy and its purveyors was enhanced by the way things were going in the world. The collectivism they hated and feared had, for their purposes, an ideal embodiment in the totalitarians, Hitler and Mussolini. The ruthlessness of dictatorship could be represented as inseparable from collectivism. This, to the Brandeis group, was very useful and they made the most of it. When Franklin turned from the collectivistic First to the atomistic Second New Deal and Corcoran became a White House favorite, the association had given Franklin the feeling of being approved by those whose

---

[8] When the utility-holding-company legislation had to be drafted Frankfurter, having introduced them, continued to be their mentor. He was a constant consultant.

opinion he valued. He liked that. Besides, as we have seen, the atomism of Brandeis was congruous with the progressive liberalism Franklin believed politically acceptable.

That there was something much deeper involved, no one, apparently, understood. But there is no doubt in my mind, as I review the subsequent years, that Franklin's turn to atomism was a deliberate long-range political choice. Collectivism would be represented by Hitler. His own position must stand in the clearest contrast with that of the man who was to be his rival for the regard of a generation. It would have been done without Brandeis, if my supposition is true, or even without the old progressives. He may have looked to a new generation.

This is a delicate and complicated matter to explore, and it lies so deep that evidence, as in most of Franklin's decision-making, is lacking. It can only be said that there is no other way to explain the attitudes and occurrences of the succeeding years. When Franklin emerged from his wrestle with Hoover in 1932, there soon waited for him, with open challenge, the figure across the sea in Germany who represented a kind of caricature of collectivism. Franklin could have used his leadership to provide an alternative kind—a democratic version, such as was developing in Britain and had definite attractions for him—or he could offer a complete alternative. The first would be difficult, not only because there would be confusion caused by similarity of social objectives, but because he would be going against an accepted American ideology with a long tradition. This was the simple, negative dependence on competitive capitalism, modified by imposed standards and minima which were the credo of progressivism. This was an attitude, a faith, well understood and accepted. Even those who fought against the regulation—and even the breaking up—of big business did not deny theoretical rightness of such measures. It was orthodox—rather like sin to a sinner.

Then there was another complication. This was Communism, long a bogey in America and very easily made to seem the promised land of all collectivists. As it was, the early New Dealers had instantly and happily been tagged as "Reds" by the hostile press, and it had been a successful kind of denigration, one Franklin had had to compromise with by letting most of them go.

Communism was even worse to become identified with than National Socialism, but both were deadly labels, speaking politically, and anyone taking a fundamental position vis-à-vis the polarizing philosophies of the time would do well to escape completely from identification with either or both. For this escape, progressivism of the Brandeis variety, with its reminders of long-rooted American attitudes and personalities —including Uncle Ted, who by no stretch could be associated with any foreign "ism"—was readily available.

To one who, like Franklin, seldom actually thought out a policy but

546

rather allowed his unconscious calculations to become gradually dominant, it could presently seem that no choosing had taken place. Rather, the only possible course had been followed; there was no alternative. A certain confusion accompanying the turn-around, such as was involved in the abandonment of NRA and the re-establishment of trust busting, could be glossed over and explained away. And this had been done. The embarrassments of 1934 were covered first by the onslaught against the utilities and then by the overwhelming ratification of the 1936 election. After that Franklin had nothing to explain. Or at least no one who commanded attention demanded an explanation.

From 1936 to 1940 there was a constantly enlarging spectacle of monstrous behavior abroad to which American eyes could be directed. At home there were smaller engagements with less powerful antagonists. These reminded everyone that businessmen had leanings toward the version of collectivism represented by Hitler and Mussolini. And they relieved Franklin of any taint of such an attitude himself, especially since those prominent in his administration who were known collectivists had departed—they were either allowed to feel unwanted or were sabotaged by Corcoran until their separation became inevitable. There was a considerable exodus.

Corcoran played a useful role in these years, fitting perfectly as he did into the large design. His talents, his energy, and his lack of scruple were just what was needed. By 1940 he had outlived that usefulness. When the third term was definitely in prospect, but before the campaign was started, he was allowed to understand what he had conveyed to so many others—that his departure would be welcome. And so he went.

Hopkins' part in this is quite understandable. Corcoran was his only remaining rival for Franklin's trust and affection. He was vigorous and ebullient. Hopkins, sick and driven, made a sorry contrast. In his mind, I think, it came to be an intolerable rivalry. So Franklin was caused to hear from many prompted visitors, as had happened once to Moley, later to me, and at other times to others, that Corcoran was a handicap. He irritated the politicians; he presumed on his White House credentials; he was a political liability. This opinion was made to flow from many sources. Of course much of it was true, but it was less true now than it had been in 1937, when Franklin had no thought of getting rid of Corcoran; and for that reason, if for no other, it can be regarded as an arranged matter.

That Hopkins planted these stories cannot be proved. But that somehow he was responsible for Corcoran's departure seems to me obvious. Moreover, it is likely that Franklin knew all about it. He was through with the contriving Irishman. Perhaps he felt himself surrounded too closely by Corcoran's picked people. Perhaps he thought there had been

547

too much Brandeis. Perhaps he felt that politics ought to be returned to the professionals who were now closely tied to him. Farley was gone, but Flynn had set up a satisfactory relationship with the party stalwarts. Corcoran was not in this picture. He had better be eliminated altogether.

There would, anyway, be less need of intriguers and hatchet men of the Corcoran type now. Franklin had, he believed, undertaken his last political campaign. Moreover, for what he had to do from now on, he could call on another kind of talent. Suddenly the businessmen who had never before been persona grata in his circle were becoming useful. The need of the moment was a vast expansion of production. For this he would find a whole new assortment of administrators.

The press, about this time, began to speak of a "business brains trust," and the phrase was some comfort to those who had been so unhappy over the academic one. At last "practical men" instead of "theorists" were close to the seat of power. William Knudsen was the Director General of the Office of Production Management. He was in and out of the presidential offices almost in the way Corcoran had recently been. Under him there were five other big businessmen whose names and connections brought a warm feeling of security to all the conservatives. These names were Biggers, Batt, Harriman, Harrison, and Johnson; and they came, respectively, from the Libbey-Owens-Ford Glass Company, the S.K.F. Industries (ball bearings), the Union Pacific Railroad, the American Telephone and Telegraph Company, and General Motors. This was a top command to be relied on. The chorus of approval was general.

As for progress, it was reported at year's end that the Army had risen from 290,000 men in June to 675,000, and the Navy from 150,000 to 200,000. Tanks were being delivered at the rate of 100 a month, planes at the rate of 800 a month, Navy ships at the rate of one every ten days—and so it went. The most significant increase, however, was in more general facilities for production, not measurable except in dollar contracts and completions. But anyone could understand that presently "production would be no problem." The period of waste and confusion was not ended—far from it—but in spite of the lost motion there was progress. And, perhaps best of all, the "bottlenecks" were one after another being broken. A system was, however agonizingly, at last emerging.

It must sometimes have seemed to Franklin that every gain in the struggle to increase capacity and translate capacity into planes, ships, tanks, and guns was torn ruthlessly out of his nervous system. In the accounts of those who were close to him at that time, there began to be evidence of exhaustion, of irritability, and of impatience. But none of this—or very little—showed in the public reports. The newsmen may have talked about it among themselves, but they had seen spells of this kind of thing before, and always it had been cured by two weeks at Warm Springs, a cruise on the *Tuscaloosa,* or some days at Hyde Park.

It cannot be wondered at if the burden began to seem a crushing one. There was the question, acute now, whether Britain, now generally looked on as America's first line of defense, would survive the coming months. Then there was the progress of the Japanese southwestward, which no force available seemed powerful enough to stop. Everywhere Franklin looked in the world there was a menace—and no adequate means for meeting it. Consider the names he must catalogue day by day and the worrying he must have done about the demands they represented: Hitler, Mussolini, Stalin, Konoye (now puppet Premier in Japan), Pétain (tool of Hitler in France)—all enemies. But there were demanding friends too: Chiang Kai-shek in China (so far away) and other lesser allies of more doubtful usefulness. And there was always Churchill, waiting impatiently in Britain for aid.

There were times when he felt that he had, as the opponents of Lend-Lease were already saying, exceeded his powers as President. There was even talk of impeachment, something he wondered about himself a little; but driven as he was, he saw no alternative to what he was doing. He was indeed being accused by interventionists of neglect for not going farther and faster. Especially Stimson felt this, and let him know how he felt.

The President of the United States, however, must not show the stresses he feels. He must turn a confident face to his public. They must rely on his leadership. Even though the isolationist wolves were now snarling at his flanks, he must not acknowledge any worry. As the year ended, a struggle with the Congress was in immediate prospect for the passage of the Lend-Lease Act. It would be sure to engage the best oratorical efforts of all his enemies. But no one must know that he was concerned.

Luckily his powers responded to the challenge. He was competent for his task. Of that I think he had no doubt.

Since I believe that in 1940 and the several succeeding years Franklin rose to a climax supremely becoming in such a career, it seems to me important that views of him at home, at work, and relaxing should be studied. It is only from this kind of examination that a more than surface understanding can be gained. There are a multitude of these available. Some of the sharpest and most gifted of contemporary newsmen are in constant contact with any President; and, as we know, they were much more than usually intrigued with Franklin. He had made himself the hero of a vast drama, and he was watched by the rest of the world as well as the United States. The demand for news about him was unprecedented because no individual in modern history had ever occupied so central a position. The only possible comparison was with Wilson in World War I, but the tenseness now was greater than then, if only because the reporting services were more universal. Actually, however, no one in 1918 had felt that the nation might be conquered if it failed; now there were many who began to understand the crisis in those terms. There was no free press in the lands controlled by the dictators, but there was curiosity even there; and to millions of the suppressed he was a man who represented hope—their only hope for release.

This magnification of their President in others' regard had its reflection in the interest of Americans. They were somewhat dazzled even though he had now a familiar and accustomed place in their lives. When they had re-elected him, he had become more than ever a symbol of their faith in the future. They did not know where they were going in those confused days, but they had a leader. They would go where he led. They watched him with a concern intensified by both fear and hope.

We have glimpses of him in many press accounts as he waited at Hyde Park for the election returns. This one is from *Time* (November 11, 1940):

The night was warm for November, still and starless; on a flagpole above the portico the blue Presidential flag, with its shield, eagle, and white stars, flapped listlessly. Hyde Park House was dark—from outside, not a crack of light showed from the library. Inside and out, the atmosphere was solemn, expectant, tense.

In station wagons and long shining limousines came people in evening clothes, neighbors and friends. Inside they assembled in the long furniture-cluttered library, chatting quietly or sitting, hands in laps, listening to the radio chattering election returns.

Apart from his household, alone at the mahogany table in the family dining room, sat the master mathematician of U.S. politics. Outside the room's closed doors was expectant silence. Inside, Franklin Roosevelt worked calmly in the midst of the nerve-tattering, incessant clacking of the three press tickers, loud in the empty room. Before him were large tally sheets with the States listed alphabetically across the top; a long row of freshly pointed pencils. His coat was off. His tie hung low under the unbuttoned collar of his soft shirt, but he had not rolled up his sleeves. His one companion was Marguerite (Missy) LeHand, who snatched the latest "takes" from the thumping tickers, put them before the President without a word, as fast as he finished charting the latest tally. He enjoyed the job.

Occasionally, the doors slid open to admit Harry Hopkins or Judge Samuel Rosenman, but even the President's wife and mother kept out of this political sanctum in this sacred hour . . .

At midnight New York was coming in fast and close, but Franklin Roosevelt, with all other big states in his bag, was in . . . Harry Hopkins went out on the porch for a breath of fresh air, happy to the bursting point. The tension in the house had relaxed. Down the Albany Post Road tootled and whammed a fife, drum and bugle corps, behind them a straggling crowd of 500 villagers, carrying red railroad flares, and Squire Roosevelt of Hyde Park, first third term President of the U.S., came out on the stone porch to joke with his friends . . .

Somehow *Time's* reporters missed what the villagers regarded as a nice touch. The foremost of the placards they carried had the inscription: *Safe on Third*—a colloquialism borrowed from baseball, and somehow very expressive. It marked a kind of relationship among neighbors that only an American would understand.

That *Time's* account was as accurate as could be expected appears from Sherwood's paragraph in *Roosevelt and Hopkins* describing the same evening:

On election night, after a stand-up supper at Mrs. Roosevelt's cottage, we drove through the Hyde Park woods, beloved by Franklin Roosevelt, to the big house to listen to the election returns. In a little room to the left off the front hall sat the President's mother with several old lady friends. They were sewing or knitting or chatting. A radio was on, softly, but they seemed to be paying little attention to it. In the big living room there was another radio going and a large gathering of weirdly assorted guests. The President was in the dining room in his shirtsleeves, with his sons and his Uncle Fred Delano and members of his staff. Large charts were littered on the dining table and news tickers were clattering in the pantry. The Roosevelt boys were excited, but not their father. Mrs. Eleanor Roosevelt moved about from one room to another, seeing to the wants of the guests, apparently never pausing to listen to the returns. If you asked her how she thought things were going she would reply, impersonally, "I heard someone say that Willkie was doing quite well in Michigan," in exactly the tone of one saying, "The gardener tells me the marigolds are apt to be a bit late this year."[9]

But Sherwood's conscience was bothering him, and perhaps more because none of the others—including Hopkins, Rosenman, and Franklin himself—seemed in the least disturbed. It was the mark of the neophyte in politics. He looked back on election night and found some excuse for what seemed to him now a looseness with people's trust that was horrifying:

Although Roosevelt had obvious advantages in this campaign . . . Willkie had one substantial advantage of his own—freedom from responsibility. The challenger could later dismiss his statements as "campaign oratory"; the President of the United States . . . could not. Willkie could say that, if Roosevelt were elected, we might well be in a war by April; Roosevelt could not truthfully say that we would not . . . Perhaps he might have done a better and more candid job of presenting his case. For my own part, I think it was a mistake for him to go so far in yielding to the hysterical demands for sweep-

[9] P. 199.

ing reassurance; but, unfortunately for my own conscience, I happened at the time to be one of those who urged him to go the limit on this, feeling as I did that any risk of future embarrassment was negligible as compared with the risk of losing the election. I burn inwardly whenever I think of those words "again—and again—and again."[10]

Sherwood, like Josephus Daniels, could not quite smother his scruples. He did not have the politicians' immunity to doubt. The proper answer to his reservations is the one so often repeated by Franklin to those around him: "We won, didn't we?" To the true professional this is justification, ample and complete. And that it is accepted in the United States as a folkway of democracy is quite evident. No one goes back of the election returns, or, when he does, expects to be taken seriously. Sherwood was speaking by the book when he referred to Willkie's dismissal of his extremism as "campaign oratory." Willkie did say to a congressional committee a little later precisely that: and he smiled—they all smiled—when he said it.

A month after election Franklin had things cleared away enough so that he could set out again for southern waters. He had missed his fall stay at Warm Springs and had had only a weekend on the *Potomac* (with Harry Hopkins and Bob Jackson) and one at Hyde Park. He was tired again. The *United States News* recorded his departure:

Age: 58 years, 10 months. Weight: 188 pounds. Pulse: normal. Respiration: normal. Appetite: normal. Complexion: pale.

That was the health log of Franklin Roosevelt last week, as, slipping into the final days of his second term, he set sail for the Caribbean . . .

On Monday, his special train heading for . . . "a Biscayne Bay rendezvous with the cruiser *Tuscaloosa,*" the President left details of his trip a tight secret. Grinning, enjoying the complete mystery surrounding his itinerary, he announced that "we are going to Christmas Island to buy Christmas cards, and to Easter Island to buy Easter eggs."

As he was piped aboard the *Tuscaloosa* in Miami Tuesday noon, with naval pomp and ceremony, the President was followed only by his closest aides and advisers: Harry Hopkins, his intimate personal friend; Maj. Edwin M. Watson ("Pa"), his secretary and military aide; Capt. Daniel J. Callaghan, naval aide, and Dr. McIntire—and Fala, a black Scotty pup, the newest addition to the Roosevelt kennels.[11]

Franklin sailed the blue Caribbean for two weeks. All seemed normal. He appeared not to have anything unusual on his mind—or, if he did, nothing was said about it to Harry. But one morning in the Mona Passage (where Ernest Hemingway, a famously successful deep-sea fisherman, had cabled that there were big ones) the mail plane brought him a four-thousand-word letter from Winston Churchill. The plane lin-

[10] Ibid., pp. 200–1.
[11] No mention, this time, of the Cherable Isles.

gered, as was the custom, until pressing signatures had been appended to papers—a matter of an hour or two—and then took off. The newsmen on the accompanying smaller vessel were aware of no change. But that letter to which he settled down on the afterdeck stirred Franklin to renewed action.

Churchill afterward described this letter as the most important he ever wrote and its result as the most generous gesture a nation ever made. For in it he described in language only he could command the plight of the British: desperate was the least word that fitted the circumstances. And it would get worse because funds and credit were now exhausted.

Franklin had been trying to think of some way to help without piling up such a debt as had resulted from World War I and had still been one of his own worst headaches as he first came to the presidency. It was no secret that he was trying to find a formula. There had been speculations about it in the press. But that he had found it, no one knew. He sprang it at the first news conference after his return. How he came to it was described in the *United States News:*

The Presidential special pulled into the yards of the Union Station at Washington in the midst of a gray December rain. At the station to meet him were Under Secretary of State Sumner Welles, Postmaster General Frank D. Walker, and Mrs. Roosevelt.

By the next day, the President was ready to spring his big news of the week, and he chose his regular Tuesday afternoon press conference as a channel for the story. Sensing that something was up—200 newsmen crowded into his oval office.

The President started off, as he often does, with an announcement of no great moment. He said he had found on returning that plans for his inaugural were getting out of hand, but he was still insisting on simplicity.

Then, saying there was no particular news, he launched into his discussion of the problem of financing aid to Britain. The tentative plan he outlined—for the loan or leasing of war supplies, to be paid later in kind—was a complete surprise . . .

The President seemed tense, as if he realized how much might depend on how well he explained his plan. He puffed hard on his cigarette . . . For illustrations, he likened this country to a householder whose neighbor's house was burning down, and whose hose was needed to extinguish the fire. In such a crisis, the President declared, the hose immediately would be attached to a hydrant and there would be no haggling over the cost. Afterward, he went on, the neighbor could return the hose, or, if it was ruined, replace it with a new one.

While Franklin had been away, Lord Lothian, British Ambassador to the United States, had died—a considerable loss, since he had been very successful in smoothing over the irritation caused by the customary British high-handedness in wartime with American ships at sea. He had

had the sense, also, to counsel a waiting policy at home. He knew as well as Churchill that Franklin must be given time. His death, together with Churchill's passionate summary of the crisis, had brought Franklin up to scratch. He knew he was asking for trouble. And he did not like trouble. He could foresee what would be done and said by such isolationist senators as Wheeler, Johnson, Clark, and Vandenberg, and such others on the outside as Lindbergh, Wood, and Hutchins. He could almost read the headlines and the editorials. But if the time was not as propitious as he could wish, there was none to be lost. It was life or death for Britain now in a matter of months. If he waited longer it would be too late.

Soon after getting back he sent Hopkins to London, but even before this he made an announcement of Lend-Lease in general terms and put Edward Foley, Oscar Cox, and Herman Oliphant, Treasury lawyers, to work at drafting. Hopkins, who was to be head man in the Lend-Lease Administration, was being educated. His British tour was the first of many such confidential missions; but, being the first, it was an experiment. He at once made his mark, because Churchill, seeing his opportunity, took him at once to his heart. It was too good a chance to miss.

This was the beginning of a strange liaison and one calculated, it must be supposed, to infuriate all the official diplomats. It probably bothered Ambassador Winant very little. He was an informal man himself. But the career men, both American and British, must have been exasperated. For there was at once set up, through Hopkins, an exchange between Churchill and Franklin which by-passed the formal routing of intergovernmental communications. Already it could be said that Hull and the career officers were treated with some neglect by the White House. Often Hull knew of important decisions just about the time they were made public, and even more often he had no part in making them. Hull had suffered much from Moley and Welles; now he had another cross to bear.

Formally Hopkins dealt only with supplies, allocations, production, and so on, not with diplomacy; but neither Franklin nor Churchill was disposed, in the circumstances, to consider protocol. They had vital matters to decide. It was fortunate that the heads of government could deal with each other in this way. Later they even got to talking by telephone, as business executives do. And what went on then was even more exasperating to the agencies involved in their decision-making.

On this January trip Hopkins, suffering all the while from cold and malnutrition, was given a firsthand view of the British plight. In his cheap crushed hat and rumpled clothes, wearing his overcoat even at dinner in British country houses, looking wan and ill, he was dragged by the Prime Minister to air installations, camps, factories, and munitions dumps. He was required to confer late into the night; he suffered formal dinners in London, but he was introduced to everyone of note as "a friend of the President," and he had to play up to his billing. Several times he had to make speeches, and he did it creditably, even if with cruel effort.[12]

When he came back to Washington he was far gone in exhaustion, but he had a knowledge of the Allied situation essential in the work he was to do. Later on he would set up a similar exchange with Stalin. For the moment, the British had to be saved from imminent German attack, although actually there was little that the United States could do. The time was now too short. Still, for what was to come, the knowledge of stiff backing was not without its uses. The Battle of Britain was won with nerve—nerve and the Spitfire—more than with munitions. Old men were drilling on village greens and learning to handle arms. Years later there could still be seen, back a little from the coasts, the gun shelters and other small works intended to be of some use in meeting the expected invasion. Every Englishman expected it, and expected to have a part in it. He would die on the beaches or in the hills. But he would never bow to Hitler. That when Churchill expressed these sentiments he spoke for all his countrymen, no one could doubt. There were many Englishmen who would always regret that the Nazis had not actually come across to meet the valor of free men.

It was the story of this resolution, backed by pitifully small resources, that Hopkins took back to Washington. Not that Franklin needed it. He, Stimson, Knox, Marshall, and a few others had already taken the resolution which would be the over-all guide during the years to come —Germany first, others afterward. They had taken it because already the choice had had to be made. The Japanese threat was looming large in the Pacific.

It had not been only to get Douglas MacArthur out of Washington —although that was a consideration—that Franklin had arranged for him to have the Philippine command when he had finally finished his double term as Chief of Staff in Washington. He had now been in Manila for several years. It was reported that he had made of the constabulary a competent small army. The islands would be defended if need should arise. The "third fleet" was in Asiatic waters too; it was small compared with the growing Japanese Navy, but put together with the British and Dutch ships, there was some force to be counted on.

It looked now, at the beginning of the year destined to end in Pearl Harbor, as though the Japanese expansion downward would soon encompass the Dutch East Indies as well as further stretches of the mainland. Once these islands were taken, several of Japan's more serious

---

[12] All this is vividly related in *Roosevelt and Hopkins*.

ortages would be relieved. There was fuel there for ships and metals
for industry. As Franklin made his calculations, he had to estimate how
soon such an attack would be made. Also, he must wonder whether
Americans would see such an event as a danger to their interests. They
had not so far reacted to Japanese effrontery in China beyond a certain
sympathy for the Chinese and a tendency to think of the Japanese as
having exceeded civilized tolerance. Still, even if this was so, it was
not a duty of the United States to do more than refuse them countenance. The Chinese were sympathized with, but not to the extent of
military interference.

It had not escaped observers that the Stimson who was now Secretary
of War had been Hoover's Secretary of State and had had a "doctrine"
named after him. That Stimson Doctrine had been directed at checking
Japan's expansion into Manchuria. It was also recalled that Franklin
had publicly approved Stimson's stand—something Hoover had not
done. Neither could be supposed to have changed. Japan had gone on,
under the direction of a clique of war lords, subjecting all the weaker
nations of Asia to her will. She intended a complete conquest. And no
one doubted that Franklin, supported by Stimson, intended to oppose
that conquest by every means at his command.

Nothing could be done, everyone knew, without the consent of Congress. And Franklin knew that consent would never be given unless and
until the Japanese expansion became a recognized threat to the nation.
It was a nice calculation whether the conquest of Dutch and British
possessions would be so considered. The Philippines, probably, although
the republic was about to become completely independent of the
United States and already was, in principle; but not so likely the possessions of the European empires. At this stage Franklin could certainly
not have judged how far the Japanese would be allowed to go by
American public opinion. Nor could he have any good estimate of time.
It was common knowledge that Japanese predations were becoming
bolder, the war lords more arrogant, and the Navy more powerful.
There was adequate attention in the press to Japanese doings, and opinion was certainly adverse and growing more so, but this was an irritation
far short of willingness to take punishing action.

Something of a recapitulation had been general late in September
when Germany and Italy had added Japan to their Axis and all three
had proclaimed a military alliance. Americans had been reminded, in
the succeeding weeks of editorial review, that a long succession of
events, all having the same orientation, had been occurring. A gift for
prophecy was not necessary to see that at some time not too far ahead
a crisis would be reached if that series was extended, and surely it would
be. Just how or where the precipitation might come was not known, but
that it would come, and before very long, no one could any longer

doubt. There was one element of uncertainty. The Japanese were complete opportunists; how far and how fast they would go would depend on events in Europe. If Britain was successfully invaded and the fleet put out of action, they would feel free to act. They obviously anticipated this.

They also anticipated, it seemed to Franklin, thinking largely as always, a pincers movement which would win North Africa, Europe, and Asia for the Axis. The Japanese share would be Asia. The preliminaries of this were already in process. The conquest of Africa seemed a matter of weeks. A huge Italian army was in position in the northern deserts, preparing a drive into Egypt. The opposing force of General Wavell was not regarded as capable of resisting—although Churchill had high hopes. The Japanese, in joining the European dictators, obviously anticipated that they would drive through the Middle East to India, where they would be met by the Emperor's armies.

Franklin himself reviewed where he stood vis-à-vis the Asiatic threat. Back in July 1939 he had gone so far as to abrogate the 1911 commercial treaty with Japan and, at the same time, to authorize a warning speech by Ambassador Joseph C. Grew. The Ambassador had said to the Japanese that the United States was quite aware of the implications of present policy; the new order in East Asia included depriving Americans of long-established rights in China; that was dangerous. He implied that further tolerance could not be expected.

There had been a certain amount of action. Boycotts, although they were unofficial, had followed the bombing of Shanghai as long ago as 1937, and in the summer of 1938 a "moral embargo" had been formally imposed. This had stopped the shipment from the United States of all munitions. The Japanese cynically seized the moment of Nazi conquest in France to demand concessions in Indochina. They also persuaded the British to close the Burma Road, the back door to China over which the resistance forces were receiving supplies. Franklin at that time had clamped licenses on a long list of essential supplies. Then Japan actually invaded Indochina. Franklin proclaimed an embargo on more materials, this time including vital scrap iron, which theretofore had been going in quantity to Japan.

It was at this time (September 1940) that the Japanese joined the Axis. As Franklin approached the celebration of Christmas that year, he had to consider how a threat in the East, almost as immediate as that in the West, could be countered.

Never had the United States seemed so hedged about with hostile forces. The German submarines and the Japanese Navy, between them, reduced the bordering oceans to doubtful protections. The very coasts of the nation were open to attack. It seemed intolerable. It lent drive to the defensive build-up if it did nothing more.

As the New York *Times*, anticipating the new term, looked at the situation, it did not pretend to have forgotten that its support of Willkie had been enthusiastic. Franklin was now the nation's leader; let him prove worthy:

The nation looks to Mr. Roosevelt—those who voted for him, and surely the greater number of those who did not—to understand its needs and give potency to its desires. He has assumed a responsibility such as has fallen to no man's lot in this continent before. He has the gifts to bear it bravely and well, and, in all friendliness let it be added, the defects of those gifts.

The press on the whole was unforgiving and not to be cajoled by Franklin's recent acceptance of assistance from more dependable sources. The Indianapolis *News* put it this way:

In the minds of a good many people, at least the 22,000,000 who did not vote for him in November, the Roosevelt election for the third term is fraught with peril. The risk is that the country will so weaken itself by the improvidence of the New Deal visionaries that it will be unable to survive as a country of free men in the inevitable reckoning.

The Columbus *Dispatch* was even more fearful:

The President owes to the American people the preservation of their popular form of government. The question of how he discharges that obligation will be the most widely debated subject during the next four years.

What the White House Christmas was like that year—the last before war actually began—we can only guess. There are accounts of the actual proceedings. They do not tell us much about the minds and hearts of those involved, but they do allow us to make some guesses. Let me quote the summary made by the *United States News*:

The master of the house stood bareheaded in the dusk before a huge red cedar on the browned turf of the ellipse, at the South End of the lawn, and listened to carols. Then he touched a silver switch, and 10,000 watts of hand-dipped stars opened the Christmas season for the good people of the United States.

A few minutes later, President Roosevelt, in a solemn but neighborly mood, told the 6,000 listeners before him, and the millions on the air: "Let us make this Christmas a merry one for the little children in our midst. For us of maturer years it cannot be merry."

Only one grandchild was there that Christmas to be made merry; that was Franklin III, son of Franklin Jr.; but Diana Hopkins was there again, and much was made of the motherless girl. The presidential Christmas schedule as the newspapers reported it was formidable. The activities of those few days—and the known ones were probably no more than half the total—seem beyond the capacity of any man to sustain over any long period. Yet this, or most of it, was the usual burden of those days:

A party in his private oval room for members of the Executive Office staff (225) with a small present for each (a miniature likeness of Fala on a silver key ring); a party in the East Room for the household staff (again a gift for everyone); two Christmas dinners at which Franklin carved; the stocking-hanging on the big bedroom mantle—one for each, including Fala; emptying of the stocking next morning; telephoning to all absent members; inspection and opening of a full truckload of gifts; a visit, with all the family, to church; a ball, this Christmas for the Morgenthaus' debutante daughter; and, not to be missed, the reading of the Carol.

But one reporter took the trouble to catalogue what he assumed was on the presidential mind:

. . . such general problems as speeding the defense program, speeding aid to Britain; such specific problems as naming a new Ambassador to London, a new governor of Puerto Rico; issuing the necessary executive orders regarding the new Office for Production Management; writing four speeches and statements, the third-term inaugural; the state-of-the-union report, to be delivered by the President in person to Congress January 7, and the first "fireside chat" to the American people since his re-election—on the "present emergency."

Franklin was a man who carried a load. If he did it with the appearance of ease and competence, it was because he was by now quite certain of his direction and of its rightness. There were trials and crises ahead, but the means for meeting them were being prepared. He had done all he could.

27

The fireside chat on "the state of the emergency" was made on December 29, 1940. This was called among the White House intimates the "arsenal of democracy" speech because of the fortunate invention and inclusion of that phrase. It was certainly one of the most telling speeches Franklin ever made, thrown as it was against the prevailing background of deepening acrimony and confusion. The interventionists were at the moment speaking softly, trying to appear reasonable, but the isolationists were actively noisy and indignant. They controlled many powerful newspapers and seemed to be carrying opinion with them. A Gallup poll showed that 60 per cent of Americans wanted to aid Britain even at the risk of war; but, on the other hand, only 12 per cent favored going to war deliberately. The inconsistency in this was typical of the time. It is no more than exact to say that many Americans were divided in their own minds, one moment intent on peace, the next indignant to the point of wanting to act.

The America First group was presently joined by others.[1] There was still a receptive audience for opponents of further involvement in "the European mess." The isolationists more savagely than ever denounced the "imperialist war" in Europe, and Franklin for being "Anglophile"; but they also continued to demand the seizure of Greenland, the Azores, Bermuda, the Bahamas, and other miscellaneous outlying possessions of the Europeans. The senators among them were especially belligerent and ready with advice. Wheeler—just re-elected and so feeling safe—told reporters that if Franklin wanted to he could make peace in Europe. Asked how, he answered that Franklin could threaten to enter

[1] The noisiest was the No Foreign War Committee headed by Verne Marshall of the Cedar Rapids (Iowa) *Gazette*, who conveniently moved into Willkie's New York headquarters as the politicians moved out. Marshall appeared to have large funds for propaganda, and much attention was paid to him and to his pronouncements.

the war on the British side unless Hitler agreed to "reasonable" terms. Other senators—McCarran, Tydings, Tobey, Vandenberg, Holt, Johnson —agreed volubly with Wheeler.

Into the muddy turbulence of contention the words of the President who knew his own mind fell like a precipitant. There were many who felt that he had said what they had been groping for words to express. There was a notable calming, even though the debate over Lend-Lease was just beginning. What Franklin told his countrymen was that the course he had chosen to follow—aid to Britain—was the way of "least risk." He did not say again that he was confident of being able to stay out; instead he pointed out the growing intransigence of the dictators. Their program, he said, involved first the domination of all life in their own country, next the enslavement of Europe, and then, using Europe as a base, the conquest of all the rest of the world.

He went directly to the attitude made most of by the isolationists— that a negotiated peace was possible but that the administration was unwilling. "The United States," he said, "has no right or reason to talk of peace, until the day shall come when there is clear intention on the part of the aggressor nations to abandon all thought of dominating or conquering the world. . . ." As to the assertion, made so often by the isolationists, that the Nazis had no interest in attacking the United States, he said, "This is the same wishful thinking which has destroyed . . . so many conquered peoples . . . The vast resources and wealth of this hemisphere constitute the most tempting loot in the world."

Before ending he indulged an anger he seldom allowed himself to show. The Nazis, he said, have "in their background the concentration camp and the servants of God in chains . . . Shootings and chains and concentration camps are not simply transient tools but the very altars of modern dictatorships. They may talk of 'a new order' . . . but what they have in mind is but a revival of the oldest and the worst tyranny. In that there is no liberty, no religion, no hope . . ."

So began the fight for Lend-Lease. It would go on into 1941 for two months. But the isolationists in opposition would be more and more aware of thinning support. Events were running against them. The Germans were penetrating deep into the Balkans, but Wavell and his army had shown initiative in North Africa. There was a growing belief that, powerful as the Nazi armies were, there was real courage and ability left in Britain. It was worth supporting. It might yet beat off the threat from the continent. Not the least stimulant to this belief was the glowing and eloquent defiance of Churchill, something Franklin watched with professional admiration—and just a touch of jealousy.

No more than a few minutes after the signing of the Lend-Lease Act supplies were freed for shipment. And four days later Franklin made another historic address, this time to the White House correspondents.

Post-war
solution
Reactionary

It was carried over the radio networks of many countries in a dozen languages and rebroadcast by the British to the *verboten* receivers in Germany. "Let not the dictators of Europe or Asia doubt our unanimity now"—was its burden. But he specified in it for the first time the responsibilities that the nation, in passing the act, had accepted, and what was implied in the way of duties for American citizens:

> We shall have to make sacrifices—every one of us. . . . Whether you are in the armed services; whether you are a steel worker or a stevedore; a machinist or a housewife, a farmer or a banker . . .—to all of you it will mean sacrifice in behalf of your country and your liberties. . . .
>
> You will have to be content with lower profits . . . You will have to work longer at your bench, or your plow, or your machine, or your desk. . . .[2]

But the most interesting passage in this speech was Franklin's first reference to his thoughts about the post-war world. They foreshadowed important things to come. It was clear that, in spite of pressures and harassments, his mind was already busy with new projects far ahead of any possible realization:

> . . . when . . . dictatorships disintegrate . . . then our country must continue to play its great part in the period of world reconstruction for the good of humanity. . . . We believe that any nationality, no matter how small, has the inherent right to its own nationhood.
>
> We believe that the men and women of such Nations . . . can, through the processes of peace, serve themselves and serve the world by protecting the common man's security; improve the standards of healthful living; provide markets for manufacture and for agriculture. Through that kind of peaceful service every Nation can increase its happiness, banish the terrors of war, and abandon man's inhumanity to man.
>
> Never, in all our history, have Americans faced a job so well worth while. May it be said of us in the days to come that our children and our children's children rise up and call us blessed.[3]

It is recorded that this speech was received with more enthusiasm by the newspapermen present than any other of Franklin's addresses at any time. And it undoubtedly appealed directly to the simple humanitarianism of his audience. It was argued later by those who believed in European integration that this was unfortunate, because it encouraged a line of policy which, in the true sense of the word, was reactionary. It was pure Wilsonianism. It called up a nostalgia for the old shibboleths, including that fatal "self-determination for small nations," which had dominated the bargaining at Paris in 1918. But it is unlikely that the approval or disapproval of the newsmen affected the issue one way or the other. It was already settled.

[2] *Public Papers*, 1941 vol., pp. 64–65.
[3] Ibid., pp. 60 ff.

Could FDR profit from WW's errors?

The principle of fractionalization in the Treaty of Versailles, according to the dissenting view, had set up the numerous non-viable but jealous and quarrelsome governments of central Europe whose bickerings and intrigues had led on to the renewed crises of the thirties. But to Wilsonian liberals, self-determination was a theory beyond the reach of fact or experience. And this first pronouncement showed that Franklin shared their dogma. In the more than a score of years since the armistice of 1917, there had been no change; the liberal mind was still fixed on smallness, on independence, on self-government.

This, it will be understood, came out of the same package of principles as the dominating ideas of the Second New Deal. It was consistent with domestic free enterprise, atomization, competition, and, wherever it existed, the breaking up of monopoly. Trust busting was appropriately having a belated revival,[4] but it is hard to believe that it was regarded by Franklin, the experienced statesman and executive, as the principle that ought to dominate future organization.

Or perhaps it was so regarded by him. I have to confess that I am unable to say whether it was or not. Franklin was extremely sensitive, all during the development of the international crisis, to the possibility that the same fatal errors which had wrecked Wilson's plans might be repeated. It is not too much to say that this fear dominated all his planning. Studying his problem with this in mind, he must have judged that Wilson had failed to commit enough influential politicians to the settlement so laboriously arrived at. This was an error that must, whatever the cost, be avoided. The United States must not be a holdout from the United Nations as it had been from the League of Nations. Beginning with the appointment of Knox and Stimson to the cabinet, he had begun to assemble the necessary support. It would continue by careful cultivation of senatorial collaboration at every step.

But Wilson's principles for the settlement had been unexceptionable from the point of view of liberal approval. Whether they were congruous with the world to which they were to be applied, or whether they were not, it was clear from this time on—the beginning of 1941—that they were to be dominant again. It was as though the intervening years had been banished by some magic. Wilson, instead of being a stubborn

---

[4] In a Department of Justice now captained by Robert H. Jackson. The enlarged and revivified Anti-Trust Division of the department had been placed under the management of Thurman Arnold, a highly competent professor of law from Yale University, who had done many smaller chores for the administration before this assignment. His activities naturally met head on the expansion of industry for war purposes which involved consolidation, co-ordination, central management, and monopoly—all the qualities anathema to the liberal progressives. Before long, trust busting was quietly put away for the duration of the crisis. But quite some stir had been made by the Arnold activities before they had to be smothered.

Scotsman, had in a new incarnation been transformed into a clever opportunist. His work was to be finished in 1945 by a junior who had learned from the failure of 1919, and finished, moreover, on the same liberal model.

Perhaps it *had* to be finished before the next stage of world development could be entered on. Nehru, the Indian leader, addressing himself to this inconsistency some years later, would remark that nations had to be *independent* before they could *co-operate*. To his mind this served as justification, at a stage, for an independence he otherwise deplored.[5] Wilsonianism, reappearing now as Rooseveltism, looked toward association, but a voluntary one, as opposed to the involuntary gathering in of neighbors and satellites by totalitarian states with the power to compel it. If that was so, it was too bad that the achieving of independence everywhere had been delayed so long. If small states had been obsolete in Wilson's time, they were far more dangerously so two decades later.

Franklin had been caught in this dilemma before—when in 1934 he had chosen atomism as against collectivism in industrial organization. So now he elected for independence as against integration. In the latter case, as in the former, it was so obviously good politics that political reasons for it are impossible to dismiss. Cheers came even from the skeptical newspapermen. It might not comport well with the historical drift, but it comported perfectly with the frustrated emotions still entertained in democratic heads.

There is no evidence that this decision—any more than others—was ever discussed with anyone while it was developing. There is every indication that it was not. Such intimates as Sherwood and Rosenman did not even recognize that any decision had been made. Neither, for instance, did Harry S. Truman, nor any others who are of record. And perhaps the truth is that none had been made. Self-determination was so much part of the accepted liberal furniture that it was taken for granted. If Franklin had chosen otherwise he would probably have had the same treatment his momentary venture into collectivism had elicited in 1933.

Here at the outset of the momentous venture given authorization by the Lend-Lease Act, it must be understood that Franklin's last grand undertaking lay beyond. War was not his object, but peace, a peace within a framework made as secure as such things can be on this earth. As to this framework, there were two alternatives, as we should recognize—not one possible choice only, but two. Franklin had chosen one.

[5] But Nehru conspicuously failed to honor the principle within India; also, he, unlike the Burmese leaders, chose to stay within the larger entity, the Commonwealth.

We must see what it was and try to understand why it was selected.[6] The alternatives can be thought of as *voluntary* and *involuntary*, perhaps, although these are loaded words, easily distorted to mean *free* or *forced*. The fact is that any majority exercises restraint on a minority, in the sense that one can do what it wants to do and the other cannot. A majority is voluntary and a minority is involuntary. It is also fact that democracies have discovered no better way of coming to collective decisions than by voting—that is, the establishment of a consensus. It is, indeed, the very essence of democracy that the larger number shall prevail and shall not be overruled by the lesser number. Any other principle has been found to result in something like anarchy. If the minority is able to prevent action, nothing is done; if it is allowed to secede, the integrity of the whole is disrupted. A reasonable protection of its rights, when they do not affect adversely the decisions of the majority, is granted, to a greater or less degree, if for no other than humanitarian reasons. And the rule is made that a dissenter shall be punished only for acting, not for thinking. But that the majority must prevail is essential.

Why Europe should not be considered as a whole, and why the United States should, rests on historical, not on moral justification. The United States enforces its union, does not permit secession, and extends majority rule even over those areas where consent would not voluntarily be given. The principle of self-determination, if applied in the United States, would long ago have broken up the nation. On one occasion it almost did.

If it is attempted to apply a standard of oppression it is impossible to distinguish between discipline in the interest of the whole and punishment beyond necessity. The matter inevitably escapes the reach of fact or logic and becomes claim and counterclaim.

There is something in human nature that reacts against pressures on individuals or groups—unless the individual happens to be on the majority side. Then he shows a high immunity to indignation, and consent to the rule of the whole, even if harsh, is granted without qualms. So Americans accepted integration at home in the name of Union but regarded the same principle when enforced by the dictators as intolerable. Franklin was subtle enough to understand that a principle might be right, even though its pursuit might be wrong. But this, like domestic collectivism, was too difficult for public debate.

These considerations were as germane to the struggling Europe of 1939–40 as they had been in 1917–18. There were those to whom it seemed possible that the conflict had arisen all over again because it

[6] This involves the question whether the world organization brought about in one or the other way would or would not be viable. But that is really a later question. Looked at from 1940, the question was how the organization should be attained.

had not been properly settled in the earlier struggle. If Europe had been integrated then, instead of divided, there might have been revolts among minorities, rising even to revolutions; but there would not have been war calling for American intervention. The majority would have had a means of expression and would have prevailed.

It was the claim of certain dissenters that war should be regretted even as a resort in extreme circumstances. Let Europe reach integration, they argued, and there would be a viable economy. Viability would bring reasonable tranquillity because there would be prosperity. This did not suit the British, it was argued, because the British wanted Europe to be divided and weak. Only when this was the case could she feel safe—the more so because she must control the seas to maintain the Empire's communications. A Europe united might be a threat. But why, asked the dissenters, should the United States enforce the British desire for a disunited Europe?

Franklin felt compelled to risk his leadership on the denial of this argument. The dictators were "aggressors"; they were oppressors of minorities; they were therefore immoral. It was protested that "aggressor" was another loaded word, a very effectual one, but invidious and selective, and so unfair. It connoted oppression of the weak and the setting up of alien rule. The entity called Czechoslovakia, for instance, took on a sacred connotation. It had not existed until the Treaty of Versailles, of course, and it had its own unhappy minorities; but sympathy for the Czechs threatened by Hitler seemed unaffected by such facts. Hitler was an aggressor. Czechoslovakia was an innocent victim.

By 1941 the whole argument was, indeed, escaping reason. There was a struggle between propagandistic claims. There were those who said that Hitler was unifying Europe belatedly and that all its peoples would be better off when the job had been done. Franklin said that ruthless force was being used to overthrow "legitimate" governments and that such lawlessness could not be condoned. He had by now gone farther. He was saying that the aggressors were intending to conquer the United States. That it was taking a long leap to claim that the United States was in the same danger from Hitler as Austria or Czechoslovakia would seem obvious to another generation, but it was hotly supported by the interventionists of 1940, and Franklin's assertions were as solemn as any he ever made.

They had more trouble—and Franklin had more trouble—about Britain. When it came to conquering and suppressing, the British record was certainly second to none—that had been the way of Empire—and the arguments for aiding Britain had to be put on other grounds. An admirable courage in defiance of threatening invasion was admitted even by the isolationists; and this could be traded on for the further contention that conquest of the isles would bring immediate danger to the United States.

The argument, as it developed in the United States, between Germans and British was pretty well confused by loose and often ridiculous charges and countercharges. In this contest the British, ably abetted by Franklin, had by far the better of it. And they deserved to. Hitler, apart from any exaggeration or distortion, was a detestable character, and the means he used were utterly indefensible. He was always cutting the ground from under those in the United States who argued for his mission as the unifier of Europe. In this he was a worthy successor to the egotistical Kaiser who had led the former German attempt to conquer the continent. But the merits of the case had nothing to do with Hitler's character or behavior. He was an unfortunate advocate.

That the differences about Europe between the isolationists and the interventionists in the United States were strictly matters of means would be amply proved by the attempts made in the years after the war to bring about the establishment of a "United States of Europe." It would then be argued that the risk of recurring war, likely to involve the United States, could be liquidated only by creating a federal union on the American model. And much diplomatic energy would be wasted in trying to force a union into being. The attempt would fail, of course; and that failure might seem to be an argument for Hitler's method— which might have succeeded if the United States had not intervened to rescue oppressed people from aggressors; that is, to enforce self-determination. The chaos of the post-war years would make independence and disunity appear very dangerous indeed. Whether this would constitute a practical justification for allowing union under the auspices of a Hitler will always be a hotly argued question. At any rate, Franklin had no doubts, although an acrimonious and confused debate made thinking difficult.

There were no more questions of substance in Franklin's mind. Nor, for that matter, were there many concerning method. But he still could not be certain of his following. Was there a majority against Hitler? Presumably he still thought not, because Lend-Lease was definitely a measure short of war and was consistently presented and defended as no more than assistance to those who were defending themselves against the aggressors. The isolationists had not yet been routed. And although their case was undermined continually by the horrors and excesses of the Nazi regime, they could always fall back on the effective argument about "the boys being sent to fight for English imperialism." Franklin's retort that American coasts were vulnerable as long as an aggressive enemy held positions bordering the seas did not convince parents with sons of an age to serve. Many of them were simply and understandably against war.

These sons were now being called into training, and the agonies of separation were affecting families all over the land. The reverberations of parents' concern were naturally felt in Washington. They reached the White House mostly by way of Capitol Hill, but they were not long delayed. Representatives, having made administration as difficult as possible, always expect perfection in the operation of their laws; and they never, under any circumstances, admit any responsibility for shortcomings. This characteristic had especially exaggerated results in the months just before and just after Pearl Harbor, when a monstrous expansion of preparatory activity was taking place. Boys were sent to half-finished camps for training. They fell ill and were not properly cared for, or they lacked all sorts of equipment and had ill-prepared officers. They wrote home to say so. Parents communicated indignantly with their congressmen, and the congressmen demanded to know from the White House why such conditions existed. The executives responsible —civilians or Army officers—dodged. It was impossible to locate any individual who was at fault.

Presently, however, one of the most remarkable of all the figures of World War II would be miraculously discovered. He was a lieutenant colonel who had been most lately in charge of the Works Progress Administration in New York. His sudden rise to a lieutenant-generalship in charge of all Army construction[7] would solve the problem in the way genius always does—by performing miracles. Brehon B. Somervell soon had camp construction in order and the famous Pentagon built. For cutting red tape and getting things done there never had been anyone like him. Many an overpassed senior and many a disgruntled property owner or contractor would gleefully have seen him boiled in oil. But he was just what Marshall needed, and so long as Marshall and the President were behind him he could not be reached.[8]

Something of the pressure and confusion of these months can be realized by studying the amazing records being made in every direction —not only in the building of camps where millions of men would be trained, but in the construction of ships to make good the frightful losses from submarine attack; in the fabulous expansion of the Navy, including the small patrol ships, resisted so long by the Navy but finally given high priority; in the building of plants and the manufacture of machines to create from nothing planes enough to darken German skies in another two years; in the making of tanks and arms of all sorts and other muni-

[7] Formally he was commanding general, Army Service Forces.
[8] When the emergency passed, the enemies he had made nearly caught up with him; but his achievement has always seemed to me one of the most remarkable of all the tremendous ones called out by the national need. He made effective use of civilian expediters, one of them the remarkable Madigan half of the Madigan-Hyland firm in New York, which was responsible for so much of Robert Moses' reputation as a builder of public works.

tions needed by armed forces expanding into the millions; in bolstering the transportation and communication facilities needed to implement all these arrangements; in providing housing and other facilities for defense areas—in doing, in fact, a thousand unaccustomed things in entirely unaccustomed ways.

When the phenomena were marshaled in figures and charts, as could be done afterward, the vastness of the achievement could be appreciated. It was without precedent. Things were done every day that could not be done. And if there seemed at the time, to those affected, more failures than successes, that is not strange. And it would be expected that, as Americans do, they would complain. In those weeks and months of turmoil, no one seems to have been praised, everyone was denounced, and the whole nation appeared to be busier with recrimination than with work. But these irritated comments must have come mostly from people annoyed because their own miracles were being prevented from occurring. They must find someone to blame. The fact is that prodigies were performed.

Whether Franklin, when he set fantastic (as it seemed) goals for every sort of expansion, actually expected them to be reached, no one can say. Very evidently Batt or Knudsen or one of the other industrialists who had some idea of the potentialities in a system of mass production which had never really been free to operate had briefed him. The goals were almost always reached and were often proved to be too low. But it was he, and no other, who had to protect the operators like Somervell and Knudsen (later Nelson, Wilson, and others). They had to be free to work until their results could show, and this was sometimes a very trying length of time. Deliberately, for once, he gathered to himself all the complaints and recriminations. But even he, used to punishment as he was, could take only so much of it before reacting. He was actually made sick by the strain along about May of 1941.

But for that near collapse there were other reasons than what was happening in Georgia, Arizona, or Michigan, as the earth was ripped up by bulldozers, as the steel mills roared and the railway trains moved back and forth across the country. He had before him every morning as he woke and every day as he worked the determination of dozens of interlocking concurrent problems, all of which affected each other and none of which could be miscalculated without momentous consequences throughout the mounting effort. What measures, for instance, should he take to check the submarine menace and protect British shipping? At the moment the proportion of goods leaving American ports which never arrived on the other side of the Atlantic was almost too frightening to calculate, and it was getting worse.[9] How far could he

[9] There would be no relief until the Quebec Conference (Quadrant) in August of 1943.

go—and by what devices—in checking Japan? The game in the Pacific was to embarrass the Japanese without precipitating a declaration of war, because such a declaration would free them for depredations in the South Pacific. What treatment of Russia would be best under the ambiguous circumstances? How ought occupied France to be regarded —as an outright enemy? It would obviously be worse if Hitler's occupation extended to the Mediterranean and the Pyrenees, or perhaps Gibraltar, than if it was limited to half of France.

Because the answers to these problems—and many others—obviously called for temporizing, even to the extent, on occasion, of humiliation, they were far more difficult to make and to defend than belligerent expressions of national aims. These problems of delays, of picking the right time for action, are hard for a politician who is under constant harassment; they are harder when they are invested with the consequence of a nation's fate.

But no one could share this responsibility. Franklin must always, himself alone, be ready with the finished calculation when the propitious moment arrived. When someday Admiral Stark (and later Admiral King) asked whether ships could fire back at attacking submarines, or General Marshall wanted to know whether, in his talks with the British mission (there had been one in Washington since last fall, publicized as little as possible lest the Anglophobes should be stirred up), a timetable of the American build-up could be furnished, he must give an answer. So, too, when it had to be decided whether the Japanese invasion of Indochina should be protested and in what degree. Should an actual threat now be resorted to with the Navy far from ready to make it good?

These instances furnish no more than the merest intimation of the content crowding Franklin's mind in these months. From the pressures and complications there was no possibility of escape and very little relief. If his problems had had an unbearable complexity before, that complexity was now infinitely increased. Every entangled item was swollen with national importance, and every decision was his alone to make.

Even the making of a speech in these circumstances had such possibilities of disaster that its preparation was extraordinarily difficult. Sherwood tells about one to be made in mid-May. The occasion was Pan American Day, always a favorite State Department occasion for emphasizing hemispheric solidarity. But it came at a time this year when even Hopkins was forgetting his chosen role and urging a bolder course. So, too, was Stimson, especially, but also others like Wallace, Ickes, and La Guardia were belligerent beyond discretion. At the same time Nazi (and Communist) propaganda was at its height. Lindbergh's radio addresses were just next to treasonable, but they had an unmistakably

570

receptive audience. Never had the nation's state of mind been in more delicate balance.

That a speech would be made had been announced, but what could a President of the United States say who at the moment wanted just not to rock the boat? He wanted production to accumulate momentum; soldiers, sailors, and airmen to be trained and to move across the seas; and the Japanese not to have an excuse for declaring war. And he wanted as little as possible to be said about any of it:

. . . It was obviously impossible for him to refer to his plans for Iceland and patrols—or to the possibility of an American occupation of the Azores—or to the fact that part of the Pacific fleet was at that moment moving into the Atlantic. . . . The tension was heightened by a number of public utterances by high officers of the government, notably Stimson and Knox, which seemed to place the United States on the very brink of war. Roosevelt had read those speeches before they were delivered. It was generally assumed that he approved the position taken . . .[10]

Caught in a dilemma he was not ready to resolve, Franklin simply postponed speaking—a craven solution, perhaps, as was hinted broadly by those it did not suit, but a sound one. He did not like what was said by either aggrieved faction, however, and he showed his irritation:

During those days in mid-May Roosevelt spent a great deal of time in bed and rarely went to his office. He said that this was one of the most persistent colds he had ever had. One day, after a long talk with him in his bedroom, I came out and said to Missy LeHand, "The President seems in fine shape to me. He didn't cough or sneeze or even blow his nose the whole time I was in there and he looked wonderfully well. What is really the matter with him?" Missy smiled and said, "What he's suffering from most of all is a case of sheer exasperation." Indeed, he seemed at the time to be exasperated with practically everyone . . .

Very few people were allowed to see the President during those days. There were a lot of very nervous men in high places in Washington wondering what was the reason for this inaccessibility and, when the President should finally emerge from it, which way he would jump. . . .

It may appear in looking back that there was a steady succession of events leading to the climax of that next December, but we understand from this—and other evidence—that the succession was not a steady one and that the participants who were living through it were far from certain how it would end. Appeasement—for the course Franklin was following seemed that to his annoyed associates—might yet avert American participation.[11]

[10] This and the following quotation are from *Roosevelt and Hopkins*, Chapter XIII.

[11] The postponed speech, mentioned by Sherwood, was finally written and was delivered on May 27. Toward its end an "unlimited national emergency" was

He got to Hyde Park for an early June weekend. But until the historic journey to Argentia in August, there were few other breaks.[12] He was kept steadily at work in Washington day after day, week after week, never escaping "from the wash," and never able to think of the old accustomed things—his trees, his stamps, Warm Springs, and all the rest.

Before going on to speak of the meeting in the far northern bay where the U.S.S. *Augusta* and H.M.S. *Prince of Wales* kept a rendezvous on a misty summer morning, I must refer to another matter—the beginning of that work which led, in 1942, to the fission of uranium in a self-sustaining reaction, and then in 1945 to the Alamogordo trial and to the destruction, some weeks later, of Hiroshima and Nagasaki. The importance to the world of this work was to be incalculable. It would not bulk large in Franklin's life because, as a project, it did not mature until after his death. But his name will forever be associated with the undertaking—and rightly so, because another kind of person would have dismissed as fanciful the suggestion that anything so fantastic should be given serious consideration. It is not irrelevant, governmental processes being what they were, to mention that before its consummation the project ate up two billions of dollars. That anything on such a scale could be done without disclosing to more than a few individuals—none of them legislators—what was going on is not the least remarkable aspect of the whole enterprise. Imagine its being done, for instance, in the pre-war months!

Perhaps the consummation was possible because the A-bomb was, in a way, a product of something larger—the systematic marshaling of scientific resources on a scale never before even contemplated. And it should be remembered, in this connection, that the bomb was only one of several tremendous advances resulting from the scientists' labors. Radar and jet engines were others.

An account of these scientific developments is to be found in *Scientists against Time;*[13] it can only be referred to here. But it is probably true to say that the peril in which the British lived for several years, and from which it was obvious they could not be rescued by conventional military means, is what gave the special organization for scientific

announced. This allowed him to go much farther in taking responsibility for deliveries to Britain. The reception of the speech was mostly favorable. The opposition had been overestimated. Still, he continued to be wary and put off asking for the further changes he had in mind for the Neutrality Act.

[12] There had been one on the *Potomac* and a cruise in Bahama waters in early spring—the last, almost, of the "fishing trips" he depended on for resuscitation when he was exhausted.

[13] By James Phinney Baxter (Boston: Little, Brown, 1946). I have written further about the development of atomic weapons and their effects in the post-war decade in *A Chronicle of Jeopardy* (University of Chicago Press, 1955).

research its start. And it should be said that, although the more spectacular of the achievements occurred under American auspices, the contributions to their development came very largely from citizens of other nations—the British, of course, but also others. For the names of Einstein, Fermi, Szilard, Wigner, Bethe, and Teller, for instance, are directly connected with the bomb—and not one of them was American by birth. Farther back, the preliminary scientific work which made it possible was done mostly abroad—in Italy, in Germany, in Denmark, in Britain.

The Americans most responsible for the beginnings of this mobilization were Vannevar Bush, Karl T. Compton, James B. Conant, and Frank B. Jewett. These, talking over the problem, proposed a National Defense Research Committee—to consist of some twelve members appointed by the President. It was to co-ordinate all scientific work and to be authorized to contract with universities and other institutions for its actual carrying out. It was this proposal that Bush took to Hopkins in 1940. Hopkins arranged an interview with Franklin. They talked only a few minutes, it is recorded, and Franklin agreed without argument.

So it was begun. Under the committee many important pieces of work were taken in hand, particularly in weaponeering, radar, sonar, and aeronautics. It was available when in 1940 the possibility of a bomb was brought to Franklin's attention. It was able to organize and distribute the research necessary so that within two years fission had been obtained.

The startling suggestion that a bomb to end all bombs might be developed was made to the Navy Department in the spring of 1939 by Enrico Fermi,[14] but it was a letter from Albert Einstein to Franklin that really started operations. Szilard, whose activities in subsequent years would be so fruitful, persuaded Einstein to write the letter and, looking about for someone who had access to the White House, hit on Alexander Sachs, an economist known to Franklin from NRA days. Sachs did his intermediary work well. Franklin, at his suggestion, appointed an Advisory Committee on Uranium with Lyman J. Briggs, Director of the Bureau of Standards, as its chairman. The committee held meetings in October of 1939 and April of 1940. By that time the scientific world was alerted, although the whole matter was hidden from laymen. Funds for development began to be found. The Carnegie Institution contributed some of them, but the armed services were soon able to find others. And by July of 1940 the scientists felt able to inform Franklin that they believed they might succeed.

From this point on the story of the bomb becomes too complex to be

[14] Fermi was an Italian Nobel Prize winner who had escaped from Fascist Italy and was a professor at Columbia University, where Urey was also working.

followed in detail. The work was now put under the OSRD.[15] Special committees for development and review were formed, and there was much going back and forth to confer with the British.[16]

By the time the United States was actually at war the project was far advanced, but there were still many problems to be solved, and no time could be set for the production of the actual bomb. It would still be a year before the last and worst bottleneck was broken and controlled fission in the atomic pile achieved at Chicago. From that time on it would be largely a question not of theoretical progress but of engineering technique.

Almost from the first, and with growing concern, the scientists anticipated a race with the German scientists. Much of the groundwork had been laid in German laboratories, and in fact it was two Germans who achieved the first reaction which pointed directly to Alamogordo. Otto Hahn and Friedrich Strassman, bombarding uranium with neutrons, had produced barium. Speculating on this, two Jewish exiles in Denmark, Lise Meitner and her nephew, Otto Frisch, guessed that what had happened was that the nucleus had split into two parts. Nils Bohr, the noted Dane, carried this news to a conference on theoretical physics held at the Carnegie Institution in Washington. This was in January 1939. Many of the physicists present hurried back to their laboratories to verify the reported result. There was, in fact, great excitement in the scientific world.

This excitement gradually focused in the later work at Chicago, then at Los Alamos and at Oak Ridge. About these possibilities, until told of it by Sachs first and then Bush, Franklin was as innocent of knowledge as any other layman. It was, however, characteristic that he should at once accept the possibility of revolutionary change and from then on follow developments with an interest rivaled only, apparently, by that of Churchill. The two were alike in their capacity to imagine results emerging from unorthodox sources; if they had not been, the war might well have ended in German victory. The bomb did not defeat the Axis; it came too late. But other scientific developments can be credited with contributions which were very possibly crucial—that which defeated the

[15] Office of Scientific Research and Development. Later the bomb was made the responsibility of the Manhattan District of the War Department and a general put in charge. It will not be further referred to here, but serious differences with the British would arise as soon as the military took charge, causing Churchill a good deal of anguish and complicating British-American relations.

[16] Churchill and the British scientists agreed that the work ought to be carried out in a more secure location, and for that purpose the leading scientists were sent to work at various centers where separate jobs were being done, all bearing on the central problem, most of them in the United States and notably at the universities of Chicago, Columbia, and California, and at Los Alamos and Oak Ridge.

submarines and mines, for instance, and enabled ships and planes to see beyond the horizon and through cloud and fog.

For our purpose here, the development of the bomb is of importance in illustrating Franklin's characteristic receptivity to what was novel. There is no better way to highlight this quality than to retell the famous remark of Admiral Leahy, who, after his service as Ambassador to Vichy France, would become Franklin's chief of staff—an office created to emphasize the authority of the Commander-in-Chief.[17] The admiral, when he heard about the bomb and who was working on it, remarked that he himself was an expert on explosives and that the idea of a super-bomb was damned professors' nonsense.

It was not in direct answer to this remark, but it might well have been, that Professor Harold Urey afterward pointed out something that Franklin instinctively knew. "No military man," Urey said, "ever invented a weapon." The military men were already getting a little above themselves in the pressure for expansion. Their inclination was to take everything into their own control. They resented any interference and any contribution from outside. It was Franklin who repeatedly forced them to accept the contributions of the scientists and other laymen. If there is one thing that can be said of him unequivocally by a biographer, it is that he knew how to make use of all the resources available; and among these, he learned very early, were the human repositories of skill and intelligence. He always had about him the best brains available. They were able to make a far larger contribution to the history of their generation because he sponsored and supported their ideas and their projects. He had to keep them isolated from politics; at least he tried to. But often they were in difficulty. From these situations he extricated himself and them as well as he could. But it was often awkward. The contribution of the scientists in wartime made intellectuals much more respectable.

The start of the research which ended in Hiroshima is, in historical perspective, a tremendous event. But, as one of the matters with which Franklin had to deal in 1940, it was not of great immediate concern; it was something for the future, something still speculative. In the present there was much else to think about. Speaking of immediate matters, it can now be understood, and it was clear to Franklin from the first moment—as it was to Churchill—that a turning point in the war was reached when Hitler invaded Russia. That this occurred even before the United States became a combatant makes it an even more notable event. It did not mean that the war would be won without the intervention of the United States, but it did mean that a situation had been created in which victory could much more hopefully be striven

[17] Leahy, for instance, as the President's representative, acted as chairman of the Joint Chiefs and was the ranking American on the Combined Chiefs.

for. If Hitler had chosen otherwise, the outcome might very well have been different. It seems now to have been an incredible stupidity. Franklin and Churchill instantly recognized it as such. But Hitler did have his reasons,[18] even if they proved to be mistaken.

The explanation is that he had not been able to reach an agreement with the Russians for the division of the world. From what has been learned since the war, it appears that Molotov was as tough with the Germans on his famous visit to Berlin in 1940 as he was to be later with Americans all during the decade of the cold war. He was, in fact, too tough; and Hitler concluded that any agreement made with him would be so costly as to be worthless to the Reich. Added to this was the Nazi antipathy to Communism. A number of times Hitler would intimate that he ought rather to be supported than opposed by the British in his Russian venture. The famous flight of his intimate, Rudolf Hess, to Britain was probably in the interest of such support. There were those in the United States who favored such a policy, and there was for some time a suspicion that Churchill had similar leanings. But from the first Franklin refused to entertain any such suggestion.

Hitler began to prepare for his Russian invasion months before it began, and almost at once British and American intelligence agents were aware of it. As a gesture of friendship—although there had been no favors to call it out—the information was passed on to the Russians. They appeared not to be impressed. Their characteristic suspicion and their preconceived distrust of "capitalist nations" would not allow them to believe that such good will was possible. They were, anyway, wide open to the German blitzkrieg. It penetrated deep into their heartland before winter set in to check it.

The German thrust toward the east, well prepared as it was, and executed with customary efficiency, was doomed to fail as Napoleon's campaign had failed, beaten by distance and winter. It was a long way to Moscow, even with motorized armies, and the hardships of campaigning in below-zero weather were immense. Presently, also, guerrillas went to work on the extended lines of communication. Altogether the difficulties were far greater than Hitler had anticipated. The effort was his nemesis.

The Russian armies fought better than the Germans expected—better, in fact, than anyone in the West expected. Franklin, Hopkins, and Churchill were very nearly alone in believing that they would hold out more than a few weeks. For the widespread adverse opinion there were several reasons. One was the singularly stupid behavior of American

---

[18] Although it still seems strange that he did not complete the British conquest before turning on Russia. The British believed that it was the defeat of the Luftwaffe by their fighter planes which made invasion impossible. But he might have come back for another battle.

Communists during the spring of 1941. Right up to the moment of the Nazi invasion, the propaganda line was that Franklin was "an imperialist warmonger." Strikes in important aircraft plants were inspired and the White House was picketed. All this had conditioned American opinion against the homeland of Communism in Russia. There was another influence as well. The Russian armies had not displayed any considerable effectiveness in the recent attack on Finland. And military men had concluded that the weakness was inherent and fatal. There would be, they thought, no very determined resistance to the German advance.

Military reports to Franklin were unanimous in predicting that the Red Army would be destroyed in about six weeks. That this belief was deep-seated and serious was confirmed by a report made by Stimson to Franklin after a day of canvassing the situation with Marshall and the War Plans Division. Russia would hold out, the generals said, for a "maximum" of three months. This time, they felt, must be utilized to "push, with the utmost vigor, our movements in the Atlantic theater of operations." Word came to Franklin that the British military had come to the same conclusion.

On the basis of these unconditional warnings, Franklin and Churchill might have made a strategic blunder of immense consequence. But they did not accept the view of the generals, and they took measures based on a directly opposite judgment. Churchill at once hailed Russia as an ally, and on June 24 Franklin announced United States support. This last determination was seriously sabotaged, and months afterward it had still not been implemented. The military were so certain that they knew best that they deliberately ignored presidential instructions. This infuriated Hopkins, and slowly he would bring about some change. But this would not be really effective until after Pearl Harbor.

The conference at Argentia[19] was prepared for in unorthodox fashion. Franklin sent Hopkins to visit Churchill. And from London, Hopkins, borrowing a Lend-Lease bomber with a British crew, flew to Moscow, by way of Archangel, for a face-to-face conference with Stalin. Hopkins was ill and the voyage was rough. When he returned to Britain and, with Churchill aboard the *Prince of Wales*, rendezvoused with Franklin on the *Augusta*, he was almost in collapse. But his mission had been accomplished. In spite of military reluctance and Russian suspicion, an alliance had been made real. He knew what the Russians needed; he had confirmed Franklin's conviction that they would hold out. If he had had doubts about the nutcracker strategy, they were dispelled by Hopkins' report.

Franklin approached Argentia with a flare-up of his old gusto. His deceit of the press was elaborate; he succeeded in concealing, until after

---

[19] Held in August 1941.

the meeting, that he was on any mission any more important than his usual recreational enjoyment of naval life.[20] Actually it was the first of several meetings with Churchill, both backed by their respective staffs, in which the principles were laid down for the conduct of the war. It was still an undeclared war[21] so far as the United States was concerned, but now that Lend-Lease was in effect and responsibility accepted for patrols at sea, it was very little short of belligerence. Nevertheless, it was somewhat removed, and the distinction was maintained by Franklin with the utmost care.

There issued from the conference the famous Atlantic Charter. But there were other topics on the agenda. These concerned the war both in the West and in the East. Yet it has to be said again that, although he joined with Churchill in a statement of war aims, Franklin did not regard American participation as necessarily following. Even though the flanks of the route across the North Atlantic had been protected by the occupation of Iceland as well as the establishment of bases in the Caribbean and the South Atlantic, full responsibility for convoying had not been accepted. The one instruction Hopkins had been given for his mission to Churchill and Stalin had been "no talk of war." And Franklin did not regard the proceedings at Argentia as inconsistent with this.

The Charter itself was a statement of principles on which the leaders "based their hopes for a better world." There were, of course, the "Four Freedoms," already set out by Franklin, but there was much more. There was, for instance, a rather surprising agreement by Churchill to freedom of the seas and to self-determination. Even though the Prime Minister had reservations, it shows how powerful a hand Franklin played that he should have gained such verbal concessions. There were, as the conference got down to work, two drafts of the "aims." One was that of Welles; the other was that of Churchill's aide, Sir Alexander Cadogan. There were several compromises. Yet who would have expected Churchill to agree to such statements as this of American-British intentions?

. . . they will endeavor, with due respect for their existing obligations, to further the enjoyment by all States, great or small, victor or vanquished, of access, on equal terms, to the trade and to the raw materials of the world . . .

Or this:

. . . after the final destruction of the Nazi tyranny, they may hope to see established a peace which will afford to all nations the means of dwelling in

[20] He sailed from New London on the *Potomac* on August 3, transferred to the *Augusta* at sea, and arrived at the rendezvous on August 10.
[21] This was, in fact, the title given their elaborate book covering this period by W. L. Langer and S. Everett Gleason (New York: Harper, 1953).

safety within their own boundaries, and which will afford assurance that
the men in all the lands may live out their lives in freedom from fear
want.

Then there was the "eighth point":

. . . all of the nations of the world, for realistic as well as spiritual reasons,
must come to the abandonment of the use of force. Since no future peace
can be maintained if land, sea or air armaments continue to be employed
by nations which threaten, or may threaten, aggression outside of their frontiers, they believe, pending the establishment of a wider and permanent
system of general security, that the disarmament of such nations is essential. . . .[22]

I have spoken before of Franklin's continual watchfulness lest Wilson's mistakes be repeated. One of these, he felt, was the inclusion of
the League in the peace treaty. In the argument over the point just
quoted, Franklin refused to accept a British version which included the
setting up of a formal organization. Such action, he felt, should wait
until some time had passed, and then be taken only if a big-power police force had created the conditions in which it might succeed. Welles'
draft made no reference to general security, and Churchill said this
omission would create opposition among the extreme internationalists.
Franklin replied simply that the time had come for "complete realism."

Considering what was to happen afterward at Dumbarton Oaks when
the permanent organization was shaped, this important principle may
seem to have been given up by Franklin between 1941 and 1944. I
think it was only modified. And it has to be remembered that he did
not live to participate in the final proceedings at San Francisco. The
historian Basil Rauch, in considering this matter, seems to have reached
conclusions similar to mine.[23] Franklin's position, in the Argentia discussions, he agrees, showed an awareness of Wilson's mistake in insisting that the League Covenant be made part of the treaty. The League
had been unequal to the task of disarming the aggressors, reconstruct-
ing the devastated areas, and re-educating peoples "corrupted with
militarism." Only the great powers were equal to such demands. Their
forces had been built up to victory strength, and their will to reconstruct would not be "restricted by other governments which, lacking
power, lacked responsibility."

It is true that, as Churchill said, the "realistic" approach—that the
great powers must first establish discipline in the world before consign-
ing it to a permanent organization—risked opposition from the extreme
internationalists. But obviously Franklin's intention was to appeal to a
much wider constituency, including even the moderate dissenters who

[22] *Public Papers*, 1941 vol., pp. 314–15.
[23] Cf. *Roosevelt from Munich to Pearl Harbor*.

were so prevalent in the United States. It is to be noted that this approach was not objected to by Churchill. It was only at the request of Cadogan that any reference at all was made to a permanent organization. When he asked Welles for reconsideration, a final compromise draft was proposed and accepted. It was in this way that the phrase "pending the establishment of a wider and permanent system of general security" was inserted.

This may seem inconsistent with Franklin's later acceptance of the Dumbarton Oaks scheme. But when the Security Council provision in the United Nations Charter is examined, at least part of this feeling disappears. The Council would go some way to center control in the great powers; it was the only agency capable of acting. And its decisions had to be unanimous. The Assembly, in which all the nations were represented, could only discuss and recommend. And it was undoubtedly, it seems to me, because of the apparent inability of the smaller powers to interfere when they had no responsibility that he agreed to the Charter. Whether he would have thought in after years that he had been wise to do so, we cannot tell. But at any rate he would be preparing for the San Francisco conference as he died, and the American proposal to that conference would be substantially what was adopted as the governing protocol for the United Nations.[24]

The picture of Franklin and Churchill meeting to confer, surrounded by their experts, on battleships in a foggy northern bay, was certainly confirmation that it was intended to back to the limit those who were fighting the aggressors. It was more than that—it was a public acknowledgment that the United States had gone all the way over to a foreign policy based on collective security. Whether or not a formal organization of nations ever came about, there would be the same result from now on in the conferring and agreeing of the great powers—provided, of course, that Russia collaborated. That was still the important unknown. But Franklin had hopes.

Franklin, better than anyone else, realized that what had been agreed to at Argentia was subject to isolationist consent at home. That sentiment was, in fact, far from dead. On the last day of the conference the House back in Washington finally passed the bill extending the draft. It had been debated for almost a month with rising tempers in both camps. And it passed with a margin of only one vote. Such a sharp reminder of the opposition's strength was not necessary to make Franklin cautious. He was already cautious. He knew, if no one else did, that some sort of outrage by the aggressors would alone make it possible to move much farther.

[24] As will be seen, the evolution of the UN organization involved no violent revisions. There would be no considerable disagreement when Stalin was consulted.

In the next few months there must have been constant speculation in Franklin's mind about what the effect of various possible enemy outrages might be. It could not be foretold where they might originate. The submarines in the Atlantic might become more offensive and so fire American tempers, or the Japanese might go too far in the Pacific. But what kind of offense would create a genuine belligerent emotion it was impossible to calculate. Attacks on British or Dutch territory in Southeast Asia would probably not be violently reacted to, but suppose the Japanese attacked the Philippines. This seemed unlikely. But even the calculation of probable reaction from such a provocation was far from easy to make in the turbulence of that summer.

It is a study in delicate presidential sensitivity concerning public opinion to observe Franklin's behavior from late August to early December 1941. In the press conference following his return from Argentia he denounced such isolationists as Borah, Fish, and MacCracken in terms he seldom used. The euphoria of the Charter's success seemed to prevail over the scare from the close vote on the draft. And two weeks later he made the rousing fireside chat known familiarly as the "rattlesnake speech." It is not necessary to wait for a snake to strike, he said; the sounding of its rattle is enough. He went on to the crisis of December 7 feeling his way, reaffirming his detestation of the dictators and his support of those who were fighting them. But there was no further action to back the talk.

During this period, however, certain dispositions were made which would be extremely useful when it was necessary to make the convulsive effort which would follow December 7.

Already in July the land and sea forces of the Philippines had been placed under United States command. In case of invasion, plans long and carefully considered would go into effect. The Japanese would find such an enterprise difficult. And Pearl Harbor itself was alerted to the intensification of Japanese pressure, although no one actually anticipated trouble. But the most careful attention had to be given to the civilian expansion. Adjustment to emergency was being made with the greatest difficulty. There was the utmost reluctance, amounting almost to congressional refusal, to entertain any thought of price regulation, thus illustrating once again the power of pressure groups to prevent any legislation averse to their interests. Controls were an absolutely essential accompaniment of expanded production and unbalanced budgets. Without them the pressures on workers and other consumers would become intolerable. Disturbance would be sure to result and it might well be serious. But the first bill was not passed until a few days before Pearl Harbor and did not become effective until the last of the January following. Even then it yielded much less authority than had been asked. Whether it would be effective was a serious question.

But a Supply Priorities and Allocations Board could be set up by executive order, and that was done. This made more certain that munitions makers would have enough materials. It was plain enough, however, that there was still a long way to go. Record numbers of civilian automobiles were being manufactured, for instance; and Miami was entertaining extravagant tourists in fantastic numbers. There arose, in fact, a sharp public controversy between the business-as-usual contenders and the all-outers. It was a bitter and unhappy time. In October, Franklin asked of the Congress authorization to arm merchant ships (some had already been sunk by submarines). A week later he announced that supplies were being sent to Russia, and on the twenty-eighth he established finally the Office of Lend-Lease and named Hopkins administrator.

The blow of December 7 fell on a nation still divided, still unwilling to accept its responsibilities in a world at war. For Franklin it would be at once a release from the bindings of political caution and a beginning failure in his tenure as Commander-in-Chief. He may have been hoping in those last weeks that something would happen to break the mounting tension. He could not have wished that it would be the destruction that occurred at Pearl Harbor, the result of carelessness, divided command, and a fatuous certainty that the Japanese would fear to venture such an expedition.

28

The diplomatic delaying game played so long with the Japanese finally reached an end. They broke into violence. Contrary to all expectation, one of their moves was against Pearl Harbor; and because this was a complete surprise, the victory was a costly one for the fleet assembled there. It very nearly became a disaster for the nation, and did not go so far partly because the Japanese themselves could not credit their own success. They might have gone on to attack the West Coast or the Canal, but they withdrew. And when they came westward again they suffered a defeat from which they never really recovered. They also assaulted other places with success on December 7—the Philippines, notably—but no other attack had the same effect. The nation was first stunned, then it boiled with rage.

Before coming to Pearl Harbor it is necessary, even if only briefly, to examine its preliminaries. Documents discovered after the war would substantiate what was plain enough to Franklin and to Hull and Welles as they dealt with the Japanese movement in progress. There was to be established a Southeast Asia Co-prosperity Sphere (the phrase was intended to attract the approval of all the Orient) under Japanese hegemony. It was a mighty venture for a small power. But there was no lack of gall in the military make-up.

Chiang Kai-shek was still resisting in China but was having almost as much trouble with the Chinese Communists as with the invaders. There could be but feeble resistance anywhere short of India to the Japanese thrust; the rich Netherlands East Indies would not hold out long, and even Australia and New Zealand were in danger. The Philippines, of course, were high on the agenda for conquest.

It has been noted that it was Franklin's early decision, agreed to by his Chiefs of Staff (with some reluctance in the Navy), that the defeat of Germany should have first priority. In order to sustain this policy it was necessary to temporize with the Japanese, keeping talks going, returning soft answers even to demands so outrageous that they amounted almost to insults. The most recent phase of this interchange had opened with the arrival of a new negotiator from Japan in February of 1941. This was Admiral Nomura, an envoy obviously selected because it was believed that he would be especially acceptable in Washington. He was a "moderate," in contrast to the military extremists who held Tokyo in their grip. When, in August, Admiral Toyoda succeeded Mitsuoka as Foreign Minister, it was thought momentarily that American opposition to aggression had had some effect. But almost at once Japanese troops invaded Indochina and it was clear that no policy change had occurred.

It had been Nomura's plea in many conversations carried on privately in Hull's apartment that Japan genuinely wanted a peaceful settlement. The proposals he had to submit never bore this out, but Hull always found something in them to justify further consideration, and his temporizing went on until Hitler invaded Russia in June. Franklin then thought it quite possible that Japan might attack Russia from the east. He sent a message to Prince Konoye, the Premier, expressing the hope that rumors of such an attack were false. Konoye, in reply, sent a message denying such an intention but in turn asking whether the United States intended to intervene in Europe. Franklin replied that American aid to the Allies "in no way threatens the security of nations which have not joined the conflict on Hitler's side." It was a standoff.

When the Japanese move into Indochina began, Nomura's protestations were so obviously a cover for aggression that Welles was instructed to tell the Ambassador that no further basis existed for continuing conversations. Nevertheless, at Nomura's urging, Franklin consented to an off-the-record interview at the White House. In this conversation Franklin told Nomura that if Japan would withdraw from Indochina he would do all he could to persuade the Allied powers to declare Indochina neutral, on the pattern of Switzerland, provided Japan would also agree to neutralization.

The Japanese answer was so slow in coming that Franklin's patience ran out and pressure was applied by freezing her assets in the United States and denouncing the commercial agreements between the two countries. A little later, when Japanese demands on Thailand became known, Franklin extended his neutralization offer to that country as well. At the same time, to emphasize the penalties, he embargoed the export of aviation gasoline. This was a serious restriction, and it got a quick reaction. Nomura on August 6 handed Hull a reply to the American proposals of July 24.

At this time Franklin was on the way to Argentia aboard the *Augusta* and in Canadian waters. Hull replied to Nomura, however, two days later, saying that the new proposal "did not seem responsive to American suggestions." Then, to everyone's surprise, Hull was asked whether it might not be possible for Franklin to meet Prince Konoye at sea. It will have to be sufficient here just to note that this meeting did not take place. Franklin agreed to it but said that Japan would first have to clarify the purpose to be served. When this was done it was evident that nothing short of American consent to Japanese hegemony of all Southeast Asia would be agreed to as the price of peace. Franklin and Hull intended to put off a showdown as long as possible, but, as they put it, they could not agree to the sacrifice of other nations' interests. The conversations with Nomura were still going on when Pearl Harbor intervened.

The matter was complicated in its later stages by British fears. At Argentia one of the matters discussed was the checking of Japan. There was reason for British concern. The Empire was by now directly threatened: Singapore and Malaya first, other areas later; and colonial resistance, Churchill suddenly realized, was not likely to offer any serious obstacle to the Japanese. It seemed desirable to adhere to the Hitler-first formula; nevertheless, the Pacific threat was immediate. What Churchill and his advisers wanted was a stern warning to Japan that any further aggressions would be cause for American intervention. This they did not get. Franklin said that in his judgment he could "baby them along" for three more months, and this he intended to do. In rather sharp conversations he stuck to this determination. There was evidently something like panic among the British.

Franklin, ably seconded by Hull throughout this period—Hull got along very well with Nomura personally, and always continued to believe that Nomura was used by the militarists without his knowledge—did "baby them along." His judgment as to time proved remarkably correct. But where the babying would end he did not foresee.

During this preliminary period, as well as that of the war, the American negotiators had one immense advantage not usually to be counted on in diplomatic exchanges. The Japanese codes for communication had been broken, and the exchanges of Nomura with his government could be read at once. Franklin knew from these that the Japanese were not negotiating in good faith. But he did not know that months before Pearl Harbor the decision to attack had been made and training for it had begun. It seems likely that Nomura did not know it either. During the last stages of the negotiations the task force was sailing toward its objective, already committed without a declaration of war. But this was not revealed in any of the dispatches. Nevertheless, it does seem that the Japanese attack ought to have been foreseen. General Marshall, as early as February, had begun to think that a Japanese surprise was not impossible. He looked for it elsewhere—Singapore or the Dutch East Indies—but he also recognized the possibility that the Philippines or even Pearl Harbor might be raided. It is suggested that he considered sabotage much more likely than outright attack.[1] These two possibilities —raid or sabotage—might have called for opposite dispositions. A raid could be minimized by dispersal; sabotage could be better prevented by concentration and close guarding. It must be sufficient here to say that sabotage must finally have seemed more likely and guarding against it the first duty. Otherwise the fleet crowded into a confined harbor is an utterly unaccountable risk.

When Marshall testified before a later congressional committee, another influence was revealed—one that undoubtedly existed in the period immediately preceding the war. Marshall was asked why a telegram of alert had been sent to General Short in Hawaii on Sunday morning (this was the telegram that arrived too late) when he might have been spoken to over the scrambler telephone. The committee report said:

General Marshall testified that among the possible factors which may have influenced him against using the scrambler telephone was the possibility that the Japanese could construe the fact that the army was alerting its garrisons in Hawaii as a hostile act. "The Japanese would have grasped at most any straw to bring to such portions of our public that doubted our integrity of action that we were committing an act that forced action on their part."

Even the military had been sensitized to the carping of the isolationists. Even though an attack was not forecast, tension was mounting throughout the preceding weeks and days. It is not too much to say that Franklin and all the others in the high command expected something to happen momentarily. Even outsiders, who knew no more than they read in the newspapers, felt the tightening of anticipation. The nervousness spread everywhere throughout the country. What Franklin himself expected was an invasion of the East Indies; this was a reasonable deduction from Japanese movements known to American intelligence. Nevertheless, Marshall and King alerted their Pearl Harbor commanders to the immediate possibility of danger and felt that they were exercising extreme caution. They also warned MacArthur in the Philippines that alertness was called for. They were, it seems, not sufficiently emphatic, or else the commanders used their own judgment. The last message, also, did not arrive in time, so that the raid occurred on essentially surprised and therefore almost defenseless installations. The devastation was very serious—most of all, of course, at Pearl Harbor, although the Philippine losses were also disastrous.

This is a very brief, inadequate, and possibly partial recitation of the preliminaries to December 7. Few events in American history have been

[1] The suggestion is made by Basil Rauch in *Roosevelt from Munich to Pearl Harbor.*

more closely examined or have been the center of such controversy. The "revisionists" at once accused Franklin of inducing the attack. The main points they made were that he had opposed legitimate Japanese aspirations, had repulsed the attempts of moderates like Prince Konoye to reach an agreement with him, and had provoked reprisal with such actions as the embargoing of gasoline. But when Pearl Harbor occurred, he was, on the other hand, accused of negligence in not anticipating it and taking proper safeguarding measures.[2]

Reading the voluminous papers and books relevant to the period and to Franklin's conduct, it seems to me that the development of events was strictly ordained in the original determination to adhere to the Stimson Doctrine. If the United States was to oppose Japanese expansion in Asia, the time would come, in spite of temporizing, when a physical clash would occur. But it seems entirely illogical that it should have begun with a raid on Pearl Harbor, and it is easy to see why this was not seriously within Franklin's calculations. In the first place, the Japanese armies were bogged down in China and making only slow progress in their vital drive southeastward; in the second place, what the economy needed most could be got only from the Netherlands East Indies. This was oil, certain minerals, and food supplies. Nothing really was to be gained by a hit-and-run raid on Pearl Harbor. The installations could not be totally destroyed, and the ships could not be harmed unless concentrated and immobile. Lacking reserves of oil, moreover, the Japanese could not follow up a victory by going on to the West Coast without grave risks. It made more sense to anticipate developments in Singapore, the East Indies, and even in the Philippines.

Franklin was often accused of exaggerating the capabilities and the intentions of both Germany and Japan. This was an instance in which he underestimated the megalomania and the suppressed rage of the Japanese militarists. For years they had been developing a fixation on the United States as the only real check to their ambitions in Asia. It was by a kind of instinct overriding reason that they were driven to strike at their chosen enemy. This could be understood afterward, but before it happened it seemed so irrational as to be beyond serious consideration.

Following the disaster, there was a series of inevitable investigations. They can be referred to here only to say that the Senate's investigating committee, after long probing, concluded: "The President, the Secretary of State, and high government officials made every possible effort,

---

[2] Various "revisionist" materials have already been cited. Perhaps the most extreme, however, is a book by C. C. Tansill of Georgetown University, *Back Door to War* (Chicago: Regnery, 1952). Perhaps the best account of the pre-Pearl Harbor developments is that of Herbert Feis, *The Road to Pearl Harbor* (Princeton University Press, 1950).

without sacrificing our national honor and endangering our security, to avert war with Japan." And it was true that in a conversation on the night before Pearl Harbor, when Harry Hopkins suggested that the United States might strike first, Franklin had replied, "No, we can't do that. We are a democracy of a peaceful people. We have a good record. We must stand on it." This remark is quoted from Jonathan Daniels' *The End of Innocence*.[3]

Daniels was pointing out another remarkable analogy with Wilson's position on the verge of war in 1917. Wilson then had said to the young Assistant Secretary of the Navy, who had suggested bringing the fleet up from its Cuban base: "I owe you an explanation. I don't want to do anything . . . by way of war preparations, that would allow the definitive historian in later days . . . to say the United States had committed an unfriendly act against the Central Powers." Daniels went on to remark what a change was represented by Franklin's attitude then contrasted with that when the nation was on the verge of war in 1941! In 1917 he had noted in the diary he kept for a short while: "White House statement that W has power to arm and *inference* that he will use it. J.D. [Josephus Daniels, Franklin's chief] says he will by Monday. Why doesn't the President say so *without equivocation?*"

Franklin had been as impatient in 1917 as the most extreme interventionists were now; equivocation seemed to him almost cowardly. But now, when the presidential leadership was his own responsibility, he found himself reacting in a way remarkably similar to the way he had once thought was craven. At any rate, on Pearl Harbor day he was in what he felt to be an unassailable moral position. As he prepared his message to the Congress asking a declaration of war, his sense of outrage caused him to change a phrase in the prepared draft referring to December 7 as "a date which will live in *history*" to "a date which will live in *infamy*." But perhaps the important point about this is that obviously there was overwhelming support all over America for such an indignant interpretation. The isolationists, those who for years had been objecting to support for China as against Japan, and those who had felt and said that the "moderates" had been forced into retirement by American refusal to negotiate were swamped by an outpouring of anger. Never within memory, never since the nation's earliest days, had so brazen an effrontery been offered. Visibly the nation closed ranks behind Franklin. The Japs should be taught a lesson. That was the instant resolve.

In the crowded hours of that day, after the news came to Franklin and Hopkins in the Oval Room where they were "talking about things

[3] P. 209 (Philadelphia: Lippincott, 1954).

far removed from war,"[4] Franklin must have had some momentary wonder whether he might not be held accountable. Would the nation's reaction be one of anger directed against the Japanese? Or would there be a general disposition to blame him for provoking the conflict which had been so reluctantly approached? We know what he did and most of what he said that day and the next. If he had any such uneasiness, it was hidden. He seemed to move naturally and instantly into the role of Commander-in-Chief, even though he began under the cloud of an admitted incompetence somewhere in the command.

It was only gradually during the long hours of the afternoon and evening that the full extent of the disaster developed. Not only the losses at Pearl Harbor grew with every report, but losses elsewhere as well. This was not just a raid on one naval base. Hong Kong, Guam, the Philippines, Wake Island, and Midway Island were involved. It became clear, as Franklin said next day in his message, that Japan had "undertaken a surprise offensive extending throughout the Pacific area." What this meant he did not try to conceal. "There is no blinking the fact," he warned the Congress, "that our people, our territory, and our interests are in grave danger."

That this was literally true, no one doubted. There had been a tragedy, but that tragedy was founded on disgrace. There was not at once that disposition to find and punish a scapegoat to which Franklin must have given some thought; that occurred to the opposition later, but it was never made effective. The first reaction was consistent with injured pride. What had given the Japanese the idea that they could affront Americans and get away with it? They would have to be punished. "Let's get down to it!" everyone said. Franklin's antennae very quickly registered the prevailing sentiment. He certainly spoke the national resolution when he said two days later in an address to the nation:

We may acknowledge that our enemies have performed a brilliant feat of deception, perfectly timed and executed with great skill. It was a thoroughly dishonorable deed, but we must face the fact that modern warfare as conducted in the Nazi manner is a dirty business. We don't like it—we didn't want to get in it—but we are in it, and we're going to fight it with everything we've got.[5]

Churchill was almost as quick as Franklin to assess the meaning of the Japanese aggression; he was almost as quick, too, to sense the American temper. Although he had recently been asking American assistance

---

[4] Hopkins took the trouble, after that day was over, to dictate a memorandum about its events. It is quoted in full in Sherwood's *Roosevelt and Hopkins*, pp. 430–34. It tells how the first news came, how Franklin conferred with his commanders, resolved on his message to the Congress, and made various emergency dispositions.

[5] *Public Papers*, 1941 vol., p. 529.

in the Pacific, his first thought now was that the prevailing indignation might cause a change in the commitment to put the Atlantic—the defeat of Hitler—first. There might well be such an urgent demand to punish Japan that the agreed strategy would be abandoned. It was at least partly this concern that brought him hurrying to the White House with all his staff. He arrived before Christmas. And there is an unforgettable picture, in contemporary accounts, of his stay there and of the close resulting intimacy of these chiefs of state. In this Hopkins was a third party, playing a strange liaison role. He and Churchill had rooms across from each other, and on the days before Christmas they stumbled over piles of gift packages as they visited each other and went together to confer with Franklin. The three were inseparable for the next few weeks, lunching and dining together most of the time and sitting together far into the night, their various aides and commanders coming and going, dispatches being received and instructions going out.

Churchill did not find the change of view he had half expected. In the first formal conference the American Chiefs of Staff presented, as the basis for the planning to take place, a statement saying that although much had happened since last February, when agreement had been reached that the European area was the decisive theater, "our view remains that Germany is still the prime enemy and her defeat is the key to victory. Once Germany is defeated, the collapse of Italy and the defeat of Japan must follow."

There were to be several general guiding decisions of similar importance made during the next few years; for instance, the decision to invade France from the British Isles, then to postpone invasion in favor of a North African campaign; to go on into Italy but not into the Balkans; and, finally, to mount the cross-Channel effort in 1944. They would all be reached in a similar way. After long staff study and argument, the principals would meet to establish policy. The forces in the field would then operate as directed. So, following Argentia, there was this White House conference in late 1941 running on into early 1942. So there would be future meetings at Quebec, at Casablanca, at Teheran, and finally, so far as Franklin would be concerned, at Yalta.

The history of the war then being entered on is now voluminous. There are official accounts from the Army, the Navy, and the Air Force. And there are many individual memoirs of generals, admirals, and other participants. There are accounts, also, of the conferences. Churchill's six-volume *Second World War* tells his side of every individual occurrence of a joint sort as well as his own part as the British leader. In weighing Franklin's role in all this it is necessary to consider that no participant, in telling his story, could ever know all that went on, even if he was scrupulously honest and had industriously tried to be complete. There were many unrecorded conversations; there was complex and secret maneuvering on the part of all the principals; there were antagonisms, irritations, bickerings, and plain differences of opinion which never got into any transcript. But the record as it does exist suggests many of these, and often much more can be inferred than was written down. It has also to be noted that we do not have an account from Franklin's point of view comparable with that written by Churchill. It is not entirely irrelevant to note also that Churchill was a practiced historian and a skillful writer. Whether justified or not, posterity is tempted to accept his view of what went on.

The war reached every spot on earth, disrupting routines, changing the lives of individuals and nations. There were wounds, illness, and suffering; there was meanness as well as courage and glory. There was also the sacrifice, for millions of men and women, of their occupations and careers and a turning for years to arduous training and then service in armies, navies, and air forces or in civilian employments to back up the military. The earth's resources were squandered, lives were used up, and the future mortgaged with a recklessness never before known. And presiding over this vast upheaval and speedy deployment for war were a few men who made policy. They were able to make it because they were positioned at the head of the powers now engaged in a struggle to the finish.

The struggle had its rationale, as Franklin had defined it in his January message to the Congress in 1941, so far as the United States was concerned, in the Four Freedoms: freedom of speech and expression; freedom of worship; freedom from want; and freedom from fear. This definition of Franklin's was, in spite of Churchill's far glossier eloquence, the most telling one of the whole war. It set the alternative to the dictators' system in the clearest contrast. It made plain, at last, why American domestic policy had been shaped as it had. For behind the Freedoms were the historic American policies of free trade, national integrity, and disarmament. The Nazis were allowed integration and collectivism. Peace and free interchange were the goals. "The world order we seek," Franklin had said, "is the co-operation of free countries, working together in a friendly, civilized society."

At Argentia there had come the first intra-Allied tussle. Those Four Freedoms comported well enough with British home policy; democracy, thus defined, was very possibly more secure as a practical reality in the United Kingdom than in the United States. But Churchill was far from having abandoned British imperialism. He had not become the King's First Minister, he said, to preside over the dissolution of the Empire. But Franklin told him plainly—so I was told by Franklin himself when he spoke to me of Argentia and of his relations with Churchill—that the dissolution of the Empire would nevertheless have to be contemplated. The United States could not and would not underwrite colonialism or undertake to defend imperialism as against the movements in various places—like India—for independence.

I am inclined, considering everything, to credit Franklin with having been immensely influential in the eventual turning of the whole British imperial system toward Commonwealth. The pattern was already established, of course, in Canada, Australia, and New Zealand. But it had not become official policy that most of the remaining colonies must be shaped into self-governing entities. The decisive movements would be delayed as long as Churchill remained the King's First Minister. It would be his successor, Clement Attlee, in 1945 and afterward, when Labor succeeded Coalition, who would arrange for free choice in India, Burma, and Ceylon, and clear the way for other Dominion movements in the West Indies, the East Indies, and in Africa. Franklin would not live to see India independent, but he would deserve much credit for its achievement.[6]

I think Franklin felt that the independence movement, so powerful in India, was latently just as insistent elsewhere and that it must eventually prevail. He had no intention of committing the United States to the impossible task of checking these aspirations. On the contrary, he was dedicated to self-determination. It was inherent in his Four Freedoms. The appeal of this call to contemporary emotions was irresistible. It might not be wise; it might run against the imperatives of technology, which certainly looked toward integration. But men wanted it. They would have it if they had to die for it. If they went on subsequently to the co-operation he talked about, it must be, as Nehru said, "voluntarily."

The conversation which makes me certain of this determination took place in Franklin's office only a few days before Pearl Harbor. It was my first visit to Washington after having become governor of Puerto Rico. As happened so often in these conversations, the lead was taken away from me. I had Puerto Rican business to discuss. I wanted answers to a number of questions important to my conduct in office. I never got them. Franklin wanted to talk about the mounting crisis. He went back to Argentia, and he had Churchill very much on his mind. "He doesn't see things as you and I do," he said. "He is amazingly unreformed. He wants this war to result, as others have, in another extension of the Empire. And he wants us to back him up. He is most frightened now about the East—Hong Kong, Malaya, India, and Burma. I had to refuse again and again to threaten Japan when I was trying my best not to give them any excuse for actual attack on us."

I may not go on quoting, because I have no transcript, just as no

---

[6] He actually advised Churchill a little later, in a carefully considered memorandum, of the stages by which India could be converted into a self-governing dominion. Churchill was furious. But not more so than when Franklin later tried to persuade the Prime Minister to give up Hong Kong voluntarily.

transcript exists of any conversation, however important, in that office or in the Oval Room. But I recall as the other matter most emphasized his confidence in Russian resistance. He ticked off on his fingers the weeks left to Hitler when he could move at all on the vast frozen, wind-swept plains. He would come to a halt until spring, Franklin said, and by then we would have got a lot of matériel to Stalin, and the German armies would have been terribly hurt by a winter of suffering. He spoke of his troubles with the military and with American civilians in charge of production and procurement. They had practically refused to obey orders, and it had been only by the most strenuous efforts that he had compelled them to make a beginning at sending aid.

Later on Harry Hopkins told me this whole story in more detail. That would be when the resistance had been more or less overcome and the Russians had defeated the Germans at Stalingrad. He would be sitting in bed in the old naval hospital, parchment-colored, wasted, obviously near his end. We would talk for hours, reviewing an old collaboration. I would not have believed that he would live longer than Franklin, who still looked so vigorous, even serene, with victory coming into sight. And I would leave him sadly—as must always be the case when an intimacy is threatened by the final termination of death.

Even now, as he and Churchill talked long into the night and quantities of spirits disappeared—more than was good for Harry, although Churchill thrived on them—he was a man doomed, husbanding what little force was left to him. He was playing a central part in historic events and was always a little awed by his role. Generals, cabinet members, heads of Allied governments, even the formidable Churchill himself—all were respectfully aware of the prestige he shared. He was nobody in himself; as Franklin's alter ego—the role he had now definitely assumed—he was a very important person.

Churchill seems never to have forgotten that Franklin outranked him. He never called him by his first name. He was always "Mr. President" —as he was to Hopkins, even in their closest exchanges. He *was* the United States, as Cleopatra had been Egypt in Shakespeare's play, or as Louis had been France when he had said, "*L'état c'est moi.*" The best account of this long White House meeting—it went on until well into January—is in Sherwood.[7] But of course the determinations arrived at and the instructions issued can be found in official accounts. The most important of all the decisions was undoubtedly that to set up a central command which should be in Washington. This became the Combined Chiefs of Staff. There was more difficulty about the matter of supply and procurement. At first a body parallel to that of the Combined Chiefs was thought of, but Marshall protested that these were military matters

[7] *Roosevelt and Hopkins.*

and ought not to be separated from command. Hopkins supported him. Eventually a Munitions Assignments Board was established and Hopkins became its head. Formally it was an organ of the Combined Chiefs of Staff; actually it centered power over supplies in Marshall and Hopkins; it thus avoided the danger that the Chiefs might order something done and find the matériel lacking.

While Churchill was in America he went north to Ottawa and addressed the Canadian Parliament. When he returned he spoke to a joint session of the United States Congress. Both speeches had tremendous effect on public opinion as well as on the legislators. By this time the two leaders had agreed on the language of a United Nations Declaration —a kind of Allied manifesto—and had secured consent to it from all the Allies. On New Year's Day the representatives of twenty-six countries gathered in the White House and signed the prepared document. There was some argument about its wording, but the final result was a reaffirmation of the Atlantic Charter, together with a pledge to pool resources and to co-operate; it further said that no signatory would make a separate peace with the enemy. This was the initiation of the United Nations.

As Franklin and Churchill continued their work, they concluded that supreme theater commanders must be appointed who would be responsible to the Combined Chiefs of Staff. They began by appointing Sir Archibald Wavell, who had done so well in North Africa, to the ABDA area (the initials representing American, British, Dutch, and Australian possessions now the center of Allied attention). Correspondingly, Chiang Kai-shek was designated to command the Chinese theater. That these dispositions came first shows the impact of the Japanese aggression. And of course as the conversations proceeded, the situation in the Pacific was degenerating with disastrous speed—so rapidly, in fact, that plans were obsolete almost before they could be made, much less carried out.

With amazing success the Japanese were fanning out through the whole Southeast Pacific. Almost at once Hong Kong fell, and the Netherlands East Indies and British Malaya were invaded. The push was headed rapidly toward Burma and seemed likely to reach India without any real fighting. The British hoped that Singapore would hold out, but when the *Prince of Wales* and the *Repulse* were sunk by aerial bombing in Malayan waters and a little later Singapore fell without serious resistance, the hollowness of these hopes was revealed. Nowhere in the whole colonial world so dear to Churchill was there courageous or effective resistance to the Japanese advance. And everywhere the emptiness of imperial pretensions to native loyalty was exposed. Wavell's Asian command never became effective. It had disappeared before it could be organized.

The Philippine disaster had more impact on American sensibilit. For some unaccountable reason the planes at Clark Field had been destroyed on the ground in the first strike, and resistance to the Japanese invasion was almost at once reduced to the battles on Bataan and Corregidor. These instances of heroic resistance would become an imperishable part of the American tradition. But that they were imposed on the brave men—Philippine and American—who fought them was no credit to the planners and commanders who allowed them to occur. The agonies of the defense were hopeless from the first. The means for relief did not exist, and Americans had the strange, unprecedented experience of standing helplessly by while military defeat was inexorably driven home. The Japanese had succeeded there as everywhere because they had been underestimated. No one was certain now that they would not soon prevail everywhere, from Australia to India. The drive ended short of its logical extension, but as it was, it constituted the most rapid and most extensive conquest in all history.

While this was going on in the Pacific, the North African situation was changing. There were German armies facing the British now, and they were a very different foe from the Italians, who had been defeated earlier. After a series of reverses Egypt seemed about to be invaded, and no one could think of any reason why it would not succumb. The British armies were apparently demoralized and incapable of further resistance. The nightmare that so often haunted British strategists now tormented the Allied planners in Washington. If the Germans pushed on into Egypt and the Japanese into India, they might presently meet. They would then have conquered Europe, Asia, and Africa. The whole world would come within their grasp. They had only to subdue Chiang Kai-shek—no very great task with so much done—to control three quarters of the world's people and more than half its land mass. The nutcracker strategy would be reversed, with the Allies being pressed from both flanks.

The only hopeful spot on the charts in Franklin's map room was the area of Russian resistance to invasion. The military had been wrong. Moscow had not fallen. Winter was doing its work, and the Russians were growing relatively stronger.

As the American and British peoples took one after another of the blows that came to them in those weeks of winter, there was some tendency at the top to worry about morale; it was, however, a worry not much shared by Franklin. His uncanny understanding of Americans was never more strikingly demonstrated than then. This turned out to be the period of greatest unity. Danger had that effect. The country's senses were tuned to the hopeless battles in the Philippines, to the sacrifice at Wake Island, and to the hopeless naval engagements in the Java Sea. Franklin refused to excite himself about public opinion; and

Churchill took heart, in the midst of his disasters, from what Franklin told him of American intentions—so much so that when the Prime Minister addressed the Congress his American mother seemed to dominate. "What kind of people do they think we are?" he cried. "Is it possible they do not realize that we shall never cease to persevere against them until they have been taught a lesson which they and the world will never forget?"

It even seems a little foolhardy for the strategists, Franklin giving the lead, to have kept as they did to long-range considerations when it really seemed likely that there might be no long range. In those deep winter months the thought must often have been entertained that the dictators might prevail. But no one from top to bottom admitted it. That prospect was too abysmal. So the strategy agreed on was one for the future:

> In 1942 the main methods of wearing down Germany's resistance would be:
> a. Ever-increasing air bombardment by British and American Forces.
> b. Assistance to Russia's offensive by all available means.
> c. The blockade.
> d. The maintenance of the spirit of revolt in the occupied countries . . .
> . . . It does not seem likely that in 1942 any large scale land offensive against Germany except on the Russian front will be possible. We must, however, be ready to take advantage of any opening that may result from the wearing down process . . .
> . . . In 1943 the way may be clear for a return to the Continent, across the Mediterranean, from Turkey into the Balkans, or by landings in Western Europe. Such operations will be the prelude to the final assault on Germany itself, and the scope of the victory program should be such as to provide means by which they can be carried out.[8]

The Christmas conference of which this minute was a part was given the identifying name "Arcadia"—singularly inappropriate, it might be thought, considering the Allied situation at that time. The records are voluminous. Each participant, with his aides, produced memoranda; these were submitted for discussion and withdrawn for revision or adopted with amendments—or perhaps discarded as impractical. The subjects were global because now the war was everywhere. But the attempt was obviously to plan the production and disposition of such manpower and matériel as would be needed for the surrounding and reduction of Germany and for containing the offensives now in progress in the Pacific, in Russia, in the Balkans, and in Africa. No one knew that it could be done or that any part of it could be done. Yet it is impressive to see how much was accomplished even under the pressures of retreat on every front.

[8] Ibid., p. 459.

American troops, such as were available, were already being disposed about the world in places unheard of to most of them a short time before. They were on their way to New Caledonia, to Aruba, Curaçao and other West Indies stations, to the Azores, to Iceland, to Brazil, to Northern Ireland, to Africa, and to the far Pacific. Planes were going to Australia, and all kinds of munitions were headed around South Africa to the Persian Gulf on the long journey to rearm Russia and the defeated British armies in Africa. New plane routes were being established across the North and South Atlantic and far out into the Pacific. Such stations as Belém, Ascension, Dakar, Brazzaville, and the Azores Islands became matters of daily discussion.

Code names, among the Arcadia conferees, included Magnet, Gymnast, and even Super-Gymnast. These were short references to ambitious undertakings it was hoped might develop. As the conference came to a close, Franklin went to the Congress and asked for what seemed an astronomical sum for implementing the effort. His figures frightened even many of the military who had worked for months on estimates.[9] His requests were made without consultation with anyone. But the Congress voted the money with a minimum of discussion. Congressmen were as reluctant to risk being held responsible for having voted against the war effort as they once had been for having voted against recovery. There was a good deal of murmuring, but it was generally well below the surface.

The possession of ample funds at once raised the question of their use. For months Franklin had been under pressure to appoint a production "czar." What was obviously hoped by the conservatives was that this large sector of activity would be taken out of his control and entrusted to a businessman who would be "sympathetic." This Franklin had no intention of doing. The nearest thing to it had been the SPAB (Supply Priorities and Allocation Board), of which Vice-President Wallace had been chairman. But now the time had come for centering at least this authority in one person. Wallace, it appeared, was receptive; so was Baruch—indeed, Baruch was waiting expectantly in a hotel room, feeling that Franklin, who had evaded so long, must now recognize his historic claim to this position.[10] Knudsen felt himself entitled to it; and so, curiously, did Morgenthau, Jesse Jones, and Ickes. It was a strange set of claims to have to resolve in the midst of crisis. But the power in prospect was enormous, and men are attracted to authority by irresistible pulls.

Franklin had decided on Donald Nelson, formerly of Sears, Roebuck

[9] In the privacy of their offices they muttered that Franklin "had fallen for a numbers racket."

[10] He had been, it will be remembered, Wilson's War Industries Board chairman.

and Company. He was an experienced production and merchandising expert; he was not an isolationist in spite of his Chicago affiliations, and he had belonged to the all-out-production group rather than the business-firsters who had been giving so much trouble; also, he seemed likely to know his place. So in mid-January the announcement was made—and everyone was relieved. The nation went on to the most astonishing feat of production ever heard of. The ships, the planes, the munitions, the food, and the fibers which supported the campaigns of the next few years were forthcoming with beginning confusion but with later ease. And when it was over Americans would realize that they had not only performed a miraculous military feat but that while they were doing it they had lived better—much better—than they had ever done before. The levels of living would rise steadily all through the war emergency.

But the year 1942, just commencing as Arcadia ended, was nevertheless the one in all recent history which ran closest to the margins of national disaster. It was a very narrow escape, far narrower than most Americans realized as they were going through it, or, at least, until it was almost over. The Japanese were denied Australia by the inconclusive battle of the Coral Sea which kept a convoy of troops from Port Moresby; and they were turned back at Midway from a westward thrust. But these were checks only, and they were on the far west and south reaches of the enormous fan spreading down across the Pacific. The Emperor's armies steadily penetrated to the borders of India, conquering Burma on the way, and held China in a vise behind their advance. The British and Dutch empires in the southeast were gone, and the Philippines had surrendered. On the other side Vichy France with her African possessions drifted farther into the Nazi orbit; the Germans flexed their muscles in Africa and in the spring took Tobruk, the last British stronghold outside Egypt.

Rosenman speaks of the comfort he felt at this time, knowing as he did how close the nation was to defeat, in seeing the military chiefs, Marshall, King, and Arnold, pacing together through the White House corridors and rooms on the way to or from these Arcadia meetings and those almost daily ones that would go on into the future. They were, indeed, three strong men. Marshall's abilities were organizational, and it was he who had the strongest planning staff—at this time it included Eisenhower—and produced the best military machine. Bradley, for instance, was an extraordinarily able general who would prove later to have statesmanlike qualities as well; Patton, Patch, and others were superb field commanders; King was a hard, shrewd, but world-minded Navy man who saw his forces deployed and moving with uncanny precision. Arnold's was the junior service, rising rapidly; as its Chief he

598

presided easily over the spectacular changes in weaponeering and tactics which went on all during the war.

Franklin, as Commander-in-Chief, relied on these and other of his military men as he had never relied on the civilians around him. He had nearly always chosen cabinet members for political reasons. More often than not they had proved to be undependable as politicians and even more often they had been incapable of carrying their administrative responsibilities. Going on now into the immense and demanding activity of war, only a few of these could be trusted in the emergency agencies. Wallace, of course, was Vice-President. He had been a useful second in the preliminary stages. He was an effective and influential speaker. If now he wanted to expand into executive responsibility, he was entitled to consideration. He was not happy presiding over the Senate. To be useful there it was necessary to have abilities altogether different from those he possessed. He had none of the demogogic arts, no friendly attractiveness, no flair for bargaining and maneuver. He was in fact unpopular in the Senate, and more and more the leading politicos were turning against him. He thought he might be useful in managing economic dispositions which were a corollary of military strategy. The enemy could be hurt and friends assisted very materially in such ways. But there soon arose conflicts with the Department of State and with Jesse Jones, who had money to dispose of in vast quantities for the purchase of materials, for the encouragement of production, and for loans and gifts to allies.[11] Some of these quarrels were compromised, but Wallace was a man of conscience, Hull was jealous and his aides more so, and Jones was arrogantly conscious of his impregnable position vis-à-vis the Congress. There was trouble that Franklin would need finally to resolve. The way he did it showed better than anything else how decidedly he had put behind him the considerations he had been governed by in other such situations—when he had had to dismiss Peek from AAA, General Johnson from NRA, or Woodring from the War Department.

Ickes was another old-timer. He was still querulous, still sorry for himself, still childishly hopeful of recognition. He had several war respon-

[11] Jones' ghost-written book, *Fifty Billion Dollars* (New York: Macmillan, 1951), is a seemingly unconscious record of flagrant and persistent disloyalty to his chief over the period running from the first days of Franklin's coming to Washington until his death. Jones boasts of following his own line of policy, of thwarting Franklin's, and of constantly conspiring against him with the Southerners in the Congress. To read his account is to realize what forces a President must contend with. Franklin probably knew all along that Jones was disloyal, though he may not have known the extent of his machinations. He nevertheless kept him in office, because, on balance, he gained more from having him there than he would have gained from his dismissal. Jones is the most extreme case. On what a loose tether all the chief administrators were held, even the more loyal ones, can be realized by studying the Ickes *Diary*.

ties. He was controller of fuels, among other things, but he had ʒd more recognition and an expanded authority. He could be trusted to do capable administrative work, but in most other ways he was more a nuisance than a help. None of the progressives who had sponsored him was by now an administration supporter. He had no special friends, and his enemies were numerous.

So it went. There obviously had to be recruiting of entirely new people for the war. Leon Henderson, one of these, proved to be a find.[12] As 1942 advanced, inflationary pressures built up, as they were bound to do, and the Congress was still adamant about price controls; there was even a disposition to revise the parity formula for agriculture in ways that might easily double the price of food.[13] Henderson was one of Hopkins' men. He was a born politician. All the arts of persuasion and trading, so woefully lacked by Wallace, he had. He was a genuine support in the fight for price controls, and when they had been adopted he would be a capable administrator. The control and rationing system would be more his than anyone else's.

In another field, that of propaganda and persuasion, several new figures emerged who proved a comfort. Besides Sherwood, who was put to work in the foreign field, there were Archibald MacLeish and Elmer Davis, very different, but each possessed of a touch of genius. MacLeish was the imaginative one, Davis the dry, caustic puncturer of the lies and deceits specialized in by the dictators. MacLeish made vocal the American dream; Davis embodied—with his Indiana accent—the common sense of honest men. Then there was Lowell Mellett, the soft-voiced, utterly loyal assistant who seemed always to be at Franklin's elbow when embarrassing questions were asked.

New personnel was not the only need. New agencies were multiplying as they had not since 1933; and in a way this period was much like that of the earlier one when the enemy had been the impalpable but terrifying depression. Franklin had, indeed, used the analogy of war at that time. He must often have been reminded now of that allusion. Certainly he went, with the same boldness, into administrative adventures which promised to be of use. He disregarded general criticism, ignored cost, and asked only whether the device would further the main objective. A partial list of the new agencies he established in this year shows how ready he was to experiment:

On January 12 he established the National War Labor Board (NWLB).
On January 16 he established the War Production Board (WPB).

[12] So did his second, Professor J. Kenneth Galbraith.
[13] Franklin was inclined not to oppose this because he wanted the support of the farm bloc for war measures. He ought by now to have realized that this group would never be available for any but self-interested efforts. Cf. Rosenman, op. cit., p. 337.

On January 26 he announced the creation of the Combined Raw Materials Board, the Munitions Assignments Board, and the Shipping Adjustment Board.

On January 30 he signed the Emergency Price Control Act.

On February 7 he established the War Shipping Administration (WSA).

On February 24 he established the National Housing Agency (NHA).

On February 28 he announced the reorganization of the Army and the War Department.

On March 9 he established the Anglo-American Caribbean Commission.

On March 11 he established the Office of Alien Property Custodian (APC).

On March 12 he announced the reorganization of the Navy Department.

On March 18 he established the War Relocation Authority to take care of Japanese aliens, principally on the West Coast (WRA).

On April 7 he established machinery for rationing.

On April 18 he established the War Manpower Commission (WMC).

On May 15 he established the Women's Auxiliary Army Corps (WAAC).

On June 9 he announced the Combined Production and Resources Board and the Combined Food Board.

On June 13 he established the Office of War Information (OWI) and also the Office of Strategic Services (OSS).

On July 24 he appointed Admiral William Leahy Chief of Staff to the Commander-in-Chief in order to be more fully equipped to take his part in over-all strategy discussions.

On July 25 he established the War Relief Control Board.

On August 6 he set up the Baruch Board to survey and report on rubber.

On October 3 he established the Office of Economic Stabilization (OES).[14]

When it is realized that each of these agencies must have been conceived for a reason, and that this reason, even if it had not been originated by Franklin, must have been discussed at length with and consented to by him, something of the organizational task he got through in this first war year can be realized. Also, once established, each agency must be manned, must be provided with appropriations, must have its activities co-ordinated with all the others so rapidly proliferating, and then it must be directed as it carried out its tasks. The effort was heroic.

The city of Washington, about this time, began to bulge; some agencies were moved to other cities, and so some relief was found; but there was much inefficiency arising from inadequate quarters. Quarrels originating in such simple competitions as those for space, for personnel, and, worst of all, for jurisdiction—because the struggle for authority was by no means adjourned for war—much too often had to be resolved at or very near the top. No man was ever busier—even if the *weight* of the busyness is not considered—than Franklin was at this time. Nevertheless, as we have seen, he frequently made contributions of reasoned

14 Rosenman, op. cit., pp. 327–28.

memoranda to the various strategy meetings and spent much time in and out of his map room studying with Marshall, King, and Arnold the progress of the American deployment. Also, as we have seen, on occasion he was beginning to allow his mind to work in and around the problems of permanent world organization.

Yet he had still another duty, and it was by no means the least. This was the exercise of the leadership essential to a democracy. It was not only expected in these months, it was depended on for reassurance as defeat followed defeat all around the American periphery. It was not an important strategic matter except as it showed a frightening weakness, but up and down the country's coasts the sea lanes were harassed by submarines, and especially the crowded passages on the Atlantic side. Publicity about the sinkings could not be suppressed. There were convoys now on the route to Britain and on through the North Sea to Murmansk and Archangel. But these used all the destroyer strength, so that ships bringing oil from Venezuela and Aruba, aluminum ores from Guiana, sugar and fruit from the West Indies, as well as the heavy goods from Central and South America, were falling prey in hundreds to these U-boat attacks. The Navy had no defense. The planners had been scornful of the small boats they could now have used. They were now converted and construction was being rushed, but it would be months before convoys could be organized and protected.

The Pacific side was not so bad. The Japanese had business elsewhere than in unprofitable long-distance submarine attacks far away from their main expansion. And they had no such numbers as the Germans possessed. They made some token appearances, and these had an exaggerated psychological effect, but actually the threat to the Coast and its shipping was not important. Californians did not think so, of course, and the outcries were loud; but actually the losses were mostly in the Atlantic. These were considerable. The islands of the West Indies were practically besieged, and food in some places—Puerto Rico for one—was very short. Along the eastern coast the devastation could be seen from city streets. The beaches were fouled by the oil from exploded tankers, and often columns of smoke from burning ships rose against the horizon. All this, together with the distressing reports from the war fronts, presented Franklin with a problem of morale. He must find ways to bolster the nation's self-confidence as well as to manage the present strategic retreat and somehow plan for future offensives. This need for reassurance was never greater than in the late winter of 1942.

A characteristic effort to stiffen the country's courage was that made on Washington's Birthday. The development of this address is described in some detail in *Working with Roosevelt*.[15] The idea was essentially

[15] Pp. 329 ff.

a democratic one. It was an explanation more than anything else. It assumed that if people knew the problem and what was being done about it they would be able to withstand any amount of battering. They needed only the reassurance that their leaders knew what they were doing and were doing it with energy. That this was a sound approach was proved by the unmistakable dissipation of discouragement that followed. In spite of the bad news of the next few months there was never again cause to believe that defeatism might overcome the will to win. For once Franklin had the co-operation of the press; publishers, too, were frightened. When he asked them to print in advance certain maps to which he would refer, they complied; and he was able to read the nation an effective lesson in geopolitics. It was not an easy lesson to prepare. There were seven drafts before it was finished, and all the available speech writers collaborated. But when it was finished it was a masterpiece.

The address began by a reference to history understood by every hearer. Washington, said Franklin, had also faced defeat and had overcome the odds against him even if only after eight years of continual fighting. Then, too, there had "existed fifth columnists—and selfish men, jealous men, fearful men, who proclaimed that Washington's cause was hopeless, and that he should ask for a negotiated peace." Franklin then went on to those who advocated an alternative strategy. They were, he said, lingering in the days of sailing ships. "They advise us to pull our warships and our planes and our merchant ships into our own home waters and concentrate solely on last-ditch defense. . . . Look," he said, "at your map." He then developed his argument. Suppose the United States, Britain, China, and Russia were to isolate themselves. Suppose, for instance, no aid were sent to China. It was the Chinese who were keeping vast armies of Japanese troops away from other theaters. If the Chinese were not aided, all the Southwest Pacific, including Australia, New Zealand, and the Dutch East Indies, would fall, and this would release ships and men to attack the Western Hemisphere, South America, Central America, North America. Also, Japan would "extend her conquests in the other direction toward India, and through the Indian Ocean to Africa, to the Near East, and try to join forces with Germany and Italy."

Likewise, if the British and Russians were not aided, Turkey, the Near East, and North and West Africa would be overrun. This would put Germany within striking distance of South America. Such a "fatuous policy" would, by exposing the North Atlantic supply line, "help to cripple the splendid counteroffensive by Russia against the Nazis," and would also deprive Britain of food and munitions.

Having exposed the defeatist ideas, he went on in a few lucid paragraphs to explain the alternative—the plan actually being followed:

. . . we reject the turtle policy and will . . . carry the war to the enemy in distant lands and distant waters—as far as possible from our own home grounds.

There are four main lines of communication now being travelled by our ships: the North Atlantic, the South Atlantic, the Indian Ocean, and the South Pacific. These routes are not one way streets—for the ships which carry our troops and munitions outbound bring back essential raw materials. . . .

The maintenance of these vital lines is a very tough job. It is a job which requires tremendous daring, tremendous resourcefulness, and, above all, tremendous production of planes and tanks and guns and also of the ships to carry them. And I speak again for the American people when I say again that we can and will do the job.

The defense of the world-wide lines of communication demands relatively safe use by us of the sea and of the air along the various routes; and this, in turn, depends upon control by the United Nations of many strategic bases along these routes.

Control of the air involves the simultaneous use of two types of planes—first, the long-range heavy bomber; and second, the light bombers, dive bombers, torpedo planes, and short-range pursuit planes, all of which are essential. . . .

Heavy bombers can fly under their own power from here to the Southwest Pacific; but the smaller planes cannot. Therefore these light planes have to be packed in crates and sent on board cargo ships. Look at your map again; and you will see that the route is long—and at many places perilous—either across the South Atlantic all the way around South Africa and the Cape of Good Hope, or from California to the East Indies direct. A vessel can make a round trip by either route in about four months, or only three round trips a year.

In spite of the length, and in spite of the difficulties . . . I can tell you that in two and a half months we already have a large number of bombers and pursuit planes, manned by American pilots and crews, which are now in daily contact with the enemy in the Southwest Pacific. And thousands of American troops are today in that area engaged in operations not only in the air but on the ground as well.[16]

On the night of this speech the Japanese offered a reply of sorts. One of their submarines surfaced and shelled a relatively uninhabited stretch of California coast—just to show, it must be supposed, that it could be done. It was not much of a reply; it was generally regarded as what Churchill had called it in advance, when he had spoken of such possibilities—an "insult." It changed nothing. Americans were already brimful of determination that the Japanese should be taught such a lesson

---

[16] *Public Papers,* 1942 vol., pp. 105 ff. The rest of it, not quoted here, was an explanation of the initial advantage possessed by the Japanese in the Pacific, a reference to Pearl Harbor, saying that even if that attack had not been made it would have been impossible to check the Japanese at once, and an affirmation that with the present strategy and a general agreement concerning post-war aims, ultimate victory was certain.

as would never be forgotten. Thanks to presidential candor, they now had a fair idea of how it would be done. Victory might be delayed, but it would come. Meanwhile the nation's first business lay in the other direction.

Franklin was extremely anxious, for all sorts of reasons—morale among them—to pass to the offensive as quickly as possible. In late March, after long discussions and careful consideration, he made his first move. Hopkins and Marshall were sent to London; their task was to persuade Churchill and the British staff that an invasion of the Continent ought to be made before 1942 was over.

Certainly the maintenance of civilian morale would have to be put very high on any list of Franklin's responsibilities in 1942. We have seen how each month matters got worse—in spite of the battle of the Coral Sea, at the time apparently inconclusive but actually of great importance, and Midway, much more clearly a victory. As the spring came on, the British completely lost control of the sea in the far Pacific. Japanese bombers sank ships at will in the Bay of Bengal; Java was invaded; Ceylon was imminently threatened; India was wide open; and, since supplies to Chiang Kai-shek in China were likely to be cut off, a Japanese turning movement would probably result in surrender.

There was still resistance in Egypt; but Auchinleck, now commanding, was not trusted by Churchill; and statesmen feared the worst. There was a kind of American front on Guadalcanal, but what a heroic and decisive defense would be staged there no one could foresee; at the moment it appeared insecure. In the Philippines the hopeless struggle to save Corregidor harrowed the spirits of everyone who could read a newspaper. When Franklin had confessed the feebleness of the effort in the South Pacific and explained how difficult the build-up for a return to the offensive would be, morale did indeed become important, but it must be said that his sustaining efforts were well timed and thoroughly effective. On April 28 he made another fireside chat. It had the same perfection of execution as the earlier one in February.[17]

But no war was ever won by enthusiasm or even determination. There has to be established a power to match the enemy's, and it has to be disposed competently. This is the first, the indispensable, duty of leadership. Franklin was deeply conscious of this. He gave occasional attention to morale. But to strategy he gave part, sometimes all, of every day and every night. As he studied and thought, it became more and more apparent that the need for going over to the offensive was imperative. Besides, he was convinced that the time was approaching when action was possible. It was only after careful consideration that he sent Hopkins and Marshall to London with instructions to press for an im-

[17] It can be found in *Public Papers,* 1942 vol.

mediate invasion of Europe, but they were as convinced as he, when they left, that it was time for a change. The mission succeeded in the sense that Churchill, with whatever mental reservations, finally agreed. The British staff, under duress, was also brought to consent. The invasion did not take place that year, but it was actually not British opposition that prevented it so much as the recognition, as the weeks went by and defense demands multiplied, that it could be done only by risking a holocaust—"rivers of blood," Hopkins admitted finally. Not enough power could be mustered. Both men and matériel were short.

The situation, the truth was, worsened everywhere more rapidly than had been thought possible. And the demands multiplied. Munitions were needed for Russia, for the British in Africa, and for doing something toward a build-up in Australia, where MacArthur had been ordered and was now waiting with fuming impatience. Besides, the landing craft for the Channel crossing took twice as long to be produced as had been planned.[18] It was in these circumstances that Churchill diverted Franklin to the African campaign—something to which he was susceptible anyway.[19]

Franklin and Churchill were always under suspicion by their military staffs of being partial to schemes best described as adventurous and bizarre. I find something very sound in this predilection of these wartime leaders. Instinctively they understood that it was better to use guile, surprise, deception, maneuver, than frontal attack, which the military men preferred when the scale was so grand. Generals tended to become lost when nations and whole peoples were the subject of maneuver. Churchill, like Franklin, was a politician, and the last thing a politician wants is to come to a showdown with the enemy which risks everything. He much prefers to win by outthinking or outguessing him, without ever committing more than relatively cheap pawns to the venture. And he is accustomed to the manipulation of masses and their political organizations.

The expenditure of lives necessarily seems more horrible to a politician than to a general. This can, of course, lead to greater losses, through softness and compromise, than a harder, more calculating policy would result in. That depends, as so often, on alternatives. The summer of 1942, when much of the subsequent war was planned, illustrates this difference. It has to be recalled that both Franklin and Churchill had

18 Afterward it could be seen that the Navy had skimped the Army project in favor of their own in the Pacific, but anyway, the craft were not ready.
19 This operation had the code name Gymnast, later Super-Gymnast. The British plan for the French invasion was first Roundup (1942), but the later (1944) operation was called Overlord. In this truncated account, not intended at all to describe the war's progress but only Franklin's experience during it, I have been reluctant to make much use of these code names. They finally became confusing even to the planners.

had experience with the military and knew their limitations. Both also, as was not true of generals and admirals, were always dependent on being upheld by majority approval. During World War I Franklin had overcome Navy opposition to a cross-Channel barrage of mines. Also, he had planned to captain an expedition of long-range naval guns at the front. Both these gave signs of the same flair for the unorthodox that was now at work outmaneuvering Hitler (who was unorthodox too, but who had a megalomania fast building up to a conviction of infallibility).

Churchill was not less inventive. He had been kept out of the premiership in Britain until the nation's last extremity because he was not thought "safe." All during the period between wars he had been dogged by identification with the failure of the Gallipoli campaign, a diversion that had been very natural to his mind but had been undertaken reluctantly by the military and not prosecuted vigorously. Even in this war he was less the bulldog his defiant speeches pictured than the adventurer determined to outguess his opponent. It has only to be considered what colossal losses the British suffered in the slaughters on the western front in the first war and how few they suffered in the second one to understand the difference his leadership made. In the first war he had been only a subordinate; in this he was the King's First Minister and could have his way. This accounts in part for his opposition to the Channel crossing so closely pressed by Marshall. He was always trying to tempt the Americans with diverting alternatives. It was afterward said that all along he had had the intention of taking the Balkans and eastern Europe before the Russians got there. This would seem very prescient after the Yalta arrangements went to pieces. He undoubtedly always wanted to safeguard the life line through the Mediterranean, but the prescience about the Russians is largely imaginary. He was much more strongly motivated to avoid the slaughter of another whole generation of British young men.

All through the tortured discussions of that summer—whose records are available—this thread can be followed. It was not always Churchill against the Americans, but it often was. Also, it should be said that it is far more interesting to follow the accommodations of the civilian leaders to each other and to the realities they faced than to read the strategic papers produced by the military men. There was a general British avoidance of cross-Channel invasion. There was a general determination on Franklin's part that American troops should be committed to action at once, and this had its basis in the long delays preceding Pearl Harbor when everyone was fighting except Americans; they must make an immediate contribution. Nothing would so foreclose further discussion as being "blooded" in battle. But the British had had that induction. They knew the value of indirection.

But there was Stalin, who, when he talked to his two colleagues, spoke from a background of survived sacrifice hardly to be matched in history. The Russians possessed the pride of martyrs and heroes. They could ask—as Stalin did ask Churchill—whether the Allies were "afraid of the Germans." This was a most terrible insult, of course, but one that Churchill swallowed in order to have his way about postponing the invasion of the continent.

But anyway, as all three statesmen realized, they must talk to each other. They were heads of vast nation-complexes and they disposed of tremendous power. In this trio Stalin had the prestige now, the upper hand; he could demand everything and give nothing. Franklin, who had potentially vaster power, must show that it could be deployed and used before he could attain equality. These two were the heads of continental and unified systems able to strike outward or to defend inward. Their resources, depending on their development, were infinite. Between them, most of the world—its richest industrialized part—was available.

Churchill, on the other hand, stood at the head of a scattered Commonwealth held together by ideas and traditions, not by the possession of a heartland. It had been a sea empire, and Churchill had the handicap of not being willing to admit its obsolescence. He was not quite an equal among the Big Three, not even among the Big Four (when Chiang Kai-shek was present), because China, too, was a continental unit. Churchill's was infinitely the more difficult task. The measure of his achievement is that the world was a long time understanding how difficult it was. He might not be ready to see the Empire go, but he knew that its survival depended on Hitler's defeat and the steady support of the United States. For the one he would join even with Russians; for the other, he invoked his American mother, called to the sympathies of Americans, and cultivated with endless care the man in the White House.

Churchill did not hesitate to make Washington the British-American headquarters, with the implication that Franklin had the Empire in his keeping. This amused Franklin, who saw through it well enough and did not allow it to affect his calculations. Stalin, however, feeling strength, never wooed anyone. He would not even go far for a meeting. He would make the short journey to Teheran when the Americans had paid their way to recognition, but mostly the others had to go to him, as for instance Churchill did in the summer of 1942, conveying the difficult confession that a second front was as yet impossible and that an African invasion (now called Torch) was to be the substitute. Stalin was quite frank with Churchill, and would continue to be for the next two years, that the African operation was a poor substitute. He may not actually have thought so—he summed up its merits himself very well on one occasion—but it was an advantage he did not let go. It tormented the others, as he knew it must.

Franklin, waiting in Washington, was relieved when Churchill was able to report Stalin's agreement; now the African adventure could be developed.

The invasion of that continent occurred almost on election day. By that time the battle of El Alamein which would free Egypt had started, and MacArthur had begun his journey across southern seas to the Philippines. For the first time in a long, long year Franklin could say (as he did to a New York audience) that the news was good. He even spoke of a "turning point." But the congressional elections had gone badly. The House majority was reduced to fourteen, hardly a workable one in other circumstances. Still Franklin was asking nothing now but backing for the military forces. He thought himself likely to get that until the dissensions of prospective peace should again arise. Toward that peace he must soon be turning openly if his larger designs were not to be lost as Wilson's had been in futile differences among Americans themselves.

29

It is time to say something more about the nation itself as it plunged into war. It will be recalled that Franklin had opted for private enterprise in war production but that numerous agencies for co-ordination, for the financing of expansion, for the allocation of scarce materials, for the conciliation of labor disputes, and so on, had been set up. The Congress, under the prevailing stress, was quite willing to vote funds for almost any war-connected project. It was far less willing to impose any kind of restriction or authorize severe restraint on any substantial private interest. The general atmosphere of rebellion against discipline and of determined demand for privileges made it difficult for the civilian agencies of control to function at all. Also, there were furious internal quarrels within most of them, sometimes very embarrassing ones, such, for instance, as those that a little later disrupted the War Production Board. Their efficiency was very slowly increased, and some never reached a decent effectiveness.

Washington had become a kind of madhouse. The streets swarmed with the newly uniformed officers, male and' female, assigned to the vastly expanded military headquarters. They alone would have crowded housing and social facilities far beyond tolerable limits. But added to these were all the new civilian employees. Then, too, there had descended on the capital flocks of businessmen and their various satellites in pursuit of profitable war contracts, or of escape from regulations, or in search of favors of other sorts. They buttonholed congressmen, made themselves at home in executive offices, entertained lavishly in hotels, and generally created confusion and sometimes near scandal. It became more and more difficult to keep the economic expansion orderly, to avoid flagrant profiteering, and to keep to the main purpose of the effort, the gathering and discharging upon the enemy of the force to compel his submission. It was one of those times when everyone was getting rich or trying to, and when the tension of speculation reduced scruples to the vanishing point and even clouded the perception that a vast and concerted effort had to be made.

Cynicism spread out from this vortex. Men who were being asked to give years of their lives—at the sacrifice of their careers—to unaccustomed military life noted with bitterness the prevailing attitude of those who had escaped or evaded similar responsibilities. And men who were asked to risk their lives had difficulty in accepting the exhortations to patriotism, offered so freely by their leaders, when they were aware of what went on at home. Men in uniform all over the world had a curious feeling about the country they had left—that somehow things had gone wrong, not only in Washington but everywhere. They were ashamed, but they were resentful too.

Franklin was aware of this demoralization. Almost at once, after the beginning of the war, he had begun to deplore it publicly. He had tried with slight success to impose disciplines of various sorts. In 1942 he did get two measures passed—a Price Control Act and a Stabilization Act. They went some way toward combating inflation and allowed a system of consumer rationing to be installed. They were, however, limited to two years. Presently the battle for them would have to be fought all over again.

It was in these circumstances that he succumbed to the pressures exerted by the conservatives for a more sympathetic White House attitude toward business. Even though Donald Nelson was already functioning as the head of the War Production Board, the demand did not diminish. Someone with more authority and with wider scope was still wanted. Nelson did not meet the requirement for an "economic czar."

Franklin's resort, characteristically, was not to a businessman but to a lifelong politician, James F. Byrnes, formerly senator from South Carolina but currently an associate justice of the Supreme Court. Byrnes very probably was not the man who would have been the choice of those who had urged the necessity of a "czar," but anyway they got him, and he was an authentic enough conservative. The reasons for the choice, from Franklin's point of view, were the same ones he had been guided by in making many of his appointments. Byrnes had the prestige of having given up the Court, he was an ex-senator, and he was a Southerner. He was, in Franklin's view, a kind of hostage. His presence in the White House (his offices were in the new east wing) silenced many unscrupulous critics—not all, by any means, but some of the worst —and his influence helped to hold the line in the Congress. There was certainly no reason to think him an administrator of any account or even to think him very wise in public affairs. Also, he had not been conspicuously loyal to Franklin; he had opposed the Court bill and on several other occasions had turned up in the enemy camp. But, like others of his sort, he was solid on the war.

Byrnes was at once spoken of as "Assistant President." His ego expanded easily to meet the expectations of the conservatives. But Franklin had had such problem assistants before. It could not be said that he always knew what to do with them, because the most embarrassing incidents of his presidency are those having to do with the disciplining, put off too long, of unruly subordinates. He never learned to dismiss them soon enough or frankly enough. But, at any rate, he felt that he had to have them. And for the moment a problem of organization as well as of politics was at least postponed.

Presently, also, a minor czar for food—now getting short—was appointed in the person of Chester C. Davis. Washington was in fact as full of commissars as Moscow—something the newspapers now began to make something of, although they had recently clamored for their creation—but Byrnes was the head commissar. Franklin could now be, he hoped, Commander-in-Chief for the duration. If domestic problems could be less demanding and he could avoid "politics," he might have time to do his part in managing the war. He had some relief. But he was still far from being as free as he would have liked.

The evidences were multiplying that the Congress, on domestic issues, was completely out of control. In June an anti-strike bill was passed under the provocation of John L. Lewis' defiant attitude in the current coal strike.[1] Franklin vetoed it, but both Senate and House at once mustered more than the necessary two-thirds majorities to override. More than half these votes were Democratic. In the next month the National Resources Planning Board was abolished. Franklin did what he could to save it, but too many of his bargaining counters had been sacrificed. He could no longer have anything the most reactionary of his party members were not willing to accept. And any kind of planning likely to limit the speculations of businessmen was not among the list of approved activities. The Board, which had existed since the first days of the Public Works Administration, was put to death.

It must sometimes have occurred to Franklin that the degeneration of the home front was a case of chickens coming home to roost. The cynical pursuit of self-interest, the indifference to the national good, so often exhibited by businessmen and their congressional friends, were in logical sequence to the compromises of former years. When Franklin gave up collectivism for atomism and failed to see to it that standards for competition were enforced; when monopolies were allowed to develop, not under the aegis of the NRA, but cloaked by the pretense that

---

[1] During which Franklin was compelled to use his wartime powers to seize the mines and operate them under federal control.

they did not exist; when the development of the war-supplies intries was opened to private exploitation, appeal was frankly ma men's base impulses, not to their higher ones. Patriotism was not a word —or a sentiment—often referred to in wartime Washington. The motives behind the prevailing selfishness were those given the cover of respectability by talk of free enterprise and the like. Actually they were a naked abandonment to self-interest.

Franklin was obviously made uneasy by the spectacle. He never admitted that his leadership was in any way responsible and that he had resorted to means which were now creating their own monstrous ends. But he did begin a repeated denunciation of the performance taking place in and out of the halls of the Congress, and it was the most unrestrained of all his castigations. One reproof would appear in his Casablanca report. He would speak then of the concern felt by the fighting men about the home front:

. . . that there is too little recognition of the realities of war; that selfish labor leaders are threatening to call strikes that would greatly curtail the output of the war industries; that some farm groups are trying to profiteer on prices, and are letting us down on food production; that many people are bitter over the hardships of rationing and priorities; and especially that there is a serious partisan quarrel over the petty things of life in our Capital City of Washington. . . .[2]

He had told them, he would say, that these were exaggerations, that "the people as a whole are in this war to see it through with heart and body and soul . . . but I could not deny that a few chiselers, a few politicians, and a few—to use a polite term—publicists . . . have placed their personal ambition and greed above the nation's interests."

He really would let himself go in his State of the Union message in 1944, just after Teheran. I anticipate that denunciation to show the development of his wrath.

. . . while the majority goes on about its work without complaint, a noisy minority maintains an uproar of demands for special favors for special groups. There are pests who swarm through the lobbies of the Congress and the cocktail bars of Washington, representing these special groups as opposed to the basic interests of the nation as a whole. They have come to look upon the war as primarily a chance to make profits for themselves at the expense of their neighbors—profits in money or political or social preferment.[3]

Whether or not he identified the phenomena as the results of his policy, Franklin plainly did not like what was going on. He would doubtless have argued that no other resort had been open to him and that

[2] Address to the White House Correspondents Association. *Public Papers*, 1943 vol., p. 74.
[3] Ibid., 1944–45 vol., p. 34.

in the end, for justification, it would be said that victory resulted; but what kind of victory it was to be and what kind of nation it was to be conferred on were matters he avoided—or rather ones, as we shall see, which he sought in other ways to shape to a nobler pattern. There was to be a so-called "G.I. Bill of Rights" for the boys who had served in the forces; there was to be, he even hoped, a Bill of Economic Rights for all citizens; and the nation, having given up isolationism, was to enter on the task of securing similar rights for all other peoples of the world. If it was a dream insecurely based on a false theory of social relationships, Franklin never acknowledged that this might be true.

Meanwhile the Commander-in-Chief was busy, in and out of his map room and his office, studying, discussing, and arranging a thousand details. Something of vast importance impended. North Africa was about to be invaded. The landings there were less than a month old when the Big Three began to exchange opinions concerning the desirability of another conference. All felt the need of a face-to-face meeting; Stalin, of course, less than the others. This mutual concern would lead to the choice of Casablanca; and Stalin would finally refuse to come, intimating that he was busy fighting and that until the others were successfully engaged they were not entitled to such Russian recognition as would be involved in a foreign journey by the Generalissimo. This was more pressure for the second front, now become an obsessive symbol haunting every Allied conversation.

Franklin set out for Casablanca two days after delivering his State of the Union speech on January 7.[4] The longest legs of the journey were made by air from Miami across the South Atlantic and up across the shoulder of Africa. This was Franklin's first plane trip as President —the first since his flight from Albany to Chicago in 1932. He was accompanied by Hopkins, by his new chief of staff, Admiral Leahy (who had finally given up his Vichy mission), and by Dr. Ross McIntire. Leahy contracted pneumonia and had to be dropped in Trinidad. The others went on down to steamy Belém and across the South Atlantic to Bathurst in shirt-sleeve comfort. Franklin, as always, was immensely interested in this new adventure. In Belém he saw an old acquaintance, Admiral Jonas Ingram, commanding the fleet in those waters, a salty character, once football coach at Annapolis, who recalled old Navy days. Ingram had been rough with Perón on occasion, and the other dictators respected him.

The Pan American clipper—these were still the days of flying boats —landed in the mouth of the Gambia River. The cruiser *Memphis* and a destroyer were in the harbor, and the cruiser's captain took the voy-

---

[4] A relatively mild address devoted mostly to a frank assessment of the military situation and of the costs involved in meeting it. It will be found in *Public Papers*, 1943 vol., pp. 21 ff.

agers on a trip around the port in a motor whaleboat. They dined and slept on the *Memphis* and next morning set out for Casablanca in an Army C-54. They detoured to Dakar so that Franklin could see from the air the place he had dealt with so often on paper and in discussions during the last year, then went on over the deserts and above the barren Atlas Mountains to the northwest coast. A memorandum of Hopkins' noted that they

suddenly came on the fertile fields of N. Africa—looking like the Garden of Eden should look and probably doesn't—camels—olive groves—oranges—wheat-fields—no cows—rain—miles of black earth. The President missed nothing.[5]

This was probably exact. No doubt Franklin's sensations were those of a well-schooled geographer making his first visit to a long-studied area. He knew what it would be like, but he was excited at the prospect of really seeing it at last.

Casablanca—ten days of it—was diverting too. For instance, Elliott was waiting for him in a suburban villa. Hopkins' boy, David, serving with Eisenhower, was there too, and Churchill was in another villa not far away. In the fine Moroccan weather the two leaders had their third series of conferences.[6]

Since their meeting in June of 1942 there had been battles everywhere, in the Atlantic and the Pacific; in Africa, in Russia, in Burma. It was time to assess the results and to take new decisions. When Africa was purged of the enemy, what should be the next move? As Franklin and Churchill met, their Chiefs of Staff, who had preceded them, were ready with a plan for the invasion of Sicily (Husky). This meant the abandonment of the European invasion (Roundup) for the year at least. Marshall had opposed any further operations from Africa, but the other Chiefs, King and Arnold, differed. Arnold was attracted by the

---

[5] Op. cit., p. 673.

[6] That of June 1942 in Hyde Park and Washington has not been mentioned here. Nothing of new importance was decided on, but the American conferees were left, as Sherwood says, with "a growing sense of alarm that the Second Front was not going to be established in 1942 or 1943 either" (op. cit., p. 594). Perhaps I should refer to the momentary thought given just afterward to revising the Germany-first formula. About this Sherwood goes on:

The disagreement at this stage gave evidence of being so acute that the U.S. Chiefs of Staff seriously considered radical revision of the long-determined strategy of Germany first. MacArthur in Australia had made his own plans for an offensive in the Southwest Pacific. These were co-ordinated with Navy plans in Washington into the conception of a major offensive against the Japanese in 1942 and 1943 along the line of eastern New Guinea to the Admiralty Islands and up through the Celebes Sea to the west of the Philippines to Camranh Bay in Indo-China and Hong Kong . . . the plan was far more than a bluff . . . Indeed, the first step in it—the assault on Guadalcanal—was approved on June 25, the last day of Churchill's short stay in Washington.

prospect of air bases in Italy; King agreed with the British—as a naval man might—that safe passage through the Mediterranean was a first consideration. Churchill had spoken of that:

The paramount task before us is, first, to conquer the African shores of the Mediterranean and set up there the naval and air installations which are necessary to open an effective passage through it for military traffic; and, secondly, using the bases on the African shore, to strike at the underbelly of the Axis in effective strength and in the shortest time.[7]

Franklin's part in this seems to have been that of consenting. The cross-Channel operation from Britain had grown more formidable as it was studied, and obviously the preparations for a Sicilian invasion would be a much smaller drain on the limited resources so pressingly needed elsewhere. The conference laid plans for further operations in the north of Burma and for the recapture, by amphibious attack, of Rangoon. The first of these had for its object the reopening of the Burma Road and the succor of Chiang Kai-shek. It resulted in one of the most dangerous and daring campaigns of the whole war, one from which tales of adventure would stem for all the future; but it had no effect on the war's outcome. The second—the Rangoon capture—was never carried out at all. The means for it could not be found.

Casablanca would, however, be recalled most often in the future for other decisions than these. Its name is linked with "unconditional surrender" as a statement of policy toward the enemy, and with the determination that France should be freed and should go to elections before any faction or leader should be recognized as representative by the Allies. Controversy would arise about the unconditional-surrender formula. It was thought at the time to be a mistake, and it has been increasingly regarded since as the most serious political error of the war. Franklin felt that the German people must be punished for their slavish following of Hitler. They must be taught not to follow irresponsible leaders. But there were numerous Americans who disagreed.

Students will recall that Franklin had felt this way in 1917 when he had said that the peace should be made "in Berlin," and that he had been disappointed in the premature armistice. Churchill, surprised, apparently consented to the commitment sprung on him in order to avoid controversy. It seems to me likely that Franklin introduced the idea as he did, in a press conference, because he was reluctant to argue the point. Churchill would afterward offer various explanations of his agreement. They would never be convincing. Franklin was severely criticized, and there were indignant assertions, among liberals particu-

[7] From a message sent to Franklin when Torch succeeded and the battle of El Alamein was concluded. He now repeated it as the guide to British policy. The "underbelly" allusion was one of those Churchillian inspirations Franklin envied so much.

larly, that revenge and punishment were poor beginnings of work for peace. He had lately offended his liberal supporters in other ways. When this year was over, he would have tried their loyalty almost beyond its limits. Aside from unconditional surrender, the worst of these trials was his attitude toward the French. For by now the generals and the diplomats were deeply involved with the reactionaries who had brought France into such disrepute.

This is a matter we cannot adequately explore here. But it must at least be referred to because it was one of those "realistic" determinations that give rise to controversy concerning principle. It will be recalled that French defeat in 1940 had been followed by German occupation in the north of France and by a virtual puppet government in the south. Franklin and Hull had considered it better to have an ambassador at Vichy than to ignore the regime, and Leahy had been designated, an old admiral who might gain the confidence of Pétain. Leahy, however, had failed either to get much valuable information or to influence policy. Pétain, Laval, Darlan, and a few others of their sort were not averse to a semi-Nazi regime and functioned not at all uncomfortably under Hitler's supervision. But General Charles de Gaulle had escaped and had set up in London a Free French organization. There had been general recognition of de Gaulle as the representative of republican France. Britain had encouraged him, for instance, and a growing resistance movement inside France acknowledged his leadership. De Gaulle, however, contracted the megalomania which so often infects exiled patriots. He identified himself with France irredenta. It became traitorous in his eyes and those of his followers to look elsewhere for an interpretation of French aspirations or for leadership in the return of France to the family of nations.

But French North Africa was not Gaullist, although some French colonies elsewhere were. In Morocco and in Algiers, especially, the Vichy regime was in control. So that when an Allied occupation was in prospect, there was a choice of trying to make a deal for collaboration with the Vichyites or of risking a fight with French forces as well as German. Franklin, Hull, and Marshall chose to try guile. They succeeded in suborning Darlan, one of the most notorious Vichyites, at the moment commanding in Algiers, and he turned over the French installations there without a fight. He also intervened to stop the fighting in Morocco at an early stage. But the price was his recognition as the head of North African France. This, of course, infuriated de Gaulle and, indeed, most of the otherwise uncommitted French. One of these was General Giraud, a much-respected military man who had been imprisoned by the Germans and had escaped. His reputation for integrity led Franklin to settle on him as the alternative to de Gaulle.

By the beginning of 1943, with the African occupation accomplished

—and Darlan dead under mysterious circumstances—there was a real problem to be solved. Franklin had by now an almost uncontrollable dislike for de Gaulle, but Churchill was committed to him. How could the difficulty be compromised so that a provisional regime could be set up in Africa but the post-liberation regime in France left for the future? The matter became acute at Casablanca and very nearly obscured all the other issues.

It had become necessary to Franklin, because of the widespread disapproval he had incurred, that some display of sympathy should be made for those French leaders who were opposed to Vichy. Why, liberals were asking, was it always necessary to be friendly only with reactionaries? And of course there were not only the Vichyites to explain, there was Franco in Spain. For now, as in the past, Franklin's administration had favored the Spanish dictator, who was in no way better and, indeed, in many ways worse than Hitler or Mussolini. Franco, like Darlan, was another instance of "realism." During the Civil War, the Catholic interest in the United States had influenced policy against the Spanish Republicans; Franklin's compromise then had been hard to explain to liberals, and he had never really tried. The present case was becoming almost as bad, and he fretted at the prospect of returning home to face those who were already accusing him of too devious a relationship with an enemy he professed on principle to abhor.

This accounts for the effort to bring de Gaulle and Giraud together at Casablanca. The tour de force succeeded; enough, at least, for Franklin's purposes. De Gaulle refused flatly to come at first, but then appeared sullenly and was photographed shaking hands with Giraud. A regime of sorts for North Africa resulted.[8] But both de Gaulle and Giraud afterward visited Washington, and Franklin escaped some of the censure he doubtless deserved for making a bargain with a regime it was difficult to distinguish from the Nazis themselves.

On January 26 Franklin—with Hopkins and McIntire—was back in Bathurst. He was looking very tired and worn, and McIntire discovered when they boarded the *Memphis* that he had a fever. Nevertheless, he insisted on a day's journey up the Gambia on a British seagoing tug (built, he noticed, in Bay City, Michigan, and transferred to the British under Lend-Lease), and on a four-hour flight next day to Monrovia for lunch with Liberian President Barclay. In Brazil again a day later, he met President Vargas. He arrived in Washington to hear the news that the battle of Stalingrad had ended in the humiliating capture of Field

---

[8] De Gaulle and Giraud did compromise enough to form a French Provisional Executive Committee made up of themselves and the following others: General Georges Catroux, René Massigli, Jean Monnet, General Alphonse Georges, and André Philip. This committee served until the liberation.

Marshal Paulus and sixteen of his generals, together with what was left of his army. Stalin's pride would now be even more inflated. Care was indicated.

Sherwood concludes his account of Casablanca with a discussion of the unconditional-surrender statement. In writing it he had consulted Churchill and had been told that Franklin had taken him by surprise, although he loyally defended the policy. "At that moment," he wrote, "no one had a right to proclaim that victory was assured. Therefore, defiance was the note. . . ." Franklin afterward said that the phrase "popped into his mind" as he sat thinking that the getting together of de Gaulle and Giraud had been as difficult as that of Grant and Lee, and that the association had called up Grant's famous phrase. This was disingenuous.[9] Franklin spoke from notes at that press conference, notes which survive. Sherwood's explanation is:

> What Roosevelt was saying was that there would be no negotiated peace, no compromise with Nazism and Fascism, no "escape clauses" provided by another Fourteen Points . . . He wanted to ensure that when the war was won it would stay won.
>
> Undoubtedly his timing . . . was attributable to the uproar over Darlan . . . and the liberal fears that this might indicate a willingness to make similar deals with a Goering in Germany or a Matsuoka in Japan.[10]

If that was Franklin's purpose, he did not succeed. Liberals took the other view, that to punish all Germans, even those who had been non-Nazis, was almost certain to prolong resistance because it refused any encouragement to dissidents who might undermine the dictators' regimes from within. Furthermore, it left no surviving group to form a government. Occupation forces would have to govern by military law during an indefinite interim period. So much was inherent in the formula.[11] Franklin's defense—that the complete extirpation of "a philosophy in Germany, Italy, and Japan which is based on the conquest and subjugation of other peoples" was necessary—is not untenable. I have indeed come to believe that this was somehow a part of the grand conception then shaping in his mind. It was during this year, I think, that the design for the world to come finally formulated itself; and unconditional surrender may well have seemed to him an indispensable preliminary. As we shall see, it came up again both at Teheran and Yalta.

When he returned from Casablanca he found domestic matters ur-

[9] Besides being mistaken; Grant demanded unconditional surrender not of Lee at Appomattox but of Buckner at Fort Donelson.
[10] Op. cit., p. 697.
[11] When the time came it would be necessary to supplement this with a division into occupation zones, and the troubles stemming from this are well enough known.

gently needing attention.[12] These had to be settled somehow before other problems could be turned to. They were embarrassing and took time, but by March he consented to a visit from Anthony Eden, British Foreign Minister, who wished to speak of many things. Eden stayed for two weeks, and the memoranda resulting from the conversations furnish the first significant glimpses of post-war arrangements.[13]

As these talks went on, it should be remembered, the American armies in North Africa were suffering their first defeats. The experiences at Kasserine Pass and elsewhere in that first full-scale campaign were valuable but costly. They seemed at first to show, among other things, that American generalship would be unequal to its responsibilities; and this must have been very disturbing. At the very least, a year or more in the field would be necessary to produce reliable fighting organizations; this was not too disconcerting, but the question whether Eisenhower and his organization had developed competence in command was not one to be taken lightly.

Stalin had not been made happy by the conclusions reached at Casablanca, and he watched the American defeats with an obvious skepticism. The Allied power, as shown so far, was not thought worthy of respect by the victors of Stalingrad. Indeed one of the worries of that whole season was that Stalin might assess the Allied effort at so low a value that he would try for a separate peace. This would be a most acute concern at the time of Churchill's next visit to Washington in early summer.

In March, when Eden was in Washington, these fears were rising but were not so demanding that some attention could not be given to post-war arrangements. In a sense the future was more important to Eden than to Hull, who was inclined to concentrate his diplomatic efforts on maneuvers strictly contributory to victory. Eden was concerned about

[12] There was acute dissension in the War Production Board. The individuals involved were Donald Nelson and Charles E. Wilson on one side and Ferdinand Eberstadt on the other. Eberstadt more or less represented the military, who were impatient with the more general considerations which influenced Nelson and Wilson. Franklin was annoyed and inclined to dismiss all of them. But Nelson was finally supported although his usefulness was greatly diminished. The controversy confirmed Franklin's feeling that businessmen in government always got into trouble by becoming more bureaucratic than the bureaucrats. Politicians, he told Nelson in reproof, know how to get along with each other. Somewhat later Nelson was exiled to China; and finally Wilson, too, had to be relieved.

[13] Many of them are noted in Sherwood. If I seem to refer often, at this stage, to *Roosevelt and Hopkins*, it is because Hopkins was the only individual who had some contact with the presidential mind as it turned over and over suggested alternatives, slowly shaped ideas, and gradually fitted together the conceptions which ultimately became policy. Hopkins had to infer much, but no one else shared the knowledge necessary to the interpretation of casual remarks and suggestions.

Europe. He found in Franklin one who spoke his language. Hopkins, who was present, made rather full notes. They reveal a wide-ranging discussion concerning the future of all the European peoples and the view the Russians might take. Litvinov, the Ambassador, was talked to but was something less than frank, probably because he did not know Stalin's mind and functioned at the end of the usual tight Russian tether.

The matter of most interest to a later generation is the suggestion of a world organization just beginning to take shape. Franklin at one time spoke of "Free Ports of Information" established at strategic points so that there would be no area where totalitarian censorship could deny access to general news. He also spoke of a system of strategic bases under the control of the Big Four, to be permanently garrisoned, and gave as examples Dakar, the tip of Tunisia, and Formosa. He also repeated to Eden his idea that France and other occupied countries should not have to bear the burden of rearmament after the war. Postwar security should be guaranteed by the already armed nations. This was obviously a hint that there must be a continuing Big Four consortium. It was plainly around this conception as a nucleus that his ideas were forming.

Eden's March visit was succeeded by a Churchill sojourn in May which was reminiscent of Arcadia in December of 1941. The Prime Minister again stayed in the White House and was again accompanied by a formidable entourage, so that Washington became as before the temporary center of the British Empire.[14] Trident was soon (in August) to be followed by Quadrant in Quebec. Taken together, these discussions resulted in decisions governing most of the rest of the war. Stalin was not present; his sardonic image was, however, very much in everyone's mind and may have been more influential for having been absent. The most consequential of the determinations was that for Overlord. This was the cross-Channel invasion which was at long last to establish the second front. The Americans were still wary of Churchill, however, being fearful that he would soon begin, as usual, to find reasons for postponement in favor of further ventures in the eastern Mediterranean. He was fascinated by the possibilities of this area. In this preoccupa-

[14] This meeting had the code name Trident. It was notable for including, for the first time, theater commanders from the East; both Wavell and Stilwell were present. Stilwell was very bitter both because he disliked and distrusted Chiang Kai-shek, to whom he was assigned as chief of staff, and because he felt that his theater was being slighted. He noted in his diary that Churchill "had Roosevelt in his hip pocket . . . the Limeys are not interested in the war in the Pacific, and with the President hypnotized they are sitting pretty." It might be noted that MacArthur felt the same way. But so also did other commanders who did not get the allocations of men and matériel they demanded. The same complaint would presently arise from Italy, for instance.

tion Marshall and Hopkins were his active counters. Their acceptance of Russia as an ally was much more sincere than that of the British, who grew increasingly shy as the Russian successes became more sweeping. They were obviously alarmed about Empire interests in the post-war world.

At the time of Quadrant—the real occasion for the meeting—Italy was about to surrender and the fixing of terms was an urgent necessity. Churchill argued for retaining the royal house. He always believed that constitutional monarchy was the best form of government. On this, too, the Americans differed with him, and especially in the Italian case. Victor Emmanuel had been a very willing co-operator with Mussolini. Franklin himself was less concerned with this than that disarmament should be complete and a military government installed for an indefinite stay. Purging was called for in Italy as well as reconstruction, but the economic situation was disastrous. People would have to be fed and industries restarted. This would have to go on while governments, from top to bottom, national, city, and on down to the smallest rural administrative unit, were being reorganized and the Fascists expelled. Occupation would be necessary for an indefinite period.

It was in this connection that Hopkins naturally thought of La Guardia, who was the most prominent of Italian-Americans and a thoroughgoing anti-Fascist. The idea was to commission La Guardia and make him the military governor. The appointment would have been in every way suitable and popular, but Stimson arbitrarily refused and the mayor of New York was once more disappointed in his effort to get into war service, preferably in uniform.[15]

Very soon after the end of the Quadrant discussions Franklin was forced to let Sumner Welles go. Hull's jealousy had been smoldering for a long time, and there is reason to believe that when he saw his chance he presented Franklin with an ultimatum. Much as he depended on Welles, and fond as he was of him, it was necessary to hold his southern support; and Hull had his way. Washington was awash just now with derogatory gossip, malicious rumor, and fantastic allegation. The game was to pick off all those who were really loyal to Franklin. The conservatives who were now gathering about Hull succeeded with Welles, who was too proud and too reserved to fight back. Hopkins was hurt, but he was tougher. When stories about his private life were circulated he fell back—as Welles could not do—on his immediate association with Franklin. He had no superior, as Welles did, who was out to get him. And so, in a welter of abuse, he went on. He remarried about this time and at least had the renewed comfort of a home for his

---

[15] The La Guardia matter had gone so far that a personal promise had been given by Franklin himself. Cf. the note to Hopkins quoted in Sherwood, p. 727.

last few years of life. But Welles was permanently lost to the government and the leader he had served so long and so ably.

It was obvious to anyone who looked at Hopkins that he was hanging onto life by the most tenuous of threads. He had not lost his sharp wit, his flair for intrigue, or his determination to stay close to Franklin. He was an ideal assistant, except for his exclusive jealousy, and there can be no doubt that Franklin was fond of him as he had never been of any other of his associates except Louis Howe. Hopkins was, moreover, as Howe had never been, a man of the wide world, one who could rise to global thinking as the nation's interests proliferated. He had no fear of responsibility and felt quite comfortable with Franklin's decisions, or, if he did not, hid his reservations with complete success. Then, too, he had that indispensable trait for one in his position, an ability to smother his scruples when they threatened to interfere with his usefulness. He had also an almost clairvoyant view of the national interest which was never clouded by his own preferences. He furthered that interest, when he was allowed, with ruthless determination. His qualities were important because he operated within a wider tolerance, had a vaster range of decision now than any other individual.

Hopkins seems to have had no difficulty in getting along with Byrnes, the mobilizer. He might not have got along as well with Baruch, who had been thought of at first. That Franklin considered Baruch and appointed Byrnes is revealing, and it may be that Hopkins influenced that decision. Baruch had been on the presidential doorstep since 1933, controlling all the time a significant bloc in the Congress and turning up to influence more or less most economic decisions. It had obviously been a decade for Franklin of holding off. He must repeatedly have given infinite pains to the thwarting of Baruch's devious maneuvers, and he had apparently made a resolve never to allow him the actual power of office. If Baruch had been in the cabinet or in any post of importance, his influence would have been as sinister as that of Jesse Jones.

It is possible that Franklin no longer cared enough about the matters Baruch might manage to go on holding him at arm's length. By the acceptance of so powerful a party man he himself might be made more free. It might indeed assist in carrying out the vast design for the nation and the world now forming in his mind. He had Hull and Jones, Democrats; and he had Stimson, Knox, and many businessmen, Republicans. He had no progressives, of course, and almost no liberals of any sort. They would not oppose him anyway. What he must have was the immunity to criticism, the majority in the Congress, the freedom to operate in international affairs, to be secured only by abandoning his defense of those welfare and equalizing objectives he had once fought for so ably. He was prepared to go as far in this sacrifice as was essential to ensure his freedom of action. So Baruch; and if not Baruch, then Byrnes, and all that either implied. But Hopkins was as vigilant as a cat when his preferential place was threatened.

We can reconstruct the progression leading to Franklin's growing detachment from lesser considerations than those great ones now dominant in his mind. He had once been an architect of houses, building several to suit himself, then the builder of a navy; gradually he had widened his scope to become a creator of institutions—Warm Springs as a prototype; then he had become a planner of nationwide improvements, and now he was a shaper of world institutions. Each stage had been left behind as he had gone on, something accomplished and done with. Similarly he had been a conservationist, a reformer of the economic system, a manipulator of forces making for national prosperity, and then of others for bringing security into people's lives. He was intent now on gaining for all peoples immunity from war and a world purged of organized brutality (*vide* unconditional surrender), in which economic prosperity would be universal and universally shared.

The sublimity of this conception is beyond any criticism. What is not beyond appraisal is whether the means chosen, the price paid, was too much. This can never be a settled matter. He did not live to establish the situation he had planned. He paid much for the privilege of being allowed to proceed. He would be stopped by death from advancing to the stage at which the great powers established their hegemony, much less the stage at which they consigned their control to a democratized institution, fostered by them through perhaps the first post-war decade until it was capable of bearing the weight it must carry. The United Nations proved to be premature. His first plans were better than his second ones, especially for a world he no longer led.

There were other concessions in this year besides those of yielding to the demand for an economic czar and the expulsion of Welles. There was, for example, a harsh judgment against Vice-President Wallace as chairman of the Board of Economic Warfare and in favor of Jesse Jones, whom Wallace had accused of negligence and contumacy. Wallace seems to me entirely justified in his wrath with Jones, but Franklin humiliated him almost beyond tolerance. Wallace had already lost favor with the politicians of the right—a loss traceable to his growing independence and progressive views—and Franklin's chastisement in effect ended his political career. It was only to be expected that he should be displaced a year later as vice-presidential candidate for a second term.[16]

The climax, however, of this line of progression occurred at the end of December 1943, when the New Deal was openly abandoned for the

[16] Cf. *Public Papers*, 1943 vol., pp. 298 ff.

duration of the war. Franklin's mood at that time is so well represented that it seems to me worth while to quote excerpts from the transcript of an exchange with reporters:[17]

Q. Mr. President, after our last meeting with you, it appears that someone stayed behind and received word that you no longer like the term "New Deal." Would you care to express any opinion to the rest of us?

The President: Oh, I supposed somebody would ask that. . . .

. . . the net of it is this—how did the New Deal come into existence? It was because there was an awfully sick patient called the United States of America, suffering from a grave internal disorder . . . And they sent for the doctor. And it was a long, long process—took several years before those ills . . . were remedied. But after a while they were remedied. . . .

Two years ago, the same patient had a very bad accident—not an internal trouble. Two years ago, on the seventh of December, he was in a pretty bad smashup—broke his hip, broke his leg in two or three places, broke a wrist and an arm, and some ribs; and they didn't think he would live, for a while. And then he began to "come to"; and he had been in charge of a partner of the old doctor. Old Dr. New Deal didn't know "nothing" about legs and arms. He knew a great deal about internal medicine, but nothing about surgery. So he got his partner, who was an orthopedic surgeon, Dr. Win-the-War, to take care of this fellow who had been in this bad accident. And the result is that the patient is back on his feet. He has given up his crutches. He isn't wholly well yet, and he won't be until he wins the war.

Here Franklin discoursed for some time on the accomplishments of the New Deal (it will be noted that he admitted no such distinction as First or Second with the implied change of policy), listing in all some thirty, beginning with "a sound banking system" and ending with "conservation." He then went on:

Well, my list just totaled up to thirty, and I probably left out half of them. But at the present time, obviously, the principal emphasis, the overwhelming first emphasis, should be on winning the war. In other words, we are suffering from that bad accident, not from an internal disease.

And when victory comes, the program of the past, of course, has got to be carried on, in my judgment, with what is going on in other countries—postwar program—because it will pay. We can't go into an economic isolationism, any more than it would pay to go into a military isolationism.

This is not just a question of dollars and cents, although some people think it is. It is a question of the long range, which ties in human beings with dollars, to the benefit of the dollars and the benefit of the human beings . . .

But, as I said about the meeting in Teheran and the meeting in Cairo, we are still in the generality stage, not in the detail stage, because we are talking about principles. Later on we will come down to the detail stage, and we can take up anything at all and discuss it then. We don't want to confuse people by talking about it now.

[17] The Nine Hundred and Twenty-ninth Press Conference (excerpts), December 28, 1943, *Public Papers,* 1943 vol., pp. 569 ff.

But it seems pretty clear that we must plan for, and help to bring about, an expanded economy which will result in more security, in more employment, in more recreation, in more education, in more health, in better housing for all of our citizens, so that the conditions of 1932 and the beginning of 1933 won't come back again.

Q. I don't mean to be picayune, but I am not clear about this parable. The New Deal, I thought, was dynamic, and I don't know whether you mean that you had to leave off to win the war and then will take up again the social program, or whether you think the patient is cured.

The President: I will explain it this way . . .

The 1933 program . . . was a program to meet the problems of 1933. Now, in time, there will have to be a new program, whoever runs the Government. We are not talking in terms of 1933's program. We have done nearly all of that, but that doesn't . . . make impossible or unneedful another program, when the time comes. When the time comes.

The reference to "Cairo and Teheran" deserves to be noted. These conferences had been concluded and will presently be discussed. But there was also a reference to the future, which suggested a fourth term. And it was true that the year about to open would again see a presidential election—not that Franklin or the nation needed any reminder. His candidacy had long been accepted.

Franklin had attained a status not unknown before in American politics. He could not be denied renomination for the presidency, because no other candidate could be nominated against his opposition and because, for the party, he was its only sure election winner. But at the same time he was unable to force the acceptance in the Congress of the program for which he stood. He had to go on, as he had been, trading his preferred domestic policy for consent to his foreign designs. And the Democratic conservatives were driving a harder and harder bargain. They would stop short of denying him the appropriations necessary to winning the war, but beyond this he must still cultivate with care consent to his plans for the peace. For these, however, he would have no strong party opposition. The "willful men" in Wilson's time had been Republicans and progressives—one of them, Hiram Johnson, was still in the Senate; the conservative Democrats had always favored international organization. He had only to hoard such good will as they still had for him and not to irritate them with domestic ventures. Thus the abandonment of Dr. New Deal and the embracing of Dr. Win-the-War.

It was with his political base secure—with more years in the presidency fairly guaranteed—that he advanced to his first meeting with the Russian potentate in Teheran. This security was important. How many times American negotiators had been unable to make commitments or had had their agreements rejected in a recalcitrant Senate was well enough known in the diplomatic world. That Stalin should be conscious of talking to the United States incarnate when he talked to the Chief of State was an immense advantage in dealing with that tough and firmly seated dictator.

To emphasize his hold on the party, and the agreement of all factions on the matters in hand, the advance preparations for Teheran were entrusted to Hull. This, following the dismissal of Welles, emphasized both at home and abroad the solidarity of left and right in the coming negotiations. Not since his Nomura conversations had Hull had any prominent part in the strategic proceedings. He had not even been present at Casablanca or Quebec.[18] Now he was sent to Moscow itself to arrange for the most fateful of all the conferences—that which for the first time would bring leaders of the world's two continental systems to the same table.

Hull's mission in October[19] had exactly the result Franklin wanted: On November 5, 1943, as the Secretary was returning, the Senate passed, by a vote of eighty-five to five, a resolution sponsored by Connally of Texas supporting post-war collaboration for the maintenance of peace and the establishment of a general international organization. No President had ever been better equipped for a negotiating session. However much the backing had cost, Franklin must have felt it worth the price. When he sailed on November 13 from Hampton Roads on the new battleship *Iowa*, he felt that he had reason to be optimistic about the momentous occasion he had so long anticipated. How momentous it was could have been guessed from the company behind him.[20] The *Iowa* was to carry them to Oran, and during the week of the crossing there would be some necessary preliminary explorations. For there was in prospect not one conference only, but three. Teheran was to be a climax. First there were matters to settle with the British; then there was scheduled Franklin's first meeting with Chiang Kai-shek. These conversations were to take place in Cairo.[21]

What was to be discussed with the British was the important matter of a commander for Overlord: also, so far as Marshall and Hopkins

[18] Hopkins had, in fact, sat with the other Foreign Ministers.

[19] Joseph C. Davies, former Ambassador to Russia, had been sent some months before to make certain that Stalin was agreeable to a meeting. Hull was already in that decline which would cause his resignation in 1944; nevertheless, the visit of an American Secretary of State to Moscow was an event, and with competent aid he lasted through the negotiations.

[20] It included all the Chiefs of Staff and, in addition, Hopkins, McIntire, Generals Somervell, Watson, and Handy, and Admirals King, Brown, and Cooke. The party would grow to seventy by the time it reached Teheran.

[21] Chiang could not meet with the Russians because they were still at peace with Japan. What their policy in the Far East would be was a matter still to be determined, but they were not disposed to commit themselves by conferring with Chiang.

were concerned, that Overlord would be mounted at all; they still half expected Churchill to talk the others out of it in favor of an eastern Mediterranean adventure. This was less likely now because Churchill, without consulting the Allies, had sent General Wilson and a formidable expedition to capture the Dodecanese Islands in preparation for a Balkan penetration and had seen it fail with terrible losses. He was somewhat chastened. Nevertheless, he did now suggest that going north to meet the Russian eastward drive somewhere in the Balkans would be a way of preventing future trouble in Europe. He also reminded the Americans that the Soviet leaders shared the old imperial dreams of warm-water ports and control of the Black Sea outlets to the Mediterranean. This was a matter of no importance in the American thinking. They were concentrated on beating the present enemy. Only Franklin among them seems to have understood thoroughly the hidden antagonisms of Churchill and Stalin.

The preliminary conference, at Cairo, served to bring Churchill up to the mark—that is, he protested his faithfulness to Overlord and confirmed the date set at Quebec—May 1944. The whole question of the Far East campaign was left, in spite of much discussion, in an unsatisfactory state. The acidulous Stilwell was there, despising Chiang and regarding Franklin, too, with a suspicious eye. He still thought the politicians were playing with forces they did not understand. He expected no good to result for his command. There was agreement on a Burma campaign under Lord Louis Mountbatten. The resources for it were scant, but the planners looked to this and to movements in North China as actions necessary to the defeat of Japan. The Japanese armies scattered throughout Southeast Asia were now of enormous size, and defeating them seemed necessary to victory. For this the Russians' help would be essential. Their armies must come down from the northeast while the other Allies came up from the southwest. Before Japan could be attacked by bombing or amphibious operations the continent must be cleared. Chiang was far from enthusiastic about this scheme. He saw Chinese manpower used prodigally in these battles and probably doubted his ability to muster it. But at any rate matters were left in this way. One thing was clear: the Burma Road must be opened so that supplies could go into China, else nothing would be possible.

Of course this strategy, as it turned out, was useless. The Japanese were eventually defeated at sea. Being an island, they could be. And the final blows came from the south and east by air and ship. Armies played little part in the climactic actions except for the insular campaigns culminating in the battle of Okinawa. The great Japanese conglomerations on the mainland surrendered in millions without a fight when they were left headless by the Tokyo capitulation. King and Arnold, and Franklin dimly, foresaw something of this. But the British were determined to preserve Burma and the rest of the Empire in the East. They had no doubt that it must be done by armies on land. For Franklin's part, he agreed with Marshall that it was a first necessity to have Russian help. He must give the demand for collaboration priority as he talked with Stalin.

The stay at Ambassador Alexander Kirk's villa was lightened by a certain amount of desert sight-seeing—the pyramids and the Sphinx were not far away, and Franklin, as always, had an active curiosity about all that went on in unaccustomed places. Then, too, Elliott and Franklin Jr. were brought in by their commanders to be with their father. Hopkins' boy, David, and Churchill's son were also present, as they had been at Casablanca. The newspapermen, as always, admired Madame Chiang, thus enhancing her ability to make mischief.[22]

Franklin had insisted on the Chiang meeting, in spite of British indifference, for what seemed to him a compelling reason. China was a great power, not by anyone's nomination, but by circumstance. Her land masses, her vast population, her situation on the Pacific border made her a central concern for the future as well as the present. He did not foresee—although he must have realized Chiang's weaknesses and the essential corruptness of the Kuomintang—that the Communists would prove to be the strongest element in post-war China. He had no doubt that, with American assistance and the Japanese driven out, some sort of satisfactory regime with Chiang at its head could be set up. For this reason he insisted that China should be accorded great-power status and her Chief of State recognized as one of the Big Four by whom the post-war world would be disciplined.

This Big Four was now Franklin's constant preoccupation. He had lost Welles, who shared his determination that the war should result in a realistic world organization; but there was a group in the Department of State, as there was one in the British Foreign Office, constantly at work on preliminaries. How much these contributed to Franklin's developing conception it is hard to say. The central ideas were his own, wherever the suggestion for them had come from; and by now, as he began seriously to prepare the way for their acceptance, he reduced them to the characteristically simple formula he always tried to reach in such matters. One day in the course of the Teheran conversations he would draw a deceptively careless diagram showing what he had in mind. Across the top of this chart there would be three circles, one labeled "40 U.N.," the next, "Executive," the third, "4 Police"; and off to one side two lines of notes, reading: "ILO—Health—Agriculture

---

[22] She was one of Franklin's most unmanageable visitors several times during the war—especially since there were so many Americans who never surrendered their conviction that the real American war was in the Pacific.

—Food." The chart would be signed "By FDR, at Teheran, Nov. 30, 1943."

This was it. This was what all the struggle had been for, all the bargaining, the compromising, the committing of a nation to global war. It could finally be put on a scrap of paper. It needed almost no explanation. Only about the middle circle marked "Executive" was there any need for detail: a few explanatory words described the membership as follows: U.S.S.R., the U.S., the U.K., and China, together with two European nations, one South American, one Middle Eastern, one Far Eastern, and one British Dominion. This Executive Committee would deal with *non-military* questions, economic and social. The four policemen would be the peace-enforcing agency, able to deal instantly with any sudden emergency. They were, for this purpose, one.

This revelation of what was in his mind was made in a conversation with Stalin. The Russian leader obviously had no more than a minor interest in Franklin's scheme, but it is known that he asked several penetrating questions. One was whether the assembly would be world-wide or merely European. Franklin said that it should be world-wide. Stalin also asked whether the Executive Committee would have the right to make decisions binding on all nations. About this Franklin could not give a decisive answer; it could only be done, so far as the United States was concerned, if the Congress agreed to be so bound. Stalin also noted shrewdly that there appeared to be involved the necessity for using American forces abroad. Franklin thought the use of naval and air units might be sufficient and might not raise many difficulties. Stalin seemed to have thought that there might be regional committees, especially since he doubted China's strength after the war or the suitability of Chinese intervention in European affairs. Franklin indicated in his reply that Churchill had been approached previously and had had a similar idea for regional committees—one for Europe, one for the Far East, and one for the Americas. He doubted that the Congress would consent to American participation in a European committee. Nevertheless, the regional organizations seem to have been acceptable to both.

The one matter not discussed between them—or at all—was the possibility that a threat of war might come from one of the four policemen. This would always be a difficulty, but, as Franklin must have conceived, a purely theoretical one. The Big Four must, in a very real sense, constitute a whole, be indivisible. That whole would be the world. Ideology apart, there would be no cause for conflict. Each would have ample resources, or access to those in each other's territories, and trade would not be widely restricted. They would not interfere with each other and they would not allow lesser peoples to interfere with any one of them. We can see how his mind was working; if such an agreement could not be made a reality, the only chance the world might have for permanent peace would be the conquest of the world by one power. It was now his final responsibility to persuade the others that they must make themselves a Committee of the Whole, abjure force among them, share resources, and provide the common means for stifling conflict before it became dangerous.

The impression given by study of the various papers resulting from Teheran is that it was Franklin to whom this seemed the paramount need. Stalin was intelligently interested, but he was still intent on more immediate problems—the second front, arrangements for the dismemberment of Germany, and the situation in the East. To Franklin these were now lesser issues. The way to victory could be seen. It was time to make that victory a glorious one: not merely a defeat for enemies, but a triumph for mankind. To paraphrase Churchill, this was Franklin's finest hour. His further statesmanship was to be not exactly anticlimactic, but something less creative, more foregone. The war could be won, but could men organize themselves for peace?

To understand the conception fully, the then situation has to be recollected, something peculiarly difficult for later generations to do. Especially it has to be recalled that there was as yet no absolute weapon from which to argue that there was no alternative to peace. This overwhelming fact would soon change the possible ambitions, and the means available for attaining them, of all the nations. But this was not mentioned at Teheran, so far as anyone knows, although the critical incident under the stands at Stagg Field in Chicago had taken place at the beginning of the last December (1942).[23]

Other conditions at the time of Teheran are also significant. The Japanese retreat from their farthest spread had not begun. And since it was still thought that they must be driven into the sea from the continent, the most indispensable aid the United States Chiefs had to ask of Stalin was Russian participation. Actually Stalin readily agreed that Japan was a common foe and that as soon as it was possible the eastern armies must be reinforced and a campaign begun. Argument about this did not last long. Doubtless the Americans felt a certain gratitude for this concession.

What Stalin was more anxious to discuss was what he evidently felt most important for Russian security. This was the disarmament, indeed

[23] Churchill had been having trouble with the American military about the development of the bomb. They were inclined to shut out the British as success approached, but most of his conversations were with Hopkins. The bomb would not even be mentioned at Yalta, a year later. The "critical event" was the first self-sustaining nuclear reaction so brilliantly brought to reality by Szilard, Fermi, and their colleagues.

the dismemberment, of Germany; and he insisted that not only within but without that nation, at strategic places, there must be strong and ready forces to suppress any further German aggression. This, he found, coincided with an area of Franklin's interest. He specifically mentioned Dakar and islands in the vicinity of Japan as such possible bases. Franklin seized on this, saying that his agreement was "one hundred per cent"; and he also mentioned China in this connection. He was sure it was better to have the four hundred million Chinese for friends than possible future enemies.

This was possibly the most important conversation of Franklin's whole life, his supreme achievement.[24] He must have felt at its end the kind of euphoria that comes to few men and on few occasions. It looked as though he and Stalin, just as he had hoped, could agree and could work together. His geopolitical sense made him very certain that if the U.S.S.R. and the U.S.A. had a firm understanding nothing else really mattered very much. That understanding was in the making.

This meeting of the two was preceded by an incident with an interest of its own: Franklin refused to lunch alone with Churchill before his conference with Stalin. He guessed that Churchill wanted to brief him, or at least to have it appear to Stalin that the two who had met so often and had so much in common—culture, language, democratic political institutions—were, for the purpose in hand, agreed, and that Stalin was a third party who could, if he too agreed, come in. Franklin saw to it, as again and again appeared in other proceedings, that no impression of Anglo-American exclusiveness should be conveyed to the Russians. The principals here were Stalin and himself. If there was a third party it was Churchill, with his obsolete imperial notions.

The most interesting other conversation of all those at Teheran was another between the Big Two. In this they crossed the lines of reserve and talked together as no two other people in the world could have talked. It was professional business. Franklin told Stalin of his political problems, those especially affected by Russian policy; and Stalin, as he expected, understood. If Franklin had been encouraged by the agreement on post-war matters, he must have had his confidence that the

[24] It is interesting to note that Stalin did not hesitate to contradict Franklin on two matters. Hitler, he said, was not deranged; he was an extremely competent leader, he had no culture and was deficient in other ways, but he had great ability. This must have surprised Franklin, who had shown some tendency to project his detestation of the German into exaggerated views of his actions. It was a healthy corrective. The other matter Stalin differed with Franklin about—and said so—was "unconditional surrender." He told Franklin plainly why it was a mistake to have made it the basis of policy. What impression it made is not evident. On this matter Franklin never changed.

two nations could work together strongly reinforced by this later exchange.[25]

Stalin had met his expectations; now Franklin went some way to meet those of the Russian. One of these was an assurance that Overlord was a firm undertaking. Stalin was at first reluctant to believe it, because, as he said, if no commander had been chosen no actual preparations could be under way. Franklin went into session with himself and decided on his man, something he had been hesitating about for months. Marshall was the candidate of Stimson and Hopkins. Eisenhower had not, in their opinion, shown the necessary stature in Africa. Besides, Marshall had earned the field command by his services in Washington. Franklin did this thing in the right way. In a man-to-man talk he told Marshall he ought to have the command but that he could not be spared as Chief of Staff. As Marshall recalled it, he was told: "I couldn't sleep nights with you out of the country." Marshall made no objection. He had hoped for, but he had not requested, the command. He acceded at once to Eisenhower's appointment. Franklin's telling this to Stalin was the one thing needed to make the conference a complete success. This, it is quite certain, all those present but Churchill felt that it had been.

It would be an exaggeration to say that the meetings had produced a friendship between Franklin and Stalin. It is, however, wholly accurate to say that they understood each other. Franklin, at least at that moment, felt that he had found one reliable colleague for that policeman group whose members were to constitute the governing body of the immediate post-war world.

The Russians had been touched by having custody, during the conference, of Franklin's person. The American Embassy, where Franklin was at first installed, was some distance from the place of meetings in the Russian compound. Stalin suggested that he move to a villa close to his own. This must have worried the American Secret Service, but Franklin nevertheless accepted. It is recorded that the well-trained servants were obviously members of the Russian police, being identifiable by conspicuous bulges at the hips if in no other way. But the arrangements were happy enough and undoubtedly tended to soften the suspicious natures of such old revolutionists on the Russian side as Molotov, Voroshilov, and Stalin himself.

When it was over, Franklin was exhausted by the prolonged discussions and the accompanying entertainment. The luncheons, dinners,

---

[25] Much has been made of the differences that seemed to be developing at the time of Franklin's death about these very matters. They had to do with Poland and other "buffer states," and Franklin had explained the political importance of the millions of people in the United States who were Poles or Balts or descendants of immigrants and who had considerable voting strength. An examination of these incipient differences suggests that with more patience and care they might have been compromised by his successor.

and other occasions at these conferences were their most formidable requirement. The rounds of toasts ran to dozens, and there was close observation of any being missed. The nationals entertained in turn and naturally tried to outdo each other in lavishness. For oldish men, under terrible and prolonged strain, to move into new quarters far from home after long travel, and then undertake not only to negotiate for their nations' futures but to outdo each other in eating, drinking, and the display of bonhomie, was a killing ordeal.[26]

The Americans continued to have trouble with Churchill, who never gave up his preoccupation with the eastern Mediterranean. He had left Casablanca to negotiate with Turkey about coming into the war; the matter came up at Teheran. Stalin was not much interested, and the American Chiefs were inclined to think that Turkish adherence would be overcostly. Much matériel would be demanded at once and there was none to spare. Franklin knew well enough how important the Middle East was likely to become, and he met with President Inonu and the Foreign Minister twice at Churchill's request; but nothing came at once of these negotiations.

Franklin got home from Teheran toward the middle of December. On the way he had to hear of Marvin McIntyre's death, a reminder that time was making inevitable inroads. He must himself have felt his age as he heard of another loss from among the old pre-presidential crowd.[27]

But when he got to Washington the whole Cabinet and many of the wartime agency heads were gathered at the south entrance of the White House to greet him. They recognized his satisfaction. He was confident that he had accomplished what he had set out to do. The two continental powers had come to an understanding. The world was by way of being made safer for future generations. The grand conception was being implemented in the only way it could be—by the mutual understanding of those statesmen to whom it was a necessity.

---

[26] After Teheran, Hopkins was prostrated; during most of the next year he was continuously in hospital. Not until the next Christmas would he reappear as a useful aide. And then he would find, as so many others had, that he had been replaced. He was never again as influential in Franklin's career as he had been until now. He would be present at Yalta, but even there he would spend most of his time in bed.

[27] Louis Howe had gone in 1936, and Missy LeHand in 1941. Now McIntyre; and on another voyage from another conference in this same part of the world, "Pa" Watson would die on shipboard.

30 On his home-coming from Teheran, Franklin seemed to the company gathered at the White House to be a bone-tired man. He gave the impression of being exhausted; he must have known also with desolate certainty what troubles lay ahead. They would not be less tormenting than those in the past. They might well be more complicated and difficult. The end was down an arduous road for one who was aging and depleted. With an even more discouraged certainty he must have thought of the domestic trials immediately in prospect. For Franklin in full vigor, these would merely have been challenges, well within his powers; he would have met them with that professional relish such tasks had always called out.

But it soon appeared that he was desperately ill. In Teheran he had developed a bronchial infection accompanied by a racking cough. It hung on and on, indicating plainly a lack of resistance. McIntire called in consultants several times; they found no chronic troubles except the bronchitis and the sinuses he had fought for years, but the symptoms refused to clear up. Those about him were so used to seeing him carry his work-horse burdens and periodically to be borne down by them, only to be rejuvenated by changes of scene, rest, and relaxation, that they naturally expected these therapies to go on working. Only they did not. The well-known resilience was gone. His weight was reduced; he cut down his smoking; he fell sometimes into unaccustomed reverie, from which he awoke with a start. The gusto had departed from many of his occupations and pursuits; his face was lined and when in repose had begun to have that drawn and melancholy look which would a little later become so marked. He still got through an incredible labor each day, but he was forcing himself and found no pleasure to lighten the evenings.[1]

[1] All of the Big Three, who were, in Franklin's conception, to bring order into a distracted world, were sick old men. Besides Franklin's illness, Stalin had the first of his "heart attacks" just after Teheran, and Churchill was down with

Weary as he was, he had to rouse himself to immediate effort. Congressional leaders had to be informed of the Teheran results; then he must hold a press conference, saying, what the newsmen already knew, that the proceedings had been "in every way a success, not only from the point of view of the conduct of the war, but also for the discussions that I hope will have a definite and very beneficial effect for the post-war period." Then he had at once to begin the arduous preparation of his State of the Union message. The opening of another session of the Congress was imminent.

It was easy enough to see where his thoughts were tending. With the surface of his mind the day-to-day matters would be dealt with, but the real care and close attention would henceforth go to the arrangements for what he thought of as "the peace." The world of which he dreamed had come to have a shape in his thoughts which was far more comprehensive than just a formal post-war organization. Something had renewed his concern for a better life for all people. I think myself that he was having a severe revulsion from the spectacle of a nation so inglorious in prospective victory as the United States undoubtedly was. I think he blamed himself, regretting almost at once his Dr. Win-the-War parable. It may even be that the press conference, so usually interpreted as abandonment of the New Deal, really expressed contrition; perhaps justification also for compromise; it may have signaled the rebirth of progressive ideas. "Now, in time," he had said, "there will have to be a *new* program . . ."

The press could not ignore the White House or its occupants, and since readers had been well schooled in making allowances during the years of their hostility, the publishers' unremitting perversions of the news were less damaging than would have been expected. There was endless curiosity concerning all the Roosevelts, and characteristically their doings were twisted to fit the accepted stereotype of irresponsibility. The Roosevelt young men, being healthy and high-spirited, were of the sort to whom escapades were natural, and even Anna had furnished the gossips with a divorce. But there was a more tolerant attitude everywhere than the detractors supposed. The boys were brave, and all of them were doing their duty. Anna was living in Seattle with her second husband (who had been White House correspondent for the Chicago *Tribune* and, as such, had manufactured as much malicious comment, probably, as any single individual); and the four sons were

---

pneumonia and its aftereffects most of the winter. Merriman Smith, who was one of the White House correspondents with the longest service and who had studied his man carefully, said later, in *Thank You, Mr. President* (New York: Harper, 1946), that the correspondents had for a year watched Franklin "die before their eyes." Both Stalin and Churchill, a year later, would have much more the appearance of health and competence than Franklin. He never came back.

in various services—Elliott in the Air Force (he was at this time on the list to become a brigadier general and Franklin was indignantly refusing advice from the politicians to delete his name), James in the Marines, Franklin and John in the Navy. None had asked for—or got—any favors, unless attendance at the historic conferences as presidential aides is regarded in that light.

Eleanor, knowing her boys, had rather more worries than most mothers of sons in the services. James was involved in the amphibious warfare of the Pacific, as risky an occupation as could be thought of. Elliott was flying from African bases, and this was a dangerous service. Franklin Jr. and John were on destroyers in the Atlantic, and these vessels were in the first line of defense against the U-boats. There was no day when the mother of four such boys might not expect dreaded news. But Eleanor was no usual woman; she was, for one thing, about the busiest one in the country. She can have had little time for exaggerated worries. Her daily column, still growing in popularity, gave her something to do every day, but this was the least of her duties. She had a full schedule of lectures, radio talks, and conferences; she moved about the country constantly, and constantly brought home the reports Franklin had long ago learned to rely on. They were prejudiced, but these were the reverse of most prejudices he had to discount. So she had a certain responsibility, along with her industriousness, to maintain equilibrium.

Eleanor was, as she always had been, an incorrigible doer of good works and would not have been ashamed to say so. Her developing streak of realism, however, saved her nowadays from being taken in as she had sometimes formerly been by self-seekers or charlatans. Her liberalism had led her to extend sympathy and protection to individuals and groups who were merely exploiting her good intentions, and not always for purposes she approved. But about these she had learned to be appraising, too, and more inclined to put first things first. She saw the war develop and displace other causes with none of the mixed and tortured feeling so many Americans had. It was surprising how many there were who were unable to give themselves over wholly to belligerence. But she was not one of them.

Gentle as she was, Eleanor had no more doubt than Franklin that this was a necessary war and that the fighting was for a justifiable cause. She worked to maintain morale and to define national purposes in simple terms that ordinary people could understand. This was something for which she had a gift. She represented to other women one who, like themselves, was called on to endure the age-old ordeal of women—sending their men out to fight. If she usually ordered her life now without much relation to Franklin's, it was because they no longer had the same need for each other that younger people have. She had her job to do.

It was no part of her remaining duty to furnish the usual submissive wifely companionship. Franklin did not tell her his troubles and ask for soothing and sustaining reassurance; she did not offer an uncritical support for all his plans. They were equals who met often and had much in common.

This was even more necessarily the arrangement when she became assistant director (under La Guardia) of the Office of Civilian Defense in September 1941. For some time she worked very hard at the duties set out for her. But Civilian Defense soon became a somewhat absurd agency in a country not likely to be attacked as Britain had been, where the idea had originated. La Guardia, pathetically eager to "get into the war," and with a politician's desire for the spotlight, attempted to blow up the importance of his new command. The result was that both he and Eleanor became the favorite subjects of a national humor that had too few outlets. Military pretensions might be absurd, but just now generals were sacred. Civilian Defense nearly ruined La Guardia; and Eleanor was a long time recovering from the reputation it gave her as an interfering busybody.[2]

It was not long before she saw that her position was impossible. Nothing she did was treated with decent toleration; and in February of 1942, just after La Guardia himself had quit in disgust, she resigned. Her own words explain:

The whole OCD episode was unfortunate. I had been reluctant to take the job and had done so only at the insistence of Harry Hopkins and another of my husband's advisers. Franklin himself was completely neutral, though he told me he thought it would help Mayor La Guardia. When the mayor found what a controversial person I became he was appalled at having me; and I did not blame him for disclaiming any responsibility for the "dreadful" things that some members of Congress felt I had done. After the mayor resigned from the OCD I was instrumental in obtaining his successor. The mounting wave of attack in Congress finally convinced me that I was not going to be able to do a real job . . . so . . . I too resigned, leaving Judge Landis a pretty prickly problem which he handled very well.[3]

Thereafter Eleanor's war work was unofficial. But she was still a very busy woman. Among other major endeavors she undertook a mission

---

[2] There is an amusing passage in *This I Remember* about Eleanor's relations with La Guardia in the Office of Civilian Defense (pp. 230–31): "I soon found that every activity which Mayor La Guardia did not want in his part of the program was thrust into my division. His work as mayor of New York prevented him from giving his full time to organizing . . . The few group meetings we had left me with an impression of great hurry and a feeling that decisions were taken which were not carefully thought out. Frequently heads of divisions, including myself, were unable to discuss with him things we hoped to get settled. I could not help realizing that the mayor was more interested in the dramatic aspects . . . than in such things as building morale."
[3] Ibid., p. 240.

to England in 1942, to the far Pacific in 1943, and around the Caribbean in 1944. Her endurance on these journeys was a marvel to everyone who saw her; she set herself a killing schedule and met all its engagements serenely and in good health. She visited thousands of military installations of all sorts, talking with everyone, asking questions, exchanging information, always interested, sympathetic, and cheerful. She made countless little speeches. She took long flights in uncomfortable planes, rode in jeeps, walked endless miles through camp streets, kitchens, hospitals, and warehouses; she busily took names and promised to see or write to families back home (and she always did). Weather did not daunt her—tropical or frigid, it was all the same. She shamed the hardiest military men by her endurance and brought to millions of homesick boys in what seemed to them the most outlandish outposts of the world an assurance that their ordeal was appreciated.

She visited us in Puerto Rico on her 1944 journey. When she arrived she had already gone through a similar program in Central America, Cuba, Haiti, and Santo Domingo; and after she left us she was going on down the islands as far as the Guianas and Brazil and then back across the top of South America. She was received on her arrival with full military and civilian honors, parades, inspections, and all the rest. She came to La Fortaleza, the Governor's Palace, through streets lined with cheering crowds; she endured an official luncheon with a full attendance of admirals, generals, and lesser officers, as well as members of my cabinet, federal officials in the island, and other appropriate notables; in the afternoon she visited hospitals, several outlying Army and Navy installations, and returned to a formal, if slightly more select, dinner followed by a reception at which she shook some three thousand hands; after that she made a several hours' visit to the USO club. Next day was a repetition; she had not covered *all* the hospitals and camps on the first day, nor visited with *all* the groups at the USO. That night she finished at about two. My wife and I saw her to her rooms in our *Mirador* with enormous relief. As we were dropping off to sleep half an hour later, we heard the typewriter clacking over our heads—the daily column was being prepared.

At six this indefatigable lady of sixty was up and packed, ready to go on to the next stop at Antigua. Malvina Thompson, her secretary and companion, was not so cheerful. She thought herself ill used. "But," she said, "I'll drop before I'll complain. Look at her! She's just as full of energy as ever." And she was.

Aside from these self-imposed duties having to do with the familial relations of the soldiers—because to them she stood for a motherhood they longed for in their rough and temporary lives—Eleanor had many social responsibilities. Washington entertainment had taken on a wartime cast. Formal dining was reduced but not altogether abolished. During the whole war there was a procession of refugee royalty, all of whom were entertained at the White House, usually for several days to give full expression to sympathy for their plight. But there were also heads of state and others of lesser rank. The White House was far from being useless; and Eleanor was—however casually—its chatelaine.

She may not have taken part in official exchanges, but she shrewdly knew what was going on. She sized up Churchill, for instance, and noted that he was going to be an unhappy man after the war when he found out what the world was going to be like. Not only Churchill but Stalin came within her reviewing mind. She went to none of the conferences, but very probably she wanted to; and about the last one—Yalta—she spoke of nearly going, although Franklin finally decided that Anna should go instead. So she did not see Stalin, but she quoted him in an interesting passage. It began with a remark by Franklin that Churchill would find the spreading socialism of the post-war world repugnant. Then about Stalin:

A remark made to him [Franklin] by Mr. Stalin in one of their talks stayed in his mind and I think gave him hope that there might be, after the war, more flexibility in communism, or at least in that particular communist leader . . . Franklin had been wondering aloud what would happen in their respective countries if anything happened to either Churchill, Stalin or himself, and Stalin said: "I have everything arranged in my country. . . ." My husband said: "So much depends in the future on how we get along together. Do you think it will be possible for the United States and the USSR to see things in similar ways?" Mr. Stalin responded: "You have come a long way in the United States from your original concept of government and its responsibilities, and your original way of life. I think it is quite possible that we in the USSR, as our resources develop and people can have an easier life, will find ourselves growing nearer to some of your concepts and you may be finding yourselves accepting some of ours."[4]

That this was the all-important consideration for the after-war world, Eleanor knew as well as Franklin. She brooded over the impermanence of life, also; and thoughts of this sort occurred to Franklin as well, and disturbed the picture he had of the Big Three keeping order at the summit while the nations got back to normal. He was an incorrigible politician. He believed that no institution could be a substitute for face-to-face dealing. He must often have wondered who would be capable of handling Stalin or his successor when he had gone.[5]

[4] Ibid., p. 253.
[5] Eleanor spoke of Franklin's confidence in his own ability to understand others and make them understand him:

I think one of his reasons for being willing to meet with the heads of other nations outside the country, when they were unwilling to come here, was his feeling that he could convince them better by personal contact . . . I have heard some statesmen say they did not think it advisable for an American president

The relationship of husband and wife in these circumstances was not —it could not be—a normal one. But that Eleanor made a dignified and useful adjustment is perfectly obvious. She remarked about this that a man with all the cares a President must have in wartime makes him an individual of a very special sort—and, she might have added, one entitled to special consideration.

But Eleanor and Franklin as joint parents had always cultivated familial closeness even though the circumstances of public life made it difficult. One means of emphasizing mutual relationships was to celebrate their annual occasions in appropriate fashion. Lesser anniversaries were never forgotten, but the national holidays were the best; and, of these, Christmas was the most precious. It was an occasion for overcoming obstacles to reunion, for appraising the grandchildren, and for retightening the bonds which years and trials inevitably tended to loosen. For eleven Christmases the family celebration had centered in the White House. It had come to be a kind of national tradition that the presidential family should gather, decorate its tree, recall the Christ child, exchange gifts, and, above all, make the children happy in the security of a gay, close circle. Franklin had always lit the White House tree in the park across the way or, later, on the south lawn, and had spoken to the nation on the eve of Christmas Day. The tree always came from the Conservation Department of New York State and might well have had its roots in soil which Franklin had been instrumental in setting apart for such a purpose. Old and well-loved customs were kept, and family solidarity was emphasized.

This year the holiday was celebrated at Hyde Park. And *Time* wrote about it. When last the family had gathered at Springwood for Christmas (in 1932) there had been four grandchildren, all present. This year there were fourteen, but only seven could come. The war had affected even the presidential gathering. Nevertheless:

Granpa Roosevelt—his hair considerably whiter than in 1932 and, as he remarked to a photographer, thinning just short of baldness—presided at a gift-unwrapping in the library, carved the turkey at dinner and read aloud, as always, Dickens' *Christmas Carol*.

At 3 P.M. on Christmas Eve the adults at the family gathering clustered in the . . . Memorial Library while the President, broadcasting to U.S. armed services around the world on what was announced as history's greatest hook-up, prosily summarized and confirmed the headline news and dope stories of the past several weeks. General Eisenhower was to command the U.S.-British invasion of Europe, heavy casualties are to be expected. Mr. Roosevelt and Joseph Stalin had got along fine at Teheran, they had agreed

to go abroad . . . . because we nearly always got the short end of the bargain. . . . I think Franklin accepted what other men in high office said, and believed that if he kept his word they would keep theirs. . . . [Ibid., p. 254.]

that in the future international peace would be kept, if necessary, by international force. This was perhaps the poorest of all the President's thousands of speeches in the past decade . . .[6]

The tone of this report, starting with the sentimental note about the grandchildren and the reading of the *Christmas Carol,* and ending by suggesting decline and incompetence, has some significance. This was more than an editorializing of news. It was an accusation of failure to achieve the leadership expected of a man who had just represented his nation at Teheran. *Time* was not alone in this; the disparagement ran through the country's press like a theme. Franklin was not being yielded the confidence and support he had hoped for. *Time* furnished an intimation of things to come. Nineteen forty-four was to be a year when victory was made certain but when it became less and less certain what the victory's significance was. The nation's dream was dim. Besides, an election was coming on and the publishers were Republicans.

This speech, spoken of so disparagingly by *Time,* is recalled in Rosenman's *Working with Roosevelt.*[7] It was, contrary to *Time's* suggestion, very carefully prepared. It went through eight revisions. Franklin's idea had been to "tie in the objective of permanent world peace discussed at Teheran with the natural message of Christmas, peace on earth, good will to men." As one who heard that speech broadcast (I was in tropical Puerto Rico), I found nothing "prosy" about it; in fact, it seemed to me to point up a purpose which hitherto had been obscure. I began, as I suspect millions of others did, to see into the depths of Franklin's mind, to understand his intention. The war, for me, as, I am sure, for others, had a sharper meaning.

Britain, Russia, China, and the United States and their allies, represent more than three-quarters of the total population of the earth. As long as these four nations with great military power stick together in determination to keep the peace there will be no possibility of an aggressor nation arising to start another world war.

But those four powers must be united with and cooperate with all the freedom-loving peoples of Europe, and Asia, and Africa, and the Americas. The rights of every nation, large or small, must be respected and guarded as jealously as are the rights of every individual within our own Republic. . . .

The well-intentioned but ill-fated experiments of former years did not work. It is my hope that we will not try them again. No—that is putting it too weakly—it is my intention to do all that I humanly can as President and Commander-in-Chief to see to it that these tragic mistakes shall not be made again. . . .[8]

[6] January 3, 1944.
[7] P. 412. Rosenman presently would give up his judgeship in New York and move into the White House to stay until the end with Franklin—and beyond, well into the administration of his successor.
[8] Rosenman, op. cit., p. 413.

Time could have it one way. Millions had it the other. These were sadly needed hopeful words. They were also informative.

It was less than two weeks later that Franklin was on the air again, this time to broadcast his State of the Union message. His illness was so serious by now that he did not go to the Capitol as usual but sent it to be read; he could, however, tell it to the nation as a fireside chat. Coming as it did immediately after the Christmas speech and, as well, after the press conference in which Dr. New Deal was dismissed in favor of Dr. Win-the-War, this message had special significance. It was another, more specific, glimpse of a materializing future. It began to show what, besides a firm organization to protect the coming peace, Franklin expected his maneuvering and management to produce in the post-war period. Peace, after all, was a negative objective. There were mighty constructive tasks to be done, although there were few in the United States besides himself who seemed to know it. He meant to arouse other ambitions than those of defeating the nation's enemies and taking suitable revenge for their effronteries.[9]

It was a stirring call to come from a sick man, and it would have reverberations far into the years ahead. Again it must be noted that its plain words, so simply yet so movingly spoken, are, in comparison with Churchill's eloquence, much less musical; but did Churchill envision any such future for mankind as was outlined in these paragraphs? Or, for that matter, was Stalin interested in such matters? We know that both of these statesmen were still thinking far more of ways to win the war and, beyond that, of ways to extend and consolidate their imperial systems. The welfare of humanity had small part in any calculation made by either. Franklin never appeared in grander guise than as he approached victory with a dream of new and loftier aims to be attained in an era of peace—not for a few, not for the victorious, but for all men. They were God's children. They were therefore brothers. He was their champion. Perhaps indeed it was an appointment. If it was late, and if he was tired and worn, it still must be done.

This is what he said:

This Republic had its beginning, and grew to its present strength, under the protection of certain inalienable political rights—among them the right of free speech, free press, free worship, trial by jury, freedom from unreasonable searches and seizures. They were our rights to life and liberty.

As our Nation has grown in size and stature, however—as our industrial

---

[9] I omit discussion of necessary immediate legislation. This will be found in *Public Papers*, 1944–45 vol., p. 37. It included: a new tax law "to reduce the ultimate cost of the war to our sons and daughters," renewed authority to renegotiate contracts ("for two long years," he said, "I have pleaded with the Congress to take undue profits out of war"), a "cost of food law"—to place a floor under farmers' prices—an extension of the stabilization authority, and a national service law to "make available . . . for essential services every able-bodied adult."

economy expanded—these political rights proved inadequate to assure us equality in the pursuit of happiness.

We have come to a clear realization of the fact that true individual freedom cannot exist without economic security and independence. "Necessitous men are not free men." People who are hungry and out of a job are the stuff of which dictatorships are made.

In our day these economic truths have become accepted as self-evident. We have accepted, so to speak, a second Bill of Rights under which a new basis of security and prosperity can be established for all—regardless of station, race, or creed.

Among these are:

The right to a useful and remunerative job in the industries or shops or farms or mines of the Nation;

The right to earn enough to provide adequate food and clothing and recreation;

The right of every farmer to raise and sell his products at a return which will give him and his family a decent living;

The right of every businessman, large and small, to trade in an atmosphere of freedom from unfair competition and domination by monopolies at home or abroad;

The right of every family to a decent home;

The right to adequate medical care and the opportunity to achieve and enjoy good health;

The right to adequate protection from the economic fears of old age, sickness, accident, and unemployment;

The right to a good education.

All of these rights spell security. And after this war is won we must be prepared to move forward, in the implementation of these rights, to new goals of human happiness and well-being.

America's own rightful place in the world depends in large part upon how fully these and similar rights have been carried into practice for our citizens. For unless there is security here at home there cannot be lasting peace in the world.

One of the great American industrialists of our day—a man who has rendered yeoman service to his country in this crisis—recently emphasized the grave dangers of "rightist reaction" in this Nation. All clear-thinking businessmen share his concern. Indeed, if such reaction should develop—if history were to repeat itself and we were to return to the so-called "normalcy" of the 1920's—then it is certain that even though we shall have conquered our enemies on the battlefields abroad, we shall have yielded to the spirit of Fascism here at home.

I ask the Congress to explore the means for implementing this economic bill of rights—for it is definitely the responsibility of the Congress so to do. Many of these problems are already before committees of the Congress in the form of proposed legislation. I shall from time to time communicate with the Congress with respect to these and further proposals. In the event that no adequate program of progress is evolved, I am certain that the Nation will be conscious of the fact.

Our fighting men abroad—and their families at home—expect such a program and have the right to insist upon it. It is to their demands that this Government should pay heed rather than to the whining demands of selfish pressure groups who seek to feather their nests while young Americans are dying.[10]

The Congress paid not the slightest attention. The session of that winter was a worse one, from Franklin's point of view—if that is possible—than that of 1937 when the Court plan had been rejected. The congressional subservience to the pressure groups in Washington had become a groveling scandal. And Franklin's disgust at the spectacle became more and more an irritation he found it hard to conceal. His annoyance reached a quick climax in February, when, instead of taxes to take the profit out of war, the reverse kind of bill was sent him to sign. With his veto he returned the sharpest rebuke of his presidency. It was, he said, "not a tax bill but a tax relief bill providing relief not for the needy but for the greedy." The senators and congressmen were furious, the more so since the rebuke was thoroughly justified and their exposure complete.[11]

This was not the only specific conflict with the legislative branch. Even more annoying was the refusal to enact the manpower legislation asked for in the opening message. There had already been long hesitation about this. It had been thought necessary as a measure for national mobilization ever since the draft had compelled young men to accept military service. The Army and Navy departments had urged it repeatedly, but Franklin had hesitated. He was reluctant, not only because it was being bitterly fought by organized labor, but because he was very conscious that a limitation on bargaining for wages and other conditions of employment was unfair when employers of all sorts were profiteering as they were allowed to do. He only recommended such legislation in correlation with a stringent law to "take the profit out of war."

The Congress, pulled this way and that by pressure groups, could find no consensus. The act was not passed, and in the annual message of 1945 Franklin would still be repeating his request for action.

On other matters there were additional quarrels with the Congress. A bill passed at the instance of the strong farm lobby would have raised the cost of living materially. A sharp veto message said so. And the request for a bill that would have allowed soldiers serving overseas to vote in the coming election was passed in a form which Franklin pub-

[10] *Public Papers,* 1944–45 vol., pp. 40–42.
[11] This was the occasion for Senator Barkley's resignation as majority leader of the Senate. Franklin recanted enough to write Barkley, hoping that he would continue—which he did after being re-elected. But the resultant relations between the two can be imagined.

licly castigated as "futile." It was an unhappy time in these respects and especially so for a President who was ill. By May he was so dangerously exhausted that McIntire intervened and sent him to spend some weeks at Baruch's Hobcaw Barony in tidewater South Carolina, the cypress and magnolia country, so soft and lovely in the early spring. There was much speculation about his disappearance from Washington.

From this time on the suggestion of failing powers was never allowed to die out in people's minds by a press obviously hoping that it might be true. This became so controversial a matter, even in subsequent discussion by historians, that Rosenman was led to comment, and of course McIntire discussed the problem in his *White House Physician*,[12] published after Franklin's death. Getting at the truth is not easy; there are those who are convinced that circulatory pressure had begun to reduce his vigor and even to affect his mental processes; there are others who say that they can tell from his photographs something even more definite. They contend that he had already begun to suffer a series of tiny strokes, which would end in the massive hemorrhage of April 1945. McIntire denied this. Concerning the spring of 1944, so difficult a one in every respect—with legislative quarrels in process, with the war reaching a climax, and with physical disability dogging both days and nights—Rosenman has written a common-sense account which I quote here:

After his return from the Teheran Conference, the President . . . contracted influenza, which prevented him from delivering his 1944 State of the Union Message to the Congress in person. A heavy bronchial cough remained as an aftermath of the "flu," and throughout the late winter and early spring of 1944 the President's resistance was further lowered by a heavy burden of legislative work . . .

In order to lessen the load on his heart, the President early in February dieted to reduce his weight about ten pounds. The President felt in such good condition, as a result, that on his own initiative he reduced his weight another five pounds in March. This loss of fifteen pounds served to lower the President's resistance even further, and he tired quickly.

He was, therefore, happy to accept the invitation . . . to spend some time at the spacious, 23,000 acre Baruch plantation, "Hobcaw Barony," near Georgetown, South Carolina. There, several miles from the nearest highway, and without a telephone, the President could really relax.

The President left Washington on April 8. Because of the beneficial effects of the rest, sunshine, and fishing, he decided to extend his stay until May 7 before returning to the White House.

On numerous occasions from the time he first campaigned for the governorship, malicious rumors were circulated concerning Roosevelt's health. Had any of these rumors been true about any man, he could not have survived the crushing burdens of the President's office during the years of almost continuous crisis as long as Roosevelt did; yet they persisted and were spread

[12] New York: Putnam, 1946.

646

by Roosevelt's enemies and by sensationalists. While the President was resting in South Carolina, more malicious accounts were passed around that he had suffered a stroke or was afflicted by some other ailment. Such rumors were completely false—both then and at any other time. Until, on the day of his death, the President suffered a cerebral hemorrhage—which no physician can predict will or will not occur—none of the responsible physicians who were called in by Dr. McIntire to examine the President expressed any apprehension of any critical ailment.[13]

One thing at least is certain. He returned from the South much rested and better prepared for what was to come. For now D-Day was approaching. Besides, with the warmer season, he could find refuge oftener at Shangri-La. This retreat represented something long wanted by Presidents but never authorized by Congresses inherently uninterested in presidential comforts. No other nation in the world, probably —certainly no large one—had failed to provide a retreat for its chief of state in addition to the central official residence in the capital. But whenever the matter had been broached in Washington the meaner demagogues had had to be dealt with, and such projects had always died.

With aerial war a present fact and the possibility that the Commander-in-Chief might be the target of a raid, it was a military necessity to find a close-by place where, if necessary, he could function. Some fifty miles northwest of Washington an isolated pile of hills furnished some altitude, woodsy surroundings, and easy security. A camp was set up—as a matter of fact, it was a recreation center first—which was inelegant but adequate, and there Franklin went often during the years when Hyde Park was too far away.[14]

Springwood was still maintained and used for entertaining visiting royalty and other dignitaries, and even for occasional weekends. But Eleanor had her own establishment now; it was back from the highway, some two miles from the old house. So, it should be noted, did Franklin, only his was somewhat farther back. He had built "hill-top cottage" just before the war, a retreat overlooking the country he loved.[15]

But most used during the rest of Franklin's presidency was the Catoctin Mountain retreat. The security officers were annoyed when a

[13] This is a note in *Public Papers*, 1944–45 vol., pp. 121–22.
[14] Eleanor, in an access of patriotic generosity, had wanted to turn Springwood into a convalescent hospital. Franklin, doubtless conscious that for her the place had far less precious associations than for him, refused. For some reason the suggestion was regretted in a memorandum; the matter ended with an unusually uppish note on her part saying that "my conscience is free." The exchange will be found in the last volume of *Personal Letters: 1928–1945*, p. 1283.
[15] There is a memorandum about this project written by Franklin himself, motivated by his natural indignation that the press should have labeled it his "dream house." In it he carefully sets out his reasons for the construction. Cf. *Personal Letters: 1928–1945*, Vol. II, p. 378.

gossip columnist, after about a year, made it much less adequate from their point of view by telling all about it. Thereafter they were not much happier when Franklin was there than when he was in the White House. Nevertheless, he continued to use it, and of course the same considerations which by then affected the need for civilian defense affected presidential security—there might be sabotage, but there would not conceivably be an attack from the air.[16]

One of the real achievements of that spring, in spite of all the dissensions, was one measure for which everyone concerned would be called blessed by a whole generation. This was the so-called G.I. Bill of Rights. Under it the returning soldiers, many of whom had been taken away from incompleted educations, were able to go back to schools, colleges, or vocational institutions and find a new start in life. This, together with health benefits, home loans, and disability payments, would avoid, as was Franklin's purpose, nearly all of the mean contentiousness over veterans' benefits which had divided the country for years after every other war.[17]

But this was an isolated achievement. Otherwise the Washington atmosphere reeked with malice. Partisan sniping more and more obscured the national interest. Franklin's health was constantly commented on, the burden of the comment being that he was incompetent. When for thirty-eight days he held no press conference while he was at Hobcaw Barony, it was slyly suggested that he had become unmanageable. He had entrained for the South, it was said, with a corps of physicians, including two psychiatrists. When he reappeared, thin, worn-looking, but brown and alert, the attack took other turns, but it never stopped. It worried the Democrats, who had no alternative but to renominate him; and it elated the Republicans, who hoped this would be their year. Their loss in 1940 had not been too discouraging; and Franklin

[16] Franklin, in his press conference of May 6, 1944, as he was leaving Hobcaw Barony, spoke of this:
. . . the matter of a vacation hide-out for the President is really a problem. Up until two years ago last December, I used to do a lot of cruising down the Potomac. Then there arose the danger of German subs, and of hostile planes flying over the Potomac . . . The navy stopped us.
I looked around for some Government property near Washington where I could spend a holiday. I tried in vain to go to Sugar Loaf Mountain. There's a place up there not far from Frederick. It belongs to a man who doesn't like me; he's going to give it to the Government some day, but he didn't want the President going up there. We found a place up on the Blue Ridge Mountains, but it was practically impossible to get to.
Then up almost to Gettysburg, I found a place . . . It was built as a recreation center, as part of the WPA. It consists of two or three separate camps. It's up in the Catoctin Mountains, near the Pennsylvania-Maryland line . . .
[17] The so-called G.I. Bill of Rights apparently originated with the National Planning Board; but as long ago as 1942 Franklin had set up an educational commission to study and report. The final result, anyway, was a credit to all concerned.

seemed to be in constant trouble now, especially with the Congress, which was sullen when it was not actively hostile. About a fourth term Franklin was saying nothing, but there was no need. His work was not yet done.

If the war panorama was looked at, the contrast with the domestic scene was striking. Everything was pointing up to victory, and soon, at least in Europe; and, if not so soon, just as certainly in the Pacific. It may have been just this prospect which had so loosened the ties of unity at home. It was no longer a matter of survival that the Commander-in-Chief should be supported. And all the irritating restrictions could now be allowed to influence expression and conduct. They would almost certainly be registered in the voting of that fall.

The Democrats seemed at first to have only one strategy open to them —to claim credit for the developing victory. And, similarly, they were reduced to one argument—"don't change horses in the middle of the stream." But gradually, under Franklin's management, the terms of the contest changed. By summer the Republicans were harping on the erosion of sovereignty inherent in Franklin's post-war intentions. He was going to revive the old League of Nations, rejected before, and stuff it down American throats. The Republicans professed not to be averse to international co-operation, but Franklin meant to take away the national power of decision. His new League would commit the armed forces to carrying out the behests of a super-national body on which United States representation would be small.

Franklin, without hesitation, and using his press-conference method, allowed it to become known that he was intending no such thing. Here he had the opposition off balance because its spokesmen had protested strongly that they were not isolationist—a term, by now, in fairly bad odor. When it was made clear that the operating organ of his United Nations was to be a Council unable to act except when the Great Powers were unanimous, Franklin appeared rather more isolationist than those who had been attacking him.[18]

In June, overshadowing everything else and distracting attention even from politics for the moment, the cross-Channel invasion was finally mounted. This had been so long expected that the relief of tension from the unsuccessful first landings was enormous. Hardly ever had so many civilians been able to participate vicariously in a battle. The build-up had been going on in Britain for more than a year, and nearly everyone had known what impended. The only secret was the specific coastal area where the landings would take place. With the warnings so plain, would not the Germans throw the invasion force back

---

[18] Cf. especially the press conference of May 30, 1944, *Public Papers*, 1944–45 vol., p. 140.

into the sea? People wondered aloud. Strategy was dinner-table talk all across the country. There was some luck. Rommel guessed wrong at first and was slow to believe that the Normandy landings were not a feint. The German air force was almost nonexistent, and the mine sweepers did an outstanding job. The weather did not turn out well, and the initial losses were even heavier than had been estimated; but within a week the penetration inland had provided a staging area sufficient for the build-up necessary to a land battle. By that time the German counterthrust was readying; but Allied confidence grew with every day. The fighting was costly. The invaders' courage was put to the test as every mile was gained. Until some time had passed, a real harbor—Cherbourg—could not be gained, and the armor prepared for a break-out. When it came it was one of the most brilliant lightning maneuvers ever executed. The Americans had learned from the German example of 1940 and from their hard lessons in Africa.

The triumphant battle of France would be an election argument superior to any Dewey could adduce. Franklin, winning the war, could hardly lose an election. Things were coming right after all. He had no hesitation in commending the invading army to God. He did it in a prayer he and Anna wrote together at Pa Watson's house and which, as the landing ships began to empty on the Normandy beaches, he read over the radio:

Almighty God: Our sons, pride of our Nation, this day have set upon a mighty endeavor, a struggle to preserve our Republic, our religion, and our civilization, and to set free a suffering humanity.

They will be sore tried, by night and by day, without rest—until the victory is won. The darkness will be rent by noise and flame. Men's souls will be shaken with the violence of war.

For these men are lately drawn from the ways of peace. They fight not for the lust of conquest. They fight to end conquest. They fight to liberate. They fight to let justice arise, and tolerance and good will among all Thy people. They yearn but for the end of battle, for their return to the haven of home.

Some will never return. Embrace these, Father, and receive them, Thy heroic servants, into Thy kingdom.

And for us at home—fathers, mothers, children, wives, sisters, and brothers of brave men overseas—whose thoughts and prayers are ever with them—help us, Almighty God, to rededicate ourselves in renewed faith in Thee in this hour of great sacrifice. . . .

Thy will be done, Almighty God.

Amen.[19]

It was a crowded summer. A few days before the invasion Rome fell. During June and July the nominating conventions were held. The

[19] Ibid., pp. 152–53.

Bretton Woods and Dumbarton Oaks meetings followed, the one to find agreement on international organization, with all the foreign offices represented, and the other to plan for an orderly economic progress into the post-war world, particularly to prevent inflation and to assist in reconstruction. To furnish further sensation, there was the generals' plot to assassinate Hitler, the failure of which did nothing to obscure the dictator's end.

There was, at this time, so much emphasis on victory and what would happen after it that there began to be worry about a letdown. Plane production dropped—in fact, workers everywhere began to take it easy. But the men in the battle lines had still their bloodiest ordeals to meet. The break-out at St. Lô did not come until July 26. Franklin began to think that he had turned people's minds to the far future somewhat too early. He was certain of it when the Stabilization Extension Act, necessary to carry on price control and rationing activities, was passed with reduced rather than increased authority. The country was going to escape from war and war restrictions just as fast as it could. That dangerous disorganization might result was a warning no one believed; there were very few who would consider seriously the fact that the war was not yet won. Everyone wanted just to have it over and go back to normalcy. No exhortation was likely to dam back the flood of abandoned responsibilities. People wanted their boys back home, restrictions lifted, and everything as it had been.

That life in 1938 had not been altogether happy was completely forgotten, perhaps because of the gains of labor and the farmers during the war. The level of living had risen steadily, even though there was a shortage of civilian goods. Unemployment had been at last abolished and every family had an income. If houses were scarce, if there were few automobiles to be had—no new ones—and fewer household appliances, there were more food and more clothing. The enormous expansion of production had taken care of that. Reconversion might bring back unemployment, and in fact the mysterious paralysis of depression; but not many had fears of this sort. Most people wanted war prosperity without war, and they would vote for the man who promised it to them. This threatened to be the theme of the year's electoral campaign.

Franklin could not avoid a good deal of political maneuvering even if mostly in the interest of victory and of post-victory plans. But mostly he was forced to keep his attention centered on the events so swiftly succeeding each other. He could not ignore the Democratic convention, but he could more or less wash his hands of it. And this he did. The hand-washing involved the sacrifice of Wallace to the bosses and the acceptance of Senator Harry S. Truman as his running mate, and of this he cannot have been very proud. But at the moment he was on his way out to the Pacific. As he journeyed by train to the San Diego naval base, and then by cruiser, he must have been telling himself that the immolation of Wallace was justified. He would have called it a contribution to party strength and so to electoral certainty, and so, in turn, to participation in the long work of making a better world. But that he had a bad conscience about it, no one can doubt who studies his behavior.

And he should have had a bad conscience. It was the worst bargain of all his long line of compromising trades. The consequences would run on into a far future and bring the nation to perils far greater than Pearl Harbor, not to mention its effect on the presidential office he himself had done so much to enhance. The Wallace execution was not a thing easily accomplished, either, as Franklin tried to pretend it would be. His weakness for escaping disagreeable situations was never more evidently just that. He accepted from Robert Hannegan, currently chairman of the Democratic National Committee, the dictum that the election depended on abandoning Wallace and finding someone more acceptable to party leaders. There is no doubt that the city bosses disliked Wallace or that the reactionary members of the Congress resented his militant liberalism. But that this meant unpopularity in the country, Franklin must have known was not true. The reverse was the fact. Franklin seems to have gone along in the interest of "party harmony"— which means that in the struggles to come he wanted the bosses committed to him.

When the decision about him was made, Wallace was just returning from a mission to China. Franklin instructed Rosenman to meet him in Seattle and put it to him that the sacrifice was necessary. The plan went awry; Rosenman did not see Wallace until he was home; and then, of all people, Ickes was allowed to be present. Ickes had, for various reasons, been critical of Wallace, and the two had become antagonistic to a degree only possible in such tense circumstances as existed in Washington that summer. Wallace did not accept the Rosenman and Ickes argument. He went straight to Franklin and told him the bosses were deceiving him. Their reasons for ditching him, he said, were quite other than the ones they admitted to. Franklin, under this pressure, became tortuous and promised Wallace to let the convention decide.[20] At the same time he instructed Hannegan otherwise in writing.

Wallace was almost nominated by delegates confused about their instructions and, when they understood them, rebellious about carrying them out. In 1940 Wallace had been accepted under protest; this time he was defeated under just as much protest. Labor and all the liberals were reluctant. But in the end the bosses had their way, and Truman,

[20] He then wrote the equivocal letter that Chairman Jackson read to the convention.

their man, was selected. Wallace was paid for his intelligence and loyalty by being required to give up the succession. It was an expensive sacrifice to the enemy. Franklin, on his way to the Pacific, held his pose of being above the battle. The whole affair was not pretty, and no amount of explaining can make it so. Nothing so tempts the biographer to suggest failing powers as this incident in July, unless it is another that happened in September. That was the acceptance of the fatuous "Morgenthau plan" at Quebec. This, however, was after Franklin returned from the Pacific. About this journey to Hawaii and the Aleutians, something must be said.

General MacArthur detested Franklin. Apart from the sense of rivalry natural in two striking contemporary figures, MacArthur resented having been ordered to Australia when the Philippines were invaded. In spite of every precaution about this, there had been in the popular mind a suggestion of a captain's abandonment of his ship. But added to MacArthur's annoyance about his personal position was his conviction that his theater was being neglected in favor of Europe. To make everything complete, there was the inevitable disagreement as to whose authority was supreme—MacArthur of the Army or Nimitz of the Navy. In the nature of amphibious operations on the scale of those in the Pacific, they had to work together. MacArthur was not one to suffer in silence when his *amour propre* was touched. And he was reported to be near explosion.

Franklin chose to ignore MacArthur's personal feeling that he and his operations had been outrageously handicapped. When it came to a showdown, MacArthur, he apparently felt, would restrain himself. If he did, then he and Nimitz, studying together, could be got to agree on a plan for future operations. MacArthur was already in New Guinea, and the prospect of an island-hopping campaign, calculated to leave many Japanese installations and Army units isolated and useless, was in prospect.[21] This seems to have been something the Japanese had not foreseen. At any rate, the Navy's power in the Pacific was already pressing in on the Japanese in their home waters; and MacArthur, with his army, was expected to make only a few landings instead of many on the way to the final invasion of the islands.

There was controversy concerning the number of islands to be taken. For instance, the Navy would have by-passed the Philippines, something that also infuriated MacArthur, who had said in his most imperious manner on leaving, "I *shall* return." The great moment of his war

[21] This possibility could only have opened as a result of the enormously accelerated shipbuilding program which was enabling the Navy to dispense with shore bases. Not only were many new warships already at work, but a complete service equipment was afloat: the sea trains supporting the fleet were of a size and complexity undreamed of until then.

would be when he again set foot on a Philippine beach and said, "I *have* returned." Now the Navy doubted the utility of such a landing and would preferably have surrounded and pressed home the attack nearer to Japan, leaving the Philippines until later.

Then there was the Chinese theater to be considered. It was not even yet apparent that all the effort being expended in the Burmese jungles and all the organization in India were not going to contribute materially to Japanese defeat. The war would be over before any significant Chinese build-up would take place. Meanwhile Stilwell's bitterness and jealousy were even more outspoken than MacArthur's. He would actually have to be relieved. But that a vast and costly campaign would not be fought in China, no one yet would have believed.

Franklin probably had an active concern about his two commanders, much more about MacArthur because of his political bent—he was already the darling of those curious "isolationists" who wanted to conquer everything in the Pacific or bordering it but had no interest in the Atlantic—a group whose preference would torment American policy for years to come. It was, after all, an election year; if MacArthur should resign, with the fireworks to be expected on such an occasion, the outcome might be affected. And Franklin, as things were going, was not too happy about the prospect anyway.

There was a very noticeable erosion of support for himself which was part of a spreading war-connected disaffection. As the final drives for victory began, the tendency to conclude that it "was all over but the shouting" was turning to resentment that the pressures for production and the restraints on consumption should be as urgent as ever. There was likely to be a big protest vote. For the first time in a national campaign Franklin was inclined to be annoyed with the electorate. It showed in his attitude. Then, too, his bad conscience about Wallace may have soured him for the moment on professional politics. Those around him were even becoming afraid that he would refuse to campaign at all. If he did refuse, the politicians felt, he might very well lose. After their success in displacing Wallace they had thought they could let down and trust the favored bosses to deliver; now they saw that they would have to go to work. And they had to persuade Franklin that he must emerge from his retirement and take the lead. He was sensitive as ever about such matters; he understood the exigency as soon as anyone else.

Political managers are apt to be poor strategists. They tend to concentrate on obvious activities and the marshaling of local support. Franklin must have figured that more was gained than lost when Truman was substituted for Wallace, but he must have known that it was a close calculation. His approach to politics had always been strategic. His weighing of the situation may have told him that if he had the war coming along toward victory, and if the nation had a high level of well-being, surely everything else could be taken for granted. But if an ungrateful nation ousted the winning Commander-in-Chief—well, he was just now inclined to say that they would deserve what they got. Of course it was his business as party leader to prevent any untoward occurrences, and the Wallace incident had not passed off too well. There had been remarkably few of these occurrences in any other campaign; no others could be allowed to happen in this. Specifically, he must see to it that the Pacific preference of the isolationists, coupled with the one politically potent military leader's resentment, was not allowed to create a fortuitous disaster. He must take care about MacArthur.

MacArthur was no political neophyte. He knew that he was not called to Hawaii from New Guinea for military reasons. He was being made use of by a political adversary, and he was resentful. Still, unless he was prepared to give up his command, he must comply. Dewey was already the Republican nominee. MacArthur could not, therefore, return home, lead a revolt, and find himself headed for the White House. If he went home, it would be to retirement. He must smother his choler and join the conferences.

As Franklin's cruiser approached Pearl Harbor there was an immense crowd, both civilian and military, on and surrounding the dock (a strange violation of security in wartime, but there it was), who cheered as the gangplank was lowered to receive on board Admiral Nimitz, General Richardson, and some fifty other high-ranking military and naval officers. They came aboard to be greeted by the Commander-in-Chief on the quarter-deck. Rosenman, who was present, has described the scene:

> One officer was conspicuously absent. It was General Douglas MacArthur. When Roosevelt asked Nimitz where the General was, there was an embarrassed silence. We learned later that the General had arrived about an hour earlier, but instead of joining the other officers to greet the Commander-in-Chief, he had gone by himself to Fort Shafter.
>
> After we had waited on the *Baltimore* some time for the General, it was decided that the President and his party would disembark and go to the quarters on shore assigned to them. Just as we were getting ready to go below, a terrific automobile siren was heard, and there raced onto the dock and screeched to a stop a motorcycle escort and the longest open car I have ever seen. In the front was a chauffeur in khaki, and in the back one lone figure —MacArthur. There were no aides or attendants. The car traveled some distance around the open space and stopped at the gangplank. When the applause of the crowd died down, the General strode rapidly to the gangplank all alone. He dashed up the gangplank, stopped halfway up to acknowledge another ovation, and soon was on deck greeting the President.[22]

[22] Op. cit., pp. 456–57.

A general with this kind of flair was no opponent to encourage. But MacArthur's flamboyancy was no surprise to Franklin: that was why he was in the Pacific. It is interesting to note that he merely said, "What are you doing in that leather jacket? It's darn hot today." MacArthur, as usual, wore a non-regulation uniform. It set him apart from other generals.

With whatever ill-concealed hostility, Franklin sat between Nimitz and MacArthur for three days. They came to the inevitable compromise. The Navy was to support the MacArthur return to the Philippines, meanwhile going on across the northern Pacific and preparing for a final assault when European victory should release the necessary forces. And that seemed not too far off. It was so close, in fact, that even as Franklin conferred in Honolulu, another high-level strategy meeting was becoming a necessity. Eisenhower had to be given orders. Many matters had been left at Teheran in an equivocal state. It remained to make them specific.

It had been seven months since the Cairo-Teheran meetings, the longest interval between Churchill-Roosevelt meetings since 1941, obviously lengthened because of Franklin's concern that Stalin should not think his allies concerting anything behind his back. Why Franklin consented to this Quebec meeting alone with Churchill, it is not at all clear. It had been projected first for Scotland, then for Bermuda, and there seems not to have been any question of Stalin's attendance.[23]

The agenda was restricted: Germany was the main subject. There had been a Russian-British-American Advisory Committee created at Teheran, and it had been meeting inconclusively in London. With the apparent imminence of victory, there must be decisions made both as to zones of occupation and as to Allied policy. It was concerning this last that the unfortunate Morgenthau plan was introduced. This scheme was straight out of the Old Testament, a pulling down of the German edifice and a sowing with salt of the ruins. The Reich was to be made a pastoral country, never again powerful enough to oppress minorities or to threaten neighbors with aggression. It was a not illogical successor to the unconditional-surrender formula announced at Casablanca. It has been suggested, although no one can say whether it is true, that Franklin, as he announced the first and consented to the later policy, was influenced by two politically potent American groups—the Catholics and the Jews—both of whom had ample cause to demand that the Nazis not only be punished but also be made impotent to begin ever again another career of brutality, aggression, and suppression of minorities. This, so far as Franklin is concerned, is sheer speculation.

Since the Morgenthau plan was initialed at Quebec and was, in fact,

[23] He may have refused to come because of his heart attack.

the most important decision of that meeting, it is interesting that Franklin almost at once, but without making any admission, abandoned it as a policy. One reason for this must have been that Stimson, Hopkins, Hull, and others, when they heard of it, broke into violent opposition. At any rate, he proceeded to pretend that he knew nothing about it. Unfortunately his initials were evidence to the contrary. But anyway, the thing never was allowed to control subsequent planning.

I am almost tempted to account for the strange aberration of consent to the Morgenthau plan by guessing that, as his strength failed, Franklin became more and more dependent upon those close to him and that Morgenthau took advantage of this. Hopkins was not at Quebec; in fact, he had reached the period, described by Sherwood, when he was no longer a constant consultant. He was too often ill. The military people who were present thought this a matter beyond their competence. So there was no one to object—until Stimson and Hull heard of the scheme.

There is another possible explanation, not, maybe, to be taken too seriously, but still possible. He may have initialed the plan absentmindedly. He may have been thinking about the peace to come. Then there is reason to believe that, close to his heart at this time, was the revivification of his old scheme for party realignment. The time had come. His waiting had been patient, but his political sense told him not to wait longer. He started his move in the midst of the campaign. Then, too, he had begun, under duress, to think more seriously of the election. Dewey had succeeded in annoying him to the point of setting up a reaction.

Quite apart from speculating as to whether preoccupation with plans for a post-war peace organization, together with those for party realignment at home, occupied him to the exclusion of other matters, these post-war designs must now be considered for their own importance. At the same time that Franklin was corresponding with Wendell Willkie, the Dumbarton Oaks and Bretton Woods meetings were in process; there were matters enough to fill his mind even if there had been no election to think of—and no war.

But this effort to enlist Willkie was part of the emerging design. Franklin was an American political leader. No one could know as well as he that what he hoped for from the war could not be secured by merely setting up an international organization. Only if he, Stalin, Churchill, Chiang, and the emerging leader in France, agreeing and solidly anchored in consent at home, could make certain that the machinery—whatever it was—would work, could they be content to turn it over to successors. Nor was it enough that leaders should agree. They must represent peoples who believed they intended not only to keep the peace but to create the conditions for increasing freedom and well-being and who had themselves chosen co-operation. He may have been better satisfied with Stalin's tenure and even Churchill's than with his own at that moment. He was experiencing the first blows of what he would afterward call the "dirtiest campaign in all history."[24]

His feeling about Dewey—he called him "that little man" and confessed afterward to his son James that "he made me pretty mad"—was that the nation would be betrayed if he should win. Elections, he suddenly felt, ought not to put the nation's future in jeopardy because some politician wanted power. Dewey represented himself as a better internationalist than Franklin; only he was, he said, not a bungler and meddler. Franklin insisted that peace, co-operation, and well-being were the vital needs and that Republicans could not be trusted on such issues. Dewey maintained that the tired old incompetents who had committed the country to do-gooding and sold it out to boondogglers ought to be ousted. The Republicans would make a shrewder peace than the soft-headed Democrats.

The wastefulness and irrelevance of the campaign, as well as the malevolence of the opposition, convinced Franklin that there must be a political realignment. No longer ought it be necessary to trade a decent welfare policy at home for international co-operation. This was what he had been forced to do for years. He was sick of it. Also, he was a little frightened lest everything he had planned should fail. He recalled the experience of 1938—the purge which had backfired. Then, and since, his own party had had a reactionary core whose bargains had grown more and more demanding. He had at last come to the shameful point of sacrificing Wallace. It might have been better had he made another try at capturing the machinery and told the reactionaries he did not want them. He could see now that they could not have kept the nomination from him. Nor, he must have felt, could they have prevented him from being elected. He might lose, but it would not be for this reason.

His bad conscience, together with his feeling about Willkie, caused him to act. Willkie had campaigned vigorously enough against him in 1940, and at the end had even allowed himself to be pushed into extreme positions. But he had repudiated them afterward and had even gone on a visit to Britain and a famous round-the-globe mission with Franklin's blessing, returning to support the foreign policy the Republicans had been attacking. He, more than Franklin himself, had dramatized the one-world concept. Since the war had begun he had been an ardent supporter of the Europe-first strategy. He was, moreover, as had become more and more clear, liberal in domestic matters, so much so that he had refused to compromise in the Wisconsin primary that

[24] In a letter to Mrs. King, *Personal Letters: 1928–1945*, p. 1563.

spring. He had been defeated by Dewey there and had in consequence withdrawn from the race for the nomination. But the liberals in the Republican party recognized him as their leader, and the reactionaries were more than ever his enemies.

Franklin thought that Willkie and he together could do what he had wanted to do so long and had not quite dared to try—they could make a progressive party. One day during the last week in June, Franklin called Rosenman into his office and said to him:

Governor Pinchot has just been in to see me. He has had a meeting recently with Willkie. They talked about the possibility of a new setup in American politics. . . . Willkie has just been beaten by the conservatives in his own party who lined up in back of Dewey. Now there is no doubt that the reactionaries in our party are out for my scalp, too. . . . I think the time has come . . .[25]

Rosenman gives a firsthand account of what followed. Willkie was willing when Rosenman saw him in New York, but, fairly enough, thought it ought to wait until after the election. Franklin was more impatient. He seems to have thought that if Willkie would join him at once they could simply transform the Democratic party. Willkie had his eye on 1948. But Willkie was dead by election time in 1944, and Franklin was dead before another liberal Republican appeared. Thus ended the tentative moves to secure progressive support for internationalism in a nation whose progressives had mostly been isolationists.

It is not necessary to say that Franklin won in November. But a comment or two on the canvass may point up its significance. Reluctant as Franklin was to become active until Dewey seemed to offer a real threat, when he did offer himself to the electorate he was irresistible. He made two appearances likely to be recalled as long as American political records are kept—the so-called "Fala speech" and the last-minute open-car journey through the five boroughs of New York in a cold October rain. The one showed him in the fighting mood his followers had been afraid had been smothered by his increasing feebleness. The other was a heart-rending demonstration that he was not the incompetent old man that Dewey said he was.

The "Fala speech" had its origin in one of the low-pitched rumors the opposition had lately resorted to with more and more frequency. Republican Representative Knutson rose one day in September and told his colleagues that Fala, Franklin's little Scotty dog, had inadvertently been left behind at the Aleutians on the President's trip, that his absence had not been discovered until the party reached Seattle, and that it was rumored that a destroyer was sent a thousand miles to fetch him. Next day Majority Leader McCormack took the floor and indi-

[25] Rosenman, op. cit., p. 463.

cated that he had checked with Admiral Leahy and found that the story was "made out of whole cloth."[26]

I have referred to the Knutson remarks rather than some of Dewey's because Franklin seized on them as the theme for his answer to detractors. It was his tactical instinct that directed him to the devastating reply he came up with. In the speech to Dan Tobin's Teamsters' Union in September he delivered it. His supporters, who had been concerned at his increasing indifference to campaigning, were delighted, and it put Dewey in a hole from which he never escaped. In itself the paragraph at the heart of the address seems trivial; yet it is not too much to say that it turned the tide of that campaign:

> The Republican leaders have not been content with attacks on me, or my wife, or on my sons . . . they now include my little dog, Fala. Well, of course, I don't resent them, and my family doesn't resent attacks, but Fala *does* resent them . . . You know Fala is Scotch . . . as soon as he learned that the Republican fiction writers . . . had concocted a story that I had left him behind on the Aleutian Islands and had sent a destroyer back to find him—at a cost to the taxpayer of two or three or eight or twenty million dollars—his Scotch soul was furious. He has not been the same dog since. . . .[27]

So Franklin climbed down from the Commander-in-Chief position to which he had been keeping and went after Mr. Dewey. There were not many speeches, but there were enough; and to give the campaign a final touch, shortly before election he started out one morning in the Borough of Brooklyn and wound up that night in Manhattan after having covered pretty much the whole city. It was a day of cold rain and driving wind. He rode in an open car, protected only by his old naval cloak and the soft felt hat he had worn through all his campaigns. He spoke a dozen times, shook innumerable hands, got thoroughly chilled, and frightened everyone responsible for him. He laughed off the exposure. He had his teeth in this effort to beat Dewey in New York. But his frailness was apparent and a protective sentiment was aroused. It seemed, however, not to occur to the voters that he might not last out the new term he was asking for; and he did defeat Dewey in New York as he had beaten Hoover, Landon, and Willkie. Sick as he was, he was still what Willkie had called him: "the old champ."

It was hard for the Republicans to deny that the war was being won.[28] It was hard also to oppose a reasoned plan for making another war

[26] Accounts of the origin and writing of the Teamsters' Union speech will be found in both Sherwood and Rosenman.

[27] Rosenman, op. cit., p. 477. *Public Papers*, 1944–45 vol., pp. 284 ff.

[28] Only a few days before the spectacular landings in Leyte Gulf, Dewey had the misfortune to claim that Franklin had willfully withheld support from MacArthur. The general could say, "I *have* returned"; but it was a terrible embarrassment to Dewey.

impossible. Franklin drove home his claim. Dewey had by now slipped lower and lower to resorts presidential aspirants may not use. When it was over he had disgraced himself, and still he had not won. Franklin had now a mandate for collective security. That—and making its acceptance secure at home—was to be the task of his next four years. This was his hope. But with Willkie dead, it cannot have been clear to whom he would turn among the Republicans for an ally. One thing only is certain. He had not given up. He intended to find a way.

31 Presidential campaigns in the United States are inhuman ordeals for the candidates even when they are comparatively tame and there are no competing responsibilities to complicate the canvass. For a man in Franklin's situation in 1944 the proceedings verged on cruelty. True, the war was going well, but it was far from over, and there was reason to fear for its further conduct if demoralization at home continued. He had intended to ignore the political campaign, believing that the Commander-in-Chief (the role which required most of his energy) ought to be more or less immune to partisan attacks. This was a mistaken estimate. The Republican candidate turned out to be reckless and irresponsible beyond anything Franklin had ever experienced. His appeal was to the disgruntled, the irritated, and the restless folk who found it difficult to sustain the long discipline of war. There were many of these, and the number grew alarmingly under Dewey's incitement.

For the later weeks of the campaign Franklin was forced to meet the challenge in the old way. The Teamsters' Union speech had an enormous effect. It encouraged the political workers to know that Franklin had returned to politics with the same skill and much the same zest as in the other contests. But it had another effect; it so disconcerted Dewey, who had thought he could undermine the Commander-in-Chief with immunity by appearing respectable while slyly suggesting incompetence, neglect, and prostitution of the national interest, that he abandoned his dignity altogether and thereafter resorted to mudslinging with a recklessness approaching the intolerable.[1]

This was hard to take while it was going on, but it could be seen

---

[1] Sherwood, op. cit., p. 829, quotes Hopkins as saying: *The President told me he meant it when he said that this was the meanest campaign of his life. He said he thought they hit him below the belt several times and that it was done quite deliberately and very viciously. He was particularly resentful about the whispering campaign which he believes was a highly organized affair.*

afterward how clever Franklin had been to provoke the "little man" to violence. There could be no doubt, when it was all over, that Dewey had contributed to his own defeat by going too far. The Republican vote was swollen by disgruntlement, but those who had not lost their balance altogether saw how incapable Dewey was of assuming the presidency. It finally became downright absurd for anyone not hard-shell Republican to think of him in the White House.

Franklin did not again use the tactics of the Teamsters' Union speech. It had served its purpose. His campaigning after that was pitched to people's intelligences. He asked them to believe that the war was not being won by accident and in spite of its commanders, but because they were competent and careful and had planned and executed a victorious strategy. He asked them further to consider how necessary it was to undertake post-war reconstruction at once to bring the world back to something approaching the normal. And he asked them to support his design for organizing the peace, in concert with the other powers, and in accord with the traditions of free men and free nations.

The result was that when he had won he had reason to argue that the result constituted a mandate—or as near that as any presidential election yields. No one knew better than he, after his many letdowns, how conditional such commitments were. He had no illusion about the incorrigible American indifference to everything beyond the seas. But something had been gained. And that something was enough for him to build on. He would have to go on leading, educating, and urging. But he had confidence that he could carry his country into a system of collective security during the next few years. And he still hoped, we must believe—even though Willkie was gone—to work out a political realignment before 1948 which would underpin the program, domestic and foreign, now identified with him.

What was most in his mind, and what he most wanted those who voted for him to understand as his policy, was made clear in his customary election-eve radio talk from Hyde Park:

When we think of the speed and long-distance possibilities of air travel . . . to the remotest corners of the earth, we must consider the devastation wrought on the people of England, for example, by the new long-range bombs. Another war would be bound to bring even more devilish and powerful instruments of destruction to wipe out civilian populations. No coastal defenses, however strong, could prevent these silent missiles of death, fired perhaps from planes or ships at sea, from crashing deep within the United States itself.

This time, this time, we must be certain that the peace-loving nations of the world band together in determination to outlaw and to prevent war.[2]

2 *Public Papers*, 1944–45 vol., p. 410.

A few years later that passage could be understood. In 1944 he was asking people to take his word for something he could not more frankly reveal. They knew about aerial bombing; he had reason to believe that someday before long the intercontinental bomber, then the manless missile, would be armed with atomic bombs. He was saying what a President just ten years later would repeat with more facts to be cited: "There is no alternative to peace." He was asking now to be supported in creating the institutions appropriate to such a recognition of the inevitable.

It was natural that when he had won he should turn at once to working for these institutions. It is in this light that his January 1945 State of the Union message is to be read. And his fourth inaugural would be keyed to a quotation from Emerson which shows the upwelling of the Christian ethic which underlay his whole design: "The only way to have a friend is to be one." Was it naïve to apply this essentially individual approach to national dealings? Did he think too simply that Russia was Stalin, and that Stalin would respond to friendship? He extended his conception this way: "We cannot live alone at peace . . . our own well-being is dependent on the well-being of nations far away . . . we have learned to be citizens of the world, members of the human community. . . ."

Rosenman watched him at the inauguration standing in the winter cold on the south portico of the White House, without coat or hat, thin now, almost emaciated, but full of Dutch determination. It seemed to this devoted helper that, oblivious of the people before him or of the people all over the world who were listening, the weary President was offering a prayer. "It was a prayer—on the eve of his departure for Yalta—that all the peoples of the world, and their leaders, be endowed with the patience and faith that could abolish war."

In all of Franklin's public appearances now there was a note almost of melancholy. The gaiety and ebullience of past years had disappeared. There was a tone of petition rather than of hope in everything he said. Immediately after the election he had gone to Warm Springs for a three-week stay and had come back brown and a little brighter. But he continued to lose weight, the seams in his thin face had deepened, and the Georgia tan could not disguise the dark discoloration of his eye sockets. Christmas came and went, and for the New Year he was back in Washington, toiling at the same old pile of "wash." But in the last month there had been plenty to worry a much more vigorous President than he was now, and he did not take it well.

That last month of 1944 was the *Dark December* of Robert E. Merriam's vivid story.[3] The Battle of the Bulge was a shock to everyone,

[3] New York: Ziff-Davis, 1947.

and more to Franklin than to anyone else not in the actual fighting. Until Von Rundstedt staged his comeback, the nation had been convinced that the war was practically over. This optimism was suddenly succeeded by a suspicion that it might go on indefinitely. There was wonder whether an inefficiency in the command had been responsible for the break-out of the Germans. A very general reduction of trust in national leadership could be sensed.

By the end of the month it was apparent that the attack had been a last convulsion of the dying Reich, but still the extent of the penetration had not been accounted for. It was one of the worst holiday seasons within the memory of living men. Franklin, reading the *Christmas Carol* to his grandchildren again and making his annual fireside chat, was distraught. His mind was on the forthcoming Big Three meeting. All he had thought won at Teheran was now in doubt. And in the nation's present mood it seemed doubtful whether the year or more of war yet to come in the Pacific would be sustained without a serious rebellion of the spirit. He must make his January State of the Union speech a morale-lifting effort, offering hope and courage; he must go to Yalta resolved on two results: to extract from Stalin a renewed promise to enter the war against Japan lest it run on for years to come, and he must persuade the Russian leader that the United Nations was a cause to be solidly supported.

It was as these responsibilities came up to test his waning strength, and as he read dispatches telling of Von Rundstedt's progress, that he composed his Christmas message, doing it himself this time, with Anna helping. The two of them worked over it on his small table in the Little White House—the winter sun gilding the pines outside. It is, I think, one of his most characteristic communications with his people. And it is so near to being the last one not linked with a special subject that it can be thought of as one among the most moving of valedictories.

It is not easy to say "Merry Christmas" to you, my fellow Americans, in this time of destructive war. Nor can I say "Merry Christmas" lightly tonight to our armed forces at their battle stations all over the world—or to our allies who fight by their side.

Here, at home, we will celebrate this Christmas Day in our traditional American way—because of its deep spiritual meaning to us; because the teachings of Christ are fundamental in our lives; and because we want our youngest generation to grow up knowing the significance of this tradition, and the story of the coming of the immortal Prince of Peace and Good Will. But, in perhaps every home in the United States, sad and anxious thoughts will be continually with the millions of our loved ones who are suffering hardships and misery, and who are risking their very lives to preserve for us and for all mankind the fruits of His teachings and the foundations of civilization itself.

The Christmas spirit lives tonight in the bitter cold of the front lines in Europe and in the heat of the jungles and swamps of Burma and the Pacific islands. Even the roar of our bombers and fighters in the air and the guns of our ships at sea will not drown out the messages of Christmas which come to the hearts of our fighting men. The thoughts of these men tonight will turn to us here at home around our Christmas trees, surrounded by our children and grandchildren and their Christmas stockings and gifts—just as our own thoughts go out to them, tonight and every night, in their distant places . . .

This generation has passed through many recent years of deep darkness, watching the spread of the poison of Hitlerism and Fascism in Europe—the growth of imperialism and militarism in Japan—and the final clash of war all over the world. Then came the dark days of the fall of France, and the ruthless bombing of England, and the desperate battle of the Atlantic, and of Pearl Harbor and Corregidor and Singapore.

Since then the prayers of good men and women and children the world over have been answered. The tide of battle has turned, slowly but inexorably, against those who sought to destroy civilization.

On this Christmas Day, we cannot yet say when our victory will come. Our enemies still fight fanatically. They still have reserves of men and military power. But, they themselves know that they and their evil works are doomed. We may hasten the day of their doom if we here at home continue to do our full share . . .

We pray that with victory will come a new day of peace on earth in which all the Nations of the earth will join together for all time. That is the spirit of Christmas, the holy day. May that spirit live and grow throughout the world in all the years to come.[4]

As the holiday approached, American forces were deployed all over the world, in many strange lands and on many distant seas, and the casualty lists were at their peak. MacArthur's campaign in the Philippines and Nimitz's attack by sea were being pressed as the Battle of the Bulge ran on to its conclusion. War correspondents on many fronts reminded those at home that Christmas to the soldiers would be just another day of exposure, exhaustion, wounds, and death. On the ships there might be a Christmas tree from home, but work and danger would be unremitting.

It says something about the nation in those days that as fear was faced down by the nation's soldiers and sailors the last two acts of the Commander-in-Chief's year should have had to be disciplinary ones for those at home who thought more of themselves than of their country. On December 27 he had to issue an order for the seizure of Montgomery, Ward and Company for refusing to comply with the law requiring the adjudication of labor disputes; and he had to veto a bill, slipped through the Congress at the behest of western cattlemen, abolishing the Jackson Hole National Monument. Both were evidences of a disaffection far more extensive and significant than the matters in-

[4] *Public Papers*, 1944–45 vol., pp. 444 ff.

volved directly in either incident. It was with this kind of selfishness in mind that he reminded the Congress in his State of the Union message that the men on the fighting fronts were entitled to a support they were not getting. They were not getting it from businessmen: but they were not getting it from workers either. Production figures were dropping month by month. Men were leaving their jobs for better ones in after-war industries, and strikes were becoming more and more numerous.

Franklin renewed his demand for a national service law, without much hope of getting it. And if the whole section of this message having to do with affairs at home seemed pessimistic, there was ample reason. It was not that the war was not being won—it was—but the winning had inglorious overtones. A peace so won would not be the peace he had hoped to see established. Naturally he spoke of the coming victory. But he began by admitting that "the nearer we come to vanquishing our enemies, the more we inevitably become conscious of differences among the victors." And he went on to warn his hearers that the United States could not always prevail in international bargaining. There must be compromise, and to compromise means to give up something desired. "Nations," he said, "like individuals, do not always see alike or think alike, and international co-operation and progress are not helped by a nation assuming that it has a monopoly of wisdom or of virtue."

This was a plea for support as he went to a new bargaining session. Yalta was just ahead.[5] Too much was to be made of Yalta during the decade after Franklin's death. It would be said that the American negotiators sold out to the Russians, ignored Churchill's sage advice, and left the way open for the Communist conquest of eastern Europe. Most of this was obvious nonsense to anyone who consulted the record rather than his prejudices. It was, for instance, the military men who were most anxious for Russian participation in the Japanese war and who felt that concessions in this interest were well worth their price. They still felt that the Japanese armies would have to be defeated in the field, even though, as they met, Iwo Jima was being taken and the Philippines were being cleared. The vast fleet under Nimitz was destroying the Japanese Navy. Nothing but Okinawa now barred the way to the home islands. But Marshall and the others had not yet concluded that there would be no mainland campaign. Nor, as a matter of fact, was Churchill any wiser.

There were, besides the military problems in the East, those having

[5] Much material concerning the Yalta Conference will be found in the memoranda published by the Department of State in 1955. But the individuals who were there are also on record. Churchill, Leahy, Hopkins (in Sherwood, op. cit.), Stettinius, Byrnes—all have published their impressions in one or another form.

to do with a defeated Germany—the American and Russian armies were now only some three hundred miles apart. Then there were others concerning the re-establishment of the governments about to emerge from Nazi occupation. But these questions, as we already know, were dwarfed in Franklin's mind by the need for final agreement on the form and functioning of the organization for peace, now known as the United Nations. He felt that Dumbarton Oaks and Bretton Woods had been good beginnings, but he had no very clear idea about Stalin's views. At Teheran all the Russians had been indifferent. Would they now have a livelier interest?

Franklin's entourage included some new personnel. Hull, having declined gradually into senility, had gone from the Department of State, and his place had been taken by Edward R. Stettinius, generally said to have been a Hopkins choice.[6] General Arnold had to send a substitute because he was in hospital with pneumonia. It was noted, too, that Franklin had invited Ed Flynn to accompany him, which seemed to indicate a need to commit the city bosses to the bargains he was about to make.[7] Besides these, there were the regulars—Hopkins and Marshall. Hopkins, still ill, would spend most of his days in bed but would still have much to say about what went on. The company was the most numerous of those at any of the conferences, and Yalta's accommodations were the most crowded. The small Crimean resort—about which Mark Twain had written years before—had been knocked to pieces and looted by the Germans; and although the Russians frantically tried to effect repairs in time, there was far from room enough for all those present. Some notes speak of generals and admirals sleeping ten or more in a room, a circumstance that would have pleased many a soldier or sailor fed up with the pompousness of the "brass." Communications were difficult. The *Catoctin* stood by some eighty miles away at Sevastopol (it could not come closer for fear of uncleared mines in Yalta waters), and the signal men had laid lines all that distance.

Franklin had journeyed to Malta on the *Quincy* and had had ten days at sea, something which would usually have brought him to a state

[6] Stettinius had brought into the Department an assortment of assistants whose appointment had been discouragedly deplored by Franklin's liberal friends—who were now in mourning for the departed New Deal. They included Joseph C. Grew as Under Secretary, and Will Clayton, Nelson Rockefeller, and James C. Dunn, Assistant Secretaries. The presence among them of Archibald MacLeish did not sufficiently sweeten the dose; they were regarded as reactionaries. Such senators as Guffey, O'Mahoney, and Maloney asked out loud if more liberal appointees could not be found; and these were Franklin's friends. But we see now that he was not pleasing friends but enemies, in preparation for the ordeal of ratification to come after Yalta.

[7] But Flynn, after all his services, had been roughly treated by the party. Franklin may have been paying him something in prestige.

of sparkling health. But Admiral King, who went on board the cruiser in the harbor of Valletta, said afterward that he had been alarmed by his evident deterioration during the two weeks since he had seen him last at the inaugural ceremonies. Ill as he looked, however, he was excited by the prospect of new experiences as he boarded his plane to make the rest of the trip by air. The night of February 2–3 must have been a busy one at Luqa airfield. Transport planes, taking off at intervals of minutes, conveyed seven hundred people across the Aegean and the Black Sea to Saki airfield in the Crimea. It was done under strict security controls; the Germans seemed to know all about the meeting.

Franklin landed on Saturday, February 3; Stalin did not come until Sunday. But when he did arrive, he and Molotov immediately came to call. The two chiefs of state at once settled down for a talk. It lasted for only about an hour in Franklin's study in the Livadia Palace; at five they moved down to the Grand Ballroom for the first of the formal meetings; but in that hour they exchanged news of the war and raised between them several questions having to do with German occupation. It seemed a good beginning.

One interesting feature of the Yalta proceedings was that there were really three meetings going on simultaneously: that of the heads of government, that of the Foreign Ministers, and that of military staffs. This was partly the result of learning by experience how to conduct such affairs; but partly, too, it was an indication of the growing confidence the various participants felt in each other. This was the first time there had been real military talks with everything—or nearly everything—laid on the table. The Americans, it must be said, withheld their approach to success with the A-bomb.[8] But otherwise there were no secrets, and the military exchanges were valuable to all three high commands. While Yalta was in progress, Manila fell and toasts were drunk in celebration; but there was no remission in the American desire for Russian assistance against Japan. As before, it was freely given and a date set—three months after German surrender.

On the diplomatic level this was paid for by certain concessions in the Far East having to do with ports, railways and off-shore islands.[9] There was, in this instance, the same easy exchange as at Teheran about political matters. Franklin understood perfectly when Stalin said that the Russian people would wonder why war was declared on Japan unless some objective of national interest was to be gained.

[8] It was suspected that the Russians knew about it, but Stettinius and Marshall thought it best to wait and see if it was mentioned. It never was.
[9] Cf. Stettinius, *Roosevelt and the Russians* (New York: Doubleday, 1949), pp. 91–92 for a convenient summary, although the same information may be found in other accounts, including the Yalta material published by the Department of State. The real author of the Stettinius book was Professor Walter Johnson of the University of Chicago.

There was cause to wonder, however, whether it was the Russian people Stalin was concerned about or whether it was his fellow members of the Politburo. The Americans were aware that he was having difficulty—the same difficulty diplomatic negotiators always have, and the same one Franklin had taken such pains to avoid for himself. He was being suspected of giving too much and getting too little. In Stalin's case this may well have accounted for intransigence about a number of issues—such as exaggerated demands for reparations and, on the Polish question, unwillingness to agree to the interim arrangements for government and for the demarcation of borders. It would be on this question that the later serious differences would arise which were pending as Franklin died and which, it appeared, only he could have straightened out.

Franklin had warned the Congress and the American people very plainly, as we have seen, that in negotiations it is necessary to give as well as to get. At Yalta he was fortunate in not being asked for concessions in any area vital to the United States. It would afterward be said that he had, but it is impossible to see anything in such claims but prejudice.[10]

As Stalin, Churchill, and Franklin talked, differences developed in several areas; but none of these seemed impossible to work out amicably, and several of them were referred to the Foreign Ministers' group —Stettinius, Molotov, and Eden—for study.[11] The central problems, in Stalin's view, had to do with Germany, with Poland, and with other eastern European countries; but Franklin's best efforts were directed toward final agreement on a structure for the permanent United Nations. What indifference remained he must convert into enthusiasm.

The German problem divided itself into questions of dismemberment, occupation zones, and territory to be taken over by Poland on the east and possibly France on the west. Before the end, agreement had been reached on all these matters. The Polish problem consumed much more time, was more difficult to compromise, and was left in the most unsatisfactory state. There were a number of reasons for this. For Russia a friendly Poland was a necessity; for Britain a free Poland was what she had entered the war against Germany to secure; for the United States there was a political sensitivity arising from the vast number of

---

[10] It is true that the agreement with the Russians about the Far East was kept secret, but that was for military reasons. It would have been foolish to notify the Japanese that they were presently to be attacked by the Russians.
[11] It should be recalled that ever since Teheran there had been a European Advisory Commission at work in London. Little was accomplished by this group, but a good deal of background work was done, and at least many differences were revealed. The real problems were known to all three governments when Yalta convened.

Polish immigrants. During the war there had been a government-in-exile in London, and the Russians sponsored another at Lwow in Poland. It seemed necessary, if there was to be a compromise, to amalgamate these governments in some way that would serve until there could be elections. An arrangement to this effect was agreed on after the Foreign Ministers had argued the matter at some length:

The Provisional Government now functioning in Poland should be reorganized on a broader democratic basis with the inclusion of democratic leaders from Poland itself and from Poles abroad. This new government should then be called the Polish Provisional Government of National Amity.

There was an arrangement in the same protocol for Molotov, Harriman (U. S. Ambassador), and Sir A. Clark Kerr (British Ambassador) to consult the Provisional Government and to work out the composition of the Government of National Amity which should be responsible for holding free elections. The Soviet Union pledged itself to recognize this reconstituted regime.

It was in the subsequent negotiations, Harriman participating, that the serious post-Yalta troubles arose which led on, after Franklin's death, to the long cold war pursued by his successor, Stalin always protesting that it was Harriman, and not he, who had caused the rift. The rift would enlarge itself rapidly once it was opened. Whether its original causes could have been compromised and the later bitterness prevented will always be matters for argument. It must be enough here to say that, as he left Yalta, Franklin anticipated no such succeeding trouble, and that as he died he was studying the means for conciliation.

All the participants, as they departed, seemed to feel that much had been accomplished. Especially, of course, the international organization had been advanced. Indeed a time and place had been fixed for its initial meeting—San Francisco, on April 25, 1945. This meant, at the least, that the differences concerning it had been resolved. They had not really been serious, anyway. The Russians had been insisting that no small nation should be able to commit the large ones—and specifically the Soviet Union—to any action. But that had been one of Franklin's first principles too. And it was agreed that, in the Security Council, resolutions should pass with seven votes, all five of the Great Powers voting in the affirmative. This meant that each had a veto and that all actions must be unanimous.[12] There was further negotiation about votes in the Assembly; the Russians had been asking for sixteen, one for each of the Soviet republics. They gracefully came down to three (one each for the Ukraine, Byelorussia, and the U.S.S.R.). It was left that the

[12] If the Russians had not insisted on this, the Americans would have. Not only Franklin but the military men as well were set against committing American forces to projects originating elsewhere.

United States might also have the same number, but Franklin decided against asking for more than one. The Assembly was, after all, only a debating group.

It has to be said that the progress made at Yalta toward establishing the United Nations was due entirely to Franklin's initiative. The British were interested mostly in the Empire, and Stalin in an alliance of the Big Three.[13]

Stalin nevertheless agreed to an organization that was much more than a Great Power consortium. For instance, there were other members of the Security Council, although the Great Powers must each consent to any action. And, much against his original wishes, Stalin also consented to full and free discussion in the Assembly. This made of the UN a forum to be used alike by small nations and great ones.

Franklin, when he spoke of the Yalta achievement to the Congress on March 1, made a modestly optimistic statement. It was obvious that he felt it to have been a good beginning, even if not more than that:

. . . For the second time, in the lives of most of us, this generation is face to face with the objective of preventing wars. To meet that objective, the nations of the world will either have a plan or they will not. The groundwork of a plan has now been furnished and has been submitted to humanity for discussion and decision. No plan is perfect. Whatever is adopted at San Francisco will doubtless have to be amended time and again over the years, just as our own Constitution has been. No one can say exactly how long any plan will last. Peace can endure only so long as humanity really insists upon it, and is willing to work for it, and sacrifice for it.

Twenty-five years ago, American fighting men looked to the statesmen of the world to finish the work of peace for which they fought and suffered. We failed them. We failed them then. We cannot fail them again, and expect the world to survive.

I think the Crimea Conference was a successful effort by the three leading nations to find a common ground for peace. It spells—and it ought to spell—the end of the system of unilateral action, exclusive alliances, and spheres of influence, and balances of power and all the other expedients which have been tried for centuries and have always failed.

We propose to substitute for all these, a universal organization in which all peace-loving nations will finally have a chance to join.

I am confident that the Congress and the American people will accept

---

[13] Stettinius reported one conversation of his own with Franklin when he was puzzled about the British attitude on the proposed Trusteeship Council. Franklin told him he had discussed the matter with Chiang Kai-shek and Churchill separately. Chiang had said that China did not want Indochina and, in fact, regarded a trusteeship as a good solution. Churchill, when he heard this, said "Nonsense!" Then Franklin said to him, "Winston, this is something which you are just not able to understand. You have 400 years of acquisitive instinct in your blood and you just do not understand how a country might not want to acquire land somewhere if they can get it. A new period has opened in the world's history and you will have to adjust yourself to it."

the results of this conference, as the beginnings of a permanent structure of peace upon which we can begin to build, under God, that better world in which our children and grandchildren—yours and mine, and the children and grandchildren of the whole world—must live, can live. . . .[14]

This appearance on Capitol Hill had been carefully prepared for. Franklin was gravely ill, as was now apparent to everyone, but the pains he took to see that the results of the Yalta meeting should have a favorable report were as meticulous as any he ever arranged. On the day the first communiqué was issued a presidential assistant carried it to the Capitol and gave senators and representatives a look at it before publication.[15] Also Mobilizer Byrnes, who had been in the party, flew straight home and at once called a press conference. He told the newsmen that Franklin had been chairman of the conference, had been responsible for the compromise on the Dumbarton Oaks voting formula, and had written the section applying to liberated countries. Later he too went to the Capitol and did a good deal of explaining.

Just one day after Yalta, Franklin announced his choices for delegates to the forthcoming San Francisco meeting. From the Republicans, he passed over both Dewey, the party's titular leader, and Hiram Johnson, ranking minority member of the Senate's Foreign Relations Committee; his choices were Senator Vandenberg, ex-Governor (of Minnesota) Stassen, and Representative Eaton. From the Democrats, he named Stettinius, Hull (this was honorific; Hull was in the Bethesda naval hospital and would never again have any part in public affairs), Senator Connally, and Representative Sol Bloom. As a woman, presumably, he also added Dean Virginia Gildersleeve of Barnard College. The appointments were well received and seemed to ensure bipartisan cooperation for what was to come. Wilson's return from Paris was distinctly not to be repeated by his successor's return from Yalta.

But if co-operation seemed assured for the final moves to establish the framework of that international organization through which, Franklin hoped, he and the others might see the world well on the way to peace and well-being, there was even less co-operation, if that was possible, for any other purpose. Even while he was away it became clear that his second attempt at a "labor draft," as his manpower bill was being called, had failed. Stimson was angry. He called the Senate's dithering on this issue "a failure of democracy" and warned the senators that "deadly shortages were looming up," a warning the legislators evidently could not hear.

There was, at the same time, an ignoble hassle about the confirmation

---

[14] *Public Papers*, 1944–45 vol., pp. 571–72.
[15] This was ex-Congressman J. M. Barnes. The communiqué was released before the meetings were over. The air by now was full of rumors being complicated by Goebbels' efforts to confuse everyone.

of Henry Wallace as Secretary of Commerce. Franklin had promised the displaced Vice-President his choice among governmental posts after election, and Wallace had chosen Commerce. Jesse Jones was Secretary at the moment, having succeeded Hopkins; it was undoubtedly painful for Franklin to dismiss Jones, who had so many close connections on the Hill. A row was certain to result. Jones had kept his RFC chairmanship by taking the Corporation into the Department of Commerce. The reactionaries made a loud protest at the thought of "that madman" Wallace having control of all the billions in loan funds which were at the disposal of the Corporation. Senator George at once concocted a bill to re-establish RFC as an independent agency. Wallace's confirmation was then made conditional on the passage of this bill. It was an insult, of course, both to Wallace and to Franklin, but in the end both were forced to swallow the reactionary ultimatum.

Franklin, on the whole, was returning to a capital more divided, more resentful of his popular strength, more determined to slough off all wartime discipline even than the one he had left. And that one had seemed about as far gone in disaffection as was possible. He must have dreaded the prospect. Nevertheless, as he journeyed homeward he made other essays toward a better world. As the *Quincy* lay in Great Bitter Lake (midway along the Suez Canal) he entertained three of the Middle East kings: Haile Selassie of Ethiopia, Farouk of Egypt, and Ibn Saud of Saudi Arabia. Newsmen, who had not been present at Yalta but had joined the party for the trip home, had a field day with the kings. Especially did Ibn Saud furnish colorful copy. The picture of Franklin, his naval cloak about his shoulders, conversing with the turbaned King in his voluminous robes, on the cruiser's deck, went some way to offset the frightening picture that had gone home from Yalta. Franklin, in the official photograph, central figure of the Big Three, had been disclosed to be a frail and wasted man between two companions who by comparison seemed well nourished and in good health. From this time on there was no doubt in anyone's mind that his was a life in extreme jeopardy. The news had got around, moreover, at least in Washington, that the Secret Service had set up a significant night-and-day watch over the Vice-President. The conclusion from this was not difficult to draw.

The other effort on the homeward journey was a conciliatory one. Considering the circumstances, it was generous, but it was not received as such. De Gaulle was asked to meet with Franklin at Algiers and refused. Franklin, de Gaulle must have known, had been largely responsible for the decision at Yalta to return France to Great Power status by giving her an occupation zone in defeated Germany—something the French contribution to the war, Stalin thought, had not merited. In fact the Russians thought the suggestion absurd. De Gaulle, however, long

674

annoyed with Franklin, chose to be miffed because he had not been asked to make the Big Three into the Big Four. Franklin shrugged off the slight, but he must have had some worry about a France whose most prominent leader could behave so haughtily when he ought to have been, as one French journal said, "on his knees with gratitude."

Yalta was received very well at first by most of the American press; but before many days had passed, the Chicago *Tribune*, the New York *Daily News*, and lesser journals of the bitter-enders had recovered their usual initiative. They found plenty of fault and even began to hint at secret agreements—"sell-outs" to the Russians. And of course there *were* two deals not mentioned in the communiqués. One was the Far East concession in exchange for Russia's entrance into the war. The memorandum about this was locked in Franklin's safe. It, however, had a military excuse. The other was the arrangement for Russia to have three votes in the UN Assembly. Why this was not mentioned, no one seems to know. It was sure to come out at San Francisco if not before, and it was an ideal morsel for the opposition press. It did presently come out, and there was a first-rate storm that seemed for a time to threaten all the good work so carefully done before. It was a matter of no importance, the Assembly being what it was, and ought not to have been concealed, as everyone but Franklin seems to have recognized. This was a delayed bomb. Otherwise even the most hostile newspapers had difficulty in presenting the conference in a bad light, and there was reason to believe that their efforts were causing a reaction. By the first of April the atmosphere, if not friendly in the press, was decidedly hopeful and friendly elsewhere, even, for the most part, on Capitol Hill.

As March ran out and the San Francisco conference began to be prepared for, it was obvious to every commentator that in spite of the failure of all his legislative program, and in spite of the sniping still in progress, Franklin had refused to be diverted from the next necessary achievement for his grand design—the firm establishment of an organization for peace. He entertained Mackenzie King, Canadian Prime Minister, and this was linked with conference arrangements. Also, it was noted, he had seen to it that the American delegates to San Francisco were adequately briefed and that they were received with due ceremony at the White House. Everything was as ready as it could be. He was reported to be cheerful about the prospect.

He could also be cheerful about the war. The Germans were still fighting—"unconditional surrender" had seen to that—but most of the battlefields were now inside Germany. The exception was Italy, where Kesselring still had some twenty-seven divisions standing off the Allied drive toward the Alps. It was reported that the Nazis were preparing a bastion in the mountains of southern Germany, but the Rhineland had fallen when the river itself was crossed, and the Russians were almost upon Berlin. The bombings of the last months, especially since the Luftwaffe had almost disappeared, had been frightful. Cities were reduced to rubble; transportation was disrupted; even the countryside was devastated. There would be no more sorties like the Battle of the Bulge. A little more time for the Allied armor to penetrate, a few more weeks of hammering from the skies, and what was left of Hitler's Reich would be prostrate before the invading armies.

Out in the Pacific, after bombing Tokyo in February, the carrier task groups were appearing closer and closer to the islands. But also the big B-29s were now raiding with a new and devastating technique—large-scale night fire-bombing, the most terrifying of all possible attacks to the flimsily built cities of Japan. Tokyo, Kobe, and Osaka had been struck again and again. MacArthur was still in the Philippines, clearing out the Japanese resistance, but he had plenty of force now at his disposal and would soon be ready to move on to Formosa, Okinawa, and then the home islands.

Everywhere, as Franklin studied his maps, it was now just a matter of time. There would be more casualties. The Chiefs of Staff thought it might cost a million lives to invade Japan and many more to defeat the armies in Manchuria and China; but not so many of these would be American lives if the Russians came in as now they were pledged to do. In Europe it was about over. The final drive was starting. And resistance was not likely to be very costly with the Russians also closing in from the east.

Yes, he had been an architect of victory, a really momentous one from which the whole world would emerge changed. It cleared the way for reconstruction. And this was the work to which he could now turn without distraction, using his talents to carry with him the reluctant Churchill and the tough but realistic Stalin. He was weary, almost too weary, we may guess, to indulge the elation over his magnificent achievement to which he was entitled. He was also thoroughly disgusted with the performance of the Congress as its tactics became meaner and meaner in the effort to show the man in the White House that the legislature was still his master. At the moment, Aubrey Williams, in New Deal days Harry Hopkins' right hand in WPA, who had been nominated to be administrator of the Rural Electrification Administration, was being subjected in confirmation hearings to intolerable humiliations at the hands of old Senator McKellar of Tennessee and his colleagues. It was done to bring Franklin to heel on domestic policy. This was a forecast, he must have thought, of the fights to come.

It may well be that he was already telling himself how he would act when the peace treaties were ratified. He would then notify the reactionaries that he would no longer trade, that compromising was done with, past. It can be imagined how he savored in prospect the occasion when they should learn that 1948 was to be different. He can be pictured smiling to himself and whispering, "A New New Deal." The progressives he had so long held at arm's length would then be ingathered; and, together at last with his natural friends, he would go forward to the work for the world yet to be done.

Aubrey Williams' nomination was rejected by the Senate, fifty-two to thirty-six. Against him were nineteen Democrats, most of them from the South, in addition to thirty-three Republicans; for him were thirty-one Democrats, four Republicans, and one Progressive. This, Franklin must have thought, is about the way it is. This was the first time in six years that the Senate had rejected one of his nominations.[16] Not that they had never wanted to, but that he had always had something to bargain with. The reason for this rejection was no mystery; as much as anyone could, Aubrey Williams personified that part of the New Deal which put welfare ahead of business, which cared when ordinary folk were hungry, insecure, and unhappy. Williams himself said it: "I'm just Joe Doaks in this thing." He was defeated, he said, because he "openly espoused the idea of getting power into the hands of the common people . . ."

The Williams issue came at a time when his old friend Hopkins was again immured in the Mayo Clinic. But even if he had been in the White House there was nothing he could have done. There was nothing Franklin or his friends had to yield any more which would appease the reactionaries. Or possibly Williams was inadvertently the last straw. It may well have been that Franklin at last had come to the end of his long immolation. San Francisco was about to occur. Ratification of the Charter had been paid for and ought to be delivered. That done, Franklin would at last be able to team up with those whose minds ran with his own—Democrats, Republicans, or Progressives.

At any rate, the nasty Williams business was about the last occurrence in Washington before Franklin went off South to meet the spring. The Little White House on the hillside in the Georgia scrub was bright in the sun of April. It must have felt good on the face of the depleted man who took up the familiar Warm Springs routine once more. It really did seem like home, and never had he needed home so much.

As he settled down, perhaps to consider what to do after San Francisco, suddenly his international arrangements seemed to go to pieces. It was disclosed—as it was bound to be—that the Russians were to have three votes in the UN. The New York *Herald Tribune* broke the story and forced a White House explanation. "Secret deal," screamed the isolationist press. It threatened to become a *cause célèbre*. Immediately

---

[16] Although the nomination of Ed Flynn to be Ambassador to Australia had been withdrawn under pressure, a surprising occurrence, considering that Flynn had been chairman of the National Democratic Committee.

Franklin heard, too, that the Russians were intending to slight San Francisco by sending a second-rate delegation. Even Molotov was not coming. But this was not the worst occurrence. That was Stalin's quarrel with Harriman in Moscow about the Polish government, the issue which had so troubled the conference at Yalta.

Then Stalin in effect demanded that the Yalta compromise be abandoned and that his puppets in Warsaw be invited as participants at San Francisco. Britain quickly refused; Franklin hesitated, then he too refused. I think, however, that this rift worried him less than other matters. He and Stalin were too practical to allow such an issue any great weight. If things could be postponed until they met again, everything could be put right.

There was a good deal of talk around Washington that the forthcoming peace conference was premature. There were many differences, it was said, yet to be resolved; also, the Russians were not to be trusted. The flurry in the press caused no change in Franklin's plans; his speech for the opening ceremony was being got ready, and he himself, as he always did, was poring over the schedules for his trip to the Coast. San Francisco simply had to happen.

Rosenman was in Europe on a mission, Eleanor was about her own affairs, Hopkins was ill, Steve Early was holding the fort at the White House. Franklin had the company of his maiden-lady cousins, Laura Delano and Margaret Suckley; and Bill Hassett, his secretary, was present to replenish the "wash" on his table as fast as it was disposed of. Spring was high in Georgia, the Judas trees were red, and mixed with the pervasive smell of pine there were hints of newly blooming shrubs. The cool mornings allowed an open fire, but later on the sun burned away the mist, and the doors could stand open to the woods.

On the morning of April 12 all was as it had been. The plane bringing the mail had been delayed so that Franklin was late getting to his papers. Hassett asked if he would rather lunch before he went to work on them; but Franklin said no, he had a busy afternoon coming up, he'd better get through. He was going to a barbecue, among other engagements, later in the day; and in the evening there was a minstrel show to be seen. It was to be in his honor, put on by the polio patients. They had practiced for weeks, and he would not have missed it for any other entertainment he could think of.

The Misses Delano and Suckley sat serenely by the fire. Miss Suckley was crocheting. Mrs. Schoumatoff, the latest of many portrait artists to ask for a sitting, was sketching in the room. Franklin signed a bill and several commissions; Hassett spread them out, remarking to the artist, "Don't mind me. I'm waiting for the laundry to dry." Presently he got his papers together and went out. It was quiet in the smallish, cozy, resinous study. Miss Suckley looked up from her crocheting; Cousin

Franklin had slumped sidewise in his chair. She ran to him. He whispered, "I have a terrific headache." Then he fell into unconsciousness and never again emerged.

Arthur Prettyman, his big valet, was used to lifting Franklin around; with some help from a Filipino messboy he got him into his arms and carried him to his bed. In the little wood-paneled room, with its characteristic naval picture on the wall and its chronometer to tell the time, and on his narrow bed, he died a few hours later—a little after half-past three. The children down the hill in the big hall had been rehearsing earnestly that morning for the minstrel show that never would be given; and Jess Long's Brunswick stew, prepared for the barbecue at Frank Alcorn's house up on the ridge, would never be eaten by the man who had once loved such good and hearty food and good and hearty company.

The news seeped across the nation. Eleanor, sent for at the Sulgrave Club on DuPont Circle, where she was attending a benefit tea for Washington's children's clinics, rode back to the White House and heard from Steve Early that her husband (of forty years; they had recently celebrated an anniversary) was dead. She thought first of the world's millions for whom, as she knew, he had had unfinished work to do, work that only he knew about. "I am more sorry," she said, "for the people of the country and the world than I am for us." She thought next, characteristically, of Harry Truman. Steve Early telephoned for him and presently he came. When he asked what *he* could do, she returned gently, "Tell us what *we* can do." She knew better than he what was about to happen to him; very likely she suspected that the advice he was likely to take would be the kind that would commit him to a reversal of the dead President's intentions. She could hardly have foreseen that the cold war would follow the intransigence toward Russia of the reactionaries in the cabinet, the Department of State, and the embassies everywhere. But she knew—no one better—that Franklin's method was a personal one and that his negotiations and maneuverings for the world he wanted were far from over. She must indeed have looked at Harry Truman with genuine pity; but she must have felt an even more overflowing concern for the vast masses whose poor lot had been made desperate by the war and for whose rehabilitation the plans had been mostly in the mind and heart now inactivated forever.

The husk which had been a husband was in Warm Springs. With Early and McIntire that night she flew down the states, arriving before dawn. She went directly in to sit beside him. When day came, the cousins, the Misses Delano and Suckley, rode with her—three quiet women in a dark limousine—behind the hearse brought to carry his body. For the last time, leaving the Springs, Franklin was allowed his custom of passing the Administration Building where the crippled victims of the disease he had fought so long lined up in their wheel chairs to see him go. As the procession paused in passing, it is recorded, Graham Jackson, a Negro accordionist who had been one of Franklin's favorites at patients' parties, stood facing the man he had loved and played "Going Home."

The casket was draped with the flag; a band from Fort Benning, with drums and brass, seemed to give notice that a nation's mourning was joined with that of the widow—and of the little dog Fala who went aboard the waiting train with her. Soldiers, sailors, and marines took up their watch and the train rolled slowly out toward Atlanta. By way of Greenville, Charlotte, and other Carolina cities, it pushed its way up toward Virginia and Washington. Along the route, men and women stood uncovered, as they had when Lincoln had rolled homeward behind a chugging engine to Springfield. In thousands they stood near the stations, and often those in the train could hear spirituals being sung; often the faces they saw were twisted with a grief that blotted away self-consciousness. People's masks were off that day.

These evidences of broken bonds and of the lost feeling as people realized that the President was gone forever from the places where he had been their surrogate were intensified as the casket—on a caisson now, young men in the nation's uniform marching with it, bands again speaking agonizingly to their ears and muffled drumbeats seeming to echo in their hearts—was drawn down Pennsylvania Avenue.

I had heard the news in Puerto Rico late the day before—too late to answer the funeral summons. My wife and I asked the Episcopal bishop of Puerto Rico to hold a memorial service. As we left La Fortaleza, in the car carrying the governor's flag, for the cathedral service, the San Juan streets, although there were crowds all along the way, were quiet. Shopkeepers had closed their doors; workmen had simply gone home. They stood to watch the governor's car go by, as if it were some kind of symbol of the man who had been their friend. The tears on their faces were, I thought, a fitting remembrance for him who was gone. It was, I knew, the same in vast reaches of every continent.

The funeral service was read in the East Room of the White House, as it had been for Lincoln. As at Lincoln's funeral, there were many uniformed mourners for the Commander-in-Chief—each had just brought the nation through a war; each had left, to an unschooled successor, problems with which he could hardly cope, for which he had no real direction, and whose advisers would not scruple to take advantage of his innocence. The civilians present had most of them served in the dead man's government in one or another way, some loyally, some with understanding; others, as would become known, without either loyalty or understanding. Steve Early was crumpled in his grief; Harry Hopkins, a fugitive from the hospital, was hardly able to stand; what was left of his withered body was racked with dry and tearing sobs. Elliott was there, and Anna. James, flying in from the Pacific, was too late; Franklin and John, serving on active ships, could not even start.

The dead President was carried out from the White House that night, and the caisson bore him again along Pennsylvania Avenue, where he had so many times ridden as he came and went on the nation's business. Slowly the train carrying him slipped through the cities and towns between Washington and New York, through the tunnel under Manhattan, over the Hell Gate Bridge, and up along the Hudson to the Hyde Park siding. On another caisson he traveled slowly up the hill to Springwood, drums beating him to the grave prepared in the high-hedged garden. April is early in the Hudson Valley. The spring was just showing as the year turned toward life from the death of winter. The aged trees Franklin had climbed as a boy were just in bud and the roses had not yet bloomed, but the grass of the lawns was green in the chilly air. The place was sweet and close as it would always be.

As the dirges died and the crowd quieted, the old rector of St. James, now seventy-eight, lifted his skullcap. The wind from the river stirred his thin white hair. His voice was suddenly heard repeating the service for committal to the grave:

Unto Almighty God we commend the soul of our brother departed . . .

He ran on to the Lord's Prayer, then, raising a frail hand in benediction, he intoned the lines from the old hymn beginning

> *Now the laborer's day is o'er,*
> *Now the battle day is past . . .*

and ending

> *Father in Thy gracious keeping,*
> *Leave we now our brother sleeping.*

One reporter noted that gentle Cousin Margaret Suckley brought Fala into the enclosure on a leash and that he whimpered when a salute was fired by a heavy gun. He rolled on the grass and barked furiously when the rifles of the cadets cracked out.

In the pictures published in the next day's papers there can be distinguished, standing sadly in the pale sunshine, not only Anna and Elliott, but the venerable Josephus Daniels from far out of the past, and Steve Early, Sam Rosenman, Harry Hopkins, Ed Flynn, Ross McIntire, Frank Walker, and Lowell Mellett. All these loyal helpers buried a good part of themselves that day. All the rest of their lives would be lived in the past.

Taps sounded sweetly within the tall hedges. The crowd dispersed. When everyone had gone but the workmen, Eleanor came back in her widow's veil and stood by the grave until the last shovelful of earth had been smoothed down. Then she too went away. A sharp-eyed reporter noted that she wore at her throat a small pearl fleur-de-lis. It had been her young husband's wedding gift.

A SELECTED LIST OF FURTHER READINGS

Allen, F. L. *Since Yesterday*. New York: Harper, 1940.

Alsop, Joseph, and Kinter, Robert. *Men around the President*. New York: Doubleday, 1939.

———— and Catledge, Turner. *The 168 Days*. New York: Doubleday, 1938.

Arnold, H. H. *Global Mission*. New York: Harper, 1949.

Arnold, Thurman. *The Folklore of Capitalism*. Yale University Press, 1937.

Barkley, Alben W. *That Reminds Me*. New York: Doubleday, 1954.

Barnes, W. R., and Littlefield, A. W. *The Supreme Court Issue and the Constitution*. New York: Barnes & Noble, 1937.

Beard, Charles A. *American Foreign Policy in the Making, 1932–1940*. Yale University Press, 1946.

Bellush, Bernard. *Franklin D. Roosevelt as Governor of New York*. Columbia University Press, 1955.

Blum, J. M. *The Republican Roosevelt*. Harvard University Press, 1954.

Bradley, Omar. *A Soldier's Story*. New York: Henry Holt, 1951.

Brogan, D. W. *The Era of Franklin D. Roosevelt*. Yale University Press, 1951.

Brownlow, Louis. *The President and the Presidency*. Chicago: Public Administration Service, 1949.

Burns, J. M. *Roosevelt: The Lion and the Fox*. New York: Harcourt, Brace, 1956.

Busch, Noel. *What Manner of Man?* New York: Harper, 1944.

Byrnes, J. F. *Speaking Frankly*. New York: Harper, 1947.

Carr, R. K. *The Supreme Court and Judicial Review*. New York: Farrar & Rinehart, 1942.

Cheever, D. S., and Haviland, H. F., Jr. *American Foreign Policy and the Separation of Powers*. Harvard University Press, 1952.

Chenery, W. L. *So It Seemed*. New York: Harcourt, Brace, 1952.

Childs, Marquis W. *They Hate Roosevelt!* New York: Harper, 1936.

Churchill, Winston S. *The Second World War*. 6 vols. Boston: Houghton Mifflin, 1948–53.

Cline, R. S. *Washington Command Post*. Washington: Office of Military History, U. S. Army, 1951.

Cox, J. M. *Journey through My Years*. New York: Simon & Schuster, 1946.

Crawford, K. G. *The Pressure Boys*. New York: Messner, 1939.

Creel, George. *Rebel at Large*. New York: Putnam, 1947.

Dahl, R. A. *Congress and Foreign Policy*. New York: Harcourt, Brace, 1950.

Daniels, Jonathan. *The End of Innocence*. Philadelphia: Lippincott, 1954.

Dows, Olin. *Franklin Roosevelt at Hyde Park*. New York: American Artists Group, 1949.

Eccles, M. S. *Beckoning Frontiers*. Ed. by Sidney Hyman. New York: Knopf, 1951.

Eisenhower, D. D. *Crusade in Europe*. New York: Doubleday, 1948.

Farley, James A. *Behind the Ballots*. New York: Harcourt, Brace, 1938.

————, with Trohan, Walter. *Jim Farley's Story*. New York: Whittlesey House, 1948.

Feis, Herbert. *The Road to Pearl Harbor*. Princeton University Press, 1950.

Flynn, E. J. *You're the Boss*. New York: Viking, 1947.

Freidel, Frank. *Franklin D. Roosevelt*. 6 vols. Boston: Little, Brown, 1950, 1954, 1956, etc.

Fusfield, Daniel R. *The Economic Thought of Franklin D. Roosevelt*. Columbia University Press, 1956.

Galbraith, J. K. *The Great Crash, 1929*. Boston: Houghton Mifflin, 1955.

Gosnell, Harold. *Champion Campaigner*. New York: Macmillan, 1952.

Gunther, John. *Roosevelt in Retrospect*. New York: Harper, 1950.

Hallgren, Mauritz. *The Gay Reformer*. New York: Knopf, 1935.

Helm, Edith Benham. *The Captains and the Kings*. New York: Putnam, 1954.

High, Stanley. *Roosevelt—And Then?* New York: Harper, 1937.

Hoover, Herbert. *Memoirs*. 3 vols. New York: Macmillan, 1951–52.

Hugh-Jones, E. M., and Radice, E. A. *An American Experiment*. Oxford University Press, 1936.

Hull, Cordell. *Memoirs*. 2 vols. New York: Macmillan, 1948.

Hyman, Sidney. *The American President*. New York: Harper, 1954.

Ickes, Jane, ed. *The Secret Diary of Harold L. Ickes*. 3 vols. New York: Simon & Schuster, 1953–54.

Johnson, Gerald. *Roosevelt: Dictator or Democrat?* New York: Harper, 1941.

Johnson, Hugh S. *The Blue Eagle from Egg to Earth*. New York: Doubleday, 1935.

Johnson, Walter. *The Battle against Isolation*. University of Chicago Press, 1944.

Jones, Jesse. *Fifty Billion Dollars*. New York: Macmillan, 1951.

Kent, Frank. *Without Grease*. New York: W. Morrow, 1936.

King, Admiral E. J. *Fleet Admiral King: A Naval Record*. New York: Norton, 1952.

Konefsky, S. J. *Chief Justice Stone and the Supreme Court*. New York: Macmillan, 1945.

Langer, W. L., and Gleason, S. E. *The Undeclared War, 1940–1941*. New York: Harper, 1953.

Laski, H. J. *The American Presidency*. New York: Harper, 1940.

Leahy, W. D. *I Was There*. New York: Whittlesey House, 1950.

Lindley, Ernest K. *Franklin D. Roosevelt*. New York: Blue Ribbon Books, 1931.

——. *Half Way with Roosevelt*. New York: Viking, 1937.

——. *The Roosevelt Revolution*. New York: Viking, 1933.

Lippmann, Walter. *Interpretations, 1933–1935*. New York: Macmillan, 1936.

Lorant, Stefan. *FDR: A Pictorial Biography*. New York: Simon & Schuster, 1950.

Lord, Russell. *The Wallaces of Iowa*. Boston: Houghton Mifflin, 1947.

Ludwig, Emil. *Roosevelt: A Study in Fortune and Power*. New York: Garden City Publishing Co., 1941.

Marshall, George C. *General Marshall's Report: The Winning of the War in Europe and the Pacific*. New York: Simon & Schuster, 1945.

McCune, Wesley. *The Farm Bloc*. New York: Doubleday, 1943.

——. *The Nine Young Men*. New York: Harper, 1947.

McIntire, Ross T. *White House Physician*. New York: Putnam, 1946.

Michelson, Charles. *The Ghost Talks*. New York: Putnam, 1944.

Millis, Walter, ed. *The Forrestal Diaries*. New York: Viking, 1951.

Mitchell, Broadus. *Depression Decade*. New York: Rinehart, 1947.

Moley, Raymond. *After Seven Years*. New York: Harper, 1939.

Moscow, Warren. *Politics in the Empire State*. New York: Knopf, 1948.

Nesbitt, Henrietta. *White House Diary*. New York: Doubleday, 1948.

Nevins, Allan. *The New Deal and World Affairs, 1933–1945*. Yale University Press, 1950.

Ogburn, W. F., ed. *American Society in Wartime*. University of Chicago Press, 1943.

Partridge, Bellamy. *Imperial Saga: The Roosevelt Family in America*. New York: Hillman-Curl, Inc., 1936.

Peel, Roy V., and Donnelly, T. C. *The 1928 Campaign*. New York: R. R. Smith, 1931.

——. *The 1932 Campaign*. New York: Farrar & Rinehart, 1935.

Perkins, Frances. *The Roosevelt I Knew*. New York: Viking, 1946.

Pratt, Fletcher. *The Navy's War*. New York: Harper, 1944.

Pritchett, C. H. *The Roosevelt Court*. New York: Macmillan, 1948.

The Public Papers of [Governor] Franklin D. Roosevelt. Albany: J. B. Lyon, 1930, 1931, 1937, 1939.

The Public Papers of [President] Franklin D. Roosevelt, 13 vols. Compiled by Samuel T. Rosenman, with notes and introduction by Franklin D. Roosevelt. New York: Random House, 5 vols., 1938; Macmillan, 4 vols., 1941; Harper, 4 vols., 1950.

Rauch, Basil. *History of the New Deal, 1933–38*. New York: Creative Age Press, 1944.

——. *Roosevelt from Munich to Pearl Harbor*. New York: Creative Age Press, 1950.

Reilly, M. F. *Reilly of the White House*. New York: Simon & Schuster, 1947.

Richberg, Donald. *My Hero*. New York: Putnam, 1954.

Roosevelt, Eleanor. *This I Remember*. New York: Harper, 1949.

——. *This Is My Story*. New York: Harper, 1937.

Roosevelt, Elliott, ed. *F.D.R.: His Personal Letters,* 4 vols. New York: Duell, Sloan & Pearce, 1947.

Roosevelt, Nicholas. *A Front Row Seat.* University of Oklahoma Press, 1953.

Roper, Daniel C. *Fifty Years of Public Life.* Duke University Press, 1941.

Rosenman, Samuel I. *Working with Roosevelt.* New York: Harper, 1952.

Rossiter, Clinton. *The American Presidency.* New York: Harcourt, Brace, 1956.

Schlesinger, A. M. *The New Deal in Action, 1933–1939.* New York: Macmillan, 1940.

———. *The Crisis of the Old Order,* the first of several volumes intended to comprise an *Age of Roosevelt.* Boston: Houghton Mifflin Co., 1957.

Schriftgiesser, Karl. *This Was Normalcy.* Boston: Little, Brown, 1948.

Schuman, Frederick L. *The Nazi Dictatorship.* New York: Knopf, 1939.

Sherwood, Robert E. *Roosevelt and Hopkins.* New York: Harper, 1948.

Smith, Merriam. *A President Is Many Men.* New York: Harper, 1948.

———. *Thank You, Mr. President.* New York: Harper, 1946.

Stettinius, E. R. *Roosevelt and the Russians.* Ed. by Walter Johnson. New York: Doubleday, 1949.

Stiles, Lela. *The Man behind Roosevelt: The Story of Louis McHenry Howe.* New York: World Publishing Co., 1954.

Stilwell, Joseph W. *The Stilwell Papers.* Ed. by Theodore White. New York: William Sloane Associates, 1948.

Stimson, Henry L., with Bundy, McGeorge. *On Active Service in Peace and War.* New York: Harper, 1948.

Swisher, C. B., ed. *Selected Papers of Homer S. Cummings.* New York: Scribner, 1939.

The Unofficial Observer. *Our Lords and Masters.* New York: Simon & Schuster, 1935.

Walker, Turnley. *Roosevelt and the Warm Springs Story.* New York: A. A. Wyn, 1953.

Wecter, Dixon. *The Age of the Great Depression, 1929–41.* New York: Macmillan, 1948.

Wehle, Louis B. *Hidden Threads of History.* New York: Macmillan, 1953.

Welles, Sumner. *Seven Decisions That Shaped History.* New York: Harper, 1951.

———. *The Time for Decision.* New York: Harper, 1944.

White, William Allen. *A Puritan in Babylon.* New York: Macmillan, 1938.

White, William S. *The Citadel.* New York: Harper, 1957.

Wilson, H. H. *Congress: Corruption and Compromise.* New York: Rinehart, 1951.

Winant, J. G. *Letter from Grosvenor Square.* Boston: Houghton Mifflin, 1947.

Zeller, Belle. *Pressure Politics in New York.* New York: Prentice-Hall, 1937.

INDEX

American political system, 72, 123, 331, 406, 434
American President, The, 373 n.
American Telephone and Telegraph Company, 548
Amsterdam, 164
Andeman Islands, 517 n.
Andrew, A. Piatt, 52, 54
Anglicanism, 31
Anglo-American Caribbean Commission, 601
Anglophobes, 521, 543, 543 n., 570
Annapolis, 25
Antioch College, 287
Anti-trust laws, 230; FDR on, 331
Appeasement, 473, 488, 571
Argentia, 572, 577–80, 584, 585, 590, 591, 592; *see also* Atlantic Charter
Arizona, 265, 403, 569
Armed forces, 573, 597; growth, 438, 568–69; *see also* under name of service
Armistice (1917), 563
Army, U.S., 279; construction, 568; growth, 548, 568–69; Secretary of, 526
Army Service Forces, 568 n.
Arnold, Henry H., 598–99, 615–16, 668
Arnold, Thurman, 563 n.
Ashurst, Senator, 403, 405
Astor, Lady, 61
Astor, Vincent, 25, 242, 264, 324 n.
Athens, 494, 496
Atlantic Charter, 578–80; *see also* Argentia
Atlee, Clement, 592
Atomism, 219, 221, 416, 564, 612; FDR, 545
Attorney General, U.S., 267–68, 399 n.
Auchinleck, Claude, 605
Augusta (U.S.S.), 572, 577, 578 n., 584
Australia, 583, 592, 606
Austria, 473, 565
Axis, 485, 519, 556, 557, 574
Azores, 499 n., 522, 560, 571

Babbitt, Irving, 47
Back Door to War, 587 n.
Bacon, Mrs. Robert, 61
Bad Nauheim, 17, 26
Bahamas, 560
Baker, Newton D., 224, 226
Balance of power, 419

Balkans, 561
"the baloney dollar," 322
Bank holiday, 272
Bankers Conference, 379–82
Bankhead, William B., 470
Banking Act of 1935, 344 n., 369, 375, 443
Banking crisis, 263–64, 294, 369; closing, 270 n.; Depression and, 262; FDR on, 243; legislation, 271–72
Barkley, Alben, 405, 451, 645 n.
Barnes, W. R., 389 n.
Barnesville, Ga., 461
Baruch, Bernard, 167, 239, 242, 265, 286, 313, 315, 327, 349, 452, 597, 597 n., 623–24, 646; Board, 601; recovery formula, 239
Bassett, Edward M., 84
Bataan, 595
Batt, Mr., 525, 548, 569
"Battle of Anacostia Flats," 271, 350
Battle of Britain, 555
Battle of the Bulge, 664–66
Baxter, James Phinney, 572
Bay of Fundy, 27, 139
Beard, Charles A., 483 n.
Beckoning Frontiers: Public and Personal Recollections, 373 n., 444 n.
Behind the Ballots, 348 n.
Belgium, 512
Belmont, August, 85
Benedum, M. L., 242
Benítez, Jaime, 16
Berle, Adolf, 215, 218, 234, 246
Berlin, 576, 616, 676
Bermuda, 522, 560
"Bible belt," 154
Biddle, Francis, 29 n.
Biddle, George, 294–95
Big business, 281, 454; FDR negation of, 420
Big Four, 621, 629, 630
Big Three, 640; health, 635 n.
Bill of Rights, 415
Biloxi, Miss., 173 n.
Biltmore Hotel (New York), 238, 249
Bismarck, N.D., 425
Black, Hugo, 283 n., 358 n., 378, 379, 406
Black, Van Lear, 134–35, 139
Black-Connery bill, 284 n., 310
Blackstone Hotel, 119
Blitzkrieg, 489, 490, 576; technique, 475

Hughes, Charles Evans, 71, 387, 396, 405–6, 416

Hughes-Wheeler alliance, 387

Hull, Cordell, 220–21, 267, 290, 313, 315–17, 323, 325, 327, 411, 463–64, 478, 490, 513 n., 516, 531, 554, 584, 585, 599, 617, 620, 622, 627, 657, 673; international laissez-faire, 231; *Memoirs*, 315 n.

Humphries case, 392, 392 n., 393 n., 400

Hundred Days, 306, 465

Hungary, 494

Hurley, Patrick J., 257 n.

Hutchins, Robert M., 499 n., 554

Hyde Park, 18, 19, 26, 31, 44, 46, 48, 56 n., 61, 66, 67, 81, 87, 88, 95, 144, 174, 193, 194, 236, 253, 264, 301, 361, 362, 431, 436, 437, 481, 482, 487, 491, 496, 502, 549, 641; British royalty visit, 493–94; changes made, 88, 88 n.; library, 14, 15; museum, 511 n.; Township, 17, 23

Hyman, Sidney, 373 n., 477 n.

Ibn Saud, 674

Ickes, Harold, 13, 162 n., 267, 319, 320, 327, 354, 359, 360, 360 n., 375, 404, 441 n., 449, 481, 538, 570, 597, 599–600, 652; *Diary*, 320, 527, 599; -FDR relations, 360

Ides of March, 468

Il Duce, 438; *see* Mussolini

Illinois, 70, 119

Imperialism, 99, 100

India, 484, 557, 564 n., 592, 594

Indiana, 538

Indianapolis *News*, 558

Indochina, 557, 570, 584

Ingram, Jonas, 614

Inspector, 206, 207, 208

Insull, Samuel, 287

Interior, U.S. Department of, 162 n., 404, 441; Secretary of, 319

International Association of Machinists, 279 n.

International bankers, 333

International Debts, 253–56, 257, 259, 260, 315

International finance, 257

International organization, 410

International Workers of the World, 121, 127, 338

Internationalism, 244, 492; FDR, 335; *see also* under Collective Security

Interstate Commerce Commission, 357 n.

Iowa, 627

Isolationism, 115, 244, 333, 338, 345, 419, 441, 469, 470, 473, 474, 478, 484, 488–89, 491–92, 498–99, 521, 549

Isolationists, 450, 470, 475, 483, 488, 491–93, 494, 495, 505, 532, 542, 560–61, 566, 567, 581, 588, 654; responsibility for war, 486 n.

Issues of 1930's, 338–39

Italy, 64, 205, 350, 494, 556, 573; Fascists, 263; policies, 347; Spanish War, 469; surrender terms, 622

IWW *see* International Workers of the World

Jackson, Andrew, 365

Jackson, Graham, 680

Jackson, Jimmy, 50

Jackson, Robert H., 399 n., 404, 405, 490, 527, 542, 552, 563 n., 652

Jamestown, 155, 158, 160, 164; speech, 160–61

"Janizaries," 542 n.

Japan, 19, 20, 473 n., 484, 489, 549, 556–57, 570; designs in Asia, 484; expansion, 555–56; in Manchuria, 257; growth of totalitarianism, 439; militarists, 484, 587; Navy, 555–57; people, 56 n., 469, 521, 581, 598, 602, 604; Southeast Asia Co-prosperity Sphere, 583; threat to U.S., 555, 557; -U.S. relations, 583–87; war lords, 556

Java Sea, 595

Jefferson, Thomas, 91, 96

Jeffersonianism, 197, 218

Jewett, Frank B., 573

Jewish Theological Seminary of America, 513

Johnson, Hiram, 71, 119, 246, 256, 267, 281, 360, 409, 479

Johnson, Hugh, 159, 232, 238–39, 284, 306 n., 307, 309, 311, 313, 319 n., 320 n., 324, 326, 327, 327 n., 330, 413, 542 n., 543 n., 599; NRA administrator, 286; resignation, 331

Johnson, Louis A., 505–6

Johnston, Tom, 213 n.

Jones, Jesse, 327, 359, 360, 378, 379,

697

tenant-governorship, 180–81; nomi-
nation, 245
Lemke, William, 429, 430
Lend-Lease, 515, 542, 549, 554, 561,
578; Act, 523, 549, 561, 564; debate,
561; Hopkins, 544
Leon, René, 272 n.
Lewis, John L., 336, 360, 403–4, 531
Libbey-Owens-Ford Glass Company,
548
Liberals, criticism of FDR, 191–92, 195
Liberty Leagues, 173, 246, 321, 322 n.,
347–48, 428
Lilienthal, David, 287, 441 n.
Lincoln, Abraham, 11, 41, 42, 166, 365,
428, 429, 469, 483, 680
Lindbergh, Charles A., 492, 520, 554,
570–71
Lindley, Ernest K., 78 n., 93 n., 163 n.,
218–19, 219 n., 241 n., 242, 315,
315 n., 408, 482, 482 n., 543 n.
Lippmann, Walter, 12, 72, 185, 187,
188, 196, 245, 268–69, 521, 522;
criticism of FDR, 191, 222
Littlefield, S. W., 389 n.
Little White House, 677
Litvinov, Maksim M., 346, 621
Lobbies, 167
Lobbyists, 160
Lodge, Henry Cabot, 115, 117, 118, 123
London, 64, 116, 260, 323, 333, 494,
495, 605
London Conference *see* World Mone-
tary and Economic Conference
Long, Huey P., 13, 246, 297, 297 n.,
298, 318, 334, 348–51, 429, 430;
assassination, 350; -FDR relations,
297, 348–49; machine (La.), 429
Longworth, Alice Roosevelt, 46 n., 52,
61, 302, 303
Los Alamos, 574
Lothian, Lord, 553–54
Louisiana, 297, 348, 350
Low Countries, 271, 438, 520; fall of,
532; *see also* under World War II
Lowell, A. Lawrence, 47
Luce, Clare Booth, 61
Luce, Henry, 537
Ludlow, Congressman, 469
Ludlow Resolution, 469–70
"Lunatic fringe," 430
Lusitania, 101 n.
Lynch, Tom, 67, 125, 128, 129

McAdoo, William G., 84 n., 94, 106,
120, 145, 191, 214, 223, 226, 233
McAllister, Dorothy, 527
MacArthur, Douglas, 12, 202 n., 297 n.,
525, 555, 586, 606, 660 n., 676; FDR
opinion, 349–50; -FDR relations, 653–
56
McCarran, Pat, 405, 533, 561
McCarthy, Joseph R., 202 n.
McCombs, William F., 84 n.
McCormick, Robert R., 25, 29 n., 492,
492 n.
MacCracken, Henry N., 499 n., 581
MacDonald, Ramsay, 290
McGuire, E. J., 84
McIntire, Dr. Ross, 355, 517, 552, 614,
618, 635, 646, 647, 679, 681
McIntyre, Marvin, 128, 271, 333, 355,
445, 455, 634
Mack, John E., 67, 69, 70, 94, 108
McKellar, Kenneth M., 676
McKinley, William, 63, 296, 483 n., 537
MacLeish, Archibald, 544, 600, 668 n.
McNary, Charles L., 388, 405 n.
McNary-Haugen Acts, 158, 174, 175,
276
McNeil, Archibald, 196–97
McNutt, Paul, 490
McReynolds, James Clark, 386
MacVeagh, Lincoln, 494, 496
Madigan-Hyland, 568 n.
Madison, James, 91, 483 n.
Madison Square Garden, 250, 409 n.
Maginot Line, 512
Mahan, Alfred T., 37, 99, 110, 440
Malaya, 585
"Malefactors of great wealth," 167
Malta, 668
Manila, 555
Man on Horseback ideal, 349–50
Manchuria, 56 n., 257, 556
Marines, U.S., 18, 110
Marshall, George C., 525, 526, 555,
598, 570, 577, 585, 586, 593–94,
602, 605–6, 607, 615, 622, 627–28,
633, 668
Marshall, John, 365, 395
Marshall, Thomas R., 124
Marshall, Verne, 560 n.
"Martin, Barton, and Fish," 540–41
Martin, Joseph W., Jr., 540
Maryland, 476
Massachusetts, 224, 476

New York *World*, 187, 191, 196
New Zealand, 583, 592
Nimitz, Chester W., 653, 655
"Nine Old Men," 372, 384; *see also* Supreme Court
NIRA *see* National Industrial Recovery Act
No Foreign War Committee, 560 n.
Nomura, Kichisaburo, 584, 585
Non-Partisan Committee for Peace through the Revision of the Neutrality Law, 492
Norfolk Navy Yard, 535
"Normalcy," 122, 128
Normandy, 20; beaches, 650
Norris, George, 220, 252, 281, 286, 287, 298, 328, 388, 451, 532, 533, 409
North Carolina, 86
North Dakota, 214
Norway, 499
Nova Scotia, 89, 522
NRA *see* National Recovery Administration
NYA *see* National Youth Administration
Nye, Gerald P., 281, 328, 360, 405 n., 478, 537

Oak Ridge, 574
O'Connor, John J., 533
O'Connor, D. Basil, 19, 186
Ochs, Adolphe S., 134
OES *see* Office of Economic Stabilization
Office of Alien Property Custodian, 601
Office of Civilian Defense, 523, 638
Office of Economic Stabilization, 523, 601
Office of Emergency Management, 523
Office of Production Management, 523, 548
Office of Scientific Research and Development, 574, 574 n.
Office of Strategic Services, 601
Office of War Information, 543 n., 601
Ogburn, William F., 202 n., 335
Ogden *vs.* Saunders (1827), 400 n.
Oglethorpe speech, 218–19, 219 n., 221, 246, 281, 329
Oglethorpe University, 218
O'Gorman, James A., 80, 84 n.
"Okies," 422, 528
Okinawa, battle of, 628

Old-Age Assistance, 504
Old Testament, 168
Olds, Leland, 183
Oliphant, Herman, 554
Olson, Floyd, 218, 296–97, 298
O'Mahoney, Joseph C., 402 n., 405
OPM *see* Office of Production Management
Oregon, 423
"Organized progress," 122
Osborne, Thomas M., 82, 84, 84 n.
Oslo, 494
OSS *see* Office of Strategic Services
Ottinger, Albert, 52, 168, 169
OWI *see* Office of War Information
Oyster Bay, 46, 86, 126

Pacific Coast, 522
Pacific Ocean, 570
Palmer, A. Mitchell, 120, 127, 338
Panama, 17, 90, 118, 345; Declaration of, 518–19
Panama Canal, 88, 100, 518; Miraflores Lock, 90; Pedro Miguel Lock, 90
Pan American Day, 570
Paris, 64, 114, 116, 254, 494, 562, 673
Peabody, Endicott, 28, 29, 31, 50, 96, 210
Peabody, George Foster, 141
Peabody, H., 49
Peace Conference, 18, 116
Parity, 230, 240
Parker, Alton B., 79 n.
Passamaquoddy, 90, 91, 366
Patch, Alexander M., 598
Patronage, 72, 76 n., 94, 106, 266, 299, 350, 402 n.
Patten, Simon N., 53 n.
Patton, George S., 598
Paulus, Friedrich, 619
Payne, Lou, 93
"Peace in our time," 473
Pearl Harbor, 19, 485, 487 n., 498, 525, 542, 555, 568, 577, 582, 585, 586–87, 589; investigations, 587; U.S. reaction to, 583, 588–89, 590
Pearson, Drew, 384 n.
Pecora, Ferdinand, 379, 537
Pendergast, Thomas J., 526
Peek, George N., 159, 167, 232, 239, 276, 313, 327, 371, 599
Peekism, 158–61
Peel, Roy V., 225 n.

702

Soldiers Bonus

p. 444